BIG DATA & HADOOP

V.K. Jain
BE(E), M.Tech, FIE, FIETE
Chartered and Consultant Engineer
Visiting Faculty

KHANNA BOOK PUBLISHING CO. (P) LTD.
Publisher of Science, Technology and Engineering Books
4C/4344, Ansari Road, Darya Ganj, New Delhi-110002
Phone: 011-23244447-48 **Mobile:** +91-99109 09320
E-mail: contact@khannabooks.com
Website: www.khannabooks.com

Dear Readers,

To prevent the piracy, this book is secured with HIGH SECURITY HOLOGRAM on the front title cover. In case you don't find the hologram on the front cover title, please write us to at contact@khannabooks.com or whatsapp us at +91-99109 09320 and avail special gift voucher for yourself.

Specimen of Hologram on front Cover title:

Moreover, there is a SPECIAL DISCOUNT COUPON for you with EVERY HOLOGRAM.

How to avail this SPECIAL DISCOUNT:

Step 1: Scratch the hologram
Step 2: Under the scratch area, your "coupon code" is available
Step 3: Logon to www.khannabooks.com
Step 4: Use your "coupon code" in the shopping cart and get your copy at a special discount
Step 5: Enjoy your reading!

ISBN: 978-93-82609-13-1

Big Data and Hadoop *by*
V.K. Jain

First Edition: 2017
Second Edition: 2023
Reprint: 2025, **2026**

To view complete list of books, Please scan the QR Code:

Published by:
Khanna Book Publishing Co. (P) Ltd.
CIN: U22110DL1998PTC095547

Visit us at: **www.khannabooks.com**
Write us at: **contact@khannabooks.com**

Printed in Bharat.

THE INSTITUTION OF ELECTRONICS AND TELECOMMUNICATION ENGINEERS

IETE, 2, Institutional Area, Lodhi Road, New Delhi-110003, India
email : dysec@iete.org Ph.: 011-43538823

Foreword

Big data is a board term for data sets so large or complex that traditional data processing applications are inadequate. Challengers include analysis, capture, data curation, search, sharing, storage, transfer, visualization, querying and information privacy.

As per International Data Corporation, the digital universe- the data we create and copy annually-is doubling in size every two years and by 2020 this digital universe will reach 44 zettabytes (1021bytes) or 44 trillion gigabytes.

Fortune 1000 companies and government bodies are starting to benefit from the innovations in field of Big Data. These organisations are defining new initiatives and re-evaluating existing strategies to examine how they can transform can transform their business using Big Data.

Over the past decade, major web companies like google, Amazon and facebook pioneered business built on monetizing massive data volumes. In the process, they invented new paradigms not only for extracting value from data, but also for managing data and compute resources from data centre design, to hardware, to software, to application provisioning. Google can detect and track the emergence of disease outbreaks through social media communications and help governments monitor and control the spread of the disease.

Big data is among the hottest trends in IT right now and hadoop stands at the forefront and centre in the discussion of how to implement a big data strategy. Apache hadoop is a distributed computing framework modelled after google Map reduce to process large amount of data in parallel.

It is not an easy task to produce a book of this size and magnitude on a highly technical subject involving skilled deep level of programming. Shri V.K. Jain is a very versatile, prolific and legendary author who evolved elementary level books much ahead of time and then DOEACC books. The book has been written by famous computer Guru Er. V.K. Jain who is credited to have written more than 100 books on various subject of Computer science and Information Technology. His books are available forpractically all computer languages like Cobol, BASIC, Pascal, C,C++, C#,, JAVA, DTP, JSP, Visual BASIC, HTML, WML, C# and comprehensive subjects like Computer Architecture, DTP, Multimedia, Networking, Cryptography, Network Security, system Analysis and design etc. He was the first author to write books as per syllabus of DOEACC "O", "A" and "B". This is his 133th book on various subjects of Engineering, IT and Management-perhaps a word record.

I have great pleasure in recommending this book to the engineering and IT fraternity. I wish him every success in all his endeavours.

Lt Gen (Dr) AKS Chandele, PVSM, AVSM (Retd),
PRESIDENT IETE (2016-17)

Preface

Big data is a broad term for data sets so large or complex that traditional data processing applications are inadequate. Challenges include analysis, capture, data curation, search, sharing, storage, transfer, visualization, querying and information privacy. The term often refers simply to the use of predictive analytics or certain other advanced methods to extract value from data, and seldom to a particular size of data set. Accuracy in big data may lead to more confident decision making, and better decisions can result in greater operational efficiency, cost reduction and reduced risk. Big Data and its driving force Hadoop is occupying entire media more than any other single subject. The Hadoop platform provides sufficient coverage in getting mass public opinion in unprecedented manner over a very wide canvas in Zettabyte range 1021.

Social media data can help a company take corrective action to retain a high-value group of customers when predictive analysis on the social media data suggests they are at risk to move to a competitor. I am chasing information Technology and computer Science right from their inception from 1968 whence I did my first computer programming at IIT Kanpur for my M.Tech. Thesis. I could not find anything more interesting and challenging than the subject Big. Data. I took training from HCL Noida and interfaced the programming portion of Hadoop. I decided to go for IBM's Infosphere BigInsight as working platform and I found that there is plenty of learning material on internet. I have taken lot of help from their tutorials for composing this book and therefore express my sincere gratitude.

I am also thankful to Abhishek Rastogi of HCL Noida and Ms. Hina Malvia M.Tech who took special interest in my subject and in designing this book. I cannot forget Mukul Seth of Khanna Book Publishing Co. (P) Ltd. who motivated me and provided lot of literature on this subject.

V.K. Jain

BE(E), M.Tech, FIE, FIETE

Chartered and Consultant Engineer

Visiting Faculty

Contents

CHAPTER 1

Overview of Big Data

1.1 BIG DATA

Big data is among the hottest trends in IT right now, and Hadoop stands at front and center in the discussion of how to implement a big data strategy. Doug Cutting's gave this (Hadoop) name to his son's toy elephant. Later on he used this name for his open source project.

Symbolic Hadoop

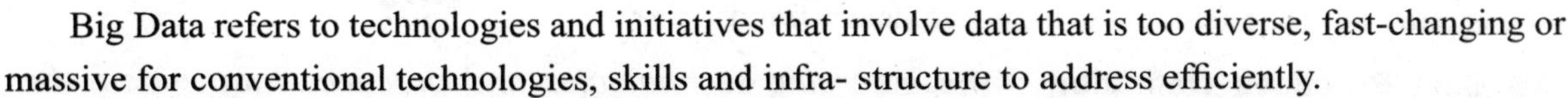

If you do a Google search on big data (1.1.16), over 746,000,000 search results are returned. The term **big data** is a relatively new IT industry term dealing with multitude of this amount of data .

Big Data refers to technologies and initiatives that involve data that is too diverse, fast-changing or massive for conventional technologies, skills and infra- structure to address efficiently.

Over the past decade, major web companies like Google, Amazon and Facebook pioneered businesses built on monetizing massive data volumes. In the process, they invented new paradigms not only for extracting value from data, but also for managing data and compute resources from data center design, to hardware, to software, to application provisioning. Governments and even Google can detect and track the emergence of disease outbreaks via social media signals. Oil and gas companies can take the output of sensors in their drilling equipment to make more efficient and safer drilling decisions. In the same way that the mission to the moon spawned a wave of innovation across multiple industries, Big Data has pushed information technology a quantum leap forward.

Hadoop is, at its core, an Apache Software Foundation project consisting of two primary subprojects

1. Hadoop MapReduce and the
2. Hadoop Distributed File System. (HDFS)

For organizations of all sizes, data management has shifted from an important competency to a critical differentiator that can determine market winners and has-beens. Fortune 1000 companies and government bodies are starting to benefit from the innovations of the web pioneers. These organizations are defining new initiatives and re-evaluating existing strategies to examine how they can transform their businesses using Big Data. In the process, they are learning that Big Data is not a single technology, technique or initiative. Rather, it is a trend across many areas of business and technology.

1.2 DEFINING BIG DATA

As per Oxford English Dictionary , the definition of Big Data is "data of a very large size, typically to the extent that its manipulation and management present significant logistical challenges."

Big Data refers to technologies and initiatives that involve data that is too diverse, fast-changing or massive for conventional technologies, skills and infrastructure to address efficiently. Said differently, the volume, velocity or variety of data is too great. "Big Data" describes data sets so large and complex they are impractical to manage with traditional software tools.

But today, new technologies make it possible to realize value from Big Data. For example, retailers can track user web clicks to identify behavioral trends that improve campaigns, pricing and stockage. Utilities can capture household energy usage levels to predict outages and to incentivize more efficient energy consumption.

Governments and even Google can detect and track the emergence of disease outbreaks via social media signals. Industrial equipment manufacturers are storing and analysing sensor data collected from connected vehicles to determine preventive maintenance programs for fleet optimization, and for the monitoring of vehicle components for design enhancements. Banking institutions are capturing tick data and customer interactions to model risk and detect fraud.

SAS Best Practices Definition :*"The emerging technologies and practices that enable the collection, processing, discovery, analysis, and storage of large volumes and disparate types of data, quickly and cost effectively."*

1.2.1 How big is the canvas of Big Data

Big data does not have to be big (peta/exabytes). Even 50 GB can be said as big data if the structure is too complex for a normal RDBMS to store. What is small data? Small data is simple data structures, e.g. numbers (be it monetary, integers, fractions or floating points), strings (names, description, types), dates, times, and all the data we used to know in the last 30 years of data warehousing history.

Big data usually includes data sets with sizes beyond the ability of commonly used software tools to capture, curate, manage, and process data within a tolerable elapsed time. Big data "size" is a constantly moving target, as of 2012 ranging from a few dozen terabytes to many petabytes of data. Big data requires a set of techniques and technologies with new forms of integration to reveal insights from datasets that are diverse, complex, and of a massive scale.

Let us see how big is petabyte. The Information size is calculated as below:

1000 (10^3) kB 1 kilobyte

1000 (10^6) MB 1 megabyte

1000 (10^9) GB 1 gigabyte

1000 (10^{12}) TB 1 terabyte

1000 (10^{15}) PB 1 petabyte

1000 (10^{18}) EB 1 exabyte

1000 (10^{21}) ZB 1 zettabyte

1000 (10^{24}) YB 1 yottabyte

We shall be soon reaching to a range which is known as पद्‌म (*padma*) 1,00,000 mahā-vanda 10^{32}.

Actually 1 KB = 1024 = 2^8 .We have to enhance each of above by this magnitude.

A processor with a 64-bit address bus can address 16 exbibytes of memory, which is over 18 exabytes.

Vedic Mathematics thought of 10^{60} as ultimate that in Sanskrit known as Mahogh

As per IBM

(a) 2.5 petabytes is Memory capacity of the human brain

(b) 13 petabytes is the amount that could be downloaded from the internet in two minutes, if every American (300M) got on a computer at the same time

(c) 4.75 exabytes : Total genome sequences of all people on the Earth about 7 billion in 2015

(d) 422 exabytes is total digital data created in 2008

(e) 1 zetabyte was World's digital storage capacity in 2013

As per IDC, Digital universe is doubling in size every two years, and by 2020 the digital universe – the data we create and copy annually – will reach 44 zettabytes, or 44 trillion gigabytes. Between 2013 and 2020 the division of the digital universe between mature and emerging markets (e.g., BRICKS) will switch – from 60% accounted for by mature markets to 60% of the data in the digital universe coming from emerging markets.

1.3 THE MANY V'S OF BIG DATA

In a 2001 research report[3] and related lectures, META Group (now Gartner) analyst Doug Laney defined data growth challenges and opportunities as being three-dimensional, i.e. increasing volume (amount of data), velocity (speed of data in and out), and variety (range of data types and sources). Gartner, and now much of the industry, continue to use this "3Vs" model for describing big data. In 2012, Gartner updated its definition as follows: "Big data is high volume, high velocity, and/or high variety information assets that require new forms of processing to enable enhanced decision making, insight discovery and process optimization." Gartner's definition of the 3Vs is still widely used, and in agreement with a consensual definition that states that "Big Data represents the Information assets characterized by such a High Volume, Velocity and Variety to require specific Technology and Analytical Methods for its transformation into Value".

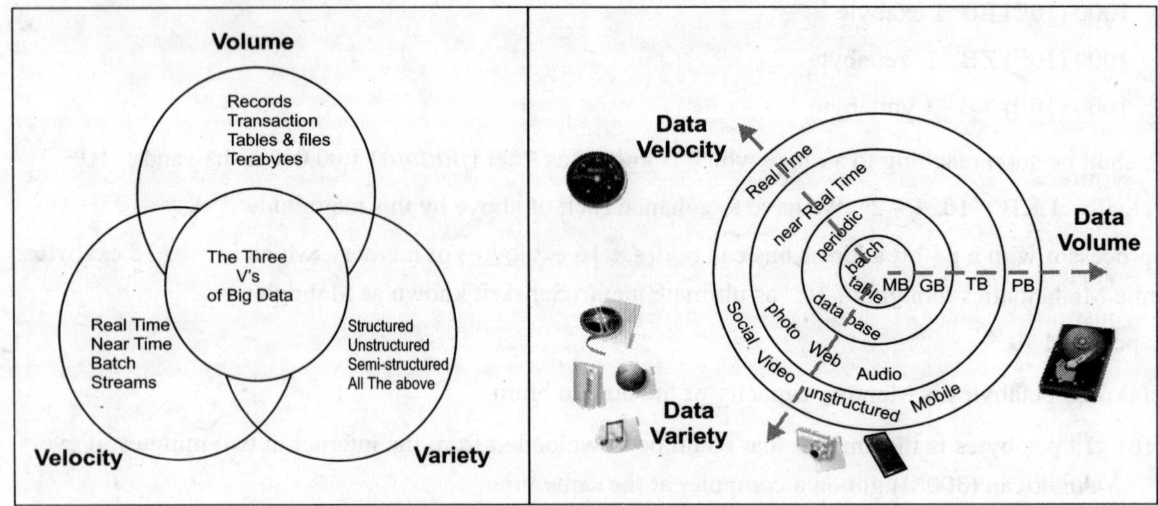

Figure. 1.1: The 3 V's of Big Data

1.3.1 The Five V's of Big Data (Coined in 2013)

Gartner term 3 V of big data (coined in 2001) is now modified as the 5 V. The 5 V's, now signifies the unique features of big data: *volume, variety, velocity , Veracity,and Value* as elaborated below:

Volume: This signifies large amounts of data. Typically when people discuss big data volumes, they discuss petabytes. But in reality, most real-life big data implementations are still in the 10's to

100's of terabytes range. Which is still a lot of data. The rapidly increasing volume data is due to cloud-computing traffic, IoT, mobile traffic etc as described in Fig. 1.2.

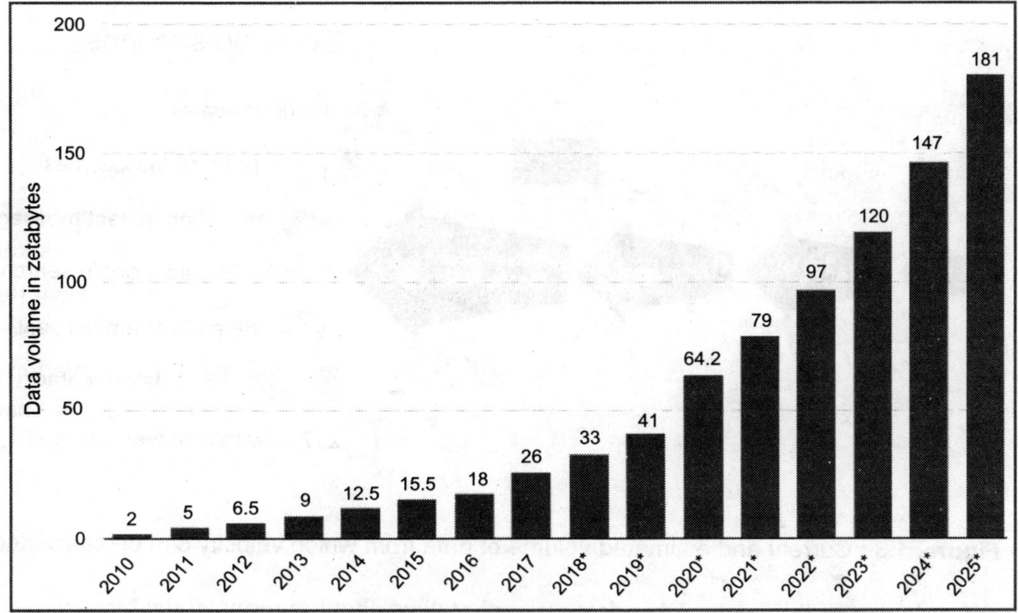

Figure. 1.2 : Increasing volume of data over the years, Source : Published by Statista Research Department, Sep 8, 2022

Variety: This refers to the evolving types and growing sources of data, including semi-structured and unstructured data. An example of semi-structured data might be an e-mail message, where the date might be in a common, structured format, but the e-mail text itself is more unstructured. An example of unstructured data would be notes that a customer support representative might type in, free-form, about a customer's trouble ticket.

Velocity: Velocity in the context of big data refers to the speed of data acquisition and processing. Big data technologies provide horsepower that accelerates these processes, thereby making data provisioning and usage faster, too. The rapidly increasing speed at which new data is being created by technological advances, and the corresponding need for that data to be digested and analyzed in near real-time is now beyond imagination. For example, Amazon captures every click of the mouse while shoppers are browsing on its website. This happens rapidly.

Velocity is important in stream processing. Think of all the data from radio-frequency identification (RFID), global positioning system (GPS), near-field communication (NFC), and Bluetooth sensors flooding in to a system. Stream processing aims to aggregate single data points from high-velocity data, in order to trigger a high-level event when a certain pattern is detected. It also focuses on deciding which data to keep from a stream, since it is unfeasible to retain all the data that is rushing in.

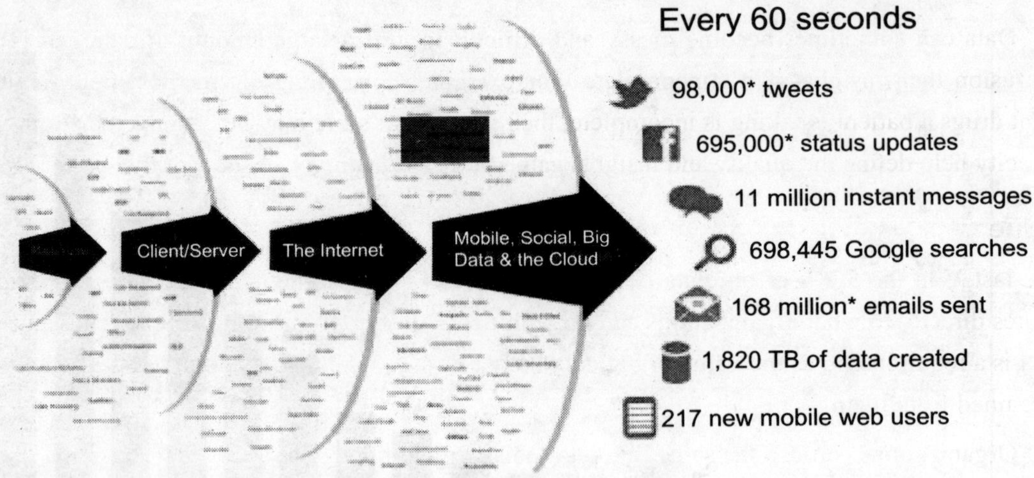

Figure. 1.3 : Current and estimated volume of data from which velocity can be calculated

In the early part of this century, big data was only talked about in terms of the three V's -- *volume, velocity and variety.* Over time, two more V's (value and veracity) have been added to help data scientists be more effective in articulating and communicating the important characteristics of big data. The number five mirrors the five basic questions every news article should answer. However, it is not specifically required that organizations follow data guideline over the other.

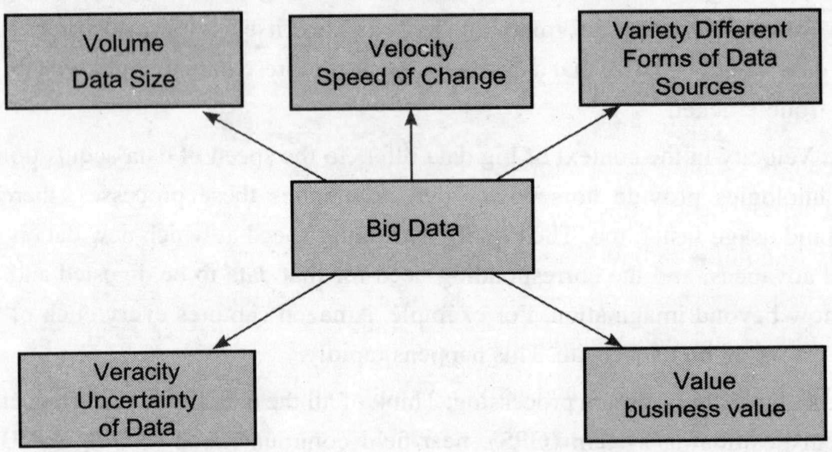

Figure. 1.4 : Current Five 'V's of Big data

Veracity : Veracity is the fourth V in the 5 V's of big data. It refers to the quality and accuracy of data. Gathered data could have missing pieces, may be inaccurate or may not be able to provide real, valuable insight. Veracity, overall, refers to the level of trust there is in the collected data.

Data can sometimes become messy and difficult to use. A large amount of data can cause more confusion than insights if it's incomplete. For example, concerning the medical field, if data about what drugs a patient is taking is incomplete, then the patient's life may be endangered. Both value and veracity help define the quality and insights gathered from data.

Value

The last V in the 5 V's of big data is value. This refers to the value that big data can provide, and it relates directly to what organizations can do with that collected data. Being able to pull value from big data is a requirement, as the value of big data increases significantly depending on the insights that can be gained from them.

Organizations can use the same big data tools to gather and analyze the data, but how they derive value from that data should be unique to them.

1.3.2 Some more V's (Coined in 2013)

Variety : Variety describes one of the biggest challenges of big data. It can be unstructured and it can include so many different types of data from XML to video to SMS. Organizing the data in a meaningful way is no simple task, especially when the data itself changes rapidly.

Variability (inconsistency in data flow) : Variability is different from variety. A coffee shop may offer 6 different blends of coffee, but if you get the same blend every day and it tastes different every day, that is variability. The same is true of data, if the meaning is constantly changing it can have a huge impact on your data homogenization.

Visualization : Visualization is critical in today's world. Using charts and graphs to visualize large amounts of complex data is much more effective in conveying meaning than spreadsheets and reports chock-full of numbers and formulas.

Volatility (durability or how long time data is valid and how long it should be stored), Especially in production systems, one has to prepare for data volatility. Data that should "never" be missing suddenly disappears, numbers suddenly contain characters!

Viability (capability to be live and active), Validity (understandable to find the hidden relationships)

Viscosity (complexity or degree of correlation),

1.4 GROWTH OF AND DIGITIZATION OF GLOBAL INFORMATION STORAGE CAPACITY

Big data is a broad term for data sets so large or complex that traditional data processing applications are inadequate. Challenges include analysis, capture, data curation, search, sharing, storage, transfer, visualization, querying and information privacy. The term often refers simply to the use of predictive analytics or certain other advanced methods to extract value from data, and seldom to a particular size of data set. Accuracy in big data may lead to more confident decision making, and better decisions can result in greater operational efficiency, cost reduction and reduced risk.

Analysis of data sets can find new correlations to "spot business trends, prevent diseases, combat crime and so on. Scientists, business executives, practitioners of medicine, advertising and governments alike regularly meet difficulties with large data sets in areas including Internet search, finance and business informatics. Scientists encounter limitations in e-Science work, including meteorology, genomics, connectomics, complex physics simulations, biology and environmental research.

Data sets are growing rapidly in part because they are increasingly gathered by cheap and numerous information-sensing mobile devices, aerial (remote sensing), software logs, cameras, microphones, radio-frequency identification (RFID) readers and wireless sensor networks. The world's technological per-capita capacity to store information has roughly doubled every 40 months since the 1980s; as of 2012, every day 2.5 exabytes (2.5×10^{18}) of data are created. One question for large enterprises is determining who should own big data initiatives that affect the entire organization. IDC and EMC project that data will grow to 40 zettabytes by 2020, resulting in a 50-fold growth from the beginning of 2010.

Relational database management systems and desktop statistics and visualization packages often have difficulty handling big data. The work instead requires "massively parallel software running on tens, hundreds, or even thousands of servers". What is considered "big data" varies depending on the capabilities of the users and their tools, and expanding capabilities make big data a moving target. "For some organizations, facing hundreds of gigabytes of data for the first time may trigger a need to reconsider data management options. For others, it may take tens or hundreds of terabytes before data size becomes a significant consideration.

1.5 DATA WAREHOUSE

As per Vincent Rainardi, a data warehouse is a system that retrieves and consolidates data periodically from the source systems into a dimensional or normalized data store. It usually keeps years of history and is queried for business intelligence or other analytical activities. It is typically updated in batches, not every time a transaction happens in the source system.

Fig. 1.5 is a diagram of a data warehouse system:

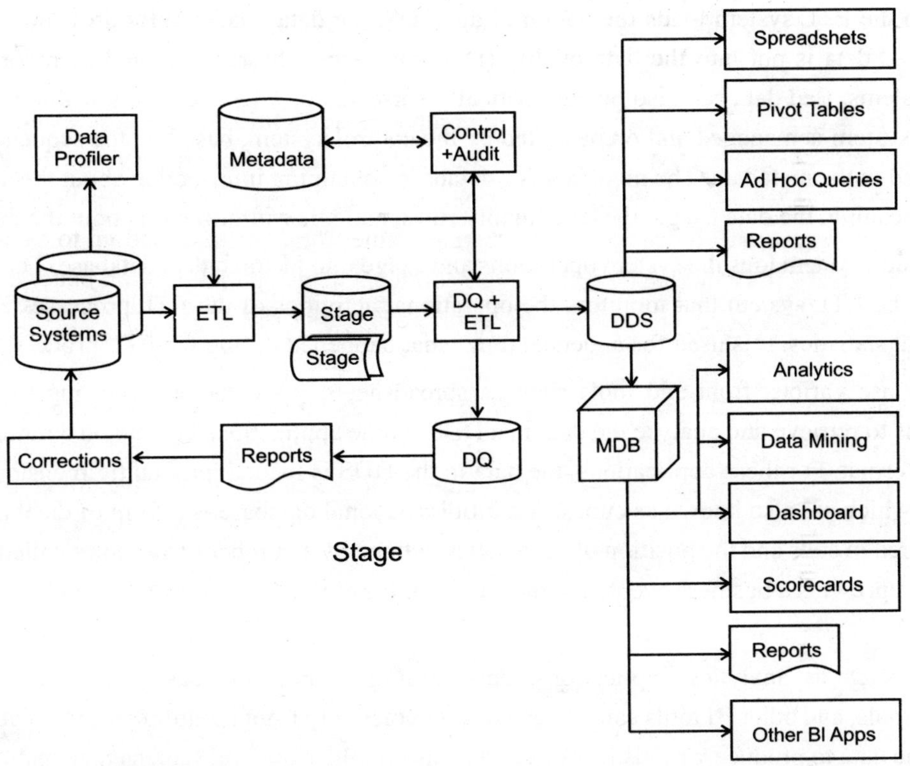

Figure.1.5: Components of Typical Data ware Housing Project

(DOS = Disk Operating System, DQ = data quality, ETL = Extract, Transform and Load)

The source systems are the OLTP systems that contain the data you want to load into the data warehouse. Online Transaction Processing (OLTP) is a system whose main purpose is to capture and store the business transactions. The source systems' data is examined using a data profiler to understand the characteristics of the data. A data profiler is a tool that has the capability to analyse data, such as finding out how many rows are in each table, how many rows contain NULL values, and so on.

The extract, transform, and load (ETL) system then brings data from various source systems into a staging area. ETL is a system that has the capability to connect to the source systems, read the data, transform the data, and load it into a target system (the target system doesn't have to be a data warehouse). The ETL system then integrates, transforms, and loads the data into a dimensional data store (DDS). A DDS is a database that stores the data warehouse data in a different format than OLTP. The reason for getting the data from the source system into the DDS and then querying the DDS instead of querying the source system directly is that in a DDS the data is arranged in a dimensional format that is more suitable for analysis. The second reason is because a DDS contains integrated data from several source systems.

When the ETL system loads the data into the DDS, the data quality rules do various data quality checks. Bad data is put into the data quality (DQ) database to be reported and then corrected in the source systems. Bad data can also be automatically corrected or tolerated if it is within a certain limit. The ETL system is managed and orchestrated by the control system, based on the sequence, rules, and logic stored in the metadata. The metadata is a database containing information about the data structure, the data meaning, the data usage, the data quality rules, and other information about the data.

The audit system logs the system operations and usage into the metadata database. The audit system is part of the ETL system that monitors the operational activities of the ETL processes and logs their operational statistics. It is used for understanding what happened during the ETL process.

Users use various front-end tools such as spreadsheets, pivot tables, reporting tools, and SQL query tools to retrieve and analyse the data in a DDS. Some applications operate on a multidimensional database format. For these applications, the data in the DDS is loaded into multidimensional databases (MDBs), which are also known as cubes. A multidimensional database is a form of database where the data is stored in cells and the position of each cell is defined by a number of variables called dimensions. Each cell represents a business event, and the values of the dimensions show when and where this event happened.

Tools such as analytics applications, data mining, scorecards, dashboards, multidimensional reporting tools, and other BI tools can retrieve data interactively from multidimensional databases. They retrieve the data to produce various features and results on the front-end screens that enable the users to get a deeper understanding about their businesses. An example of an analytic application is to analyse the sales by time, customer, and product. The users can analyse the revenue and cost for a certain month, region, and product type.

1.6 DATA MINING

Data mining is the process of exploring data to find the patterns and relationships that describe the data and to predict the unknown or future values of the data. The key value of data mining is the ability to understand why some things happened in the past and the ability to predict what will happen in the future. To refer to predicting the future with regard to data mining, some people use the term forecasting, and some call it predictive analytics. On the other hand, when data mining is used to explain the current or past situation, it is called descriptive modeling, descriptive analytics, or knowledge discovery.

Implementing data mining in the business is growing by the day, both through descriptive and predictive analytics. Using data mining, we can find the correlation between purchase patterns and customer demographics. For example, in our Amadeus Entertainment case study, we can find whether there is a relation between the sales of a music product type and the customer interest or occupation. In the financial services industry, data mining is traditionally used for credit scoring, for example, to predict the ability and willingness to pay the loan based on (each country has different factors) payment behavior, past delinquency, current debt, credit history, number of inquiries, address, bankruptcies filed, and customer demography.

In business intelligence, popular applications of data mining are for fraud detection (credit card industry), forecasting and budgeting (finance), cellular/mobile package development by analyzing call patterns (telecommunication industry), market basket analysis (retail industry), customer risk profiling (insurance industry), usage monitoring (energy and utilities), and machine service times (manufacturing industry).

1.7 DATA LAKES

We are now moving into the era of data lakes. Every industry has a potential data lake use case. A data lake can be a way to gain more visibility or put an end to data silos. Many companies see data lakes as an opportunity to capture a 360-degree view of their customers or to analyze social media trends.

Medical Centers maintain millions of records for more than a million patients, including radiology images and other semi-structured reports, unstructured physicians' notes, plus volumes of spreadsheet data. To solve the challenge the hospital faced with data storage, integration, and accessibility, the hospital created a data lake based on a Hadoop architecture, which enables distributed big data processing by using broadly accepted open software standards and massively parallel commodity hardware.

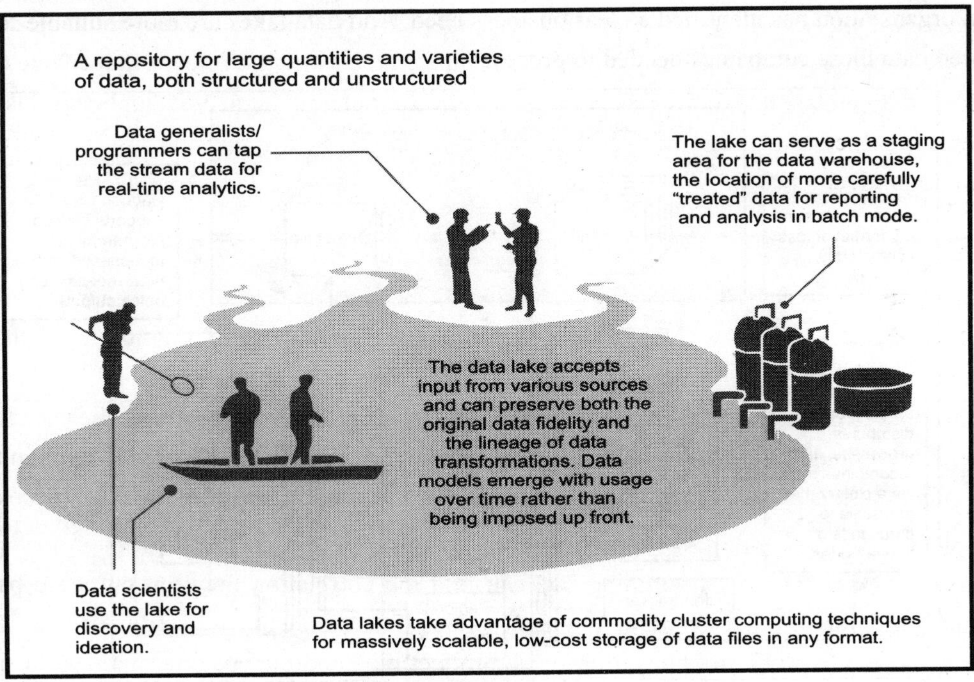

Figure. 1.6 : The Concept of Data Lakes

Hadoop allows the hospital's disparate records to be stored in their native formats for later parsing, rather than forcing all-or-nothing integration up front as in a data warehousing scenario. Preserving the native format also helps maintain data provenance and fidelity, so different analyses can be performed using different contexts. The data lake has made possible several data analysis projects, including the ability to predict the likelihood of readmissions and take preventive measures to reduce the number of readmissions.

A data repository is a storage space for researchers to deposit data sets associated with their research. And if you're an author seeking to comply with a journal data sharing policy, you'll need to identify a suitable repository for your data.

Like the hospital, enterprises across industries are starting to extract and place data for analytics into a single Hadoop-based repository without first transforming the data the way they would need to for a relational data warehouse. The basic concepts behind Hadoop3 were devised by Google to meet its need for a flexible, cost-effective data processing model that could scale as data volumes grew faster than ever. Yahoo, Facebook, Netflix, and others whose business models also are based on managing enormous data volumes quickly adopted similar methods. Costs were certainly a factor, as Hadoop can be 10 to 100 times less expensive to deploy than conventional data warehousing. Another driver of adoption has been the opportunity to defer labour-intensive schema development and data cleanup until an organization has identified a clear business need. And data lakes are more suitable for the less-structured data these companies needed to process.

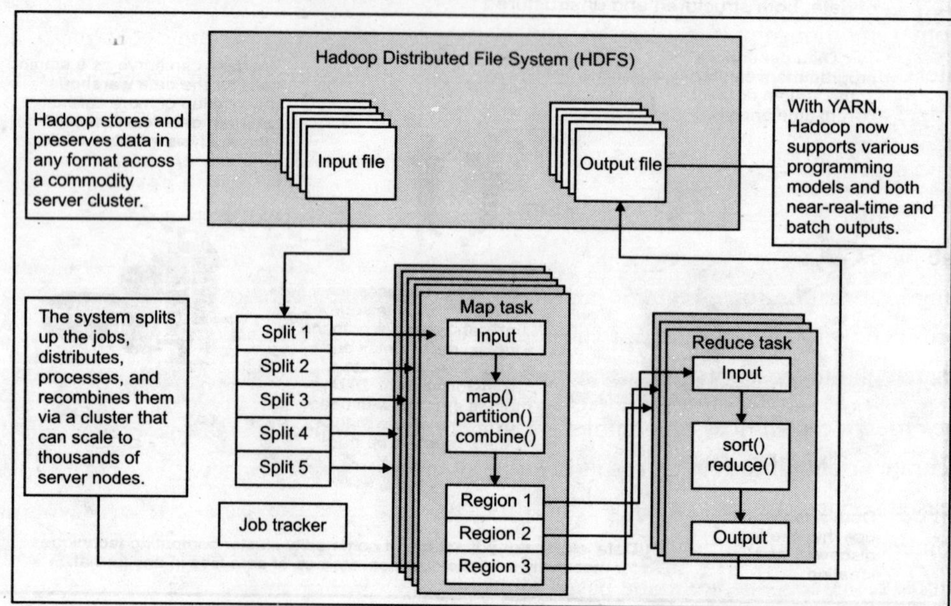

Figure. 1.7: A basic Hadoop architecture for scalable data lake infrastructure

The contents of fig. 1.7 shall be better grasped when reader goes through the contents of of 3 and 4 of this book. The approach to data lakes is simple: instead of organising data in a siloed (like storing of food items in silo), prescriptive store, you can retain all types of data together in their original formats. Data lakes store both structured data – as contained in relational databases and spreadsheets - and unstructured data - such as social media, email and text documents. It can then be used far more rapidly and flexibly. This system allows users to run ad hoc queries, perform cross-source navigation, and make analytical decisions, all based on real-time information.

1.8 BIG DATA AND BUSINESS INTELLIGENCE (BI)

BI refers to the procedural and technical infrastructure that collects, stores, and analyzes the data produced by a company's activities. BI is a broad term that encompasses data mining, process analysis, performance benchmarking, and descriptive analytics.

Leveraging business intelligence to create business value is about aligning the BI capabilities with the core business processes of the firm to significantly improve business performance and profitability.

Business intelligence can help organizations transform data into insight and achieve higher levels of performance by:

1. Providing insights that can help pinpoint new revenue-generating opportunities and improve operational efficiencies and visibility across the organization Optimizing the return on existing business and IT investments such as data management, data mining, customer intelligence, customer relationship management and enterprise resource planning technology achieving greater compliance with government and regulatory guidelines. Enabling faster problem-solving and decision making at the strategic, operational and tactical levels by internal and external users.
2. Data quality has a direct and measurable impact on business process efficiency.
3. In the purchase to pay process, poor quality vendor data causes missing purchase contracts or pricing information for important materials leading to delays in the procuring vital goods. This can result in production material short-ages, use of non approved procurement channels and ultimately higher costs of goods sold.
4. In the order to cash process, incomplete or inaccurate customer records, incorrect credit limits, or inaccurate pricing information result in lower overall customer service, lost or delayed revenue, increased service costs and a huge effort by the customer service team to resolve without losing customers. Furthermore, inaccurate data result in incorrect management reporting meaning that vital business decisions are made based upon incorrect information.

5. Data is deemed of high quality if it correctly represents the real world to which it refers and meets business-driven metrics. Data quality is essential, but the level of quality and the related investment depends on an understanding of business and investment priorities. High-quality data must be complete, timely, accurate, consistent, relevant and reliable. Initiatives that only address portions of the data quality strategy are ineffective and costly in the long term and tend not to be aligned with overall business priorities. What is required is an ongoing program of improvements in all aspect of the enterprise ranging from data entry standards and measures to technical data validation routines to how business organization and structure changes are implemented.
6. The systematic analysis of data, or data profiling, gathers actionable and measurable information about its quality. Information gathered from data profiling activities is used to assess the overall health of the data and determine the direction of data quality initiatives.
7. Data cleansing is a continuous process that requires corrective actions throughout the data life-cycle. Data cleansing activities must have adequate and dedicated resources from both the business and technical support organizations. Business resources are critical to provide context and insight into potential data anomalies.
8. Data compliance consists of the ongoing processes to ensure adherence of data to both enterprise business rules, and to legal and regulatory requirements. Data compliance includes four areas, controls, audit, regulatory compliance and legal compliance.

1.8.1 Difference between BI and Big Data

Simply stated, the means to achieve the same end goal of data-driven decisions and greater business insight will most likely be different – such as the technologies, platforms, tools, models, processes, and skills. Some may argue that big data offers greater insights than BI because there's more data to work with, and there's some truth to that. However, be mindful that if you're still struggling to make BI "work" with your smaller data sets ("smaller" being a relative term), those struggles will only be amplified when you add big/more data. And as the old saying goes ' We must learn to walk before we can run.

1.8.2 Difference Between Big Data and Data Ware Housing

There is a lot of talk both within and outside the big data community: "What does the big data trend mean for my existing data warehouse?" The short answer is: Use the best tool for the job.

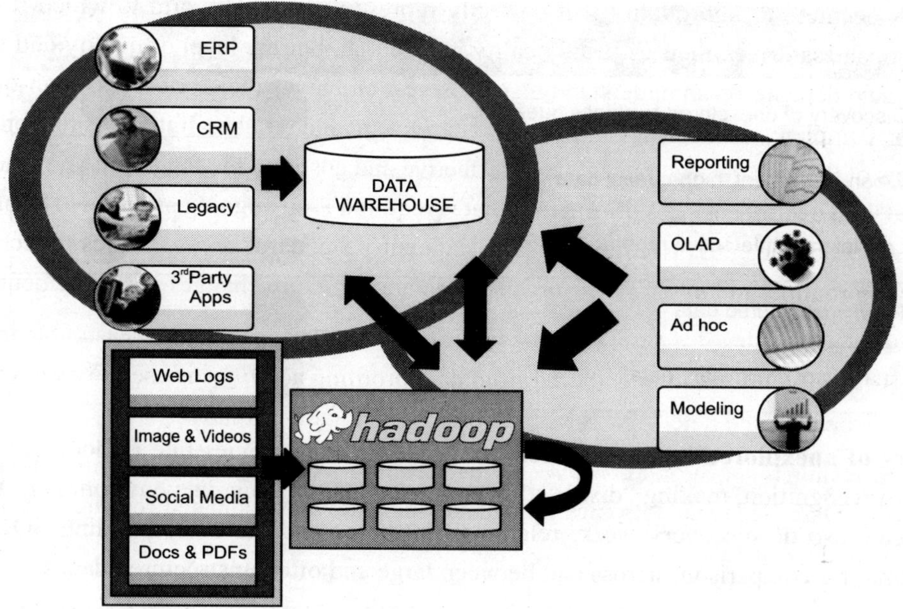

Figure. 1.8 : Difference Between Big data and Data Ware housing

The figure 1.8 illustrates how the data warehouse and big data environments can come together in an integrated and very complementary way. In this scenario, the Hadoop system can perform quickly. For instance, a high-tech company might decide to pull data from its social networking site and combine it with data from the data warehouse to update a customer's social network circle of friends. The environment might also use Hadoop to quickly "score" that person's social influence. Then that data will be provisioned back to the data warehouse so that, say, a campaign manager can view that person's influence score and re-segment him (or her) accordingly.

The example here is one of many potential uses for Hadoop and the data warehouse working together. The point to make here is that each system is doing what it's best designed to do. In the case of Hadoop, it's processing large amounts of social networking data quickly and in parallel. In the case of the data warehouse, it's availing that data to business users, knowledge workers, or data scientists who are using that data—and other data as well—to make business decisions.

While there are exceptions to every rule, big data and data warehouse technologies are optimized for different purposes. Again, the goal is to use these solutions for what they were designed to do. In other words: Use the best tool for the job.

BUSINESS REQUIRMENT	BIG DATA	DATA WAREHOUSE
Discovery of unexplored business question	●	●
Clean, consistent, high-quality data	◒	●
Low latency, interactive reports, OLAP	◒	●
Raw, unstructured data	●	
Analysis of preliminary data	●	

Discovery of unexplored business questions. Big data technologies like Hadoop are very good for fast pattern recognition, making "discovery" work very fast in a big data environment. While data warehouses can also do discovery work, relational databases and the corresponding SQL language aren't as optimal for comparisons across and between large and often unstructured data sets.

Clean, consistent, high-quality data. In terms of data quality, many data warehouses have integrated data quality functions built-in. The data used for analytics must be meaningful to end users. In big data environments, however, there could be a reason to provision data in its "raw" or unstructured format. Data quality can happen inside Hadoop—but, as of this writing, there aren't many data quality solutions for Hadoop so data cleansing might involve manual coding. For now, most companies prefer to make data quality a function of their analytics environment.

Low latency, interactive reports, OLAP. Data warehouses have typically been known as the answer for low-latency or interactive reporting. But with new data visualization tools, big data technologies are presenting an interesting new alternative for reporting directly against big data platforms.

Raw, unstructured data. Big data technologies are primed to process raw, unstructured data. They cannot only process it quickly, but they can store it cheaply and avail it to a range of projects locally. Data warehouses, on the other hand, often deal with aggregated data (which might have been aggregated using big data technologies and provisioned to the data warehouse). The process of "late binding" means that Hadoop can actually keep raw data and make it meaningful at the time of the query, meaning it might apply different rules to the data for different purposes.

1.9 BIG DATA TYPES

Thus Big Data includes huge volume, high velocity, and extensible variety of data. The data in it will be of three types.

1. Structured data : Relational data.

2, Semi Structured data : XML data.

3. Unstructured data : Word, PDF, Text, Media Logs.

1.9.1 Structured Data

It concerns all data which can be stored in database SQL in table with rows and columns. They have relational key and can be easily mapped into pre-designed fields. Today, those data are the most processed in development and the simplest way to manage information.

Structured data is often managed using Structured Query Language (SQL) – a programming language created for managing and querying data in relational database management systems. Originally developed by IBM in the early 1970s and later developed commercially by Relational Software, Inc. (now Oracle Corporation).

Structured data was a huge improvement over strictly paper-based unstructured systems, but life doesn't always fit into neat little boxes. As a result, the structured data always had to be supplemented by paper or microfilm storage. As technology performance has continued to improve, and prices have dropped, it was possible to bring into computing systems unstructured and semi-structured data.

1.9.2 Characteristics of Structured Data

Structured data first depends on creating a data model – a model of the types of business data that will be recorded and how they will be stored, processed and accessed. This includes defining what fields of data will be stored and how that data will be stored: data type (numeric, currency, alphabetic, name, date, address) and any restrictions on the data input (number of characters; restricted to certain terms such as Mr., Ms. or Dr.; M or F).

Structured data has the advantage of being easily entered, stored, queried and analyzed. At one time, because of the high cost and performance limitations of storage, memory and processing, relational databases and spreadsheets using structured data were the only way to effectively manage data. Anything that couldn't fit into a tightly organized structure would have to be stored on paper in a filing cabinet. But structured datas represent only 5 to 10% of all informatics data.

1.9.3 Structured Data Technology Standards

SQL has been a standard of the American National Standards Institute since 1986. It is managed by Inter National Committee for Information Technology Standards (INCITS) Technical Committee DM 32 – Data Management and Interchange. The committee has two task groups, one for databases and the other for metadata. HP, CA, IBM, Microsoft, Oracle, Sybase (SAP) and Tera-data all participate, as well as several federal government agencies. Both of the committee project documents have links to further information on each project. SQL became an International Organization for Standards (ISO) standard in 1987. The published standards are available for purchase from the ANSI Standards Store, under the INCITS/ISO/IEC 9075 classification.

1.9.4 Semistructured Data

Semi-structured data is information that doesn't reside in a relational database but that does have some organizational properties that make it easier to analyze. With some process you can store them in relation database (it could be very hard for some kind of semi structured data), but the semi structure exist to ease space, clarity or compute…

Examples of semi-structured : CSV , XML and JSON documents are semi structured documents, **NoSQL databases are considered as semi structured.**

1.9.5 Unstructured Data

Unstructured Data (or unstructured information) refers to information that either does not have a pre-defined data model or is not organized in a pre-defined manner. Unstructured information is typically text-heavy, but may contain data such as dates, numbers, and facts as well. This results in irregularities and ambiguities that make it difficult to understand using traditional programs as compared to data stored in fielded form in databases or annotated (semantically tagged) in documents.

Techniques such as data mining, Natural Language Processing(NLP), and text analytics provide different methods to find patterns in, or otherwise interpret, this information. Common techniques for structuring text usually involve manual tagging with metadata or part-of-speech tagging for further text mining-based structuring.

Examples of "unstructured data" may include books, journals, documents, metadata, health records, audio, video, analog data, images, files, and unstructured text such as the body of an e-mail message, Web page, or word-processor document.

Unstructured data is data that does not follow a specified format for big data. If 20 percent of the data available to enterprises is structured data, the other 80 percent is unstructured. Unstructured data is really most of the data that you will encounter.

The unstructured data growing quickiest than the other, and their exploitation could help in business decision.

1.9.6 Standards on Unstructured Data

A group called the Organization for the Advancement of Structured Information Standards (OASIS) has published the Unstructured Information Management Architecture (UIMA) standard. The UIMA « defines platform-independent data representations and interfaces for software components or services called **analytics**, which analyze unstructured information and assign semantics to regions of that unstructured information. »

Many industry watchers say that Hadoop has become the de facto industry standard for managing Big Data.

1.9.7 Sources of unstructured big data

Unstructured data is everywhere. In fact, most individuals and organizations conduct their lives around unstructured data. Just as with structured data, unstructured data is either machine generated or human generated.

Here are some examples of machine-generated unstructured data:

1. **Satellite images**: This includes weather data or the data that the government captures in its satellite surveillance imagery. Just think about Google Earth, and you get the picture.
2. **Scientific data**: This includes seismic imagery, atmospheric data, and high energy physics.
3. **Photographs and video**: This includes security, surveillance, and traffic video.
4. Radar or sonar data: This includes vehicular, meteorological, and oceanographic seismic profiles.

The following list shows a few examples of human-generated unstructured data:

- **Text internal to your company**: Think of all the text within documents, logs, survey results, and e-mails. Enterprise information actually represents a large percent of the text information in the world today.
- **Social media data:** This data is generated from the social media platforms such *as YouTube, Facebook, Twitter, LinkedIn, and Flickr.*
- **Mobile data**: This includes data such as text messages and location information.
- **Website content**: This comes from any site delivering unstructured content, like *YouTube, Flickr, or Instagram.*

Of the useful data, IDC estimates that in 2013 perhaps 5% was especially valuable, or "target rich." That percentage should more than double by 2020 as enterprises take advantage of new Big Data and analytics technologies and new data sources, and apply them to new parts of the organization.

1.10 ANALYTICS

Analytics is the discovery and communication of meaningful patterns in data. Especially valuable in areas rich with recorded information, analytics relies on the simultaneous application of statistics, computer programming and operations research to quantify performance. Analytics often favors data visualization to communicate insight.

Firms may commonly apply analytics to business data, to describe, predict, and improve business performance. Specifically, areas within analytics include predictive analytics, enterprise decision management, retail analytics, store assortment and stock-keeping unit optimization, marketing optimization and marketing mix modeling, web analytics, sales force sizing and optimization, price and promotion modeling, predictive science, credit risk analysis, and fraud analytics. Since analytics can require extensive computation (see big data), the algorithms and software used for analytics harness the most current methods in computer science, statistics, and mathematics.

In a nutshell, analytics is the scientific process of transforming data into insight for making better decisions.

By using techniques such as mathematical modeling to analyze complex situations, analytics gives executives the power to make more effective decisions and build more productive systems based on:

1. More complete data
2. Consideration of all available options
3. Careful predictions of outcomes and estimates of risk
4. The latest decision tools and techniques

To achieve these results, analytics professionals draw upon the latest analytical technologies, including:

1. Simulation Giving you the ability to try out approaches and test ideas for improvement
2. Optimization Narrowing your choices to the very best when there are virtually innumerable feasible options and comparing them is difficult
3. Probability and Statistics Helping you measure risk, mine data to find valuable connections and insights, test conclusions, and make reliable forecasts

Data warehousing has been around for thirty years providing business intelligence for structured operational data. The source of this data, for all intents and purposes, comes from Relational Database

Management Systems (RDBMS). Warehousing is generally costly and proprietary where many of the RDBMS providers also offer such solutions. Data Lakers on the contrary are relatively new (around five years) and are routinely based on commodity hardware and open-source projects (e.g. Hadoop). Typically, the source of this data is, well… anything and everything, but primarily semi-structured than unstructured respectively.

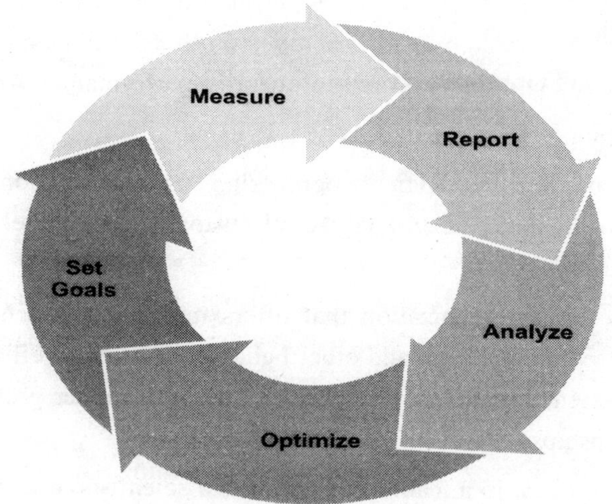

The goal of Data Analytics (big and small) is to get actionable insights resulting in smarter decisions and better business outcomes. How you architect business technologies and design data analytics processes to get valuable, actionable insights varies.

It is critical to design and build a data warehouse / business intelligence (BI) architecture that provides a flexible, multi-faceted analytical ecosystem, optimized for efficient ingestion and analysis of large and diverse datasets.

There are three types of data analysis:

1. Predictive (forecasting)
2. Descriptive (business intelligence and data mining)
3. Prescriptive (optimization and simulation)

1.10.1 Predictive Analytics

Predictive analytics turns data into valuable, actionable information. Predictive analytics uses data to determine the probable future outcome of an event or a likelihood of a situation occurring.

Predictive analytics encompasses a variety of statistical techniques from modelling, machine learning, data mining and game theory that analyze current and historical facts to make predictions about future events.

In business, predictive models exploit patterns found in historical and transactional data to identify risks and opportunities. Models capture relationships among many factors to allow assessment of risk or potential associated with a particular set of conditions, guiding decision making for candidate transactions.

Three basic cornerstones of predictive analytics are:

1. Predictive modelling
2. Decision Analysis and Optimization
3. Transaction Profiling

An example of using predictive analytics is optimizing customer relationship management systems. They can help enable an organization to analyze all customer data therefore exposing patterns that predict customer behavior.

Another example is for an organization that offers multiple products, predictive analytics can help analyze customers' spending, usage and other behavior, leading to efficient cross sales, or selling additional products to current customers. This directly leads to higher profitability per customer and stronger customer relationships.

An organization must invest in a team of experts (data scientists) and create statistical algorithms for finding and accessing relevant data. The data analytics team works with business leaders to design a strategy for using predictive information.

1.10.2 Descriptive Analytics

Descriptive analytics looks at data and analyzes past events for insight as to how to approach the future. Descriptive analytics looks at past performance and understands that performance by mining historical data to look for the reasons behind past success or failure. Almost all management reporting such as sales, marketing, operations, and finance, uses this type of post-mortem analysis.

Descriptive models quantify relationships in data in a way that is often used to classify customers or prospects into groups. Unlike predictive models that focus on predicting a single customer behavior (such as credit risk), descriptive models identify many different relationships between customers or products. Descriptive models do not rank-order customers by their likelihood of taking a particular action the way predictive models do.

Descriptive models can be used, for example, to categorize customers by their product preferences and life stage. Descriptive modelling tools can be utilized to develop further models that can simulate large number of individualized agents and make predictions.

For example, descriptive analytics examines historical electricity usage data to help plan power needs and allow electric companies to set optimal prices.

1.10.3 Prescriptive Analytics

Prescriptive analytics automatically synthesizes big data, mathematical sciences, business rules, and machine learning to make predictions and then suggests decision options to take advantage of the predictions.

Prescriptive analytics goes beyond predicting future outcomes by also suggesting actions to benefit from the predictions and showing the decision maker the implications of each decision option. Prescriptive analytics not only anticipates what will happen and when it will happen, but also why it will happen.

Further, prescriptive analytics can suggest decision options on how to take advantage of a future opportunity or mitigate a future risk and illustrate the implication of each decision option. In practice, prescriptive analytics can continually and automatically process new data to improve prediction accuracy and provide better decision options.

Prescriptive analytics synergistically combines data, business rules, and mathematical models. The data inputs to prescriptive analytics may come from multiple sources, internal (inside the organization) and external (social media, et al.). The data may also be structured, which includes numerical and categorical data, as well as unstructured data, such as text, images, audio, and video data, including big data. Business rules define the business process and include constraints, preferences, policies, best practices, and boundaries. Mathematical models are techniques derived from mathematical sciences and related disciplines including applied statistics, machine learning, operations research, and natural language processing.

For example, prescriptive analytics can benefit healthcare strategic planning by using analytics to leverage operational and usage data combined with data of external factors such as economic data, population demographic trends and population health trends, to more accurately plan for future capital investments such as new facilities and equipment utilization as well as understand the trade-offs between adding additional beds and expanding an existing facility versus building a new one.

Another example is energy and utilities. Natural gas prices fluctuate dramatically depending upon supply, demand, econometrics, geo-politics, and weather conditions. Gas producers, transmission (pipeline) companies and utility firms have a keen interest in more accurately predicting gas prices so that they can lock in favorable terms while hedging downside risk. Prescriptive analytics can accurately predict prices by modelling internal and external variables simultaneously and also provide decision options and show the impact of each decision option.

1.11 INDUSTRY EXAMPLES OF BIG DATA

Big data involves the data produced by different devices and applications. Here are four powerful Big Data application examples that can help you on your way.

1.11.1 Fraud detection

For businesses whose operations involve any type of claims or transaction processing, fraud detection is one of the most compelling Big Data application examples. Historically, fraud detection on the fly has proven an elusive goal. In most cases, fraud is discovered long after the fact, at which point the damage has been done and all that's left is to minimize the harm and adjust policies to prevent it from happening again. Big Data platforms that can analyze claims and transactions in real time, identifying large-scale patterns across many transactions or detecting anomalous behavior from an individual user, can change the fraud detection game.

1.11.2 IT log analytics

IT solutions and IT departments generate an enormous quantity of logs and trace data. In the absence of a Big Data solution, much of this data must go unexamined: organizations simply don't have the manpower or resource to churn through all that information by hand, let alone in real time. With a Big Data solution in place, however, those logs and trace data can be put to good use. Within this list of Big Data application examples, IT log analytics is the most broadly applicable. Any organization with a large IT department will benefit from the ability to quickly identify large-scale patterns to help in diagnosing and preventing problems. Similarly, any organization with a large IT department will appreciate the ability to identify incremental performance optimization opportunities.

1.11.3 Call Center Analytics

Now we turn to the customer-facing Big Data application examples, of which call center analytics are particularly powerful. What's going on in a customer's call center is often a great barometer and influencer of market sentiment, but without a Big Data solution, much of the insight that a call center can provide will be overlooked or discovered too late. Big Data solutions can help identify recurring problems or customer and staff behavior patterns on the fly not only by making sense of time/quality resolution metrics, but also by capturing and processing call content itself.

1.11.4 Social Media Analysis

Of the customer-facing Big Data application examples we could discuss, analysis of social media activity is one of the most important. Everyone and their mothers are on social media these days, whether they're "liking" company pages on Facebook or tweeting complaints about products on Twitter. A Big Data solution built to harvest and analyze social media activity, like IBM's Cognos Consumer Insights, a point solution running on IBM's BigInsights Big Data platform, can make sense of the chatter. Social media can provide real-time insights into how the market is responding to products and campaigns. With those insights, companies can adjust their pricing, promotion, and campaign placement on the fly for optimal results.

1.11.5 Improving Healthcare and Public Health

The computing power of big data analytics enables us to decode entire DNA strings in minutes and will allow us to find new cures and better understand and predict disease patterns. Just think of what happens when all the individual data from smart watches and wearable devices can be used to apply it to millions of people and their various diseases. The clinical trials of the future won't be limited by small sample sizes but could potentially include everyone! Big data techniques are already being used to monitor babies in a specialist premature and sick baby unit. By recording and analyzing every heart beat and breathing pattern of every baby, the unit was able to develop algorithms that can now predict infections 24 hours before any physical symptoms appear. That way, the team can intervene early and save fragile babies in an environment where every hour counts. What's more, big data analytics allow us to monitor and predict the developments of epidemics and disease outbreaks. Integrating data from medical records with social media analytics enables us to monitor flu outbreaks in real-time, simply by listening to what people are saying, i.e. "Feeling rubbish today - in bed with a cold".

1.11.6 The Role of Big Data in Medicine

The data generated by medical care and medically relevant research are rapidly becoming bigger and more complex, particularly with the advent of new technologies. Our ability to advance medical care and efficiently translate science into modern medicine is bounded by our capacity to access and process these big data. From human genetics and pathogen genomics to routine clinical documentation, from internal imaging to motion capture, from digital epidemiology to pharmacokinetics, and from treatment pathways to life course assessment, the big Vs of Big Data - volume, variety, velocity and veracity - abound in medicine. Statistical, mathematical, visualisation, and computational approaches, from a wide range of disciplines, as well systems for innovative ICT-based interventions are needed to keep apace of the complexity in Big Data and to advance medicine.

The role of big data in medicine is one where we can build better health profiles and better predictive models around individual patients so that we can better diagnose and treat disease.

As per Dr. Eric Schadt (the founding director of the Icahn Institute for Genomics and Multiscale Biology at New York's Mount Sinai Health System), one of the main limitations with medicine today and in the pharmaceutical industry is our understanding of the biology of disease. Big data comes into play around aggregating more and more information around multiple scales for what constitutes a disease—from the DNA, proteins, and metabolites to cells, tissues, organs, organisms, and ecosystems. Those are the scales of the biology that we need to be modeling by integrating big data. If we do that, the models will evolve, the models will build, and they will be more predictive for given individuals.

Wearable devices and engagement through mobile health apps represent the future—not just of the research of diseases, but of medicine. A normal individual who is generally healthy spends maybe ten minutes in front of a physician every year. What that physician can possibly score you on to assess the state of your health is very minimal. Unless something catastrophic is going on within you—lipid levels that are way off the charts or glucose levels or something extreme—they're not doing much to assess what your state of well-being is, and the information stored in medical records is not extensive enough.

What the wearable-device revolution provides is a way to longitudinally monitor your state—with respect to many different dimensions of your health—to provide a much better, much more accurate profile of who you are, what your baseline is, and how deviations from that baseline may predict a disease state or sliding into a disease state. That means we'll be able to intervene sooner to prevent you from that kind of slide. That sort of modeling would be impossible unless you could phenotype individuals on a longitudinal and long-term basis.

And while the wearable devices today are in this more recreational-grade state, they're changing incredibly rapidly into research grade and ultimately clinical grade. There are already glucose monitors. Individuals can wear and that interface with digital apps, which then connect directly with healthcare providers based on what they're seeing with your glucose profiles. You'll see that kind of sensoring get better and better, providing higher and higher grades and better and better profiles on individuals over time.

1.11.7 Science and Technology

The Large Hadron Collider experiments represent about 150 million sensors delivering data 40 million times per second. There are nearly 600 million collisions per second. After filtering and refraining from recording more than 99.99995% of these streams, there are 100 collisions of interest per second.

As a result, only working with less than 0.001% of the sensor stream data, the data flow from all four LHC experiments represents 25 petabytes annual rate before replication (as of 2012). This becomes nearly 200 petabytes after replication.

If all sensor data were recorded in LHC, the data flow would be extremely hard to work with. The data flow would exceed 150 million petabytes annual rate, or nearly 500 exabytes per day, before replication. To put the number in perspective, this is equivalent to 500 quintillion (5×1020) bytes per day, almost 200 times more than all the other sources combined in the world.

The Square Kilometre Array is a radio telescope built of thousands of antennas. It is expected to be operational by 2024. Collectively, these antennas are expected to gather 14 exabytes and store one petabyte per day. It is considered one of the most ambitious scientific projects ever undertaken.[citation needed]

Big data sets come with algorithmic challenges that previously did not exist. Hence, there is a need to fundamentally change the processing ways.

Given below are some other fields that come under the umbrella of Big Data.

1. Stock Exchange Data : The stock exchange data holds information about the 'buy' and 'sell' decisions made on a share of different companies made by the customers.
2. Power Grid Data : The power grid data holds information consumed by a particular node with respect to a base station.
3. Metrological and Transport Data : Transport data includes model, capacity, distance and availability of a vehicle.
4. Search Engine Data and Social Web Data : Search engines retrieve lots of data from different databases.
5. Social, Census and Meta-morphical Data
6. Financial Services organizations are using data mined from customer interactions to slice and dice their users into finely tuned segments. This enables these financial institutions to create increasingly relevant and sophisticated offers.
7. Advertising and marketing agencies are tracking social media to understand responsiveness to campaigns, promotions, and other advertising mediums.
8. Insurance companies are using Big Data analysis to see which home insurance applications can be immediately processed, and which ones need a validating in-person visit from an agent.
9. By embracing social media, retail organizations are engaging brand advocates, changing the perception of brand antagonists, and even enabling enthusiastic customers to sell their products.
10. Hospitals are analyzing medical data and patient records to predict those patients that are likely to seek readmission within a few months of discharge. The hospital can then intervene in hopes of preventing another costly hospital stay.
11. Web-based businesses are developing information products that combine data gathered from customers to offer more appealing recommendations and more successful coupon programs.

12. Managing data coming from multiple sources can be very challenging. Data must be linked, connected, and correlated so users can query and process it effectively.
13. Factory work and Cyber-physical systems may have a 6C system:
14. Connection (sensor and networks)
15. Cloud (computing and data on demand)
16. Cyber (model and memory)
17. Content/context (meaning and correlation)
18. Community (sharing and collaboration)
19. Customization (personalization and value)

1.12 BIG DATA AND DATA RISK

According to Bernard Marr (strategic performance consultant, and analytics, KPI, and big data guru) "As with any business initiative, a big data project involves an element of risk. Any project can fail for any number of reasons: bad management, under-budgeting, or a lack of relevant skills. However, big data projects bring their own specific risks."

Due to the advanced technology often needed and the relative newness of the skillsets required to truly "think big" (or as I prefer to say, "think smart") with data, care must be taken at every step of a big data project to ensure you don't stumble into pitfalls which could lead to wasted time and money, or even legal trouble.

1. **Data Security**

   This risk is obvious and often uppermost in our minds when we are considering the logistics of data collection and analysis. Data theft is a rampant and growing area of crime – and attacks are getting bigger and more damaging. In fact five of the six most damaging data thefts of all time (eBay, JP Morgan Chase, Adobe, Target, and Evernote) were carried out within the last two years.

   The bigger your data, the bigger the target it presents to criminals with the tools to steal and sell it. In the case of Target, hackers stole credit and debit card information of 40 million customers, as well as personal identifying information such as email and geographical addresses of up to 110 million people. In March, a federal judge approved a settlement in which Target would pay $10 million into a settlement fund, from which payments of up to $10,000 would be made to everyone affected by the breach.

2. **Data Privacy**

   Closely related to the issue of security is privacy. But in addition to ensuring that people's personal data are safe from criminals, you need to be sure that the sensitive information you are storing and collecting isn't going to be divulged through less malevolent but equally damaging misuse by yourself or by people to whom you have delegated responsibility for analyzing and reporting on it.

   Failing to follow applicable data protection laws can lead to expensive lawsuits and even prison, depending on what sort of data you are using and the jurisdiction you are in. Last year,

3. **Costs**

   Data collection, aggregation, storage, analysis, and reporting all cost money. On top of this, there will be compliancy costs – to avoid falling foul on the issues I raised in the previous point. These costs can be mitigated by careful budgeting during the planning stages, but getting it wrong at that point can lead to spiralling costs, potentially negating any value added to your bottom line by your data-driven initiative. This is why "starting with strategy" is so vital. A well-developed strategy will clearly set out what you intend to achieve and the benefits that can be gained so they can be balanced against the resources allocated to the project. One bank that I worked with was worried about the costs of storing and maintaining all the data it was collecting to the point that it was considering pulling the plug on one particular analytics project, as the costs looked likely to exceed any potential savings. By identifying and eliminating irrelevant data from the project, the bank was able to bring costs back under control and achieve its objectives.

4. **Bad Analytics**

   Aka "getting it wrong." Misinterpreting the patterns shown by your data and drawing causal links where there is in fact merely random coincidence is an obvious pitfall. Sales data may show a rise following a major sporting event, prompting you to draw a link between sports fans and your products or services, when in fact the rise is based on there being more people in town, and the rise would be equally dramatic after a large live music event.

   In addition, care must be taken to avoid confirmation bias – easily imposed when an analyst comes to a project with predetermined ideas about what they are looking for and is blinded to insights from the data that go against these preconceived notions. The only way to protect against this is to ensure that you are implementing all best practice procedures from top to bottom throughout your project.

5. **Bad Data**

   Many data projects that start off on the wrong foot by collecting irrelevant, out of date, or erroneous data gets impounded heavily. This usually comes down to insufficient time being spent on designing the project strategy. The big data gold rush has led to a "collect everything and think about analyzing it later" approach at many organizations. This not only adds to the growing cost of storing the data and ensuring compliance, it leads to large amounts of data that can become outdated very quickly.

   The real danger here is falling behind your competition. If you are not analyzing the right data, you won't be drawing the right insights that will provide value. Meanwhile, your competitors most likely will be running their own data projects. And if they are getting it right, they'll take the lead. A healthcare client I recently worked with created a 217-page report for senior management. A lot of the data in the report would have been useful, but it was drowned out by irrelevant background noise. Working with them, I was able to show them how to cut the report down to 20 pages, mostly infographics, which clearly showed the relevant data while omitting a lot of the noise.

6. **Rules and Regulations**

   The regulatory climate has evolved in response to these events, which in turn increases the compliance risk associated with big data. For example, the most recent European Union Data Protection Regulation, released in January 2012, extends the scope of the EU data protection law to all foreign companies that process personal data of European Union residents.6 In an increasingly globalized economy, the rules are becoming ever more complex for financial institutions – and, for that matter, all organizations with customers or operations in more than one country – that must now comply with multiple regulations about how they store, access, and share personal information.

1.12.1 Risk Management

From a risk management perspective, any effort to improve the management of today's large reservoirs of data must approach the challenge on both fronts:

1. it must mitigate the strategic risks associated with using big data initiatives to boost performance, improve sales, and achieve other strategic goals; and
2. it must develop ways to use big data to perform the risk, audit, and compliance functions more efficiently. In other words, the objective is to both "increase the gain" and "reduce the pain."

While Big Data is already being embraced in many fields, risk managers have yet to harness its power. Big Data technology has revolutionary potential. It can improve the predictive power of risk models, exponentially improve system response times and effectiveness, provide more extensive risk coverage, and generate significant cost savings.

Over 90% of the world's data has been created in the last two years . Forward-thinking industries and organisations have already begun to capitalise on this gold mine.

Big Data technologies can help Risk teams gain more accurate risk intelligence, drawn from a variety of data sources, in almost real-time.

Within the financial services industry, they can allow asset managers, banks and insurance ompanies to proactively detect potential risks, react faster and more effectively, and make robust decisions informed by thousands of risk variables. Already used widely across other sectors - particularly in eCommerce -- Big Data is a true game changer.

The era of data warehouses - with their static structures and limited interaction paths - is over. The complexity and variety of sources now available (including social media, email, sensor data, business apps, archives and documents), and the speed required for retrieval and analysis, demand fresh new approaches.

1.12.2 Applying Big Data to Risk Management : 'Noise' or 'Signal'

For example: imagine you want to conduct a credit check on a new customer. Data lakes allow a risk profile to be developed based on a range of data - including customer credit reports, spending habits, social media profiles, and credit card repayment rates – in seconds.

Rather than manually - and laboriously - track staff trading actions, data lakes allow the retrieval of an instant snapshot of activity, including information from chat room sites, mobile phones, and even door swipe cards. Suspicious activity can be identified and stopped as it is happening, before incurring fines and devastating damage to your bank's reputation.

Big Data technologies will allow the development of models that will support everyday Risk Officer decision-making. Able to process enormous amounts of data in fast timeframes, the technologies can also accommodate new requirements for scenario stress tests at the trade, counterparty and portfolio levels.

The majority of benefits – and challenges - offered by Big Data stem from its massive volume and variety (Fig.1.5). However, different risk domains stand to benefit from Big Data technologies in diverse ways. Big Data can be targeted to an organisation's particular needs - whether they are for greater volume, variety, velocity or veracity - and strategically applied to enhance different risk domains. Big data offers significant opportunities in most risk domains.

Risk Area	Volume	Velocity	Variety	Veracity
Credit Risk				
Market Risk				
Operational Risk				
Compilance Risk				
Asset-Liability Risk Management				
Integrated Risk Management				

Figure. 1.8 : Impact of Big. Data in various risk domains.

Each organization will develop its own particular approach for doing this. According to Richard Anderson (Managing Director of Crowe Horwath Global Risk Consulting in London) in general, however, a successful approach will occur over the course of five broad phases. Note, that these five phases often overlap and do not necessarily occur in a step-by-step sequence. In addition, both risk management professionals and the organization's senior management have specific tasks they must accomplish in each phase in order to make the process work.

Phase 1: Identify Roles and Responsibilities

The roles of risk, audit, and compliance professionals in supporting and developing big data approaches should be clearly defined at the outset. As new strategic, marketing, customer-service, and operational initiatives are launched and championed by other groups, it is essential that risk and compliance professionals be engaged in the process of determining if there are issues that require C-suite or board-level attention. Just as a manufacturer would not launch a new product without extensive testing, any new information-driven initiative should be thoroughly tested to identify potential strategic and regulatory compliance risk.

Concurrent with this role, risk and compliance professionals should engage education and awareness building in order to develop a proper focus on risk among marketing, research and development, and other functions that use big data. At the same time, they should tap into the capabilities of these groups to help them to exploit available data to improve the efficiency of the audit and compliance processes. Finally, the organization's senior executive and management team must exercise leadership so that risk management professionals are prepared to address both sides of the risk-related uses of big data. At the same time, they are responsible for making sure the board understands these issues, so that the next phase can be performed effectively.

Phase 2: Define Goals and Priorities

Another critical early step is clearly defining and prioritizing the goals the organization hopes to achieve by using big data. As with any high-level function, this definition must be directed at the executive level with general board oversight, but its success ultimately will depend on those who are actually involved in developing the big data approach for input and expertise. These contributors include the potential users of big data – strategists, marketers, researchers, and operational managers – as well as the IT team and the risk and compliance professionals.

Phase 3: Assess Critical Data Issues

With goals and priorities established, a closely related activity is assessing the critical data-related issues that are likely to arise as these initiatives are undertaken. These issues may include matters such as privacy concerns, the degree of transparency required for regulatory compliance, existing data silos, necessary firewalls that either exist or must be constructed, and existing firewalls that should be removed. Both the risk management and executive teams should be actively involved in this effort – the risk management professionals providing hands-on expertise and counsel and the executive teams making sure the issues are being addressed in ways that comply with the organization's long-term strategies and governing principles.

Phase 4: Identify Key Risk Indicators

As big data initiatives are developed, the critical data issues that were identified upfront will help to inform the risk management team as it identifies key risk indicators to be monitored. The goals are to spot troublesome trends as they start to emerge in the data and to get ahead of the curve before performance problems arise. In this effort, risk management professionals should be particularly alert to the need to play both reactive and proactive roles in managing big data risk. In addition to monitoring and mitigating risks associated with the use of big data in various business functions such as marketing, hiring, and product development, they should be alert to opportunities to employ big data proactively as risk managers. For example, internal auditors and risk managers in financial institutions can effectively use big data techniques to identify fraud, money laundering, or other prohibited activities by identifying connections among various third parties that might not otherwise be apparent.

Phase 5: Identify Opportunities to Add Value

In businesses that are inherently data-intensive, it is possible to generate added value in the risk management element by finding new ways to derive meaningful analysis from large quantities of data. For example, one insurance brokerage recently uncovered a large-scale, yet still developing, insurance fraud scheme by employing big data techniques to discover that various individuals – with completely different names and no apparent relationship – were all connected to known fraudsters by way of interconnected telephone numbers, addresses, and company names. This ability to capture several sets of data, cross-check across various data types, and then match both internal and external data would not have been available to the brokerage just a few years ago. Post-crisis, financial institutions are now expected to have thorough knowledge of their clients. Increasingly, forward-thinking banks - for example - will harness Big Data to develop more robust predictive indicators in the credit risk domain. New data sources - including social media and marketing databases -can be used to gain greater visibility into customer behaviour.

These sources can reveal startling information: a costly divorce, an Following several recent scandals, the industry has zero tolerance for money laundering/terrorism financing. Fines have been huge, recently reaching a record $8.9bn for one French bank found to be working with countries subject to US sanctions.

The high cost of money laundering cases has prompted banks to seek new ways to address the severe limitations in current anti-money laundering risk management.

Traditional approaches to antimony laundering remain dependent on rule-based, descriptive analytics to process structured data. This system clearly has limitations - without automated algorithms, detecting information within the wealth of data requires laborious keyword searches and Credit Risk: Better Predictive Power expensive purchase, a gambling problem.

Drawn from data lakes, this information can augment traditional data sources including financial, socio-demographic, internal payments and externals loss data. Together, the datasets can produce a highly robust, comprehensive risk indicator.

Rather than waiting to review loan clients' financial reports to discover loan-servicing problems, firms can utilise Big Data technologies to detect early warning signals by observing clients' on-going behaviours, and act in time.

1.13 BIG DATA TECHNOLOGIES

Big data technologies are important in providing more accurate analysis, which may lead to more concrete decision-making resulting in greater operational efficiencies, cost reductions, and reduced risks for the business. To harness the power of big data, you would require an infrastructure that can manage and process huge volumes of structured and unstructured data in real time and can protect data privacy and security.

There are various technologies in the market from different vendors including Amazon, IBM, Microsoft, etc., to handle big data. While looking into the technologies that handle big data, we examine the following two classes of technology:

1.13.1 Operational Big Data

NoSQL Big Data systems are designed to take advantage of new cloud computing architectures that have emerged over the past decade to allow massive computations to be run inexpensively and efficiently. This makes operational big data workloads much easier to manage, cheaper, and faster to implement. Some NoSQL systems can provide insights into patterns and trends based on real-time data with minimal coding and without the need for data scientists and additional infrastructure.

This include systems like ***MongoDB*** that provide operational capabilities for real-time, interactive workloads where data is primarily captured and stored. These are discussed in detail in chapter 2 of this book.

1.13.2 Analytical Big Data

This includes systems like Massively Parallel Processing (MPP) database systems and Map Reduce that provide analytical capabilities for retrospective and complex analysis that may touch most or all of the data.

MapReduce provides a new method of analyzing data that is complementary to the capabilities provided by SQL, and a system based on Map Reduce that can be scaled up from single servers to thousands of high and low end machines. This aspect is discussed in detail in chapter 3 of this Book.20

These two classes of technology are complementary and frequently deployed together. The major challenges associated with big data are as follows:

1. Capturing data Curation
2. Storage
3. Searching
4. Sharing
5. Transfer
6. Analysis
7. Presentation

Machine Learning: big data often doesn't ask why and simply detects patterns

Digital footprint: big data is often a cost-free by product of digital interaction

The growing maturity of the concept more starkly delineates the difference between big data and Business Intelligence:

- Business Intelligence uses descriptive statistics with data with high information density to measure things, detect trends, etc..

- Big data uses inductive statistics and concepts from nonlinear system identification to infer laws (regressions, nonlinear relationships, and causal effects) from large sets of data with low information density to reveal relationships and dependencies, or to perform predictions of outcomes and behaviors.

1.14 THE EVOLUTION OF BIG DATA ARCHITECTURE

1941 "Information explosion" (a term first used in 1941, according to the Oxford English Dictionary.

1958 IBM researcher Hans Peter Luhn defines Business Intelligence as "the ability to apprehend the interrelationships of presented facts in such a way as to guide action towards a desired goal."

1989 Possibly the first use of the term Big Data (without capitalization) in the way it is used today. International best-selling author Erik Larson pens an article for Harpers Magazine speculating on the origin of the junk mail he receives. He writes: "The keepers of big data say they are doing it for the consumer's benefit. But data have a way of being used for purposes other originally intended."

October 2000 Peter Lyman and Hal R. Varian at UC Berkeley publish "How Much Information?" It is the first comprehensive study to quantify, in computer storage terms, the total amount of new and original information (not counting copies) created in the world annually and stored in four physical media: paper, film, optical (CDs and DVDs), and magnetic. The study finds that in 1999, the world produced about 1.5 exabytes of unique information, or about 250 megabytes for every person on earth.

November 2000 Francis X. Diebold presents to the Eighth World Congress of the Econometric Society a paper titled "'Big Data' Dynamic Factor Models for Macroeconomic Measurement and Forecasting.."

In 2000, Seisint Inc. (now LexisNexis Group) developed a C++-based distributed file-sharing framework for data storage and query. The system stores and distributes structured, semi-structured, and unstructured data across multiple servers. Users can build queries in a C++ dialect called ECL. ECL uses an "apply schema on read" method to infer the structure of stored data when it is queried, instead of when it is stored. In 2004, LexisNexis acquired Seisint Inc. and in 2008 acquired ChoicePoint, Inc. and their high-speed parallel processing platform. The two platforms were merged into HPCC (or High-Performance Computing Cluster) Systems and in 2011, HPCC was open-sourced under the Apache v2.0 License. Currently, HPCC and Quantcast File System are the only publicly available platforms capable of analyzing multiple exabytes of data.

In 2004, Google published a paper on a process called MapReduce that uses a similar architecture. The MapReduce concept provides a parallel processing model, and an associated implementation was released to process huge amounts of data. With MapReduce, queries are split and distributed across parallel nodes and processed in parallel (the Map step). The results are then gathered and delivered (the Reduce step). The framework was very successful, so others wanted to replicate the algorithm. Therefore, an implementation of the MapReduce framework was adopted by an Apache open-source project named Hadoop.

MIKE2.0 is an open approach to information management that acknowledges the need for revisions due to big data implications identified in an article titled "Big Data Solution Offering".[38] The methodology addresses handling big data in terms of useful permutations of data sources, complexity in interrelationships, and difficulty in deleting (or modifying) individual records.[39]

Recent studies show that a multiple-layer architecture is one option to address the issues that big data presents. A distributed parallel architecture distributes data across multiple servers; these parallel execution environments can dramatically improve data processing speeds. This type of architecture inserts data into a parallel DBMS, which implements the use of MapReduce and Hadoop frameworks. This type of framework looks to make the processing power transparent to the end user by using a front-end application server.

Big Data Analytics for Manufacturing Applications can be based on a 5C architecture (connection, conversion, cyber, cognition, and configuration).

The data lake allows an organization to shift its focus from centralized control to a shared model to respond to the changing dynamics of information management. This enables quick segregation of data into the data lake, thereby reducing the overhead time.

February 2001 Doug Laney, an analyst with the Meta Group, publishes a research note titled "3D Data Management: Controlling Data Volume, Velocity, and Variety." A decade later, the "3Vs" have become the generally-accepted three defining dimensions of big data, although the term itself does not appear in Laney's note.

2005 Commentators announce that we are witnessing the birth of "Web 2.0" – the user-generated web where the majority of content will be provided by users of services, rather than the service providers themselves. This is achieved through integration of traditional HTML-style web pages with vast back-end databases built on SQL. 5.5 million people are already using Facebook, launched a year earlier, to upload and share their own data with friends.

This year also sees the creation of Hadoop – the open source framework created specifically for storage and analysis of Big Data sets. Its flexibility makes it particularly useful for managing the unstructured data (voice, video, raw text etc) which we are increasingly generating and collecting.

September 2005 Tim O'Reilly publishes "What is Web 2.0" in which he asserts that "data is the next Intel inside." O'Reilly: and 'SQL is the new HTML.' Database management is a core competency of Web 2.0 companies, so much so that we have sometimes referred to these applications as 'infoware' rather than merely software."

March 2007 John F. Gantz, David Reinsel and other researchers at IDC release a white paper titled "The Expanding Digital Universe: A Forecast of Worldwide Information Growth through 2010 " It is the first study to estimate and forecast the amount of digital data created and replicated each year. IDC estimates that in 2006, the world created 161 exabytes of data and forecasts that between 2006 and 2010, the information added annually to the digital universe will increase more than six fold to 988 exabytes, or doubling every 18 months. According to the 2010 and 2012 releases of the same study, the amount of digital data created annually surpassed this forecast, reaching 1227 exabytes in 2010, and growing to 2837 exabytes in 2012.

June 2008 Cisco releases the "Cisco Visual Networking Index – Forecast and Methodology, 2007–2012 " estimates IP traffic in 2012 at just over half a zettabyte and notes it "has increased eightfold over the past 5 years."

December 2008 Randal E. Bryant, Randy H. Katz, and Edward D. Lazowska publish "Big-Data Computing: Creating Revolutionary Breakthroughs in Commerce, Science and Society ." They write: "Just as search engines have transformed how we access information, other forms of big-data computing can and will transform the activities of companies, scientific researchers, medical practitioners, and our nation's defense and intelligence operations….

February 2010 Kenneth Cukier publishes in The Economist a Special Report titled, "Data, data everywhere." Writes Cukier: "…the world contains an unimaginably vast amount of digital information which is getting ever vaster more rapidly… The effect is being felt everywhere, from business to science, from governments to the arts. Scientists and computer engineers have coined a new term for the phenomenon: 'big data.'"

May 2011 James Manyika, Michael Chui, Brad Brown, Jacques Bughin, Richard Dobbs, Charles Roxburgh, and Angela Hung Byers of the McKinsey Global Institute publish "Big data: The next frontier for innovation, competition, and productivity."

2014 : The rise of the mobile machines – as for the first time, more people are using mobile devices to access digital data, than office or home computers. 88% of business executives surveyed by GE working with Accenture report that big data analytics is a top priority for their business.

1.15 SELECTING A BIG DATA TECHNOLOGY: OPERATIONAL VS. ANALYTICAL

The Big Data landscape is dominated by two classes of technology: systems that provide operational capabilities for real-time, interactive workloads where data is primarily captured and stored; and systems that provide analytical capabilities for retrospective, complex analysis that may touch most or all of the data. These classes of technology are complementary and frequently deployed together.

Operational and analytical workloads for Big Data present opposing requirements and systems have evolved to address their particular demands separately and in very different ways. Each has driven the creation of new technology architectures. Operational systems, such as the NoSQL databases, focus on servicing highly concurrent requests while exhibiting low latency for responses operating on highly selective access criteria. Analytical systems, on the other hand, tend to focus on high throughput; queries can be very complex and touch most if not all of the data in the system at any time. Both systems tend to operate over many servers operating in a cluster, managing tens or hundreds of terabytes of data across billions of records.

1.15.1 Operational Big Data

For operational Big Data workloads, NoSQL Big Data systems such as document databases have emerged to address a broad set of applications, and other architectures, such as key-value stores, column family stores, and graph databases are optimized for more specific applications. NoSQL technologies, which were developed to address the shortcomings of relational databases in the modern computing environment, are faster and scale much more quickly and inexpensively than relational databases.

Critically, NoSQL Big Data systems are designed to take advantage of new cloud computing architectures that have emerged over the past decade to allow massive computations to be run inexpensively and efficiently. This makes operational Big Data workloads much easier to manage, and cheaper and faster to implement.

In addition to user interactions with data, most operational systems need to provide some degree of real-time intelligence about the active data in the system. For example in a multi-user game or financial application, aggregates for user activities or instrument performance are displayed to users to inform their next actions. Some NoSQL systems can provide insights into patterns and trends based on real-time data with minimal coding and without the need for data scientists and additional infrastructure.

1.15.2 Analytical Big Data

Analytical Big Data workloads, on the other hand, tend to be addressed by MPP database systems and MapReduce. These technologies are also a reaction to the limitations of traditional relational databases and their lack of ability to scale beyond the resources of a single server. Furthermore, MapReduce provides a new method of analyzing data that is complementary to the capabilities provided by SQL.

As applications gain traction and their users generate increasing volumes of data, there are a number of retrospective analytical workloads that provide real value to the business. Where these workloads involve algorithms that are more sophisticated than simple aggregation, MapReduce has emerged as the first choice for Big Data analytics. Some NoSQL systems provide native MapReduce functionality that allows for analytics to be performed on operational data in place. Alternately, data can be copied from

NoSQL systems into analytical systems such as Hadoop for MapReduce.

Table 1.1 Overview of Operational vs. Analytical Systems

	Operational	Analytical
Latency	1 ms - 100 ms	1 min - 100 min
Concurrency	1000 - 100,000	1 - 10
Access Pattern	Writes and Reads	Reads
Queries	Selective	Unselective
Data Scope	Operational	Retrospective
End User	Customer	Data Scientist
Technology	NoSQL MapReduce,	MPP Database

1.16 CLOUD COMPUTING

Cloud computing refers to a broad set of computing and software products that are sold as a service, managed by a 3rd-party provider and delivered over a network. **Infrastructure-as-a-Service** (IaaS) is a flavour of cloud computing in which on-demand processing, storage or network resources are provided to the customer. Sold on-demand with limited or no upfront investment for the end-user, consumption is readily scalable to accommodate spikes in usage. Customers pay only for the capacity that is actually used (like a utility), as opposed to self-hosting, where the user pays for system capacity it is are used or not.

As compared to self-hosting, IaaS is:

1. **Inexpensive.** To self-host an application, one has to pay for enough resources to handle peak load on an application, at all times. Amazon discovered that before launching its cloud offering it was using only about 10% of its server capacity the vast majority of the time.
2. **Tailored.** Small applications can be run for very little cost by taking advantage of spare capacity. Bandwidth, processing and storage capability can be added in relatively small increments.
3. **Elastic.** Computing resources can easily be added and released as needed, making it much easier to deal with unexpected traffic spikes.
4. **Reliable.** With the cloud, it's easy and inexpensive to have servers in multiple geographic locations, allowing content to be served locally to users, and also allowing for better disaster recovery and business continuity.

Overall, cloud computing provides better agility and scalability, together with lower costs and faster time to market. However, it does require that applications be engineered to take advantage of this new infrastructure; applications built for the cloud need to be able to scale by adding more servers, for example, instead of adding capacity to existing servers.

It is true that around the world the telephone took almost 70 years to reach 50 per cent of households, radio took around 28 years and the Internet took 10 years. The new technology is out-pacing the old. In the near future it may take weeks or days instead of years to adopt new technology. For instance, social media services which connects people in the virual space such as Google plus which was launched by google it took 16 days to reach 10 million users, compared to 780 days for Twitter and 852 days for Facebook14. It took 10 years for the Internet to become a basic and essential part of daily life15. Today's society is digitally connected, which has a direct impact on the social, economic and political aspects of the nation.

The GoI has taken an initiative to come up with the National Fiber Optic Network with a maximum speed of 100 Mbps by investing 210 billions rupees. The government hopes that this investment will make a difference at a the grassroots level. India has the ability to launch various IT services, and even an average Indian villager is able to consume various services using CC. These services are available through desktop, laptop or mobile phone access. In today's rural India, more people have mobile phones than radio sets, which makes it very convenient for them to access government services using CC. The cloud can reach around 900 millions of rural Indians, with the ability to empower them socially and financially. The cloud can provide an effective service in critical areas such as agriculture, banking, healthcare and sanitation, education, and e-Panchayath (local self government in the villages connected through e-goverance).

Below, we set out the benefits CC services can offer rural Indian citizens.

On the storage layer, traditional relational databases were not designed to take advantage of horizontal scaling. A class of new database architectures, dubbed NoSQL databases, are designed to take advantage of the cloud computing environment. NoSQL databases are natively able to handle load by spreading data among many servers, making them a natural fit for the cloud computing environment. Part of the reason NoSQL databases can do this is that related data is always stored together, instead of in separate tables. This document data model, used in MongoDB and other NoSQL databases, makes them a natural fit for the cloud computing environment.

In fact, MongoDB is built for the cloud. Its native scale-out architecture, enabled by "sharding," aligns well with the horizontal scaling and agility afforded by cloud computing. Sharding automatically distributes data evenly across multi-node clusters and balances queries across them. In addition, MongoDB automatically manages sets of redundant servers, called "replica sets," to maintain availability and data integrity even if individual cloud instances are taken offline. To ensure high availability, for instance, users can spin up multiple members of a replica set as individual cloud instances across different availability zones and/or data centers. MongoDB has also partnered with a number of leading cloud computing providers, including Amazon Web Services, Microsoft and SoftLayer.

1.17 BIG DATA AND E-GOVERNANCE

The use and adoption of Big Data within governmental processes is beneficial and allows efficiencies in terms of cost, productivity, and innovation. That said, this process does not come without its flaws. Data analysis often requires multiple parts of government (central and local) to work in collaboration and create new and innovative processes to deliver the desired outcome. Below are the thought leading examples within the Governmental Big Data space.

Over the last two decades there has been a dramatic shift regarding the notion of a citizen's right to information. Now the right to information is considered as a right that all human beings should have access to, and ultimately government is considered as the guardian of all public information. As in other countries, the relationship between Indian citizens and government is mediated by ICT. This system introduced the concept of open government data and led to the adoption of the RTI, which provided a unique opportunity for citizens to access governmental data. This development led to an increased demand for data digitalization, with the ICT providing a digital opportunity to modernize the government and create a digital democracy.

The ICT initiative the National e-Governance Plan (NeGP) and its institutional framework, has been successful in providing timely service, eradicating corruption and reaching those who had previously no access, all at a much lower cost. Data collected from social media sites,e-commerce websites, e-government online services and sensor networks comprise a significant part of data that is being stored and transmitted over the Internet using cloud infrastructure. This data is growing at an exponential rate. This huge volume of data is being turned into information, which can be utilized for both economic and social benefits of citizens, enterprises, governmental and public sector organizations. It is very challenging to manage such huge volumes of data without the "big data" framework, advanced technology and data researchers.

The results of a global study commissioned by CA Technologies has revealed that Enterprise Big Data strategies are delivering key benefits to organizations, despite noted challenges in implementation. 44 percent of the Indian respondents have already implemented a Big Data project while 36 percent plan to implement one in the coming year. In addition to this, 12 percent of the Indian respondents have stated that they have implemented four Big Data projects to date.

The study, titled The State of Big Data Infrastructure: Benchmarking Global Big Data Users to Drive Future Performance, revealed the top five major obstacles Indian organizations need to overcome for successful big data project implementation. These include: insufficient existing infrastructure (33 percent), organizational complexity (25 percent), security/compliance concerns (28 percent), lack of budget/resources (25 percent), and lack of visibility into information and processes (21 percent).

Despite the challenges, majority of Indian organizations have or are in the process of adopting big data strategies since the benefits clearly outweigh the challenges. Indian organizations have listed the following reasons for implementing Big Data strategy: improve customer experience (67 percent), need to enter new markets (52 percent) and need to get new customers (49 percent).

The results of a global study commissioned by CA Technologies has revealed that Enterprise Big Data strategies are delivering key benefits to organizations, despite noted challenges in implementation. 44 percent of the Indian respondents have already implemented a Big Data project while 36 percent plan to implement one in the coming year. In addition to this, 12 percent of the Indian respondents have stated that they have implemented four Big Data projects to date.

The study, titled The State of Big Data Infrastructure: Benchmarking Global Big Data Users to Drive Future Performance, revealed the top five major obstacles Indian organizations need to overcome for successful big data project implementation. These include: insufficient existing infrastructure (33 percent), organizational complexity (25 percent), security/compliance concerns (28 percent), lack of budget/resources (25 percent), and lack of visibility into information and processes (21 percent).

Despite the challenges, majority of Indian organizations have or are in the process of adopting big data strategies since the benefits clearly outweigh the challenges. Indian organizations have listed the following reasons for implementing Big Data strategy: improve customer experience (67 percent), need to enter new markets (52 percent) and need to get new customers (49 percent).

"There is a huge potential for Big Data technologies in India. This is a high growth economy and organizations depend on insights from raw data, to plan their future course.

As per survey done by EY on Big data and enterprise mobility in India with 110 IT leaders across industry sectors to understand the relevance of Big data and enterprise mobility in the Indian context :

1. More than 60% of organizations define Big data as large volumes of unstructured data. Less than 20% of organizations consider Big data as "hype" or the latest technology buzzword.

2. About 60% acknowledge that unstructured information is growing out of control and is driving Big data explosion, with unstructured data expected to grow at a faster rate (30-40%) than structured data (30%) over the next 3-5 years.

3. Half of the large organizations plan to use data from social networks for sentiment analysis and customer tracking.

4. About 80% of organizations are in the early stages of Big data initiatives and 60% are still at the "exploratory stage" of evolution.
5. Concerns relating to availability of skillsets, low levels of technology awareness and lack of management sponsorship are limiting Big data adoption.
6. Data complexity will continue to increase in future and less than 10% of organizations are currently equipped to manage these unstructured data sources effectively.
7. 75% of organizations are confident of driving new revenue streams using Big data. However, only 35% plan to invest in building Big data capabilities related to analytics, security software and real-time applications.

"There is a huge potential for Big Data technologies in India. This is a high growth economy and organizations depend on insights from raw data, to plan their future course.Big data analysis helped in parts, responsible for the NDA to win Indian General Election 2014.

The Indian Government utilises numerous techniques to ascertain how the Indian electorate is responding to government action, as well as ideas for policy augmentation.

Numerous global big data players have sprouted in India over the past two years. Sears, for instance, established wholly-owned subsidiary MetaScale to service healthcare and entertainment customers with revenues between US$1 million and US$10 million. A @WalmartLabs facility also opened in Bangalore in April to develop social media and analytics and big data infrastructure. And in July, Yahoo set up a grid computing lab at the IIT-Madras campus.

On the supply side, India churns out more than 2.5 million university graduates and 750,000 post-graduates every year, of which 700,000 graduate in maths and science.

Governments, despite being data rich, have often been careful in how they leverage Big Data since they don't want to be seen as acting in a "Big Brother" fashion. This probably has been a major impediment to adoption of Big Data for Public Sector, along with the paucity of funds and know-how.

Big data services provider Mu Sigma, though, has already tapped Indian resources to meet U.S. demand for data analytics. Three quarters of its 2,500 data scientists are based in Bangalore, India, and according to founder Dhiraj Rajaram, its clients include 75 Fortune 500 companies, including Microsoft.

Some of the areas where big data can transform government agencies are as follows:

Improving service delivery – Big-data technologies are helping local and state agencies to provide timely, accurate, complete, and customizable information to their employees, residents and businesses. A case in point is the use of big data tools by many organizations at the state level to monitor transportation systems. Analysis of these systems can help officials in anticipating problems that could lead to traffic jams and address the transit related issues. Agencies can analyze the data sets related to nutrition, crime, obesity, employment, drug safety, healthcare etc. and deliver better services or make decisions that support their mission. Agencies can also use big-data technologies to enahnce their disaster response and management by collecting the data shared though different communication sources like text messages, phone calls and social media posts.

Preventing fraud in Tax compliance – Tax organizations lose a lot of money through fraud and unpaid taxes. There is a huge pressure on tax departments to collect more revenue, reduce operational costs and improve collections. Agencies can analyze huge amounts of data available for corporate entities as well as individuals to increase tax collections. They can study various parameters like expenditure, people's lifestyle and travel patterns to identify those who could be evading taxes. Even for people travelling abroad and buying expensive goods the department can track their digital footprints through online shopping statistics and piece together a their lifestyle to create a taxable database. Thus big data can enable tax departments to minimize the tax gap by proactively detecting & determining frauds and unpaid taxes.

Crime prevention and prediction – Increase in the number of crimes and the way these crimes are being executed, make it necessary for government agencies to adopt a fresh approach for managing crime-related information. Agencies require increased volume, variety and velocity of data to identify the threats to anticipate criminal activity and take corrective measures, enhancing the level of response. Big data can also be used for fighting against terrorism and organized crime, fraud detection, and maintaining internal and external security. Government organizations can analyze various data sets and use advanced real-time analytics to gather deeper understanding of crime, criminals and incident patternsin order to prevent and predict crime. By examining patterns in past crime data along with the environmental characteristics, analysts can forecast the crime location and deploy officers accordingly.

Inspite of privacy and security related challenges the opportunities that big data opens for agencies are endless. Government organizations around the world are going for big data adoption and similar analytical tools for predictive analysis to improve the quality of decisions and enable betterment of society at large.

eBay.com uses two data warehouses at 7.5 petabytes and 40PB as well as a 40PB Hadoop cluster for search, consumer recommendations, and merchandising. Inside eBay's 90PB data warehouse

Amazon.com handles millions of back-end operations every day, as well as queries from more than half a million third-party sellers. The core technology that keeps Amazon running is Linux-based and as of 2005 they had the world's three largest Linux databases, with capacities of 7.8 TB, 18.5 TB, and 24.7 TB.

1.18 THE BENEFITS OF BIG DATA

1.18.1 The Benefits of Big Data Proposition for IT

Big data tec1hnologies promise a multitude of improvements for IT organizations that understand how to leverage them.

IT transformation: Many IT organizations, especially those at older companies, recognize the promise of big data platforms to modernize outdated mainframes and antiquated code bases. One bank we know is replacing some of its core banking systems with Hadoop platforms.

Reduced cost: Most big data solutions are based on the open-source technology model and leverage commodity hardware, thus minimizing capital investments in new platforms. While Hadoop is far from ultimately "free," it introduces lower barriers to entry and faster time-to-deployment. As the Big Data Comes of Age research report emphasizes, "Inexpensive is not free."

Faster processing: Source data is more complex. Third-party data is often cryptic. Data is arriving at the corporate doorstep with increased speed. IT's ability to acquire that data and process it in the way it needs to be processed is only as good as the slowest node on the platform. With big data technologies being inherently high-horsepower and parallelized, faster processing means faster time to deployment.

1.18.2 The Big Data Proposition for the Business

The following are the big data business benefits:

Increased operational efficiencies: When big data is first mentioned, it's usually in the context of faster analytics or data mining. But many companies are also leveraging big data solutions to simply do what they've already been doing, only faster. For instance, I might be running a fraud algorithm against a data set, the result of which might be a list of individuals who exhibit attributes of fraudulent behavior. This list might be calculated nightly and pushed to data scientists the next day. With big data technologies and their ability to process those algorithms more quickly, the lists can be provisioned at regular intervals throughout the day.

Economies of scale: Likewise, a big data environment could conceivably aggregate the processing work done by multiple systems in a company into a single platform, providing not only economies of scale and process efficiencies, but reducing overall costs.

Improved customer intelligence: To business people, the promise of big data is really in what the integrated data types and growing data volumes about customers can mean to customer retention, customer attrition, sales uplift, and revenues. The more we understand about an individual customer—and her often complex relationships, preferences, and interaction history with our company—the more relevant and timely our marketing outreach can be. For a sales or marketing executive, this means higher

Return on Marketing Investment (and perhaps, higher bonuses!). For a data scientist in the compliance organization, this could mean better data tracking and audit-ability to support regulatory compliance. The business possibilities for big data are only limited by a company's ability to acquire and process that data!

1.18.3 Big Data for the Enterprise

With Big Data databases, enterprises can save money, grow revenue, and achieve many other business objectives, in any vertical.

1. Build new applications: Big data might allow a company to collect billions of real-time data points on its products, resources, or customers – and then repackage that data instantaneously to optimize customer experience or resource utilization. For example, a major US city is using MongoDB to cut crime and improve municipal services by collecting and analyzing geospatial data in real-time from over 30 different departments.
2. Improve the effectiveness and lower the cost of existing applications: Big data technologies can replace highly-customized, expensive legacy systems with a standard solution that runs on commodity hardware. And because many big data technologies are open source, they can be implemented far more cheaply than proprietary technologies. For example, by migrating its reference data management application to MongoDB, a Tier 1 bank dramatically reduced the license and hardware costs associated with the proprietary relational database it previously ran, while also bringing its application into better compliance with regulatory requirements.
3. Realize new sources of competitive advantage: Big data can help businesses act more nimbly, allowing them to adapt to changes faster than their competitors. For example, MongoDB allowed one of the largest Human Capital Management (HCM) solution providers to rapidly build mobile applications that integrated data from a wide variety of disparate sources.
4. Increase customer loyalty: Increasing the amount of data shared within the organization – and the speed with which it is updated – allows businesses and other organizations to more rapidly and accurately respond to customer demand. For example, a top 5 global insurance provider, MetLife, used MongoDB to quickly consolidate customer information from over 70 different sources and provide it in a single, rapidly-updated view.

1.18.4 Application of Big Data in Other Areas

In an excellent research report called Big Data Comes of Age,(written by Dr. Barry Devlin, Shawn Rogers, and John Myers, and published by Enterprise Management Associates (EMA) and 9sight Consulting in November 2012.) provides the big data adoption curve.

The report (Fig. 1.9) shows industries that are using big data technologies strategically to innovate. It's no surprise that the media/PR, retail, and leisure industries are leading the pack. Google, Yahoo, and Facebook laid the groundwork for the new big data technologies, and Walmart and Macy's have successfully made big data a part of their DNA.

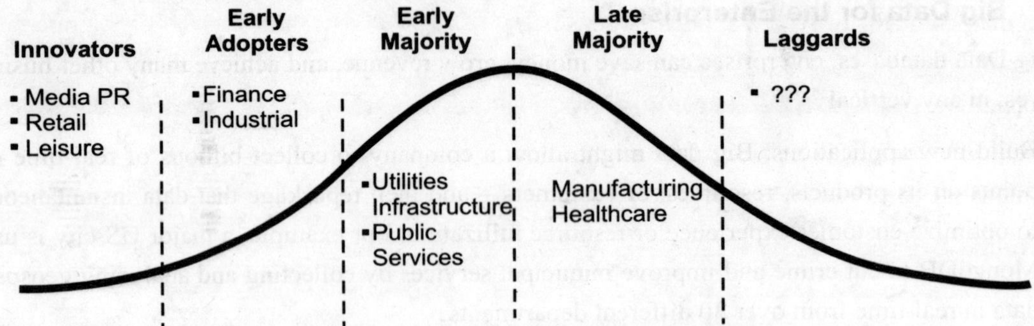

Figure. 1.9: Application spectrum of big Data

Analysis of preliminary data. This refers to data that might be in the midst of being processed, as in a staging area or sandbox. You might be pre-processing the data before it gets stored in the data wareh1ouse or Hadoop. You might simply want to explore the data before loading it into another environment. Hadoop offers a standalone environment for structured and unstructured exploration, whereas with data warehouses, the data modeling, acquisition, cleansing, structuring, and loading of the data might take more time.

1.19 MOBILE BUSINESS INTELLIGENCE (MBI)

Business intelligence (BI) refers to computer-based techniques used in spotting, digging-out, and analyzing business data, such as sales revenue by products and/or departments or associated costs and incomes. Mobile Business Intelligence (Mobile BI or Mobile Intelligence) is defined as "The capability that enables the mobile workforce to gain business insights through information analysis using applications optimized for mobile devices" Verkooij (2012).

Mobile business intelligence is the ability to access BI-related data such as KPIs, business metrics, and dashboards on mobile devices. The concept of mobile BI dates back to the early 1990s when mobile phone use first began to become widespread. Early advocates of mobile BI immediately grasped the potential of mobile phones to simplify the distribution of business-critical data to mobile or remote workers. However, it wasn't until the advent of the smartphone that mobile BI began to generate widespread attention.

In 2002, Research in Motion released the first BlackBerry smartphone optimized for wireless email use. Wireless e-mail proved to be the "killer app" that accelerated the popularity of the smartphone market. By the mid-2000s, Research in Motion's BlackBerry had solidified its hold on the smartphone market with both corporate and governmental organizations. The BlackBerry smartphones eliminated the obstacles to mobile business intelligence. The BlackBerry offered a consistent treatment of data across its many models, provided a much larger screen for viewing data, and allowed user interactivity via the thumbwheel and keyboard. BI vendors re-entered the market with offerings spanning different mobile operating systems (BlackBerry, Windows, Symbian) and data access methods. The two most popular data access options were:

Mobile BI applications can be defined/segregated as follows:

1. **Mobile Browser Rendered App**: Almost any mobile device enables Web-based, thin client, HTML-only BI applications. However, these apps are static and provide little data interactivity. Data is viewed just as it would be over a browser from a personal computer. Little additional effort is required to display data but mobile browsers can typically only support a small subset of the interactivity of a web browser.
2. **Customized App:** A step up from this approach is to render each (or all) reports and dashboards in device-specific format. In other words, provide information specific to the screen size, optimize usage of screen real estate, and enable device-specific navigation controls. Examples of these include thumb wheel or thumb button for BlackBerry, up/down/left/right arrows for Palm, gestural manipulation for iPhone. This approach requires more effort than the previous but no additional software.
3. **Mobile Client App:** The most advanced, the client app provides full interactivity with the BI content viewed on the device. In addition, this approach provides periodic caching of data which can be viewed and analyzed even offline to use the mobile browser to access data, similar to desktop computer, and to create a native application designed specifically for the mobile device

1.19.1 IBM Cognos Business Intelligence translates

Formatted and interactive dashboards feature highly scalable distribution and scheduling capabilities, with custom visualizations. There's a broad offering of analysis tools, including what-if analysis, advanced analysis, trend analysis and analytical reporting. Self-service functionality means users can interact with reports on mobile devices or while disconnected. Social networking features aid collaboration within teams and allow companies to render useful the aggregate intelligence of their entire organization.

IBM Cognos Business Intelligence presents information in a personalized format; users can analyze, share and collaborate on content in one dashboard. Language and location are no longer barriers to access and interaction with dashboards.

The IBM Cognos Business Intelligence mobile app allows users to access information via iPhone, iPad, Android tablet or smartphone.

These business intelligence capabilities can be deployed on-premise, Web or on mobile. While buyers can choose to implement any of the applications standalone, we recommend evaluating the fully integrated platform for maximum visibility and insight.

1.19.2 Oracle Business Intelligence Mobile

The only mobile app that gives you a full range of BI functionally, from interactive dashboards to location intelligence, and lets you initiate business processes right from your mobile device.

1.19.3 SAP Business Objects

With its consolidated approach, SAP Business Objects gives organizations a set of tools to manage and optimize Business Intelligence. From a centralized portal, companies handle everything from ETL and data cleansing to predictive dashboards and a variety of reports - Crystal Reports, OLAP, and ad hoc. SAP Business Objects provides solutions for medium to large enterprises, and is configurable to a number of industries, including manufacturing and distribution, financial services, and nonprofits.

Users are able to mine, analyze and report information from most data sources and present in a number of formats both internally and externally. SAP Business Objects Mobile gives users access to reports, metrics and other data from smartphones and connected mobile devices. The Business Objects platform uses a common semantic layer, avoiding report duplication and ensuring data is accurate and consistent across the organization. The solution can also be integrated with other enterprise solutions, including Salesforce and Microsoft Office.

1.20 INDIAN BIG DATA COMPANIES

As per EMMANUEL AMBERBER following are 15 Indian Big Data companies to watch out for:

1. **Heckyl:** TechSparks 2011 winner company in financial data analytics space. Founded by Mukund Mudras, Som Sagar, Abhijit Vedak and Jaison Mathews.

2. **Sigmoid Analytics:** A TechSparks 2014 company, based out of Bangalore, Sigmoid is in the area of real-time Big Data warehousing, streaming and ETL (extract, transform and load) on Apache Spark. They have a technology infrastructure which companies can use to store their data in a desired format, perform operations on it and generate insights.

3. **Flutura:** Mines Big Data to perform analytics and gives hidden insights from huge chunks of machine generated data for global oil and gas majors to bring in efficiency and safety. Flutura was founded by Krishnan Raman, Derick Jose and Srikanth Muralidhara.

4. **Indix:** Computes real-time data to give product insights for decision makers on an intuitive dashboard. Founded by Sanjay Parthasarathy, the company has its product engineering center based out of Chennai.

5. **Fractal Analytics:** Helps companies in predictive analytics and decision sciences to understand, predict and shape consumer behavior through advanced analytics, harmonize data, tell visual stories and forecast business performance.

6. **Crayon Data:** An algorithms called the WhiteBox, Simpler Choices, takes massive data, cleans it up and presents only actionable insights to banking, hospitality and, telecom sectors. It was founded by Srikant Sastri, Suresh, Shankar and Vijay Kumar.

7. **Germin8:** It is a leading Data Analytics company that helps brands with social media measurement and monitoring solutions by analysing conversations in real time. The Mumbai-based company was founded in 2007 by Raj Nair and his son Ranjit Nair.

8. **Aureus Analytics:** With its platform called ASAP (Aureus Statistical and Analytics Platform) it produces insights by mining enterprise data. Aureus was founded by technology professionals Anurag Shah, Ashish Tanna and Nitin Purohit.

9. **Dataswft:** A product of Bizosys Technologies Pvt Ltd, it has a customized search engine that can decode technical information and return search queries within milliseconds. It was founded by Sunil Guttula, Abinasha Karana and Sridhar Dhulipala.

10. **C360:** Corporate360 Pvt Ltd provides IT sales intelligence data services to enterprises. The startup was founded by college dropout Varun Chandran. Prior to founding Corporate360, Varun was working as sales and marketing executive with the likes of SAP, Oracle, Dell and NetApp. C360 is based in India and Singapore. Another similarly located Big Data company is Antuit holdings, which raised $56 million from Goldman Sachs and Zodius Capital.

11. **Metaome:** It is a health care Big Data company focused on life sciences, founded by Kalpana Krishnaswami and Ramkumar Nandkumar. Metaome's products DistilBio a free version web-based graph search and enterprise version platform that accrues a variety of data from difference sources (laboratory data management systems, private and public databases) and makes it structured to help in identifying a pattern.

12. **Frrole:** It is a Social intelligence startup with a media and brands focused offering, which allows its customers to integrate real-time Twitter data into their digital properties and TV shows. The startup was founded by Amarpreet Kalkat, Nishith Sharma and Abhishek Vaid.

13. **Bridgei2i:** It focuses on user-centric applications of Big Data. Founders are Prithvijit Roy, Ashish Sharma, Pritam Kanti Paul.

14. **Formcept:** Focused on making data analysis accessible to everyone; founders are Suresh Srinivasan and Anuj Kumar.

15. PromptCloud has been founded by Prashant Kumar. PromptCloud is a DaaS (Data-as-a-Service) platform; it crawls the websphere for data extraction and has been founded by Prashant Kumar.

1.21 CRITIQUE OF THE BIG DATA PARADIGM

Critiques of the big data paradigm come in two flavors, those that question the implications of the approach itself, and those that question the way it is currently done.

"A crucial problem is that we do not know much about the underlying empirical micro-processes that lead to the emergence of the[se] typical network characteristics of Big Data".[14] In their critique, Snijders, Matzat, and Reips point out that often very strong assumptions are made about mathematical properties that may not at all reflect what is really going on at the level of micro-processes. Mark Graham has leveled broad critiques at Chris Anderson's assertion that big data will spell the end of theory: focusing in particular on the notion that big data must always be contextualized in their social, economic, and political contexts. Even as companies invest eight- and nine-figure sums to derive insight from information streaming in from suppliers and customers, less than 40% of employees have sufficiently mature processes and skills to do so. To overcome this insight deficit, "big data", no matter how comprehensive or well analyzed, must be complemented by "big judgment," according to an article in the Harvard Business Review.

Much in the same line, it has been pointed out that the decisions based on the analysis of big data are inevitably "informed by the world as it was in the past, or, at best, as it currently is".Fed by a large number of data on past experiences, algorithms can predict future development if the future is similar to the past. If the systems dynamics of the future change, the past can say little about the future. For this, it would be necessary to have a thorough understanding of the systems dynamic, which implies theory. As a response to this critique it has been suggested to combine big data approaches with computer simulations, such as agent-based models and Complex Systems. Agent-based models are increasingly getting better in predicting the outcome of social complexities of even unknown future scenarios through computer simulations that are based on a collection of mutually interdependent algorithms. In addition, use of multivariate methods that probe for the latent structure of the data, such as factor analysis and cluster analysis, have proven useful as analytic approaches that go well beyond the bi-variate approaches (cross-tabs) typically employed with smaller data sets.

In health and biology, conventional scientific approaches are based on experimentation. For these approaches, the limiting factor is the relevant data that can confirm or refute the initial hypothesis. A new postulate is accepted now in biosciences: the information provided by the data in huge volumes (omics) without prior hypothesis is complementary and sometimes necessary to conventional approaches based on experimentation.[citation needed] In the massive approaches it is the formulation of a relevant hypothesis to explain the data that is the limiting factor.

Privacy advocates are concerned about the threat to privacy represented by increasing storage and integration of personally identifiable information; expert panels have released various policy recommendations to conform practice to expectations of privacy.

1.21.1 Critiques of Big Data Execution

Big data has been called a "fad" in scientific research and its use was even made fun of as an absurd practice in a satirical example on "pig data". Researcher danah boyd has raised concerns about the use of big data in science neglecting principles such as choosing a representative sample by being too concerned about actually handling the huge amounts of data. This approach may lead to results bias in one way or another. Integration across heterogeneous data resources—some that might be considered "big data" and others not—presents formidable logistical as well as analytical challenges, but many researchers argue that such integrations are likely to represent the most promising new frontiers in science. In the provocative article "Critical Questions for Big Data", the authors title big data a part of mythology: "large data sets offer a higher form of intelligence and knowledge [...], with the aura of truth, objectivity, and accuracy". Users of big data are often "lost in the sheer volume of numbers", and "working with Big Data is still subjective, and what it quantifies does not necessarily have a closer claim on objective truth".[130] Recent developments in BI domain, such as pro-active reporting especially target improvements in usability of Big Data, through automated filtering of non-useful data and correlations.

CHAPTER

2

Basics of Hadoop

2.1 BIG DATA AND HADOOP

Due to the advent of new technologies, devices, and communication means like social networking sites, the amount of data produced by mankind is growing rapidly every year. The amount of data produced by us from the beginning of time till 2003 was 5 billion gigabytes. If you pile up the data in the form of disks it may fill an entire football field. The same amount was created in every two days in 2011, and in every ten minutes in 2012. This rate is still growing enormously.

Hadoop was created by Doug Cutting and Mike Cafarella in 2005. Cutting, who was working at Yahoo! at the time, named it after his son's toy elephant. It was originally developed to support distribution for the Nutch search engine project. This team took the solution provided by Google and started an Open Source Project called HADOOP in 2005 and Doug named it after his son's toy elephant. Now Apache Hadoop is a registered trademark of the Apache Software Foundation.

Apache Hadoop is an open-source software framework written in Java for distributed storage and distributed processing of very large data sets on computer clusters built from commodity hardware.

Hadoop allows to store and process big data in a distributed environment across clusters of computers using simple programming models. It is designed to scale up from single servers to thousands of machines, each offering local computation and storage. All the modules in Hadoop are designed with a fundamental assumption that hardware failures are common and should be automatically handled by the framework.

For many years, users who want to store and analyze data would store the data in a database and process it via SQL queries. The Web has changed most of the assumptions of this era. On the Web, the data is unstructured and large, and the databases can neither capture the data into a schema nor scale it to store and process it.

2.2 HADOOP ARCHITECTURE

The core of Apache Hadoop consists of a storage part, known as Hadoop Distributed File System (HDFS), and a processing part called MapReduce. Hadoop splits files into large blocks and distributes them across nodes in a cluster. To process data, Hadoop transfers packaged code for nodes to process in parallel based on the data that needs to be processed. This approach takes advantage of data locality—nodes manipulating the data they have access to— to allow the dataset to be processed faster and more efficiently than it would be in a more conventional supercomputer architecture that relies on a parallel file system where computation and data are distributed via high-speed networking.

Thus base Apache Hadoop framework is composed of the following modules:

Hadoop Common – contains libraries and utilities needed by other Hadoop modules. These are Java libraries and utilities required by other Hadoop modules. These libraries provides filesystem and OS level abstractions and contains the necessary Java files and scripts required to start Hadoop.;

1. **Hadoop Distributed File System (HDFS)** – a distributed file-system that stores data on commodity machines, providing very high aggregate bandwidth across the cluster;
2. **Hadoop YARN** – a resource-management platform responsible for managing computing resources in clusters and using them for scheduling of users' applications; and
3. **Hadoop MapReduce (either MapReduce/MR1 or YARN/MR$_2$**– an implementation of the MapReduce programming model for large scale data processing.

Figure 2.1 depicts these four components available in Hadoop framework.

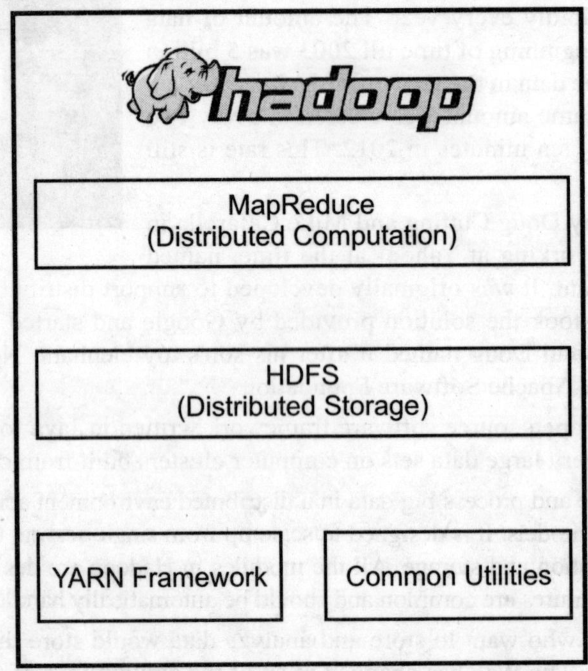

Figure. 2.1: Four components of Hadoop framework

Since 2012, the term Hadoop has come to refer not just to the base modules above, but also to the ecosystem, or collection of additional software packages that can be installed on top of or alongside Hadoop, such as Apache Pig, Apache Hive, Apache HBase, Apache Phoenix, Apache Spark, Apache ZooKeeper, Cloudera Impala, Apache Flume, Apache Sqoop, Apache Oozie, Apache Storm. Apache Spark etc

2.3 MAIN COMPONENTS OF HADOOP FRAMEWORK

Hadoop has a family of projects that are either built on top of Hadoop or work very closely with Hadoop. These projects have given rise to an ecosystem that focuses on large-scale data processing, and often users can use several of these projects in combination to handle their use cases.

There are a number of supporting projects that leverage HDFS and MapReduce as detailed below.

HDFS: If you want 4000+ computers to work on your data, then you'd better spread your data across 4000+ computers. HDFS does this for you. HDFS has a few moving parts. The Datanodes store your data, and the Namenode keeps track of where stuff is stored. There are other pieces, but you have enough to get started.

1. **MapReduce**: This is the programming model for Hadoop. There are two phases, not surprisingly called Map and Reduce. To impress your friends tell them there is a shuffle-sort between the Map and Reduce phase. The JobTracker manages the 4000+ components of your MapReduce job. The TaskTrackers take orders from the JobTracker. If you like Java then code in Java. If you like SQL or other non-Java languages you are still in luck, you can use a utility called Hadoop Streaming.

2. **Jaql** : A query language designed for use with data in a JSON format and designed to work with semi-structured data. It has High-level querie system that results in low-level MapReduce jobs.

3. **Hive and Hue**: A data warehouse system for Hadoop that uses an SQL-like language to access its data. If you like SQL, you can write SQL and have Hive convert it to a MapReduce job although you don't get a full ANSI-SQL environment, but you do get 4000 notes and multi-Petabyte scalability. Hue gives you a browser-based graphical interface to do your Hive work.
4. **Pig**: A higher-level programming environment (ie easy) to do MapReduce coding. The Pig language is called Pig Latin. You may find the naming conventions somewhat unconventional, but you get incredible price-performance and high availability.
5. **Sqoop**: Provides bi-directional data transfer between Hadoop and your favorite relational database. Transfers bulk data between Hadoop and structured datastores
6. **Flume : Hadoop Streaming** : A distributed system designed to collect, aggregate, and move log data from different sources to a central location. It is in effect a utility to enable MapReduce code in any language: C, Perl, Python, C++, Bash, etc. The examples include a Python mapper and an AWK reducer.
7. **Oozie**: Manages Hadoop workflow. This doesn't replace your scheduler or BPM tooling, but it does provide if-then-else branching and control within your Hadoop jobs.
8. **HBase**: A super-scalable key-value store. It works very much like a persistent hash-map (for python fans think dictionary). It is not a relational database despite the name HBase.
9. **FlumeNG**: A real time loader for streaming your data into Hadoop. It stores data in HDFS and HBase. You'll want to get started with FlumeNG, which improves on the original flume.
10. **Whirr**: Cloud provisioning for Hadoop. You can start up a cluster in just a few minutes with a very short configuration file.
11. **Mahout**: Machine learning for Hadoop. Used for predictive analytics and other advanced analysis.
12. **Fuse**: Makes the HDFS system look like a regular file system so you can use ls, rm, cd, and others on HDFS data
13. **Zookeeper**: A centralized system for maintaining configuration information , Naming and providing distributed synchronization and group services. Used to manage synchronization for the cluster. You won't be working much with Zookeeper, but it is working hard for you.

Hadoop is open source frame work for other applications as well like :

- **Lucene :** – high-performance, full-featured text search engine library
  - Fast indexing
  - Ranked searching
  - Date range searching
- **HBase**
  - Non-relational, distributed database
  - Runs on top of HDFS
  - Allow for updates to Hadoop data
- **Avro :** A remote procedural call and data serialization framework
- **Chukwa :** – A data collection system for monitoring.

Social media has gained immense popularity with marketing teams, and Twitter is an effective tool for a company to get people excited about its products. Twitter makes it easy to engage users and communicate directly with them, and in turn, users can provide word-of-mouth marketing for companies by discussing the products. Given limited resources, and knowing we may not be able to talk to everyone we want to target directly, marketing departments can be more efficient by being selective about whom we reach out to.

2.4 ANALYSING BIG DATA WITH HADOOP

To understand whom we should target, let's take a step back and try to understand the mechanics of Twitter. A user – let's call him Amit – follows a set of people, and has a set of followers. When Amit sends an update out, that update is seen by all of his followers. Amit can also retweet other users' updates. A retweet is a repost of an update, much like you might forward an email. If Amit sees a tweet from Smita, and retweets it, all of Amit's followers see Smita's tweet, even if they don't follow Smita. Through retweets, messages can get passed much further than just the followers of the person who sent the original tweet. Knowing that, we can try to engage users whose updates tend to generate lots of retweets. Since Twitter tracks retweet counts for all tweets, we can find the users we're looking for by analyzing Twitter data.

SQL queries can be used to answer this question: We want to look at which users are responsible for the most retweets, in descending order of most retweeted. However, querying Twitter data in a traditional RDBMS is inconvenient, since the Twitter Streaming API outputs tweets in a JSON format which can be arbitrarily complex. In the Hadoop ecosystem, the Hive project provides a query interface which can be used to query data that resides in HDFS. The query language looks very similar to SQL, but allows us to easily model complex types, so we can easily query the type of data we have. Seems like a good place to start. So how do we get Twitter data into Hive? First, we need to get Twitter data into HDFS, and then we'll be able to tell Hive where the data resides and how to read it.

2.4.1 Traditional Approach

In this approach, an enterprise will have a computer to store and process big data. Here data will be stored in an RDBMS like Oracle Database, MS SQL Server or DB2 and sophisticated softwares can be written to interact with the database, process the required data and present it to the users for analysis purpose.

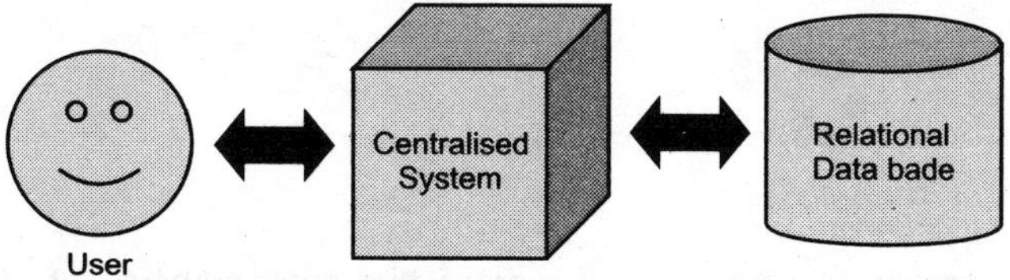

Figure. 2.3: A basic Relational Data base Approach

This approach works well where we have less volume of data that can be accommodated by standard database servers, or up to the limit of the processor which is processing the data. But when it comes to dealing with huge amounts of data, it is really a tedious task to process such data through a traditional database server.

Relational data model is the primary data model, which is used widely around the world for data storage and processing. This model is simple and it has all the properties and capabilities required to process data with storage efficiency.

Tables – In relational data model, relations are saved in the format of Tables. This format stores the relation among entities. A table has rows and columns, where rows represents records and columns represent the attributes.

Tuple – A single row of a table, which contains a single record for that relation is called a tuple.

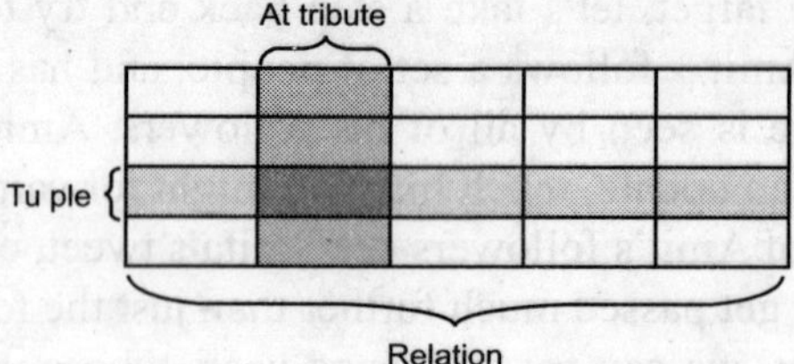

Figure. 2.4: Relational Database : Tuple and attributes

2.4.2 Google's Solution

Google solved this problem using an algorithm called MapReduce. This algorithm divides the task into small parts and assigns those parts to many computers connected over the network, and collects the results to form the final result dataset.

The Fig. 2.5 shows various commodity hardwares which could be hooked to single CPU machines or servers with higher capacity to make the system more versatile.

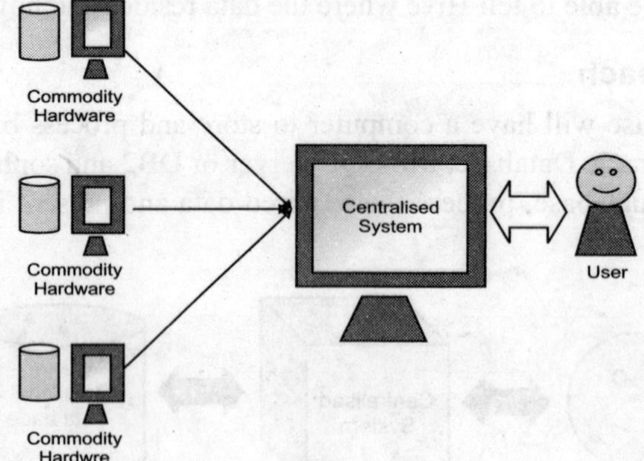

Figure. 2.5: Another Approach :Commodity hardwares which could be hooked to single CPU machines

2.4.3 Hadoop MapReduce Style

Google was one of the first organizations to face the problem, where they wanted to download the whole of the Internet and index it to support search queries. They built a framework for large-scale data processing borrowing from the "map" and "reduce" functions of the functional programming paradigm. They called the paradigm MapReduce. Hadoop is the most widely known and widely used implementation of the MapReduce paradigm.

Hadoop MapReduce is a software framework for easily writing applications which process big amounts of data in-parallel on large clusters (thousands of nodes) of commodity hardware in a reliable, fault-tolerant manner.

The term MapReduce actually refers to the following two different tasks that Hadoop programs perform:

- **The Map Task:** This is the first task, which takes input data and converts it into a set of data, where individual elements are broken down into tuples (key/value pairs).
- **The Reduce Task:** This task takes the output from a map task as input and combines those data tuples into a smaller set of tuples. The reduce task is always performed after the map task.

Typically both the input and the output are stored in a file-system. The framework takes care of scheduling tasks, monitoring them and re-executes the failed tasks.

The MapReduce framework consists of a single master **JobTracker** and one slave **TaskTracker** per cluster-node. The master is responsible for resource management, tracking resource consumption/ availability and scheduling the jobs component tasks on the slaves, monitoring them and re-executing the failed tasks. The slaves TaskTracker execute the tasks as directed by the master and provide task-status information to the master periodically.

The JobTracker is a single point of failure for the Hadoop MapReduce service which means if JobTracker goes down, all running jobs are halted.

Hadoop installation consists of four types of nodes—a NameNode , DataNodes , a JobTracker , and TaskTracker HDFS nodes (NameNode and DataNodes) provide a distributed filesystem where the JobTracker manages the jobs and TaskTrackers..

Hadoop runs applications using the MapReduce algorithm, where the data is processed in parallel on different CPU nodes. In short, Hadoop framework is capabale enough to develop applications capable of running on clusters of computers and they could perform complete statistical analysis for a huge amounts of data.

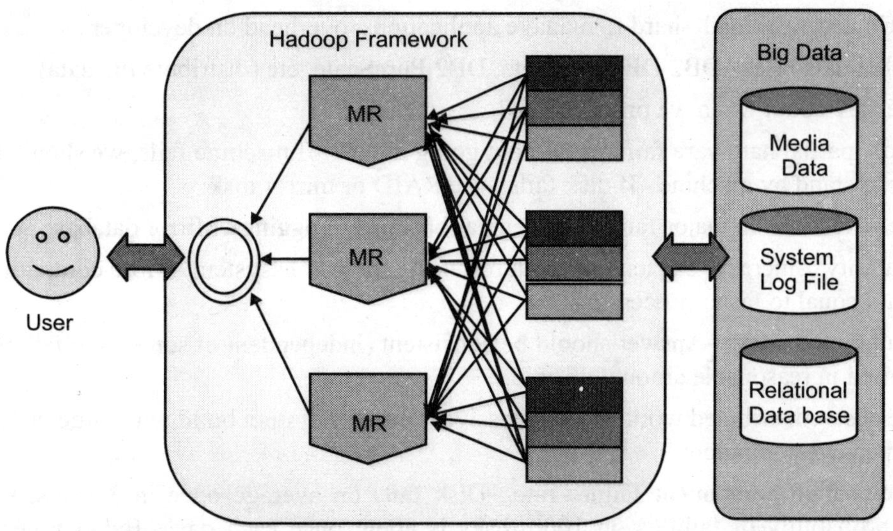

Figure. 2.6: MapReduce Hadoop

MapReduce is the parallel-processing engine that allows Hadoop to go through large data sets in relatively short order. HDFS is the distributed file system that lets Hadoop scale across commodity servers and, importantly, store data on the compute nodes in order to boost performance (and potentially save money). These are the two must-have components for any Hadoop distribution.

2.5 DISTRIBUTED APPLICATION CONCEPT

A distributed application can run on multiple systems in a network at a given time (simultaneously) by coordinating among themselves to complete a particular task in a fast and efficient manner. Normally, complex and time-consuming tasks, which will take hours to complete by a non-distributed application (running in a single system) can be done in minutes by a distributed application by using computing capabilities of all the system involved.

The time to complete the task can be further reduced by configuring the distributed application to run on more systems. A group of systems in which a distributed application is running is called a Cluster and each machine running in a cluster is called a Node.

How long it will take to read 1TB of data?

1TB (at 80Mb / sec):

- 1 disk -3.4 hours
- 10 disks -20 min
- 100 disks -2 min
- 1000 disks -12 sec

As such for dealing very high amount of data, parallel data processing is the answer! Thanks to exceptionally high speed of transfer of data.

It has been with us for a while:

1. GRID computing -spreads processing load
2. Distributed workload -hard to manage applications, overhead on developer
3. Parallel databases –DB2 DPF, Teradata, DB2 PureScale, etc (distribute the data)

What do we care about when we process data?

1. Handle partial hardware failures without going down: –If machine fails, we should be switch over to stand by machine –If disk fails –use RAID or mirror disk
2. Able to recover on major failures: –Regular backups –Logging –Mirror database at different site
3. Capability: –Increase capacity without restarting the whole system –More computing power should equal to faster processing
4. Result consistency: –Answer should be consistent (independent of something failing) and returned in reasonable amount of time.
5. Save costs -distributed workload on massively parallel system build with large numbers of inexpensive computers
6. Tolerate high component failure rate –Disk fails on average once in 3 years, which means that probability of failures on 1000 disks is about once each day. –Balance between power consumption and machine failure rates

7. Throughput is given higher priority over the response time –Batch operation, response will not be immediate
8. Large streaming scans (reads) -no random access
9. Large files preferred over small
10. Reliability provided though replication

Why Hadoop when we have relational databases?

1. One copy of data: –Exchanging data requires synchronization (consistency levels)
   - Deadlocks can become a problem
   - Need for backups –Need for recovery (based on logs or high availability)
2. RDBMS systems are very strong in transactional processing –What if you need to look at all the records in the database? How long will it take to do a relational scan on 100 TB?
3. RDBMS systems works extremely well with structured data –Some do a go job supporting XML data –Not as strong with other unstructured data 80% of all data is currently unstructured
4. Reliability requires expensive hardware

   RDBMS and Hadoop are complementary but not competing.

Table 2.1 Coparison of two data dealing methods RDBMS and Hadoop

Parameter	RDBMS	Hadoop
Type of Data	Structured data with known schemas	Unstructured and structured
Data Groups	Records, long fields, objects, XML	Files
Data Modification	Updates allowed	Only inserts and deletes (hdfs)
Programs	SQL & XQuery	Hive, Pig, Jaql
Access	Quick response, random access	Random access (indexing)
Data loss	Data loss is not acceptable	Data loss can happen sometimes
Security and auditing	Yes	Not yet
Encryption	Yes	Not yet
Compression Method	Sophisticated data compression	Simple file compression
Hardware requirement	Enterprise hardware	Commodity hardware
Evolution (for 2016)	30+ years of innovation	5-8 years old technology
Data Processing	Batch processing	Streaming Access to full files
Acceptance	Large DBA and Application development community, widely used	Small number of companies using it in production, many startups

A distributed application has two parts, Server and Client application. Server applications are actually distributed and have a common interface so that clients can connect to any server in the cluster and get the same result. Client applications are the tools to interact with a distributed application.

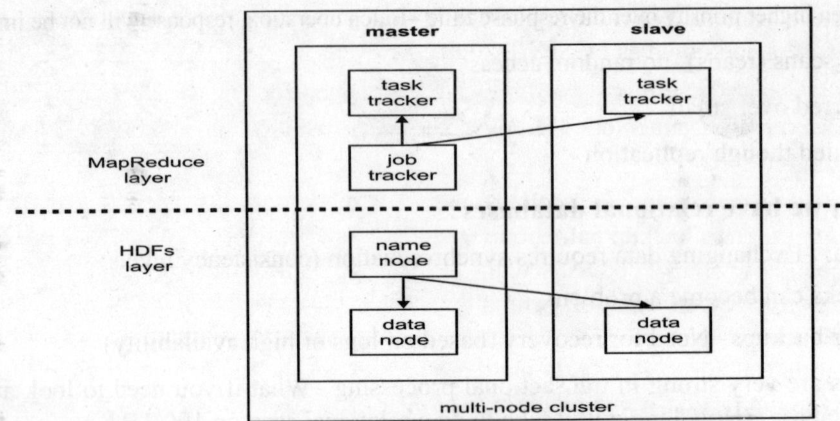

Figure. 2.7: Distributed Applications

2.5.1 Benefits of Distributed Applications

1. **Reliability** – Failure of a single or a few systems does not make the whole system to fail.
2. **Scalability** – Performance can be increased as and when needed by adding more machines with minor change in the configuration of the application with no downtime.
3. **Transparency** – Hides the complexity of the system and shows itself as a single entity / application.

2.6 HADOOP DISTRIBUTED FILE SYSTEM

The Hadoop distributed file system (HDFS) is a distributed, scalable, and portable file-system written in Java for the Hadoop framework. A Hadoop cluster has nominally a single namenode plus a cluster of datanodes, although redundancy options are available for the namenode due to its criticality. Each datanode serves up blocks of data over the network using a block protocol specific to HDFS. The file system uses TCP/IP sockets for communication. Clients use remote procedure call (RPC) to communicate between each other.

HDFS stores large files (typically in the range of gigabytes to terabyte across multiple machines. It achieves reliability by replicating the data across multiple hosts, and hence theoretically does not require RAID storage on hosts (but to increase I/O performance some RAID configurations are still useful). With the default replication value, 3, data is stored on three nodes: two on the same rack, and one on a different rack. Data nodes can talk to each other to rebalance data, to move copies around, and to keep the replication of data high. HDFS is not fully POSIX-compliant, because the requirements for a POSIX file-system differ from the target goals for a Hadoop application. The trade-off of not having a fully POSIX-compliant file-system is increased performance for data throughput and support for non-POSIX operations such as Append.

Unix was selected as the basis for a standard system interface partly because it was "manufacturer-neutral." However, several major versions of Unix existed so there was a need to develop a common denominator system. The POSIX specifications for Unix-like operating systems originally consisted of a single document for the core programming interface, but eventually grew to 19 separate documents (POSIX.1, POSIX.2, etc.) POSIX also defines a standard threading library API which is supported by most modern operating systems. Nowadays, most of POSIX parts are combined into a single standard, IEEE Std 1003.1-2008, also known as POSIX.1-2008.

HDFS added the high-availability capabilities, as announced for release 2.0 in May 2012, letting the main metadata server (the NameNode) fail over manually to a backup. The project has also started developing automatic fail-over.

The HDFS file system includes a so-called secondary namenode, a misleading name that some might incorrectly interpret as a backup namenode for when the primary namenode goes offline. In fact, the secondary namenode regularly connects with the primary namenode and builds snapshots of the primary namenode's directory information, which the system then saves to local or remote directories. These checkpointed images can be used to restart a failed primary namenode without having to replay the entire journal of file-system actions, then to edit the log to create an up-to-date directory structure. Because the namenode is the single point for storage and management of metadata, it can become a bottleneck for supporting a huge number of files, especially a large number of small files. HDFS Federation, a new addition, aims to tackle this problem to a certain extent by allowing multiple namespaces served by separate namenodes.

An advantage of using HDFS is data awareness between the job tracker and task tracker. The job tracker schedules map or reduce jobs to task trackers with an awareness of the data location. For example: if node A contains data (x,y,z) and node B contains data (a,b,c), the job tracker schedules node B to perform map or reduce tasks on (a,b,c) and node A would be scheduled to perform map or reduce tasks on (x,y,z). This reduces the amount of traffic that goes over the network and prevents unnecessary data transfer. When Hadoop is used with other file systems, this advantage is not always available. This can have a significant impact on job-completion times, which has been demonstrated when running data-intensive jobs.

HDFS was designed for mostly immutable files and may not be suitable for systems requiring concurrent write-operations.

HDFS can be mounted directly with a Filesystem in Userspace (FUSE) virtual file system on Linux and some other Unix systems.

File access can be achieved through the native Java application programming interface (API), the Thrift API to generate a client in the language of the users' choosing (C++, Java, Python, PHP, Ruby, Erlang, Perl, Haskell, C#, Cocoa, Smalltalk, and OCaml), the command-line interface, browsed through the HDFS-UI Web application (webapp) over HTTP, or via 3rd-party network client libraries.[18]We will read in detail about HDFS in chapter 4 of this book.

2.7 HADOOP CLUSTERING

Apache Hadoop's MapReduce and HDFS components were inspired by Google papers on their MapReduce and Google File System.

The Hadoop framework itself is mostly written in the Java programming language, with some native code in C and command line utilities written as shell scripts. Though MapReduce Java code is common, any programming language can be used with "Hadoop Streaming" to implement the "map" and "reduce" parts of the user's program. Other projects in the Hadoop ecosystem expose richer user interfaces.

For effective scheduling of work, every Hadoop-compatible file system should provide location awareness: the name of the rack (more precisely, of the network switch) where a worker node is. Hadoop applications can use this information to execute code on the node where the data is, and, failing that, on the same rack/switch to reduce backbone traffic. HDFS uses this method when replicating data for data redundancy across multiple racks. This approach reduces the impact of a rack power outage or switch failure; if one of these hardware failures occurs, the data will remain available.

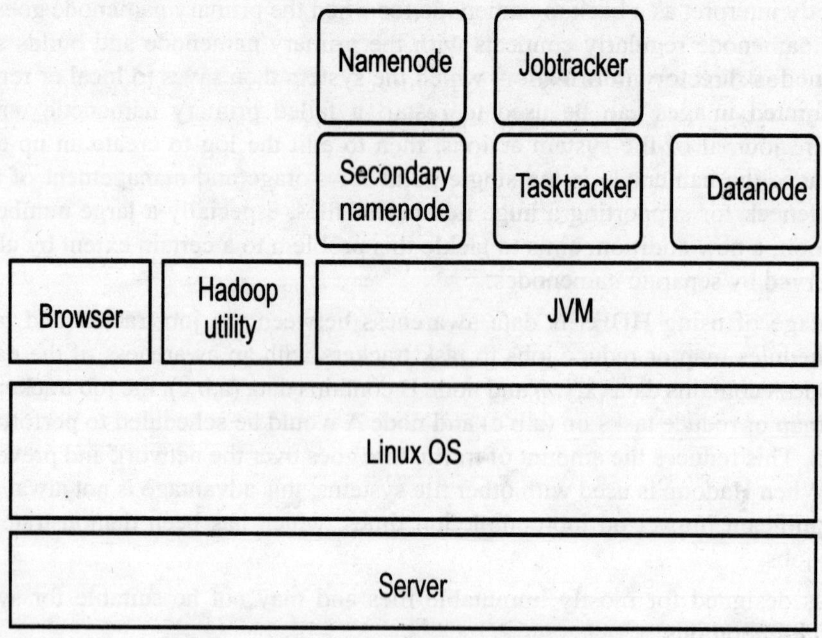

Figure. 2.8: A Multi-node Hadoop Cluster

A small Hadoop cluster includes a single master and multiple worker nodes. The master node consists of a Job Tracker, Task Tracker, NameNode, and DataNode. A slave or *worker node* acts as both a DataNode and TaskTracker, though it is possible to have data-only worker nodes and compute-only worker nodes. These are normally used only in nonstandard applications.[14]

Hadoop requires Java Runtime Environment (JRE) 1.6 or higher. The standard startup and shutdown scripts require that Secure Shell (ssh) be set up between nodes in the cluster.[19]

In a larger cluster, HDFS nodes are managed through a dedicated NameNode server to host the file system index, and a secondary NameNode that can generate snapshots of the namenode's memory structures, thereby preventing file-system corruption and loss of data. Similarly, a standalone JobTracker server can manage job scheduling across nodes. When Hadoop MapReduce is used with an alternate file system, the NameNode, secondary NameNode, and DataNode architecture of HDFS are replaced by the file-system-specific equivalents.

Hierarchical clustering is the process or finding bigger clusters, and also the smaller clusters inside the bigger clusters.In Apache Mahout, separate algorithms can be used for finding clusters at different levels.

2.7.1 Daemon Services of Hadoop

1. Namenodes
2. Secondary Namenodes
3. Jobtracker
4. Datanodes
5. Tasktracker

JobTracker and TaskTracker are coming into picture when we required processing to data set. The relationship between server and various components of HDFS system are shown in Fig. 2.9 where as the role of server is shown in Fig. 2.10.

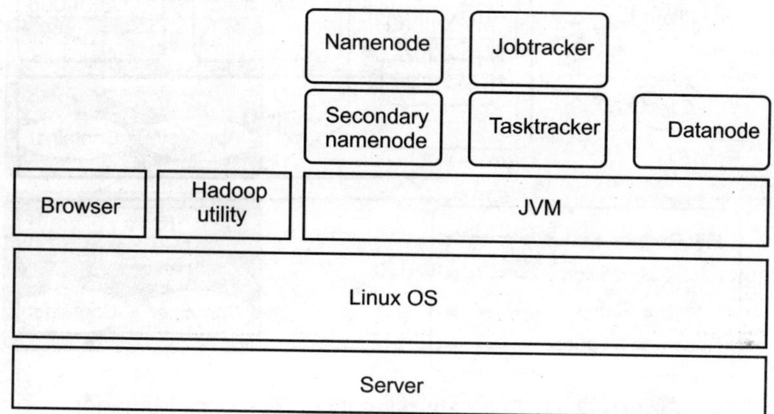

Figure. 2.9: The relationship between server and various components of HDFS

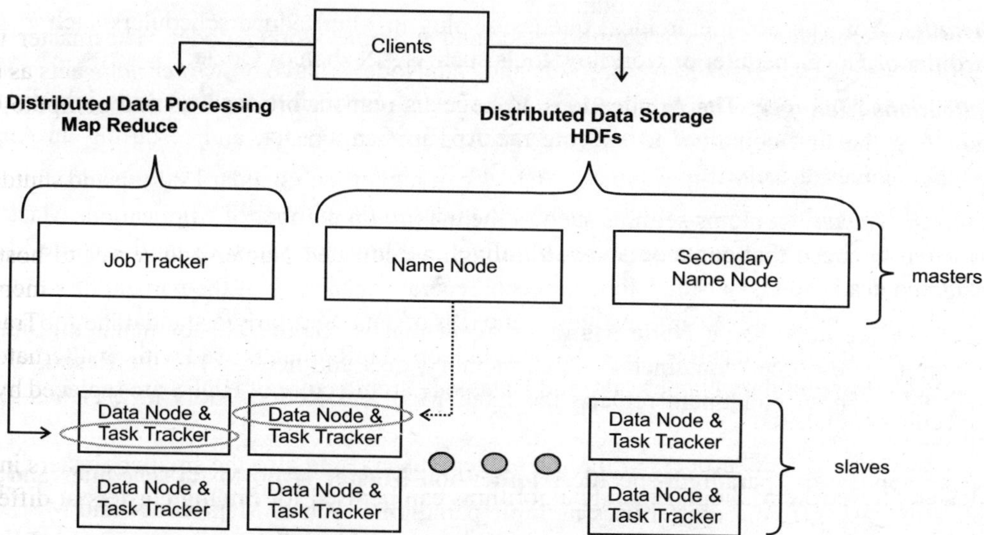

Figure. 2.10: The role of Hadoop Server

2.8 YARN (NEXT-GENERATION MAPREDUCE)

MapReduce job tracking uses the following components and sub-components:

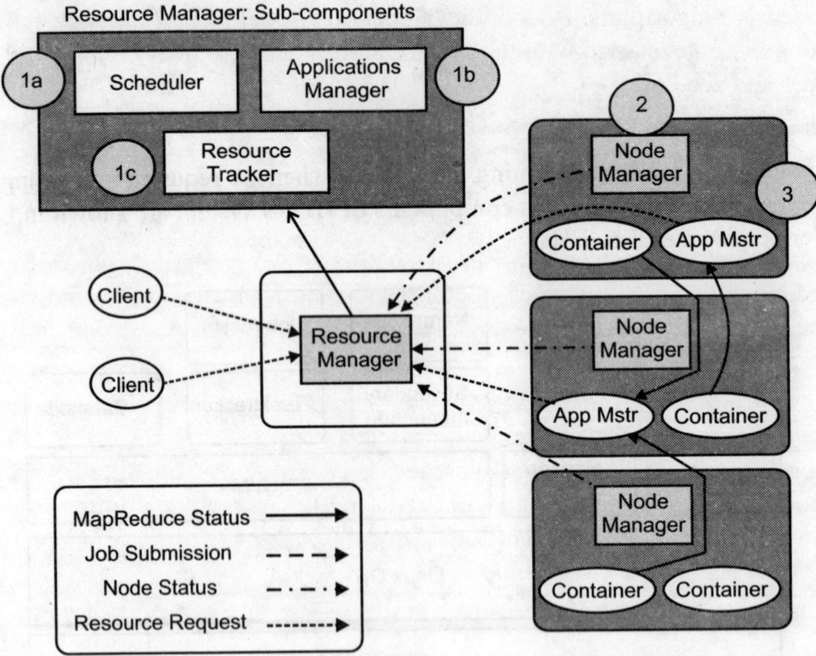

Figure. 2.11: Sub Components of Resource Manager

(1) Resource Manager:

(a) ***Scheduler***: You can use hierarchical queues or plug in MapReduce schedulers such as Capacity Scheduler or Fair Scheduler or workflow tools such as Azkaban or Oozie.

(b) ***Applications Manager***: The Applications Manager is responsible for accepting job submissions, negotiating the first container to execute the Application Master, and restarting an Application Master container on failure.

(c) ***Resource Tracker***: Contains settings such as the maximum number of Applications Master retries, how often to check that containers are still alive, and how long to wait until a Node Manager is considered dead.

(2) Each hardware node has a **Node Manager** agent that is responsible for managing, monitoring and reporting resource "containers" (CPU, memory, disk and network) to the Resource Manager / Scheduler. These containers replace the fixed Map and Reduce slots in previous-generation MapReduce.

(3) The per-application, paradigm-specific **Application Master** (App Mstr) schedules and executes application tasks. If your cluster uses multiple paradigms such as MapReduce and MPI, each will have its own Applications Master, such as the MapReduce Application Master and MPI (message passing interface) Application Master.

2.8.1 Hadoop 1

Hadoop 1 popularized MapReduce programming for batch jobs and demonstrated the potential value of large scale, distributed processing. MapReduce, as implemented in Hadoop 1, can be I/O intensive, not suitable for interactive analysis, and constrained in support for graph, machine learning and on other memory intensive algorithms. Hadoop developers rewrote major components of the file system to produce Hadoop 2. To get started with the new version, it helps to understand the major differences between Hadoop 1 and 2.

Two of the most important advances in Hadoop 2 are the introduction of HDFS federation and the resource manager YARN.

2.8.2 Hadoop 2:

HDFS is the Hadoop file system and comprises two major components: namespaces and blocks storage service. The namespace service manages operations on files and directories, such as creating and modifying files and directories. The block storage service implements data node cluster management, block operations and replication.

In Hadoop 1, a single Namenode managed the entire namespace for a Hadoop cluster. With HDFS federation, multiple Namenode servers manage namespaces and this allows for horizontal scaling, performance improvements, and multiple namespaces. The implementation of HDFS federation allows existing Namenode configurations to run without changes. For Hadoop administrators, moving to HDFS federation requires formatting Namenodes, updating to use the latest Hadoop cluster software, and adding additional Namenodes to the cluster.

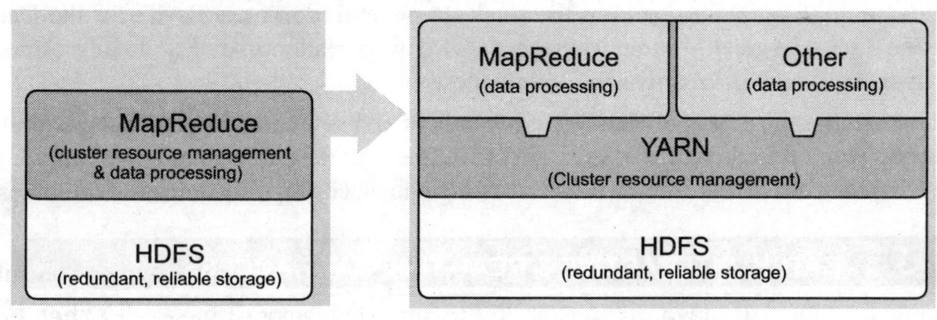

Figure. 2.12: (a) Hadoop 1 (b) Hadoop 2

2.8.3 Hadoop 2: YARN

HDFS federation brings important measures of scalability and reliability to Hadoop. YARN, the other major advance in Hadoop 2, brings significant performance improvements for some applications, supports additional processing models, and implements a more flexible execution engine.

YARN is a resource manager that was created by separating the processing engine and resource management capabilities of MapReduce as it was implemented in Hadoop 1. YARN is often called the operating system of Hadoop because it is responsible for managing and monitoring workloads, maintaining a multi-tenant environment, implementing security controls, and managing high availability features of Hadoop.

Like an operating system on a server, YARN is designed to allow multiple, diverse user applications to run on a multi-tenant platform. In Hadoop 1, users had the option of writing MapReduce programs in Java, in Python, Ruby or other scripting languages using streaming, or using Pig, a data transformation language. Regardless of which method was used, all fundamentally relied on the MapReduce processing model to run.

YARN supports multiple processing models in addition to MapReduce. One of the most significant benefits of this is that we are no longer limited to working the often I/O intensive, high latency MapReduce framework. This advance means Hadoop users should be familiar with the pros and cons of the new processing models and understand when to apply them to particular use cases.

As with terminology such as namespace, you'll often see these YARN components written as *ResourceManager*, *NodeManager* and *ApplicationMaster*. It is possible for the ApplicationMaster to communicate with more than one hardware node, so it is not a requirement to replicate the Application Master on every node. As shown on this chart, some nodes may only have containers, with the Application Master (App Mstr) residing on an adjacent node (for a example a node in the same rack using rack awareness).

Current-generation Hadoop does not support IPV6. For organizations with IPv6, investigate using machine names with a DNS server instead of IP addresses to label each node. While organizations in quickly growing markets such as China have been early adopters to IPv6 due to historical allocations of IPv4 addresses, IPv6 is started to get more attention in North America and other regions too.

For the **DataNodes**, expect failure. With HDFS, when a DataNode crashes, the cluster does not crash, but performance degrades in proportion to the amount of lost storage and processing capacity as the still-functioning DataNodes pick up the slack. In general, don't use RAID for the DataNodes, and avoid using Linux Logical Volume Manager (LVM) with Hadoop. HDFS already offers built-in redundancy by replicating blocks across multiple nodes.

YARN also extends the power of Hadoop to incumbent and new technologies found within the data center so that they can take advantage of cost effective, linear-scale storage and processing. It provides ISVs and developers a consistent framework for writing data access applications that run in Hadoop.

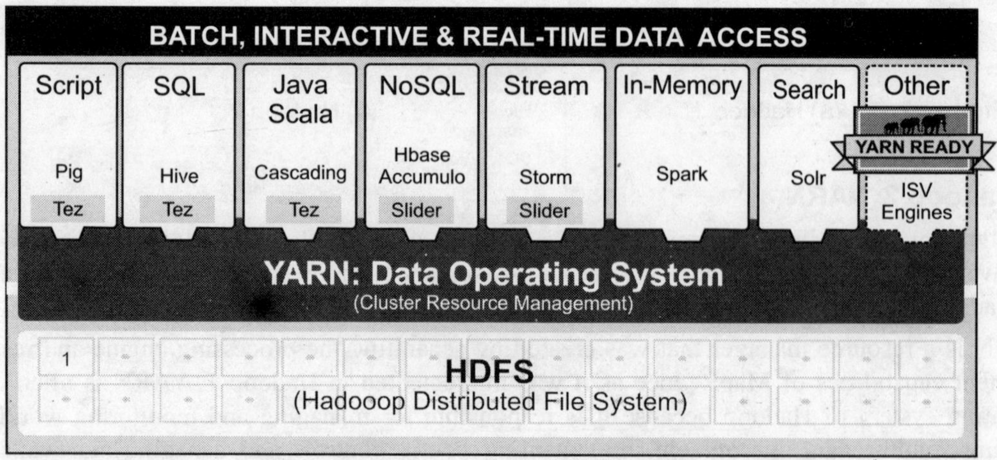

Figure. 2.13: Yarn : The next Generation MapReduce of Hadoop

YARN's original purpose was to split up the two major responsibilities of the JobTracker/ TaskTracker into separate entities:

1. A global ResourceManager
2. A per-application ApplicationMaster
3. A per-node slave NodeManager
4. A per-application Container running on a NodeManager

The ResourceManager and the NodeManager formed the new generic system for managing applications in a distributed manner. The ResourceManager is the ultimate authority that arbitrates resources among all applications in the system. The ApplicationMaster is a framework-specific entity that negotiates resources from the ResourceManager and works with the NodeManager(s) to execute and monitor the component tasks.

The ResourceManager has a scheduler, which is responsible for allocating resources to the various applications running in the cluster, according to constraints such as queue capacities and user limits. The scheduler schedules based on the resource requirements of each application.

Each ApplicationMaster has responsibility for negotiating appropriate resource containers from the scheduler, tracking their status, and monitoring their progress. From the system perspective, the ApplicationMaster runs as a normal container.

The NodeManager is the per-machine slave, which is responsible for launching the applications' containers, monitoring their resource usage (cpu, memory, disk, network) and reporting the same to the ResourceManager.

2.9 GENERAL PARALLEL FILE SYSTEM (IBM'S GPFS™)

General Parallel File System (GPFS) is an enterprise file system that InfoSphere® BigInsights™ supports as an alternative to HDFS. GPFS was developed by IBM in the 1990s for high-performance computing applications. It has been used in many of the world's fastest computers (including Blue Gene and Watson).

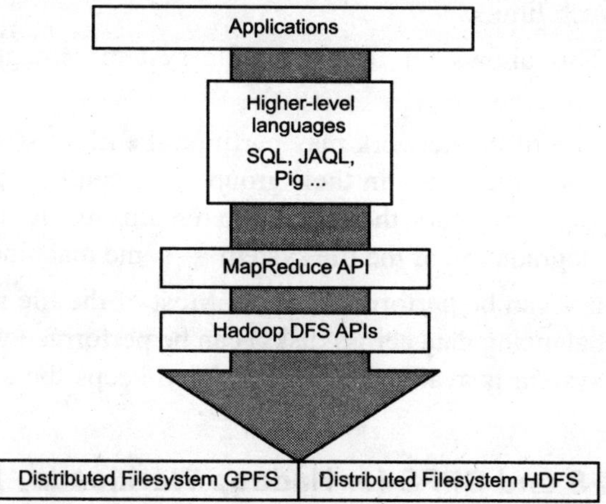

Figure. 2.14: Working of General Parallel File System (IBM's GPFS™)

GPFS supports local disks on cluster nodes and storage area networks (SANs). Logical isolation and physical isolation are supported so that file sets can be separate file systems inside of a file system (logical isolation), or can be part of separate storage pools (physical isolation). InfoSphere BigInsights uses a customized version of GPFS that supports all existing GPFS commands and provides additional interfaces and commands.

GPFS supports thousands of nodes and peta bytes of storage so that you can modify the scale to meet your most demanding needs. Data is replicated on multiple nodes so that no single point of failure exists, whereas the NameNode is a single point of failure in HDFS. You can push updates synchronously or asynchronously, allowing you to choose how you want to manage changes from a primary system to a secondary system.

If a node fails, changes are replicated to other nodes. When the failed node is operational, GPFS quickly determines which blocks must be recovered. Changes that occurred while the node was down are copied to the previously failed node so that the node is synchronized with other nodes in the cluster.

Applications define their own logical block size by segmenting data into file blocks. Each file block is determined based on the effective block size or chunk size. Applications can also determine replication layout by using either wide striping over the network, write affinity on a local disk, or a combination of both layouts. Allowing applications to dictate block size and replication layout provides greater performance and efficiency over HDFS.

GPFS was the file system of the ASC Purple Supercomputer which was composed of more than 12,000 processors and has 2 petabytes of total disk storage spanning more than 11,000 disks.

In common with typical cluster file systems, GPFS provides concurrent high-speed file access to applications executing on multiple nodes of clusters.

Other features of the GPFS files system include:

1. Distributed metadata, including the directory tree. There is no single "directory controller" or "index server" in charge of the file system.
2. Efficient indexing of directory entries for very large directories. Many file systems are limited to a small number of files in a single directory (often, 65536 or a similar small binary number). GPFS does not have such limits.
3. Distributed locking. This allows for full Posix file system semantics, including locking for exclusive file access.
4. Partition Aware. A failure of the network may partition the file system into two or more groups of nodes that can only see the nodes in their group. This can be detected through a heartbeat protocol, and when a partition occurs, the file system remains live for the largest partition formed. This offers a graceful degradation of the file system — some machines will remain working.
5. File system maintenance can be performed online. Most of the file system maintenance chores (adding new disks, rebalancing data across disks) can be performed while the file system is live. This ensures the file system is available more often, so keeps the supercomputer cluster itself available for longer.

2.9.1 Similarties of HDFS and GPFS for Hadoop Workloads

IBM General Parallel File System (GPFS) is similar to HDFS in the following ways:

1. Data inside the file system must appear as if it is coming from HDFS.
2. The /tmp and /user directories as well as the application frameworks that are supplied byInfoSphere BigInsights are owned by the HDFS user.

On the Linux command line shell, the file system permission for the /tmp directory on GPFS is associated with the HDFS user instead of the GPFS or root user.

2.9.2 Comparision of HDFS and GPFS for Hadoop Workloads

It is interesting to compare this with Hadoop's HDFS files ystem, which is designed to store similar or greater quantities of data on commodity hardware — that is, data centers without RAID disks and a Storage Area Network (SAN).

1. HDFS also breaks files up into blocks, and stores them on different filesystem nodes.
2. HDFS does not expect reliable disks, so instead stores copies of the blocks on different nodes. The failure of a node containing a single copy of a block is a minor issue, dealt with by re-replicating another copy of the set of valid blocks, to bring the replication count back up to the desired number. In contrast, while GPFS supports recovery from a lost node, it is a more serious event, one that may include a higher risk of data being (temporarily) lost.
3. GPFS supports full Posix file system semantics. HDFS and GFS do not support full Posix compliance.
4. GPFS distributes its directory indices and other metadata across the filesystem. Hadoop, in contrast, keeps this on the Primary and Secondary Namenodes, large servers which must store all index information in-RAM.
5. GPFS breaks files up into small blocks. Hadoop HDFS likes blocks of 64 MB or more, as this reduces the storage requirements of the Namenode. Small blocks or many small files fill up a file system's indices fast, so limit the file system's size.

Recently 2015 or so, IBM extended GPFS to develop GPFS-SNC, which is suitable for Hadoop environments. A key difference between GPFS-SNC and HDFS is that GPFS-SNC is a kernel-level file system, whereas HDFS runs on top of the operating system. This means that GPFS-SNC offers several advantages over HDFS, including:

1. Better performance
2. Storage flexibility
3. Concurrent read/write
4. Improved security

A 10-node GPFS-SNC-based Hadoop cluster can match the performance of a 16-node HDFS-based Hadoop cluster.

2.10 THE MAPREDUCE'S ENGINES : JOBTRACKER AND TASKTRACKER

Above the file systems, comes the MapReduce Engine, which consists of one *JobTracker*, to which client applications submit MapReduce jobs. The JobTracker pushes work out to available *TaskTracker* nodes in the cluster, striving to keep the work as close to the data as possible. With a rack-aware file system, the JobTracker knows which node contains the data, and which other machines are nearby. If the work cannot be hosted on the actual node where the data resides, priority is given to nodes in the same rack. This reduces network traffic on the main backbone network. If a TaskTracker fails or times out, that part of the job is rescheduled. The TaskTracker on each node spawns a separate Java Virtual Machine process to prevent the TaskTracker itself from failing if the running job crashes its JVM. A heartbeat is sent from the TaskTracker to the JobTracker every few minutes to check its status. The Job Tracker and TaskTracker status and information is exposed by Jetty and can be viewed from a web browser.

Known limitations of this approach are:

- The allocation of work to TaskTrackers is very simple. Every TaskTracker has a number of available *slots* (such as "4 slots"). Every active map or reduce task takes up one slot. The Job Tracker allocates work to the tracker nearest to the data with an available slot. There is no consideration of the current system load of the allocated machine, and hence its actual availability.
- If one TaskTracker is very slow, it can delay the entire MapReduce job—especially towards the end of a job, where everything can end up waiting for the slowest task. With speculative execution enabled, however, a single task can be executed on multiple slave nodes.

2.10.1 Scheduling

By default Hadoop uses FIFO scheduling, and optionally 5 scheduling priorities to schedule jobs from a work queue. In version 0.19 the job scheduler was refactored out of the JobTracker, while adding the ability to use an alternate scheduler (such as the Fair scheduler or the Capacity scheduler, described next).

2.10.2 Fair Scheduler

The fair scheduler was developed by Facebook. The goal of the fair scheduler is to provide fast response times for small jobs and QoS for production jobs. The fair scheduler has three basic concepts.

1. Jobs are grouped into pools.
2. Each pool is assigned a guaranteed minimum share.
3. Excess capacity is split between jobs.

By default, jobs that are uncategorized go into a default pool. Pools have to specify the minimum number of map slots, reduce slots, and a limit on the number of running jobs.

2.10.3 Capacity Scheduler

The capacity scheduler was developed by Yahoo. The capacity scheduler supports several features that are similar to the fair scheduler.

- Queues are allocated a fraction of the total resource capacity.
- Free resources are allocated to queues beyond their total capacity.

Within a queue a job with a high level of priority has access to the queue's resources.

There is no preemption once a job is running.

2.11 PROMINENT USERS

On February 19, 2008, Yahoo! Inc. launched what it claimed was the world's largest Hadoop production application. The Yahoo! Search Webmap is a Hadoop application that runs on a Linux cluster with more than 10,000 cores and produced data that was used in every Yahoo! web search query.[30] There are multiple Hadoop clusters at Yahoo! and no HDFS file systems or MapReduce jobs are split across multiple datacenters. Every Hadoop cluster node bootstraps the Linux image, including the Hadoop distribution. Work that the clusters perform is known to include the index calculations for the Yahoo! search engine. In June of 2009, Yahoo! made the source code of the Hadoop version it runs available to the public via the open-source community.

In 2010, Facebook claimed that they had the largest Hadoop cluster in the world with 21 PB of storage. In June of 2012, they announced the data had grown to 100 PB[33] and later that year they announced that the data was growing by roughly half a PB per day.

As of 2013[update], Hadoop adoption had become widespread: more than half of the Fortune 50 used Hadoop.

2.12 HADOOP HOSTING IN THE CLOUD

Hadoop can be deployed in a traditional onsite datacenter as well as in the cloud. The cloud allows organizations to deploy Hadoop without hardware to acquire or specific setup expertise. Vendors who currently have an offer for the cloud include Microsoft, Amazon, and Google.

2.12.1 Hadoop on Microsoft Azure

Azure HDInsight is a service that deploys Hadoop on Microsoft Azure. HDInsight uses a Windows-based Hadoop distribution that was jointly developed with Hortonworks and allows programming extensions with .NET (in addition to Java). HDInsight also supports creation of Hadoop clusters using Linux with Ubuntu. By deploying HDInsight in the cloud, organizations can spin up the number of nodes they want and only get charged for the compute and storage that is used. Hortonworks implementations can also move data from the on-premises datacenter to the cloud for backup, development/test, and bursting scenarios. It is also possible to run Cloudera or Hortonworks Hadoop clusters on Azure Virtual Machines.

2.12.2 Hadoop on Amazon EC2/S3 services

It is possible to run Hadoop on Amazon Elastic Compute Cloud (EC2) and Amazon Simple Storage Service (S3). As an example, The New York Times used 100 Amazon EC2 instances and a Hadoop application to process 4 TB of raw image TIFF data (stored in S3) into 11 million finished PDFs in the space of 24 hours at a computation cost of about $240 (not including bandwidth).

There is support for the S3 object store in the Apache Hadoop releases, though this is below what one expects from a traditional POSIX filesystem. Specifically, operations such as rename() and delete() on directories are not atomic, and can take time proportional to the number of entries and the amount of data in them.

2.12.3 Amazon Elastic MapReduce

Elastic MapReduce (EMR) was introduced by Amazon.com in April 2009. Provisioning of the Hadoop cluster, running and terminating jobs, and handling data transfer between EC2(VM) and S3(Object Storage) are automated by Elastic MapReduce. Apache Hive, which is built on top of Hadoop for providing data warehouse services, is also offered in Elastic MapReduce.

Support for using Spot Instances was later added in August 2011. Elastic MapReduce is fault tolerant for slave failures, and it is recommended to only run the Task Instance Group on spot instances to take advantage of the lower cost while maintaining availability

2.13 HOW DOES HADOOP WORK?

Stage 1

A user/application can submit a job to the Hadoop (a hadoop job client) for required process by specifying the following items:

1. The location of the input and output files in the distributed file system.
2. The java classes in the form of jar file containing the implementation of map and reduce functions.
3. The job configuration by setting different parameters specific to the job.

Stage 2

The Hadoop job client then submits the job (jar/executable etc) and configuration to the JobTracker which then assumes the responsibility of distributing the software/configuration to the slaves, scheduling tasks and monitoring them, providing status and diagnostic information to the job-client.

Stage 3

The TaskTrackers on different nodes execute the task as per MapReduce implementation and output of the reduce function is stored into the output files on the file system.

Hadoop is supported by GNU/Linux platform and its flavors. Therefore, we have to install a Linux operating system for setting up Hadoop environment. In case you have an OS other than Linux, you can install a Virtualbox software in it and have Linux inside the Virtualbox.

2.14 SETTING HADOOP FRAMEWORK

2.14.1 Pre-installation Setup

Before installing Hadoop into the Linux environment, we need to set up Linux using ssh (Secure Shell). Follow the steps given below for setting up the Linux environment.

(a) Creating a User

At the beginning, it is recommended to create a separate user for Hadoop to isolate Hadoop file system from Unix file system. Follow the steps given below to create a user:

- Open the root using the command "su".
- Create a user from the root account using the command "useradd username".
- Now you can open an existing user account using the command "su username".

Open the Linux terminal and type the following commands to create a user.

```
$ su
  password:
# useradd hadoop
# passwd hadoop
  New passwd:
  Retype new passwd
```

(b) SSH Setup and Key Generation

SSH setup is required to do different operations on a cluster such as starting, stopping, distributed daemon shell operations. To authenticate different users of Hadoop, it is required to provide public/private key pair for a Hadoop user and share it with different users.

The following commands are used for generating a key value pair using SSH. Copy the public keys form id_rsa.pub to authorized_keys, and provide the owner with read and write permissions to authorized_keys file respectively.

```
$ ssh-keygen -t rsa
$ cat ~/.ssh/id_rsa.pub >> ~/.ssh/authorized_keys
$ chmod 0600 ~/.ssh/authorized_keys
```

(c) Installing Java

Java is the main prerequisite for Hadoop. First of all, you should verify the existence of java in your system using the command "java -version". The syntax of java version command is given below.

```
$ java -version
```

If everything is in order, it will give you the following output.

```
java version "1.7.0_71"
Java(TM) SE Runtime Environment (build 1.7.0_71-b13)
Java HotSpot(TM) Client VM (build 25.0-b02, mixed mode)
```

If java is not installed in your system, then follow the steps given below for installing java.

Step 1

Download java (JDK <latest version> - X64.tar.gz) by visiting the following link http://www.oracle.com/technetwork/java/javase/downloads/jdk7-downloads1880260.html.

Then jdk-7u71-linux-x64.tar.gz will be downloaded into your system.

Step 2

Generally you will find the downloaded java file in Downloads folder. Verify it and extract the jdk-7u71-linux-x64.gz file using the following commands.

```
$ cd Downloads/
$ ls
jdk-7u71-linux-x64.gz
$ tar zxf jdk-7u71-linux-x64.gz
$ ls
jdk1.7.0_71   jdk-7u71-linux-x64.gz
```

Step 3

To make java available to all the users, you have to move it to the location "/usr/local/". Open root, and type the following commands.

```
$ su
password:
# mv jdk1.7.0_71 /usr/local/
# exit
```

Step 4

For setting up PATH and JAVA_HOME variables, add the following commands to ~/.bashrc file.

```
export JAVA_HOME=/usr/local/jdk1.7.0_71
export PATH=$PATH:$JAVA_HOME/bin
```

Now apply all the changes into the current running system.

```
$ source ~/.bashrc
```

Step 5

Use the following commands to configure java alternatives:

```
# alternatives --install /usr/bin/java java usr/local/java/bin/java 2
# alternatives --install /usr/bin/javac javac usr/local/java/bin/javac 2
# alternatives --install /usr/bin/jar jar usr/local/java/bin/jar 2
# alternatives --set java usr/local/java/bin/java
# alternatives --set javac usr/local/java/bin/javac
# alternatives --set jar usr/local/java/bin/jar
```

Now verify the java -version command from the terminal as explained above.

(d) Downloading Hadoop

Download and extract Hadoop 2.4.1 from Apache software foundation using the following commands.

```
$ su
password:
# cd /usr/local
# wget http://apache.claz.org/hadoop/common/hadoop-2.4.1/
hadoop-2.4.1.tar.gz
# tar xzf hadoop-2.4.1.tar.gz
# mv hadoop-2.4.1/* to hadoop/
# exit
```

2.14.2 Hadoop Operation Modes

Once you have downloaded Hadoop, you can operate your Hadoop cluster in one of the three supported modes:

- **Local/Standalone Mode** : After downloading Hadoop in your system, by default, it is configured in a standalone mode and can be run as a single java process.
- **Pseudo Distributed Mode** : It is a distributed simulation on single machine. Each Hadoop daemon such as hdfs, yarn, MapReduce etc., will run as a separate java process. This mode is useful for development.
- **Fully Distributed Mode** : This mode is fully distributed with minimum two or more machines as a cluster. We will come across this mode in detail in the coming chapters.

(1) Installing Hadoop in Standalone Mode

Here we will discuss the installation of **Hadoop 2.4.1** in standalone mode.

There are no daemons running and everything runs in a single JVM. Standalone mode is suitable for running MapReduce programs during development, since it is easy to test and debug them.

Setting Up Hadoop

You can set Hadoop environment variables by appending the following commands to **~/.bashrc** file.

```
export HADOOP_HOME=/usr/local/hadoop
```

Before proceeding further, you need to make sure that Hadoop is working fine. Just isSmita the following command:

```
$ hadoop version
```

If everything is fine with your setup, then you should see the following result:

```
Hadoop 2.4.1
Subversion https://svn.apache.org/repos/asf/hadoop/common -r 1529768
Compiled by hortonmu on 2013-10-07T06:28Z
Compiled with protoc 2.5.0
From source with checksum 79e53ce7994d1628b240f09af91e1af4
```

It means your Hadoop's standalone mode setup is working fine. By default, Hadoop is configured to run in a non-distributed mode on a single machine.

Hadoop Pipes has a generic Java class for handling the mapper and reducer (PipesMapRunner and PipesReducer). They fork off the application program and communicate with it over a socket. The communication is handled by the C++ wrapper library and the PipesMapRunner and PipesReducer.

Example

Let's check a simple example of Hadoop. Hadoop installation delivers the following example MapReduce jar file, which provides basic functionality of MapReduce and can be used for calculating, like Pi value, word counts in a given list of files, etc.

```
$HADOOP_HOME/share/hadoop/mapreduce/hadoop-mapreduce-examples-
2.2.0.jar
```

Let's have an input directory where we will push a few files and our requirement is to count the total number of words in those files. To calculate the total number of words, we do not need to write our MapReduce, provided the .jar file contains the implementation for word count. You can try other examples using the same .jar file; just isSmita the following commands to check supported MapReduce functional programs by hadoop-mapreduce-examples-2.2.0.jar file.

```
$ hadoop jar $HADOOP_HOME/share/hadoop/mapreducé/hadoop-
mapreduceexamples-2.2.0.jar
```

Step 1

Create temporary content files in the input directory. You can create this input directory anywhere you would like to work.

```
$ mkdir input
$ cp $HADOOP_HOME/*.txt input
$ ls -l input
```

It will give the following files in your input directory:

```
total 24
-rw-r--r-- 1 root root 15164 Feb 21 10:14 LICENSE.txt
-rw-r--r-- 1 root root   101 Feb 21 10:14 NOTICE.txt
-rw-r--r-- 1 root root  1366 Feb 21 10:14 README.txt
```

These files have been copied from the Hadoop installation home directory. For your experiment, you can have different and large sets of files.

Step 2

Let's start the Hadoop process to count the total number of words in all the files available in the input directory, as follows:

```
$    hadoop     jar     $HADOOP_HOME/share/hadoop/mapreduce/hadoop-
mapreduceexamples-2.2.0.jar  wordcount input ouput
```

Step 3

Step-2 will do the required processing and save the output in output/part-r00000 file, which you can check by using:

```
$cat output/*
```

It will list down all the words along with their total counts available in all the files available in the input directory.

```
"AS      4
"Contribution" 1
"Contributor" 1
"Derivative 1
"Legal 1
"License"      1
"License");      1
"Licensor"       1
"NOTICE"         1
"Not       1
"Object"         1
"Source"         1
"Work"     1
"You"      1
"Your")    1
"[]"       1
"control"        1
"printed         1
"submitted"      1
(50%)      1
(BIS),     1
(C)        1
(Don't)    1
(ECCN)     1
(INCLUDING       2
(INCLUDING,      2
............
```

2.14.3 Installing Hadoop in Pseudo Distributed Mode

Follow the steps given below to install Hadoop 2.4.1 in pseudo distributed mode.

Step 1: Setting Up Hadoop

You can set Hadoop environment variables by appending the following commands to **~/.bashrc** file.

```
export HADOOP_HOME=/usr/local/hadoop
export HADOOP_MAPRED_HOME=$HADOOP_HOME
export HADOOP_COMMON_HOME=$HADOOP_HOME
export HADOOP_HDFS_HOME=$HADOOP_HOME
export YARN_HOME=$HADOOP_HOME
export HADOOP_COMMON_LIB_NATIVE_DIR=$HADOOP_HOME/lib/native
export PATH=$PATH:$HADOOP_HOME/sbin:$HADOOP_HOME/bin
export HADOOP_INSTALL=$HADOOP_HOME
```

Now apply all the changes into the current running system.

```
$ source ~/.bashrc
```

Step 2: Hadoop Configuration

You can find all the Hadoop configuration files in the location "$HADOOP_HOME/etc/hadoop". It is required to make changes in those configuration files according to your Hadoop infrastructure.

```
$ cd $HADOOP_HOME/etc/hadoop
```

In order to develop Hadoop programs in java, you have to reset the java environment variables in **hadoop-env.sh** file by replacing **JAVA_HOME** value with the location of java in your system.

```
export JAVA_HOME=/usr/local/jdk1.7.0_71
```

The following are the list of files that you have to edit to configure Hadoop.

core-site.xml

The **core-site.xml** file contains information such as the port number used for Hadoop instance, memory allocated for the file system, memory limit for storing the data, and size of Read/Write buffers.

Open the core-site.xml and add the following properties in between <configuration>, </configuration> tags.

```
<configuration>
  <property>
     <name>fs.default.name </name>
     <value> hdfs://localhost:9000 </value>
  </property>

</configuration>
```

hdfs-site.xml

The **hdfs-site.xml** file contains information such as the value of replication data, namenode path, and datanode paths of your local file systems. It means the place where you want to store the Hadoop infrastructure.

Let us assume the following data.

```
dfs.replication (data replication value) = 1
(In the below given path /hadoop/ is the user name.
hadoopinfra/hdfs/namenode is the directory created by hdfs file system.)
namenode path = //home/hadoop/hadoopinfra/hdfs/namenode
(hadoopinfra/hdfs/datanode is the directory created by hdfs file system.)
datanode path = //home/hadoop/hadoopinfra/hdfs/datanode
```

Open this file and add the following properties in between the <configuration> </configuration> tags in this file.

```
<configuration>
  <property>
     <name>dfs.replication</name>
     <value>1</value>
  </property>
     <property>
    <name>dfs.name.dir</name>
     <value>file:///home/hadoop/hadoopinfra/hdfs/namenode </value>
  </property>
      <property>
     <name>dfs.data.dir</name>
     <value>file:///home/hadoop/hadoopinfra/hdfs/datanode </value>
  </property>

</configuration>
```

Note: In the above file, all the property values are user-defined and you can make changes according to your Hadoop infrastructure.

yarn-site.xml

This file is used to configure yarn into Hadoop. Open the yarn-site.xml file and add the following properties in between the <configuration>, </configuration> tags in this file.

```
<configuration>

  <property>
     <name>yarn.nodemanager.aux-services</name>
     <value>mapreduce_shuffle</value>
  </property>

</configuration>
```

mapred-site.xml

This file is used to specify which MapReduce framework we are using. By default, Hadoop contains a template of yarn-site.xml. First of all, it is required to copy the file from **mapred-site,xml.template** to **mapred-site.xml** file using the following command.

```
$ cp mapred-site.xml.template mapred-site.xml
```

Open mapred-site.xml file and add the following properties in between the <configuration>, </configuration>tags in this file.

```
<configuration>

  <property>
     <name>mapreduce.framework.name</name>
     <value>yarn</value>
  </property>

</configuration>
```

2.15 VERIFYING HADOOP INSTALLATION

The following steps are used to verify the Hadoop installation.

Step 1: Name Node Setup

Set up the namenode using the command "hdfs namenode -format" as follows.

```
$ cd ~
$ hdfs namenode -format
```

The expected result is as follows.

```
10/24/14 21:30:55 INFO namenode.NameNode: STARTUP_MSG:
/************************************************************
STARTUP_MSG: Starting NameNode
STARTUP_MSG:   host = localhost/192.168.1.11
STARTUP_MSG:   args = [-format]
STARTUP_MSG:   version = 2.4.1
...
...
10/24/14 21:30:56 INFO common.Storage: Storage directory
/home/hadoop/hadoopinfra/hdfs/namenode has been successfully formatted.
10/24/14 21:30:56 INFO namenode.NNStorageRetentionManager: Going to
retain 1 images with txid >= 0
10/24/14 21:30:56 INFO util.ExitUtil: Exiting with status 0
10/24/14 21:30:56 INFO namenode.NameNode: SHUTDOWN_MSG:
/************************************************************
SHUTDOWN_MSG: Shutting down NameNode at localhost/192.168.1.11
************************************************************/
```

Step 2: Verifying Hadoop dfs

The following command is used to start dfs. Executing this command will start your Hadoop file system.

```
$ start-dfs.sh
```

The expected output is as follows:

```
10/24/14 21:37:56
Starting namenodes on [localhost]
localhost: starting namenode, logging to /home/hadoop/hadoop
2.4.1/logs/hadoop-hadoop-namenode-localhost.out
localhost: starting datanode, logging to /home/hadoop/hadoop
2.4.1/logs/hadoop-hadoop-datanode-localhost.out
Starting secondary namenodes [0.0.0.0]
```

Step 3: Verifying Yarn Script

The following command is used to start the yarn script. Executing this command will start your yarn daemons.

```
$ start-yarn.sh
```

The expected output as follows:

```
starting yarn daemons
starting resourcemanager, logging to /home/hadoop/hadoop
2.4.1/logs/yarn-hadoop-resourcemanager-localhost.out
localhost: starting nodemanager, logging to /home/hadoop/hadoop
2.4.1/logs/yarn-hadoop-nodemanager-localhost.out
```

Step 4: Accessing Hadoop on Browser

The default port number to access Hadoop is 50070. Use the following url to get Hadoop services on browser.

```
http://localhost:50070/
```

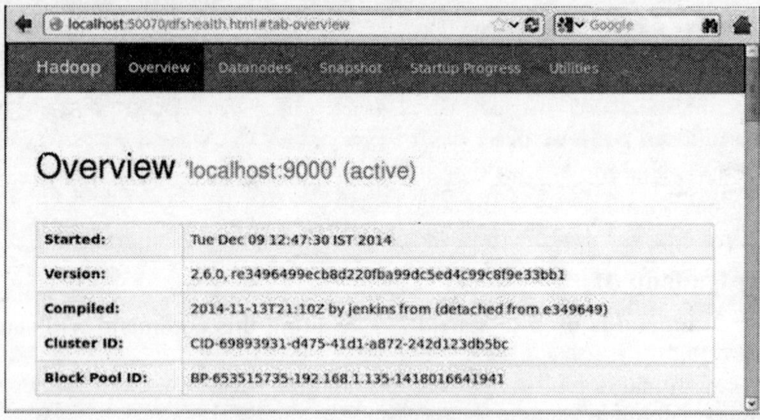

Step 5: Verify All Applications for Cluster

The default port number to access all applications of cluster is 8088. Use the following url to visit this service.

```
http://localhost:8088/
```

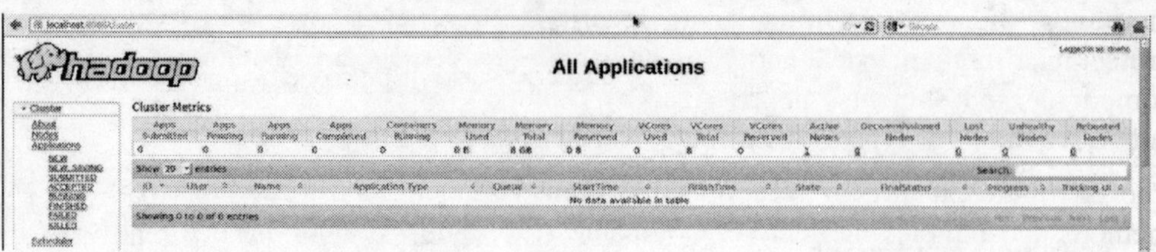

2.16 ADVANTAGES OF HADOOP

- Hadoop framework allows the user to quickly write and test distributed systems. It is efficient, and it automatic distributes the data and work across the machines and in turn, utilizes the underlying parallelism of the CPU cores.

- Hadoop does not rely on hardware to provide fault-tolerance and high availability (FTHA), rather Hadoop library itself has been designed to detect and handle failures at the application layer.
- Servers can be added or removed from the cluster dynamically and Hadoop continues to operate without interruption.
- Another big advantage of Hadoop is that apart from being open source, it is compatible on all the platforms since it is Java based.

There are also a number of Apache projects related to Hadoop, often built atop either Hadoop MapReduce or HDFS. These include — but are not limited to — Hive and Pig, two SQL-like query languages to provide data-warehouse-like capabilities to a Hadoop cluster, and HBase, a NoSQL database that leverages HDFS as its distributed storage engine.

2.17 HADOOP SECURITY CONCERNS

Some points have been raised against security over Hadoop Operations which needs to be carefully thought over :

(1) According to ITBusinessEdge website, Hadoop was originally adopted to manage publicly available information, not enterprise data. Like many ground-breaking technologies (for instance, TCP/IP or UNIX), Hadoop wasn't originally built with the enterprise in mind, let alone security. Hadoop's original purpose was to manage publicly available information like Web links, and was designed to format large amounts of unstructured data within a distributed computing environment, specifically Google's. It was not written to support hardened security, compliance, encryption, policy enablement, and risk management.

Companies leveraging Big Data are mostly on their own when it comes to security. Best practices for companies with Hadoop clusters include implementing additional access controls and limiting the number of personnel allowed to access the Hadoop cluster.

(2) Hadoop's security relies entirely on Kerberos Hadoop does utilize Kerberos for authentication. However, this protocol can be difficult to implement and it doesn't cover a number of other enterprise security requirements, like role-based authentication, LDAP, and Active Directory for policy enablement. Hadoop also doesn't support encryption on nodes or on data in transit between nodes.

(3) As a data store, a Hadoop cluster is not a single physical entity, but consists of hundreds, sometimes thousands, of nodes.Traditional data security technologies have been built on the concept of protecting a single physical entity (like a database or server), not the uniquely distributed Big Data computing environments characterized by Hadoop clusters. Traditional security technologies are not effective in this type of distributed, large-scale environment.

The distributed nature of Hadoop clusters also renders many traditional backup and recovery methods and policies ineffective. Companies leveraging Hadoop need to replicate, back up and store data in a separate, secured environment.

(4) To reap the benefits of Big Data, Hadoop is used in conjunction with other technologies such as Hive, HBase or Pig. While these tools make Big Data accessible and useable, most also lack any real enterprise-grade security. Hardening Hadoop itself is only one part of the Big Data security challenge.

2.18 IBM HADOOP TECHNOLOGIES

In addition to open source software, one of the IBMs technologies known as BigInsights includes a number of IBM-developed technologies to help you become productive quickly. Examples include a text analysis engine and supporting development tool, a data exploration tool for business analysts, enterprise software integration, and various platform enhancements to simplify administration and help improve runtime performance. I had designed this book's exercises based on IBM's BigInsights Hadoop. Take a closer look.

2.18.1 Text-based Analytics and Tooling

As previously mentioned, BigInsights is designed to help firms analyze a diverse range of data, including data that's loosely structured or largely unstructured. Various types of text data fall into this category. Indeed, financial documents, legal documents, marketing collateral, emails, blogs, news reports, press releases, and social media websites contain text-based data that firms may want to process and assess.

For this reason, BigInsights Enterprise Edition includes a text processing engine and library of annotators that enable developers to query and identify items of interest in documents and messages. Examples of business entities that BigInsights can extract from text-based data include persons, email addresses, street addresses, phone numbers, URLs, joint ventures, alliances, and others.

In addition, programmers can use the Eclipse-based plug-in to build their own library of text analytic functions for BigInsights. This plug-in includes an expression builder, pattern discovery technology, a test environment, and a results explorer to promote rapid prototyping and refinement of complex text analytic functions tailored to specific application requirements.

2.18.2 Basic and Enterprise Editions

By now, you may be wondering about the technologies that comprise the BigInsights platform. A number of IBM and open source technologies are part of BigInsights, which is available in two editions: Basic and Enterprise. As shown in Figure 2.15, both editions include Apache Hadoop and other open source software, which are explained in more detail later.

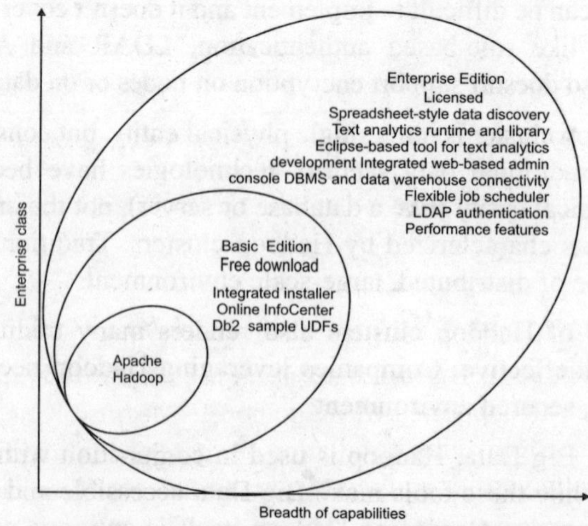

Figure. 2.15: InfoSphere BigInsights 1.2 Basic and Enterprise Editions

This figure shows the InfoSphere BigInsights 1.2 Basic and Enterprise Editions

Basic Edition is available for free download and can manage up to 10 TB of data. As such, it's suitable for pilot projects and exploratory work. The Enterprise Edition is a fee-based offering with no licensing restrictions on the quantity of data that can be managed. It includes all the features of the Basic Edition and offers additional analytic, administrative, and software integration capabilities. As such, Enterprise Edition is suitable for production applications.

2.18.3 Open source technologies

You may already be familiar with certain open source projects, so explore these first. Open source projects included with BigInsights 1.2 Basic and Enterprise Editions are:

1. Apache Hadoop (including the Hadoop Distributed File System (HDFS), MapReduce framework, and common utilities), a software framework for data-intensive applications that exploit distributed computing environments Pig, a high-level programming language and runtime environment for Hadoop Jaql, a high-level query language based on JavaScript Object Notation (JSON), which also supports SQL.
2. Hive, a data warehouse infrastructure designed to support batch queries and analysis of files managed by Hadoop HBase, a column-oriented data storage environment designed to support large, sparsely populated tables in Hadoop Flume, a facility for collecting and loading data into Hadoop
3. Lucene, text search and indexing technology Avro, data serialization technology ZooKeeper, a coordination service for distributed applications Oozie, workflow/job orchestration technology

2.18.4 Spreadsheet-Like Data Discovery And Exploration

To help business analysts and non-programmers work with "big data," BigInsights Enterprise Edition provides a spreadsheet-like data analysis tool. Launched through a Web browser, BigSheets enables business analysts to create collections of data to explore. To create a collection, an analyst specifies the desired data source(s), which might include the BigInsights distributed file system, a local file system, or the output of a Web crawl. BigSheets provides built-in support for popular data formats, such as JSON data, comma-separated values (CSV), tab-separated values (TSV), character-delimited data, and others. If desired, programmers can create plug-ins to process additional data formats and execute custom functions.

When an analyst executes (or runs) the collection's definition, BigSheets generates MapReduce jobs behind the scenes to retrieve and process the necessary data. Analysts can also review and manipulate the collection's data using built-in functions and macros. Such work is done through a traditional spreadsheet-like interface,.

2.18.5 Integrated installation and administration tools

To help firms get off to a quick start, BigInsights Basic and Enterprise editions provide a Web-based tool that installs and configures all supported IBM and non-IBM software selected by an administrator. Details about the progress of a BigInsights installation are reported in real time, and a built-in "health check" mechanism automatically verifies and reports on the success of the installation.

By contrast, those working with individual open source offerings would need to iteratively download, configure, and test each software project they wanted to use. Furthermore, they would need to be sensitive to any software pre-requisites and incompatibilities that might exist among the desired projects.

Once BigInsights is installed, Enterprise administrators can work with a Web-based management console to inspect the status of their BigInsights environment at any time. Through this console, they can start and stop nodes, investigate the status of MapReduce jobs, review log records, assess the overall health of the system, start and stop optional components, navigate the distributed file system, and more.

2.18.6 Enterprise software integration

Many organizations are concerned about introducing yet another information management platform into their existing IT infrastructure. Quite commonly, IT architects worry about integrating information managed by the new system with other important data they already have in their enterprise.

To address this concern, BigInsights Enterprise Edition provides Jaql developers with JDBC connectivity to Netezza and DB2 so they can transfer data to and from these sources in a manner that exploits the native parallel processing capabilities of those platforms. Such support is useful for BigInsights developers who want to join reference data stored in a relational DBMS with data managed by BigInsights. To access other relational data sources, BigInsights provides a generic JDBC connector.

In addition, both BigInsights Basic and Enterprise Editions provide sample DB2 user-defined functions (UDFs) that allow DB2 programmers to launch Jaql queries in BigInsights, join the output with DB2 data, and present the results to DB2 users and applications. These UDFs can be registered with a DB2 9.7 server for Linux, Unix, and Windows platforms.

Figure 2.16 illustrates the DBMS and data warehouse connectivity provided through BigInsights 1.2.

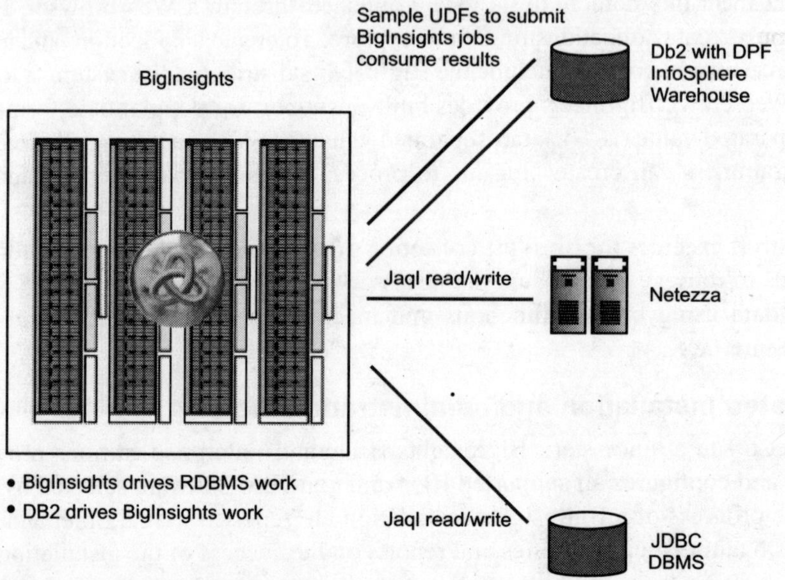

Figure. 2.16: DBMS and data warehouse connectivity for BigInsights 1.2

The figure 2.16 shows the DBMS and data warehouse connectivity for BigInsights 1.2

Platform enhancements and performance features

While BigInsights uses open source technologies that offer strong runtime performance and high levels of scalability, the Enterprise Edition also employs IBM-specific software to further enhance administration and performance.

For example, BigInsights offers an optional job scheduling mechanism for fine tuning resource allocation among long-running and short-running jobs. Administrators can use a property setting to allocate maximum resources to small jobs to help ensure they complete quickly. This job scheduling option is available in addition to Hadoop's first in/first out (FIFO) and "fair" scheduling approaches.

In addition, BigInsights provides enhanced security by supporting LDAP authentication to its Web console. LDAP and reverse proxy support help administrators restrict access to users with appropriate authorization.

Performance enhancements include efficient processing of text-based compressed data through the use of IBM LZO-based compression technology. BigInsights also includes adaptive runtime techniques for Jaql jobs that can help improve runtime performance of target applications. When IBM's adaptive MapReduce technology is turned on (through a property setting or a Jaql option), Map tasks communicate through ZooKeeper to understand the global state of the job. When it makes sense to do so, Map tasks can dynamically take on additional work, which can lead to improved runtime performance for the overall job.

2.18.7 How Biginsights Fits Into An Enterprise Data Architecture

Working with big data is becoming an integral part of the enterprise data strategy at many firms. Indeed, a number of organizations are looking to deploy a software platform such as BigInsights so that they can manage big data from the moment it enters their enterprise. After storing the raw data in BigInsights, firms can manipulate, analyze, and summarize the data to gain new insights as well as feed downstream systems. In this manner, both the original (raw) data and modified forms are accessible for further processing.

One potential deployment approach involves using BigInsights as a source for a data warehouse. BigInsights can sift through large volumes of unstructured or semi-structured data, capturing relevant information that can augment existing corporate data in a warehouse. Figure 2.11 illustrates such a scenario, which offers firms the ability to broaden their analytic coverage without creating an undue burden for their existing systems. Once in the warehouse, traditional business intelligence and query/report writing tools can work with the extracted, aggregated, and transformed portions of raw data stored in BigInsights.

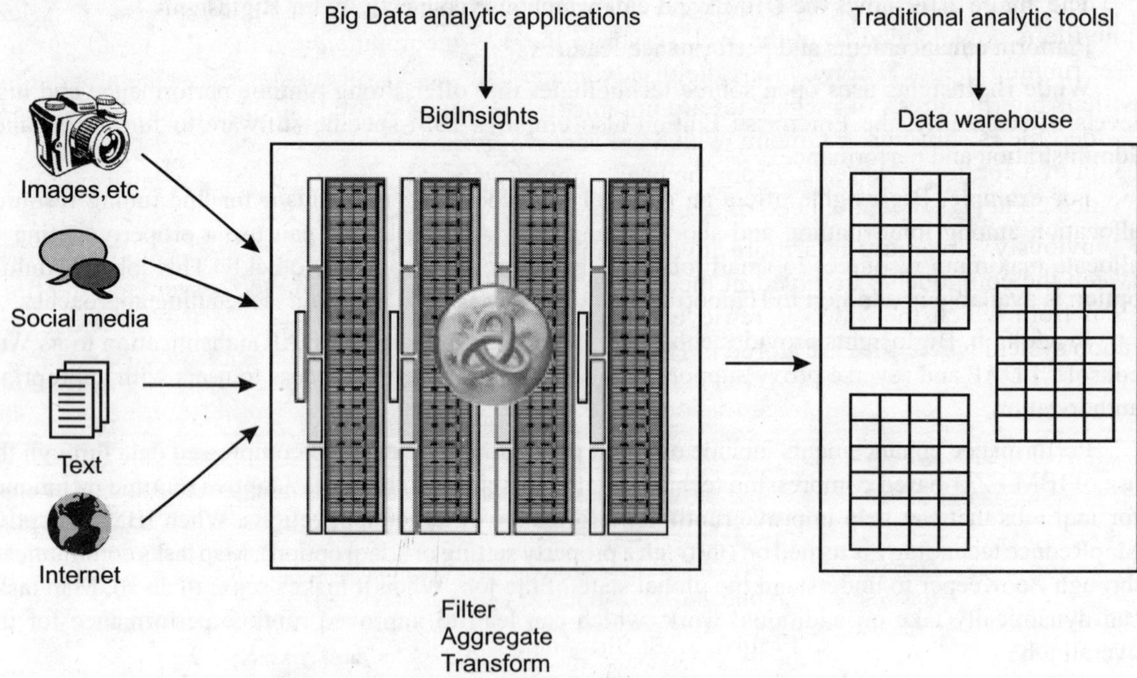

Figure. 2.17: Using BigInsights to filter and summarize big data for the warehouse

The figure 2.17 shows how to use BigInsights to filter and summarize big data for the warehouse

Another potential deployment approach involves using BigInsights as a query-ready archive for a data warehouse. With this approach, frequently accessed data can be maintained in the warehouse while "cold" or outdated information can be offloaded to BigInsights. This allows firms to manage the size of their existing data management platforms while servicing the well-established needs of their existing applications. Offloading rarely queried data to BigInsights allows that data to remain accessible to applications that may have an occasional or unpredictable need to work with it.

2.19 HADOOP STREAMING

Internet Memory supplies a service to browse archived Web pages, including multimedia content. We use Hadoop, HDFS and HBase for storing and indexing our data, and associates this storage with a Web server that lets users navigate through the archive and retrieve documents. In the present post, we focus on *videos* and detail the solution adopted to serve true streaming from HDFS storage.

2.19.1 Basics

Many video formats are found on the Web, including Windows Media (.wmv), RealMedia (.rm), Quicktime (.mov), MPEG, Adobe Flash (.flv), etc. In order to display a video, we need a *player*, which can be incorporated in the Web browser. The player depends on the specific video format, but most browsers are able to detect the format and choose the appropriate player. Firefox for instance comes with a lot of plugins, which can be quickly integrated in the presence of a specific video to display it content.

There are basically two ways to play a video. The simplest one is a two-steps process: first the whole file is downloaded from the Web server to the user's computer, and then displayed by the player running the local copy. It has the disadvantage that the download step may take a while is the file is big (hundreds of megabytes are not uncommon). The second one uses (true) *streaming*: the video file is split into fragments which are sent from the Web server to the player, giving the illusion of a continuous stream. From the user point of view, it looks as if a window is swept over the video content, saving the need of a full initial download of the whole file.

Obviously, streaming is a more involved method because it requires a strong coordination between the components involved in the process, namely the player, the Web server, and the file system from which the video is retrieved. We examine this technical issue in the context of a Hadoop system where files are stored in HDFS, a file system dedicated to large distributed storage.

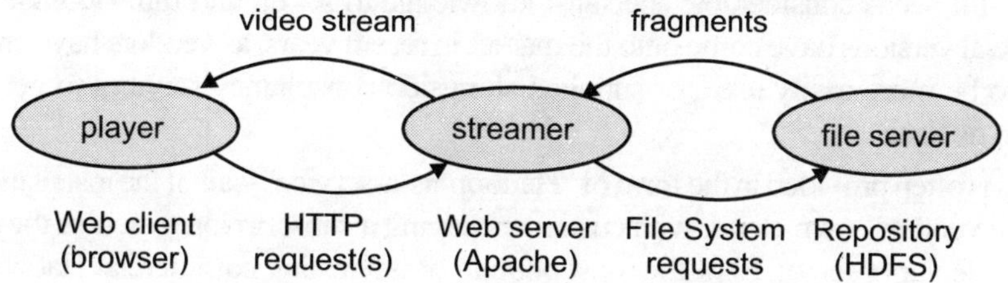

Figure. 2.18: Streaming and HDFS

2.19.2 File Seeking with HDFS

At explained above, streaming requires a strong coordination between the Web server and the file system. The former produces requests to access chunks of the video file (think to what happens when the user suddenly requires a move to a specific part of the video), whereas the later must be able to seek in the file to position the cursor at a specific location. When using HDFS, enabling such a close cooperation turns out to be a problem because HDFS can in principle only be accessed through a Hadoop client, which the standard Apache server is not. We investigated two possible solutions: Hoop, the Hadoop web server, and Apache/FUSE.

Hoop is an HTTP-HDFS-Connector. It allows the HDFS file system to be accessed via HTTP. A working local prototype has been developed using JW Player and a large video file. Streaming works, but seeking in an unbuffered part results in the playback stopping. It seems that the Hoop API does not support seeking in a file, so we had to give up this approach.

The second solution is based on HDFS/FUSE. FUSE (File System in User Space) is an API that captures the file system operations and allows to implement them with ad-hoc functions running in the the user's processus space (thereby saving the need to change the operating system kernel, a tricky and dangerous option). FUSE is provided in Hadoop as a component named "Mountable HDFS" (see http://wiki.apache.org/hadoop/MountableHDFS). It lets the standard file system user or program see the HDFS name space as a locally mounted directory. All file system operations, including directory browsing, file opening and content access, are enabled over HDFS content through the FUSE interface.

2.19.3 Apache Server Configuration

It remained to configure Apache to access the mounted FUSE system and load content from video files. How this is done depends on the video format. At the moment, we tested and validated *.mp4* files and Flash video files. For the first format we use H264 Streaming Module , an Apache plugin, which enables adaptive streaming. For FLV we used pseudo-stream module for Apache named "mod_flv". Both behave nicely and go along with the mountable HDFS without problem.

2.20 Ten big Hadoop Platforms

Hadoop the software framework that provides the necessary tools to carry out big data analysis, is widely used in industry and commerce for many big data related tasks.It is open source, essentially meaning that it is free for anyone to use for any purpose, and can be modified for any use. While designed to be user-friendly, in its "raw" state it still needs considerable specialist knowledge to set up and run. Because of this, a large number of commercial versions have come onto the market in recent years, as vendors have created their own versions designed to be more easily used, or supplied alongside consultancy services to get you crunching through your data in no time.

These days, this is often provided in the form of "Hadoop-as-a-service" – all of the installation will actually take place within the vendor's own cloud, with customers paying a subscription to access the services.Here's a rundown, in no particular order, of 10 of the most popular or interesting commercial Hadoop platforms on the market today.

2.20.1 IBM InfoSphere BigInsights

IBM has deep roots in the computing industry, particularly in distributed computing and data management. Its BigInsights package adds the company's proprietary analytics and visualization algorithms to the core Hadoop infrastructure.

InfoSphere BigInsights 1.2 is a software platform designed to help firms discover and analyze business insights hidden in large volumes of a diverse range of data—data that's often ignored or discarded because it's too impractical or difficult to process using traditional means. Examples of such data include log records, click streams, social media data, news feeds, electronic sensor output, and even some transactional data. To help firms derive value from such data in an efficient manner, BigInsights incorporates several open source projects (including Apache™ Hadoop™) and a number of IBM-developed technologies.

Figure 2.19 illustrates IBM's big data platform, which includes software for processing streaming data and persistent data. BigInsights supports the latter, while InfoSphere Streams supports the former. The two can be deployed together to support real-time and batch analytics of various forms of raw data, or they can be deployed individually to meet specific application objectives. The remainder of this article focuses on BigInsights.

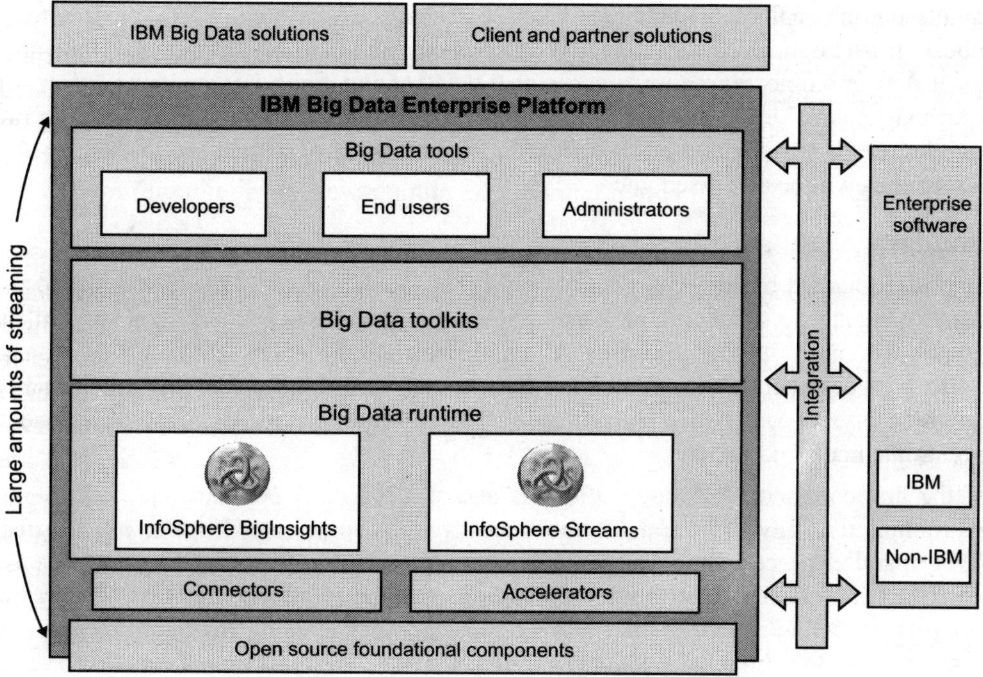

Figure. 2.19: IBM's platform and vision for big data

This figure 2.19 shows the IBM's platform and vision for big data. IBM developed BigInsights to help firms process and analyze the increasing volume, variety, and velocity of data of interest to many enterprises. Consider that industry analysts expect the quantity of digital data to increase rapidly in the coming years. Indeed, one firm, International Data Corporation, expects volumes to grow up to 44 times by 2020 when compared with 2009 levels, and most of that data will be in unstructured or semi-structured formats. As a result, many IT professionals anticipate new data processing challenges; they often use the term "Big Data" (or "big data") to refer to this issue.

However, many firms recognize that analyzing large volumes of raw data can reveal patterns and insights important to their organizations. Application areas span many domains, including customer retention, customer service, market intelligence, business planning and operations, scientific research, security, and other areas. Such applications may require analyzing application, system, or sensor log data; consumer or public sentiment expressed through various electronic venues; text-rich data, including documents, emails, and messages; and various other sources of data. Unfortunately, the sheer effort involved to collect, process, analyze, and manage this data can seem daunting.

To make sifting through large volumes of diverse data practical, BigInsights provides built-in analytic technologies and exploits shared-nothing hardware clusters. It transparently distributes data stored in files across disks attached to various nodes in a cluster, directing subtasks of applications to processors that are close to the target subsets of your data. This approach minimizes network traffic and improves runtime performance. For fault tolerance, BigInsights automatically replicates each portion of your data on multiple disks based on parameters specified by an administrator. Such replication enables BigInsights to automatically recover from a disk or node failure by redirecting work elsewhere.

BigInsights doesn't replace a relational database management system (DBMS) or a traditional data warehouse. It isn't optimized for interactive queries over tabular data structures, online analytical processing (OLAP), or online transaction processing (OLTP) applications. Rather, it's a platform that can augment your existing analytic infrastructure, enabling you to filter through high volumes of raw data and combine the results with structured data stored in your DBMS or warehouse, if desired. Potential integration scenarios will be discussed later.

2.20.2 Cloudera

Cloudera Inc. was founded by big data geniuses from Facebook, Google, Oracle and Yahoo in 2008. It was the first company to develop and distribute Apache Hadoop-based software and still has the largest user base with most number of clients. Although the core of the distribution is based on Apache Hadoop, it also provides a proprietary Cloudera Management Suite to automate the installation process and provide other services to enhance convenience of users which include reducing deployment time, displaying real time nodes' count, etc.

One of the first commercial Hadoop offerings and still the most popular, reportedly with more installations running than any of its competitors. Cloudera also contributes Impala, which offers real-time massively parallel processing of big data to Hadoop. Cloudera's open-source Apache Hadoop distribution, CDH (Cloudera Distribution Including Apache Hadoop), targets enterprise-class deployments of that technology.CDH, the world's most popular Hadoop distribution, is Cloudera's 100% open source platform. It includes all the leading Hadoop ecosystem components to store, process, discover, model, and serve unlimited data, and it's engineered to meet the highest enterprise standards for stability and reliability.

CDH is based entirely on open standards for long-term architecture. And as the main curator of open standards in Hadoop, Cloudera has a track record of bringing new open source solutions into its platform (such as Apache Spark, Apache HBase, and Apache Parquet) that are eventually adopted by the entire ecosystem. Cloudera is preparing to launch major new open-source software storage engine, Kudu, that is meant as an alternative to the widely used Hadoop Distributed File System and the Hadoop-oriented HBase NoSQL database, borrowing characteristics from both.

Kudu could present a new threat to data warehouses from Teradata and IBM's PureData (formerly Netezza), and other vendors. It may also be used as a highly scalable in-memory database that can handle massively parallel processing (MPP) workloads, not unlike HP's Vertica and VoltDB, the sources say. And one day Kudu — which works across multiple data centers with RAM and fast solid-state drives (SSDs) — could even play a part in backup and disaster recovery.

It's "nearly as fast as raw HDFS for scans" and, at the same time, "nearly as fast as HBase for random access but Kudu is not meant to be a drop-in substitute for HDFS or HBase. Kudu could be used for time-series data, or real-time reporting, or model building, Kudu isn't a SQL query engine for pulling up specific data. Cloudera has Impala for that, and others have Hive for that.

2.20.3 Hortonworks

Hortonworks, founded in 2011, has quickly emerged as one of the leading vendors of Hadoop. The distribution provides open source platform based on Apache Hadoop for analysing, storing and managing big data. Hortonworks is the only commercial vendor to distribute complete open source Apache Hadoop without additional proprietary software. Hortonworks' distribution HDP2.0 can be directly downloaded from their website free of cost and is easy to install. The engineers of Hortonworks are behind most of Hadoop's recent innovations including Yarn, which is better than MapReduce in the sense that it will enable inclusion of more data processing frameworks.

Of the vendors listed here, Horton is one of the few that offers 100 percent open source Hadoop technology without any proprietary (non-open) modifications. It also was the first to integrate support for Apache HCatalog, which creates "metadata" – data within data, simplifying the process of sharing your data across other layers of service such as Apache Hive or Pig.

2.20.4 MapR

MapR replaces HDFS component and instead uses its own proprietary file system, called MapRFS. MapRFS helps incorporate enterprise-grade features into Hadoop, enabling more efficient management of data, reliability and most importantly, ease of use. In other worlds, it is more production ready than its other two competitors.

MapR uses some differing concepts, such as native support for UNIX file systems rather than HDFS, meaning it will be more familiar to DBAs used to working in a UNIX environment. MapR technologies also is spearheading development of the Apache Drill project, which provides advanced tools for interactive real-time querying of big data sets.

2.20.5 Microsoft HDInsight

Engineered to run on Microsoft's Azure cloud platform, Microsoft's Hadoop package is based on that of Hortonworks and has the distinction of being the only big commercial Hadoop offering that runs in a Windows environment.

2.20.6 Intel Distribution for Apache Hadoop

Intel is another giant of the tech world that has recently turned its attention toward Hadoop. Intel's distribution adds the company's Graph Builder and Analytics Toolkit functions to Hadoop, and claims that security updates to the infrastructure mean that its solution offers added security for your data.

2.20.7 Datastax Enterprise Analytics

Datastax offers its own distribution of the Apache Cassandra database management system on top of its Hadoop installation. It also includes custom proprietary systems to handle security, search, dashboard, and visualization.

2.20.8 Teradata Enterprise Access for Hadoop

Teradata offers hardware and software for implementing big data solutions, as well as its own Hadoop package, which also is based on the Hortonworks distribution. Proprietary technology supplied alongside the open-source components include the company's QueryGrid analytics engine and Viewpoint dashboard.

2.20.9 Pivotal HD

Pivotal was formed as a joint venture between storage system provider EMC and virtualization specialist VMware. Pivotal HD (Hadoop distribution) forms part of the company's Big Data Suite, which also includes database tools Greenplum and analytics platform Gemfire. Customers include China's national rail operator, China Railway.

2.21 SECURITY OVER HADOOP

As Hadoop became a more popular platform for data analytics and processing, security professionals began to express concerns about the insider threat of malicious users in a Hadoop cluster. A malicious developer could easily write code to impersonate other users' Hadoop services (e.g. writing a new TaskTracker and registering itself as a Hadoop service, or impersonating the hdfs or mapred users, deleting everything in HDFS, etc.). Because DataNodes enforced no access control, a malicious user could read arbitrary data blocks from DataNodes, bypassing access control restrictions, or writing garbage data to DataNodes, undermining the integrity of the data to be analyzed. Anyone could submit a job to a JobTracker and it could be arbitrarily executed.

Because of these security concerns, the Hadoop community realized that more robust security controls were needed, and as a result, a team at Yahoo! decided to focus on authentication, and chose Kerberos as the authentication mechanism for Hadoop, documented in their 2009.

CHAPTER

3

IBM's InfoSphere BigInsights

3.1 IBM'S INFOSPHERE BIGINSIGHTS

IBM® InfoSphere® BigInsights™, is a platform for the analysis and visualization of Internet-scale data volumes that is powered by Apache Hadoop, an open source distributed computing platform.

InfoSphere® BigInsights™ is a flexible software platform that provides capabilities to discover and analyze business insights that are hidden in large volumes of structured and unstructured data, giving value to previously dormant data.

3.1.1 IBM InfoSphere BigInsights Version 2.1.2

InfoSphere BigInsights helps your organization to understand and analyze massive volumes of unstructured information as easily as smaller volumes of information. The flexible platform is built on an Apache Hadoop open source framework that runs in parallel on commonly available, low-cost hardware. You can easily scale the platform to analyze hundreds of terabytes, petabytes, or more of raw data that is derived from various sources. As information grows, you add more hardware to support the influx of data.

InfoSphere BigInsights helps *application developers, data scientists, and administrators* in your organization quickly build and deploy custom analytics to capture insight from data. This data is often integrated into existing databases, data warehouses, and business intelligence infrastructure. By using InfoSphere BigInsights, users can extract new insights from this data to enhance knowledge of your business.

InfoSphere BigInsights incorporates tooling for numerous users, speeding time to value and simplifying development and maintenance:

- Software developers can use the Eclipse-based plug-in to develop custom text analytic functions to analyze loosely structured or largely unstructured text data.

- Administrators can use the web-based management console to inspect the status of the software environment, review log records, assess the overall health of the system, and more.
- Data scientists and business analysts can use the data analysis tool to explore and work with unstructured data in a familiar spreadsheet-like environment.

3.2 INTRODUCTION TO INFOSPHERE BIGINSIGHTS ENVIRONMENT

InfoSphere® BigInsights™ is a software platform for discovering, analyzing, and visualizing data from disparate sources. You use this software to help process and analyze the volume, variety, and velocity of data that continually enters your organization every day.

InfoSphere BigInsights helps your organization to understand and analyze massive volumes of unstructured information as easily as smaller volumes of information. The flexible platform is built on an Apache Hadoop open source framework that runs in parallel on commonly available, low-cost hardware. You can easily scale the platform to analyze hundreds of terabytes, petabytes, or more of raw data that is derived from various sources. As information grows, you add more hardware to support the influx of data.

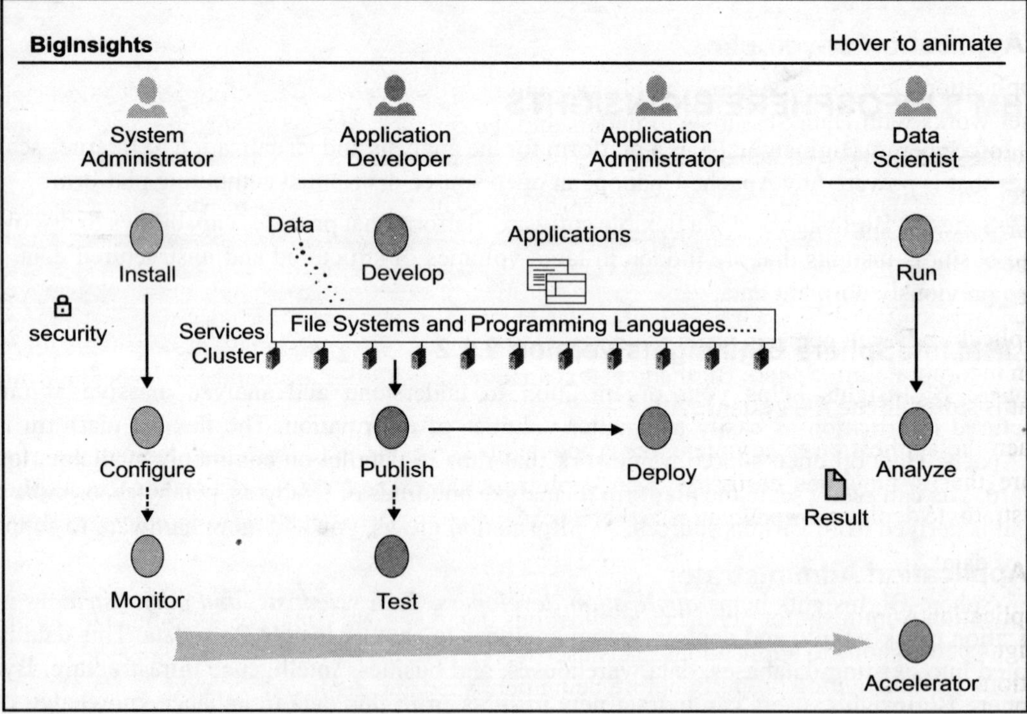

InfoSphere BigInsights helps application developers, data scientists, and administrators in your organization quickly build and deploy custom analytics to capture insight from data. This data is often integrated into existing databases, data warehouses, and business intelligence infrastructure. By using InfoSphere BigInsights, users can extract new insights from this data to enhance knowledge of your business.

3.2.1 System Administrator

The System Administrator installs, configures, and backs up InfoSphere® BigInsights™ components on the system. This user also monitors the cluster to ensure that the InfoSphere BigInsights environment is healthy and running at optimum capacity.

To help administer your Hadoop cluster, InfoSphere BigInsights includes administrative capabilities in the web-based console that provide a real-time, interactive view of your cluster. The System Administrator uses the web console to examine the health of the InfoSphere BigInsights environment, health of nodes in the cluster, and contents of the Hadoop Distributed File System (HDFS).

A dashboard in the web console summarizes the health of the system. The System Administrator can drill into this dashboard to view details about the health and status of individual components. The System Administrator can complete other tasks such as adding and removing nodes, inspecting the status of MapReduce jobs, and navigating the HDFS directory structure to view files and to create new files.

Both the System Administrator and the Application Administrator can stop applications from running.

3.2.2 Application Developer

The Application Developer develops, publishes, and tests applications for InfoSphere® BigInsights™. This user works with Data Scientists to understand the function of each application, and the business problem that the application helps to solve.

After collecting specifications and requirements, Application Developers write applications to meet particular business needs. Application Developers can create custom applications, use one of the InfoSphere BigInsights applications, or run one of the sample applications that are included with the product.

Application Developers can write their application in one of several languages, such as Jaql or Pig, and then incorporate InfoSphere BigInsights text analytic capabilities to summarize, query, and analyze data that is stored in the file system.

When the application is complete, the Application Developer publishes it in the test environment to ensure that it functions correctly. The Application Developer then works with the Application Administrator to deploy the application so that it is available for Data Scientists to complete data analysis.

3.2.3 Application Administrator

The Application Administrator publishes applications in the system, deploys applications to the cluster, and assigns permissions to applications. This user works with the Application Developer to ensure that applications are functioning properly before being published and deployed.

The Application Administrator handles all tasks related to applications after they are developed, including removing existing applications from the cluster. Configuring icons, adding descriptions to applications, changing user permissions, and modifying application categories are all completed by the Application Administrator.

By using the dashboard in the InfoSphere® BigInsights™ web console, the Application Administrator can view the status of individual applications, such as the progress of the application, when it started and ended, and when it was modified last.

After applications are deployed to the cluster, the Application Administrator works with the Data Scientist to ensure that the necessary applications are available in the InfoSphere BigInsights web console.

Both the Application Administrator and the System Administrator can stop applications from running.

3.2.4 Data Scientist

The Data Scientist collects data, completes analysis, and visualizes insights to provide answers to specific business questions. This user determines which applications and data sources to aggregate information from, and how to present the results to the intended audience.

Data Scientists understand business problems and use available data to determine potential solutions. They can connect business requirements with data trends, and use relevant data to derive insights from analytics. These insights can be used to create business intelligence reports, or used as input for further analysis.

Data Scientists work with Application Developers to determine what the goals of each application are. In conjunction, Data Scientists specify data sources to collect information from, depending on the business problem that they are trying to solve, or the question that they need to answer.

After collecting the appropriate information, Data Scientists use BigSheets to complete data analysis and derive insights from multiple data sources. These insights can be visualized as tag clouds, bar charts, maps, and pie charts, providing consumable information out of previously unstructured data.

3.2.5 Reference Architecture

Before you install InfoSphere® BigInsights®, a reference architecture is helpful to understand how to configure services in your cluster.

The goal of the recommended reference architectures is to reduce single points of failure in different topologies where InfoSphere BigInsights is installed. Each of the following topologies indicates the number of machines and racks that are required in addition to how services are structured across the cluster. The service structure depends on the size of the cluster, the distributed file system, and whether high availability is required.

In the following topologies, public nodes are nodes that are exposed to data sources (public network), whereas private nodes are included in data targets (private network). The Install Console exists in the same network that you use to manage machines in your cluster. When two tiers of networks exist, the data target (private network) and the Install Console (backplane) are typically merged into a single network. Private nodes refer to a node that is included in both a trusted network and the backplane. When three tiers of networks exist, the backplane is typically 10 times slower than the data target (private network). When you install InfoSphere BigInsights, ensure that you do not install the product into the backplane.

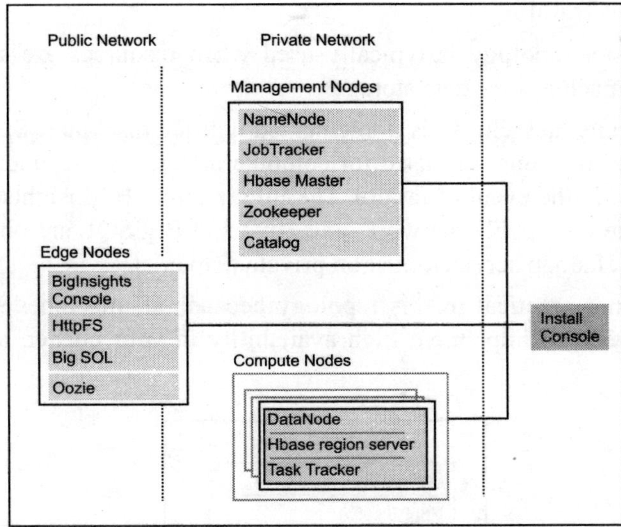

Figure. 3.1: Network Topology for InfoSphere BigInsights Services

(a) Multiple Node Cluster Topology

The *five node* cluster topology is typically used for proof of concept and sandbox environments.

Five nodes is the recommended minimum requirement to implement InfoSphere® BigInsights®. Three data nodes improve data reliability and performance by distributing work on three replica servers. All services run on the two management nodes, and data processing occurs on the three compute nodes. This topology is typically used for proof of concept (POC) and sandbox environments.

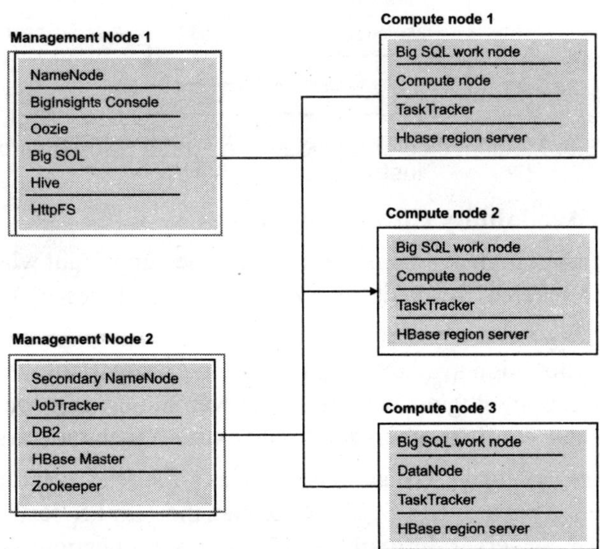

Figure. 3.2: Multiple Node Cluster Topology

(b) Single Rack Cluster Topology

The Single rack cluster topology is typically used when resources are a constraint. The main importance is to allocate machines for data storage.

In this typology, a single rack cluster is implemented with 20 machines. Six machines are used as management nodes and 14 machines are used for compute nodes. The Secondary NameNode is used to back up the NameNode in the event of failure. The InfoSphere® BigInsights® Console and HttpFS server are on one machine on a public network, and Hive and Big SQL are on another machine on a public network. All other Hadoop services exist on private networks.

High availability is not practical in this topology because all machines share power source or network switch. If you want to implement high availability in your cluster, at least three racks are required.

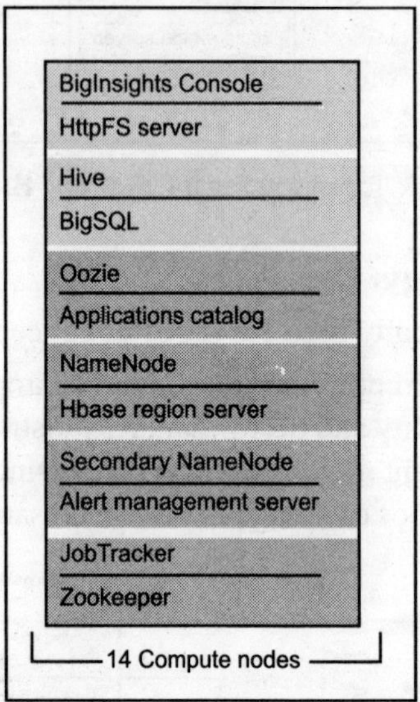

Figure. 3.3: Medium cluster topology in a Single Rack Environment

(c) Multiple Rack High Availability Cluster Topologies

In a typical Hadoop cluster, high availability (HA) becomes important when the cluster size grows beyond a single rack. InfoSphere® BigInsights® supports three types of multiple rack HA cluster configurations.

In a typical Hadoop cluster, high availability (HA) becomes important when the cluster size grows beyond a single rack. In these topologies, one HttpFS server should exist on more than one rack for bandwidth load balancing, and ZooKeeper servers should exist on each rack to support high availability.

In each of the HA cluster topologies, HBase master nodes are spread over three racks for redundancy. The InfoSphere BigInsights Console, Big SQL, Hive, and the HttpFS server are not configured for failover. The Alert Management server, InfoSphere BigInsights applications catalog, and Oozie run on separate racks to minimize impact to the cluster in the event of a failure. Data is spread across 80 data nodes to manage data in the cluster.

(c) GPFS High Availability Cluster Topology

A GPFS cluster that uses GPFS high availability (HA) instead of a Network File System (NFS) to support high availability for the JobTracker component.

In a GPFS cluster, Adaptive MapReduce is used to manage high availability. The GPFS cluster requires three system pool machines that share disks for the high availability manager component, which provide high availability for Adaptive MapReduce. At a minimum, the ZooKeeper service must have a dedicated local disk to provide I/O transactions of ZooKeeper snapshots.

In the following diagram, the HBase master nodes are spread over three racks of machines for redundancy. Data is distributed across 176 data nodes to manage data in a large cluster.

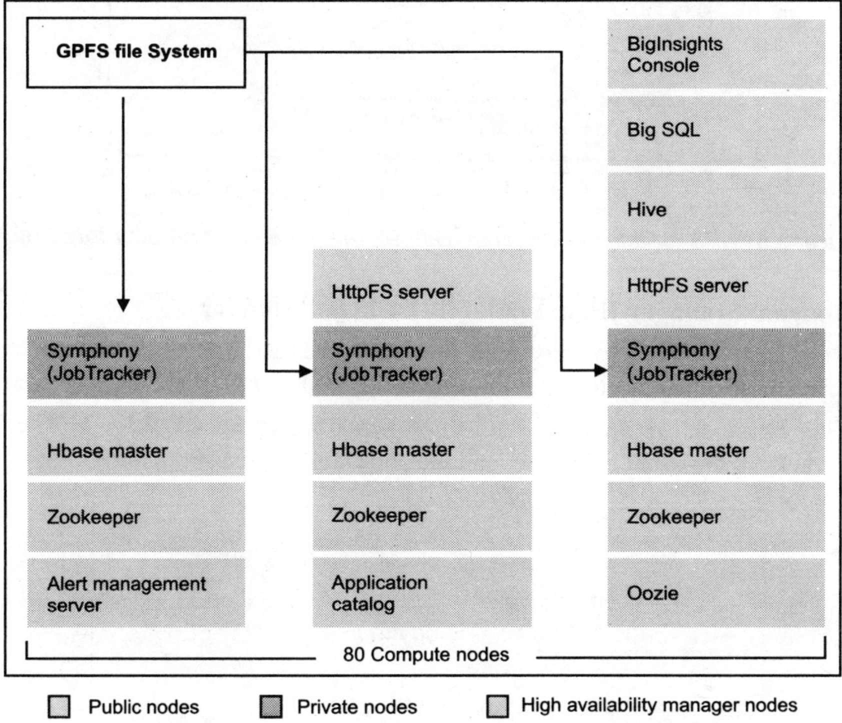

Figure. 3.4: GPFS HA cluster topology with 97 machines spread over three racks

(d) Network File System High Availability Cluster Topology

The NFS high availability (HA) cluster topology is a hybrid solution of open source technology plus MapReduce framework (Adaptive MapReduce) that is enhanced by IBM.

The NFS HA topology uses HDFS as the distributed file system and a Network File System (NFS) for high availability. The high availability manager and the NameNode service share resources on the same machine, and these components are replicated across each rack in the cluster.

The InfoSphere® BigInsights® Console, Big SQL, Hive, and HttpFS server exist on one rack, but are backed up in the NFS that is highly available.

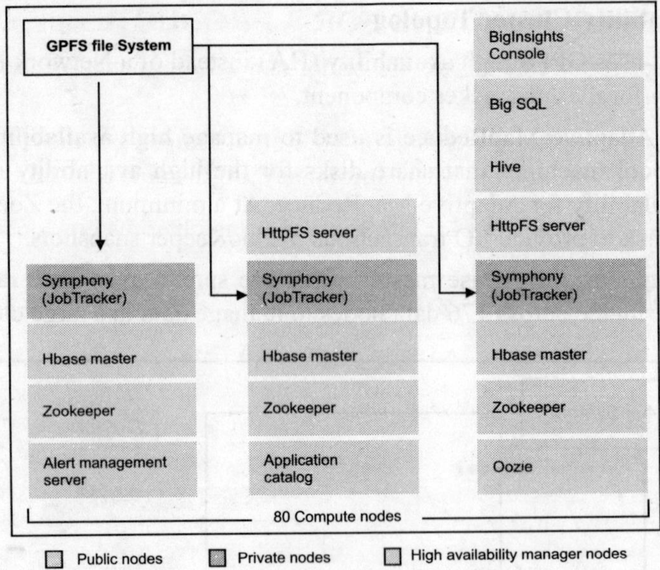

Figure. 3.5: *NFS HA cluster topology with 97 machines spread over three racks*

(e) Quorum Journal Manager High Availability Cluster Topology

The following large cluster topology uses the Hadoop Distributed File System (HDFS) as the distributed file system and the Quorum Journal Manager (QJM) for NameNode high availability (HA).

The following figure shows a cluster with three racks that utilizes QJM HA. The NameNode is spread over two racks in the event of failure, and the JobTracker exists on a third rack.

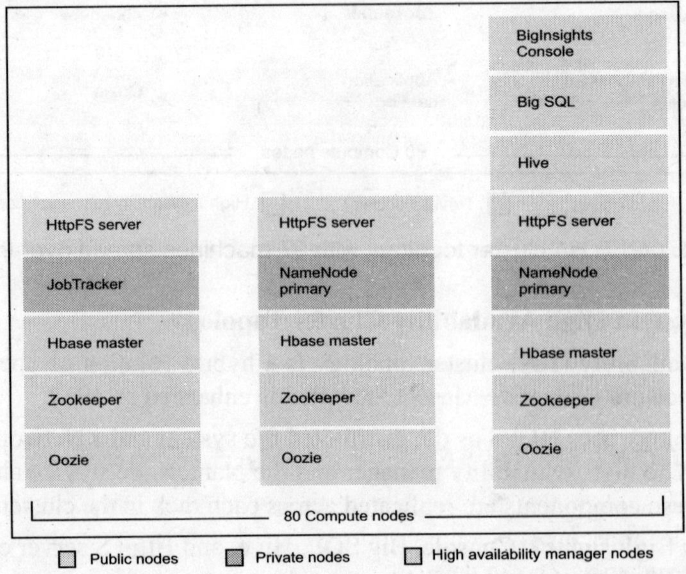

Figure. 3.6: QJM HA Cluster Topology with 98 machines spread over three racks

3.3 HARDWARE SPECIFICATIONS FOR A PRODUCTION ENVIRONMENT

The following hardware requirements are the minimum requirements to implement InfoSphere® BigInsights® in a production environment.

Your requirements might differ depending on your environment, but these hardware requirements are typical for production environments where InfoSphere BigInsights is installed.

Table 3.1. Hardware requirements for InfoSphere BigInsights in a production environment

InfoSphere BigInsights Console node	128 GB RAM	64-bit CPU with 2.4 Ghz Processor	2 TB disk space • */tmp = 50 GB • */hadoop = 1.9 TB • */ = 50 GB • Two hard drives (with RAJD) • Redundant power supplies
Secondary NameNode	128 GB RAM	64-bit CPU with 2.4 Ghz Processor	2 TB disk space • */tmp = 50 GB • */hadoop = 1.9 TB • */ = 50 GB • Two hard drives (with RAJD) • Redundant power supplies
NameNode	128 GB RAM	64-bit CPU with 2.0 Ghz Processor	2 TB disk space • */tmp = 50 GB • */hadoop = 900 GB • */ = 50 GB • Two hard drives (with RAJD) • Redundant power supplies
JobTracker	132 GB RAM	64-bit CPU with 2.0 Ghz Processor	2 TB disk space • */tmp = 50 GB • */hadoop = 900 GB • */ = 50 GB • Two hard drives (with RAJD) • Redundant power supplies
DataNode	48 GB RAM	64-bit CPU with 2.4 Ghz Processor	3.1 TB disk space • */tmp = 50 GB

InfoSphere BigInsights incorporates tooling for numerous users, speeding time to value and simplifying development and maintenance:

- Software developers can use the Eclipse-based plug-in to develop custom text analytic functions to analyze loosely structured or largely unstructured text data.
- Administrators can use the web-based management console to inspect the status of the software environment, review log records, assess the overall health of the system, and more.
- Data scientists and business analysts can use the data analysis tool to explore and work with unstructured data in a familiar spreadsheet-like environment.

3.4 INTRODUCTION TO IBM ACCELERATORS FOR BIG DATA

IBM® offers analytic applications that accelerate the development and implementation of big data solutions. These applications, or accelerators, address specific data types or operations, such as analytics for machine log data and social media data.

Accelerators provide business logic, data processing capabilities, and visualization for specific use cases. By using accelerators, you can apply advanced analytics to help integrate and manage the variety, velocity, and volume of data that constantly enters your organization. Accelerators also provide a development environment for building new analytic applications that are tailored to the specific needs of your organization.

Two accelerators are shipped with InfoSphere® BigInsights™, IBM Accelerator for Machine Data Analytics and IBM Accelerator for Social Data Analytics, and two accelerators are shipped with InfoSphere Streams, IBM Accelerator for Social Data Analytics and IBM Accelerator for Telecommunications Event Data Analytics.

3.5 IBM ACCELERATOR FOR MACHINE DATA ANALYTICS

IBM® Accelerator for Machine Data Analytics can ingest, extract, index, search, transform, and analyze a variety of machine data from sources such as machine data files, smart devices, and telemetry, and help process that data in minutes instead of days and weeks.

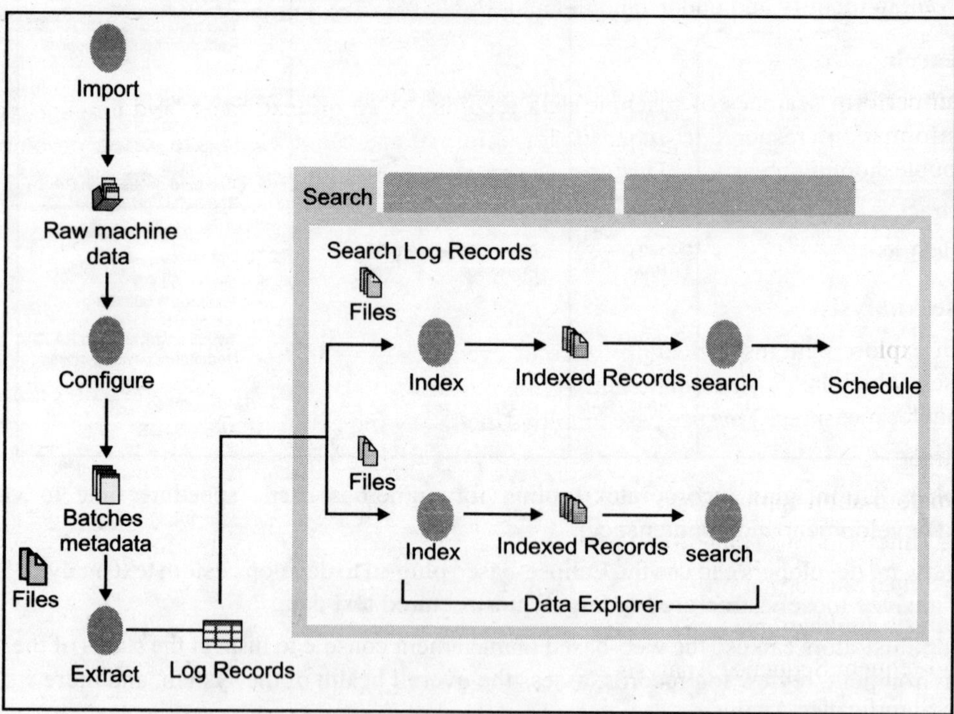

Figure. 3.7: IBM Accelerator for Machine Data Analytics

By using IBM Accelerator for Machine Data Analytics, organizations gain insights into operations, customer experience, transactions, and behavior. The resulting information can be used to proactively boost operational efficiency, troubleshoot problems, investigate security incidents, and monitor end-to-end infrastructure to avoid service degradation or outages.

With IBM Accelerator for Machine Data Analytics, you can:

- Search within and across multiple machine data entries based on a text search, faceted search, or a timeline-based search to find events
- Enrich the context of machine data by adding and extracting log types into the existing repository
- Link and correlate events across systems
- Uncover patterns.

A typical introductory workflow of IBM Accelerator for Machine Data Analytics consists of organizing batches of data, copying those batches to the distributed file system, and then extracting, indexing, searching, transforming, and analyzing the data.

Use cases

IBM Accelerator for Machine Data Analytics supports use cases for faceted search and root cause analysis. A *faceted search* is useful when you need to search and filter your data. Under this model, each information unit is classified by multiple dimensions, allowing the faceted search to extract and structure results according to your goals and your data. On the other hand, *root cause analysis* is useful when you want to identify and understand the underlying cause of a problem, not just its symptoms.

Faceted search

You can perform searches of machine data records, based on text, facet, and timeline, to locate pertinent information, respond to requests for information, acknowledge reported problems, and expedite troubleshooting measures. This use case employs the following applications:

- Extract
- Indexing

Root Cause Analysis

You can explore patterns and significance of events to expedite and broaden your understanding of root causes, which helps you isolate underlying reasons for an event and respond with efficient and effective counter measures. This use case employs the following applications:

- Extract
- Transformation applications:
  - Time Window Transformation
  - Join Transformation
- Analysis applications:
  - Frequent Sequence Analysis
  - Significance Analysis

3.6 IBM ACCELERATOR FOR SOCIAL DATA ANALYTICS

Data from social media forums contains valuable information about user preferences. However, accessing and working with that information requires large-scale import, configuration, and analysis. IBM® Accelerator for Social Data Analytics, a set of end-to-end applications, extracts relevant information from tweets, boards, and blogs and then builds social profiles of users based on specific use cases and industries.

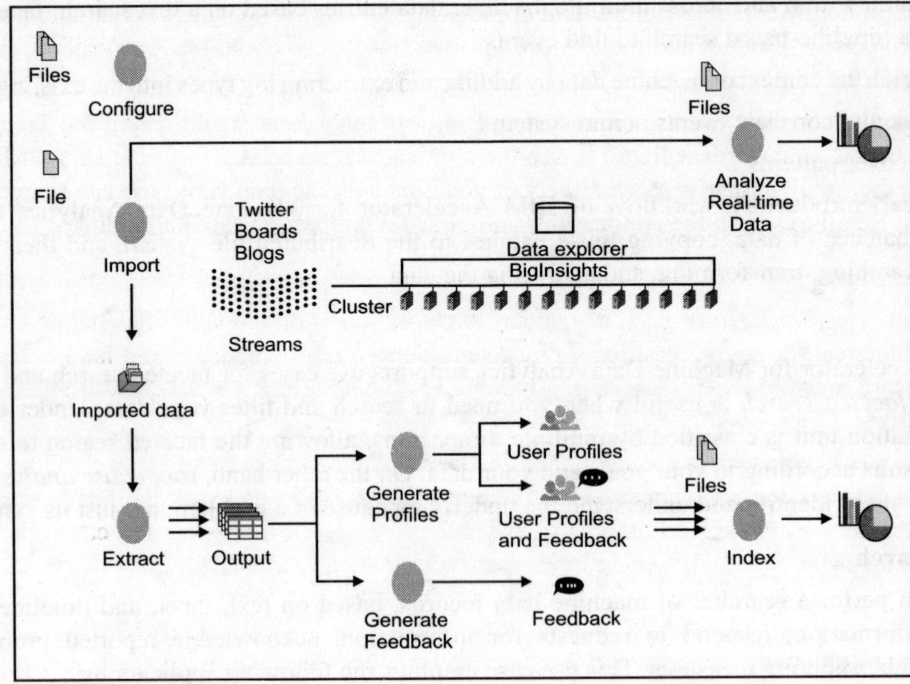

With IBM Accelerator for Social Data Analytics, you can:

- Import and analyze social media data, identifying user characteristics like gender, locations, names, and hobbies
- Develop comprehensive user profiles across messages and sources
- Associate profiles with expressions of sentiment, buzz, intent, and ownership around brands, products, and companies.

A typical workflow of IBM Accelerator for Social Data Analytics consists of importing your data files and then configuring, indexing, and analyzing the data.

Use cases

IBM Accelerator for Social Data Analytics supports use cases for brand management and lead generation. It also offers generic applications that you can customize for your use case and industry. *Brand management* is useful when you want to understand how your brand (company, product, etc.) is perceived in the marketplace. Accurate brand management can help enterprises make informed decisions as to the marketing and sales of their brands. On the other hand, *lead generation* is useful when you want to generate interest in your brand. Lead generation can have direct impact on consumer consumption and overall revenue.

Brand Management

You can track user dimensions, such as gender, location, parental status, and marital status, through measures such as sentiment, buzz, ownership, customer status, intent to purchase (for Retail and Finance), and intent to attend (for Media and Entertainment). This use case enables enterprises in the

Finance, Retail, and Media and Entertainment industries to assess the nature and amount of feedback around a company or product and make more informed decisions about how to position, market, and sell their products.

For example, suppose you are interested in Brand Management Retail. From the Tree view, you can expand Brand Management Retail to see the applications associated with the Brand Management use case and the Retail industry. Alternatively, if you are using the Icon view, you can search for Brand Management Retail to see all the applications associated with that use case and industry.

Lead Generation

You can track user dimensions, such as gender, location, parental status, marital status, employment, and product interest, through measures such as sentiment, buzz, ownership, and intent. This use case enables enterprises in the Finance and Retail industries to identify and generate leads in the Finance and Retail industries.

For example, suppose you are interested in Lead Generation Finance. From the Tree view, you can expand Lead Generation Finance to see the applications associated with the Lead Generation use case and the Finance industry. Alternatively, if you are using the Icon view, you can search for Lead Generation Finance to see all the applications associated with that use case and industry.

Generic

You can customize the generic IBM Accelerator for Social Data Analytics applications to meet the needs of your specific use cases and industries by:

- Updating the application configuration files
- Updating the data in the dictionaries used by the applications.

This customization is similar to the customization that can be performed for other use case and industry combinations. This use case employs the following applications:

- Configuration
- Local Analysis
- Global Analysis
- Real-time Analysis
- Generic Configure - Local - Global Analysis (chained application)

3.7 MANAGING YOUR BIG DATA ENVIRONMENT

EXERCISE 3.1: Overview and Getting Started

In this hands-on exercise, you will learn how to work with Big Data using Apache Hadoop and InfoSphere BigInsights 3.0, IBM's Hadoop-based platform. In particular, you'll learn the basics of working with the Hadoop Distributed File System (HDFS) and see how to administer your Hadoop-based environment using the BigInsights Web console. After launching a sample MapReduce application, you'll explore a more sophisticated scenario involving social media data. In doing so, you'll learn how to use a spreadsheet-style interface to discover insights about the global coverage of a popular brand without writing any code. Finally, you'll learn how to apply industry standard SQL to data managed by BigInsights through IBM's Big SQL technology. Indeed, you'll have a chance to create tables and execute complex queries over data in HDFS, including data derived from a relational data warehouse.

Considerable help has been derived from lab. Work done by Cynthia M. Saracco, of IBM Silicon Valley Lab.

1.1 ABOUT YOUR ENVIRONMENT

We shall work on InfoSphere BigInsights 3.0 Quick Start Edition VMware image. You should, download and install the single-node cluster VMware image from this site: http://www-01.ibm.com/software/data/infosphere/biginsights/quick-start/downloads.html

Note1 : About the screen captures, sample code, and environment configuration

Screen captures in this book depict examples and results that may vary from what you see when you complete the exercises. In addition, some code examples may need to be customized to match your environment. For example, you may need to alter directory path information or user ID information.

The VMware image is set up in the following manner:

	User	Password
VM Image root account	root	password
VM Image lab user account	biadmin	password
BigInsights Administrator	biadmin	biadmin
Big SQL Administrator	bigsql	bigsql
Lab user	biadmin	password

Property	Value
Host name	bivm.ibm.com
BigInsights Web Console URL	http://bivm.ibm.com:8080
Big SQL database name	bigsql
Big SQL port number	51000

1.2 GETTING STARTED

To get started with the lab exercises, you need to install and launch the VMware image as well as start the required services.

1. Follow the instructions provided to decompress (unzip) the file and install the image on your computer. Note that there is a README file with additional information.

2. Launch the VMware image. When logging in for the first time, use the root ID (with a password of password). Follow the instructions to configure your environment, accept the licensing agreement, and enter the passwords for the root and biadmin IDs (root/password and biadmin/biadmin) when prompted. **This is a one-time only requirement.**

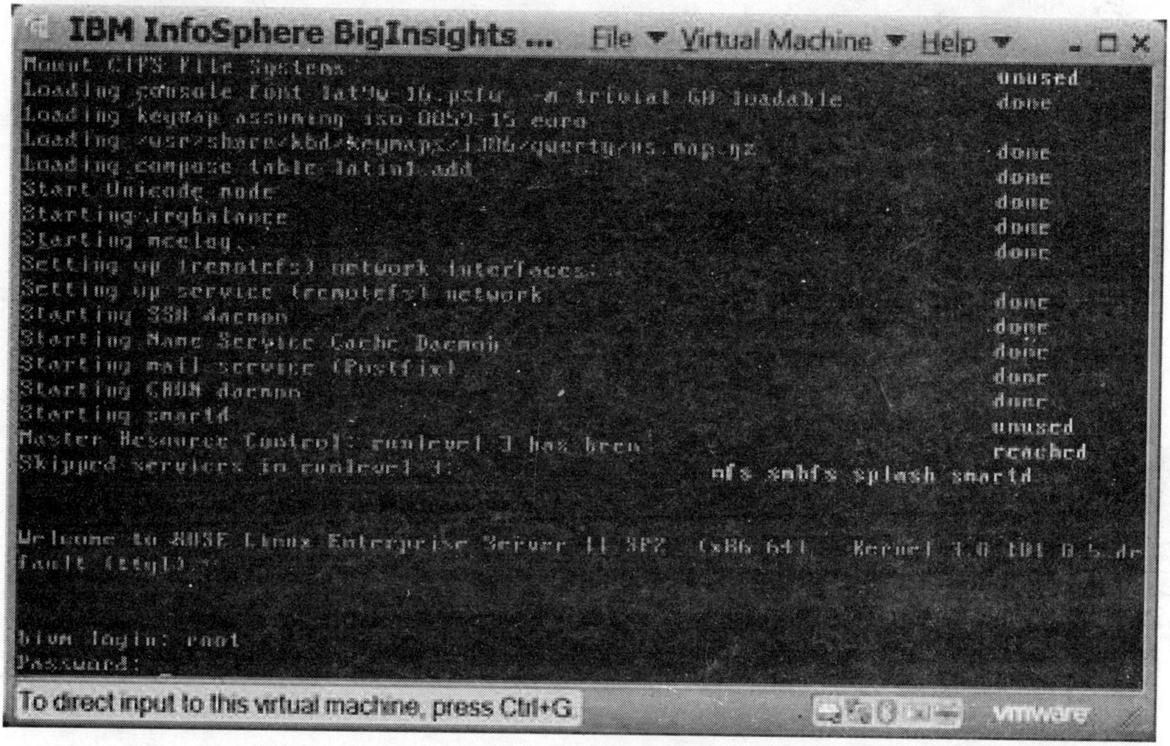

IBM InfoSphere BigInsights ... File ▾ Virtual Machine ▾ Help ▾

```
Mount CIFS File Systems                                            unused
Loading console font lat9w-16.psfu -m trivial G0:loadable          done
Loading keymap assuming iso-8859-15 euro
Loading /usr/share/kbd/keymaps/i386/qwerty/us.map.gz               done
Loading compose table latin1.add                                   done
Start Unicode mode                                                 done
Starting irqbalance                                                done
Starting mcelog..                                                  done
Setting up (remotefs) network interfaces:                          done
Setting up service (remotefs) network
Starting SSH daemon                                                done
Starting Name Service Cache Daemon                                 done
Starting mail service (Postfix)                                    done
Starting CRON daemon                                               done
Starting smartd                                                    done
Master Resource Control: runlevel 3 has been                       unused
Skipped services in runlevel 3:                                    reached
                                            nfs smbfs splash smartd


Welcome to SUSE Linux Enterprise Server 11 SP2 (x86_64) - Kernel 3.0.101-0.5-de
fault (tty1).


bivm login: root
Password:
```

To direct input to this virtual machine, press Ctrl+G vmware

3. When the one-time configuration process is completed, you will be presented with a SUSE Linux log in screen. Log in as `biadmin` with a `password` of password.

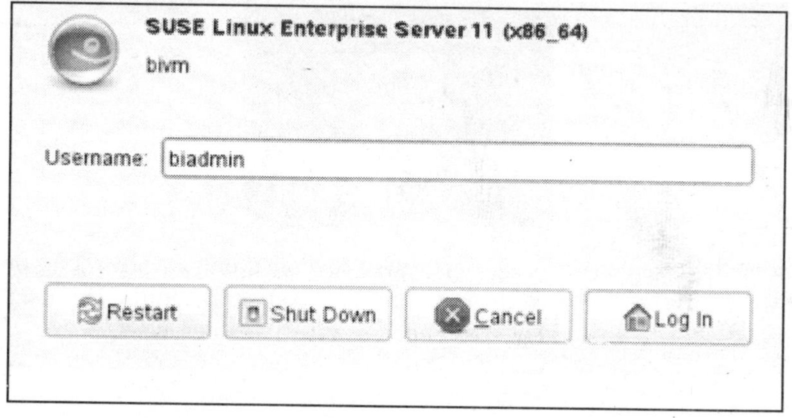

4. Verify that your screen appears similar to this:

5. Click **Start BigInsights** to start all required services. (Alternatively, you can open a terminal window and issue this command: `$BIGINSIGHTS_HOME/bin/start-all.sh`

Wait until the operation completes.This may take several minutes, depending on your machine's resources. Alternatively , for starting BigInsight you may hoover-on on the BigInsight icon and right click to see a popup from which you may select open as illustrated below.

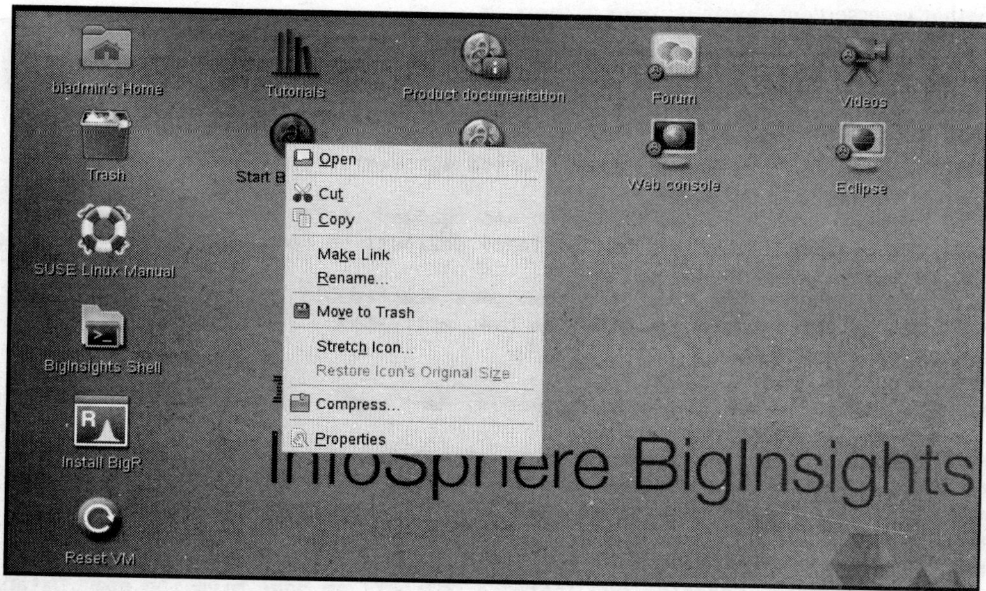

7. Verify that all required BigInsights services are up and running. From a terminal window, issue this command:`$BIGINSIGHTS_HOME/bin/status.sh.`
8. Inspect the results, a subset of which are shown below. Verify that, at a minimum, the following components started successfully:hdm, zookeeper, hadoop, catalog, hive, bigsql, oozie, console, and httpfs. I have tried to give four screen-shots one beneath another but they actually shows the starting process.

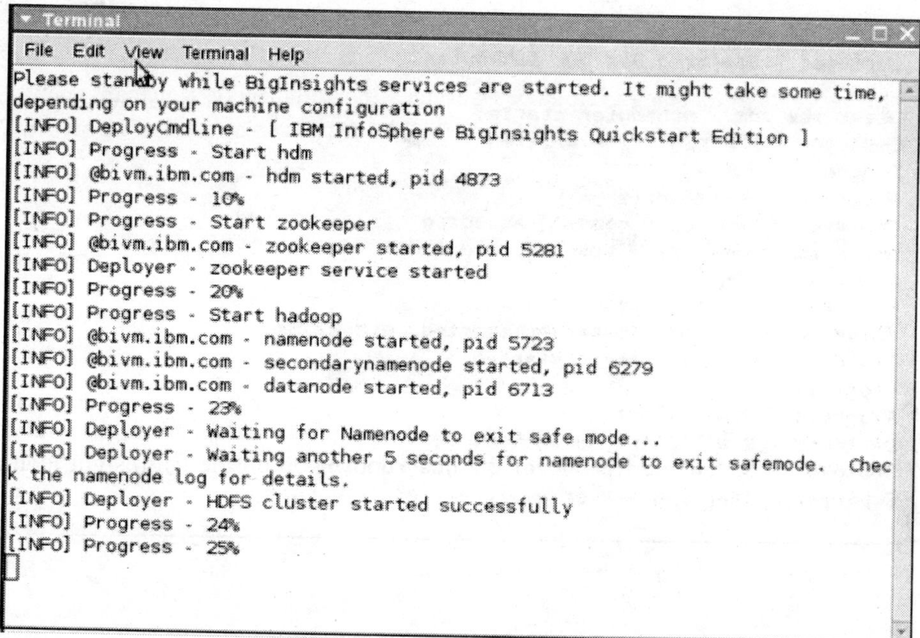

```
Terminal
File  Edit  View  Terminal  Help
[INFO] @bivm.ibm.com - tasktracker started, pid 8184
[INFO] Progress - 30%
[INFO] Deployer - MapReduce cluster started successfully
[INFO] Progress - Start catalog
[INFO] HdmUtil - Install configuration has changed in the system, reloading...
[INFO] DB2Operator - Starting DB2 Instance db2inst1 on node bivm.ibm.com .Databa
se to be activated BIDB
[INFO] DB2Operator - DB2 node bivm.ibm.comis started9018
[INFO] DB2Operator - Database BIDB has been activated
[INFO] Progress - 40%
[INFO] Progress - Start hbase
[INFO] Deployer - check zookeeper services, make sure zookeeper service is start
ed before start hbase service
[INFO] @bivm.ibm.com - hbase-master(active) started
[INFO] @bivm.ibm.com - hbase-regionserver started
[INFO] Deployer - hbase service started
[INFO] Progress - 50%
[INFO] Progress - Start hive
[INFO] DB2Operator - Starting DB2 Instance db2inst1 on node bivm.ibm.com .Databa
se to be activated BIDB
[INFO] DB2Operator - DB2 Instance db2inst1 is already running on node bivm.ibm.c
om Process ID9018
[INFO] DB2Operator - Database BIDB has already been activated
[INFO] Deployer - Starting Big SQL v1              : OK (pid 13333)

[INFO] @bivm.ibm.com - bigsql1 started
[INFO] Deployer - Starting Big SQL                 : OK

[INFO] @bivm.ibm.com - head-node started
[INFO] Deployer - Starting Big SQL Scheduler       : OK

[INFO] @bivm.ibm.com - scheduler started
[INFO] Deployer - FMP pids file written
[INFO] Progress - 70%
[INFO] Progress - Start oozie
[INFO] Deployer - Run oozie command as:oozie
[INFO] @bivm.ibm.com - oozie started, pid 21489
[INFO] Progress - 80%
[INFO] Progress - Start httpfs
[INFO] @bivm.ibm.com - httpfs-server started, pid 22058
[INFO] Deployer - httpfs service started
[INFO] Progress - 90%
[INFO] Progress - Start alert
[INFO] Deployer - start alert management service...
[INFO] Deployer - Server waslp-server is not running.
[INFO] Deployer - Starting server waslp-server.
^[[3~
```

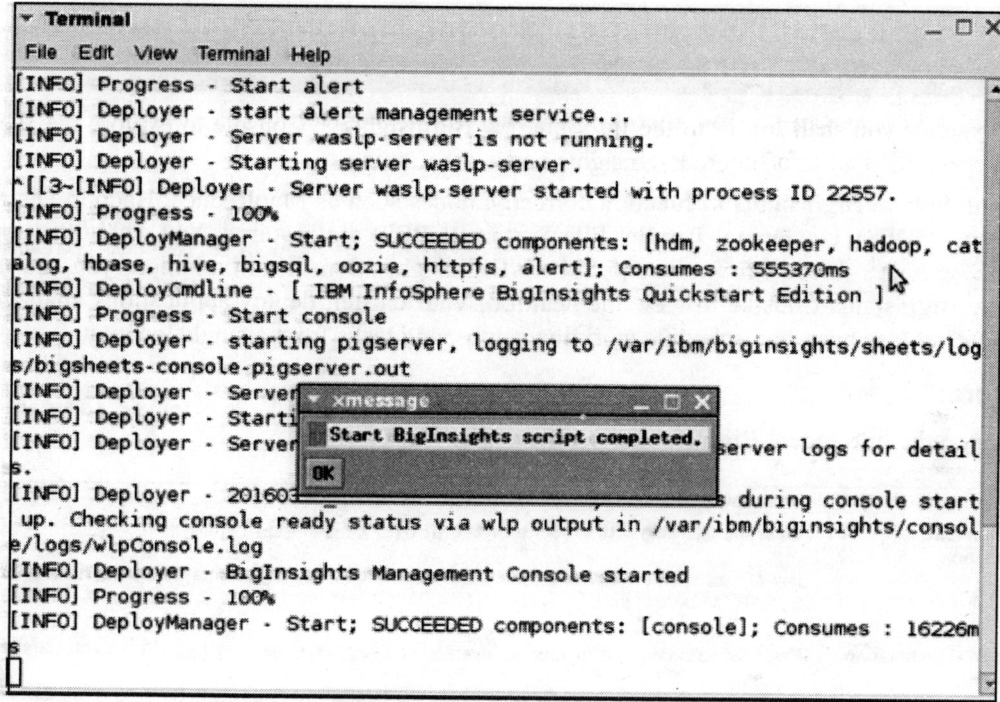

At last you may see above message that BigInsight script is completed.

The list includes the following hadoop program components or clusters:

1. namenode
2. HDFS
   jobtracker
   tasktracker
3. MapReduce
4. Catalog
5. DB-2
6. hbase
   zookeeper
7. hive
8. bigsql
9. Oozie
10. Console
11. httpfs

Now you're ready to start working with big data!

EXERCISE 3.2: Starting To Use The InfoSphere BigInsights Console

For this exercise you shall log in to the InfoSphere® BigInsights™ Console to explore the Welcome page and ensure that all InfoSphere BigInsights nodes are running.

For InfoSphere BigInsights to function correctly, nodes such as MapReduce, Hadoop Distributed File System (HDFS), or General Parallel File System (GPFS) are required. You can start, stop, and manage these nodes directly from the InfoSphere BigInsights Console. In addition, you can use the InfoSphere BigInsights Console to view the health of your cluster, deploy applications, manage your files and cluster instances, and schedule workflows, jobs, and tasks from a single location.

Procedure:

1. Log in to the InfoSphere BigInsights Console.

Option	Description
In a non-SSL installation	Enter the following URL in your browser: `http://host_name:8080` `host_name` is the name of the host where the InfoSphere BigInsights Console is running, and `8080` is the default port.
In an SSL installation	Enter the following URL in your browser: `https://host_name:8443` `host_name` is the name of the host where the InfoSphere BigInsights Console is running, and `8443` is the default port.

Explore each section of the Welcome tab to learn more about the tasks and resources that are available.

Option	Description
Understand IBM® Big Data Tools	An interactive model that describes an overview of the product capabilities in the InfoSphere BigInsights Knowledge Center.
Tasks	Quick access to commonly used InfoSphere BigInsights tasks.
Quick Links	Links to internal and external quick links and downloads to enhance your environment.
Learn More	Online resources available to learn more about InfoSphere BigInsights.

Exploring the InfoSphere BigInsights Console

You shall learn to navigate into the different sections of the InfoSphere® BigInsights™ Console to familiarize yourself with its capabilities.

Administrators use the InfoSphere BigInsights Console to inspect the overall health of the system. They also use InfoSphere BigInsights Console to complete basic functions such as starting and stopping specific servers and components, and adding nodes to the cluster. Other users can interact with files in the distributed file system and manage applications.

Procedure:

1. On the Welcome tab, select Access secure cluster servers under the Quick Links section.

   A pop-up window appears with a list of URLs and the alias for each URL. For example, click the hive link, which opens the Hive Web Interface into a new browser window. You see an open source tool that is provided with Hive for administration purposes, such as browsing the database schema and creating a session. Close the browser window to return to the InfoSphere BigInsights Console home page.

2. On the Cluster Status tab, ensure that all InfoSphere BigInsights nodes are running. If any node is not running, select it, and then click Start. If you would like to see more information about a node, select it. From this view, you can also stop a node if it is running. After you start these nodes, they should remain active for the remainder of this tutorial.

By default, monitoring is unavailable to optimize performance

1. To explore your distributed file system, select the Files tab. Here, you can see contents of the distributed file system, create new subdirectories, upload small files for test purposes, and complete other file-related functions.

2. Become familiar with the functions that are provided by using the icons at the top of the pane in the Files page. These icons are used throughout the tutorials. Hover over an icon with your cursor to learn its function.

3. Expand the directory tree in the left navigation. Here, you can locate files that were uploaded and explore existing files. To learn how to upload files, you can use the "Importing data for analysis" tutorial. .

4. On the Applications tab, click Manage. Here, you can view applications that are available in your cluster, deploy applications to the cluster, and delete applications that you no longer need.

5. In the Manage applications panel, deploy an application. For example, you can use the BoardReader application in a later module to import current web data into the distributed file system. Select the BoardReader application and then click Deploy. In the Deploy Application window, click Deploy. The status of this application changes to deployed, and the application is available for use from the Run applications panel.

6. To view the status of applications, click the Applications Status tab. If this is the first use of the InfoSphere BigInsights Console, no applications, workflows or jobs are listed. After you run applications, workflows, or jobs, you can view their status from this page.

Importing data for analysis

7. Learn how to import data into your distributed file system from your local system or network by using the InfoSphere® BigInsights™ Console and IBM® provided applications.

8. Business data is stored in various formats and sources. Before you import your data into the InfoSphere BigInsights distributed file system, you must determine what questions you want to answer through analysis, identify the data type of your sources, and use the tools and procedures that best fit your business need. You can use InfoSphere BigInsights with your existing infrastructure or data warehouse to import data and content in its original formats, or you can import huge volumes of at-rest (static) data or incoming data in motion (continually updated data). After you import your data, you can explore the data separately or combine the data to complete exploration and analysis.

9. Many businesses might want to examine the popularity of a specific brand or service in social media. The data that is provided for this Exerciseis the result of a BoardReader application search for the instances of the phrase "IBM Watson™" on the Internet. This search is detailed in the developerWorks® article, Analyzing social media and structured data with InfoSphere BigInsights: Get a quick start with BigSheets. IBM Watson is a research project that uses complex analytics to answer questions that are presented in a natural language.
10. For this tutorial, and the related tutorial on BigSheets, only news and blog data that was returned by the search is used. The returned data was slightly modified to contain only a subset of the information that the BoardReader application collects from blogs and news feeds. The full-text/HTML content of posts, news items, and certain metadata, was removed to keep the size of each file manageable.

EXERCISE 3.3 : Managing Your Data

Before you import your data, it is important to determine how you want to manage your data in the InfoSphere® BigInsights™ distributed file system.

For this module, there are two options for gathering your data. However, to best manage your information you should first create a folder to store the data.

Procedure:

1. Open the **InfoSphere BigInsights** Console.
2. From the **Files** tab, select the **DFS Files** tab.
3. Create a directory to store this data in the distributed file system. Click the **Create Directory folder** icon ( ) in the **Files** toolbar.
4. Name your directory. For this exercise, in the DFS Files tab, create the directory bi_sample_data. If you are using the InfoSphere BigInsights Quick Start Edition, the home directory is /user/biadmin/.
5. In the bi_sample_data directory, create a subdirectory named bigsheets where you can store and access this same IBM Watson™ data for the BigSheets tutorial.

Results:

You now have a directory to store all of your source data files and application results.

EXERCISE 3.4 : Importing Data By Using The Distributed File Copy Application

The Distributed File Copy application copies files to and from a remote source to the InfoSphere® BigInsights™ distributed file system by using Hadoop Distributed File System (HDFS), GPFS™, FTP, or SFTP. You can also copy files to and from your local file system.

Before you begin:

To use the Distributed File Copy application with SFTP, you can create a credential file. There are private and public files in the credentials store. The private credentials store contains the private information for each user that is in the /user/username/credstore/private directory. The following is an example of what the properties file for SFTP might look like:

```
database=db2inst2
dbuser=pascal
password=[base64]LDo8LTor
```

Note 2: The Distributed File Copy application is designed to move large amounts of data. This application is designed to run on a Linux platform. To upload smaller data sets (less than 2G), you can use the Upload function from the Files tab in the InfoSphere BigInsights Console.

Procedure:

1. Deploy the Distributed File Copy application to make it available for your use.
   a. In the InfoSphere BigInsights Console, in the Applications tab, click Manage.
   b. From the navigation tree, expand the Import directory.
   c. Select the Distributed File Copy application, and click the Deploy button (Deploy).
   d. In the Deploy Application window, select Deploy.
2. From the toolbar on the top of the hierarchy tree window, select Run.
3. Select the Distributed File Copy application.
4. Define your application parameters.
   1) Specify an Execution name. This step creates a project, and you can track the results and reuse the project later. Name the execution dc_ibmwatson.
   2) In the Input path field, specify the fully qualified path to the article_sampleData file on your local file system. For example, sftp://*username*:*password*@localhost/file/path/article_sampleData/blogs-data.txt If you provide just the directory name as input, all of the files in the local directory will be uploaded. The default is HDFS, if an SFTP or FTP connection, or a GPFS file system, is not specified.
   3) In the Output path field, specify the fully qualified path to where you want to store the data, for example /bi_sample_data/bigsheets/article_sampleData. If you are using the InfoSphere BigInsights Quick Start Edition, the directory is /user/biadmin/bi_sample_data/bigsheets/article_sampleData. Make sure to include the name of the file that you want to import in the file path to prevent the folder from being mistaken as the name of the data file.
   4) Optional: If you are using SFTP to connect to your local file system, use the Browse button to specify the fully qualified path to your properties file in the InfoSphere BigInsights credentials store.
5. Select **Run** to import the file.
6. Repeat steps 4 and 5 for the news-data.txt file.
7. Verify that the Distributed File Copy application conducted a successful import. To verify the import, you can examine the status in the **Application History** panel. Return to the **Files** tab, and locate the /bi_sample_data/bigsheets directory to locate your import results. If you are using the InfoSphere BigInsights Quick Start Edition, the directory is **/user/biadmin/bi_sample_data/bigsheets/article_sampleData**.

CHAPTER

4

Hadoop Distributed File System

4.1 HADOOP DISTRIBUTED FILE SYSTEM (HDFS)

The Hadoop distributed file system (HDFS) is a distributed, scalable, and portable file-system written in Java for the Hadoop framework. A Hadoop cluster has nominally a single namenode plus a cluster of datanodes, although redundancy options are available for the namenode due to its criticality. Each datanode serves up blocks of data over the network using a block protocol specific to HDFS. The file system uses TCP/IP sockets for communication. Clients use remote procedure call (RPC) to communicate between each other.

HDFS stores large files (typically in the range of gigabytes to terabytes across multiple machines. It achieves reliability by replicating the data across multiple hosts, and hence theoretically does not require RAID storage on hosts (but to increase I/O performance some RAID configurations are still useful). With the default replication value, 3, data is stored on three nodes: two on the same rack, and one on a different rack. Data nodes can talk to each other to rebalance data, to move copies around, and to keep the replication of data high. HDFS is not fully POSIX-compliant, because the requirements for a POSIX file-system differ from the target goals for a Hadoop application. The trade-off of not having a fully POSIX-compliant file-system is increased performance for data throughput and support for non-POSIX operations such as Append.

HDFS added the high-availability capabilities, as announced for release 2.0 in May 2012, letting the main metadata server (the NameNode) fail over manually to a backup. The project has also started developing automatic fail-over.

The HDFS file system includes a so-called *secondary namenode*, a misleading name that some might incorrectly interpret as a backup namenode for when the primary namenode goes offline. In fact, the secondary namenode regularly connects with the primary namenode and builds snapshots of the primary namenode's directory information, which the system then saves to local or remote directories. These check-pointed images can be used to restart a failed primary namenode without having to replay the entire journal of file-system actions, then to edit the log to create an up-to-date directory structure. Because the namenode is the single point for storage and management of metadata, it can become a bottleneck for supporting a huge number of files, especially a large number of small files. HDFS Federation, a new addition, aims to tackle this problem to a certain extent by allowing multiple namespaces served by separate namenodes.

An advantage of using HDFS is data awareness between the job tracker and task tracker. The job tracker schedules map or reduce jobs to task trackers with an awareness of the data location. For example: if node A contains data (x,y,z) and node B contains data (a,b,c), the job tracker schedules node B to perform map or reduce tasks on (a,b,c) and node A would be scheduled to perform map or reduce tasks on (x,y,z). This reduces the amount of traffic that goes over the network and prevents unnecessary data transfer. When Hadoop is used with other file systems, this advantage is not always available. This can have a significant impact on job-completion times, which has been demonstrated when running data-intensive jobs.

HDFS was designed for mostly immutable files[21] and may not be suitable for systems requiring concurrent write-operations.

HDFS can be mounted directly with a Filesystem in Userspace (FUSE) virtual file system on Linux and some other Unix systems.

File access can be achieved through the native Java application programming interface (API), the Thrift API to generate a client in the language of the users' choosing (C++, Java, Python, PHP, Ruby, Erlang, Perl, Haskell, C#, Cocoa, Smalltalk, and OCaml), the command-line interface, browsed through the HDFS-UI Web application (webapp) over HTTP, or via 3rd-party network client libraries.[24]

4.2 ARCHITECTURE OF APACHE HADOOP HDFS

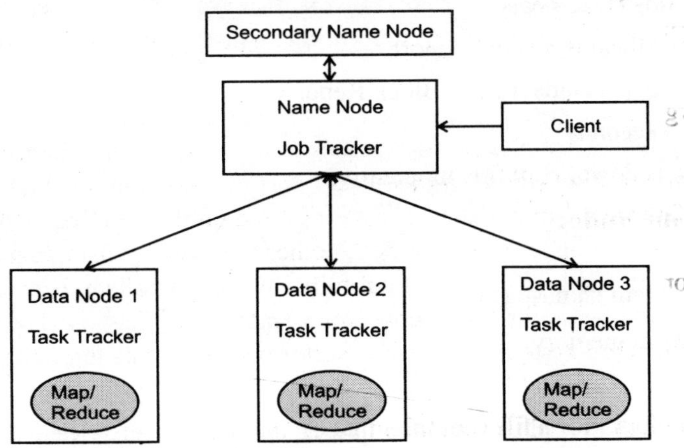

Figure. 4.1: The architecture of Apache Hadoop HDFS

HDFS or Hadoop Distributed File System is a block-structured file system where each file is divided into blocks of a predetermined size. Default size of these blocks is 64MB. These blocks are stored across a cluster of one or several machines. Apache Hadoop HDFS Architecture follows a Master/ Slave Architecture, where a cluster comprises of a single NameNode (Master node) and a number of DataNodes (Slave nodes). In hadoop system there are five services always running in background (called hadoop daemon services).

4.2.1 NameNode:

Namenode is the master of HDFS that maintains and manages the blocks present on the DataNodes (slave nodes). Namenode is a very high-availability server that manages the file system namespace and controls access to files by clients. There is just one Namenode in Gen1 Hadoop which is the single point of failure in the entire Hadoop HDFS cluster.

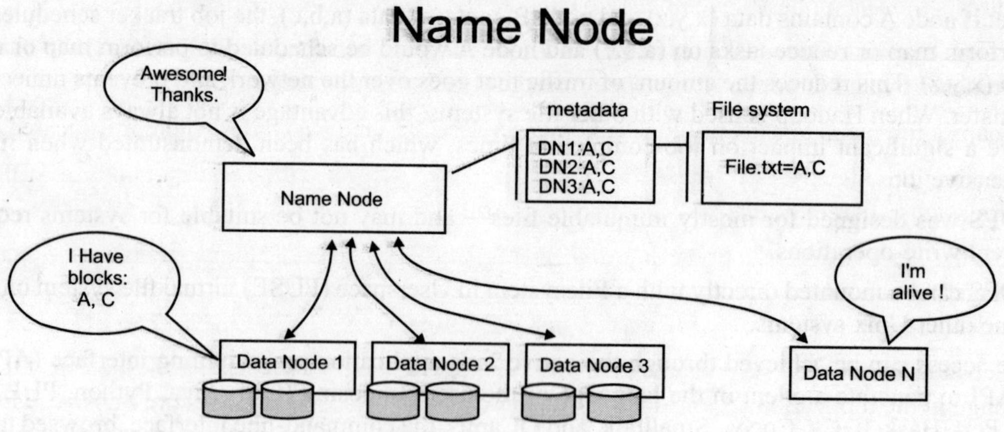

Figure. 4.2: Functions of a NameNode

- Data Node sends Heaerbeats
- Every 10th heartbeat is a Block report.
- NameNode builds metadata from Block Reports
- TCP – every 3 seconds
- If Name node is down, HDFS is inoperative

Functions of a NameNode:

1. Manages the filesystem namespace
2. Stores all metadata in memory
   1. File name
   2. Location of all blocks for a file (not in fsimage)
   3. Permissions
   4. Owner
   5. Group
3. Metadata is maintained in RAM to serve read requests –Size of metadata is limited to available RAM storage –Running out of RAM can cause the NameNode to crash
4. Single NameNode per cluster

5. File data never goes through or stored on NameNode
6. Needs to be explicitly formatted (hadoop-namenodeformat)
7. The NameNode maintains and executes the file system namespace. If there are any modifications in the file system namespace or in its properties, this is tracked by the NameNode.
8. It directs the Datanodes(Slave nodes) to execute the low-level I/O operations.
9. It keeps a recordof how the files in HDFS are divided into blocks, in which nodes these blocks are stored and by and large the NameNode manages cluster configuration.
10. It maps a file name to a set of blocksand maps a block to the DataNodes where it is located.
11. It records the metadata of all the files stored in the cluster, e.g. the location, the size of the files, permissions, hierarchy, etc.
12. With the help of a transactional log, that is, the EditLog, the NameNode records each and every changethat takes place to the file system metadata. For example, if a file is deleted in HDFS, the NameNode will immediately record this in the EditLog.
13. The NameNode is also responsible to take care of the replication factorof all the blocks. If there is a change in the replication factor of any of the blocks, the NameNode will record this in the EditLog.
14. NameNode regularly receives a Heartbeat and a Blockreportfrom all the DataNodes in the cluster to make sure that the datanodes are working properly. A Block Report contains a list of all blocks on a DataNode.
15. In case of a datanode failure, the Namenode chooses new datanodes for new replicas, balances disk usage and also manages the communication traffic to the datanodes.

4.2.2 DataNodes:

Datanodes are the slave nodes in HDFS. Unlike NameNode, datanode is a commodity hardware, that is, a non-expensive system which is not of high quality or high-availability. Datanode is a block server that stores the data in the local file ext3 or ext4. Functions of DataNodes:

1. Storage for file blocks
2. Different blocks from the same file are stored on different DataNodes
3. Replication factor is configurable
4. Size of the blocks is configurable
5. DataNode communicates with NameNode and other DataNodes
6. DataNode does not need to be explicitly formatted as does the NameNode
7. Multiple disks on DataNode:
   1. Controlled by dfs.data.dir
   2. Blocks written to each in round-robin fashion
   3. Datanodes perform the low-level read and write requestsfrom the file system's clients.
8. They are also responsible for creating blocks, deleting blocks and replicating the same based on the decisions taken by the NameNode.

9. They regularly send a reporton all the blocks present in the cluster to the NameNode.
10. Datanodes also enablespipelining of data.
11. Theyforward data to other specified DataNodes.
12. Datanodes send heartbeats to the NameNodeonce every 3 seconds, to report the overall health of HDFS.
13. The DataNodestores each block of HDFS data in separate files in its local file system.
14. When the Datanodes gets started, they scan through its local file system, creates a list of all HDFS data blocks that relate to each of these local files and send a Block report to the NameNode.

4.2.3 Secondary NameNode

In the HDFS Architecture, the name – Secondary NameNode gives an impression that it is a substitute of the NameNode. We know that NameNode stores vital information related to the Metadata of all the blocks stored in HDFS. This data is not only stored in the main memory, but also in the disk. The two associated files are:

- **Fsimage:** An image of the file system on starting the NameNode.
- **EditLogs:** A series of modifications done to the file system after starting the NameNode.

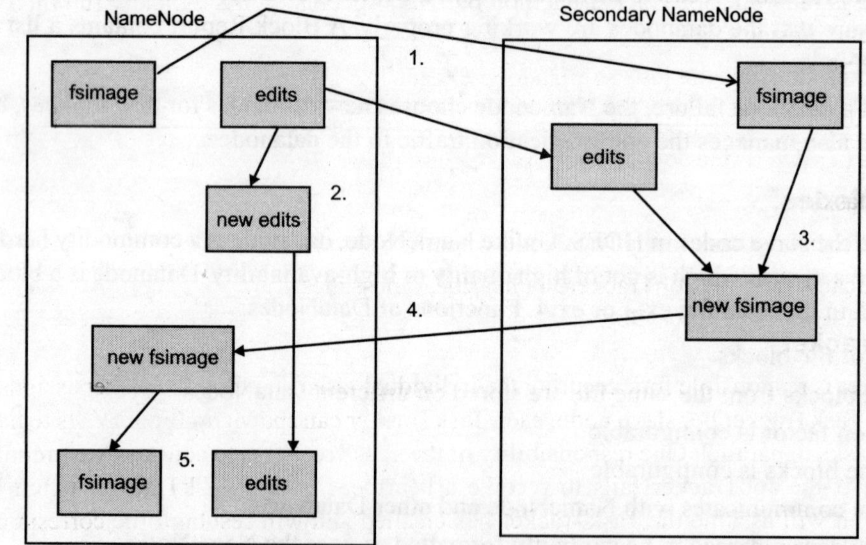

Figure. 4.3: Secondary NameNodes

Remember that Secondary NameNode are not used as hot standby or mirror node

- Memory requirements are the same as NameNode Typically runs on a separate machine Directory structure is same as NameNode
- It also keeps previous checkpoint version in addition to current It can be used to restore a failed NameNode.

–Just copies current directory to new NameNode

The Secondary NameNode is one which constantly reads all the file systems and metadata from the RAM of the NameNode and writes it into the hard disk or the file system. It is responsible for combining the editlogs with fsimage from the NameNode. It downloads the EditLogs from the NameNode at regular intervals and applies to fsimage. The new fsimage is copied back to the NameNode, which is used whenever the Namenode is started the next time.

However, as the secondary NameNode is unable to process the metadata onto the disk, it is not a substitute to the NameNode. So if the NameNode fails, the entire Hadoop HDFS goes down, in this case we have to start Secondary Name node manually which acts like the master for the cluster.

As with the storage daemons, the computing daemons also follow a master/slave architecture: the JobTracker is the master overseeing the overall execution of a MapReduce job and the TaskTrackers manage the execution of individual tasks on each slave node.

4.2.4 Job Tracker

The JobTracker daemon is the liaison between your application and Hadoop. Once you submit your code to your cluster, the JobTracker determines the execution plan by determining which files to process, assigns nodes to different tasks, and monitors all tasks as they're running. Should a task fail, the JobTracker will automatically relaunch the task, possibly on a different node, up to a predefined limit of retries. There is only one JobTracker daemon per Hadoop cluster. It's typically run on a server as a master node of the cluster.

- JobTacker manages the jobs in a Hadoop cluster

– Only one JobTracker can exist

- JobTracker determines which TaskTrackers are to handle which tasks

– Attempts to direct a task to the DataNode where the data exists

– Communicates with the JobTracker via heartbeat messages

4.2.5 Task Tracker

Each TaskTracker is responsible for executing the individual tasks that the JobTracker assigns. Although there is a single TaskTracker per slave node, each TaskTracker can spawn multiple JVMs to handle many map or reduce tasks in parallel. One responsibility of the TaskTracker is to constantly communicate with the JobTracker. If the JobTracker fails to receive a heartbeat from a TaskTracker within a specified amount of time, it will assume the TaskTracker has crashed and will resubmit the corresponding tasks to other nodes in the cluster.

- TaskTrackers manage jobs on DataNodes

– One TaskTracker per DataNode

- TaskTrackers run the MapReduce tasks in JVMs

– Have a set number of slots used to run tasks

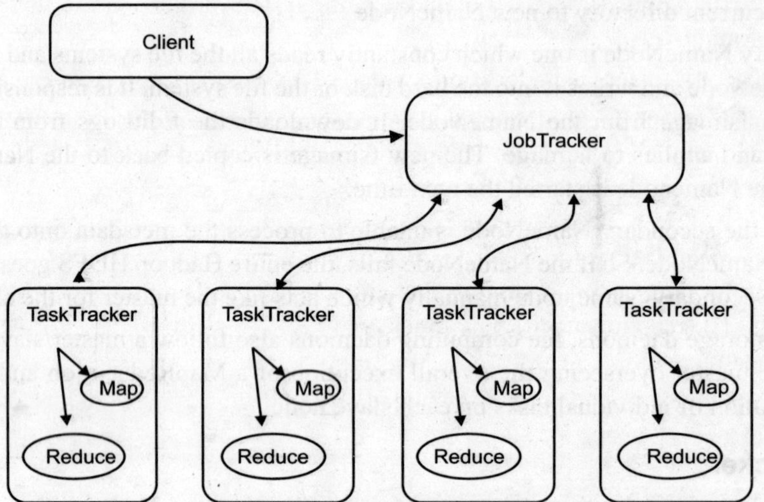

Figure. 4.4: Interaction between JobTracker and TaskTracker

After a Clint calls the JobTracker to begin a data processing job, the JobTrackerpartions the work and assigns different maps and reduce the task each time.

4.3 OTHER FILE SYSTEMS

Hadoop works directly with any distributed file system that can be mounted by the underlying operating system simply by using a file:// URL; however, this comes at a price: the loss of locality. To reduce network traffic, Hadoop needs to know which servers are closest to the data; this is information that Hadoop-specific file system bridges can provide.

In May 2011, the list of supported file systems bundled with Apache Hadoop were:

- HDFS: Hadoop's own rack-aware file system. This is designed to scale to tens of petabytes of storage and runs on top of the file systems of the underlying operating systems.
- FTP File system: this stores all its data on remotely accessible FTP servers.
- Amazon S3 (Simple Storage Service) file system. This is targeted at clusters hosted on the Amazon Elastic Compute Cloud server-on-demand infrastructure. There is no rack-awareness in this file system, as it is all remote.
- Windows Azure Storage Blobs (WASB) file system. WASB, an extension on top of HDFS, allows distributions of Hadoop to access data in Azure blob stores without moving the data permanently into the cluster.
- A number of third-party file system bridges have also been written, none of which are currently in Hadoop distributions. However, some commercial distributions of Hadoop ship with an alternative filesystem as the default—specifically IBM and MapR.
- In 2009, IBM discussed running Hadoop over the IBM General Parallel File System. The source code was published in October 2009.
- In April 2010, Parascale published the source code to run Hadoop against the Parascale file system.

- In April 2010, Appistry released a Hadoop file system driver for use with its own CloudIQ Storage product.
- In June 2010, HP discussed a location-aware IBRIX Fusion file system driver.
- In May 2011, MapR Technologies, Inc. announced the availability of an alternative file system for Hadoop, which replaced the HDFS file system with a full random-access read/write file system.

4.4 HDFS FILE BLOCKS

File blocks are not the same as the operating system's file blocks. Default size is 64MB, but for larger files should be 128MB (recommended). File blocks are stored on DataNodes in 3 (default) locations – one of them on separate rack.

The name of file blocks and location is managed by NameNode. If a chunk of the file is smaller than the HDFS blocksize, only the needed space is used.

128MB	128MB	128MB	66MB

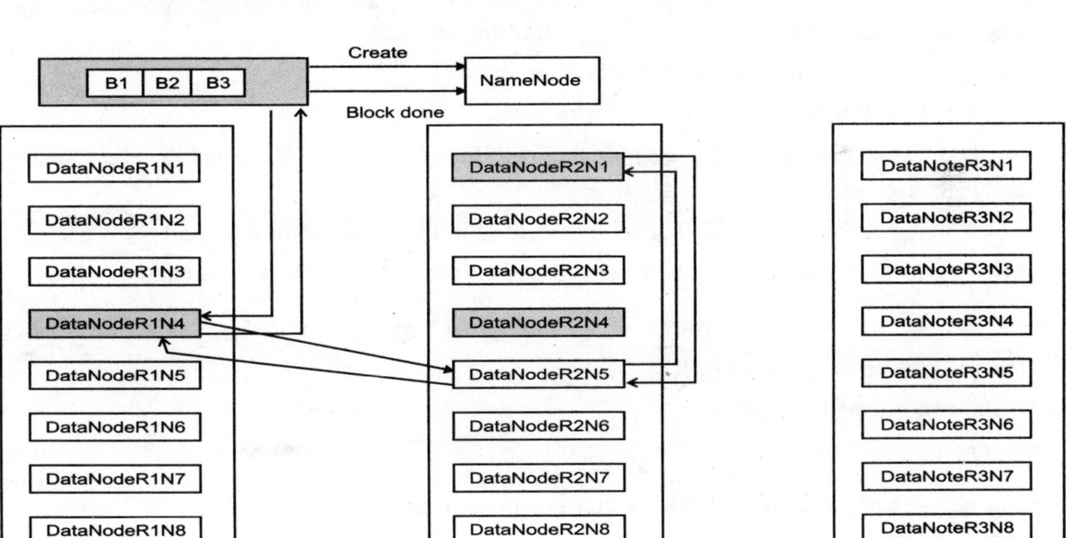

Figure. 4.5: Storing file blocks into HDFS from client machine

4.4.1 Rack Arrangement

Default installation assumes that all nodes belong to one rack in which replication factor is normally 3 and can be set by dfs.replication parameter. Computers belonging to the same rack are on the same network switch. Cluster administrator determines which computer belongs to which rack and sets the topology using topology.script.file.name. Each node's position in the cluster is represented by a string with syntax similar to a file name.

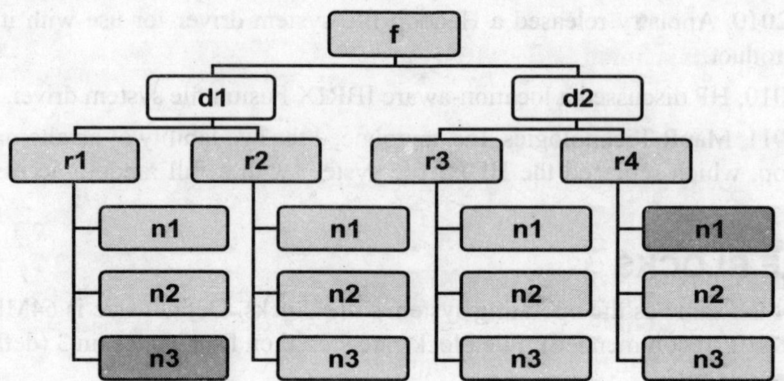

The DataNode sends its location to the NameNode as part of the registration information. A distance between two computers can be calculated by summing up their distances to their closest common ancestor.

Distance between above nodes is - f/d1/r1/n3, f/d2/r4/n1

4.5 HDFS FILE COMMANDS

- The FileSystem (FS) shell is invoked by **"hadoop fs <args>"**
- All FS shell commands take path URIs as arguments.
  - The URI format is scheme://authority/path
- For HDFS the scheme is hdfs, and for the local filesystem the scheme is file. The scheme and authority are optional.
  - If not specified, the default scheme specified in the configuration is used
- Most of the commands in FS shell behave like corresponding UNIX commands

cat

- Usage: hadoop fs -cat URI [URI …]
- Copies source paths to stdout.

Example:

hadoop fs -cat hdfs:/mydir/test_file1 hdfs:/mydir/test_file2
hadoop fs -cat file:///file3 /user/hadoop/file4

chgrp

- Usage: hadoop fs -chgrp [-R] GROUP URI [URI …]
- Change group association of files
- With -R, make the change recursively through the directory structure

chmod

- Usage: **hadoop fs -chmod [-R] <MODE[,MODE]... | OCTALMODE>** URI [URI …]
- Change the permissions of files.
- With -R, make the change recursively through the directory structure

chown

- **Usage: hadoop fs -chown [-R] [OWNER][:[GROUP]] URI [URI]**
- Change the owner of files.
- With -R, make the change recursively through the directory structure.
- **copyFromLocal**
  - Usage: hadoop fs -copyFromLocal <localsrc> URI:
- **copyToLocal**
  - Usage: hadoop fs -copyToLocal [-ignoreCrc] [-crc] URI <localdst>
- **count**
  - Usage: hadoop fs -count [-q] <paths>
- Count the number of directories, files and bytes under the paths that match the specified file pattern.
- The output columns are:
  DIR_COUNT, FILE_COUNT, CONTENT_SIZE FILE_NAME.
- The output columns with -q are:
  QUOTA, REMAINING_QUATA, SPACE_QUOTA, REMAINING_SPACE_QUOTA, DIR_COUNT, FILE_COUNT, CONTENT_SIZE, FILE_NAME.
  - Example:

hadoop fs -count hdfs:/mydir/test_file1 hdfs:/mydir/test_file2

hadoop fs -count -q hdfs:/mydir/test_file1

- **cp**
- **Usage: hadoop fs -cp URI [URI …] <dest>**
- Copy files from source to destination.
- This command allows multiple sources as well in which case the destination must be a directory.

Example:

hadoop fs -cp hdfs:/mydir/test_file file:///home/hdpadmin/foo

hadoop fs -cp file:///home/hdpadmin/foo file:///home/hdpadmin/boo hdfs:/mydir

du

- ♦ Usage: hadoop fs -du URI [URI …]
- Displays aggregate length of files contained in the directory or the length of a file in case its just a file.

Example:

hadoop fs -du file:///home/hdpadmin/test_file hdfs:/mydir

dus

- ♦ Usage: hadoop fs -dus <args>
- Displays a summary of file lengths.

expunge

- ♦ Usage: hadoop fs -expunge
- Empty the Trash

get

- ♦ Usage: hadoop fs -get [-ignoreCrc] [-crc] <src> <localdst>
- Copy files to the local file system.

– Files that fail the CRC check may be copied with the -ignoreCrc option.

– Files and CRCs may be copied using the -crc option.

- Example:

  hadoop fs -get hdfs:/mydir/file file:///home/hdpadmin/localfile

getmerge

- ♦ Usage: hadoop fs -getmerge <src> <localdst> [addnl]
- Takes a source directory and a destination file as input and concatenates files in the source into the destination local file.
- An additional option can be set to enable adding a newline character at the end of each file.

ls

- ♦ Usage: hadoop fs -ls <args>
- For a file returns statistics on the file with the following format:

– permissions number_of_replicas userid groupid filesize modification_date modification_time filename

- For a directory it returns list of its direct children as in UNIX .A directory is listed as:

– permissions userid groupid modification_date modification_time dirname

Example:

hadoop fs -ls hdfs:/mydir/test_file

lsr

- Usage: hadoop fs -lsr <args>
- Recursive version of ls. Similar to Unix ls -R.

Example:

hadoop fs -lsr hdfs:/mydir

mkdir

- **Usage: hadoop fs -mkdir <paths>**
- Takes path uri's as argument and creates directories. The behavior is much like unix mkdir -p creating parent directories along the path.

Example:

hadoop fs -mkdir hdfs:/mydir/foodir hdfs:/mydir/boodir

mv

- **Usage: hadoop fs -mv URI [URI …] <dest>**
- Moves files from source to destination.
- This command allows multiple sources. In which case the destination needs to be a directory.
- Moving files across file systems is not permitted.

Example:

hadoop fs -mv file:///home/hdpadmin/test_file file:///home/hdpadmin/test_file1

hadoop fs –mv hdfs:/mydir/file1 hdfs:/mydir/file2 hdfs:/mydir2

put

- **Usage: hadoop fs -put <localsrc> ... <dst>**
- Copy a single source, or multiple sources from local file system to the destination file system
- Reads input from stdin and writes to destination file system

– Notice that it can be the same file system.

Examples:

– hadoop fs -put file:///home/hdpadmin/test_file hdfs:/mydir

– hadoop fs -put localfile1 localfile2 hdfs:/mydir

– hadoop fs -put - hdfs://mydir/input_file1 (reads input from stdin)

rm

- **Usage: hadoop fs -rm [-skipTrash] URI [URI …]**
- Delete files specified as args
- Only deletes non empty directory and files.

Example:

hadoop fs -rm hdfs:/home/hdpadmin/test_file file:///home/hdpadmin/test_file

rmr

- **Usage: hadoop fs -rmr [-skipTrash] URI [URI …]**
- Recursive version of delete

Example:

hadoop fs -rmr file:///home/hdpadmin/mydir

hadoop fs -rmr –skipTrash hdfs:/mydir

setrep

- **Usage: hadoop fs –setrep [-w] [-R] <path>**
- Changes the replication factor of a file

Example:

– **hadoop fs -setrep -w 5 -R hdfs:/user/hadoop/dir1**

stat

- **Usage: hadoop fs -stat URI [URI …]**
- Returns the statistical information on the path.

Example:

– **hadoop fs –stat hdfs:/mydir/test_file**

tail

- Uyys last kilobyte of the file to stdout. -f option can be used as in Unix.
- Example:

– **hadoop fs -tail hdfs:/mydir/test_file**

test

- **Usage: hadoop fs -test -[ezd] URI**
- Options:

  -e check to see if the file exists. Return 0 if true.

  -z check to see if the file is zero length. Return 0 if true.

  -d check to see if the path is directory. Return 0 if true.

Example:

hadoop fs -test –e hdfs:/mydir/test_file

text

- **Usage: hadoop fs -text <src>**
- Takes a source file and outputs the file in text format.

touchz

- **Usage: hadoop fs -touchz URI [URI]**
- Creates a file of zero length.
- Example:

  hadoop fs -touchz hdfs:/mydir/test_file

EXERCISE 4.1 Exploring Hadoop Distributed File System

Hadoop Distributed File System

Technically, Hadoop consists of two key services:

(a Data storage using the ***Hadoop Distributed File System*** (HDFS) and

(b large-scale parallel data processing using a technique called ***MapReduce***.

Throughout this Exercise you will be using the following account login information:

Username	Password
Linux biadmin	biadmin
VM image setup screen root	password

1.1 GETTING STARTED

To prepare for the contents of this Exercise, you must go through the process of getting all of the Hadoop components started

1. Start the VMware image by clicking the Play virtual machine button in the VMware Player if it is not already on.
2. Log in to the VMware virtual machine using the following credentials.

   User: biadmin

   Password: password
3. After you log in, your screen should look similar to the one shown below :

Before we can start working with Hadoop Distributed File system, we must first start all the Biginsights components. There are two ways of doing this, through terminal and through simply double-clicking an icon. Both of these methods will be shown in the following steps.

First Method

4. Now open the terminal by double clicking the *BigInsights Shell* icon.

And you shall find following screen

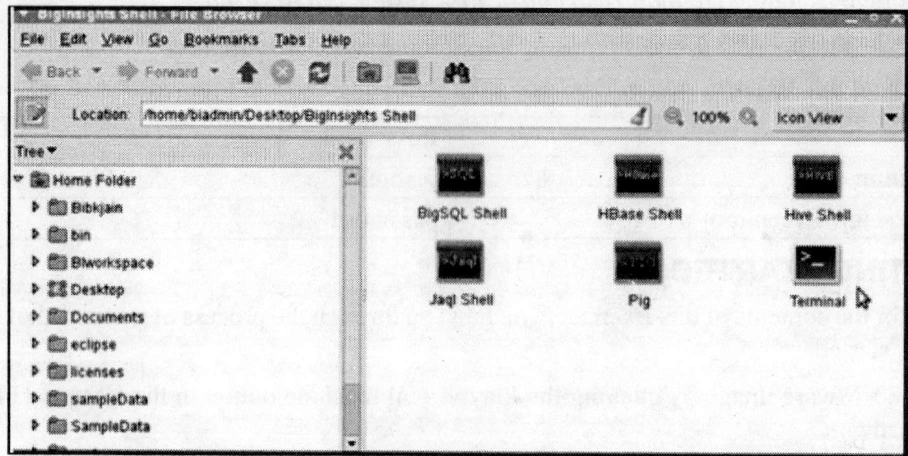

5. Click on the *Terminal* icon or you can right click over the icon and click over the option open.

Terminal

6. Once the terminal has been opened change to the $BIGINSIGHTS_HOME/bin directory (which by default is /opt/ibm/biginsights)

```
cd $BIGINSIGHTS_HOME/bin
```

or

```
cd /opt/ibm/biginsights/bin
```

While entering any command, beware that these commands and filenames are case sensitive.

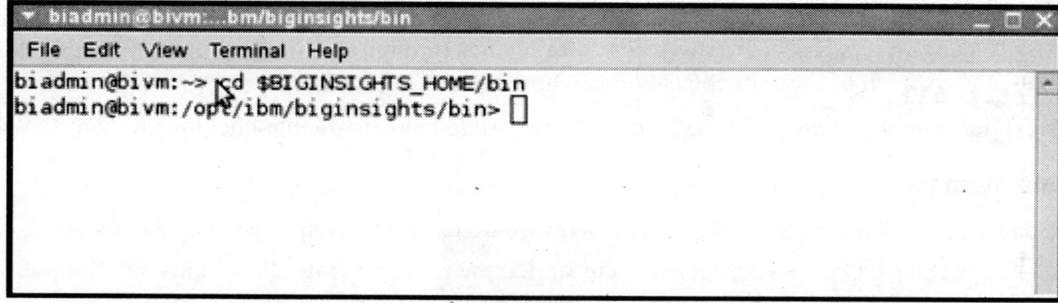

7. Start the Hadoop components (otherwise known as daemons) on the BigInsights server. You can practice starting all components with these commands. Please note that they will take a few minutes to run.

```
./start-all.sh
```

This command will cause all the components programs of Hadoop to get listed the way IBM's Biginsight has arranged them.The listing shall look like as shown below.

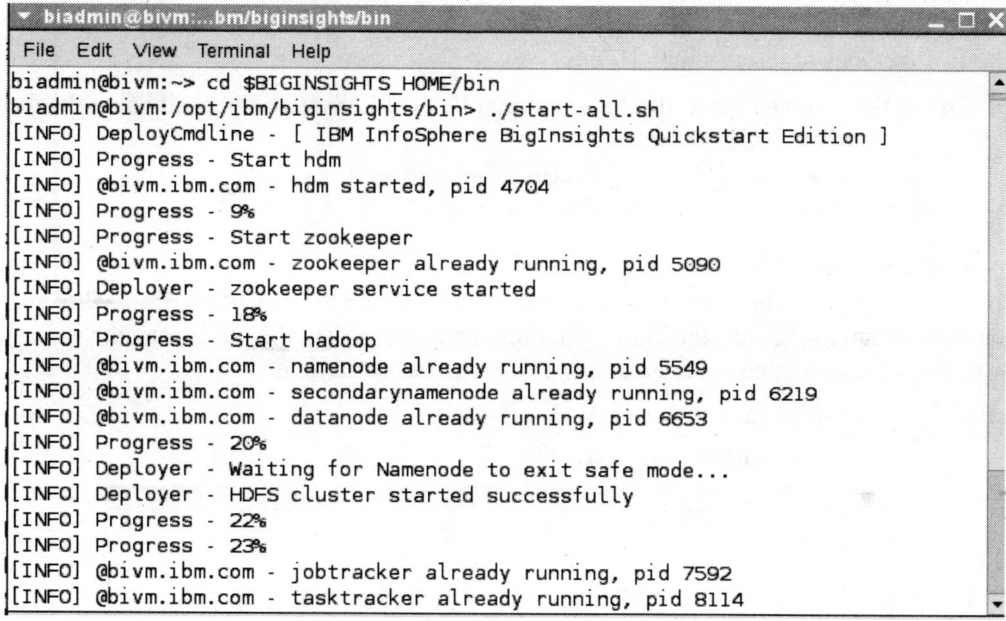

8. Sometimes certain hadoop components may fail to start. You can start and stop the failed components one at a time by using **start.sh** and **stop.sh** respectively. For example to start and stop Hive use:

```
./start.sh hive
./stop.sh hive
```

Notice that since Hive did not initially fail, the terminal is telling us that Hive is already running.

9. Once all components have started successfully you may move on.

10. If you would like to stop all components execute the command below. However, for this Exercise please leave all components started.

```
./stop-all.sh
```

Next, let us look at how you would start all the components by double-clicking an icon.

Second Method

11. Double-clicking on the *Start BigInsights* icon would execute a script that does the above mentioned steps. Once all components are started the terminal exits and you are set. Simple.
12. We can stop the components in a similar manner, by double-clicking on the *Stop Biginsights* icon. (To the right of *Start BigInsights* icon)

EXERCISE 4.2 Exploring Hadoop Distributed File System (Terminal)

Hadoop Distributed File System (HDFS) allows user data to be organized in the form of files and directories. It provides a command line interface called FS shell that lets a user interact with the data in HDFS accessible to Hadoop MapReduce programs.

There are two methods to interact with HDFS:

1. You can use the command-line approach and invoke the FileSystem (fs) shell using the format:

```
hadoop fs <args>
```

2. You can also manipulate HDFS using the BigInsights Web Console.
   We will be using both methods in this Exercise.

4.2.1 Using the command line Interface

We will start with the **hadoop fs -ls** command, which returns the list of files and directories with permission information. Ensure the Hadoop components are all started, and from the same terminal window as before (and logged on as biadmin), follow these instructions

1. List the contents of the root directory.

```
hadoop fs -ls /
```

```
biadmin@bivm:~
File Edit View Terminal Help
biadmin@bivm:~> hadoop fs -ls /
Found 5 items
drwxrwxr-x   - hdfs  biadmin          0 2016-02-26 02:40 /biginsights
drwxr-xr-x   - hdfs  biadmin          0 2014-07-24 17:23 /hadoop
drwxr-xr-x   - hbase biadmin          0 2016-02-29 06:05 /hbase
drwxrwxrwt   - hdfs  biadmin          0 2014-07-24 18:24 /tmp
drwxrwxrwx   - hdfs  biadmin          0 2016-02-15 07:37 /user
biadmin@bivm:~>
```

2. To list the contents of the /user/biadmin directory, execute:

```
hadoop fs -ls
```

```
biadmin@bivm:~
File Edit View Terminal Help
Found 9 items
drwx------   - biadmin biadmin          0 2016-02-29 17:39 .staging
drwxr-xr-x   - biadmin biadmin          0 2016-02-12 06:36 Demo
drwx--x--x   - biadmin biadmin          0 2016-02-12 06:56 Demo2
drwxr-xr-x   - biadmin biadmin          0 2016-02-15 07:31 Dummy1
drwxr-xr-x   - biadmin biadmin          0 2014-07-24 20:38 WordCount
drwxr-xr-x   - biadmin biadmin          0 2014-07-24 20:36 credstore
drwx--x--x   - biadmin biadmin          0 2016-02-15 07:44 dummy1Out
drwx--x--x   - biadmin biadmin          0 2016-02-15 07:44 oozie-oozi
-rw-r--r--   1 biadmin biadmin         10 2016-02-22 12:56 test.csv
biadmin@bivm:~>
```

or

`hadoop fs -ls /user/biadmin`

```
biadmin@bivm:~
File Edit View Terminal Help
biadmin@bivm:~> hadoop fs -ls /user/biadmin
Found 9 items
drwx------   - biadmin biadmin          0 2016-02-29 17:39 /user/biadmin/.stagin
g
drwxr-xr-x   - biadmin biadmin          0 2016-02-12 06:36 /user/biadmin/Demo
drwx--x--x   - biadmin biadmin          0 2016-02-12 06:56 /user/biadmin/Demo2
drwxr-xr-x   - biadmin biadmin          0 2016-02-15 07:31 /user/biadmin/Dummy1
drwxr-xr-x   - biadmin biadmin          0 2014-07-24 20:38 /user/biadmin/WordCou
nt
drwxr-xr-x   - biadmin biadmin          0 2014-07-24 20:36 /user/biadmin/credsto
re
drwx--x--x   - biadmin biadmin          0 2016-02-15 07:44 /user/biadmin/dummy1O
ut
drwx--x--x   - biadmin biadmin          0 2016-02-15 07:44 /user/biadmin/oozie-o
ozi
-rw-r--r--   1 biadmin biadmin         10 2016-02-22 12:56 /user/biadmin/test.cs
v
biadmin@bivm:~>
```

Note that in the first command there was no director referenced, but it is equivalent to the second command where /user/biadmin is explicitly specified. Each user will get its own home directory under /user. For example, in the case of user biadmin, the home directory is /user/biadmin. Any command where there is no explicit directory specified will be relative to the user's home directory. User space in the native file system (Linux) is generally found under /home/biadmin or /usr/biadmin, but in HDFS user space is /user/biadmin (spelled as "user" rather than "usr").

3. To create the directory **testing** you can issue the following command:

   `hadoop fs -mkdir testing`

4. Issue the ls command again to see the subdirectory **testing**:

   `hadoop fs -ls /user/biadmin`

```
biadmin@bivm:~
File  Edit  View  Terminal  Help
biadmin@bivm:~> hadoop fs -mkdir testing
biadmin@bivm:~> hadoop fs -ls /user/biadmin
Found 10 items
drwx------   - biadmin biadmin          0 2016-02-29 17:39 /user/biadmin/.staging
drwxr-xr-x   - biadmin biadmin          0 2016-02-12 06:36 /user/biadmin/Demo
drwx--x--x   - biadmin biadmin          0 2016-02-12 06:56 /user/biadmin/Demo2
drwxr-xr-x   - biadmin biadmin          0 2016-02-15 07:31 /user/biadmin/Dummy1
drwxr-xr-x   - biadmin biadmin          0 2014-07-24 20:38 /user/biadmin/WordCount
drwxr-xr-x   - biadmin biadmin          0 2014-07-24 20:36 /user/biadmin/credstore
drwx--x--x   - biadmin biadmin          0 2016-02-15 07:44 /user/biadmin/dummy1Out
drwx--x--x   - biadmin biadmin          0 2016-02-15 07:44 /user/biadmin/oozie-oozi
-rw-r--r--   1 biadmin biadmin         10 2016-02-22 12:56 /user/biadmin/test.csv
drwxr-xr-x   - biadmin biadmin          0 2016-03-03 02:05 /user/biadmin/testing
biadmin@bivm:~>
```

The result of *ls* here is similar to that found with Linux, except for the second column (in this case either "1" or "-"). The "1" indicates the replication factor (generally "1" for pseudo-distributed clusters and "3" for distributed clusters); directory information is kept in the namenode and thus not subject to replication (hence "-").

To use HDFS commands recursively generally you add an "r" to the HDFS command.

5. For example, to do a recursive listing we'll use the -lsr command rather than just -ls, like the example below.

   `hadoop fs -ls /user`

```
biadmin@bivm:/
File  Edit  View  Terminal  Help
biadmin@bivm:/> hadoop fs -ls /user
Found 3 items
drwxr-xr-x   - biadmin biadmin          0 2016-02-26 03:26 /user/applications
drwx--x--x   - biadmin biadmin          0 2016-03-03 02:05 /user/biadmin
drwxr-xr-x   - hive    biadmin          0 2014-07-24 17:41 /user/hive
biadmin@bivm:/>
```

   `hadoop fs -lsr /user`

6. You can pipe (using the | character) any HDFS command to be used with the Linux shell. For example, you can easily use *grep* with HDFS by doing the following.

   `hadoop fs -mkdir /user/biadmin/test2`
   `hadoop fs -ls /user/biadmin | grep test`

```
biadmin@bivm:/
File  Edit  View  Terminal  Help
biadmin@bivm:/>         hadoop fs -mkdir /user/biadmin/test2
biadmin@bivm:/> hadoop fs -ls /user/biadmin | grep test
-rw-r--r--   1 biadmin biadmin         10 2016-02-22 12:56 /user/biadmin/test.csv
drwxr-xr-x   - biadmin biadmin          0 2016-03-03 13:44 /user/biadmin/test2
drwxr-xr-x   - biadmin biadmin          0 2016-03-03 02:05 /user/biadmin/testing
biadmin@bivm:/>
```

As you can see the grep command only returned the lines which had "test" in them (thus removing the "Found x items" line and the other directories from the listing.

7. To move files between your regular Linux file system and HDFS you can use the put and get commands. For example, move the text file README to the hadoop file system:

```
hadoop fs -put /home/biadmin/README README
hadoop fs -ls /user/biadmin
```

```
biadmin@bivm:~
File  Edit  View  Terminal  Help
biadmin@bivm:~>        hadoop fs -put /home/biadmin/README README
put: `/home/biadmin/README': No such file or directory
biadmin@bivm:~> hadoop fs -put /home/biadmin/demo.txt DEMo
biadmin@bivm:~> hadoop fs -ls /user/biadmin
Found 12 items
drwx------   - biadmin biadmin          0 2016-02-29 17:39 /user/biadmin/.stagin
g
-rw-r--r--   1 biadmin biadmin      21555 2016-03-04 09:16 /user/biadmin/DEMo
drwxr-xr-x   - biadmin biadmin          0 2016-02-12 06:36 /user/biadmin/Demo
drwx--x--x   - biadmin biadmin          0 2016-02-12 06:56 /user/biadmin/Demo2
drwxr-xr-x   - biadmin biadmin          0 2016-02-15 07:31 /user/biadmin/Dummy1
drwxr-xr-x   - biadmin biadmin          0 2014-07-24 20:38 /user/biadmin/WordCou
nt
drwxr-xr-x   - biadmin biadmin          0 2014-07-24 20:36 /user/biadmin/credsto
re
drwx--x--x   - biadmin biadmin          0 2016-02-15 07:44 /user/biadmin/dummy1O
ut
drwx--x--x   - biadmin biadmin          0 2016-02-15 07:44 /user/biadmin/oozie-o
ozi
-rw-r--r--   1 biadmin biadmin         10 2016-02-22 12:56 /user/biadmin/test.cs
v
drwxr-xr-x   - biadmin biadmin          0 2016-03-03 13:44 /user/biadmin/test2
drwxr-xr-x   - biadmin biadmin          0 2016-03-03 02:05 /user/biadmin/testing
biadmin@bivm:~>
```

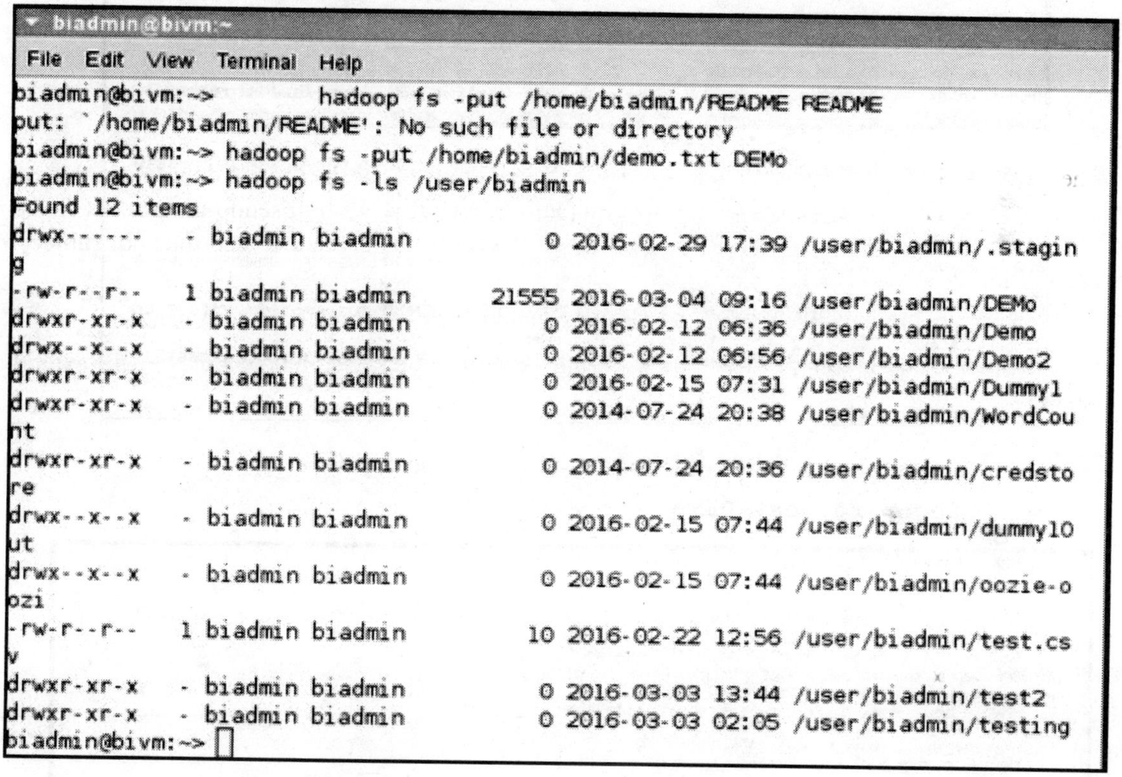

You should now see a new file called /user/biadmin/README is not available as shown above. Now let us move another file demo.txt (which is available) as DEMo by entering following at command line (remember that these names are case sensitive):

```
biadmin@bivm:~> hadoop fs -put /home/biadmin/demo.txt DEMo
   biadmin@bivm:~> hadoop fs -ls /user/biadmin
```

```
biadmin@bivm:~
File  Edit  View  Terminal  Help
biadmin@bivm:~>      hadoop fs -put /home/biadmin/README README
put: `/home/biadmin/README': No such file or directory
biadmin@bivm:~> hadoop fs -put /home/biadmin/demo.txt DEMo
biadmin@bivm:~> hadoop fs -ls /user/biadmin
Found 12 items
drwx------   - biadmin biadmin          0 2016-02-29 17:39 /user/biadmin/.stagin
g
-rw-r--r--   1 biadmin biadmin      21555 2016-03-04 09:16 /user/biadmin/DEMo
drwxr-xr-x   - biadmin biadmin          0 2016-02-12 06:36 /user/biadmin/Demo
drwx--x--x   - biadmin biadmin          0 2016-02-12 06:56 /user/biadmin/Demo2
drwxr-xr-x   - biadmin biadmin          0 2016-02-15 07:31 /user/biadmin/Dummy1
drwxr-xr-x   - biadmin biadmin          0 2014-07-24 20:38 /user/biadmin/WordCou
nt
drwxr-xr-x   - biadmin biadmin          0 2014-07-24 20:36 /user/biadmin/credsto
re
drwx--x--x   - biadmin biadmin          0 2016-02-15 07:44 /user/biadmin/dummy1O
ut
drwx--x--x   - biadmin biadmin          0 2016-02-15 07:44 /user/biadmin/oozie-o
ozi
-rw-r--r--   1 biadmin biadmin         10 2016-02-22 12:56 /user/biadmin/test.cs
v
drwxr-xr-x   - biadmin biadmin          0 2016-03-03 13:44 /user/biadmin/test2
drwxr-xr-x   - biadmin biadmin          0 2016-03-03 02:05 /user/biadmin/testing
biadmin@bivm:~>
```

8. In order to view the contents of this file use the -cat command as follows:

    hadoop fs -cat DEMo

```
IBM/HP
HP/Sharp
Delton/Fussion/as approved by the main vendor.
76      Ozone Injection system  Ruks/Trimed
77      Bus Ducting     L&T/Schneider/C&S Electric/Godrej/Zeta
78      Tube Axial Fans Kruger,Nocotra,Comefree,Flakwood/Wolter
79      Pressure independent
Balancing valve Danfoss/Flowcan/TA/Belimo
80      Heat Recovery Wheels    Desiicant Rotors(DRI), Novelair Technology,
Eventus(osterberg),Flakwood, Bryair
81      Heat Exchanger  Heatx X, Mark, Alfa lavel
82      Thermal storage tank    Crystopia, Dynambush, Calmac

83      Spiral duct     Sevenstar
84      Deep Freezer    Voltas/bLUESTAR

Note:

1. The contractor will use one of the approved makes with the prior approval of the engineer-in-charge.
2. Order will be placed with the prior approval of the engineer-in-charge.
3. When certain makes are missing in the above list, the make will be decided in consultation with the Engineer In Charge

biadmin@bivm:~>
```

You should see the output of the demo.txt file (that is stored in HDFS). We can also use the linux diff command to see if the file we put in HDFS is actually the same as the original on the local filesystem.

9. Execute the commands below to use the diff command.

```
cd /home/biadmin/
diff <( hadoop fs -cat DEMo ) demo.txt
```

```
▾ biadmin@bivm:~
File  Edit  View  Terminal  Help
biadmin@bivm:~> cd /home/biadmin/;
biadmin@bivm:~> diff <( hadoop fs -cat DEMo ) demo.txt
biadmin@bivm:~>
```

Since the diff command produces no output we know that the files are the same (the diff command prints all the lines in the files that differ). To find the size of files you need to use the -du or -dus commands. Keep in mind that these commands return the file size in bytes.

10. To find the size of the demo.txt file use the following command.

    hadoop fs -du DEMo

```
▾ biadmin@bivm:~
File  Edit  View  Terminal  Help
biadmin@bivm:~> hadoop fs -du DEMo
21555   DEMo
biadmin@bivm:~>
```

11. To find the size of all files individually in the /user/biadmin directory use the following command:

    hadoop fs -du /user/biadmin

```
▾ biadmin@bivm:~
File  Edit  View  Terminal  Help
biadmin@bivm:~> hadoop fs -du /user/biadmin
41310878   /user/biadmin/.staging
21555      /user/biadmin/DEMo
21555      /user/biadmin/Demo
110048     /user/biadmin/Demo2
21555      /user/biadmin/Dummy1
30         /user/biadmin/WordCount
122        /user/biadmin/credstore
115943     /user/biadmin/dummy1Out
0          /user/biadmin/oozie-oozi
10         /user/biadmin/test.csv
0          /user/biadmin/test2
0          /user/biadmin/testing
biadmin@bivm:~>
```

12. To find the size of all files in total of the /user/biadmin directory use the following command.

    hadoop fs -dus /user/biadmin

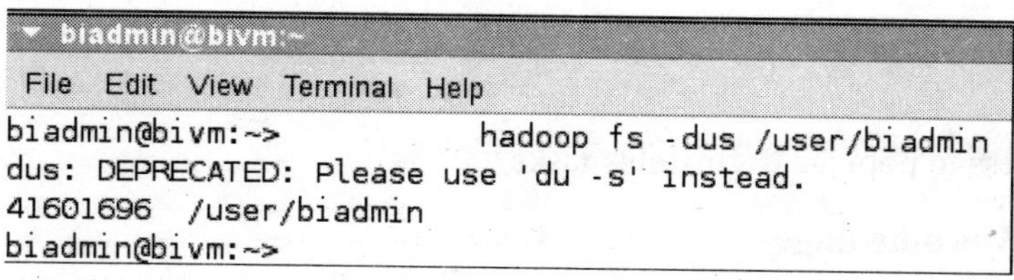

13. If you would like to get more information about hadoop fs commands, invoke -help as follows.

```
hadoop fs -help
```

14. For specific help on a command, add the command name after help. For example, to get help on the dus command you'd do the following.

```
hadoop fs -help dus
```

We are now done with the terminal section, you may close the terminal.

4.3 EXPLORING HADOOP DISTRIBUTED FILE SYSTEM (WEB CONSOLE)

The first step to accessing the BigInsights Web Console is to launch all of the BigInsights processes (Hadoop, Hive, Oozie, Map/Reduce etc.) They should have been started at the beginning of this Exercise.

EXERCISE 4.3 Using The Web Console

1. Start the Web Console by double-clicking on the *BigInsights WebConsole icon*.

2. Verify that your Web console appears similar to this, and note each section:

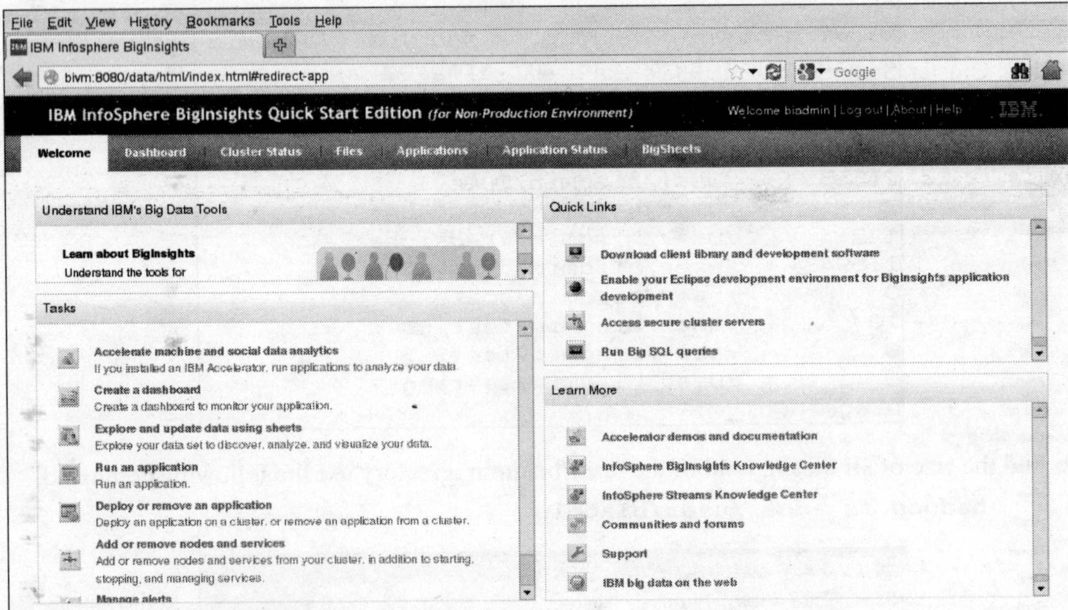

Tasks: quick access to popular BigInsights tasks,

Working with the Welcome page

This section introduces you to the Web console's main page displayed through the Welcome tab. The

Welcome page features links to common tasks, many of which can also be launched from other areas of the console. In addition, the Welcome page includes links to popular external resources, such as the BigInsights InfoCenter (product documentation) and community forum. You'll explore several aspects of this page.

3. In the Welcome Tab, the Tasks pane allows you to quickly access common tasks.

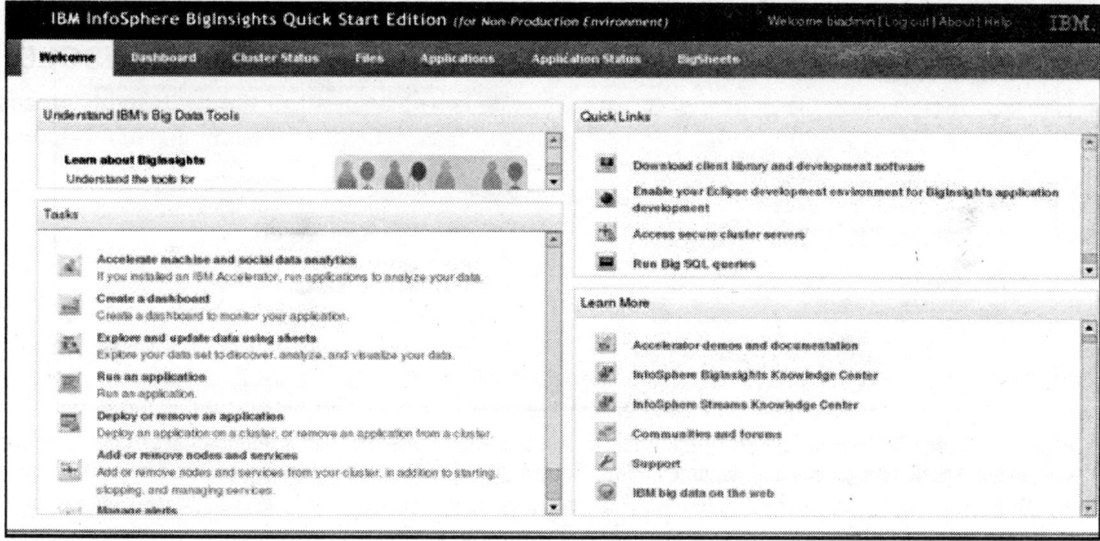

4. Click Cluster Status Tab. This takes you to the **Cluster Status** tab. Here, you can stop and start Hadoop services, as well as gain additional information as shown in the next section

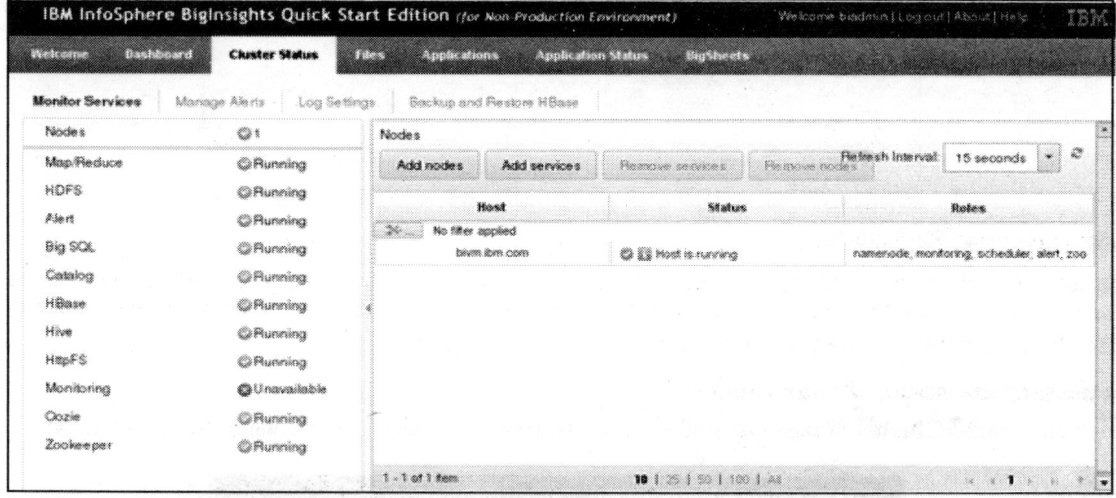

5. Click on the on the **Welcome** *tab* to return back to the main page.

6. Inspect the **Quick Links** pane at top right and use its vertical scroll bar (if necessary) to become familiar with the various resources accessible through this pane. The first several links simply activate different tabs in the Web console, while subsequent links enable you to perform set-up functions, such as adding BigInsights plug-ins to your Eclipse development environment.

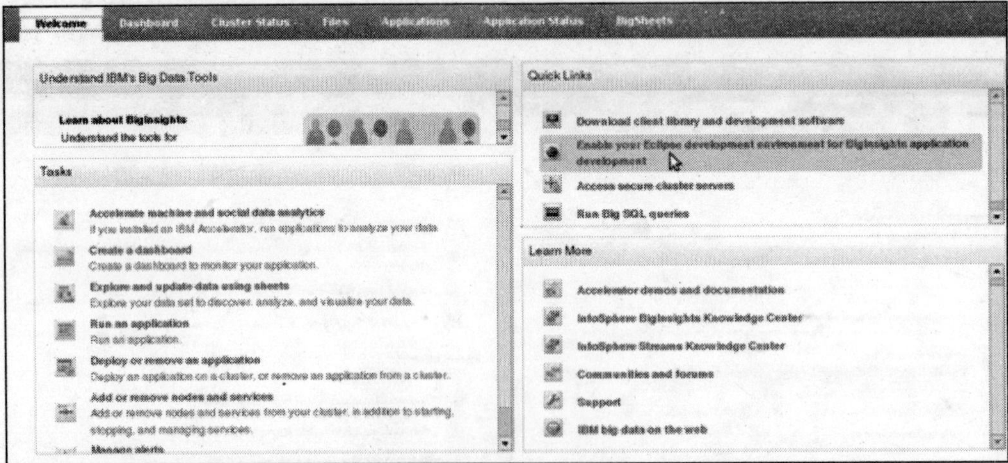

7. Inspect the **Learn More** pane at lower right. Links in this area access external Web resources that you may find useful, such as the Accelerator demos and documentation, BigInsights InfoCenter, a public discussion forum, IBM support, and IBM's BigInsights product site. If desired, click on one or more of these links to see what's available to you.

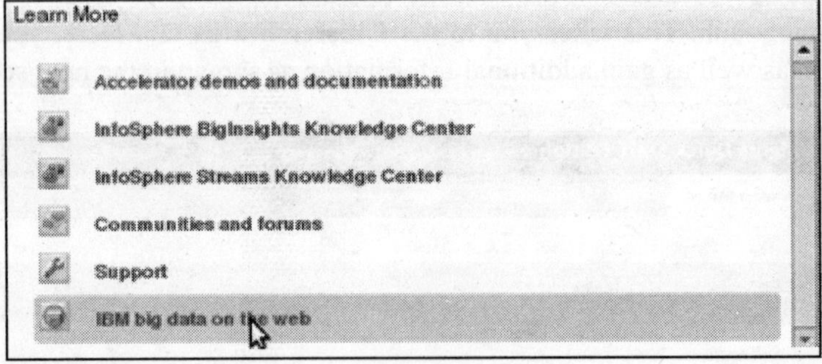

Administering BigInsights

The console allows administrators to inspect the overall health of the system as well as perform basic functions, such as starting and stopping specific servers (or components), adding nodes to the cluster, a nd so on. You'll explore a subset of these capabilities here.

Inspecting the status of your cluster

8. Click on the **Cluster Status** tab at the top of the page to return to the Cluster Status window

9. Inspect the overall status of your cluster. The figure below was taken on a single-node cluster that had several services running. One service – Monitoring -- was unavaiExercisele. (If you installed and started all BigInsights services on your cluster, your display will show all services to be running)
10. Click on the Hive service and note the detailed information provided for this service in the pane at right. From here, you can start or stop the hive service (or any service you select) depending on your needs. For example, you can see the URL for Hive's Web interface and its process ID.

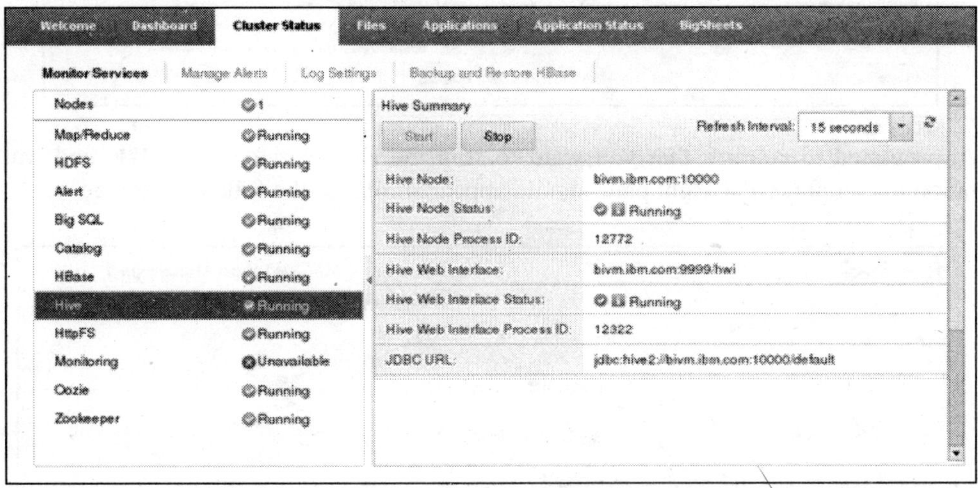

11. Optionally, cut-and-paste the URL for Hive's Web interface into a new tab of your browser. You'll see an open source tool provided with Hive for administration purposes, as shown below.

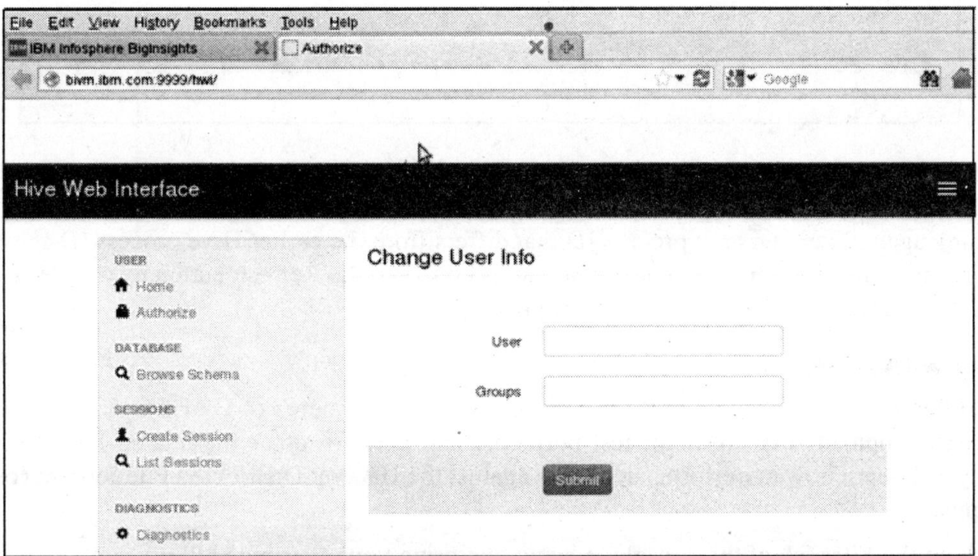

12. Close this tab and return to the **Cluster Status** section of the BigInsights Web console

Starting and stopping a component

13. If necessary, click on the Hive service to display its status.
14. In the pane to the right (which displays the Hive status), click the Stop button to stop the service

15. When prompted to confirm that you want to stop the Hive service, click **OK** and wait for the operation to complete. The right pane should appear similar to the following image

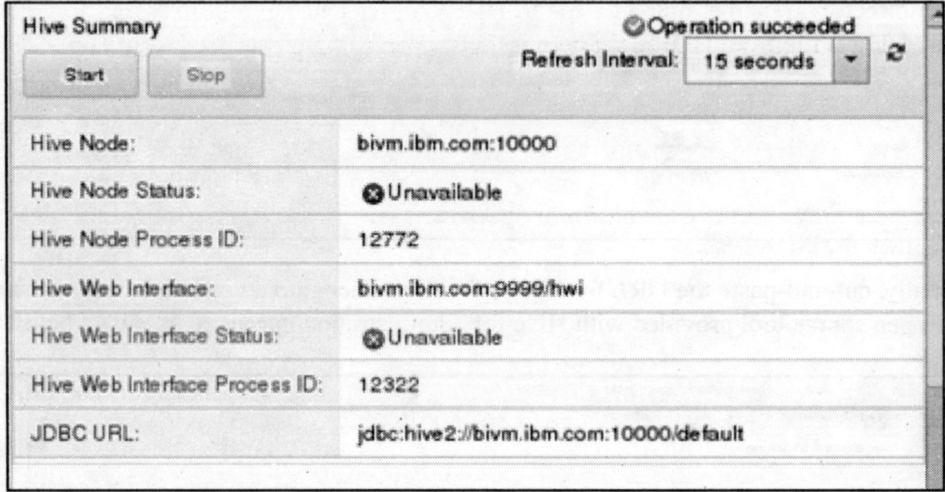

16. Restart the Hive service by clicking on the Start arrow just beneath the Hive Status heading. (See the previous figure.) When the operation completes, the Web console will indicate that Hive is running again, likely under a process ID that differs from the earlier Hive process ID shown at the beginning of this Exercise module. (You may need to use the Refresh button of your Web browser to reload information displayed in the left pane.)

Working with Files

The **Files** tab of the console enables you to explore the contents of your file system, create new subdirectories, upload small files for test purposes, and perform other file-related functions. In this module, you'll learn how to perform such tasks against the Hadoop Distributed File System (HDFS) of BigInsights.

17. Click on the **Files** tab of the console to begin exploring your distributed file system.

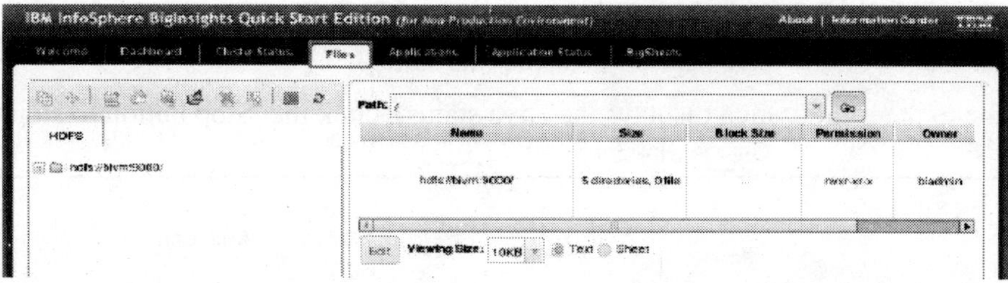

18. Expand the directory tree shown in the pane at left (**/user/biadmin**). If you already uploaded files to HDFS, you'll be able to navigate through the directory to locate them.
19. Become familiar with the functions provided through the icons at the top of this pane, as we'll refer to some of these in subsequent sections of this module. Simply point your cursor at the icon to learn its function. From left to right, the icons enable you to Copy a file or directory, move a file, create a directory, rename, upload a file to HDFS, download a file from HDFS to your local file system, delete a file from HDFS, set permissions, open a command window to launch HDFS shell commands, and refresh the Web console page.

20. Position your cursor on the **user/biadmin** directory and click the **Create Directory** icon to create a subdirectory for test purposes

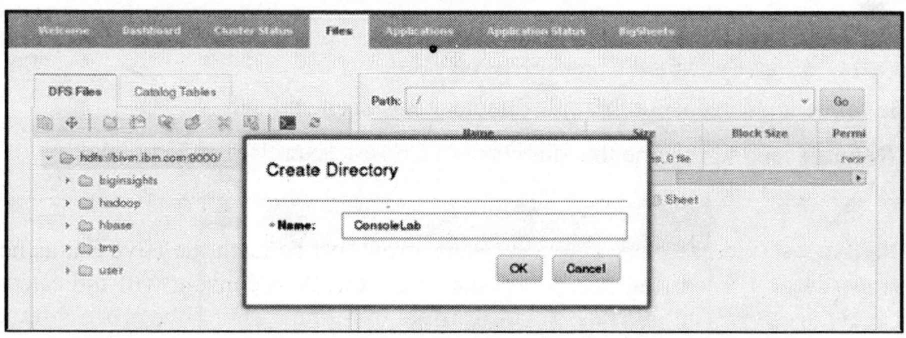

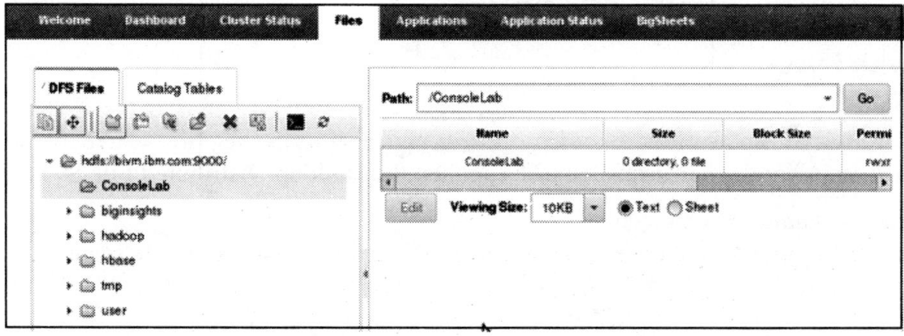

21. When a pop-up window appears prompting you for a directory name, enter **ConsoleExercise** and click **OK**

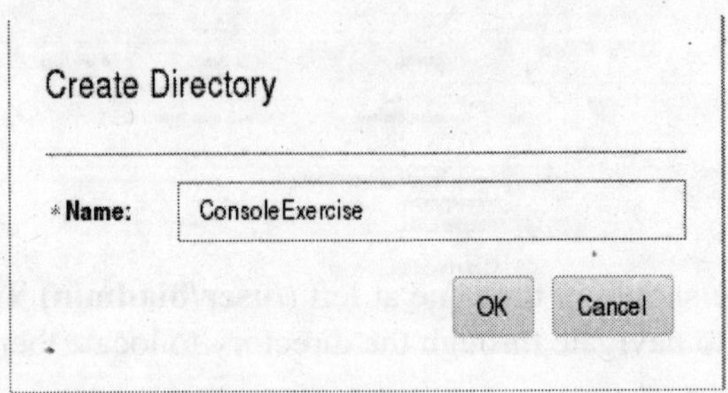

22. Expand the directory hierarchy to verify that your new subdirectory was created.

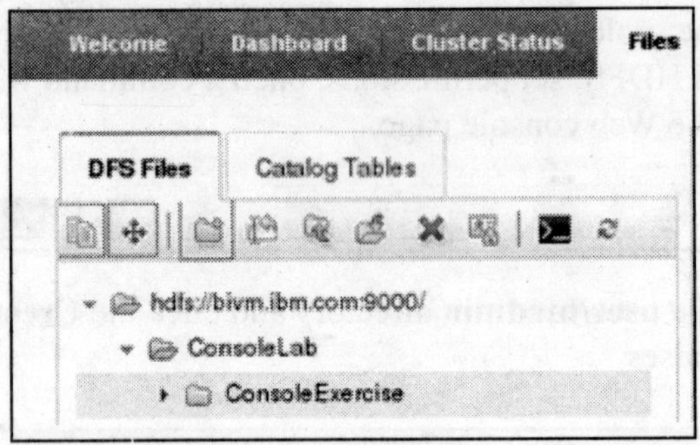

23. Create another directory named ConsoleExerciseTest.

    See in the following screenshot that this directory has been created.

24. Use the **Rename** icon to rename this directory to ConsoleExerciseTest2

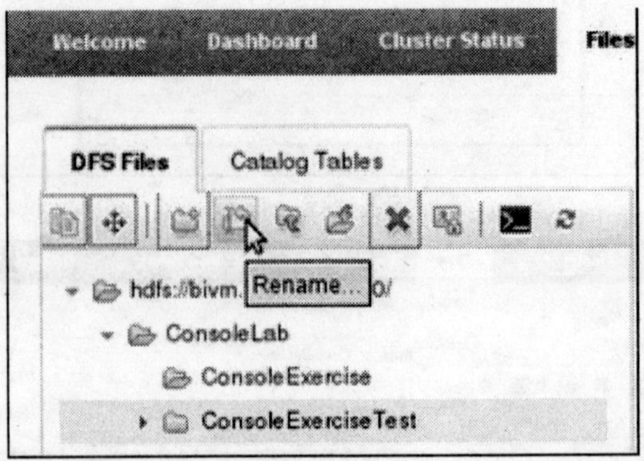

Verify that the name has changed.

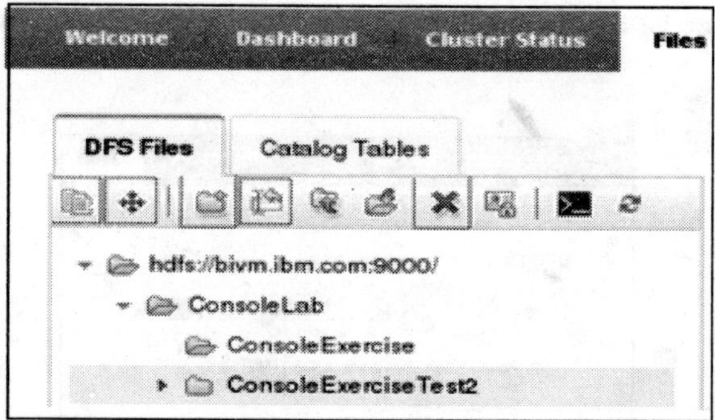

25. Click the **Move** icon, when the pop up **Move** screen appears select the ConsoleExercise directory and click **OK**.

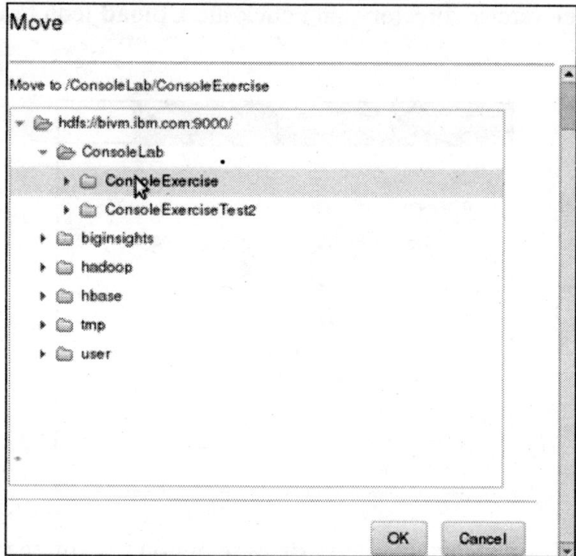

26. Using the **set permission** icon, you can change the permission settings for your directory. When finished click **OK**.

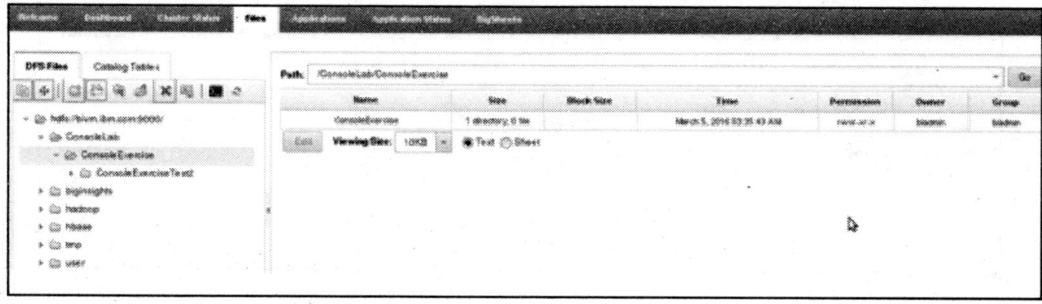

27. While highlighting the ConsoleExerciseTest2 folder, select the **Remove** icon and delete the directory.

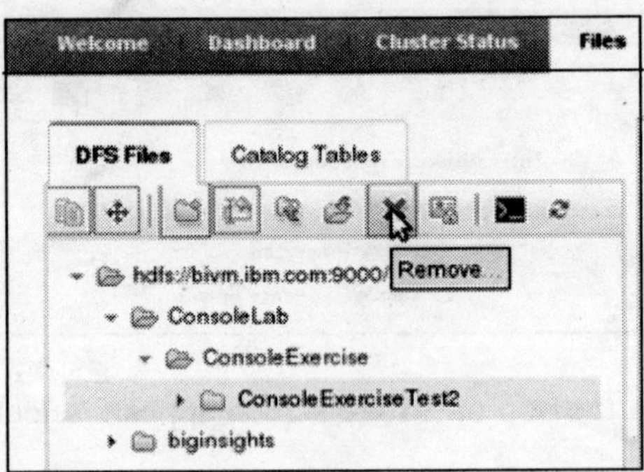

28. Remain in the ConsoleExercise directory, and click the **Upload** icon to upload a small sample file for test purposes.

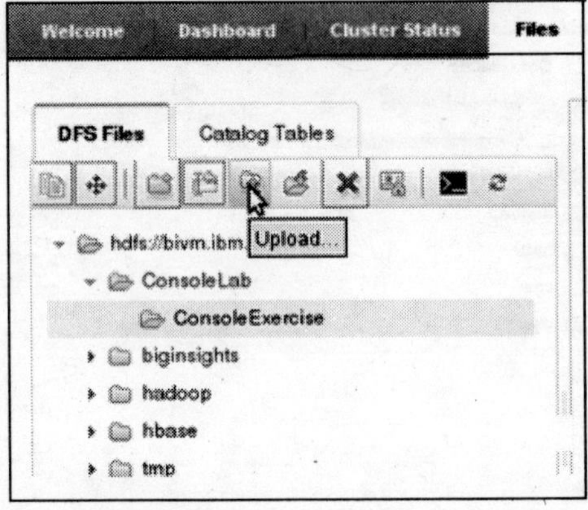

29. When the pop-up window appears, click the **Browse** button to browse your local file system for a sample file.

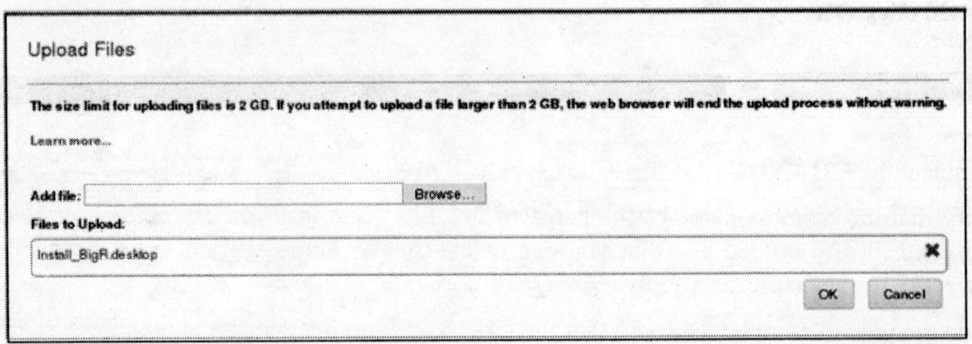

30. Navigate through your local file system to the directory where BigInsights was installed. For the IBM-provided VMWare image, BigInsights is installed in file system: ***/opt/ibm/biginsights***.

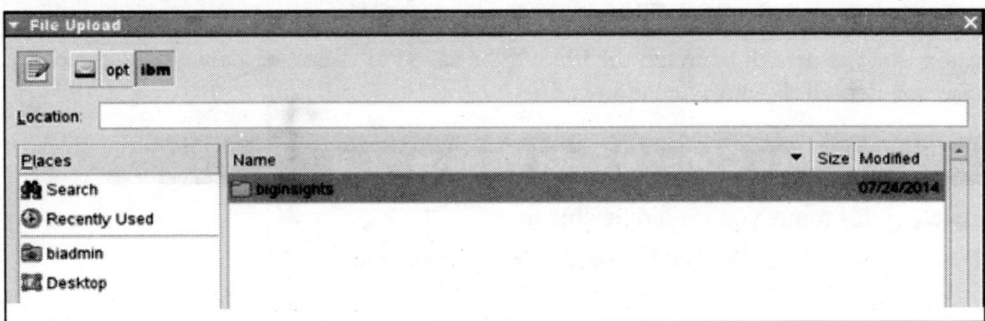

See the menu at the top of screenshot.

Locate the ***.../IHC*** subdirectory

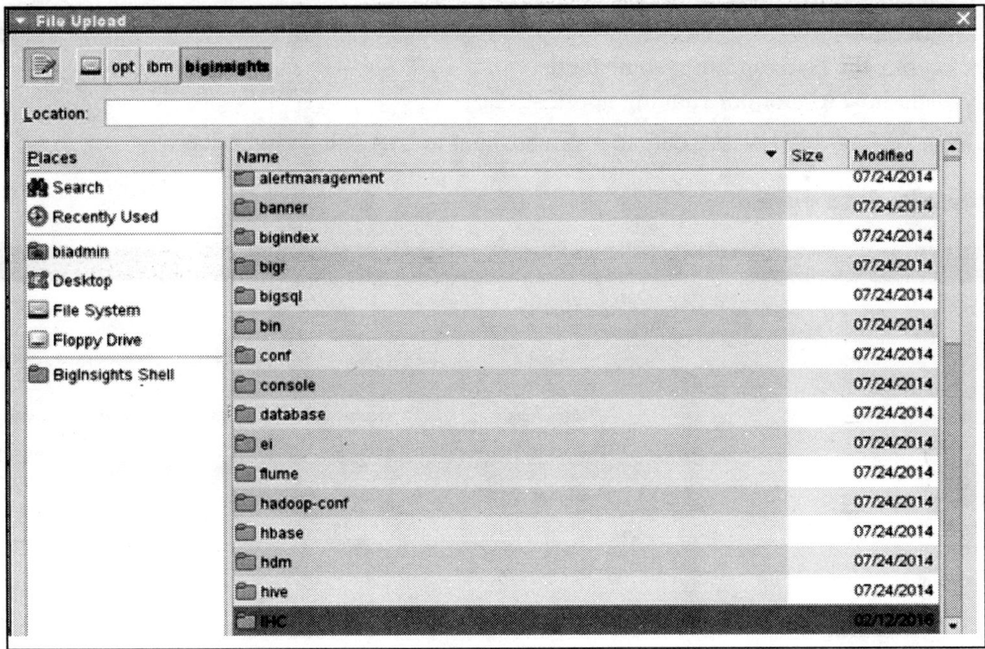

and select the **CHANGES.txt** file. Click **Open.**

31. Verify that the window displays the name of this file. Note that you can continue to **Browse** for additional files to upload and that you can delete files as upload targets from the displayed list. However, for this exercise, simply click **OK**

32. When the upload completes, verify that the CHANGES.txt file appears in the directory tree at left, If it is not immediately visible click the refresh button. On the right, you should see a subset of the

file's contents displayed in text format

33. Highlight the CHANGES.txt file in your ConsoleExercise directory and click the **Download** button.
34. When prompted, click the **Save File** button. Then select **OK**.
35. If Firefox is set as default browser, the file will be saved to your user Downloads directory. Forthis exercise, the default directory location is fine

EXERCISE 4.4 : Web Console Data Management

After completing this topic, you should be able to:

- Describe how to use the Data tab in the Web Console to
  1. Upload to HDFS
  2. Download data from HDFS
  3. Add directories to the HDFS system
  4. Move files
  5. Rename files
  6. Change permissions
  7. Edit data
  8. Invoke the Hadoop file system shell
- Explain how to monitor running applications
- Describe how to view big data in a spreadsheet format using BigSheets

Web Console data view

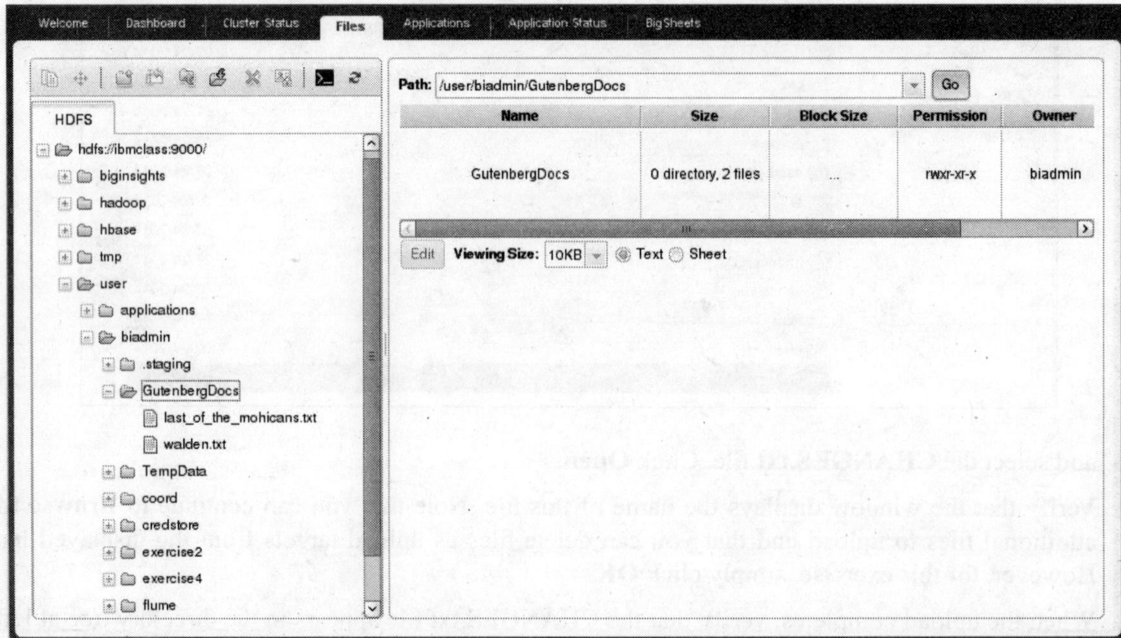

Working with files and directories

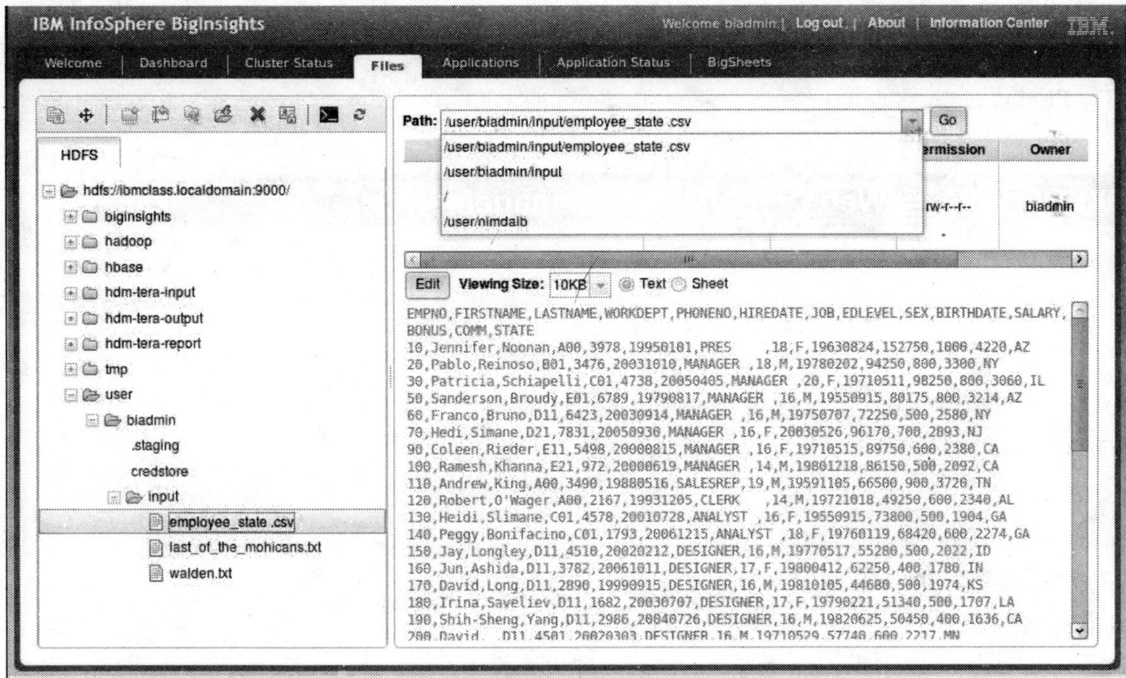

Changing permissions

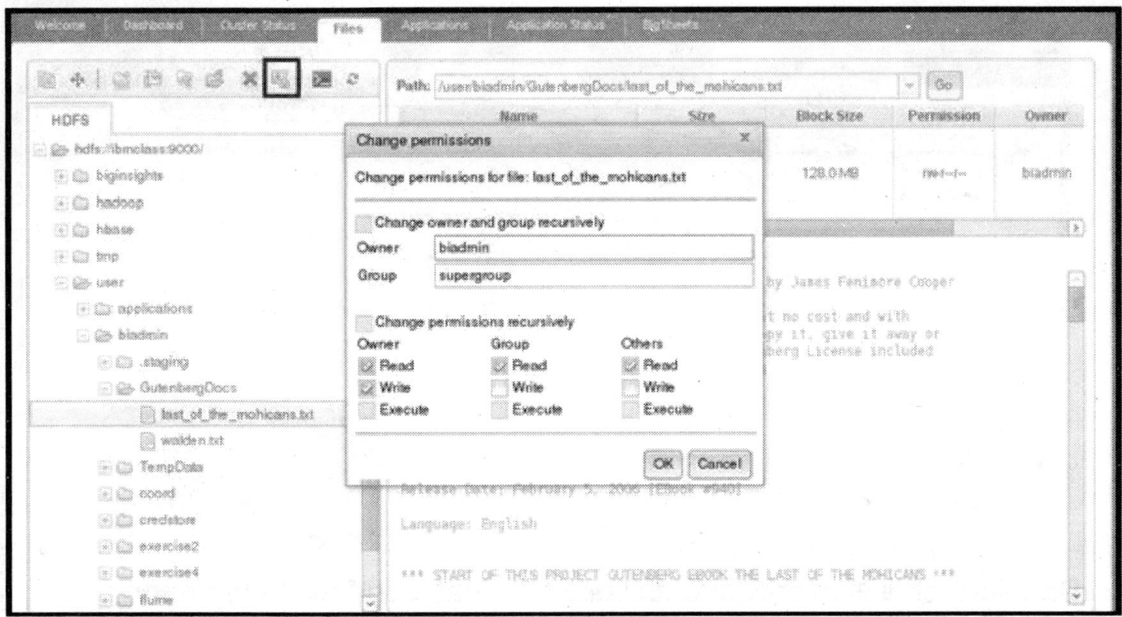

Hadoop shell command

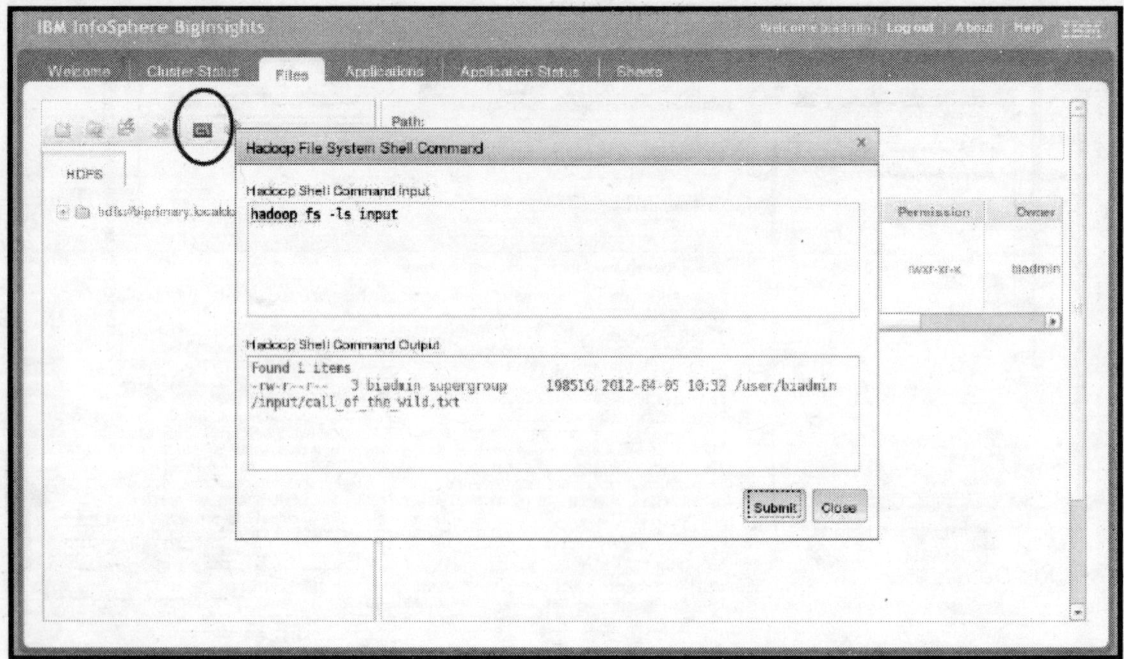

Application status

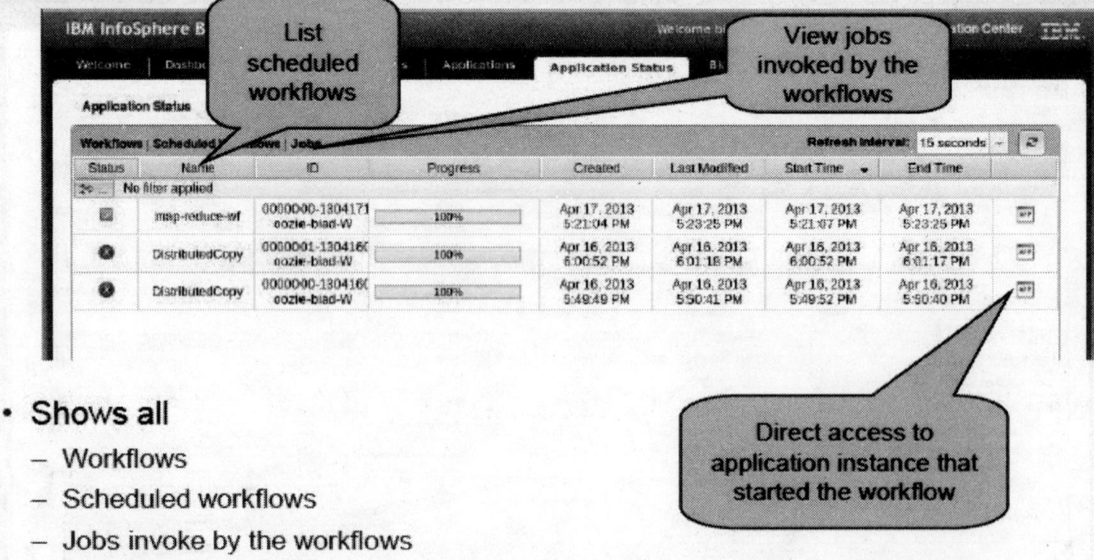

- Shows all
  - Workflows
  - Scheduled workflows
  - Jobs invoke by the workflows
- Double-click a workflow and drill down to that workflow's summary

Workflows tab

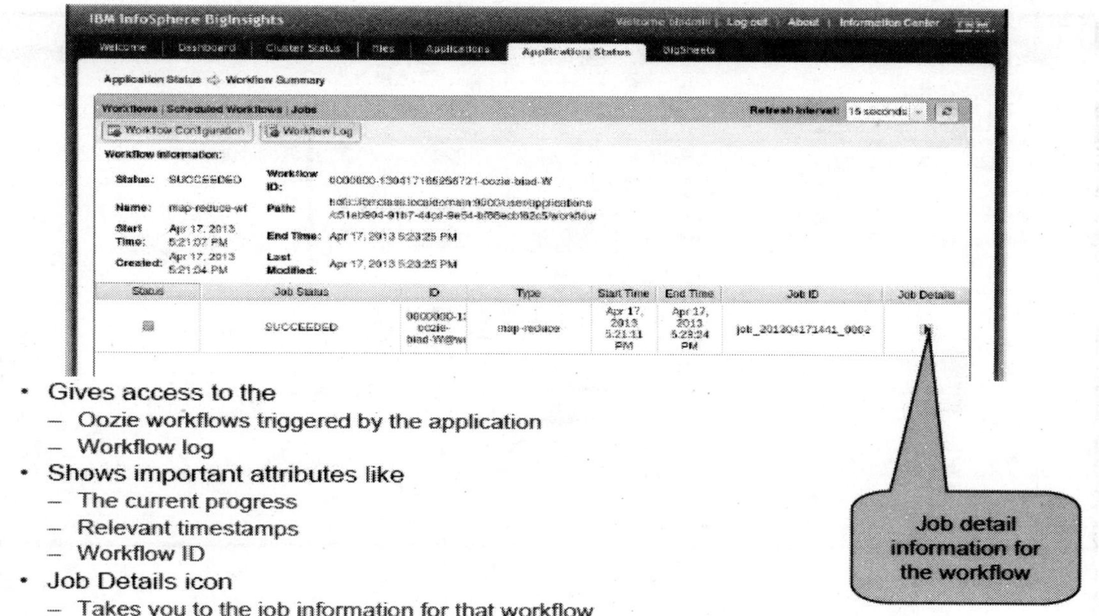

- Gives access to the
  - Oozie workflows triggered by the application
  - Workflow log
- Shows important attributes like
  - The current progress
  - Relevant timestamps
  - Workflow ID
- Job Details icon
  - Takes you to the job information for that workflow

Application Running Status

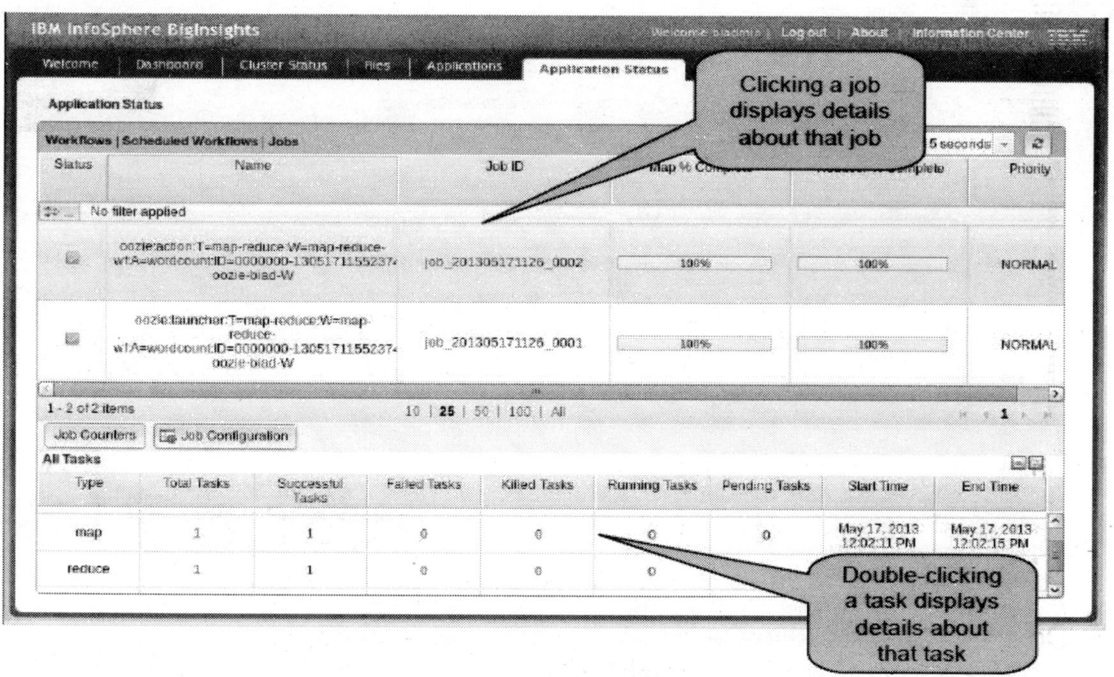

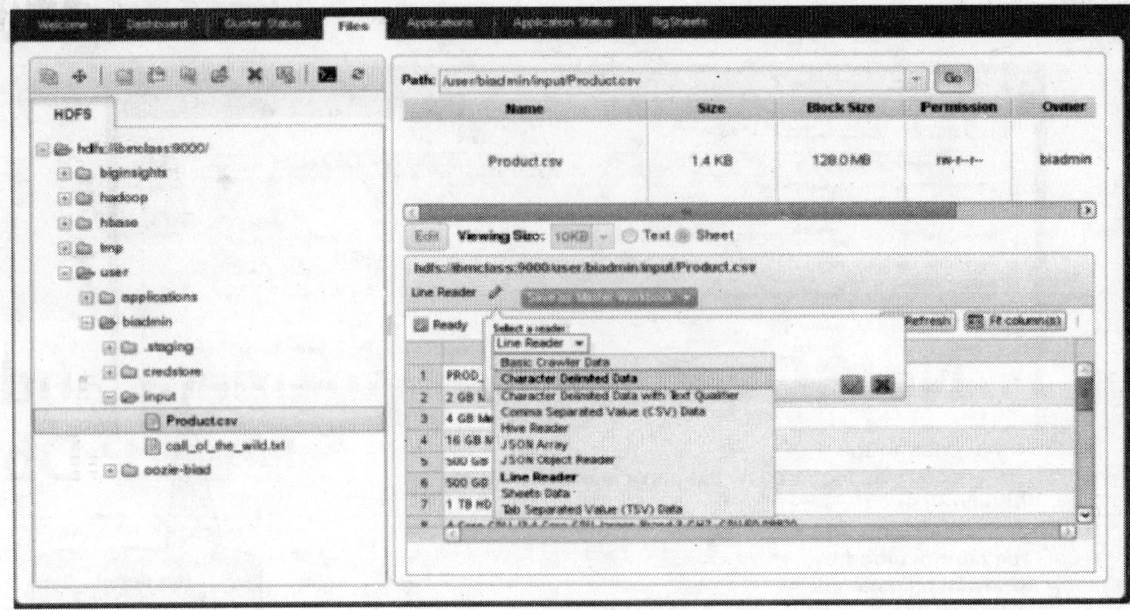
Welcome
Dashboard
Cluster Status
Files
Applications
Application Status
BigSheets
HDFS
hdfs://ibmclass:9000/
biginsights
hadoop
hbase
tmp
user
applications
biadmin
.staging
credstore
input
Product.csv
call_of_the_wild.txt
oozie-biad
Path: /user/biadmin/input/Product.csv
Go
Name
Size
Block Size
Permission
Owner
Product.csv
1.4 KB
128.0 MB
rw-r--r--
biadmin
Edit
Viewing Size: 10KB
Text
Sheet
hdfs://ibmclass:9000/user/biadmin/input/Product.csv
Line Reader
Ready
Select a reader:
Line Reader
Basic Crawler Data
Character Delimited Data
Character Delimited Data with Text Qualifier
Comma Separated Value (CSV) Data
Hive Reader
JSON Array
JSON Object Reader
Line Reader
Sheets Data
Tab Separated Value (TSV) Data
Refresh
Fit column(s)

CHAPTER

5

No SQL Data Management and MongoDb

5.1 NO SQL DATA MANAGEMENT

For over a decade, the de facto standard for database design was relational models. Relational databases use primary and foreign keys and have strict constraints when you manipulate the tables' data. These databases are good for smaller data storage requirements, but you need "big data" capabilities to manage large queries. This is the goal of NoSQL.

The term "NoSQL" was coined over a decade ago, funnily enough as a name to yet-another relational database. However, this database had a different idea behind it: eliminating the use of the standardised SQL. In the next years to come, others picked up and continued to grow this thought, by referring to various other non-relational databases as NoSQL databases.

By design, NoSQL databases and management systems are relation-less (or schema-less). They are not based on a single model (e.g. relational model of RDBMSs) and each database, depending on their target-functionality, adopt a different one.

NoSQL databases work entirely different than relational databases, so you need to learn how to work with NoSQL to properly manage big data queries. If you don't implement NoSQL properly, you can actually slow down your website or applications that use the NoSQL database system.

If you believe you need to gather large sets of data, it's probably worth looking into a NoSQL database solution. You'll also be up on the latest database languages and technology. To be a good programmer, you need to know the latest technology and languages. NoSQL is a trending type of application that is taking over from relational database systems.

But organizations are increasingly considering alternatives to legacy relational infrastructure. In some cases the motivation is technical — such as a need to handle new, multi-structured data types or scale beyond the capacity constraints of existing systems — while in other cases the motivation is driven by the desire to identify viable alternatives to expensive proprietary database software and hardware. A third motivation is agility or speed of development, as companies look to adapt to the market more quickly and embrace agile development methodologies.

These motivations apply both to analytical and operational applications. Companies are shifting workloads to Hadoop for their bulk analytical workloads, and they are building online, operational applications with a new class of so-called "NoSQL" or non-relational databases. "NoSQL" is often used as an umbrella category for all non-relational databases.

5.2 TYPES OF NOSQL DATABASES

There are several types of NoSQL database systems although a couple of them are more popular than the others. The primary way in which non-relational databases differ from relational databases is the data model. Although there are dozens of non-relational databases, they primarily fall

into one of the following three categories:

1. Document Models
2. Key Value and and Wide Column Models
3. Graph and
4. Wide column stores.

5.2.1 Document Models

The first type is the most common. Document type NoSQL databases use structures called documents to store data. The document is given an ID and you can also link these documents together using IDs just like relational databases. This type of structure is used with MongoDB, which is a common open source database system. You can think of the document system in the same way you think of a regular document. You "file" the document in the database. The document can contain any amount of data and any data types. The next document can also contain any data and any data types. There are no constraints for the data these documents contain.

Whereas relational databases store data in rows and columns, document databases store data in documents. These documents typically use a structure that is like JSON (JavaScript Object Notation), a format popular among developers. Documents provide an intuitive and natural way to model data that is closely aligned with object-oriented programming – each document is effectively an object. Documents contain one or more fields, where each field contains a typed value, such as a string, date, binary, or array. Rather than spreading out a record across multiple columns and tables connected with foreign keys, each record and its associated (i.e., related) data are typically stored together in a single document.

This simplifies data access and, in many cases, eliminates the need for expensive JOIN operations and complex, multi-record transactions. Document databases provide the ability to query on any field within a document. Some products, such as MongoDB, provide a rich set of indexing options to optimize a wide variety of queries, including text indexes, geospatial indexes, compound indexes, sparse indexes, time to live (TTL) indexes, unique indexes, and others. Furthermore, some of these products provide the ability to analyze data in place, without it needing to be replicated to dedicated analytics or search engines. MongoDB, for instance, provides both the Aggregation Framework for providing real-time analytics (along the lines of the SQL GROUP BY functionality), and a native MapReduce implementation for other types of sophisticated analyses. To update data, MongoDB provides a find and modify method so that values in documents can be updated in a single statement to the database, rather than making multiple round trips.

In a document database, the notion of a schema is dynamic: each document can contain different fields. This flexibility can be particularly helpful for modeling unstructured and polymorphic data. It also makes it easier to evolve an application during development, such as adding new fields. Additionally, document databases generally provide the query robustness that developers have come to expect from relational databases. In particular, data can be queried based on any combination of fields in a document.

Applications:

Document databases are general purpose, useful for a wide variety of applications due to the flexibility of the data model, the ability to query on any field and the natural mapping of the document data model to objects in modern programming languages.

1. Extension of key-value model, where value is a structured document
2. Documents can be highly complex, hierarchical data structures without requiring pre-defined "schema"
3. Supports queries on structured documents
4. Search platforms are also document-oriented
5. Applications that need to manage a large variety of objects that differ in structure
6. Large product catalogs in e-commerce, customer profiles, content management applications
7. No standard query syntax
8. Query performance not linearly scalable
9. Join queries across collections not efficient

Applications

Some popular use cases for document based data stores are:

- **Nested information:** Document-based data stores allow you to work with deeply nested, complex data structures.
- **JavaScript friendly:** One of the most critical functionalities of document-based data stores are the way they interface with applications: Using JS friendly JSON.

Examples:

1. **MongoDB:** An extremely popular and highly-functional database,
2. **CouchDB:** A ground-breaking document-based data store.
3. **Couchbase DB:** JSON-based, Memcached-compatible document-based data store.
4. **And Apache Solr**

5 **Elastic Search**

5.2.1.1 JSON (JavaScript Object Notation) format.

JSON's benefits and challenges: Agility, structure, and interactivity. JSON is the data structure of the Web. It's a simple data format that allows programmers to store and communicate sets of values, lists, and key-value mappings across systems.

As JSON adoption has grown, database vendors have sprung up offering JSON-centric document databases. Now, increasingly, traditional relational-style databases are integrating JSON features, resulting in a best-of-both worlds benefit to developers and database administrators.

JSON started as the "serialized object notation" for JavaScript, the programming language of the Web. With a nice combination of simplicity (the essentials of the format are specified in five grammar diagrams at JSON.org) and "just enough structure," JSON has quickly expanded beyond the Web into applications and services. For example, JSON is displacing the more complex XML format as the serialization format for exchanging data between applications.

Application developers must manage both code and data. Code is verbs, or the instructions and descriptions of how to perform a task. Code is the recipe. Data are the nouns: users, locations, recordings, amounts -- the ingredients the recipe combines. As more application developers adopt JSON as their preferred data format, the need is growing for JSON-friendly databases. Few coding tasks are more annoying or more bug prone than mechanically translating information between formats.

As a consequence, several NoSQL document store database vendors have chosen JSON as their primary data representation in a stark break from traditional relational schemes used by MySQL, PostgreSQL, VoltDB, MS SQL Server, Oracle and others. This is a natural fit for developers who use JSON as the data interchange format in their applications.

Additionally, the relative agility of JSON (JSON records are well structured but easily extended) has attracted developers looking to avoid painful database schema migrations in agile environments. Data and schema, in volume, can be hard to change. Rewriting a large dataset stored on disk while keeping the associated applications online can be time consuming. It can take days of background processing, in moderate to large examples, to upgrade data.

In contrast, JSON's lack of a predefined schema makes upgrades easy. Developers can store and update documents without restrictions.

5.2.2 Key/Value

The next popular data system is the key-value scheme. If you are used to programming languages, the key-value system will be familiar to you. The key-value stores a key, which is the identifier for the value. You can look up data using the key or the value. Again, there are no constraints with the data, because you simply have key-value pairs for each element.

From a data model perspective, key-value stores are the most basic type of non-relational database. Every item in the database is stored as an attribute name, or key, together with its value. The value, however, is entirely opaque to the system; data can only be queried by the key. This model can be useful for representing polymorphic and unstructured data, as the database does not enforce a set schema across key-value pairs.

We will begin our NoSQL modeling journey with key / value based database management simply because they can be considered the most basic and backbone implementation of NoSQL.

These type of databases work by matching keys with values, similar to a dictionary. There is no structure nor relation. After connecting to the database server (e.g. Redis), an application can state a key (e.g. the_answer_to_life) and provide a matching value (e.g. 42) which can later be retrieved the same way by supplying the key.

Key / value DBMSs are usually used for quickly storing basic information, and sometimes not-so-basic ones after performing, for example, a CPU and memory intensive computation. They are extremely performant, efficient and usually easily scalable.

These systems provide the ability to retrieve and update data based only on a single or a limited range of primary keys. For querying on other values, users are encouraged to build and maintain their own indexes. Some products provide limited support for secondary indexes, but with several caveats. To perform an update in these systems, multiple round trips may be necessary: first find the record, then update it, then update the index. In these systems, the update may be implemented as a complete rewrite of the entire record irrespective of whether a single attribute has changed, or the entire record.

Characteristic Features

- The biggest difference between non-relational databases lies in the ability to query data efficiently.
- Document databases provide the richest query functionality, which allows them to address a wide variety of operational and real-time analytics applications.
- Key-value stores and wide column stores provide a single means of accessing data: by primary key. This can be fast, but they offer very limited query functionality and may impose additional development costs and application-level requirements to support anything more than basic query patterns.
- The simplest model where each object is retrieved with a unique key, with values having no inherent model
- Utilize in-memory storage to provide fast access with optional persistence
- Other data models built on top of this model to provide more complex objects
- Applications requiring fast access to a large number of objects, such as caches or queues
- Applications that require fast-changing data environments like mobile, gaming, online ads

Weaknesses

- Cannot update subset of a value
- Does not provide querying
- As number of objects becomes large, generating unique keys could become complex

Applications: Key value stores and wide column stores are useful for a narrow set of applications that only query data by a single key value. The appeal of these systems is their performance and scalability, which can be highly optimized due to the simplicity of the data access patterns and opacity of the data itself.

Some popular use cases for key / value based data stores are:

1. Caching;Quickly storing data for - sometimes frequent - future use.
2. Queue-ing:Some K/V stores (e.g. Redis) supports lists, sets, queues and more.
3. Distributing information / tasks:They can be used to implement Pub/Sub.
4. Keeping live information:Applications which need to keep a state cane use K/V stores easily.

Examples: Riak : Riak KV is a distributed NoSQL database that is highly available, scalable and easy to operate. It automatically distributes data across the cluster to ensure fast performance and fault-tolerance. Riak KV Enterprise includes multi-cluster replication ensuring low-latency and robust business continuity, and Redis, MemcacheDB, BerkleyDB, MemcacheDB, DynamoDB etc.

5.2.3 Column or Wide Column Based Models

Column based NoSQL database management systems work by advancing the simple nature of key / value based ones. Despite their complicated-to-understand image on the internet, these databases work very simply by creating collections of one or more key / value pairs that match a record.

Unlike the traditional defines schemas of relational databases, column-based NoSQL solutions do not require a pre-structured table to work with the data. Each record comes with one or more columns containing the information and each column of each record can be different.

Basically, column-based NoSQL databases are two dimensional arrays whereby each key (i.e. row / record) has one or more key / value pairs attached to it and these management systems allow very large and un-structured data to be kept and used (e.g. a record with tons of information).

These databases are commonly used when simple key / value pairs are not enough, and storing very large numbers of records with very large numbers of information is a must. DBMS implementing column-based, schema-less models can scale extremely well.

Wide column stores, or column family stores, use a sparse, distributed multi-dimensional sorted map to store data. Each record can vary in the number of columns that are stored. Columns can be grouped together for access in column families, or columns can be spread across multiple column families. Data is retrieved by primary key per column family.

Characteristic Features

- The wide column model provides more granular access to data than the key value model, but less flexibility than the document data model.
- Extension of key-value model, where the value is a set of columns (column-family)
- A column can have multiple time-stamped versions
- Columns can be generated at run-time and not all rows need to have all columns
- Storing a large number of time-stamped data like event logs, sensor data
- Analytics that involve querying entire columns of data such as trends or time series analytics

Weakness:

- No join queries or sub-queries
- Limited support for aggregation
- Ordering is done per partition, specified at table creation time

Applications

Some popular use cases for column based data stores are:

- Keeping unstructured, non-volatile information: If a large collection of attributes and values needs to be kept for long periods of time, column-based data stores come in extremely handy.
- Scaling: Column based data stores are highly scalable by nature. They can handle an awful amount of information.

1. ***HBase*** Data store for Apache Hadoop based on ideas from BigTable
2. ***Cassandra*** Column based data store based on BigTable and
3. DynamoDB. ,
4. Apache Accumulo

5.2.4 Graph Store Model

The other two types of NoSQL are graph and wide column stores. A graph store keeps data about network systems, which can grow to several terabytes of data. Wide column stores are used for big data that stored across several data sets. These systems are mainly used for reporting.

Graph databases use graph structures with nodes, edges and properties to represent data. In essence, data is modeled as a network of relationships between specific elements. While the graph model may be counter-intuitive and takes some time to understand, it can be useful for a specific class of queries. Its main appeal is that it makes it easier to model and navigate relationships between entities in an application. These systems tend to provide rich query models where simple and complex relationships can be interrogated to make direct and indirect inferences about the data in the system. Relationship-type analysis tends to be very efficient in these systems, whereas other types of analysis may be less optimal. As a result, graph databases are rarely used for more general purpose operational applications.

One common graph store NoSQL database is XML databases. Most developers are familiar with XML, because it's an older schema that supports data queries and storage. You can more easily store XML in NoSQL databases, but XML is also a bit out of style. Most developers are working more towards JSON as a data model schema, so it might be more difficult to fit an XML database into your current systems.

Characteristics Features

1. Models graphs consisting of nodes and edges with properties (meta-data) describing them
2. Implement very fast graph traversal operations
3. Also support indexing of meta data to enable graph traversal combined with search queries
4. Applications that deal with objects with a large number of inter-relations
5. Applications like social networking friends-networks, hierarchical role based permissions, complex decision trees, maps, network topologies
6. Weakness
7. Difficult to scale for large data sets for generic graphs
8. Giraph uses the Bulk Synchronous Parallel model to overcome some of the scalability limitations

Applications:

Graph databases are useful in cases where traversing relationships are core to the application, like navigating social network connections, network topologies or supply chains.

Some popular use cases for graph based data stores are:

- Handling complex relational information: As explained in the introduction, graph databases make it extremely efficient and easy to use to deal with complex but relational information, such as the connections between two entities and various degrees of other entities indirectly related to them.
- Modelling and handling classifications: Graph databases excel in any situation where relationships are involved. Modelling data and classifying various information in a relational way can be handled very well using these type of data stores.

Some popular graph based data stores are:

1. OrientDB: A very fast graph and document based hybrid NoSQL data store written in Java that comes with different operational modes.
2. Neo4J: A schema-free, extremely popular and powerful Java graph based data store.
3. OrientDB,
4. Apache Giraph,
5. AllegroGraph

5.2.5 Relational

1. Conventional RDBMS structure consisting of fixed schema with ACID properties
2. Provides well documented and widely supported SQL syntax
3. Capable of complex queries including subqueries and joins
4. Transactional data applications like ERP, CRM, Banking etc.
5. Applications where data volume is limited and schema are by and large fixed
6. Lacks horizontal scalability and hence limited in handling "big data"
7. Not efficient at handling complex multi-level nested data
8. Cannot handle "unstructured" data where structure is not known at design time

Example

MySql, PostgreSQL, MariaDB, Oracle, SQL Server

5.3 CHOOSING A QUERY MODEL FOR BIG DATA

Each application has its own query requirements. In some cases, it may be acceptable to have a very basic query model in which the application only accesses records based on a primary key. For most applications, however, it is important to have the ability to query based on several different values in each record. For instance, an application that stores data about customers may need to look up not only specific customers, but also specific companies, or customers by a certain size, or aggregations of customer sales value by zip code or state.

It is also common for applications to update records, including one or more individual fields. To satisfy these requirements, the database needs to be able to query data based on secondary indexes. In these cases, a document database will often be the most appropriate solution.

5.3.1 Consistency Model

Most non-relational systems typically maintain multiple copies of the data for availability and scalability purposes. These databases can impose different guarantees on the consistency of the data across copies. Non-relational databases tend to be categorized as either consistent or eventually consistent.

With a consistent system, writes by the application are immediately visible in subsequent queries. With an eventually consistent system writes are not immediately visible. As an example, when reflecting inventory levels for products in a product catalog, with a consistent system each query will see the current inventory as inventory levels are updated by the application, whereas with an eventually consistent system the inventory levels may not be accurate for a query at a given time, but will eventually become accurate. For this reason application code tends to besomewhat different for eventually consistent systems - rather than updating the inventory by taking the current inventory and subtracting one, for example, developers are encouraged to issue idempotent queries that explicitly set the inventory level.

Each application has different requirements for data consistency. For many applications, it is imperative that the data be consistent at all times. As development teams have worked under a model of consistency with relational databases for decades, this approach is more natural and familiar. In other cases, eventual consistency is an acceptable trade-off for the flexibility it allows in the system's availability.

Document databases and graph databases can be consistent or eventually consistent. MongoDB provides tunable consistency. By default, data is consistent — all writes and reads access the primary copy of the data. As an option, read queries can be issued against secondary copies where data maybe eventually consistent if the write operation has not yet been synchronized with the secondary copy; the consistency choice is made at the query level.

5.4 BENEFITS OF NOSQL

There are several reasons to use big data databases. The main and most popular reason is the amount of data you can handle with your queries and reports. Relational databases can store and handle tables with millions of records. This was a large data amount a decade ago. However, these database systems are not so good when your tables grow to billions or trillions of rows. With a relational database, your only option is to store data using the same setup as your tables, and any manipulated data must adhere to any strict constraints. This doesn't allow much room for dynamic information. NoSQL databases are typically able to retrieve large data sets more efficiently than relational databases.

NoSQL databases are also able to allow for quicker code releases and work better with object oriented programming. For instance, when you create an object oriented program in a language such as C#, you have more freedom with your database creation. NoSQL lets you create database tables using your OO classes. When these classes store data, they represent a document and store in the database dynamically. If you change the class models, NoSQL databases will let you store the new data without needing to change your entire database model. Older programs know that to change your code, you needed to change your tables, any constraints and then refresh your database and your code. With NoSQL databases, the tables update automatically.

With older relational databases, developers remember first changing the database then refactoring code to work with the new changes. Large changes were sometimes not scalable with old relational databases. NoSQL is dynamic, so changes to the code are reflected in the database. You don't need to change the database several times during the development process.

5.4.1 Sharding

NoSQL databases also offer a concept called "sharding." With relational databases, you need to scale vertically. This means that when you host a database, you typically host it on one server. When you need more resources, you add another database server or more resources to the current server. With NoSQL, you can "shard" your database files. This basically means that you can share database files across multiple servers. Sharding is using done on very fast storage hardware such as a SAN and a NAS. Using several database servers at once speeds up your queries especially when you have millions of rows in your data sets.

You can implement cloud computing along with sharding. This makes your queries especially fast when you need reports available for several different locations. Using old techniques, your users would log in to the network and pull reports from miles away, sometimes in other countries. The result was that the user sometimes needed to wait several minutes for a report to render. With cloud computing, reporting data is served up from the closest data center to your users. The result is faster data processing and rendering.

Not only does NoSQL support manual sharding, but NoSQL servers will also do automatic sharding. The database server will automatically spread a dynamic amount of data across several servers, so the load on each server individually is reduced.

5.4.2 Cloud computing

In addition to using NoSQL in a cloud computing environment for performance, it's also beneficial when it comes to cost. Cloud computing hosts only charge you for the resources you use, so the costs scale with the growth of your business.

Replication with NoSQL is an option. When you gather data, you probably need to replicate that data to other servers. For instance, you probably want to replicate data to a reporting server for performance reasons on your main production server. NoSQL supports automatic replication, so you can send data to several servers as your database collects data real-time.

You can also use NoSQL with more current languages. For instance, NoSQL works with Node.js for your real-time network communication web applications. Just give the table name and schema name and you can pull data directly from your NoSQL database. With the weak typing in the newer languages and the dynamic way NoSQL stores and implements data, you can create very powerful dynamic apps with your web applications.

5.4.3 CRUD Queries

NoSQL still supports common CRUD queries. CRUD is the name giving to "create, read, update and delete" query procedures. These procedures are the four major ways you work with data in any database. The create statement creates a new record, the read (select) statement retrieves the data for your application, the update statement changes and edits the data already stored in your database and the delete statement removes a record from the database.

NoSQL statements are dependent on the type of database structure you incorporate. In most cases, you'll use a programming language to create apps that interface with your NoSQL server. Statements are much different than the statements you're used to with relational databases. Even if you had different SQL servers, the statements were still similar between the platforms (Oracle, MySQL or SQL Server). Because NoSQL is dynamic and works more with documents or entities completely different than relational tables, you have a different structure for your queries. However, when you use different programming languages, there are plugins that you can use to retrieve data from your databases. These plugins help minimize the need to learn raw query information.

5.4.4 NoSQL DBMSs In Comparison To Relational DBMSs

In order to draw a clear picture of how NoSQL solutions differ from relational database management systems, let's create a quick comparison list:

When To Use NoSQL Databases

- **Size matters:** If will be working with very large sets of data, consistently scaling is easier to achieve with many of the DBMS from NoSQL family.
- **Speed:** NoSQL databases are usually faster - and sometimes extremely speedier - when it comes to writes. Reads can also be very fast depending on the type of NoSQL database and data being queried.
- **Schema-free design:** Relational DBMSs require structure from the beginning. NoSQL solutions offer a large amount of flexibility.
- **Automated (or easy) replications/scaling:** NoSQL databases are growing rapidly and they are being actively built today - vendors are trying to tackle common issues and one of them clearly is replication and scaling. Unlike RDBMSs, NoSQL solutions can easily scale and work with(in) clusters.
- **Multiple choices:** When it comes to choosing a NoSQL data store, there are a variety of models, as we have discussed, that you can choose from to get the most out of the database management system - depending on your data type.

5.5 MONGODB

MongoDB is an open-source document database, and leading NoSQL database. MongoDB is written in c++.MongoDB is a cross-platform, document oriented database that provides, high performance, high availability, and easy scalability. MongoDB works on concept of collection and document.

Database

Database is a physical container for collections. Each database gets its own set of files on the file system. A single MongoDB server typically has multiple databases.

Collection

Collection is a group of MongoDB documents. It is the equivalent of an RDBMS table. A collection exists within a single database. Collections do not enforce a schema. Documents within a collection can have different fields. Typically, all documents in a collection are of similar or related purpose.

Document

A document is a set of key-value pairs. Documents have dynamic schema. Dynamic schema means that documents in the same collection do not need to have the same set of fields or structure, and common fields in a collection's documents may hold different types of data.

Below given table shows the relationship of RDBMS terminology with MongoDB

RDBMS Database	MongoDB Database
Table	Collection
Tuple/Row	Document
Column	Field
Table Join	Embedded Documents
Primary Key	Primary Key (Default key _id provided by
mongodb itself)	
Database Server and Client	
Mysqld/Oracle	mongod
mysql/sqlplus	mongo

Data As Documents

MongoDB stores data as documents in a binary representation called BSON (Binary JSON). Documents that share a similar structure are typically organized as collections. You can think of collections as being analogous to a table in a relational database: documents are similar to rows, and fields are similar to columns.

MongoDB documents tend to have all data for a given record in a single document, whereas in a relational database information for a given record is usually spread across many tables.

For example, consider the data model for a blogging application. In a relational database, the data model would comprise multiple tables such as Categories, Tags, Users, Comments and Articles. In MongoDB the data could be modeled as two collections, one for users, and the other for articles. In each blog document there might be multiple comments, multiple tags, and multiple categories, each expressed as an embedded array.

"Data as documents: simpler for developers, faster for users."

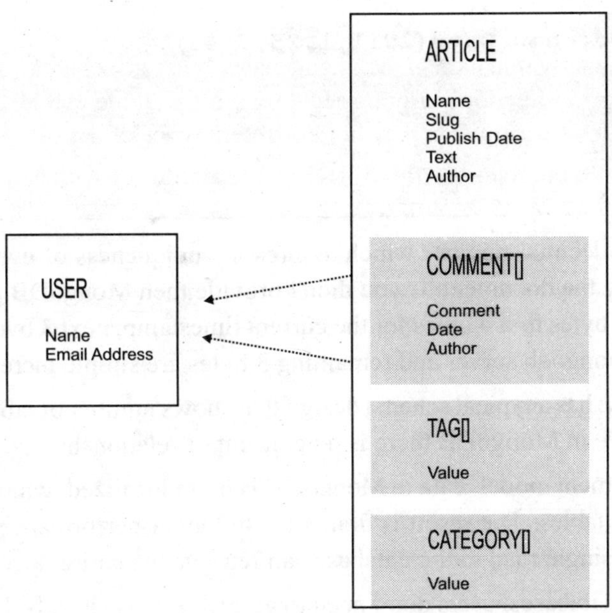

Sample document

Below given example shows the document structure of a blog site which is simply a comma separated key value pair.

```
{
  _id: ObjectId(7df78ad8902c)
  title: 'MongoDB Overview',
  description: 'MongoDB is no sql database',
  by: 'tutorials point',
  url: 'http://www.tutorialspoint.com',
  tags: ['mongodb', 'database', 'NoSQL'],
  likes: 100,
  comments: [
     {
        user:'user1',
        message: 'My first comment',
        dateCreated: new Date(2011,1,20,2,15),
        like: 0
     },
     {
        user:'user2',
message: 'My second comments',
```

```
        dateCreated: new Date(2011,1,25,7,45),
          like: 5
      }
   ]
   }
```

_id is a 12 bytes hexadecimal number which assures the uniqueness of every document. You can provide _id while inserting the document. If you didn't provide then MongoDB provide a unique id for every document. These 12 bytes first 4 bytes for the current timestamp, next 3 bytes for machine id, next 2 bytes for process id of mongodb server and remaining 3 bytes are simple incremental value.

Any relational database has a typical schema design that shows number of tables and the relationship between these tables. While in MongoDB there is no concept of relationship

As a result of the document model, data in MongoDB is more localized, which dramatically reduces the need to JOIN separate tables. The result is dramatically higher performance and scalability across commodity hardware as a single read to the database can retrieve the entire document.

Unlike many NoSQL databases, users don't need to give up JOINs entirely. For additional analytics flexibility, MongoDB preserves left-outer JOIN semantics with the $lookup operator, enabling users to get the best of both relational and non-relational data modeling.

In addition, MongoDB documents are more closely aligned to the structure of objects in the programming language. This makes it simpler and faster for developers to model how data in the application will map to data stored in the database.

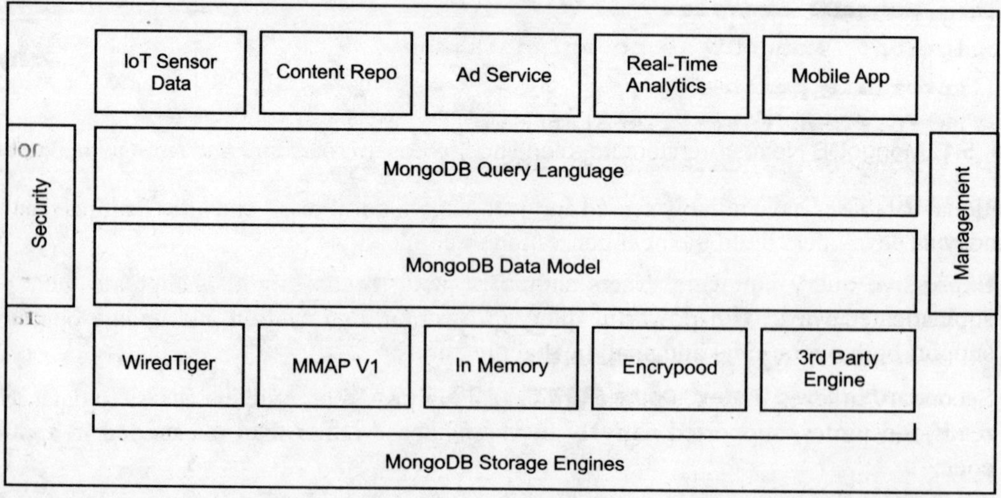

MongoDB 3.2 ships with four supported storage engines, all of which can coexist within a single MongoDB replica set. This makes it easy to evaluate and migrate between them, and to optimize for specific application requirements – for example combining the in-memory engine for ultra-low latency operations with a disk-based engine for persistence. The supported storage engines include:

1. The default WiredTiger storage engine. For many applications, WiredTiger's granular concurrency control and native compression will provide the best all round performance and storage efficiency for the broadest range of applications.
2. The Encrypted storage engine protecting highly sensitive data, without the performance or management overhead of separate filesystem encryption. (Requires MongoDB Enterprise Advanced)
3. The In-Memory storage engine delivering the extreme performance coupled with real time analytics for the most demanding, latency-sensitive applications. (Requires MongoDB Enterprise Advanced)
4. The MMAPv1 engine, an improved version of the original storage engine used in pre-3.x MongoDB **releases.**

MongoDB's design philosophy is focused on combining the critical capabilities of relational databases with the innovations of NoSQL technologies. Our vision is to leverage the work that Oracle and others have done over the last 40 years to make relational databases what they are today. Rather than discard decades of proven database maturity, MongoDB is picking up where they left off by combining key relational database capabilities with the work that Internet pioneers have done to address the requirements of modern applications.

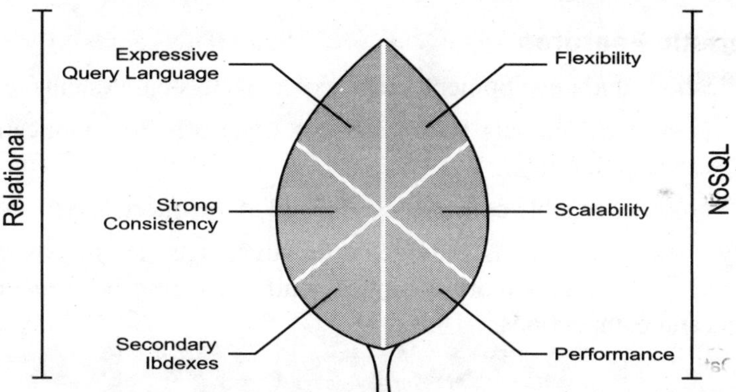

Figure. 5.1: MongoDB Nexus Architecture, blending the best of relational and NoSQL technologies

Relational databases have reliably served applications for many years, and offer features that remain critical today as developers build the next generation of applications :

- Expressive query language. Users should be able to access and manipulate their data in sophisticated ways with powerful query, projection, aggregation and update operators, to support both operational and analytical applications.
- Secondary indexes. Indexes play a critical role in providing efficient access to data, for both reads and writes, supported natively by the database rather than maintained in application code.
- Strong consistency. Applications should be able to immediately read what has been written to the database. It is much, much more complicated to build applications around an eventually consistent model, imposing significant work on the developer, even for the most sophisticated development teams. However, modern applications impose requirements not addressed by

relational databases, and this has driven the development of NoSQL databases which offer:

- Flexible Data Model. NoSQL databases emerged to address the requirements for the data we see dominating modern applications. Whether document, graph, key-value or wide-column, all of them offer a flexible data model, making it easy to store and combine data of any structure and allow dynamic modification of the schema without downtime.
- Elastic Scalability. NoSQL databases were all built with a focus on scalability, so they all include some form of sharding or partitioning, allowing the database to scale-out on commodity hardware deployed on-premise or in the cloud, allowing for almost unlimited growth.
- High Performance. NoSQL databases are designed to deliver great performance, measured in terms of both throughput and latency at any scale.

While offering these innovations, NoSQL systems have sacrificed the critical capabilities that people have come to expect and rely upon from relational databases. MongoDB offers a different approach. With its Nexus Architecture, MongoDB is the only database that harnesses the innovations of NoSQL while maintaining the foundation of relational databases.

5.5.1 Characteristic Features

- Most applications and development teams expect consistent systems.
- Different consistency models pose different trade-offs for applications in the areas of consistency anda vailability.
- MongoDB provides tunable consistency, defined at the query level.
- Eventually consistent systems provide some advantages for inserts at the cost of making reads, updates and deletes more complex, while incurring performance overhead through read repairs and compactions.

5.5.2 APIs

There is no standard for interfacing with non-relational systems. Each system presents different designs and capabilities for application development teams. The maturity of the API can have major implications for the time and cost required to develop and maintain the application and database.

5.5.3 Idiomatic Drivers

There are a number of popular programming languages, and each provides different paradigms for working with data and services. Idiomatic drivers are created by development teams that are experts in the given language and that know how programmers prefer to work within that language. This approach can also benefit from its ability to leverage specific features in a programming language that might provide efficiencies for accessing and processing data.

For programmers, idiomatic drivers are easier to learn and use, and they reduce the onboarding time for teams to begin working with the underlying database. For example, idiomatic drivers provide direct interfaces to set and get documents or fields within documents. With other types of interfaces it may be necessary to retrieve and parse entire documents and navigate to specific values in order to set or get a field.

MongoDB supports idiomatic drivers in over ten languages: Java, .NET, Ruby, Node.js, Perl, Python, PHP, C, C++, C#, Javascript, and Scala. 30+ other drivers are supported by the community.

5.5.4 Thrift or RESTful APIs

Some systems provide RESTful interfaces. This approach has the appeal of simplicity and familiarity, but it relies on the inherent latencies associated with HTTP. It also shifts the burden of building an interface to the developers; and this interface is likely to be inconsistent with the rest of their programming interfaces. Similarly, some systems provide a Thrift interface, a very low level paradigm that shifts the burden to developers to develop more abstract interfaces within their applications.

5.5.5 SQL-Like APIs

Some non-relational databases have attempted to add a SQL-like access layer to the database, in the hope this will reduce the learning curve for those developers and DBAs already skilled in SQL. It is important to evaluate these implementations before serious development begins, considering the following:

- Most of these implementations fall a long way short compared to the power and expressivity of SQL, and will demand SQL users learn a feature-limited dialect of the language.
- Most support queries only, with no support for write operations. Therefore developers will still need to learn the database's native query language.
- SQL-based BI, reporting, and ETL tools will not be compatible with a custom SQL implementation.
- While some of the syntax may be familiar to SQL developers, data modeling will not be. Trying to impose a relational model on any non-relational database will have disastrous consequences for performance and application maintenance.

5.5.6 The Nexus Architecture

Relational databases have reliably served applications for many years, and offer features that remain critical today as developers build the next generation of applications :

- **Expressive query language.** Users should be able to access and manipulate their data in sophisticated ways with powerful query, projection, aggregation and update operators, to support both operational and analytical applications.
- **Secondary indexes.** Indexes play a critical role in providing efficient access to data, for both reads and writes, supported natively by the database rather than maintained in application code.
- **Strong consistency.** Applications should be able to immediately read what has been written to the database. It is much, much more complicated to build applications around an eventually consistent model, imposing significant work on the developer, even for the most sophisticated development teams.

However, modern applications impose requirements not addressed by relational databases, and this has driven the development of NoSQL databases which offer:

- **Flexible Data Model.** NoSQL databases emerged to address the requirements for the data we see dominating modern applications. A flexible data model makes it easy to store and combine data of any structure, and allow dynamic modification of the schema without downtime.
- **Elastic Scalability.** NoSQL databases were all built with a focus on scalability, so they all include some form of sharding or partitioning, allowing the database to scale-out on commodity hardware, allowing for almost unlimited growth.
- **High Performance.** NoSQL databases are designed to deliver great performance, measured in terms of both throughput and latency at any scale.

5.5.7 Storage Efficiency With Compression

MongoDB supports native compression when configured with the WiredTiger or Encrypted storage engines, reducing physical storage footprint by as much as 80%. In addition to reduced storage space, compression enables much higher storage I/O scalability as fewer bits are read from disk. Administrators have the flexibility to configure specific compression algorithms for collections, indexes and the journal.

5.5.8 MongoDB Consistency & Availability

(1) Transaction model

MongoDB provides ACID properties at the document level. One or more fields may be written in a single operation, including updates to multiple sub-documents and elements of an array. The ACID guarantees provided by MongoDB ensure complete isolation as a document is updated; any errors cause the operation to roll back so that clients receive a consistent view of the document.

Developers can use MongoDB's Write Concerns to configure operations to commit to the application only after they have been flushed to the journal file on disk. **This is the same model used by many traditional relational databases to provide durability guarantees.** As a distributed system, MongoDB presents additional flexibility that helps users to achieve their desired availability SLAs. Each query can specify the appropriate write concern, such as writing to at least two replicas in one data center and one replica in a second data center.

(2) Replica sets

MongoDB maintains multiple copies of data called replica sets using native replication. A replica set is a fully self-healing shard that helps prevent database downtime. **Replica failover is fully automated,** eliminating the need for administrators to intervene manually.

The number of replicas in a MongoDB replica set is configurable: a larger number of replicas provide increased data availability and protection against database downtime (e.g., in case of multiple machine failures, rack failures, data center failures, or network partitions). Optionally, operations can be configured to write to multiple replicas before returning to the application, thereby providing functionality that is similar to synchronous replication.

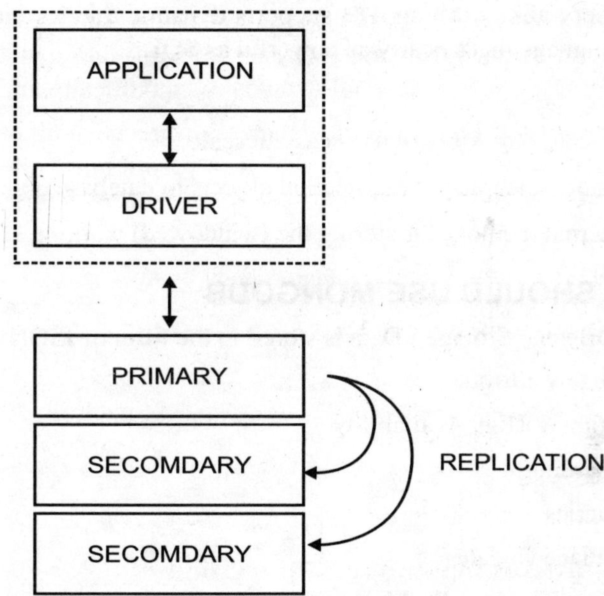

"MongoDB replica sets deliver fault tolerance and disaster recovery. Multi-data center awareness enables global data distribution and separation between operational and analytical workloads.

Replica sets also provide operational flexibility by providing a way to upgrade hardware and software without requiring the database to go offline."

(3) In-memory performance with on-disk capacity

With the addition of the new In-Memory storage engine, MongoDB users can now realize the performance advantages of in-memory computing for operational and real-time analytics workloads. The In-Memory storage engine delivers the extreme throughput and predictable latency demanded by the most performance-intensive applications in AdTech, finance, telecoms, IoT, eCommerce and more, eliminating the need for separate caching layers.

MongoDB replica sets allow for hybrid in-memory and on-disk database deployments. Data managed by the In-Memory engine can be processed and analyzed in real time, before being automatically replicated to MongoDB instances configured with one of the persistent disk-based storage engines. Lengthy ETL cycles typical when moving data between different databases are avoided, and users no longer have to trade away the scalable capacity or durability guarantees offered by disk storage.

5.6 ADVANTAGES OF MONGODB OVER RDBMS

1. Schema less : MongoDB is document database in which one collection holds different different documents. Number of fields, content and size of the document can be differ from one document to another.
2. Structure of a single object is clear
3. No complex joins

4. Deep query-ability. MongoDB supports dynamic queries on documents using a document-based query language that's nearly as powerful as SQL
5. Tuning
6. Ease of scale-out: MongoDB is easy to scale
7. Conversion / mapping of application objects to database objects not needed
8. Uses internal memory for storing the (windowed) working set, enabling faster access of data

5.7 WHY SHOULD USE MONGODB

Document Oriented Storage : Data is stored in the form of JSON style documents

Index on any attribute

1. Replication & High Availability
2. Auto-Sharding
3. Rich Queries
4. Fast In-Place Updates
5. Professional Support By MongoDB
6. Where should use MongoDB?
7. Big Data
8. Content Management and Delivery
9. Mobile and Social Infrastructure
10. User Data Management
11. Data Hub

5.8 INSTALLING MONGODB ON WINDOWS

To install the MongoDB on windows, first download the latest release of MongoDB from http://www.mongodb.org/downloads Make sure you get correct version of MongoDB depending upon your windows version. To get your windows version open command prompt and execute following command.

```
C:\>wmic os get osarchitecture
OSArchitecture
64-bit
C:\>
```

32-bit versions of MongoDB only support databases smaller than 2GB and suitable only for testing and evaluation purposes.

Now extract your downloaded file to c:\ drive or any other location. Make sure name of the extracted folder is mongodb-win32-i386-[version] or mongodb-win32-x86_64-[version]. Here [version] is the version of MongoDB download.

Now open command prompt and run the following command

```
C:\>move mongodb-win64-* mongodb
1 dir(s) moved.
C:\>
```

In case you have extracted the mongodb at different location, then go to that path by using command **cd FOOLDER/DIR** and now run the above given process.

MongoDB requires a data folder to store its files. The default location for the MongoDB data directory is c:\data\db. So you need to create this folder using the Command Prompt. Execute the following command sequence.

```
C:\>md data
C:\md data\db
```

If you have install the MongoDB at different location, then you need to specify any alternate path for **\data\db** by setting the path dbpath in mongod.exe. For the same issue following commands.

In command prompt navigate to the bin directory present into the mongodb installation folder. Suppose my installation folder is **D:\set up\mongodb**

```
C:\Users\XYZ>d:
D:\>cd "set up"
D:\set up>cd mongodb
D:\set up\mongodb>cd bin
D:\set up\mongodb\bin>mongod.exe --dbpath "d:\set up\mongodb\data"
```

This will show **waiting for connections** message on the console output indicates that the mongod. exe process is running successfully.

Now to run the mongodb you need to open another command prompt and issue the following command.

```
D:\set up\mongodb\bin>mongo.exe
MongoDB shell version: 5.4.6
connecting to: test
>db.test.save( { a: 1 } )
>db.test.find()
{ "_id" : ObjectId(5879b0f65a56a454), "a" : 1 }
>
```

This will show that mongodb is installed and run successfully. Next time when you run mongodb you need to issue only commands.

```
D:\set up\mongodb\bin>mongod.exe --dbpath "d:\set up\mongodb\data"
D:\set up\mongodb\bin>mongo.exe
```

5.9 PIPELINE CONCEPT

In UNIX command shell pipeline means the possibility to execute an operation on some input and use the output as the input for the next command and so on. MongoDB also support same concept in aggregation framework. There is a set of possible stages and each of those is taken a set of documents as an input and is producing a resulting set of documents (or the final resulting JSON document at the end of the pipeline). This can then in turn again be used for the next stage an so on.

Possible stages in aggregation framework are following:

- **$project:** Used to select some specific fields from a collection.
- **$match:** This is a filtering operation and thus this can reduce the amount of documents that are given as input to the next stage.
- **$group:** This does the actual aggregation as discussed above.
- **$sort:** Sorts the documents.
- **$skip:** With this it is possible to skip forward in the list of documents for a given amount of documents.
- **$limit:** This limits the amount of documents to look at by the given number starting from the current position.s
- **$unwind:** This is used to unwind document that are using arrays. when using an array the data is kind of pre-joinded and this operation will be undone with this to have individual documents again. Thus with this stage we will increase the amount of documents for the next stage.

Replication is the process of synchronizing data across multiple servers. Replication provides redundancy and increases data availability with multiple copies of data on different database servers, replication protects a database from the loss of a single server. Replication also allows you to recover from hardware failure and service interruptions. With additional copies of the data, you can dedicate one to disaster recovery, reporting, or backup.

5.10 WHY REPLICATION?

- To keep your data safe
- High (24×7) availability of data
- Disaster Recovery
- No downtime for maintenance (like backups, index rebuilds, compaction)
- Read scaling (extra copies to read from)
- Replica set is transparent to the application

5.10.1 How replication works in MongoDB

MongoDB achieves replication by the use of replica set. A replica set is a group of **mongod** instances that host the same data set. In a replica one node is primary node that receives all write operations. All other instances, secondaries, apply operations from the primary so that they have the same data set. Replica set can have only one primary node.

1. Replica set is a group of two or more nodes (generally minimum 3 nodes are required).
2. In a replica set one node is primary node and remaining nodes are secondary.
3. All data replicates from primary to secondary node.
4. At the time of automatic failover or maintenance, election establishes for primary and a new primary node is elected.
5. After the recovery of failed node, it again join the replica set and works as a secondary node.

A typical diagram of mongodb replication is shown in which client application always interact with primary node and primary node then replicate the data to the secondary nodes.

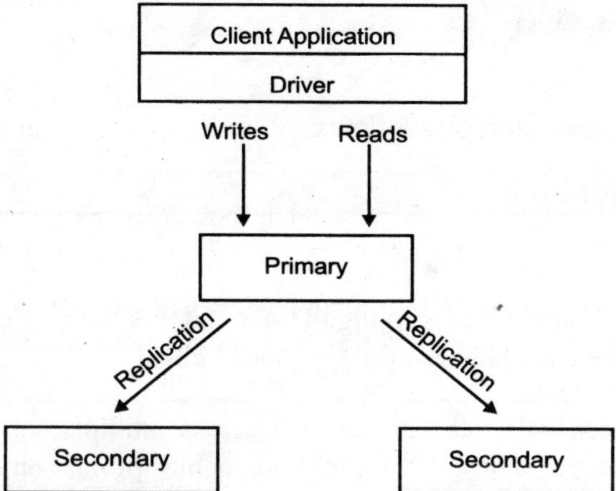

Replica set features

- A cluster of N nodess
- Anyone node can be primary
- All write operations goes to primary
- Automatic failover
- Automatic Recovery
- Consensus election of primary

Set up a replica set

In this tutorial we will convert standalone mongod instance to a replica set. To convert to replica set follow the below given steps:

- Shutdown already running mongodb server.

Now start the mongodb server by specifying **--replSet** option. Basic syntax of **--replSet** is given below:

```
mongod --port "PORT" --dbpath "YOUR_DB_DATA_PATH" --replSet "REPLICA_
SET_INSTANCE_NAME"
```

Example

```
mongod --port 27017 --dbpath "D:\set up\mongodb\data" --replSet rs0
```

It will start a mongod instance with the name rs0, on port 27017. Now start the command prompt and connect to this mongod instance. In mongo client issue the command **rs.initiate()** to initiate a new replica set. To check the replica set configuration issue the command **rs.conf()**. To check the status of replica sete issue the command **rs.status()**.

Add members to replica set

To add members to replica set, start mongod instances on multiple machines. Now start a mongo client and issue a command **rs.add()**.

Syntax:

Basic syntax of **rs.add()** command is as follows:

```
>rs.add(HOST_NAME:PORT)
```

Example

Suppose your mongod instance name is **mongod1.net** and it is running on port **27017**. To add this instance to replica set issue the command **rs.add()** in mongo client.

```
>rs.add("mongod1.net:27017")
>
```

You can add mongod instance to replica set only when you are connected to primary node. To check whether you are connected to primary or not issue the command **db.isMaster()** in mongo client.

5.11 SHARDING

Sharding is the process of storing data records across multiple machines and it is MongoDB's approach to meeting the demands of data growth. As the size of the data increases, a single machine may not be sufficient to store the data nor provide an acceptable read and write throughput. Sharding solves the problem with horizontal scaling. With sharding, you add more machines to support data growth and the demands of read and write operations.

5.11.1 Why Sharding?

1. In replication all writes go to master node
2. Latency sensitive queries still go to master
3. Single replica set has limitation of 12 nodes
4. Memory can't be large enough when active dataset is big
5. Local Disk is not big enough
6. Vertical scaling is too expensive

Sharding in MongoDB

Below given diagram shows the sharding in MongoDB using sharded cluster.

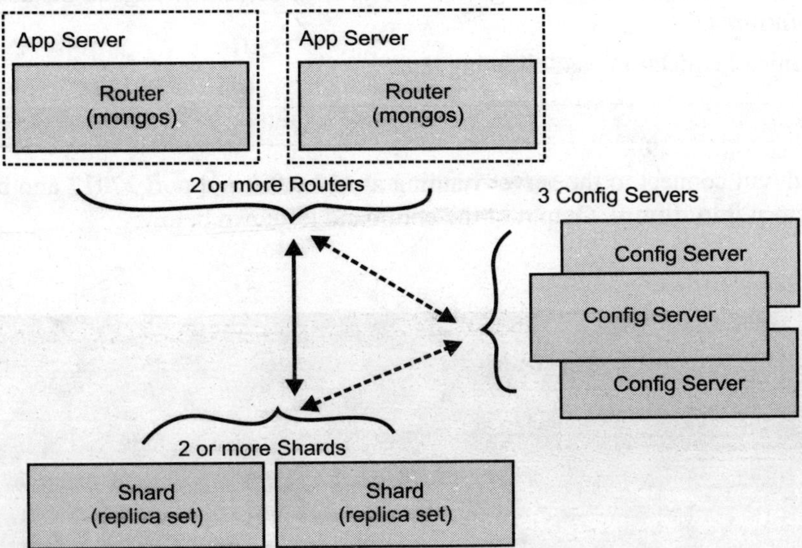

In the above given diagram there are three main components which are described below:

1. **Shards:** Shards are used to store data. They provide high availability and data consistency. In production environment each shard is a separate replica set.
2. **Config Servers:** Config servers store the cluster's metadata. This data contains a mapping of the cluster's data set to the shards. The query router uses this metadata to target operations to specific shards. In production environment sharded clusters have exactly 3 config servers.
3. **Query Routers:** Query Routers are basically mongos instances, interface with client applications and direct operations to the appropriate shard. The query router processes and targets operations to shards and then returns results to the clients. A sharded cluster can contain more than one query router to divide the client request load. A client sends requests to one query router. Generally a sharded cluster have many query routers.

Dump MongoDB Data

To create backup of database in mongodb you should use **mongodump** command. This command will dump all data of your server into dump directory. There are many options available by which you can limit the amount of data or create backup of your remote server.

Syntax:

Basic syntax of **mongodump** command is as follows

```
>mongodump
```

Example

Start your mongod server. Assuming that your mongod server is running on localhost and port 27017. Now open a command prompt and go to bin directory of your mongodb instance and type the command **mongodump**

Consider the mycol collection has following data.

```
>mongodump
```

The command will connect to the server running at **127.0.0.1** and port **27017** and back all data of the server to directory **/bin/dump/**. Output of the command is shown below:

```
C:\Windows\system32\cmd.exe
D:\set up\mongodb\bin>mongodump
connected to: 127.0.0.1
Sat Oct 05 10:01:12.789 all dbs
Sat Oct 05 10:01:12.793 DATABASE: test   to     dump\test
Sat Oct 05 10:01:12.795          test.system.indexes to dump\test\system.indexes.
bson
Sat Oct 05 10:01:12.797                   4 objects
Sat Oct 05 10:01:12.800          test.my to dump\test\my.bson
Sat Oct 05 10:01:12.803                   0 objects
Sat Oct 05 10:01:12.803          Metadata for test.my to dump\test\my.metadata.js
on
Sat Oct 05 10:01:12.807          test.cool1 to dump\test\cool1.bson
Sat Oct 05 10:01:12.810                   1 objects
Sat Oct 05 10:01:12.812          Metadata for test.cool1 to dump\test\cool1.metad
ata.json
Sat Oct 05 10:01:12.814          test.mycol to dump\test\mycol.bson
Sat Oct 05 10:01:12.817                   2 objects
Sat Oct 05 10:01:12.819          Metadata for test.mycol to dump\test\mycol.metad
ata.json
```

There are a list of available options that can be used with the **mongodump** command.

Syntax	Description	Example
mongodump --host HOST_ NAME --port PORT_NUMBER	This commmand will backup all databases of specified mongod instance.	mongodump --host tutorialspoint. com --port 27017
mongodump --dbpath DB_PATH --out BACKUP_ DIRECTORYThis command will backup only specified database at specified path		mongodump --dbpath /data/db/ --out /data/backup/
mongodump --collection COLLECTION --db DB_NAME	This command will backup only specified collection of specified database.	mongodump --collection mycol --db test

Restore data

To restore backup data mongodb's **mongorestore** command is used. This command restore all of the data from the back up directory.

Syntax

```
>mongorestore
```

Basic syntax of **mongorestore** command is

Output of the command is shown below:

C:\Windows\system32\cmd.exe

```
D:\set up\mongodb\bin>mongorestore
connected to: 127.0.0.1
Sat Oct 05 10:06:40.922 dump\test\cool1.bson
Sat Oct 05 10:06:40.924         going into namespace [test.cool1]
Sat Oct 05 10:06:40.933 warning: Restoring to test.cool1 without dropping. Resto
red data will be inserted without raising errors; check your server log
1 objects found
Sat Oct 05 10:06:41.003         Creating index: { key: { _id: 1 }, ns: "test.coo
l1", name: "_id_" }
Sat Oct 05 10:06:41.058 dump\test\my.bson
Sat Oct 05 10:06:41.058         going into namespace [test.my]
Sat Oct 05 10:06:41.062 warning: Restoring to test.my without dropping. Restored
 data will be inserted without raising errors; check your server log
Sat Oct 05 10:06:41.063 file dump\test\my.bson empty, skipping
Sat Oct 05 10:06:41.063         Creating index: { key: { _id: 1 }, ns: "test.my"
, name: "_id_" }
Sat Oct 05 10:06:41.066 dump\test\mycol.bson
Sat Oct 05 10:06:41.067         going into namespace [test.mycol]
Sat Oct 05 10:06:41.070 warning: Restoring to test.mycol without dropping. Resto
red data will be inserted without raising errors; check your server log
2 objects found
Sat Oct 05 10:06:41.077         Creating index: { key: { _id: 1 }, ns: "test.myc
ol", name: "_id_" }
Sat Oct 05 10:06:41.079         Creating index: { key: { name: 1 }, ns: "test.my
col", name: "name_1" }
```

CHAPTER 6

HBase and Cassendra

6.1 INTRODUCTION TO HBASE

HBase is a column-oriented database that's an open-source implementation of Google's Big Table storage architecture. It can manage structured and semi-structured data and has some built-in features such as scalability, versioning, compression and garbage collection. Since its uses write-ahead logging and distributed configuration, it can provide fault-tolerance and quick recovery from individual server failures. HBase built on top of Hadoop / HDFS and the data stored in HBase can be manipulated using Hadoop's MapReduce capabilities.

HBase is an open source, non-relational, distributed database modeled after Google's BigTable and written in Java. It is developed as part of Apache Software Foundation's Apache Hadoop project and runs on top of HDFS (Hadoop Distributed Filesystem), providing BigTable-like capabilities for Hadoop. That is, it provides a fault-tolerant way of storing large quantities of sparse data (small amounts of information caught within a large collection of empty or unimportant data, such as finding the 50 largest items in a group of 2 billion records, or finding the non-zero items representing less than 0.1% of a huge collection).

A **sparse file** is a type of computer file that attempts to use file system space more efficiently when the file itself is mostly empty. This is achieved by writing brief information (metadata) representing the empty blocks to disk instead of the actual "empty" space which makes up the block, using less disk space. The full block size is written to disk as the actual size only when the block contains "real" (non-empty) data..

When reading sparse files, the file system transparently converts metadata representing empty blocks into "real" blocks filled with zero bytes at runtime. The application is unaware of this conversion.

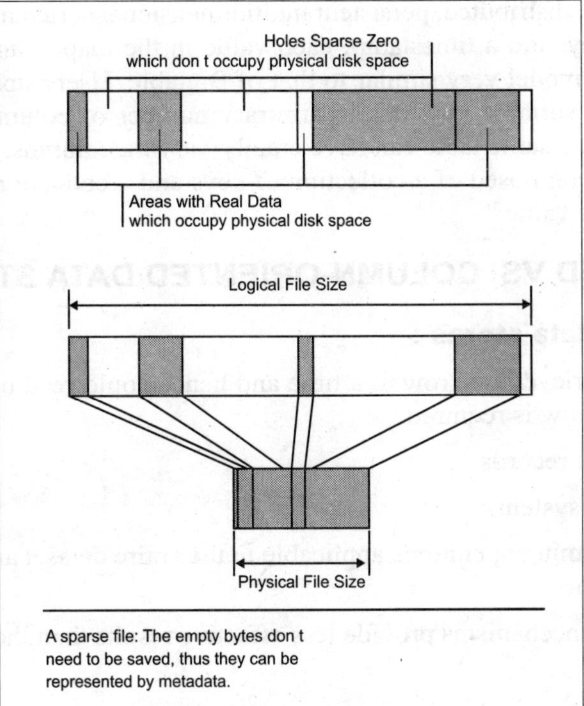

Figure. 6.1: Sparsh File

Let's now take a look at how HBase (a column-oriented database) is different from some other data structures and concepts that we are familiar with.. As shown in Fig. 6.2, in a row-oriented data store, a row is a unit of data that is read or written together. In a column-oriented data store, the data in a column is stored together and hence quickly retrieved.

Row Key	Customer		Sales	
Customer Id	Name	City	Product	Amount
101	Abbash Ahmad	Amritsar	Chairs	R5000.00
102	Vijay Agrawal	Mumbai	Lamps	R615.00
103	Sameer Gulati	Itarsi	Desk	R7000.00
104	Sapna Khanna	Kanpur	Bed	R3200.00

column Families

Figure. 6.2: Row and Column Based Tables

A Bigtable is a sparse, distributed, persistent multidimensional sorted map. The map is indexed by a row key, column key, and a timestamp; each value in the map is an uninterpreted array of bytes. HBase uses a data model very similar to that of Bigtable. Users store data rows in labelled tables. A data row has a sortable key and an arbitrary number of columns. The table is stored sparsely, so that rows in the same table can have crazily-varying columns, if the user likes. A map is "an abstract data type composed of a collection of keys and a collection of values, where each key is associated with one value."

6.2 ROW-ORIENTED VS. COLUMN-ORIENTED DATA STORES

6.2.1 Row-oriented data stores :

1. Data is stored and retrieved one row at a time and hence could read unnecessary data if only some of the data in a row is required.
2. Easy to read and write records
3. Well suited for OLTP systems
4. Not efficient in performing operations applicable to the entire dataset and hence aggregation is an expensive operation
5. Typical compression mechanisms provide less effective results than those on column-oriented data stores

6.2.2 Column-oriented data stores :

1. Data is stored and retrieved in columns and hence can read only relevant data if only some data is required
2. Read and Write are typically slower operations
3. Well suited for OLAP systems
4. Can efficiently perform operations applicable to the entire dataset and hence enables aggregation over many rows and columns
5. Permits high compression rates due to few distinct values in columns
6. Introduction Relational Databases vs. HBase

When talking of data stores, we first think of Relational Databases with structured data storage and a sophisticated query engine. However, a Relational Database incurs a big penalty to improve performance as the data size increases. HBase, on the other hand, is designed from the ground up to provide scalability and partitioning to enable efficient data structure serialization, storage and retrieval. Broadly, the differences between a Relational Database and HBase are:

6.2.3 Relational Database :

1. Is Based on a Fixed Schema
2. Is a Row-oriented datastore

3. Is designed to store Normalized Data
4. Contains thin tables
5. Has no built-in support for partitioning.

6.2.4 HBase :

1. Is Schema-less
2. Is a Column-oriented datastore
3. Is designed to store Denormalized Data
4. Contains wide and sparsely populated tables
5. Supports Automatic Partitioning

6.3 HDFS VS. HBASE

HDFS is a distributed file system that is well suited for storing large files. It's designed to support batch processing of data but doesn't provide fast individual record lookups. HBase is built on top of HDFS and is designed to provide access to single rows of data in large tables. Overall, the differences between HDFS and HBase are

HDFS :

1. Is suited for High Latency operations batch processing
2. Data is primarily accessed through MapReduce
3. Is designed for batch processing and hence doesn't have a concept of random reads/writes

HBase :

1. Is built for Low Latency operations
2. Provides access to single rows from billions of records
3. Data is accessed through shell commands, Client APIs in Java, REST, Avro or Thrift

6.4 HBASE ARCHITECTURE

The HBase Physical Architecture consists of servers in a Master-Slave relationship as shown in Fig. 6.3. Typically, the HBase cluster has one Master node, called HMaster and multiple Region Servers called HRegionServer. Each Region Server contains multiple Regions – HRegions.

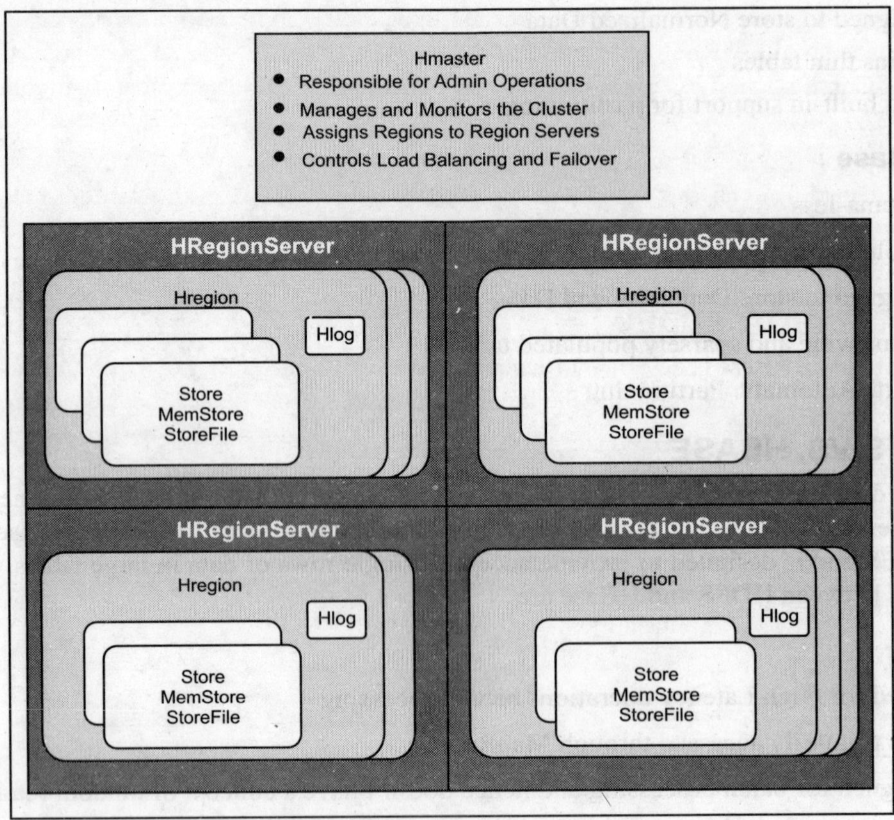

Figure. 6.3: Architecture of HBase

Just like in a Relational Database, data in HBase is stored in Tables and these Tables are stored in Regions. When a Table becomes too big, the Table is partitioned into multiple Regions. These Regions are assigned to Region Servers across the cluster. Each Region Server hosts roughly the same number of Regions.

The HMaster in the HBase is responsible for

1. Performing Administration
2. Managing and Monitoring the Cluster

Assigning Regions to the Region Servers

3. Controlling the Load Balancing and Failover

On the other hand, the HRegionServer perform the following work

1. Hosting and managing Regions
2. Splitting the Regions automatically
3. Handling the read/write requests
4. Communicating with the Clients directly

Each Region Server contains a Write-Ahead Log (called HLog) and multiple Regions. Each Region in turn is made up of a MemStore and multiple StoreFiles (HFile). The data lives in these StoreFiles in the form of Column Families (explained below). The MemStore holds in-memory modifications to the Store (data).

The mapping of Regions to Region Server is kept in a system table called .META. When trying to read or write data from HBase, the clients read the required Region information from the .META table and directly communicate with the appropriate Region Server. Each Region is identified by the start key (inclusive) and the end key (exclusive)

6.5 HBASE DATA MODEL

The Data Model in HBase is designed to accommodate semi-structured data that could vary in field size, data type and columns. Additionally, the layout of the data model makes it easier to partition the data and distribute it across the cluster. The Data Model in HBase is made of different logical components such as Tables, Rows, Column Families, Columns, Cells and Versions.

Row Key	Customer		Sales	
Customer Id	Name	City	Product	Amount
101	Abbash Ahmad	Amritsar	Chairs	R5000.00
102	Vijay Agrawal	Mumbai	Lamps	R615.00
103	Sameer Gulati	Itarsi	Desk	R7000.00
104	Sapna Khanna	Kanpur	Bed	R3200.00

column Families

Tables: The HBase Tables are more like logical collection of rows stored in separate partitions called Regions. As shown above, every Region is then served by exactly one Region Server. The figure above shows a representation of a Table.

Rows: A row is one instance of data in a table and is identified by a rowkey. Rowkeys are unique in a Table and are always treated as a byte[].

Column Families: Data in a row are grouped together as Column Families. Each Column Family has one more Columns and these Columns in a family are stored together in a low level storage file known as HFile. Column Families form the basic unit of physical storage to which certain HBase features like compression are applied. Hence it's important that proper care be taken when designing Column Families in table. The table above shows Customer and Sales Column Families. The Customer Column Family is made up 2 columns – Name and City, whereas the Sales Column Families is made up to 2 columns – Product and Amount.

Columns: A Column Family is made of one or more columns. A Column is identified by a Column Qualifier that consists of the Column Family name concatenated with the Column name using a colon – example: columnfamily:columnname. There can be multiple Columns within a Column Family and Rows within a table can have varied number of Columns.

Cell: A Cell stores data and is essentially a unique combination of rowkey, Column Family and the Column (Column Qualifier). The data stored in a Cell is called its value and the data type is always treated as byte[].

Version: The data stored in a cell is versioned and versions of data are identified by the timestamp. The number of versions of data retained in a column family is configurable and this value by default is 3.

6.6 UNDERSTANDING HBASE DATA MODEL

At Internet Memory, we use HBase as a large-scale repository for our collections, holding terabytes of web documents in a distributed cluster. This article presents the data model of HBase, and explains how it stands between relational DBs and the "No Schema" approach.

In 2006, the Google Labs team published a paper entitled BigTable: A Distributed Storage System for Structured Data. It describes a distributed index designed to manage very large datasets (``petabytes of data") in a cluster of data servers. BigTable supports key search, range search and high-throughput file scans, and also provides a flexible storage for structured data. HBase is an open-source clone of BigTable, and closely mimics its design. At Internet Memory, we use HBase as a large-scale repository for our collections, holding terabytes of web documents in a distributed cluster. HBase is often assimilated to a large, distributed relational database. It actually presents many aspects common to "NoSQL" systems: distribution, fault tolerance, flexible modeling, absence of some features deemed essential in centralized DBMS (e.g., concurrency), etc. This article presents the data model of HBase, and explains how it stands between relational DBs and the "No Schema" approach. It will be completed by an introduction to both the Java and REST APIs, and a final article on system aspects.

(1) The *map* structure: representing data with key/value pairs

We start with an idea familiar to Lisp programmers of *association lists*, which are nothing more than key-value pairs. They constitute a simple and convenient way of representing the properties of an object. We use as a running example the description of a Web document. For instance, using the JSON notation:

```
{
  'url': 'http://internetmemory.org', type: 'text/html', content: 'my
document content'
}
```

One obtains what is commonly called an associative array, a dictionary, or a *map*. Given a context (the object/document), the structure associates *values* to *keys*. We can represent such data as a graph, as shown by the figure below. The key information is captured by edges,whereas data values reside at leaves.

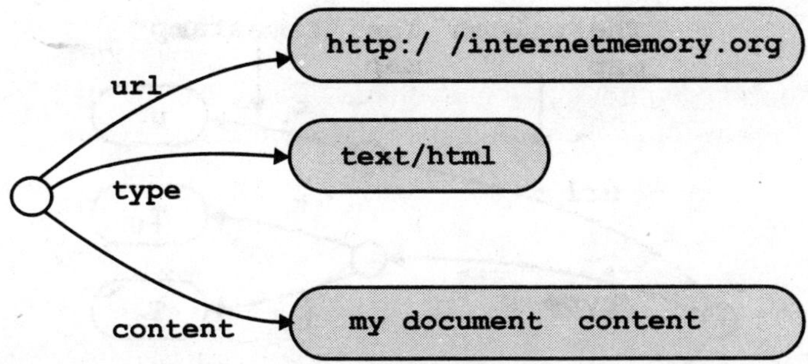

There exists many possible representations for a *map*. We showed a JSON example above, but XML is of course an appropriate choice. At first glance, a *map* can also be represented by a table. The above example is equivalently viewed as

url	Type	content
http://internetmemory.org	text/html	my document content

However, this often introduces some confusion. It is worth understanding several important differences that make a *map* much more flexible than the strict (relational) *table* structure. In particular,

- there is no *schema* that constrains the list of keys (unlike relational table where the schema is fixed and uniform for all rows),
- the *value* may itself be some complex structure.

HBase, following BigTable, builds on this flexibility. First, we can add new key-value pair to describe an object, if needed.This does not require any pre-declaration at the 'schema' level, and the new key remains local. Other objects stored in the same HBase instance remain unaffected by the change. Second, a value can be another *map*, yielding a *multi-map* structure which is exemplified below.

(2) An HBase "table" is a multi-map structure

Instead of keeping one value for each property of an object, HBases allows the storage of several *versions*. Each version is identified by a timestamp. How can we represent such a multi-versions, key-value structure? HBase simply replaces atomic values by a *map* where the key is the timestamp. The extended representation for our example is shown below. It helps to figure out the power and flexibility of the data representation. Now, our document is built from two nested maps,

- a first one, called "*column*" in HBase terminology (an unfortunate choice, since this is hardly related to the column relational concept),
- a second "*timestamp*" (each map is named after its key).

Our document is globally viewed as a *column* map. If we choose a *column* key, say, *type*, we obtain a value which is itself a second *map* featuring as many keys as there are timestamps for this specific column. In our example, there is only one timestamp for *url* (well, we can assume that the URL of the document does not change much). Looking at, respectively, *type* and *content*, we find the former has two versions and the latter three. Moreover, they only have one timestamp (t_1) in common. Actually, the "*timestamp*" maps are completely independent from one another.

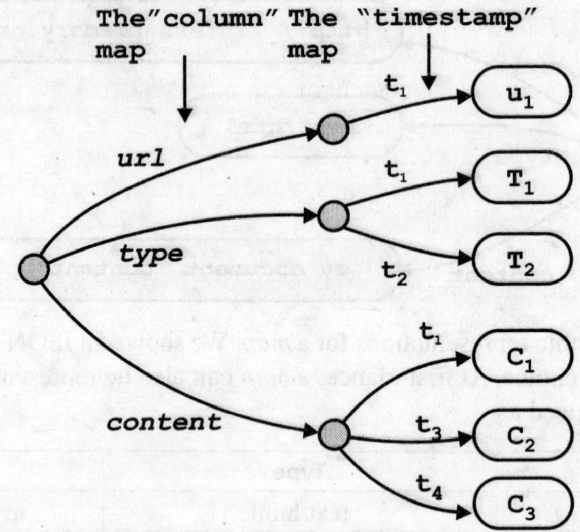

Note that we can add as many *timestamps* (hence, as many keys in one of the second-level maps) as we wish. And, in fact, this is true for the first-level map as well: we can add as many *columns* as we wish, at the document level, without having to impose such a change to *all* other documents in a same HBase instance. In essence, each object is just a self-described piece of information (think again to the flexible representation of semi-structured data formats like XML or JSON). In this respect, HBase is in the wake of other 'NoSQL' systems, and its data model shares many aspects that characterize this trend: no schema and self-description of objects. We are not completely done with the multi-map levels of HBase. Columns are grouped in *column families*, and a family is actually a key in a new map level, referring to a group of columns. In the Figure below, we define two families: *meta*, grouping *url* and *type*, and *data* representing the content of a document.

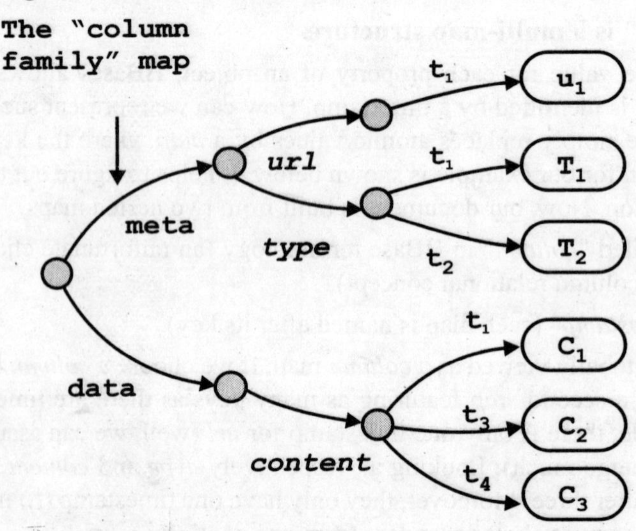

Important: Unlike the *column* and *timestamp* maps, the keys if a *family* map is *fixed*. We cannot add new families to a table once it is created. The *family* level constitutes therefore the equivalent of a relational schema, although, as we saw, the content of a family value may be a quite complex structure.

The full picture: rows and tables

So, now, we know how to represent our objects with the HBase data model. It remains to describe how we can put many objects (potentially, millions or even billions of object) in HBase. This is where HBase borrows some terminology to relational databases: objects are called "*rows*", and rows are stored in a "*table*". Although one could find some superficial similarities, this comparison is a likely source of confusion. Let us try to list the differences:

1. a "table" is actually a *map* where each row is a value, and the key is chosen by the table designer.
2. we already explained that the structure of a "row" has little to do with the flat representation of relational row.
3. regarding data manipulation, the nature of a "table" implies that two basic operations are available: *put(key, row)* and *get(key): row*. Nothing comparable to SQL here!

Finally, it is worth noting that the "table" map is a *sorted* map: rows are grouped on the key value, and two rows close from one another (with respect to the keys order) are stored is the same physical area. This make possible (and efficient) *range queries* of keys. We further explore this feature is the article devoted to the system aspects of HBase. The following Figures summarize our structure for an hypothetical *webdoc* HBase table storing a large collection of web documents. Each document is indexed by its url (which is therefore the key of the highest level map). A *row* is itself a local map featuring a fixed number of keys defined by the family names (f_1, f_2, etc.), associated to values which are themselves maps indexed by columns. Finally, column values are versioned, and represented by a timestamp-index map. Columns and timestamps do no obey to a global schema: they are defined on a row basis. The columns may vary arbitrarily from one row to another, and so do the timestamps for columns.

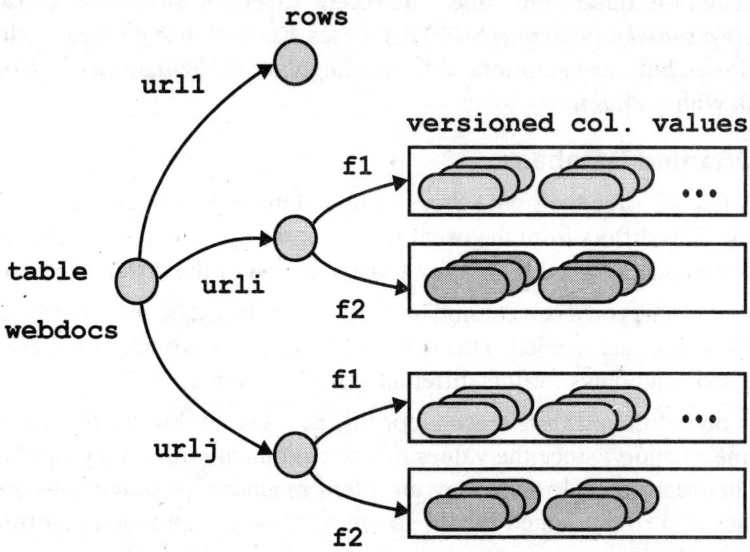

The multi-map structure of a HBase table can thus be summarized as

```
key -> family -> column -> timestamp -> value
```

It should be clear that the intuitive meaning of common concepts such as "table", "row", and "column" must be revisited when dealing with HBase data. In particular, considering HBase as a kind of large relational database is clearly a misleading option. HBase is essentially a key-value store with efficient indexing on key access, a semi-structured data model for value representation, and range-search capabilities supported by key ordering.

6.7 HBASE : AN ON-DISK COLUMN STORAGE FORMAT

Google and Amazon are prominent examples of companies that realized the value of data and started developing solutions to fit their needs. For instance, in a series of technical publications, Google described a scalable storage and processing system based on commodity hardware. These ideas were then implemented outside of Google as part of the open source Hadoop project: *HDFS* and *MapReduce*.

Hadoop excels at storing data of arbitrary, semi-, or even unstructured formats, since it lets you decide how to interpret the data at analysis time, allowing you to change the way you classify the data at any time: once you have updated the algorithms, you simply run the analysis again.

Hadoop also complements existing database systems of almost any kind. It offers a limitless pool into which one can sink data and still pull out what is needed when the time is right. It is optimized for large file storage and batch-oriented, streaming access. This makes analysis easy and fast, but users also need access to the final data, not in batch mode but using random access—this is akin to a full table scan versus using indexes in a database system.

We are used to querying databases when it comes to random access for structured data. RDBMSes are the most prominent, but there are also quite a few specialized variations and implementations, like object-oriented databases. Most RDBMSes strive to implement *Codd's 12 rules,* which forces them to comply to very rigid requirements. The architecture used underneath is well researched and has not changed significantly in quite some time. The recent advent of different approaches, like *column-oriented* or *massively parallel processing* (MPP) databases, has shown that we can rethink the technology to fit specific workloads, but most solutions still implement all or the majority of Codd's 12 rules in an attempt to not break with tradition.

6.7.1 Column-Oriented Database

Column-oriented databases save their data grouped by columns. Subsequent column values are stored contiguously on disk. This differs from the usual row-oriented approach of traditional databases, which store entire rows contiguously—see Fig. 6.4 for a visualization of the different physical layouts.

The reason to store values on a per-column basis instead is based on the assumption that, for specific queries, not all of the values are needed. This is often the case in analytical databases in particular, and therefore they are good candidates for this different storage schema.

Reduced I/O is one of the primary reasons for this new layout, but it offers additional advantages playing into the same category: since the values of one column are often very similar in nature or even vary only slightly between logical rows, they are often much better suited for compression than the heterogeneous values of a row-oriented record structure; most compression algorithms only look at a finite window.

Specialized algorithms—for example, delta and/or prefix compression—selected based on the type of the column (i.e., on the data stored) can yield huge improvements in compression ratios. Better ratios result in more efficient bandwidth usage.

> **NOTE**
>
> **Note**, though, HBase is *not* a column-oriented database in the typical RDBMS sense, but utilizes an on-disk column storage format. This is also where the majority of similarities end, because although HBase stores data on disk in a column-oriented format, it is distinctly different from traditional columnar databases: whereas columnar databases excel at providing real-time analytical access to data, HBase excels at providing key-based access to a specific cell of data, or a sequential range of cells.

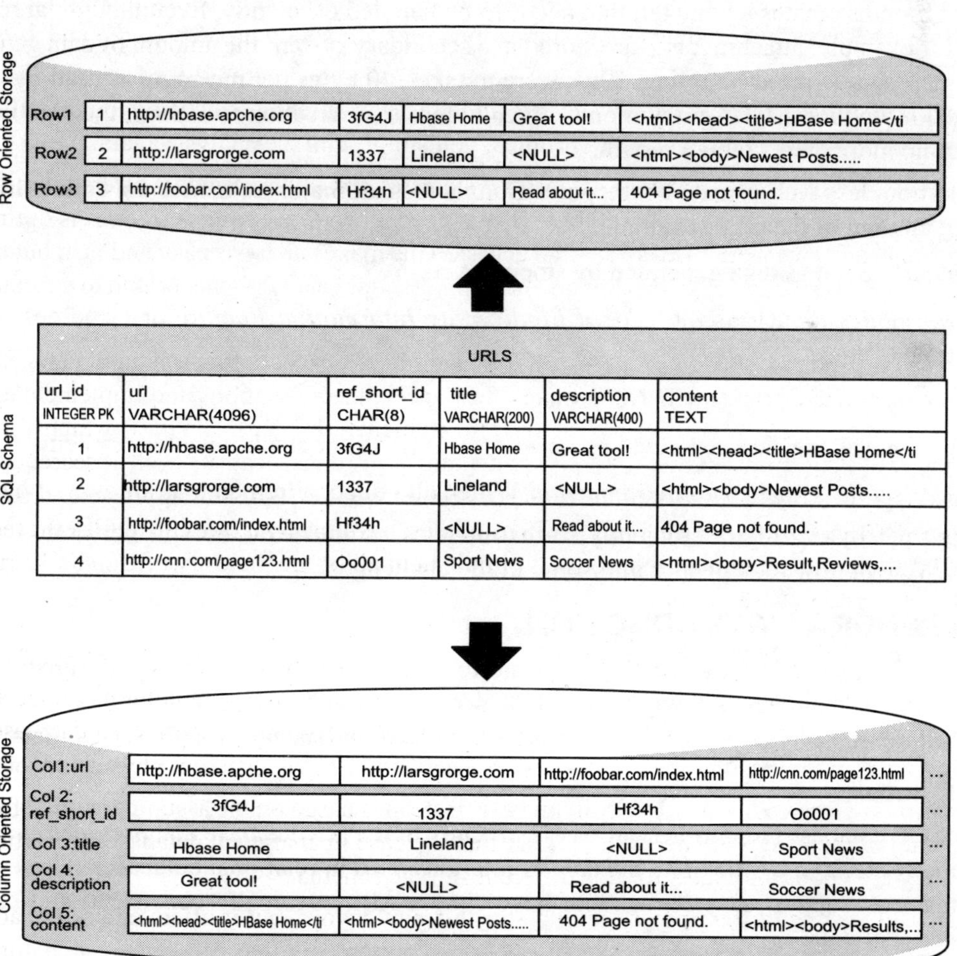

Figure. 6.4: Column-oriented and row-oriented storage layouts

The speed at which data is created today is already greatly increased, compared to only just a few years back. We can take for granted that this is only going to increase further, and with the rapid pace of globalization the problem is only exacerbated. Websites like Google, Amazon, eBay, and Facebook now reach the majority of people on this planet. The term *planet-size web application* comes to mind, and in this case it is fitting.

Facebook, for example, is adding more than 15 TB of data into its Hadoop cluster every dayand is subsequently processing it all. One source of this data is click-stream logging, saving every step a user performs on its website, or on sites that use the social plug-ins offered by Facebook. This is an ideal case in which batch processing to build machine learning models for predictions and recommendations is appropriate.

Facebook also has a real-time component, which is its messaging system, including chat, wall posts, and email. This amounts to 135+ billion messages per month,and storing this data over a certain number of months creates a huge tail that needs to be handled efficiently. Even though larger parts of emails—for example, attachments—are stored in a secondary system,the amount of data generated by all these messages is mind-boggling. If we were to take 140 bytes per message, as used by Twitter, it would total more than 17 TB every month. Even before the transition to HBase, the existing system had to handle more than 25 TB a month.

In addition, less web-oriented companies from across all major industries are collecting an ever-increasing amount of data. For example:

1. *Financial :* Such as data generated by stock tickers
2. *Bioinformatics :* Such as the *Global Biodiversity Information Facility* or Genomes of various species
3. *Smart grid :*Such as the *OpenPDC* project
4. *Sales :* Such as the data generated by *point-of-sale* (POS) or stock/inventory systems
5. *Cellular services, military, environmental* Which all collect a tremendous amount of data as well

Storing petabytes of data efficiently so that updates and retrieval are still performed well is no easy feat. We will now look deeper into some of the challenges.

6.8 CASANDRA : INTRODUCTION

Apache Cassandra is a highly scalable, high-performance distributed database designed to handle large amounts of data across many commodity servers, providing high availability with no single point of failure. It is a type of NoSQL database. Let us first understand what a NoSQL database does.

NoSQLDatabase

A NoSQL database (sometimes called as Not Only SQL) is a database that provides a mechanism to store and retrieve data other than the tabular relations used in relational databases. These databases are schema-free, support easy replication, have simple API, eventually consistent, and can handle huge amounts of data.

The primary objective of a NoSQL database is to have

- simplicity of design,

- horizontal scaling, and
- finer control over availability.

NoSql databases use different data structures compared to relational databases. It makes some operations faster in NoSQL. The suitability of a given NoSQL database depends on the problem it must solve.

Besides Cassandra, we have the following NoSQL databases that are quite popular:

- Apache HBase - HBase is an open source, non-relational, distributed database modeled after Google's BigTable and is written in Java. It is developed as a part of Apache Hadoop project and runs on top of HDFS, providing BigTable-like capabilities for Hadoop.
- MongoDB - MongoDB is a cross-platform document-oriented database system that avoids using the traditional table-based relational database structure in favor of JSON-like documents with dynamic schemas making the integration of data in certain types of applications easier and faster.

6.8.1 What is Apache Cassandra?

Apache Cassandra is an open source, distributed and decentralized/distributed storage system (database), for managing very large amounts of structured data spread out across the world. It provides highly available service with no single point of failure.

Listed below are some of the notable points of Apache Cassandra:

- It is scalable, fault-tolerant, and consistent.
- It is a column-oriented database.
- Its distribution design is based on Amazon's Dynamo and its data model on Google's Bigtable.
- Created at Facebook, it differs sharply from relational database management systems.

Cassandra implements a Dynamo-style replication model with no single point of failure, but adds a more powerful "column family" data model. Cassandra is being used by some of the biggest companies such as *Facebook, Twitter, Cisco, Rackspace, ebay, Twitter, Netflix*, and more.

The design goal of Cassandra is to handle big data workloads across multiple nodes without any single point of failure. Cassandra has peer-to-peer distributed system across its nodes, and data is distributed among all the nodes in a cluster.

All the nodes in a cluster play the same role. Each node is independent and at the same time interconnected to other nodes. Each node in a cluster can accept read and write requests, regardless of where the data is actually located in the cluster. When a node goes down, read/write requests can be served from other nodes in the network.

6.9 FEATURES OF CASSANDRA

Cassandra has become so popular because of its outstanding technical features. Given below are some of the features of Cassandra:

1. **Elastic scalability** - Cassandra is highly scalable; it allows to add more hardware to accommodate more customers and more data as per requirement.

2. **Always on architecture** - Cassandra has no single point of failure and it is continuously available for business-critical applications that cannot afford a failure.

3. **Fast linear-scale performance** - Cassandra is linearly scalable, i.e., it increases your throughput as you increase the number of nodes in the cluster. Therefore it maintains a quick response time.

4. **Flexible data storage** - Cassandra accommodates all possible data formats including: structured, semi-structured, and unstructured. It can dynamically accommodate changes to your data structures according to your need.

5. **Easy data distribution** - Cassandra provides the flexibility to distribute data where you need by replicating data across multiple data centers.

6. **Transaction support** - Cassandra supports properties like Atomicity, Consistency, Isolation, and Durability (ACID).

7. **Fast writes** - Cassandra was designed to run on cheap commodity hardware. It performs blazingly fast writes and can store hundreds of terabytes of data, without sacrificing the read efficiency.

Cassandra was the daughter of King Priam (Priamos) and Queen Hecuba (Hekabe) and the fraternal twin sister of Helenus and a princess of Troy.Cassandra is in use at Constant Contact, CERN, Comcast, eBay, GitHub, GoDaddy, Hulu, Instagram, Intuit, Netflix, Reddit, The Weather Channel, and over 1500 more companies that have large, active data sets.

One of the largest production deployments is Apple's, with over 75,000 nodes storing over 10 PB of data. Other large Cassandra installations include Netflix (2,500 nodes, 420 TB, over 1 trillion requests per day), Chinese search engine Easou (270 nodes, 300 TB, over 800 million reqests per day), and eBay (over 100 nodes, 250 TB).

6.10 HISTORY OF CASSANDRA

Cassandra was developed at Facebook for inbox search. It was open-sourced by Facebook in July 2008. Cassandra was accepted into Apache Incubator in March 2009. It was made an Apache top-level project since February 2010.

6.11 DATA REPLICATION IN CASSANDRA

In Cassandra, one or more of the nodes in a cluster act as replicas for a given piece of data. If it is detected that some of the nodes responded with an out-of-date value, Cassandra will return the most recent value to the client. After returning the most recent value, Cassandra performs a read repair in the background to update the stale values.

The following figure shows a schematic view of how Cassandra uses data replication among the nodes in a cluster to ensure no single point of failure.

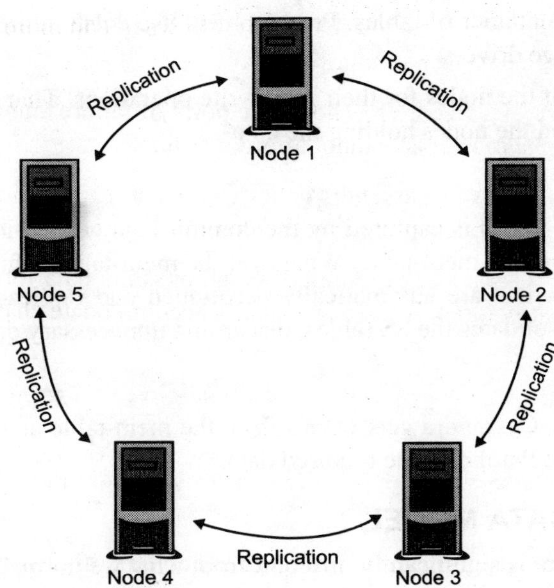

NOTE

Note – Cassandra uses the Gossip Protocol in the background to allow the nodes to communicate with each other and detect any faulty nodes in the cluster.

6.12 COMPONENTS OF CASSANDRA

The key components of Cassandra are as follows –

1. **Node** – It is the place where data is stored.
2. **Data center** – It is a collection of related nodes.
3. **Cluster** – A cluster is a component that contains one or more data centers.
4. **Commit log** – The commit log is a crash-recovery mechanism in Cassandra. Every write operation is written to the commit log.
5. **Mem-table** – A mem-table is a memory-resident data structure. After commit log, the data will be written to the mem-table. Sometimes, for a single-column family, there will be multiple mem-tables.
6. **SSTable** – It is a disk file to which the data is flushed from the mem-table when its contents reach a threshold value.
7. **Bloom filter** – These are nothing but quick, nondeterministic, algorithms for testing whether an element is a member of a set. It is a special kind of cache. Bloom filters are accessed after every query.

6.13 CASSANDRA QUERY LANGUAGE (CQL)

Users can access Cassandra through its nodes using Cassandra Query Language (CQL). CQL treats the database (Keyspace) as a container of tables. Programmers use cqlsh: a prompt to work with CQL or separate application language drivers.

Clients approach any of the nodes for their read-write operations. That node (coordinator) plays a proxy between the client and the nodes holding the data.

Write Operations

Every write activity of nodes is captured by the commit logs written in the nodes. Later the data will be captured and stored in the mem-table. Whenever the mem-table is full, data will be written into the SStable data file. All writes are automatically partitioned and replicated throughout the cluster. Cassandra periodically consolidates the SSTables, discarding unnecessary data.

Read Operations

During read operations, Cassandra gets values from the mem-table and checks the bloom filter to find the appropriate SSTable that holds the required data.

8.14 CASSANDRA DATA MODEL

The data model of Cassandra is significantly different from what we normally see in an RDBMS. This chapter provides an overview of how Cassandra stores its data.

Cluster

Cassandra database is distributed over several machines that operate together. The outermost container is known as the Cluster. For failure handling, every node contains a replica, and in case of a failure, the replica takes charge. Cassandra arranges the nodes in a cluster, in a ring format, and assigns data to them.

Keyspace

Keyspace is the outermost container for data in Cassandra. The basic attributes of a Keyspace in Cassandra are –

- **Replication factor:** It is the number of machines in the cluster that will receive copies of the same data.
- **Replica placement strategy:** It is nothing but the strategy to place replicas in the ring. We have strategies such as simple strategy (rack-aware strategy), old network topology strategy (rack-aware strategy), and network topology strategy (datacenter-shared strategy).
- **Column families:** Keyspace is a container for a list of one or more column families. A column family, in turn, is a container of a collection of rows. Each row contains ordered columns. Column families represent the structure of your data. Each keyspace has at least one and often many column families.

The syntax of creating a Keyspace is as follows

```
CREATE KEYSPACE Keyspace name
WITH replication = {'class': 'SimpleStrategy', 'replication_factor' :
3};
```

The following illustration shows a schematic view of a Keyspace.

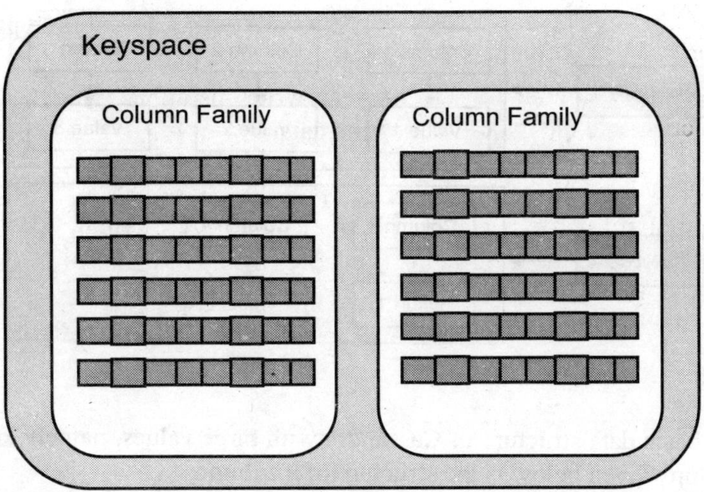

Column Family

A column family is a container for an ordered collection of rows. Each row, in turn, is an ordered collection of columns. The following table lists the points that differentiate a column family from a table of relational databases.

Relational Table	Cassandra column Family
A schema in a relational model is fixed. Once we define certain columns for a table, while inserting data, in every row all the columns must be filled at least with a null value.	In Cassandra, although the column families are defined, the columns are not. You can freely add any column to any column family at any time.
Relational tables define only columns and the user fills in the table with values.	In Cassandra, a table contains columns, or can be defined as a super column family.

A Cassandra column family has the following attributes –

1. keys_cached – It represents the number of locations to keep cached per SSTable.
2. rows_cached – It represents the number of rows whose entire contents will be cached in memory.
3. preload_row_cache – It specifies whether you want to pre-populate the row cache.

Note – Unlike relational tables where a column family's schema is not fixed, Cassandra does not force individual rows to have all the columns.

The following figure shows an example of a Cassandra column family.

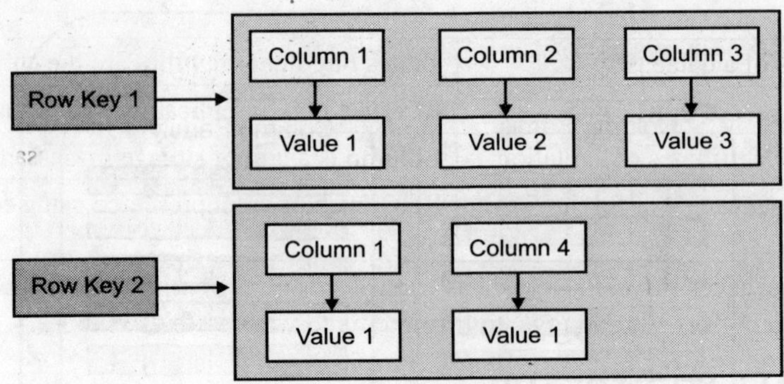

Column

A column is the basic data structure of Cassandra with three values, namely key or column name, value, and a time stamp. Given below is the structure of a column.

Column		
name : byte[]	value : byte[]	clock : clock[]

SuperColumn

A super column is a special column, therefore, it is also a key-value pair. But a super column stores a map of sub-columns.

Generally column families are stored on disk in individual files. Therefore, to optimize performance, it is important to keep columns that you are likely to query together in the same column family, and a super column can be helpful here.Given below is the structure of a super column.

Super Column	
name : byte[]	Cols : map<byte[], column>

6.15 DATA MODELS OF CASSANDRA AND RDBMS

The following table lists down the points that differentiate the data model of Cassandra from that of an RDBMS.

RDBMS	Cassandra
RDBMS deals with structured data.	Cassandra deals with unstructured data.
It has a fixed schema.	Cassandra has a flexible schema.
In RDBMS, a table is an array of arrays. (ROW x COLUMN)	In Cassandra, a table is a list of "nested key-value pairs". (ROW x COLUMN key x COLUMN value)
Database is the outermost container that contains data corresponding to an application.	Keyspace is the outermost container that contains data corresponding to an application.

Tables are the entities of a database.	Tables or column families are the entity of a keyspace.
Row is an individual record in RDBMS.	Row is a unit of replication in Cassandra.
Column represents the attributes of a relation.	Column is a unit of storage in Cassandra.
RDBMS supports the concepts of foreign keys, joins.	Relationships are represented using collections.

Cassandra can be accessed using cqlsh as well as drivers of different languages. This chapter explains how to set up both cqlsh and java environments to work with Cassandra.

6.16 PRE-INSTALLATION SETUP

Before installing Cassandra in Linux environment, we require to set up Linux using **ssh**(Secure Shell). Follow the steps given below for setting up Linux environment.

Create a User

At the beginning, it is recommended to create a separate user for Hadoop to isolate Hadoop file system from Unix file system. Follow the steps given below to create a user.

1. Open root using the command "su".
2. Create a user from the root account using the command "useradd username".
3. Now you can open an existing user account using the command "su username".

   Open the Linux terminal and type the following commands to create a user.

```
$ su
password:
# useradd hadoop
# passwd hadoop
New passwd:
Retype new passwd
```

SSH Setup and Key Generation

SSH setup is required to perform different operations on a cluster such as starting, stopping, and distributed daemon shell operations. To authenticate different users of Hadoop, it is required to provide public/private key pair for a Hadoop user and share it with different users.

The following commands are used for generating a key value pair using SSH:

1. copy the public keys form id_rsa.pub to authorized_keys,
2. and provide owner,
3. read and write permissions to authorized_keys file respectively.

```
$ ssh-keygen -t rsa
$ cat ~/.ssh/id_rsa.pub >> ~/.ssh/authorized_keys
$ chmod 0600 ~/.ssh/authorized_keys
```

- Verify ssh:

```
ssh localhost
```

Download Cassandra

Apache Cassandra is available at Download Link Cassandra using the following command.

```
$ wget http://supergsego.com/apache/cassandra/2.1.2/apache-cassandra-2.1.2-bin.tar.gz
```

Unzip Cassandra using the command **zxvf** as shown below.

```
$ tar zxvf apache-cassandra-2.1.2-bin.tar.gz.
```

Create a new directory named cassandra and move the contents of the downloaded file to it as shown below.

```
$ mkdir Cassandra
$ mv apache-cassandra-2.1.2/* cassandra.
```

Configure Cassandra

Open the **cassandra.yaml:** file, which will be available in the **bin** directory of Cassandra.

```
$ gedit cassandra.yaml
```

Note: If you have installed Cassandra from a deb or rpm package, the configuration files will be located in **/etc/cassandra** directory of Cassandra.

The above command opens the **cassandra.yaml** file. Verify the following configurations. By default, these values will be set to the specified directories.

- data_file_directories "/var/lib/cassandra/data"
- commitlog_directory "/var/lib/cassandra/commitlog"
- saved_caches_directory "/var/lib/cassandra/saved_caches"

Make sure these directories exist and can be written to, as shown below.

Create Directories

As super-user, create the two directories /var/lib/cassandra and /var./lib/Cassandra into which Cassandra writes its data.

```
[root@linux cassandra]# mkdir /var/lib/cassandra
[root@linux cassandra]# mkdir /var/log/cassandra
```

Give Permissions to Folders

Give read-write permissions to the newly created folders as shown below.

```
[root@linux /]# chmod 777 /var/lib/cassandra
[root@linux /]# chmod 777 /var/log/cassandra
```

Start Cassandra

To start Cassandra, open the terminal window, navigate to Cassandra home directory/home, where you unpacked Cassandra, and run the following command to start your Cassandra server.

```
$ cd $CASSANDRA_HOME
$./bin/cassandra -f
```

Using the –f option tells Cassandra to stay in the foreground instead of running as a background process. If everything goes fine, you can see the Cassandra server starting.

Programming Environment

To set up Cassandra programmatically, download the following jar files:

- slf4j-api-1.7.6.jar
- cassandra-driver-core-2.0.2.jar
- guava-16.0.1.jar
- metrics-core-3.0.2.jar
- netty-3.9.0.Final.jar

Place them in a separate folder. For example, we are downloading these jars to a folder named **"Cassandra_jars"**.

Set the classpath for this folder in **".bashrc"**file as shown below.

```
[hadoop@linux ~]$ gedit ~/.bashrc
//Set the following class path in the .bashrc file.
export CLASSPATH = $CLASSPATH:/home/hadoop/Cassandra_jars/*
```

Eclipse Environment

Open Eclipse and create a new project called Cassandra _Examples.

Right click on the project, select **Build Path→Configure Build Path** as shown below.

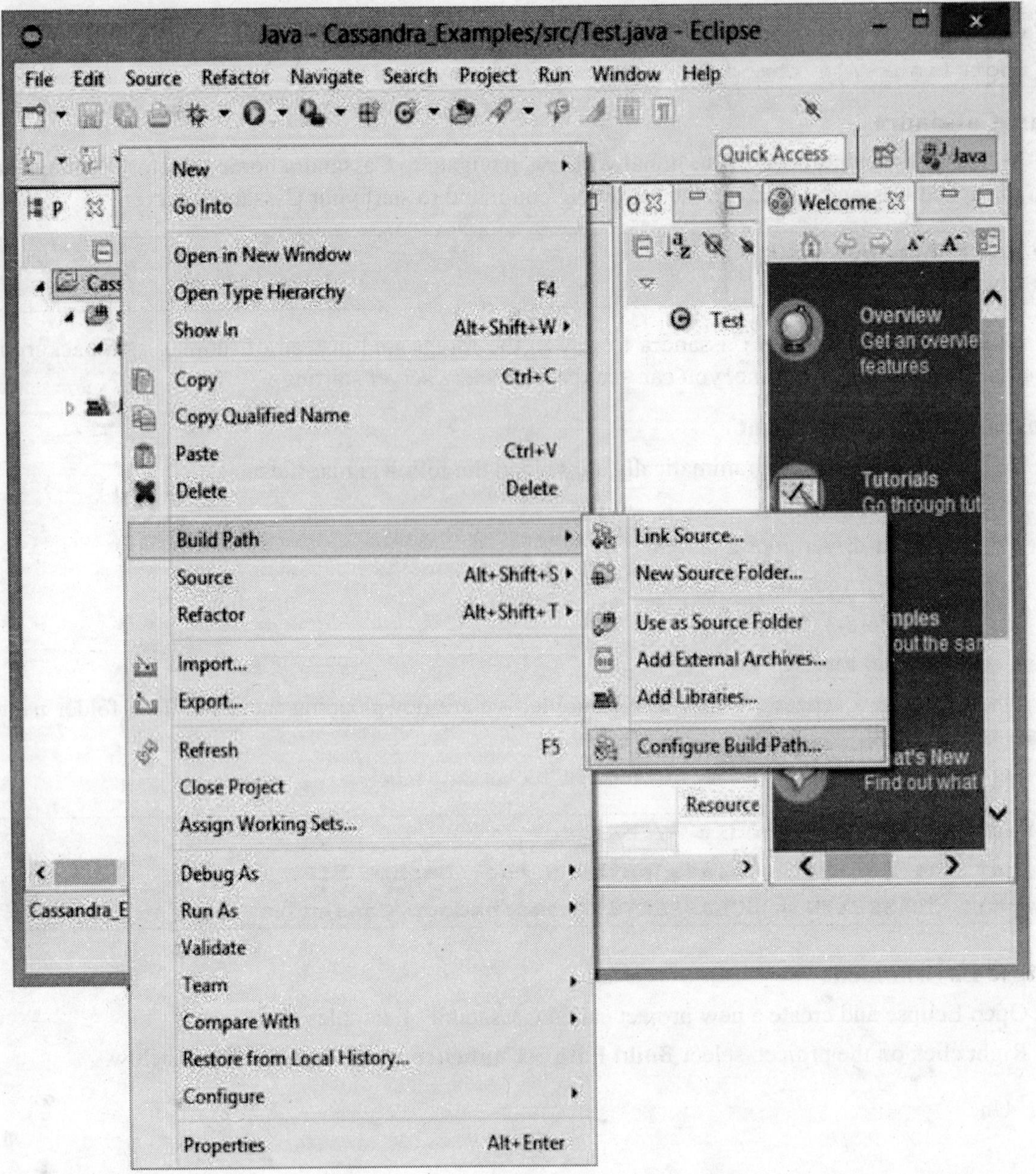

It will open the properties window. Under Libraries tab, select **Add External JARs**. Navigate to the directory where you saved your jar files. Select all the five jar files and click OK as shown below.

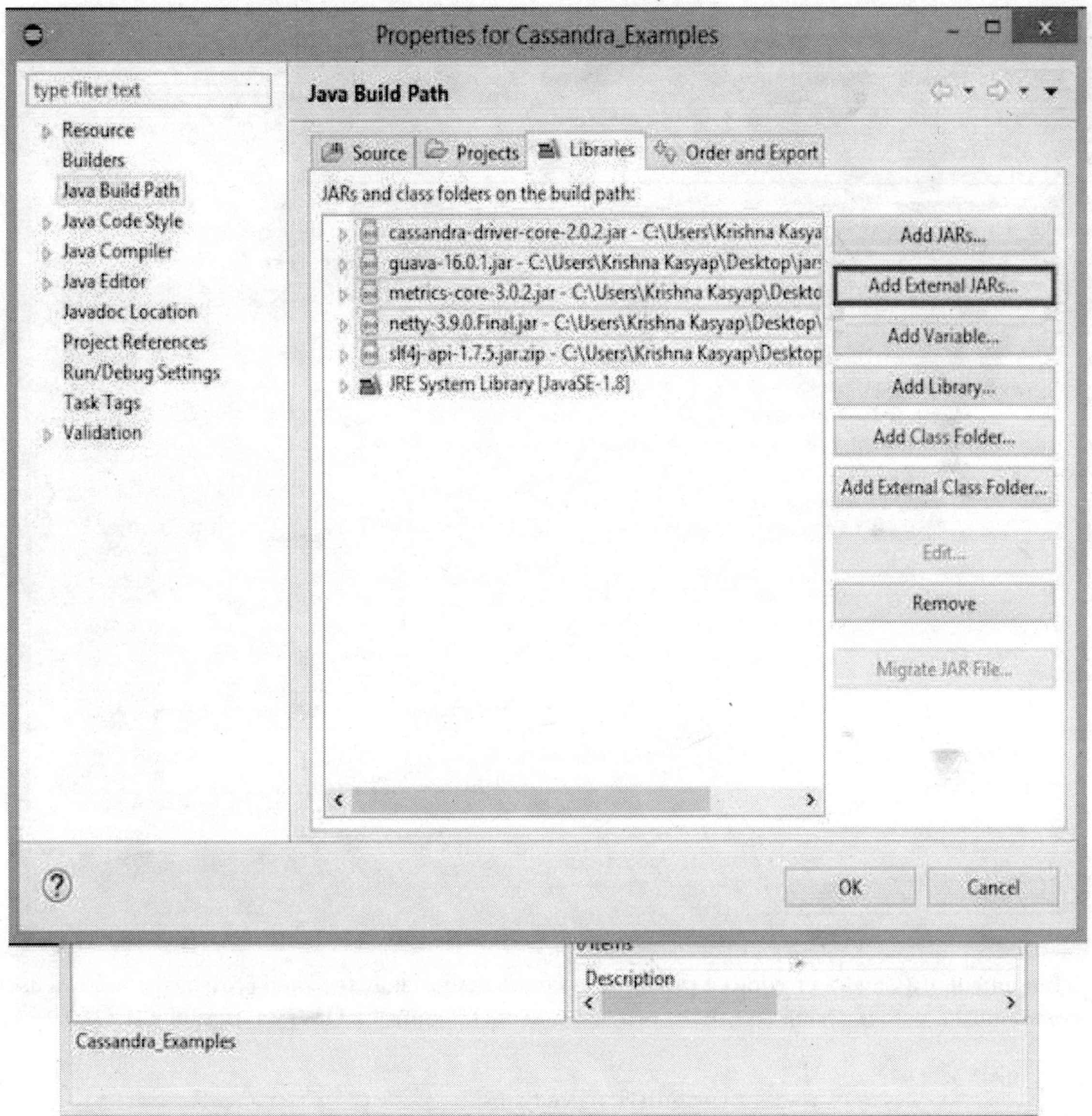

Under Referenced Libraries, you can see all the required jars added as shown below:

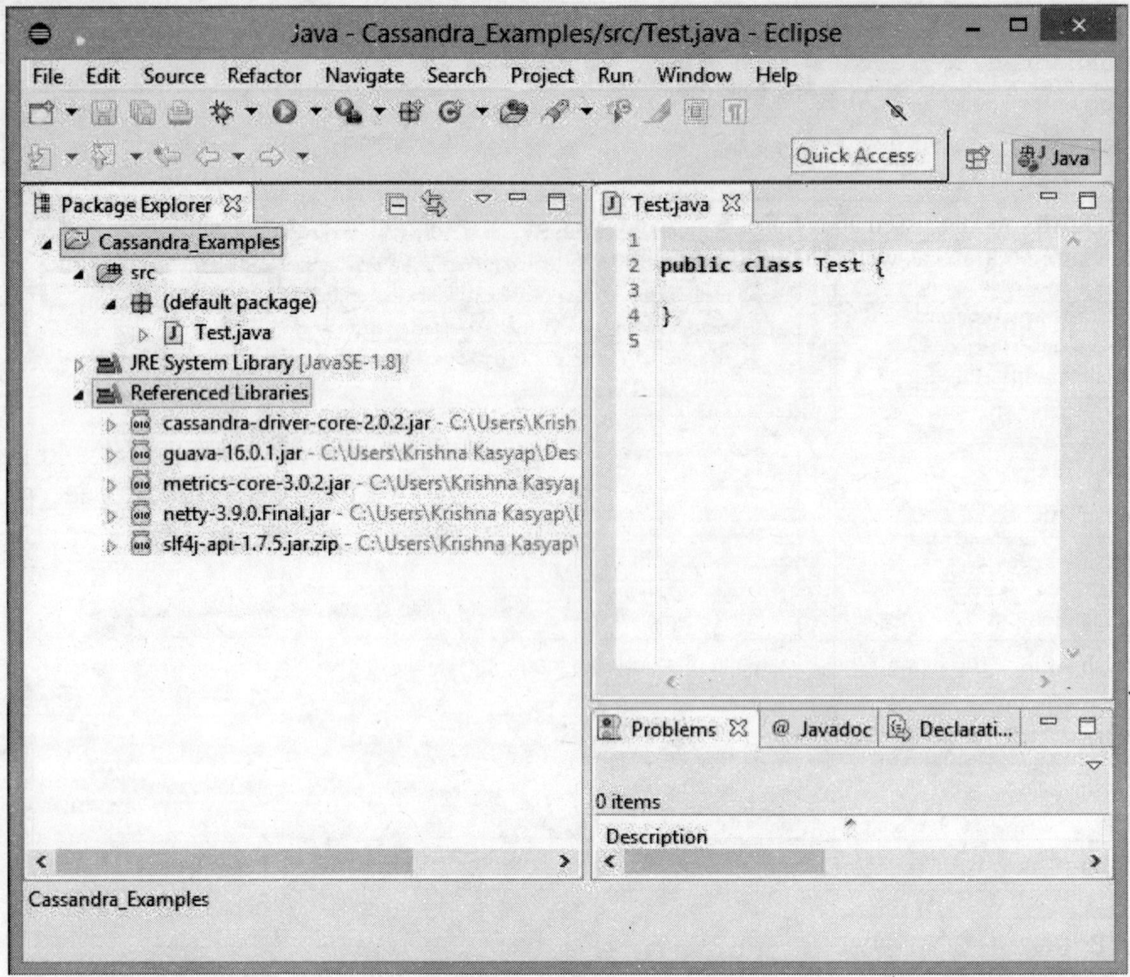

By default, Cassandra provides a prompt Cassandra query language shell **(cqlsh)** that allows users to communicate with it. Using this shell, you can execute **Cassandra Query Language (CQL)**.

Using cqlsh, you can

1. define a schema,
2. insert data, and
3. execute a query.

6.17 STARTING CQLSH

Start cqlsh using the command **cqlsh** as shown below. It gives the Cassandra cqlsh prompt as output.

```
[hadoop@linux bin]$ cqlsh
Connected to Test Cluster at 127.0.0.1:9042.
[cqlsh 6.0.1 | Cassandra 2.1.2 | CQL spec 3.2.0 | Native protocol v3]
Use HELP for help.
cqlsh>
```

Cqlsh - As discussed above, this command is used to start the cqlsh prompt. In addition, it supports a few more options as well. The following table explains all the options of **cqlsh**and their usage.

Options	Usage
cqlsh --help	Shows help topics about the options of cqlsh commands.
cqlsh --version	Provides the version of the cqlsh you are using.
cqlsh --color	Directs the shell to use colored output.
cqlsh --debug	Shows additional debugging information.
cqlsh --execute cql_statement	Directs the shell to accept and execute a CQL command.
cqlsh --file= "file name"	If you use this option, Cassandra executes the command in the given file and exits.
cqlsh --no-color	Directs Cassandra not to use colored output.
cqlsh -u "user name"	Using this option, you can authenticate a user. The default user name is: cassandra.
cqlsh-p "pass word"	Using this option, you can authenticate a user with a password. The default password is: cassandra.

6.18 CQLSH COMMANDS

Cqlsh has a few commands that allow users to interact with it. The commands are listed below.

Documented Shell Commands

Given below are the Cqlsh documented shell commands. These are the commands used to perform tasks such as displaying help topics, exit from cqlsh, describe,etc.

- **HELP** - Displays help topics for all cqlsh commands.
- **CAPTURE** - Captures the output of a command and adds it to a file.
- **CONSISTENCY** - Shows the current consistency level, or sets a new consistency level.
- **COPY** - Copies data to and from Cassandra.
- **DESCRIBE** - Describes the current cluster of Cassandra and its objects.
- **EXPAND** - Expands the output of a query vertically.
- **EXIT** - Using this command, you can terminate cqlsh.
- **PAGING** - Enables or disables query paging.

- **SHOW** - Displays the details of current cqlsh session such as Cassandra version, host, or data type assumptions.
- **SOURCE** - Executes a file that contains CQL statements.
- **TRACING** - Enables or disables request tracing.

CQL Data Definition Commands

- **CREATE KEYSPACE** - Creates a KeySpace in Cassandra.
- **USE** - Connects to a created KeySpace.
- **ALTER KEYSPACE** - Changes the properties of a KeySpace.
- **DROP KEYSPACE** - Removes a KeySpace
- **CREATE TABLE** - Creates a table in a KeySpace.
- **ALTER TABLE** - Modifies the column properties of a table.
- **DROP TABLE** - Removes a table.
- **TRUNCATE** - Removes all the data from a table.
- **CREATE INDEX** - Defines a new index on a single column of a table.
- **DROP INDEX** - Deletes a named index.

CQL Data Manipulation Commands

- **INSERT** - Adds columns for a row in a table.
- **UPDATE** - Updates a column of a row.
- **DELETE** - Deletes data from a table.
- **BATCH** - Executes multiple DML statements at once.

CQL Clauses

- **SELECT** - This clause reads data from a table
- **WHERE** - The where clause is used along with select to read a specific data.
- **ORDERBY** - The orderby clause is used along with select to read a specific data in a specific order.
- Cassandra provides documented shell commands in addition to CQL commands. Given below are the Cassandra documented shell commands.

6.19 CASSANDRA DOCUMENTED SHELL COMMANDS

Cassandra provides documented shell commands in addition to CQL commands. Given below are the Cassandra documented shell commands.

Help

The HELP command displays a synopsis and a brief description of all cqlsh commands. Given below is the usage of help command.

```
cqlsh> help
Documented shell commands:
===========================
CAPTURE COPY DESCRIBE EXPAND PAGING SOURCE
CONSISTENCY DESC EXIT HELP SHOW TRACING.
CQL help topics:
================
ALTER               CREATE_TABLE_OPTIONS        SELECT
ALTER_ADD           CREATE_TABLE_TYPES          SELECT_COLUMNFAMILY
ALTER_ALTER         CREATE_USER                 SELECT_EXPR
ALTER_DROP          DELETE                      SELECT_LIMIT
ALTER_RENAME        DELETE_COLUMNS              SELECT_TABLE
```

Capture

This command captures the output of a command and adds it to a file. For example, take a look at the following code that captures the output to a file named **Outputfile**.

```
cqlsh> CAPTURE '/home/hadoop/CassandraProgs/Outputfile'
```

When we type any command in the terminal, the output will be captured by the file given. Given below is the command used and the snapshot of the output file.

```
cqlsh:tutorialspoint> select * from emp;
```

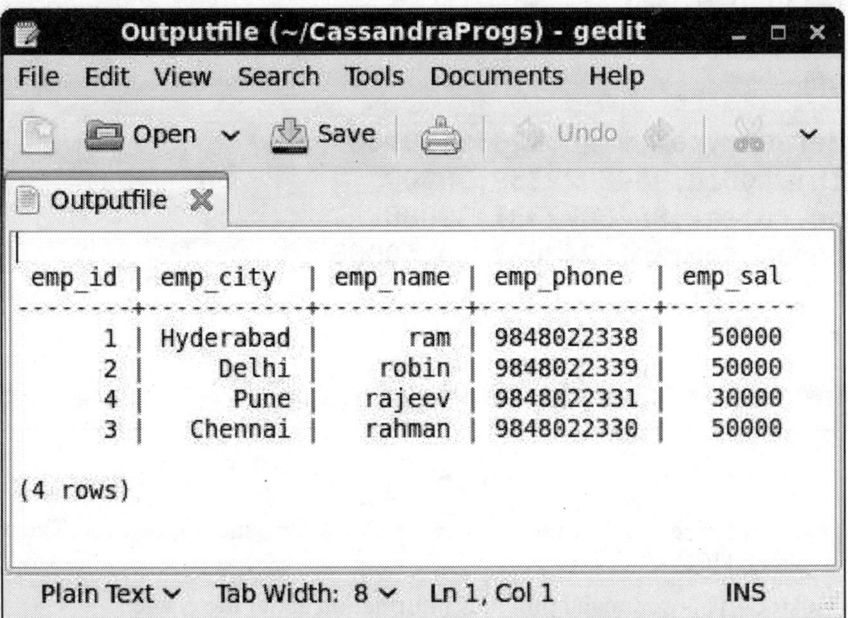

You can turn capturing off using the following command.

```
cqlsh:tutorialspoint> capture off;
```

Consistency

This command shows the current consistency level, or sets a new consistency level.

```
cqlsh:tutorialspoint> CONSISTENCY
Current consistency level is 1.
```

Copy

This command copies data to and from Cassandra to a file. Given below is an example to copy the table named **emp** to the file **myfile**.

```
cqlsh:tutorialspoint> COPY emp (emp_id, emp_city, emp_name, emp_
phone,emp_sal) TO 'myfile';
4 rows exported in 0.034 seconds.
```

If you open and verify the file given, you can find the copied data as shown below.

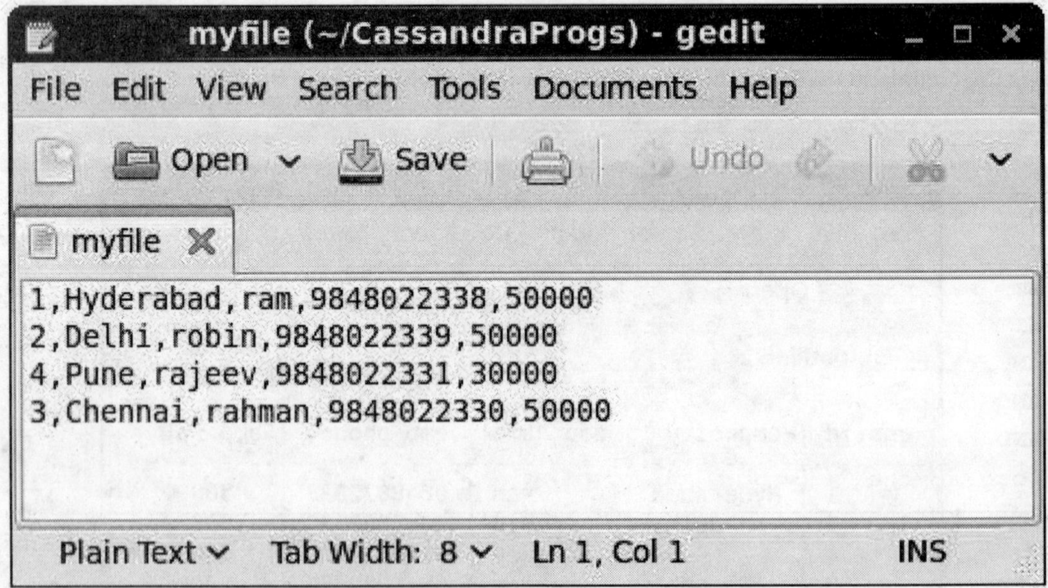

Describe

This command describes the current cluster of Cassandra and its objects. The variants of this command are explained below.

Describe cluster - This command provides information about the cluster.

```
cqlsh:tutorialspoint> describe cluster;
Cluster: Test Cluster
Partitioner: Murmur3Partitioner
Range ownership:
                 -658380912249644557 [127.0.0.1]
                 -2833890865268921414 [127.0.0.1]
                 -6792159006375935836 [127.0.0.1]
```

Describe Keyspaces - This command lists all the keyspaces in a cluster. Given below is the usage of this command.

```
cqlsh:tutorialspoint> describe keyspaces;
system_traces system tp tutorialspoint
```

Describe tables - This command lists all the tables in a keyspace. Given below is the usage of this command.

```
cqlsh:tutorialspoint> describe tables;
emp
```

Describe table - This command provides the description of a table. Given below is the usage of this command.

```
cqlsh:tutorialspoint> describe table emp;
CREATE TABLE tutorialspoint.emp (
  emp_id int PRIMARY KEY,
  emp_city text,
  emp_name text,
  emp_phone varint,
  emp_sal varint
) WITH bloom_filter_fp_chance = 0.01
  AND caching = '{"keys":"ALL", "rows_per_partition":"NONE"}'
  AND comment = ''
  AND compaction = {'min_threshold': '4', 'class':
  'org.apache.cassandra.db.compaction.SizeTieredCompactionStrategy',
  'max_threshold': '32'}

  AND compression = {'sstable_compression':
  'org.apache.cassandra.io.compress.LZ4Compressor'}

  AND dclocal_read_repair_chance = 0.1
 AND default_time_to_live = 0
  AND gc_grace_seconds = 864000
```

```
   AND max_index_interval = 2048
   AND memtable_flush_period_in_ms = 0
   AND min_index_interval = 128
   AND read_repair_chance = 0.0
   AND speculative_retry = '99.0PERCENTILE';
CREATE INDEX emp_emp_sal_idx ON tutorialspoint.emp (emp_sal);
```

Describe Type

This command is used to describe a user-defined data type. Given below is the usage of this command.

```
cqlsh:tutorialspoint> describe type card_details;
CREATE TYPE tutorialspoint.card_details (
  num int,
  pin int,
  name text,
  cvv int,
  phone set<int>,
  mail text
);
```

Given below is the usage of this command. Assume there are two user-defined data types: **card** and **card_details**.

```
cqlsh:tutorialspoint> DESCRIBE TYPES;
card_details card
```

Expand

This command is used to expand the output. Before using this command, you have to turn the expand command on. Given below is the usage of this command.

```
cqlsh:tutorialspoint> expand on;
cqlsh:tutorialspoint> select * from emp;
@ Row 1
-------------------------
   emp_id | 1
 emp_city | Hyderabad
 emp_name | ram
emp_phone | 9848022338
  emp_sal | 50000
```

```
@ Row 2
-----------+------------
    emp_id | 2
  emp_city | Delhi
  emp_name | robin
emp_phone | 9848022339
   emp_sal | 50000

@ Row 3
-----------+------------
    emp_id | 4
  emp_city | Pune
  emp_name | rajeev
emp_phone | 9848022331
   emp_sal | 30000

@ Row 4
-----------+------------
    emp_id | 3
  emp_city | Chennai
  emp_name | rahman
emp_phone | 9848022330
   emp_sal | 50000
(4 rows)
```

Note: You can turn the expand option off using the following command.

```
cqlsh:tutorialspoint> expand off;
Disabled Expanded output.
```

Exit

This command is used to terminate the cql shell.

Show

This command displays the details of current cqlsh session such as Cassandra version, host, or data type assumptions. Given below is the usage of this command.

```
cqlsh:tutorialspoint> show host;
Connected to Test Cluster at 127.0.0.1:9042.
cqlsh:tutorialspoint> show version;
[cqlsh 5.0.1 | Cassandra 2.1.2 | CQL spec 3.2.0 | Native protocol v3]
```

Source

Using this command, you can execute the commands in a file. Suppose our input file is as follows:

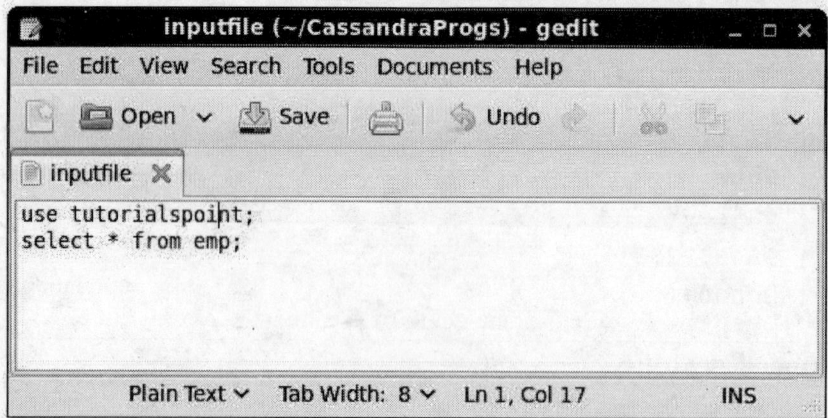

Then you can execute the file containing the commands as shown below.

```
cqlsh:tutorialspoint> source '/home/hadoop/CassandraProgs/inputfile';
emp_id |  emp_city | emp_name |  emp_phone | emp_sal
--------+-----------+----------+------------+---------
     1 | Hyderabad |   ram    | 9848022338 | 50000
     2 | Delhi     |   robin  | 9848022339 | 50000
     3 | Pune      |   rajeev | 9848022331 | 30000
     4 | Chennai   |   rahman | 9848022330 | 50000
(4 rows)
```

Creating a Keyspace using Cqlsh

A keyspace in Cassandra is a namespace that defines data replication on nodes. A cluster contains one keyspace per node. Given below is the syntax for creating a keyspace using the statement **CREATE KEYSPACE**.

Syntax

```
CREATE KEYSPACE <identifier> WITH <properties>
```

i.e.

```
CREATE KEYSPACE "KeySpace Name"
WITH replication = {'class': 'Strategy name', 'replication_factor' :
'No.Of   replicas'};
CREATE KEYSPACE "KeySpace Name"
WITH replication = {'class': 'Strategy name', 'replication_factor' :
'No.Of  replicas'}
AND durable_writes = 'Boolean value';
```

The CREATE KEYSPACE statement has two properties: replication and durable_writes.

Replication

The replication option is to specify the **Replica Placement strategy** and the number of replicas wanted. The following table lists all the replica placement strategies.

Strategy name	Description
Simple Strategy'	Specifies a simple replication factor for the cluster.
Network Topology Strategy	Using this option, you can set the replication factor for each data-center independently.
Old Network Topology Strategy	This is a legacy replication strategy.

Using this option, you can instruct Cassandra whether to use **commitlog** for updates on the current KeySpace. This option is not mandatory and by default, it is set to true.

Example

Given below is an example of creating a KeySpace.

- Here we are creating a KeySpace named TutorialsPoint.
- We are using the first replica placement strategy, i.e.., Simple Strategy.
- And we are choosing the replication factor to 1 replica.

```
cqlsh.> CREATE KEYSPACE tutorialspoint
WITH replication = {'class':'SimpleStrategy', 'replication_factor' :
3};
```

Verification

You can verify whether the table is created or not using the command **Describe**. If you use this command over keyspaces, it will display all the keyspaces created as shown below.

```
cqlsh> DESCRIBE keyspaces;
tutorialspoint system system_traces
```

Here you can observe the newly created KeySpace **tutorialspoint.**

Durable_writes

By default, the durable_writes properties of a table is set to **true,** however it can be set to false. You cannot set this property to **simplex strategy.**

Example

Given below is the example demonstrating the usage of durable writes property.

```
cqlsh> CREATE KEYSPACE test
... WITH REPLICATION = { 'class' : 'NetworkTopologyStrategy',
'datacenter1' : 3 }
... AND DURABLE_WRITES = false;
```

Verification

You can verify whether the durable_writes property of test KeySpace was set to false by querying the System Keyspace. This query gives you all the KeySpaces along with their properties.

```
cqlsh> SELECT * FROM system.schema_keyspaces;
 keyspace_name | durable_writes |                          strategy_
class | strategy_options
----------------+----------------+---------------------------------
-------------------+----------------------------
           test |          False | org.apache.cassandra.locator.
NetworkTopologyStrategy | {"datacenter1" : "3"}
tutorialspoint |           True |         org.apache.cassandra.locator.
SimpleStrategy | {"replication_factor" : "4"}
        system |           True |         org.apache.cassandra.locator.
LocalStrategy | { }
 system_traces |           True |         org.apache.cassandra.locator.
SimpleStrategy | {"replication_factor" : "2"}
(4 rows)
```

Here you can observe the durable_writes property of test KeySpace was set to false.

Using a Keyspace

You can use a created KeySpace using the keyword **USE**. Its syntax is as follows:

```
Syntax:USE <identifier>
```

Example

In the following example, we are using the KeySpace tutorialspoint.

```
cqlsh> USE tutorialspoint;
cqlsh:tutorialspoint>
```

Creating a Keyspace using Java API

You can create a Keyspace using the execute() method of Session class. Follow the steps given below to create a keyspace using Java API.

Step1: Create a Cluster Object

First of all, create an instance of Cluster.builder class of com.datastax.driver.core package as shown below.

```
//Creating Cluster.Builder object
Cluster.Builder builder1 = Cluster.builder();
```

Add a contact point (IP address of the node) using addContactPoint() method of Cluster. Builderobject. This method returns Cluster.Builder.

```
//Adding contact point to the Cluster.Builder object
Cluster.Builder builder2 = build.addContactPoint( "127.0.0.1" );
```

Using the new builder object, create a cluster object. To do so, you have a method called **build()** in the **Cluster.Builder** class. The following code shows how to create a cluster object.

```
//Building a cluster
Cluster cluster = builder.build();
```

You can build a cluster object in a single line of code as shown below.

```
Cluster cluster = Cluster.builder().addContactPoint("127.0.0.1").
build();
```

Step 2: Create a Session Object

Create an instance of **Session** object using the **connect()** method of **Cluster** class as shown below.

```
Session session = cluster.connect( );
```

This method creates a new session and initializes it. If you already have a keyspace, you can set it to the existing one by passing the keyspace name in string format to this method as shown below.

```
Session session = cluster.connect(" Your keyspace name " );
```

Step 3: Execute Query

You can execute **CQL** queries using the **execute()** method of **Session** class. Pass the query either in string format or as a **Statement** class object to the **execute()** method. Whatever you pass to this method in string format will be executed on the **cqlsh**.

In this example, we are creating a KeySpace named **tp.** We are using the first replica placement strategy, i.e., Simple Strategy, and we are choosing the replication factor to 1 replica.

You have to store the query in a string variable and pass it to the execute() method as shown below.

```
String query = "CREATE KEYSPACE tp WITH replication "
  + "= {'class':'SimpleStrategy', 'replication_factor':1}; ";
session.execute(query);
```

Step4 : Use the KeySpace

You can use a created KeySpace using the execute() method as shown below.

```
execute(" USE tp " );
```

Given below is the complete program to create and use a keyspace in Cassandra using Java API.

```
import com.datastax.driver.core.Cluster;
import com.datastax.driver.core.Session;
public class Create_KeySpace {

  public static void main(String args[]){

     //Query
    String query = "CREATE KEYSPACE tp WITH replication "
        + "= {'class':'SimpleStrategy', 'replication_factor':1};";

     //creating Cluster object
     Cluster cluster = Cluster.builder().addContactPoint("127.0.0.1").
build();

     //Creating Session object
     Session session = cluster.connect();

     //Executing the query
     session.execute(query);

     //using the KeySpace
     session.execute("USE tp");
     System.out.println("Keyspace created");
  }
}
```

Save the above program with the class name followed by .java, browse to the location where it is saved. Compile and execute the program as shown below.

```
$javac Create_KeySpace.java
$java Create_KeySpace
```

Under normal conditions, it will produce the following output:

```
Keyspace created
```

Alter Keyspace using Cqlsh

ALTER KEYSPACE can be used to alter properties such as the number of replicas and the durable_writes of a KeySpace. Given below is the syntax of this command.

Syntax

```
ALTER KEYSPACE <identifier> WITH <properties>
```

i.e.

```
ALTER KEYSPACE "KeySpace Name"
WITH replication = {'class': 'Strategy name', 'replication_factor' :
'No.Of  replicas'};
```

The properties of **ALTER KEYSPACE** are same as CREATE KEYSPACE. It has two properties: **replication** and **durable_writes**.

Durable_writes

Using this option, you can instruct Cassandra whether to use commitlog for updates on the current KeySpace. This option is not mandatory and by default, it is set to true.

Example

Given below is an example of altering a KeySpace.

- Here we are altering a KeySpace named TutorialsPoint.
- We are changing the replication factor from 1 to 3.

```
cqlsh.> ALTER KEYSPACE tutorialspoint
WITH replication = {'class':'NetworkTopologyStrategy', 'replication_
factor' : 3};
```

Altering Durable_writes

You can also alter the durable_writes property of a KeySpace. Given below is the durable_writes property of the **test**KeSpace.

```
SELECT * FROM system.schema_keyspaces;
 keyspace_name | durable_writes |     strategy_class | strategy_options
------------- +---------------+------------------+-----------------
             test |                False | org.apache.cassandra.locator.
NetworkTopologyStrategy | {"datacenter1":"3"}
tutorialspoint |            True |          org.apache.cassandra.locator.
SimpleStrategy | {"replication_factor":"4"}
       system |            True |           org.apache.cassandra.locator.
LocalStrategy | { }
 system_traces |           True |          org.apache.cassandra.locator.
SimpleStrategy | {"replication_factor":"2"}
(4 rows)
ALTER KEYSPACE test
WITH REPLICATION = {'class' : 'NetworkTopologyStrategy', 'datacenter1'
: 3}
AND DURABLE_WRITES = true;
```

Once again, if you verify the properties of KeySpaces, it will produce the following output.

```
SELECT * FROM system.schema_keyspaces;
 keyspace_name | durable_writes |     strategy_class | strategy_options
 -------------+---------------+------------------+-----------------
             test |                 True | org.apache.cassandra.locator.
NetworkTopologyStrategy | {"datacenter1":"3"}
tutorialspoint |            True |          org.apache.cassandra.locator.
SimpleStrategy | {"replication_factor":"4"}
       system |            True |           org.apache.cassandra.locator.
LocalStrategy | { }
 system_traces |           True |          org.apache.cassandra.locator.
SimpleStrategy | {"replication_factor":"2"}
 (4 rows)
```

Altering a Keyspace using Java API

You can alter a keyspace using the **execute()** method of **Session** class. Follow the steps given below to alter a keyspace using Java API

Step1: Create a Cluster Object

First of all, create an instance of **Cluster.builder** class of **com.datastax.driver.core** package as shown below.

```
//Creating Cluster.Builder object
Cluster.Builder builder1 = Cluster.builder();
```

Add a contact point (IP address of the node) using the **addContactPoint()** method of **Cluster.Builder** object. This method returns **Cluster.Builder**.

```
//Adding contact point to the Cluster.Builder object
Cluster.Builder builder2 = build.addContactPoint( "127.0.0.1" );
```

Using the new builder object, create a cluster object. To do so, you have a method called **build()** in the **Cluster.Builder** class. The following code shows how to create a cluster object.

```
//Building a cluster
Cluster cluster = builder.build();
```

You can build the cluster object using a single line of code as shown below.

```
Cluster   cluster   =   Cluster.builder().addContactPoint("127.0.0.1").
build();
```

Step 2: Create a Session Object

Create an instance of **Session** object using the **connect()** method of **Clusterclass** as shown below.

```
Session session = cluster.connect( );
```

This method creates a new session and initializes it. If you already have a keyspace, you can set it to the existing one by passing the keyspace name in string format to this method as shown below.

```
Session session = cluster.connect(" Your keyspace name " );
```

Step 3: Execute Query

You can execute CQL queries using the execute() method of Session class. Pass the query either in string format or as a**Statement** class object to the execute() method. Whatever you pass to this method in string format will be executed on the**cqlsh**.

In this example,

- We are altering a keyspace named tp. We are altering the replication option from Simple Strategy to Network Topology Strategy.
- We are altering the durable_writes to false

You have to store the query in a string variable and pass it to the execute() method as shown below.

```
//Query
String  query  =  "ALTER  KEYSPACE  tp  WITH  replication  "  +  "=
{'class':'NetworkTopologyStrategy', 'datacenter1':3}" +" AND DURABLE_
WRITES = false;";

session.execute(query);
```

Given below is the complete program to create and use a keyspace in Cassandra using Java API.

```
import com.datastax.driver.core.Cluster;
import com.datastax.driver.core.Session;
public class Alter_KeySpace {
  public static void main(String args[]){
     //Query
        String query = "ALTER KEYSPACE tp WITH replication " + "=
{'class':'NetworkTopologyStrategy', 'datacenter1':3}"
        + "AND DURABLE_WRITES = false;";
     //Creating Cluster object
     Cluster cluster = Cluster.builder().addContactPoint("127.0.0.1").
build();

     //Creating Session object
     Session session = cluster.connect();

     //Executing the query
     session.execute(query);

     System.out.println("Keyspace altered");
  }
}
```

Save the above program with the class name followed by .java, browse to the location where it is saved. Compile and execute the program as shown below.

```
$javac Alter_KeySpace.java
$java Alter_KeySpace
```

Under normal conditions, it produces the following output:

```
Keyspace Altered
```

Example of a music service

This example of a social music service requires a songs table having a title, album, and artist column, plus a column (called data) for the actual audio file itself. The table uses a UUID as a primary key.

```
CREATE TABLE songs (
 id uuid PRIMARY KEY,
 title text,
 album text,
 artist text,
 data blob
);
```

In a relational database, you would create a playlists table with a foreign key to the songs, but in Cassandra, you denormalize the data because joins are not performant in a distributed system. Later, this document covers how to use a collection to accomplish the same goal as joining the tables to tag songs. To represent the playlist data, you can create a table like this:

```
CREATE TABLE playlists (
 id uuid,
 song_order int,
 song_id uuid,
 title text,
 album text,
 artist text,
 PRIMARY KEY  (id, song_order ) );
```

The combination of the id and song_order in the playlists table uniquely identifies a row in the playlists table. You can have more than one row with the same id as long as the rows contain different song_order values.

Note: The UUID is handy for sequencing the data or automatically incrementing synchronization across multiple machines. For simplicity, an int song_order is used in this example.

Here's an example of inserting a single record into the playlist: inserting the example data into playlists

```
INSERT INTO playlists (id, song_order, song_id, title, artist, album)
 VALUES (62c36092-82a1-3a00-93d1-46196ee77204, 4,
 7db1a490-5878-11e2-bcfd-0800200c9a66,
 'Ojo Rojo', 'Fu Manchu', 'No One Rides for Free');
```

After inserting the remaining records, use the following SELECT query to display the table's data:

```
SELECT * FROM playlists;
```

```
id           | song_order | album         | artist         | song_id     | title
-------------+------------+---------------+----------------+-------------+--------------------
62c36092...  |          1 | Tres Hombres  |         ZZ Top | a3e63f8f... |           La Grange
62c36092...  |          2 | We Must Obey  |      Fu Manchu | 8a172618... |   Moving in Stereo
62c36092...  |          3 |    Roll Away  | Back Door Slam | 2b09185b... | Outside Woman Blues
```

The example below illustrates how to create a query that uses the artist as a filter:

```
SELECT album, title FROM playlists WHERE artist = 'Fu Manchu';
```

Cassandra will reject this query because the query requires a sequential scan across the entire playlists dataset, because artist is not a partition key or clustering column. By creating an index on artist, Cassandra can now pull out the records.

```
CREATE INDEX ON playlists( artist );
```

Now, you can query the playlists for songs by Fu Manchu. The output looks like this:

```
album                  | title
-----------------------+------------------
We Must Obey           | Moving in Stereo
No One Riddes for Free | Ojo Rojo
```

Hector is a high level Java client for Apache Cassandra currently in use on a number of production systems some of which have node counts into the hundreds. Issues generally are fixed as quickly as possbile and releases done frequently.

CHAPTER

7

MapReduce

7.1 INTRODUCTION TO MAPREDUCE

MapReduce is a programming model and an associated implementation for processing and generating large data sets with a parallel, distributed algorithm on a cluster.[1][2] Conceptually similar approaches have been very well known since 1995 with the Message Passing Interface [3] standard having reduce [4] and scatter operations.

A MapReduce program is composed of a **Map()** procedure (method) that performs filtering and sorting (such as sorting students by first name into queues, one queue for each name) and a **Reduce()** method that performs a summary operation (such as counting the number of students in each queue, yielding name frequencies). The "MapReduce System" (also called "infrastructure" or "framework") orchestrates the processing by marshalling the distributed servers, running the various tasks in parallel, managing all communications and data transfers between the various parts of the system, and providing for redundancy and fault tolerance.

The model is inspired by the map and reduce functions commonly used in functional programming, although their purpose in the MapReduce framework is not the same as in their original forms. The key contributions of the MapReduce framework are not the actual map and reduce functions, but the scalability and fault-tolerance achieved for a variety of applications by optimizing the execution engine once. As such, a single-threaded implementation of MapReduce will usually not be faster than a traditional (non-MapReduce) implementation, any gains are usually only seen with multi-threaded implementations. The use of this model is beneficial only when the optimized distributed shuffle operation (which reduces network communication cost) and fault tolerance features of the MapReduce framework come into play. Optimizing the communication cost is essential to a good MapReduce algorithm.

MapReduce libraries have been written in many programming languages, with different levels of optimization. A popular open-source implementation that has support for distributed shuffles is part of Apache Hadoop. The name MapReduce originally referred to the proprietary Google technology, but has since been genericized. By 2014, Google were no longer using MapReduce as a Big Data processing model, and development on Apache Mahout had moved on to more capable and less disk-oriented mechanisms that incorporated full map and reduce capabilities.

7.1.1 Overview

MapReduce is a framework for processing parallelizable problems across huge datasets using a large number of computers (nodes), collectively referred to as a cluster (if all nodes are on the same local network and use similar hardware) or a grid (if the nodes are shared across geographically and administratively distributed systems, and use more heterogenous hardware). Processing can occur on data stored either in a filesystem (unstructured) or in a database (structured). MapReduce can take advantage of locality of data, processing it on or near the storage assets in order to reduce the distance over which it must be transmitted.

- "Map" step: Each worker node applies the "map()" function to the local data, and writes the output to a temporary storage. A master node orchestrates that for redundant copies of input data, only one is processed.
- "Shuffle" step: Worker nodes redistribute data based on the output keys (produced by the "map()" function), such that all data belonging to one key is located on the same worker node.
- "Reduce" step: Worker nodes now process each group of output data, per key, in parallel.

MapReduce allows for distributed processing of the map and reduction operations. Provided that each mapping operation is independent of the others, all maps can be performed in parallel – though in practice this is limited by the number of independent data sources and/or the number of CPUs near each source. Similarly, a set of 'reducers' can perform the reduction phase, provided that all outputs of the map operation that share the same key are presented to the same reducer at the same time, or that the reduction function is associative. While this process can often appear inefficient compared to algorithms that are more sequential, MapReduce can be applied to significantly larger datasets than "commodity" servers can handle – a large server farm can use MapReduce to sort a petabyte of data in only a few hours.[12] The parallelism also offers some possibility of recovering from partial failure of servers or storage during the operation: if one mapper or reducer fails, the work can be rescheduled – assuming the input data is still available.

Another way to look at MapReduce is as a 5-step parallel and distributed computation:

1. **Prepare the Map() input** – the "MapReduce system" designates Map processors, assigns the input key value *K1* that each processor would work on, and provides that processor with all the input data associated with that key value.
2. **Run the user-provided Map() code** – Map() is run exactly once for each *K1* key value, generating output organized by key values *K2*.
3. **"Shuffle" the Map output to the Reduce processors** – the MapReduce system designates Reduce processors, assigns the *K2* key value each processor should work on, and provides that processor with all the Map-generated data associated with that key value.
4. **Run the user-provided Reduce() code** – Reduce() is run exactly once for each *K2* key value produced by the Map step.
5. **Produce the final output** – the MapReduce system collects all the Reduce output, and sorts it by *K2* to produce the final outcome.

These five steps can be logically thought of as running in sequence – each step starts only after the previous step is completed – although in practice they can be interleaved as long as the final result is not affected. In many situations, the input data might already be distributed ("sharded") among many different servers, in which case step 1 could sometimes be greatly simplified by assigning Map servers that would process the locally present input data. Similarly, step 3 could sometimes be sped up by assigning Reduce processors that are as close as possible to the Map-generated data they need to process.

7.2 HOW MAPREDUCE WORKS?

The MapReduce algorithm contains two important tasks, namely Map and Reduce.

- The Map task takes a set of data and converts it into another set of data, where individual elements are broken down into tuples (key-value pairs).
- The Reduce task takes the output from the Map as an input and combines those data tuples (key-value pairs) into a smaller set of tuples.

The reduce task is always performed after the map job.

Let us now take a close look at each of the phases and try to understand their significance.

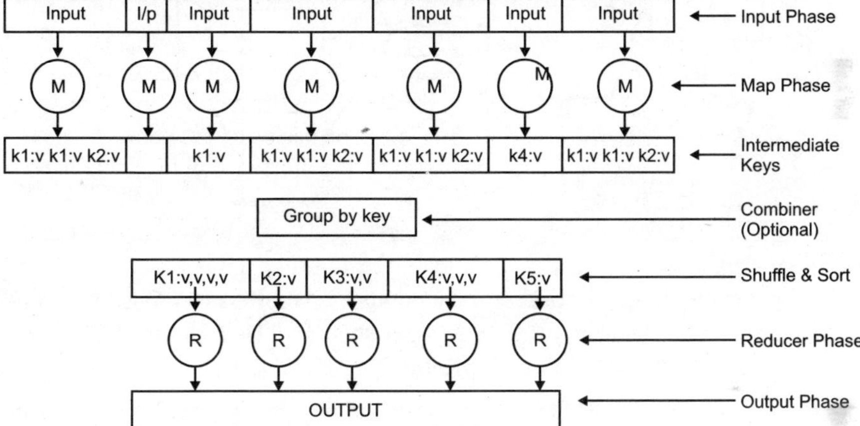

- **Input Phase** – Here we have a Record Reader that translates each record in an input file and sends the parsed data to the mapper in the form of key-value pairs.
- **Map** – Map is a user-defined function, which takes a series of key-value pairs and processes each one of them to generate zero or more key-value pairs.
- **Intermediate Keys** – The key-value pairs generated by the mapper are known as intermediate keys.
- **Combiner** – A combiner is a type of local Reducer that groups similar data from the map phase into identifiable sets. It takes the intermediate keys from the mapper as input and applies a user-defined code to aggregate the values in a small scope of one mapper. It is not a part of the main MapReduce algorithm; it is optional.
- **Shuffle and Sort** – The Reducer task starts with the Shuffle and Sort step. It downloads the grouped key-value pairs onto the local machine, where the Reducer is running. The individual key-value pairs are sorted by key into a larger data list. The data list groups the equivalent keys together so that their values can be iterated easily in the Reducer task.
- **Reducer** – The Reducer takes the grouped key-value paired data as input and runs a Reducer function on each one of them. Here, the data can be aggregated, filtered, and combined in a number of ways, and it requires a wide range of processing. Once the execution is over, it gives zero or more key-value pairs to the final step.

- **Output Phase** – In the output phase, we have an output formatter that translates the final key-value pairs from the Reducer function and writes them onto a file using a record writer.

Let us try to understand the two tasks Map & Reduce with the help of a small diagram –

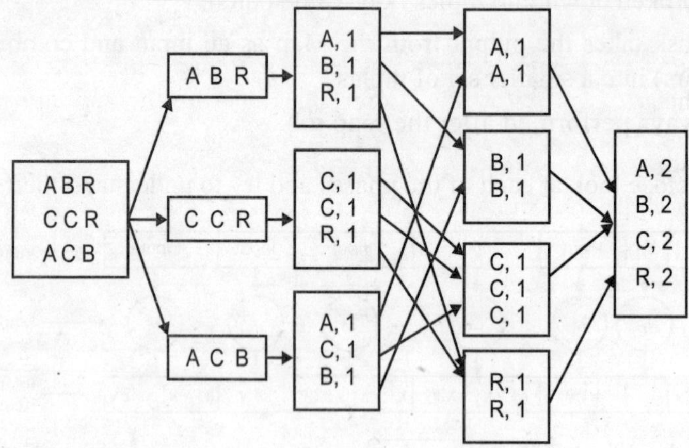

7.2.1 MapReduce-Example

Let us take a real-world example to comprehend the power of MapReduce. Twitter receives around 500 million tweets per day, which is nearly 3000 tweets per second. The following illustration shows how Tweeter manages its tweets with the help of MapReduce.

As shown in the illustration, the MapReduce algorithm performs the following actions –

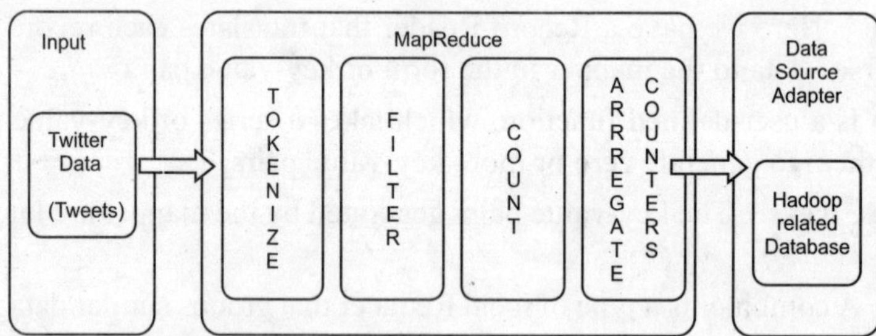

- **Tokenize** – Tokenizes the tweets into maps of tokens and writes them as key-value pairs.
- **Filter** – Filters unwanted words from the maps of tokens and writes the filtered maps as key-value pairs.
- **Count** – Generates a token counter per word.
- **Aggregate Counters** – Prepares an aggregate of similar counter values into small manageable units.

7.2.2 Hadoop's MapReduce

MapReduce applications can process large data sets in parallel by using a large number of computers, known as clusters.

In this programming paradigm, applications are divided into self-contained units of work. Each of these units of work can be run on any node in the cluster. In a Hadoop cluster, a MapReduce program is known as a job. A job is run by being broken down into pieces, known as tasks. These tasks are scheduled to run on the nodes in the cluster where the data exists.

Applications submit jobs to a specific node in a Hadoop cluster, which is running a program known as the JobTracker. The JobTracker program communicates with the NameNode to determine where all of the data required for the job exists across the cluster. The job is then broken into map tasks and reduce tasks for each node in the cluster to work on. The JobTracker program attempts to schedule tasks on the cluster where the data is stored, rather than sending data across the network to complete a task. The MapReduce framework and the Hadoop Distributed File System (HDFS) typically exist on the same set of nodes, which enables the JobTracker program to schedule tasks on nodes where the data is stored.

7.2.3 JobTracker

The JobTracker is the service within Hadoop that farms out MapReduce tasks to specific nodes in the cluster, ideally the nodes that have the data, or at least are in the same rack.

1. Client applications submit jobs to the Job tracker.
2. The JobTracker talks to the NameNode to determine the location of the data
3. The JobTracker locates TaskTracker nodes with available slots at or near the data
4. The JobTracker submits the work to the chosen TaskTracker nodes.
5. The TaskTracker nodes are monitored. If they do not submit heartbeat signals often enough, they are deemed to have failed and the work is scheduled on a different TaskTracker.
6. A TaskTracker will notify the JobTracker when a task fails. The JobTracker decides what to do then: it may resubmit the job elsewhere, it may mark that specific record as something to avoid, and it may may even blacklist the TaskTracker as unreliable.
7. When the work is completed, the JobTracker updates its status.
8. Client applications can poll the JobTracker for information.

The JobTracker is a point of failure for the Hadoop MapReduce service. If it goes down, all running jobs are halted.

As the name MapReduce implies, the reduce task is always completed after the map task. A MapReduce job splits the input data set into independent chunks that are processed by map tasks, which run in parallel. These bits, known as *tuples*, are key/value pairs. The reduce task takes the output from the map task as input, and combines the tuples into a smaller set of tuples.

A set of programs that run continuously, known as *TaskTracker* agents, monitor the status of each task. If a task fails to complete, the status of that failure is reported to the JobTracker program, which reschedules the task on another node in the cluster.

This distribution of work enables map tasks and reduce tasks to run on smaller subsets of larger data sets, which ultimately provides maximum scalability. The MapReduce framework also maximizes parallelism by manipulating data stored across multiple clusters. MapReduce applications do not have to be written in Java™, though most MapReduce programs that run natively under Hadoop are written in Java.

Hadoop MapReduce runs on the JobTracker and TaskTracker framework from Hadoop version 1.1.1, and is integrated with the new Common and HDFS features from Hadoop version 2.2.0. The MapReduce APIs used in InfoSphere® BigInsights™ are compatible with Hadoop version 2.2.0.

7.3 MAP OPERATIONS

7.3.1 What is a Map operation?

Doing something to every element in an array is a common operation:

```
var a = [1,2,3];
for (i = 0; i < a.length; i++)
a[i] = a[i] * 2;
```

New value for variable **a** would be:

```
var a = [2,4,6];
Let us repeat above and see:
```

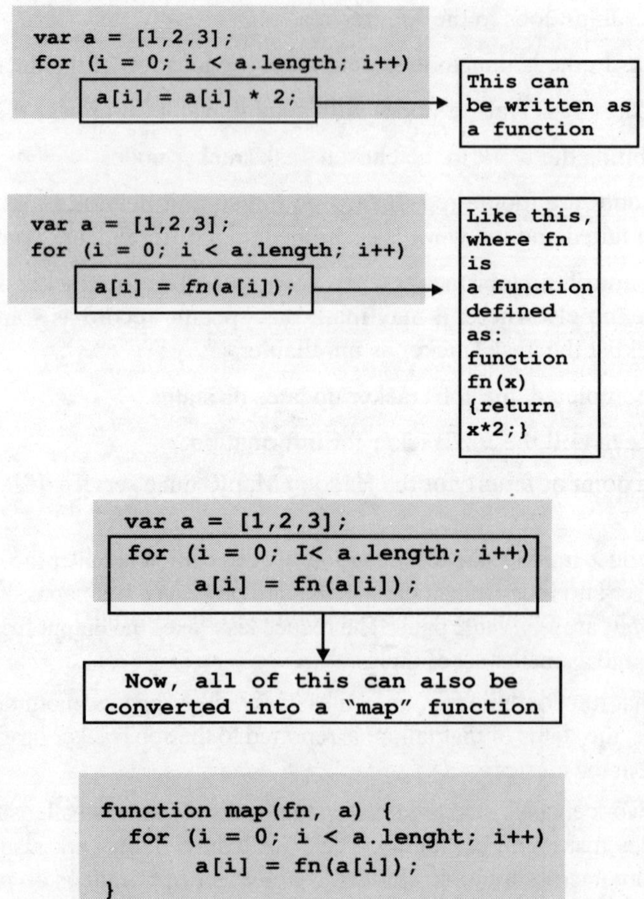

- ...like this, wher `fn` is a function passed as an argument:

```
function map(fn, a) {
  for (i = 0; i < a.length; i++)
       a[i] = fn(a[i]);
}
```

- You can invoke this map function like this:

```
map(function(x){return x*2;}, a);
```

```
map(function(x){return x*2;}, a);
```

This is function fn whose definition is included in the call

- In summary, now you can rewrite:

```
for (i = 0; i < a.length; i++)
       a[i] = a[i] * 2;
}
```

as a map operation

```
map(function (x){return x*2;}, a);
```

7.3.2 What is a Reduce Operation?

MapReduce operation has following characteristic features:

- Submitting a MapReduce job
- Distributed Mergesort Engine
- Two fundamental data types
- Fault tolerance
- Scheduling
- Task execution

Another common operation on arrays is to combine all their values:

```
function sum(a) {
  var s = 0;
  for (i  = 0; i < a.length, i++)
       s += a[i];
  return s;
}
```

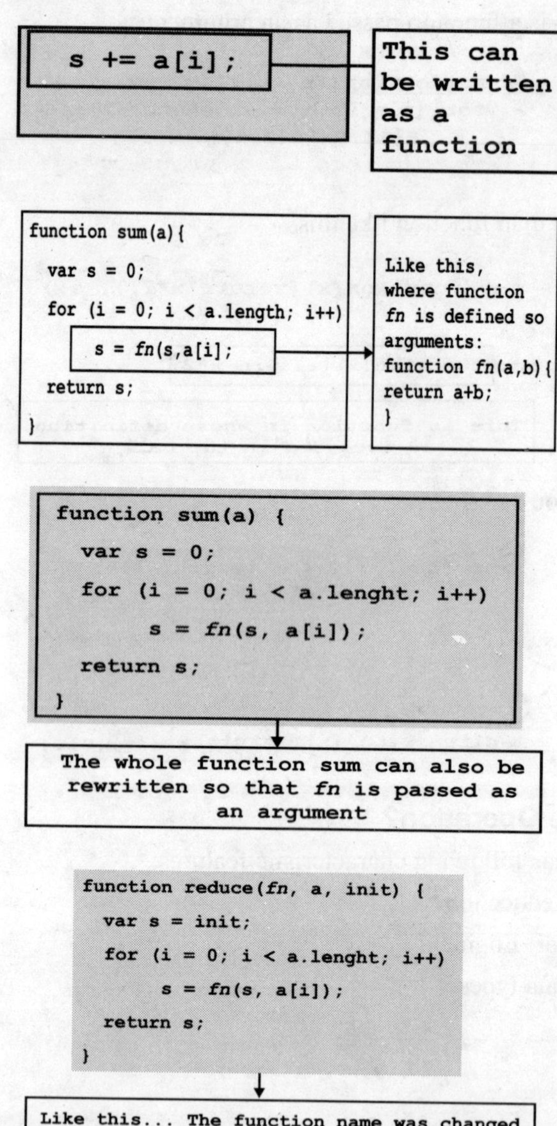

as a reduce operation:

```
reduce(function(a,b){return a+b;},a,0);
```

7.3.3 Submitting a MapReduce Job

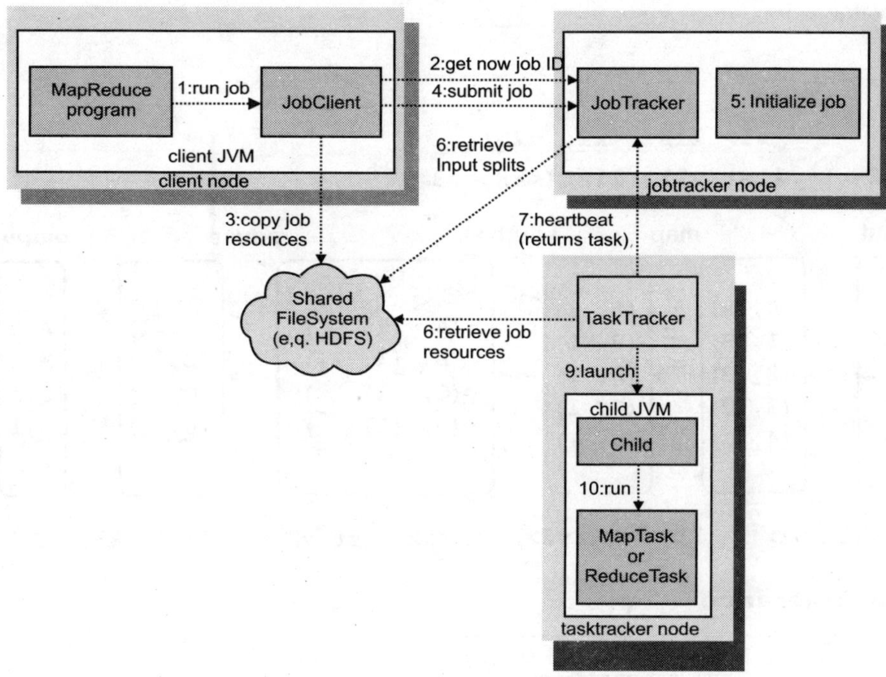

7.3.4 MapReduce – Disributed Mergesort Engine

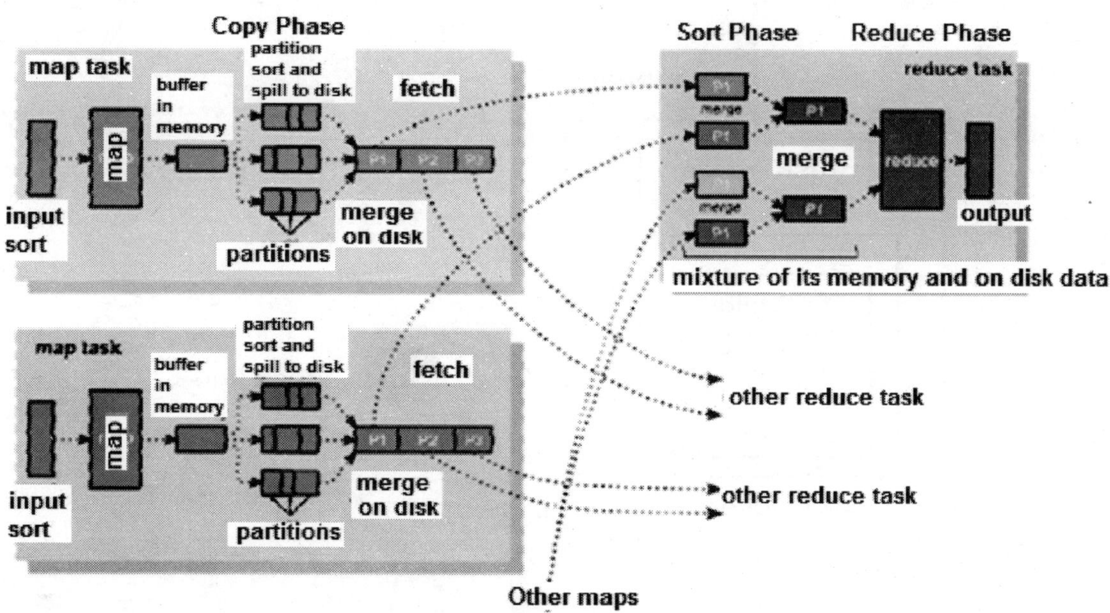

7.3.5 Two Fundamental data types

- Key/value pairs
- Lists

Input Output

```
map <k1,          v1> list(<k2, v2>)
reduce <k2,    list(v2)> list(<k3, v3>)
```

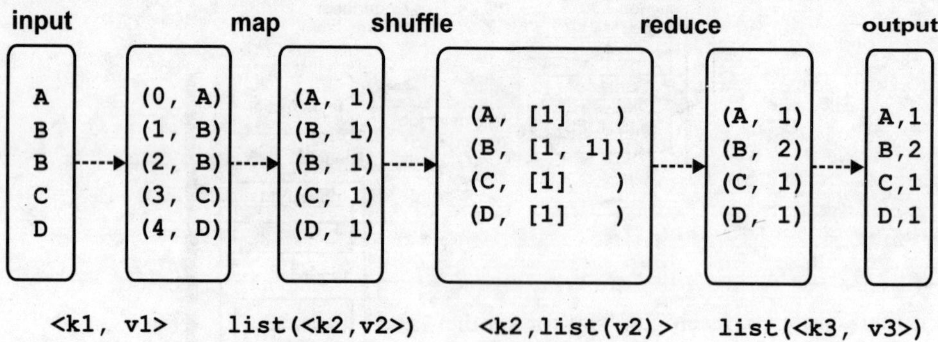

Fault Tolerance

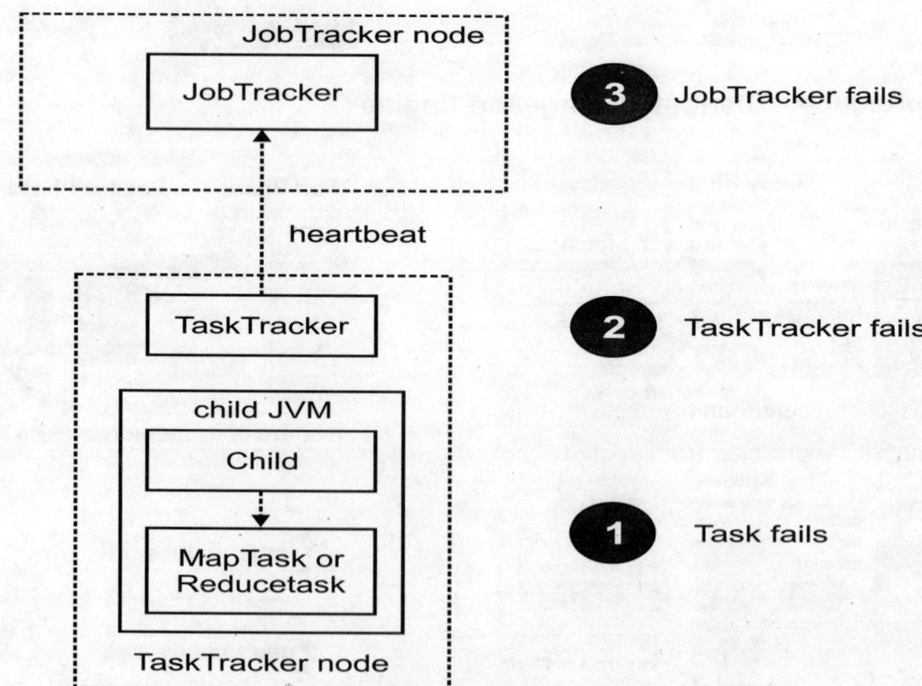

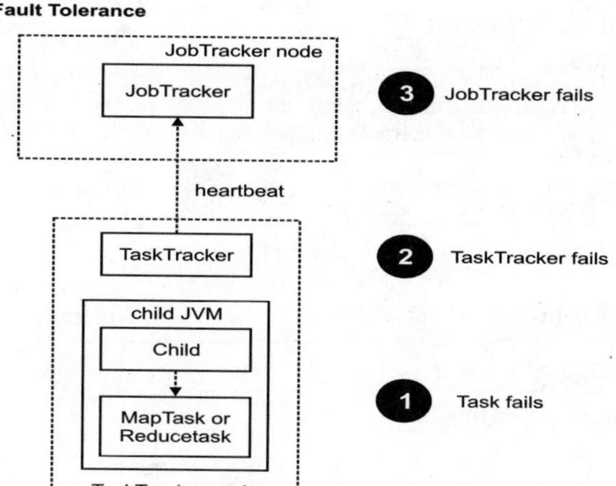

- Task Failure
- If a child task fails, the child JVM reports to the TaskTracker before it exits. Attempt is marked failed, freeing up slot for another task.
- If the child task hangs, it is killed. JobTracker reschedules the task on another machine.
- If task continues to fail, job is failed.

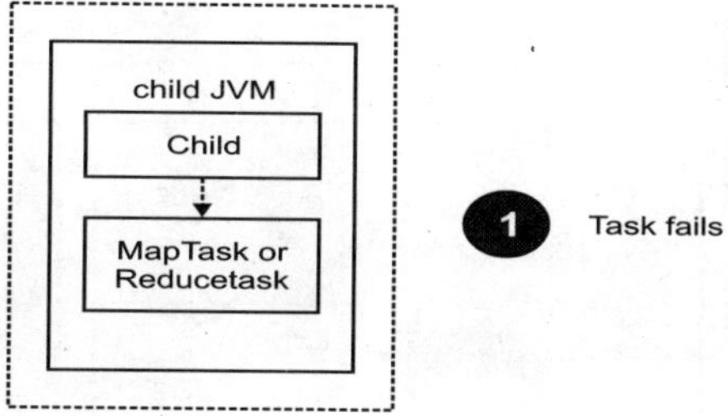

1) **TaskTracker Failure**
   - JobTracker receives no heartbeat
   - Removes TaskTracker from pool of TaskTrackers to schedule tasks on.

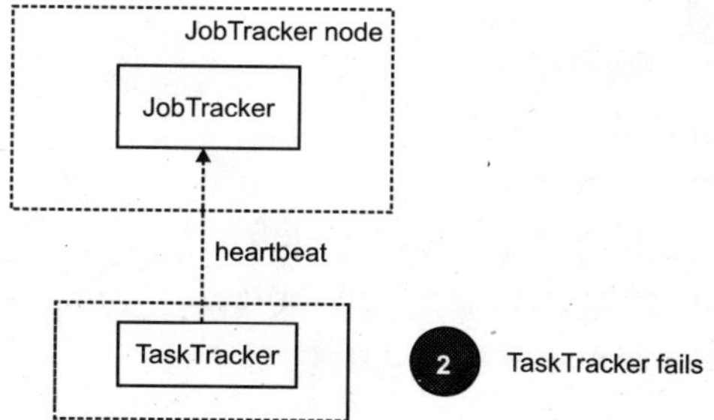

- JobTracker Failure
- Singe point of failure. Job fails

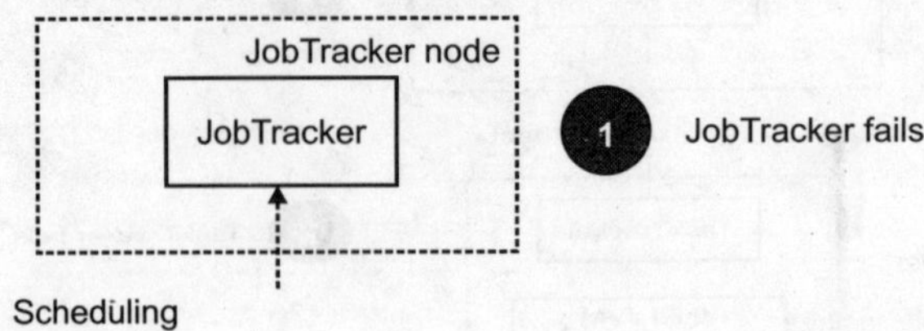

2) **Scheduling**
   - FIFO scheduler (with priorities)
   - Fair scheduler
   - Capacity scheduler

3) **Scheduling - FIFO scheduler (with priorities)**
   - Each job uses the whole cluster, so jobs wait their turn.
   - Can set priorities for the jobs in the queue (5 queues with priorities)
   - Preemption is not supported

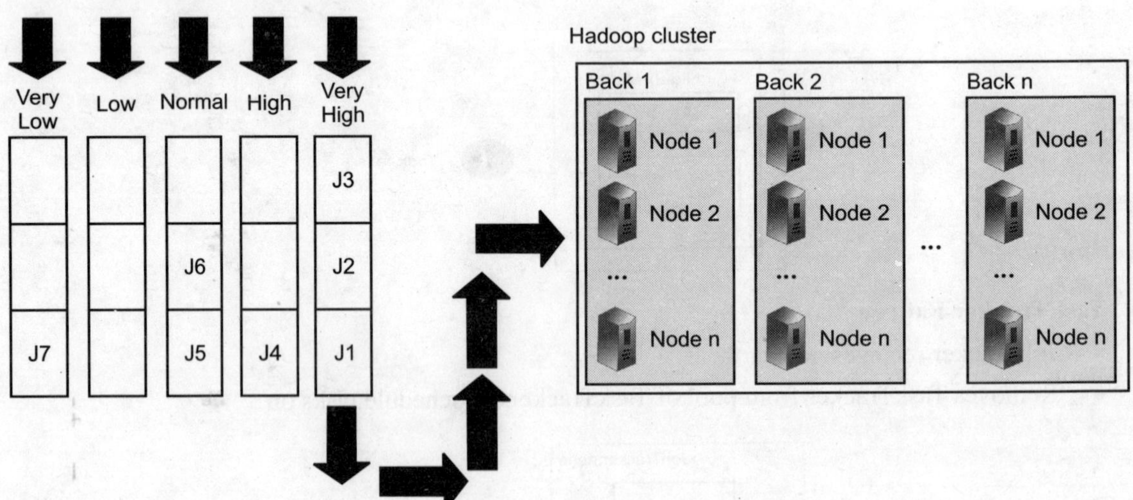

4) **Scheduling – Fair scheduler**
   - Jobs are assigned to pools (1 pool per user by default)
   - A user job pool is a number of slots assigned for tasks for that user
   - Each pool gets the same number of task slots by default

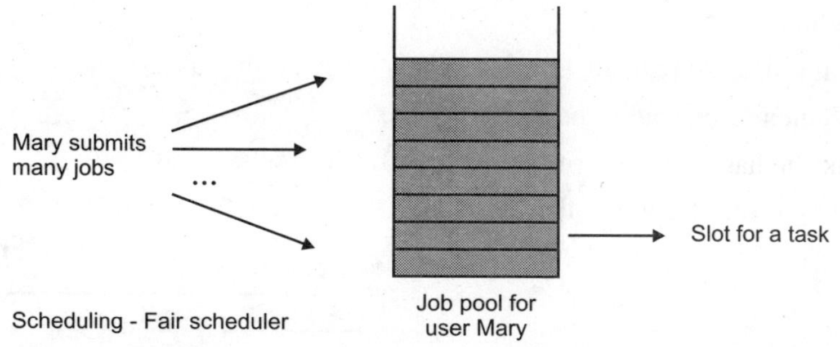

5) **Scheduling – Fair scheduler**

- Multiple users can run jobs on the cluster at the same time
- Example:
- Mary, John, Peter submit jobs that demand 80, 80, and 120 tasks

respectively

- Say the cluster has a limit to allocate 60 tasks at most
- Default behavior: Distribute task fairly among 3 users (each get 20)

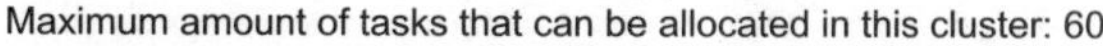

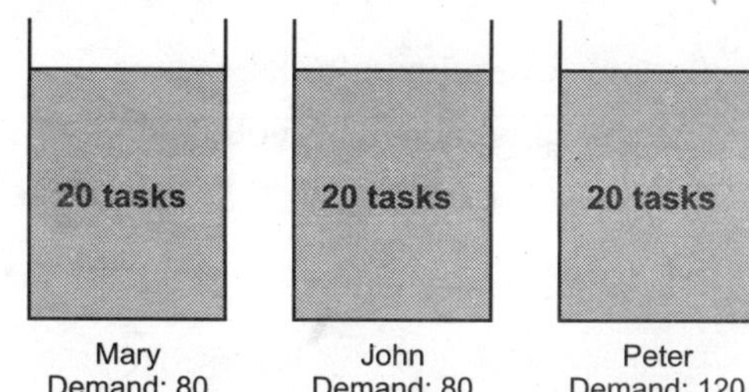

Minimum share can be set for a pool

- In the previous example, say Mary has a minimum share of 40
- Mary would be allocated 40, then the rest is distributed evenly to other pools

Maximum amount of tasks that can be allocated in this cluster: 60

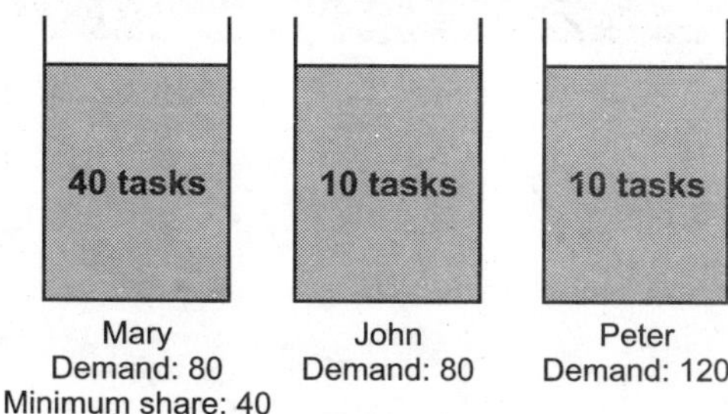

6) **Capacity scheduler**

- Similar goal to Fair scheduler: Distribute jobs fairly among users
- Works with queues instead of pools
- A user thinks he has the cluster to himself with FIFO scheduling, but actually is sharing resources with other users

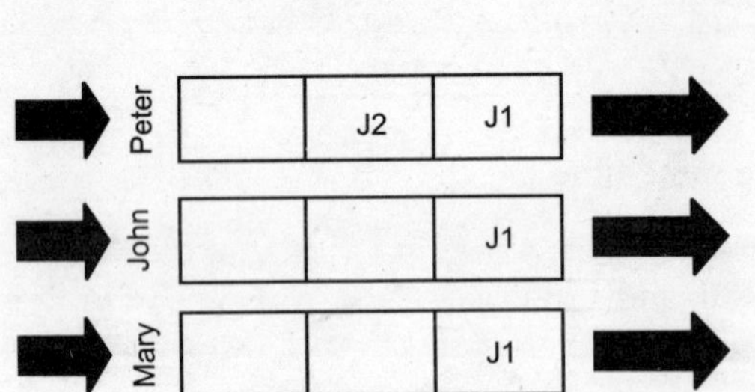

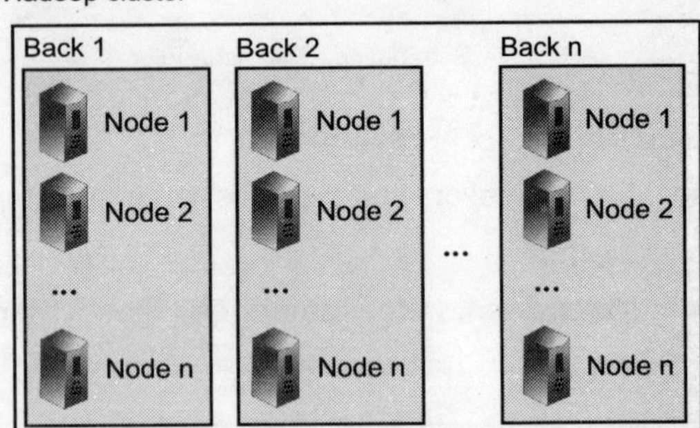

7) **Improving performance**

Speculative Execution

- Job execution is time sensitive to slow-running tasks.
- Hadoop detects slow-running tasks and launches another, equivalent

task as a backup.

- The output from the first of these tasks to finish is used.

Task JVM Reuse

- Tasks run in their own JVMs for isolation.
- Starting up a JVM is relatively expensive if jobs are short
- In these cases when jobs have many short tasks, improve

Now we shall move to actual MapReducing.

EXERCISE 7.1: RUNNING A MAPREDUCING PROGRAM (TERMINAL)

First Open up Infosphere BigInsights interface as per procrdure illustrated in Chapter 3, Exercise 3.1.

Click on BigInsight Shell and you will have following screen:

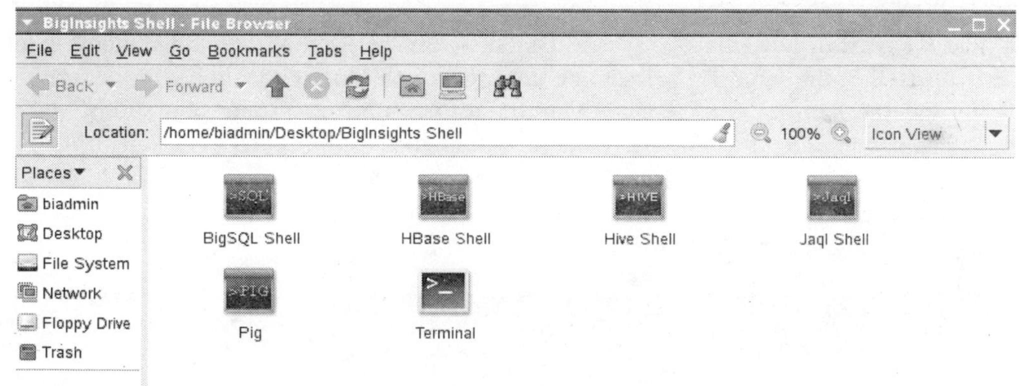

Click on Terminal. You will find Biginsight's DOS based working terminal .

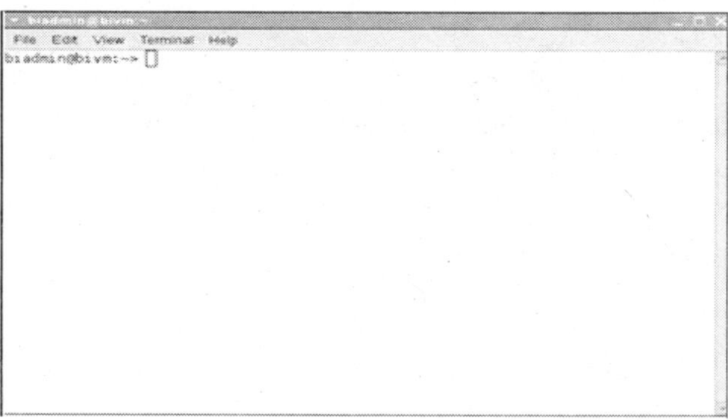

At command prompt type dir and you will find dir listing as per figure below.

```
biadmin@bivm:~
File  Edit  View  Terminal  Help
biadmin@bivm:~> dir
total 344
drwxr-xr-x  4 biadmin biadmin   4096 Feb 14 02:59 Bibkjain
drwxr-xr-x  2 biadmin biadmin   4096 Jan 31  2014 bin
drwxr-xr-x 14 biadmin biadmin   4096 Jul 15  2014 BIworkspace
-rwxrw-rw-  1 biadmin biadmin    367 May 21  2014 Clean Local BI.desktop
-rw-------  1 biadmin biadmin  21555 Feb 12 06:34 demo.txt
drwxr-xr-x  3 biadmin biadmin   4096 Jul 25  2014 Desktop
drwx------  2 biadmin biadmin   4096 Jan 31  2014 Documents
drwxr-xr-x  9 biadmin biadmin   4096 Feb 14 02:57 eclipse
-rw-r--r--  1 biadmin biadmin  12154 Jun  1  2014 fullinstall.xml
drwxr-xr-x  2 biadmin biadmin   4096 Jun 15  2014 licenses
drwxrwxrwx  4 biadmin biadmin   4096 Feb 12 06:48 sampleData
-rw-r--r--  1 root    root    269[illegible]30 Mar 22  2014 wlpConsole.log
-rw-r--r--  1 biadmin biadmin     30 Mar 22  2014 WordCount.txt
biadmin@bivm:~> 
```

Now that we've seen how the FileSystem (fs) shell can be used to execute Hadoop commands to interact with HDFS, the same fs shell can be used to launch MapReduce jobs. In this exercise, we will walk through the steps required to run a MapReduce program. The source code for a MapReduce program is contained in a complied .jar file. Hadoop will load the JAR into HDFS and distribute it to the data nodes, where the individual tasks of the MapReduce job will be executed. Hadoop ships with some example MapReduce programs to run. One of these is a distributed WordCount program that reads text files and counts the frequency of each word.

7.4 RUNNING A MAPREDUCE PROGRAM (TERMINAL)

First we need to copy the data files from the local file system to HDFS.

1. Open a Terminal and enter cd $BIGINSIGHTS_HOME/bin

Insert following at command line to invoke hadoop:

biadmin@bivm:-> hadoop fs –ls

to see the directories. Here bi represents BigInsight and vm represents Virtual Machine that generates the interface. Following screen may appear:

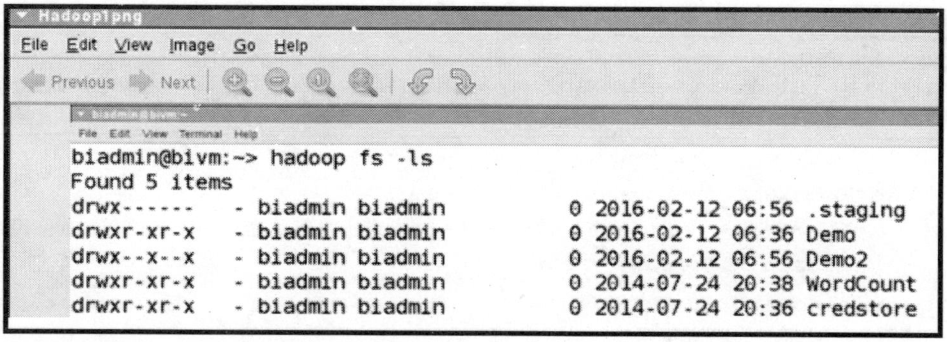

```
Hadoop1png
File Edit View Image Go Help
Previous Next
biadmin@bivm:~
File Edit View Terminal Help
biadmin@bivm:~> hadoop fs -ls
Found 5 items
drwx------   - biadmin biadmin          0 2016-02-12 06:56 .staging
drwxr-xr-x   - biadmin biadmin          0 2016-02-12 06:36 Demo
drwx--x--x   - biadmin biadmin          0 2016-02-12 06:56 Demo2
drwxr-xr-x   - biadmin biadmin          0 2014-07-24 20:38 WordCount
drwxr-xr-x   - biadmin biadmin          0 2014-07-24 20:36 credstore
```

Create a new directory (folder) by name Dummy1 at this level by entering following code at command line:

hadoop fs -mkdir Dummy1

and press enter. Beware of case sensitivity in writing the names and commands.

New list of directory shall appear as shown below indicating that a folder by name Dummy1 has been created;

```
biadmin@bivm:~> hadoop fs -mkdir Dummy1
biadmin@bivm:~> hadoop fs -ls
Found 6 items
drwx------   - biadmin biadmin          0 2016-02-12 06:56 .staging
drwxr-xr-x   - biadmin biadmin          0 2016-02-12 06:36 Demo
drwx--x--x   - biadmin biadmin          0 2016-02-12 06:56 Demo2
drwxr-xr-x   - biadmin biadmin          0 2016-02-15 07:23 Dummy1
drwxr-xr-x   - biadmin biadmin          0 2014-07-24 20:38 WordCount
drwxr-xr-x   - biadmin biadmin          0 2014-07-24 20:36 credstore
```

Type following at command prompt:

hadoop fs -put /home/biadmin/Demo.txt /user/biadmin/Dummy1

and press enter, to see following message:

```
biadmin@bivm:~> hadoop fs -put /home/biadmin/Demo.txt /user/biadmin/Dummy1
put: `/home/biadmin/Demo.txt': No such file or directory
```

This because we have entred the name of file Demo.txt with capital D in the name of file, so correct it and write like this:

hadoop fs -put /home/biadmin/demo.txt /user/biadmin/Dummy1

to see following on screen:

```
biadmin@bivm:~> hadoop fs -put /home/biadmin/demo.txt /user/biadmin/Dummy1
```

Now enter following at command line to verify whether The new directory has been created.:

Hadoop fs -ls Dummy1

```
biadmin@bivm:~> hadoop fs -ls Dummy1
Found 1 items
-rw-r--r--   1 biadmin biadmin      21555 2016-02-15 07:31 Dummy1/demo.txt
biadmin@bivm:~>
```

2. Execute the commands below to copy the input files into HDFS.

```
hadoop fs -mkdir /user/biadmin/input hadoop fs -put  /home/biadmin/
  sampleData/IBMWatson/*.txt
  /user/biadmin/input
```

Note: The above command is in a continuous line.

```
biadmin@bivm:~
File  Edit  View  Terminal  Tabs  Help
[biadmin@bivm ~]$ hadoop fs -mkdir /user/biadmin/input
[biadmin@bivm ~]$ hadoop fs -put /home/biadmin/sampleData/IBMWatson/*.txt /user/biadmin/input
[biadmin@bivm ~]$
```

3. Review the files have been copied with the following command:

```
hadoop fs -ls input
```

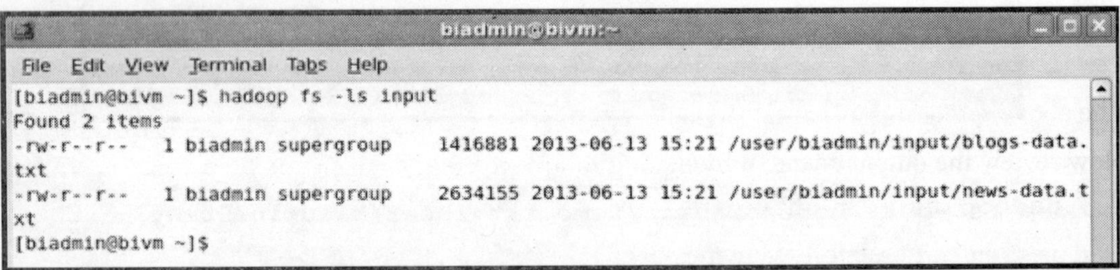

4. Now we can run the wordconut job with the command below.

```
Hadoop jar / opt/ibm/biginsights/IHC/hadoop-examples-1.1.1.jar wordcount/
user/biadmin/input output
```

Note: if the output folder already exists or if you try to rerun a successful Mapper job with the same parameters, the default behavior of MapReduce is to abort the processing.You should see an output error like this:

```
13/05/16 08:38:41 ERROR security. UserGroupInformation:
PriviledgedActionException as :biadmin
Cause : org.apache.hadoop.Mapred.FileAlreadyExistsException:
Output directory output already exists
```

```
bladmin@bivm:~
File Edit View Terminal Tabs Help
[biadmin@bivm ~]$ hadoop jar /opt/ibm/biginsights/IHC/hadoop-examples-1.1.1.jar
wordcount /user/biadmin/input output
13/06/14 11:44:27 INFO input.FileInputFormat: Total input paths to process : 2
13/06/14 11:44:28 INFO mapred.JobClient: Running job: job_201306141141_0001
13/06/14 11:44:29 INFO mapred.JobClient:  map 0% reduce 0%
13/06/14 11:44:37 INFO mapred.JobClient:  map 50% reduce 0%
13/06/14 11:44:38 INFO mapred.JobClient:  map 100% reduce 0%
13/06/14 11:44:45 INFO mapred.JobClient:  map 100% reduce 33%
13/06/14 11:44:47 INFO mapred.JobClient:  map 100% reduce 100%
13/06/14 11:44:49 INFO mapred.JobClient: Job complete: job_201306141141_0001
13/06/14 11:44:49 INFO mapred.JobClient: Counters: 29
13/06/14 11:44:49 INFO mapred.JobClient:   Job Counters
13/06/14 11:44:49 INFO mapred.JobClient:     Data-local map tasks=2
13/06/14 11:44:49 INFO mapred.JobClient:     SLOTS_MILLIS_MAPS=13083
13/06/14 11:44:49 INFO mapred.JobClient:     Launched map tasks=2
13/06/14 11:44:49 INFO mapred.JobClient:     Total time spent by all reduces wai
ting after reserving slots (ms)=0
13/06/14 11:44:49 INFO mapred.JobClient:     Total time spent by all maps waitin
g after reserving slots (ms)=0
13/06/14 11:44:49 INFO mapred.JobClient:     Launched reduce tasks=1
13/06/14 11:44:49 INFO mapred.JobClient:     SLOTS_MILLIS_REDUCES=9220
13/06/14 11:44:49 INFO mapred.JobClient:   File Input Format Counters
13/06/14 11:44:49 INFO mapred.JobClient:     Bytes Read=4051036
13/06/14 11:44:49 INFO mapred.JobClient:   File Output Format Counters
```

The above screenshot is partial, actually you may see a long output screen.

5. Now review the output of step 3 by issuing following command:

   `hadoop fs -ls output`

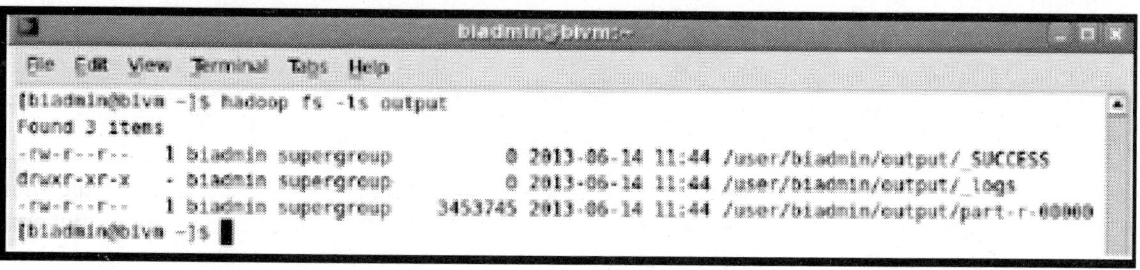

In this case, the output was not split into multiple files (i.e. part-r-00001, part-r-00002, etc)

6. To view the contents of *part-r-0000* file issue the command below:

   `hadoop fs -cat output/*00`

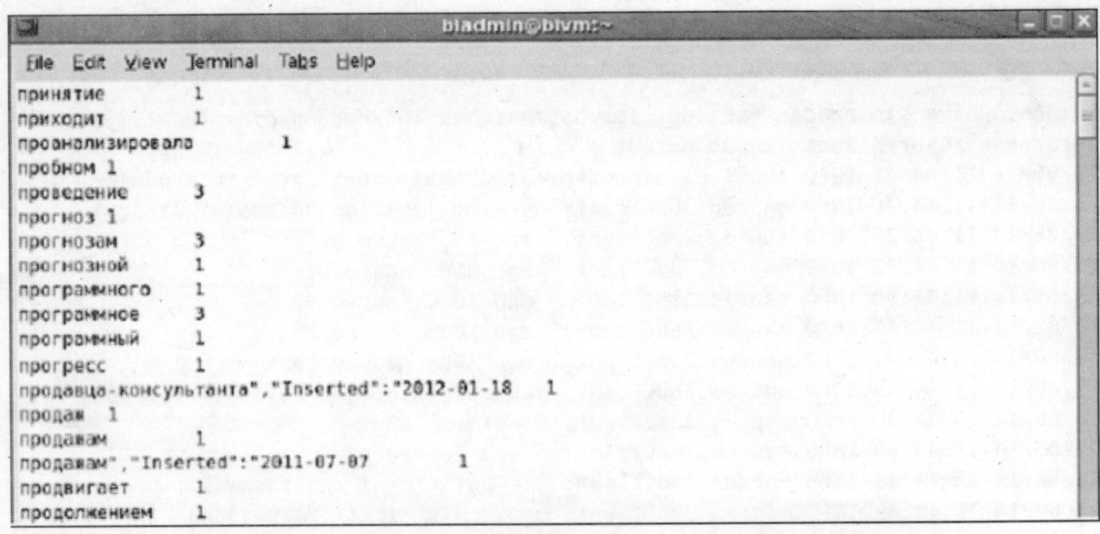

EXERCISE 7.2: RUNNING A MAPREDUCE PROGRAM (WEB CONSOLE)

1. Launch the Web Console by clicking on the BigInsights WebConsole icon

2. Click on the **Applications** tab. An application catalog is displayed in the pane at left. As you can see there are currently no deployed applications on this VM. (Administrators can upload and "publish" in-house or third-party applications as desired, as well as remove sample applications).

3. Click on the **Manage** link. The left pane is a tree of folders that contain sample applications. The right pane is a list of the actual sample applications. Notice how they all say not deployed.

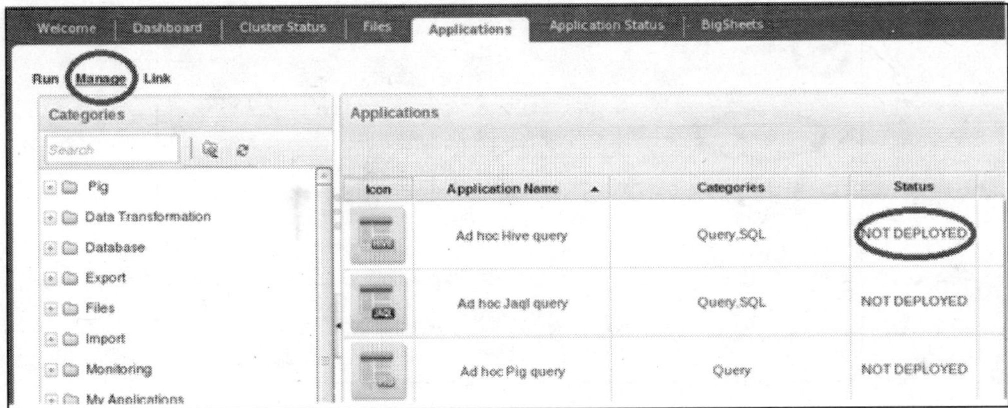

4. In the search box, type in **Word Count** to search for the word count applications. Once you see the application in the right pane select it. The Web Console displays information about this applications and status in the pane at right. If it is not yet deployed, click on the **Deploy** button as shown below, then click Deploy on the modal dialog that pops up.

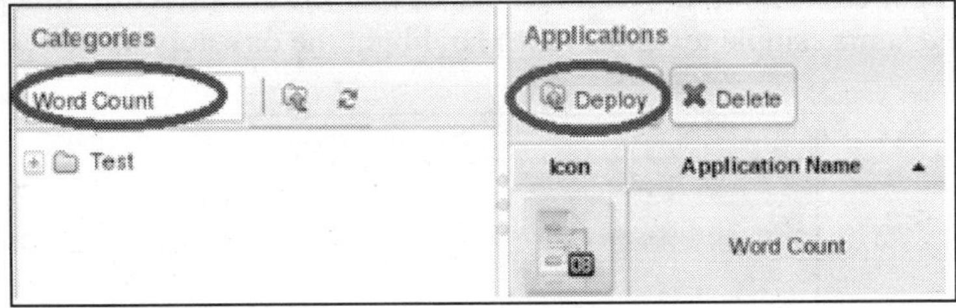

5. When the operation completes, verify that the Web console indicates that the application was successfully deployed. Specifically, confirm that the button in the upper right corner has changed to **Undeploy** and that the **Delete** button beside it is no longer active. (Deployed applications can't be deleted; they must be "undeployed" first, and then they can be deleted from the catalog.) You're now ready to run this application.

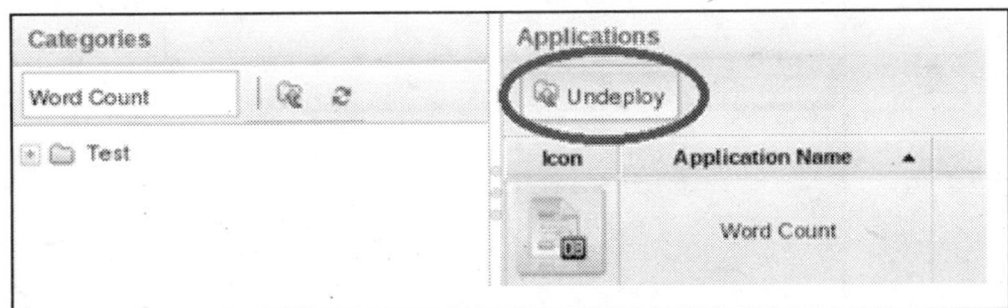

6. Click on the **Run** link to view deployed applications including the Word Count application you just deployed. If desired, you can begin to type “Word Count” into the search box to quickly access it when you are in the Run pane.

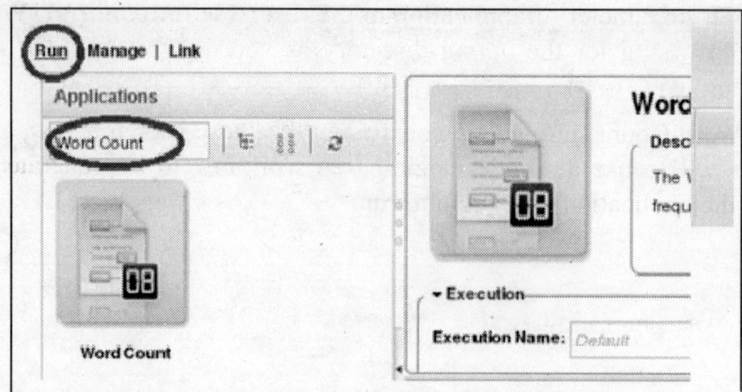

7. Once you have selected the Word Count Application shown above, in the **Execution Name** box, enter **MapReduceTest**. Do NOT click the **Run** button yet.
8. In the **Parameters** area, specify the **Input path** directory by clicking on the **Browse** button.
9. When a pop-up window appears, expand the HDFS directory tree to locate the /user/biadmin/input directory. (As you'll recall, you created this directory in a previous module of this lab and uploaded some sample text files to it.) Highlight the directory and click **OK.**

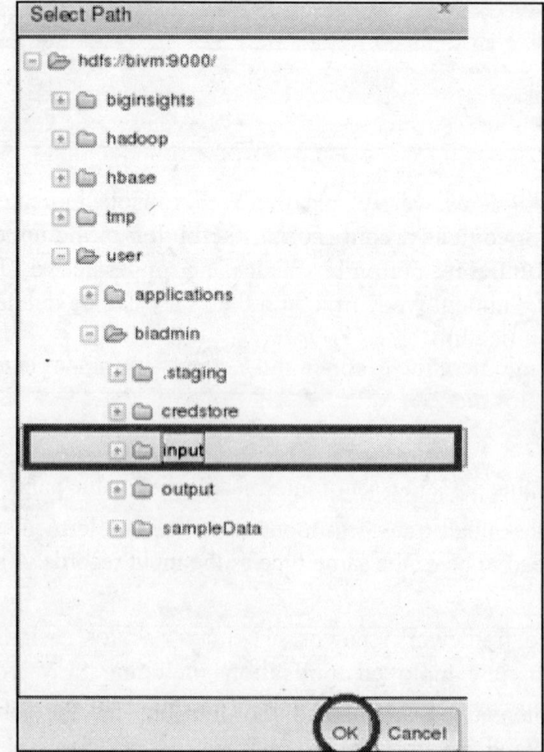

10. Set the **Output path** parameter of application to the **/user/biadmin/output_WC** (You can create this directory by browsing for the *output* directory as you did for the *input* directory and then manually appending **_WC** to it).
11. Verify that your Word Count settings are consistent with those shown below, and press the green **Run** button. This will cause a simple Oozie-based workflow to be generated for your job (or application), and the application will begin to run.

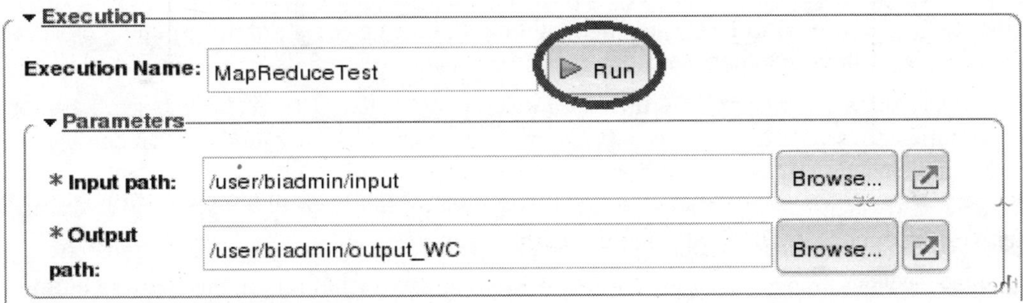

7.5 MAPREDUCE - USER INTERFACES

This section provides a reasonable amount of detail on every user-facing aspect of the MapReduce framework. This should help users implement, configure and tune their jobs in a fine-grained manner. However, please note that the javadoc for each class/interface remains the most comprehensive documentation available; this is only meant to be a tutorial.

Let us first take the Mapper and Reducer interfaces. Applications typically implement them to provide the map and reduce methods.

We will then discuss other core interfaces including JobConf, JobClient, Partitioner, OutputCollector, Reporter, InputFormat, OutputFormat, OutputCommitter and others.

Finally, we will wrap up by discussing some useful features of the framework such as the DistributedCache, IsolationRunner etc.

Payload

Applications typically implement the Mapper and Reducer interfaces to provide the map and reduce methods. These form the core of the job.

(a) Mapper

Mapper maps input key/value pairs to a set of intermediate key/value pairs.

Maps are the individual tasks that transform input records into intermediate records. The transformed intermediate records do not need to be of the same type as the input records. A given input pair may map to zero or many output pairs.

The Hadoop MapReduce framework spawns one map task for each InputSplit generated by the InputFormat for the job.

Overall, Mapper implementations are passed the JobConf for the job via the JobConfigurable. configure(JobConf) method and override it to initialize themselves. The framework then calls map(WritableComparable, Writable, OutputCollector, Reporter) for each key/value pair in the InputSplit for that task. Applications can then override the Closeable.close() method to perform any required cleanup.

Output pairs do not need to be of the same types as input pairs. A given input pair may map to zero or many output pairs. Output pairs are collected with calls to OutputCollector.collect(WritableComparable,Writable).

Applications can use the Reporter to report progress, set application-level status messages and update Counters, or just indicate that they are alive.

All intermediate values associated with a given output key are subsequently grouped by the framework, and passed to the Reducer(s) to determine the final output. Users can control the grouping by specifying a Comparator via JobConf.setOutputKeyComparatorClass(Class).

The Mapper outputs are sorted and then partitioned per Reducer. The total number of partitions is the same as the number of reduce tasks for the job. Users can control which keys (and hence records) go to which Reducer by implementing a custom Partitioner.

Users can optionally specify a combiner, via JobConf.setCombinerClass(Class), to perform local aggregation of the intermediate outputs, which helps to cut down the amount of data transferred from the Mapper to the Reducer.

The intermediate, sorted outputs are always stored in a simple (key-len, key, value-len, value) format. Applications can control if, and how, the intermediate outputs are to be compressed and the CompressionCodec to be used via the JobConf.

How Many Maps?

The number of maps is usually driven by the total size of the inputs, that is, the total number of blocks of the input files.

The right level of parallelism for maps seems to be around 10-100 maps per-node, although it has been set up to 300 maps for very cpu-light map tasks. Task setup takes awhile, so it is best if the maps take at least a minute to execute.

Thus, if you expect 10TB of input data and have a blocksize of 128MB, you'll end up with 82,000 maps, unless setNumMapTasks(int) (which only provides a hint to the framework) is used to set it even higher.

(b) Reducer

Reducer reduces a set of intermediate values which share a key to a smaller set of values.

The number of reduces for the job is set by the user via JobConf.setNumReduceTasks(int).

Overall, Reducer implementations are passed the JobConf for the job via the JobConfigurable. configure(JobConf) method and can override it to initialize themselves. The framework then calls reduce(WritableComparable, Iterator, OutputCollector, Reporter) method for each <key, (list of values)> pair in the grouped inputs. Applications can then override the Closeable.close() method to perform any required cleanup.

Reducer has 3 primary phases: shuffle, sort and reduce.

- Shuffle

Input to the Reducer is the sorted output of the mappers. In this phase the framework fetches the relevant partition of the output of all the mappers, via HTTP.

- Sort

The framework groups Reducer inputs by keys (since different mappers may have output the same key) in this stage.

The shuffle and sort phases occur simultaneously; while map-outputs are being fetched they are merged.

The major advantage of MapReduce is that it is easy to scale data processing over multiple computing nodes. Under the MapReduce model, the data processing primitives are called mappers and reducers. Decomposing a data processing application into mappers and reducers is sometimes nontrivial. But, once we write an application in the MapReduce form, scaling the application to run over hundreds, thousands, or even tens of thousands of machines in a cluster is merely a configuration change. This simple scalability is what has attracted many programmers to use the MapReduce model.

The Algorithm

- Generally MapReduce paradigm is based on sending the computer to where the data resides!
- MapReduce program executes in three stages, namely map stage, shuffle stage, and reduce stage.
  - ♦ **Map stage** : The map or mapper's job is to process the input data. Generally the input data is in the form of file or directory and is stored in the Hadoop file system (HDFS). The input file is passed to the mapper function line by line. The mapper processes the data and creates several small chunks of data.
  - ♦ **Reduce stage** : This stage is the combination of the **Shuffle** stage and the **Reduce** stage. The Reducer's job is to process the data that comes from the mapper. After processing, it produces a new set of output, which will be stored in the HDFS.
- During a MapReduce job, Hadoop sends the Map and Reduce tasks to the appropriate servers in the cluster.
- The framework manages all the details of data-passing such as issuing tasks, verifying task completion, and copying data around the cluster between the nodes.
- Most of the computing takes place on nodes with data on local disks that reduces the network traffic.
- After completion of the given tasks, the cluster collects and reduces the data to form an appropriate result, and sends it back to the Hadoop server.

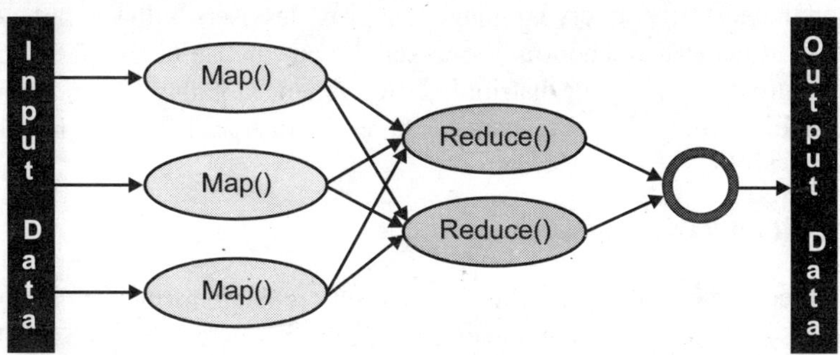

CHAPTER

8

JAQL : JSON based Query Language

8.1 INTRODUCTION TO JAQL

Jaql is a query language for JavaScript Object Notation or JSON. Although Jaql has been designed specifically for JSON, The firm has tried to borrow some of the best features of SQL, XQuery, LISP, and PigLatin. Jaql high-level design objectives include:

1. Semi-structured analytics: easy manipulation and analysis of JSON data
2. Parallelism: Jaql queries that process large amounts of data must be able to take advantage of scaled-out architectures
3. Extensibility: users must be able to easily extend Jaql

Jaql is a functional, declarative query language that provides users with a simple, declarative syntax to process large sets of structured and nontraditional data. You can use Jaql to perform activities such as select, filter, join, and group data in your distributed file system. Jaql also allows user-defined functions to be written and used in expressions. For parallel functionality, Jaql rewrites high-level queries into lower-level MapReduce jobs.

8.2 INTRODUCTION TO JSON

JSON (JavaScript Object Notation) is a lightweight data-interchange format. It is easy for humans to read and write. It is easy for machines to parse and generate. It is based on a subset of the JavaScript Programming Language, Standard ECMA-262 3rd Edition - December 1999. JSON is a text format that is completely language independent but uses conventions that are familiar to programmers of the C-family of languages, including C, C++, C#, Java, JavaScript, Perl, Python, and many others. These properties make JSON an ideal data-interchange language.

JSON is built on two structures:

- A collection of name/value pairs. In various languages, this is realized as an object, record, struct, dictionary, hash table, keyed list, or associative array.
- An ordered list of values. In most languages, this is realized as an array, vector, list, or sequence.

These are universal data structures. Virtually all modern programming languages support them in one form or another. It makes sense that a data format that is interchangeable with programming languages also be based on these structures.

In JSON, they take on these forms:

An *object* is an unordered set of name/value pairs. An object begins with { (left brace) and ends with } (right brace). Each name is followed by : (colon) and the name/value pairs are separated by , (comma).

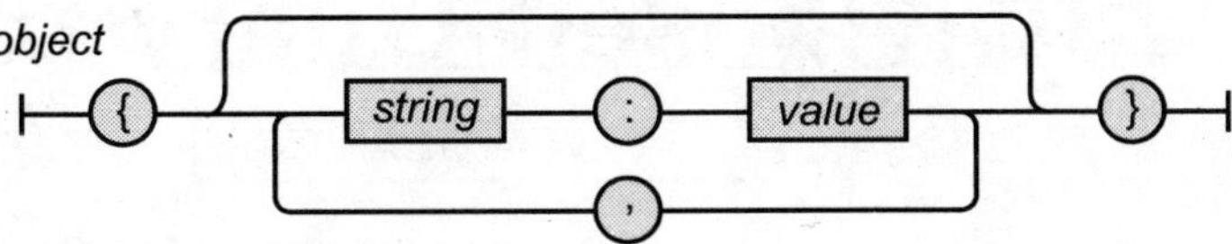

An *array* is an ordered collection of values. An array begins with [(left bracket) and ends with] (right bracket). Values are separated by , (comma).

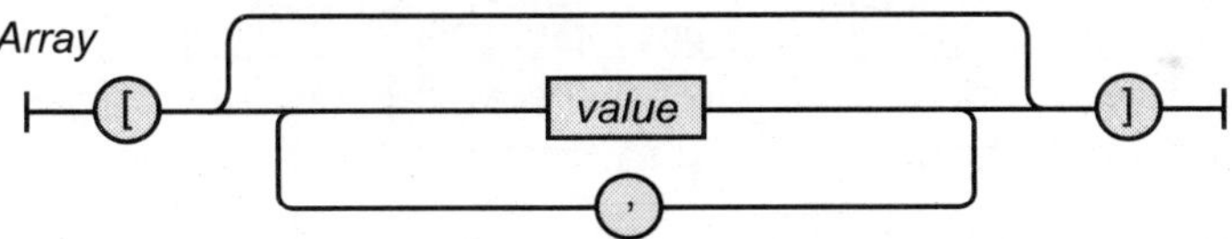

A *value* can be a *string* in double quotes, or a *number*, or `true` or `false` or `null`, or an *object* or an *array*. These structures can be nested.

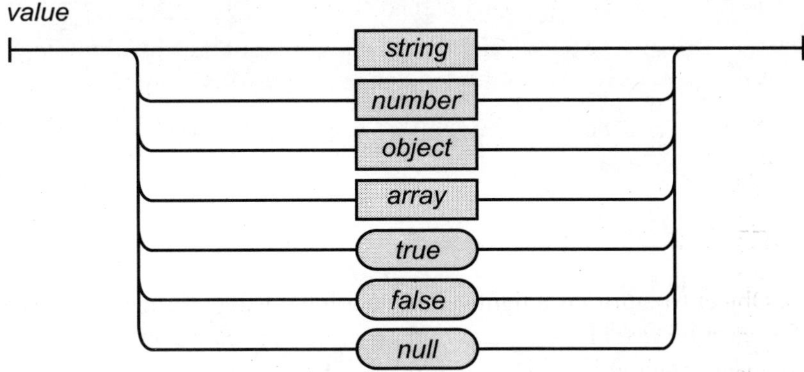

A *string* is a sequence of zero or more Unicode characters, wrapped in double quotes, using backslash escapes. A character is represented as a single character string. A string is very much like a C or Java string.

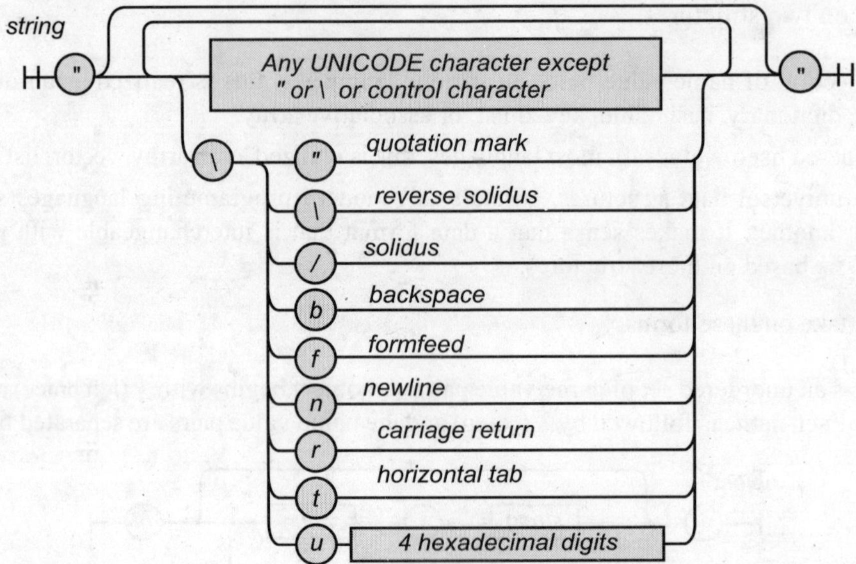

A *number* is very much like a C or Java number, except that the octal and hexadecimal formats are not used.

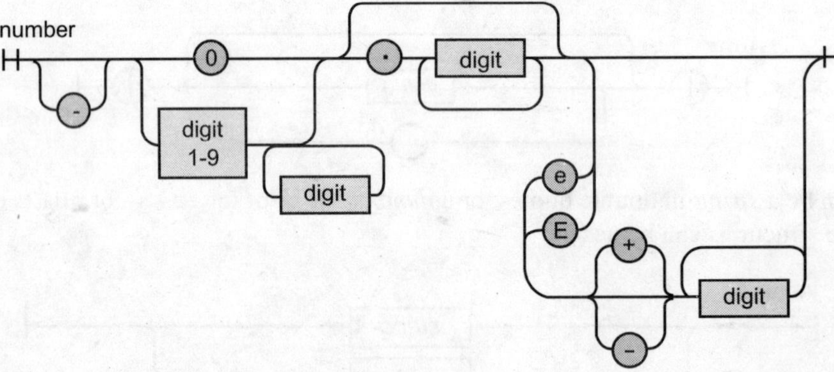

Whitespace can be inserted between any pair of tokens. Excepting a few encoding details, that completely describes the language.

8.3 COMPONENTS OF JAQL

The high-level architecture components for Jaql are:

1. A declarative scripting language
2. A shell for interactive queries
3. Support for the web and clients from many languages
4. A query processor
5. An input/output storage layer

Individual statements (or a script that is basically a sequence of statements), can be passed into the system from the interpreter in the Jaql shell or from and application. These statements are then compiled by the parser and rewrite engine to the input/output storage layer.

Jaql (JAQL) is a functional data processing and query language most commonly used for JSON query processing on BigData. It started as an Open Source project at Google but the latest release was on 7/12/2010. IBM took it over as primary data processing language for their Hadoop software package BigInsights. Although having been developed for JSON it supports a variety of other data sources like CSV, TSV, XML.

EXERCISE 8.1: Accessing JSON's Arrays and Records Using Jaql

1.1 START THE BIGINSIGHTS COMPONENTS

In this exercise you will access JSON arrays and records using Jaql.After completing this hands-on lab, you'll be able to Manipulate arrays and records using Jaql

1. Log into your BigInsights image with a userid of **biadmin** and a password of **password.**

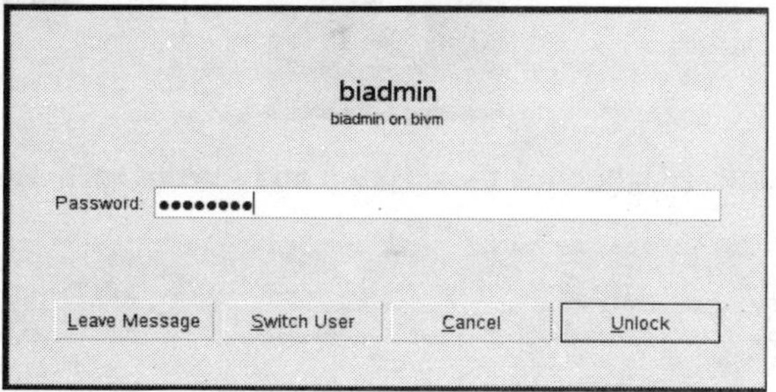

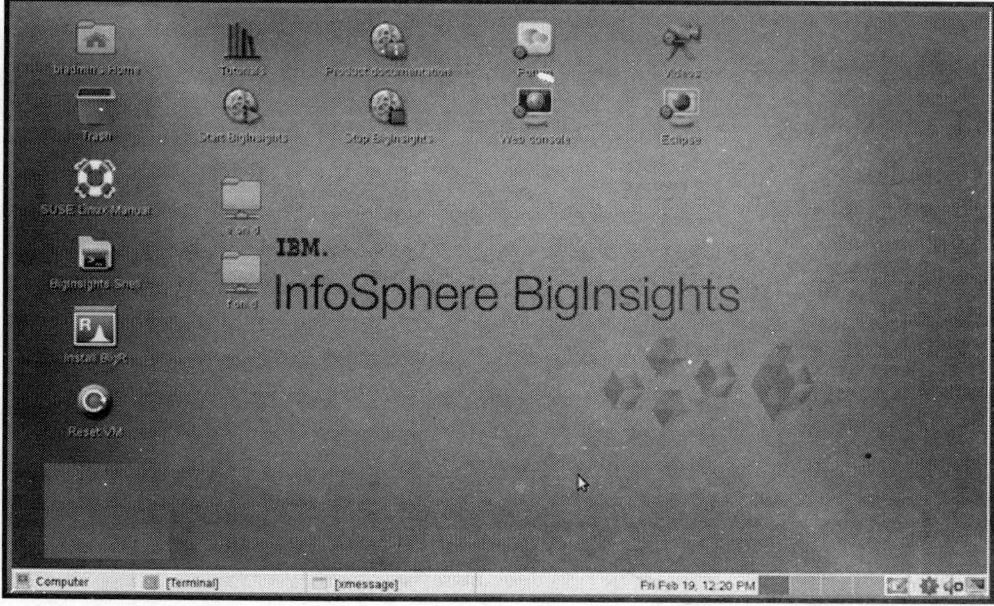

2. Start Hadoop and its components using the icon on the desktop. When done you will see following message:

1.2 SETUP TO RUN JAQL

You have two choices for your Jaql environment. You can start your Jaql shell from a command prompt or you can use the Eclipse environment. The nice thing about using the Eclipse environment is that you can cut and paste previously executed Jaql commands into the Jaql command prompt. We will use the Eclipse environment.

1. If you want to run Jaql from a command window, do the following steps.

a. Open a command window. (Right click the desktop and select **Open Terminal**.)

b. Change to the Jaql bin directory.

```
cd $BIGINSIGHTS_HOME/jaql/bin
```

```
biadmin@bivm:...ginsights/jaql/bin
File Edit View Terminal Help
Directory: /home/biadmin/Desktop
Fri Feb 19 12:49:32 EST 2016
biadmin@bivm:~/Desktop> cd $BIGINSIGHTS_HOME/jaql/bin
biadmin@bivm:/opt/ibm/biginsights/jaql/bin>
```

c. Start the Jaql shell.

```
./jaqlshell
```

```
biadmin@bivm:/opt/ibm/biginsights/jaql/bin> ./jaqlshell

Initializing Jaql - < version: unknown; no manifest >
```

Note:

You can code your Jaql script in a text file and then execute the jaqlshell command, passing one or more script files.

```
./jaqlshell script1 script2 ...
```

Note:

If you do not have a BigInsights server defined to your Eclipse system, do the following to create one:

1. In the **BigInsights Servers** frame, right-click BigInsights Servers and select New.
2. Type in the URL of the BigInsights server. For this exercise it is *http://bivm:8080*.
3. You can keep the default Server name.
4. User ID is *biadmin*.
5. *Password* is password.
6. Select to save the password.
7. Test your connection. If the test is successful, click OK and the Finish.
8. If prompted to enter a password, enter password.
9. If asked, click No on the Secure Storage dialog.
10. Click **Finish**.

2. To run Jaql from within the Eclipse environment, do the following steps.

   (a)Start Eclipse

and when prompted for a workspace, click **OK.**

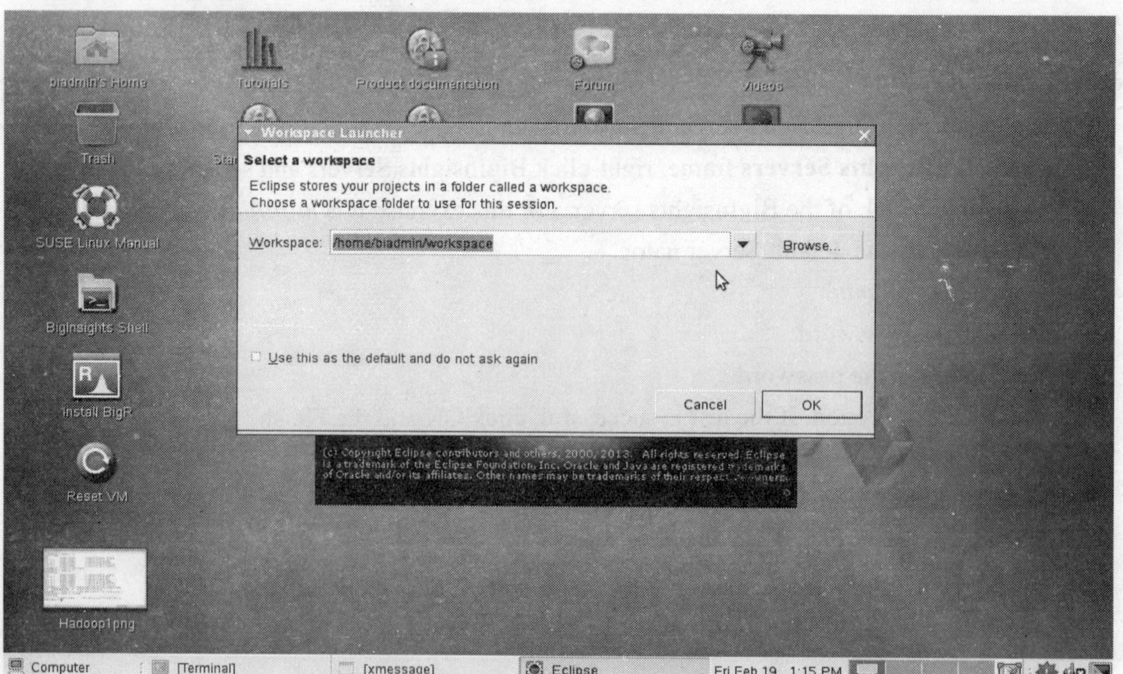

(b) Make sure that you are using the BigInsights perspective.

Click **Window->Open Perspective->Other**.

Select **BigInsights** and click **OK.**

(c) A BigInsights Server has already been defined.

(d) In the BigInsights Servers view, expand BigInsights Servers.

(e) Right click **bivm-bivm:8080...** and select Open **JAQL Shell.**

NOTE

Note: If you want to create a Jaql application that you would later publish to a igInsights erver, then you would want to create a BigInsights project and a Jaql program.

1. In the Overview tab of the Task Launcher for Big Data, click Create a new BigInsights project. Give your project a name and click Finish.
2. Click the **Develop** tab of the Task Launcher for Big Data and click **Create a BigInsights program**. Then you can select either JAQL Script or JAQL Module, depending on your needs. Then click **OK.**

8.4 STATEMENT, ASSIGNMENT AND COMMENTS

Double and single quotes are treated the same. Semicolon terminates a statement.

```
jaql> "Hello India";
```

```
jaql> 'Hello India';
```

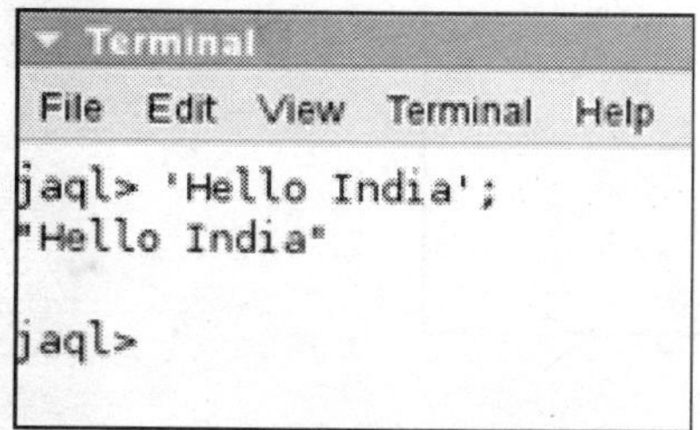

Enter following and press enter after every

```
jaql> a = 15*2;  jaql> a;
```

```
Terminal
File  Edit  View  Terminal  Help
jaql> a = 15*2;

jaql> a;
30
```

```
jaql> // This is a comment  jaql> /* and this is also  a comment */
```

8.5 DATA TYPES

Jaql is a loosely typed functional language, with lazy evaluation. Type is usually inferred by how a value is provided. Many types have a function of the same name to force conversions of a value or variable (e.g. `string()`, `double()`).

1. null – null
2. boolean – true, false
3. string – "hi"
4. long – 10
5. double – 10.2, 10d, 10e-2
6. array – [1, 2, 3]
7. record – {a : 1, b : 2}
8. others as jaql extensions – decfloat, binary, date, schema, function, comparator, regex

   Enter following:

```
jaql> array = [1, 2, 3, "hello", 4, {color: "red"}];
jaql> array;
```

```
Terminal
File  Edit  View  Terminal  Help
jaql> array = [1, 2, 3, "hello", 4, {color: "red"}];

jaql> array;
[
  1,
  2,
  3,
  "hello",
  4,
  {
    "color": "red"
  }
]
```

Operators

- arithmetic (+, -, /, *)
- boolean (and, or, not)
- comparison (==, !=, <, >, in, isnull)

Arrays

Arrays can be accessed with the [] operator.

```
jaql> a = [1, 2, 3];
jaql> a[1]; //retrieves start from zero
jaql> a[1:2]; //retrieve a range/subset
[2,3]
```

```
Terminal
File Edit View Terminal Help
jaql> a = [1, 2, 3];

jaql> a[1]; //retrieves start from zero
2

jaql> a[1:2]; //retrieve a range/subset
[
  2,
  3
]
```

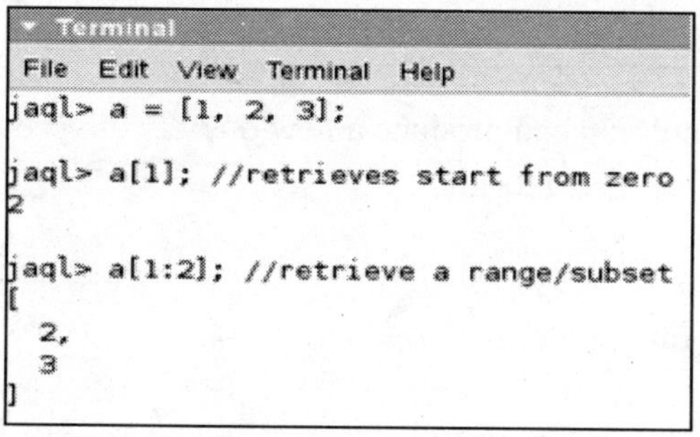

But you can't change a value, you need to use function `replaceElement()`.

```
jaql> a = replaceElement(a, 1, 10);
jaql> a[1];
```

```
jaql> a = replaceElement(a, 1, 10);

jaql> a[1];
10
```

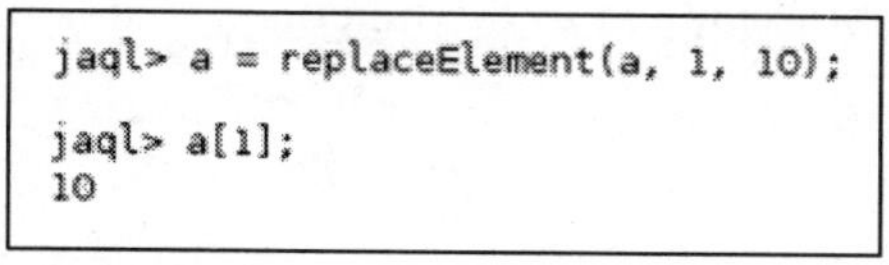

Other array functions

- count() – count(['a', 'b', 'c']); returns 3
- index() – index(['a', 'b', 'c'], 1); returns "b"
- replaceElement() – replaceElement(['a', 'b', 'c'], 1, 'z'); returns ["a", "z", "c"]
- slice() – index(['a', 'b', 'c', 'd'], 1, 2); returns ["b", "c"]
- reverse() – reverse(['a', 'b', 'c']); returns ["c", "b", "a"]
- range() – range(2, 5); returns [2, 3, 4, 5]

Records

Records are delineated by {} and contains a comma separated list of name:value pairs. Fields are then accessed by "." operator. Enetr following and press enter :

```
jaql> a = { name : "amit", age : 42, children : ["jaya", "abhishek"] };
jaql> a.name;
jaql> a.children[0];
```

The following will appear :

```
jaql> a = { name : "amit", age : 42, children : ["jaya", "abhishek"] };
jaql> a.name;
"amit"

jaql> a.children[0];
"jaya"

jaql> a.children[1];
"abhishek"
```

Again you cannot change an existing record, but you can produce a new one:

```
jaql> a = { a.name, age : 37, a.children };
```

The -> operator

The -> operator "streams" an array through a function or core operator.

```
jaql> range(10) -> batch(5);
[
 [0, 1, 2, 3, 4],
 [5, 6, 7, 8, 9]
]
```

The array on the left is implicitly passed as the first argument to the function. This is identical to the above:

```
jaql> batch(range(10), 5);
```

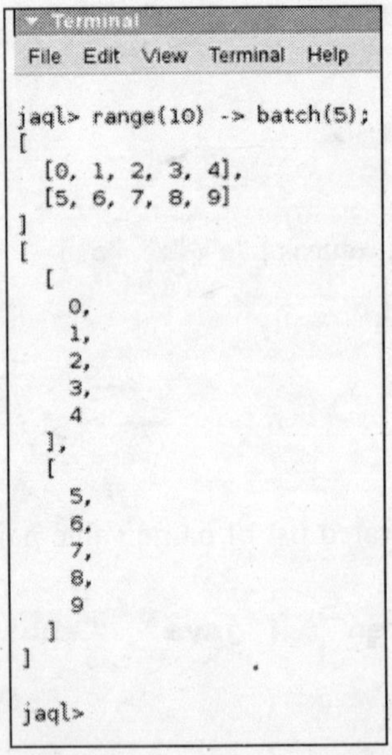

```
Terminal
File  Edit  View  Terminal  Help

jaql> range(10) -> batch(5);
[
  [0, 1, 2, 3, 4],
  [5, 6, 7, 8, 9]
]
[
  [
    0,
    1,
    2,
    3,
    4
  ],
  [
    5,
    6,
    7,
    8,
    9
  ]
]

jaql>
```

Operator -> is just a "syntactic sugar" that can dramatically improve readability when multiple operations are involved on your data.

Input/Output with Jaql

Input/Output operations are performed through I/O adapters. Adapters are a description of how to access and process a data source. I/O adapter is then passed into I/O function (e.g. read() or write()). Following is an example of writing array into a (comma-)delimited csv file where we used delimited file I/O adapter:

Eneter following :

```
jaql> [1, 2, 3, 4, 5] -> write(del("test.csv"));
```

The following shall be output of above :

```
Terminal
File  Edit  View  Terminal  Help
jaql> [1, 2, 3, 4, 5] -> write(del("test.csv"));
{
  "location": "test.csv",
  "inoptions": {
    "adapter": "com.ibm.jaql.io.hadoop.DelInputAdapter",
    "format": "com.ibm.biginsights.compress.mapred.CompressedTextInputFormat",
    "configurator": "com.ibm.jaql.io.hadoop.FileInputConfigurator",
    "converter": "com.ibm.jaql.io.hadoop.converter.FromDelConverter",
    "delimiter": ",",
    "quoted": true,
    "doubleq": true,
    "ddquote": true,
    "escape": true
  },
  "outoptions": {
    "adapter": "com.ibm.jaql.io.hadoop.DelOutputAdapter",
    "format": "org.apache.hadoop.mapred.TextOutputFormat",
    "configurator": "com.ibm.jaql.io.hadoop.FileOutputConfigurator",
    "converter": "com.ibm.jaql.io.hadoop.converter.ToDelConverter",
    "delimiter": ",",
    "quoted": true,
    "doubleq": true,
    "ddquote": true,
    "escape": true
  },
  "options": {}
}
```

Now enter following at command prompt:

```
jaql> read(del("test.csv"));
```

```
Terminal
File  Edit  View  Terminal  Help
jaql> read(del("test.csv"));
[
  [
    "1"
  ],
  [
    "2"
  ],
  [
    "3"
  ],
  [
    "4"
  ],
  [
    "5"
  ]
]

jaql>
```

Local files or HDFS are then accessed by specyfing the full path as URI:

```
jaql> read(del("file:///home/user/test.csv")); // for local file system
jaql> read(del("hdfs://localhost:9000/user/test.csv")); // for hdfs file system
```

To read a JSON data from a URL, you can use jaglGet() function:

```
jaqlGet("file:///tmp/test.txt");
```

Information about how to read from or write to different file types (like delimited, sequence, binary or JSON) and how to use I/O adapters and schemas can be found at IBM BigInsights Infocenter.

More information about I/O functions is available at IBM BigInsights Infocenter.

1. Some Jaql basics
2. At your Jaql prompt, create an array;

   ```
   a1 = [10,20,30,40];
   ```

2. Access the last element in the array.

   ```
   a1[3];
   ```

```
Terminal
File  Edit  View  Terminal  Help

Initializing Jaql - < version: unknown; no manifest >

jaql> a1 = [10,20,30,40];

jaql> a1[3];
40

jaql> 
```

3. Access the first three elements in the array by executing following:

```
a1[0:2];
```

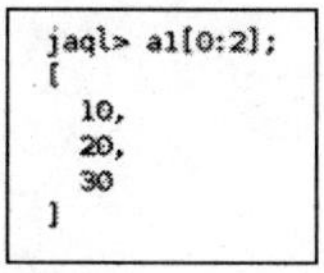

```
jaql> a1[0:2];
[
  10,
  20,
  30
]
```

4. Next update the first element in the array 10 by 9. Try the following and see what happens.

```
a1[0]=9;
```

5. Well, that did not work successfully, so try it the correct way using **replace**.

```
a1 = replaceElement(a1,0,9);
a1;
```

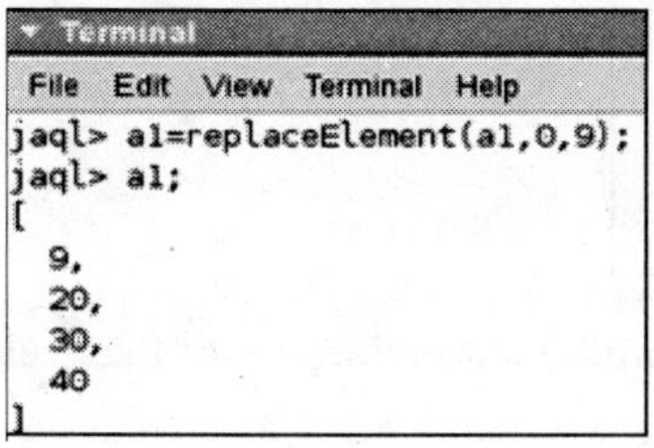

```
Terminal
File Edit View Terminal Help
jaql> a1=replaceElement(a1,0,9);
jaql> a1;
[
  9,
  20,
  30,
  40
]
```

6. Create an array, a2, whose values range from 1 to 15.

```
a2 = range(1,15);
a2;
```

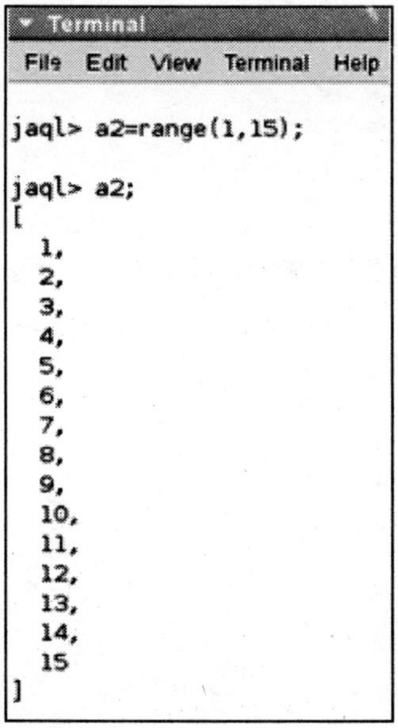

```
Terminal
File Edit View Terminal Help

jaql> a2=range(1,15);

jaql> a2;
[
  1,
  2,
  3,
  4,
  5,
  6,
  7,
  8,
  9,
  10,
  11,
  12,
  13,
  14,
  15
]
```

7. Next reverse all of the values in that array.

```
reverse(a2);
```

```
Terminal
File Edit View Terminal Help
jaql>
jaql> reverse(a2);
[
  15,
  14,
  13,
  12,
  11,
  10,
  9,
  8,
  7,
  6,
  5,
  4,
  3,
  2,
  1
]
```

8. And finally determine the number of elements in the array and what is the sum of these elements.

```
count(a2);
```

```
jaql> count(a2);
15

jaql> sum(a2);
120
```

Enter following at the command prompt;

```
[{name:'Vijay',age:35,children:['Aja','Sanjay','Jaya']},
{name:'Maya',age:21}];
```

and press enter to see following components of the above noted object.

```
jaql> [{name:'Vijay',age:35,children:['Aja','Sanjay','Jaya']},{name:'Maya',age:2
1}];
[
  {
    "name": "Vijay",
    "age": 35,
    "children": [
      "Aja",
      "Sanjay",
      "Jaya"
    ]
  },
  {
    "name": "Maya",
    "age": 21
  }
]

jaql> a3=[{name:'Vijay',age:35,children:['Aja','Sanjay','Jaya']},{name:'Maya',ag
e:21}];
```

If we make above statement equal to an object a3 by entering following :

A3= [{name:'Vijay',age:35,children:['Aja','Sanjay','Jaya']},{name:'Maya',age:21}];

2. What happens if you access the field called name?

   a3.name;

```
jaql> a3.name;
[
  "Vijay",
  "Maya"
]
```

3. Both name field values were displayed. The student guide also stated that there was another way of getting all values of a field that was more self-documenting.

   a3[*].name;

```
jaql> a3[*].name;
[
  "Vijay",
  "Maya"
]
```

4. What if you only wanted the value of the name field for the first record?

   a3[0].name;

```
jaql> a3[0];
{
  "name": "Vijay",
  "age": 35,
  "children": [
    "Ajay",
    "Sanjay",
    "Jaya"
  ]
}
```

5. And if you wanted the name of the second child from the first record:

   a3[0].children[0];

```
jaql> a3[0].children[0];
"Ajay"
```

6. List only the name and age fields for the first record.

   a3[0]{.name,.age};

```
jaql> a3[0]{.name,age};
{
  "name": "Vijay",
  "age": 35
}
```

7. Add a new field called gender to the second record and give it a value of 'F';

   {a3[1].*,gender:'F'};

```
jaql> a3=[{name:'Vijay',age:35,children:['Ajay','Sanjay','Jaya']},{name:'Maya',age:21},{a3[1].*,gender:'F'}];
```

8. Remove the age field from the first record.

   a3[0]{*-.age};

```
jaql> a3[0]{*-.age};
{
  "name": "Vijay",
  "children": [
    "Ajay",
    "Sanjay",
    "Jaya"
  ]
}
```

9. Remove the age field from the first record and at the same time add a new field called gender with a value of 'M';

   {a3[0]{*-.age},gender:'M'};

```
jaql> {a3[0]{*-.age},gender:'M'};
{
  "name": "Vijay",
  "children": [
    "Ajay",
    "Sanjay",
    "Jaya"
  ],
  "gender": "M"
}
```

10. List the field names in the first record;

    names(a3[0]);

```
jaql> names(a3[0]);
[
  "age",
  "children",
  "name"
]
```

8.6 DATA MANIPULATION (CORE OPERATORS)

Core operators manipulate streams (arrays) of data, much in the way SQL clauses interact with data.

Filter

Enter following two lines at command prompt and press enter after each entry

```
jaql> data = [1, 2, 3, 4, 5, 6, 7, 8, 9];
jaql> data -> filter 3 <= $ <= 6;
```

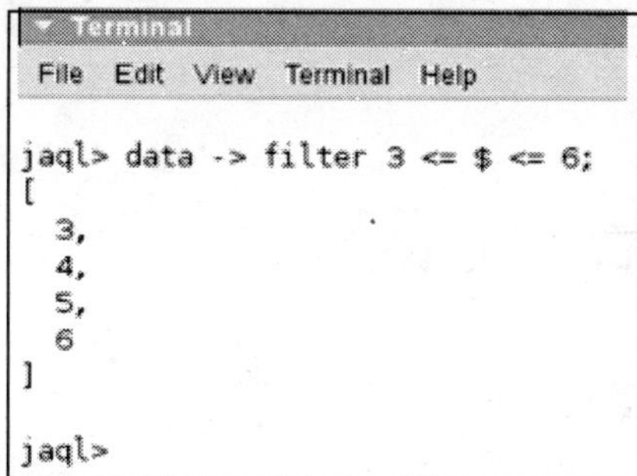

Alternatively, the each clause can be used to provide a name different than $:

Enter following two lines at command prompt and press enter after each entry

```
jaql> data = [11, 12, 13, 14, 15, 16, 17, 18, 19];
jaql> data -> filter each num (13 <= num <= 16);
```

The following shall be returned on monitor:

```
Terminal
File  Edit  View  Terminal  Help
jaql> data = [11, 12, 13, 14, 15, 16, 17, 18, 19];

jaql> data -> filter each num (13 <= num <= 16);
[
  13,
  14,
  15,
  16
]

jaql>
```

Transform

The transform operator allows you to manipulate the values in an array. An expression is applied to each element in the array. Enter following two lines at command prompt and press enter after each entry

```
jaql> recs = [ {a: 1, b: 4}, {a: 2, b: 5}, {a: -1, b: 4} ];
jaql> recs -> transform $.a + $.b;
```

```
Terminal
File  Edit  View  Terminal  Help
jaql> recs = [ {a: 1, b: 4}, {a: 2, b: 5}, {a: -1, b: 4} ];

jaql> recs -> transform $.a + $.b;
[
  5,
  7,
  3
]

jaql>
```

Enter following commands:

```
recs -> transform { sum: $.a + $.b };
```

```
jaql> recs -> transform { sum: $.a + $.b };
[{ sum: 5 }, { sum: 7 }, { sum: 3 }]
jaql>
```

Sort

```
jaql> read(del("file:///path/to/people.txt")) -> sort by [$.age asc];
```

Other data manipulation operators

Other data manipulation operators are ***expand, group, join, top***.

Jaql core operators

Use Jaql core operators to perform activities such as filter, join, and group JSON data.

Expand

Use the EXPAND expression to flatten nested arrays. This expression takes as input an array of nested arrays [[T]]. It produces an output array [T] by promoting the elements of each nested array to the top-level output array.

Syntax

In addition, the EXPAND expression can be used in a manner similar to TRANSFORM, whereby an expression is applied to each nested array. The expression must return an array. When EXPAND is used in this way, it takes as input [[T1]] and outputs [T2].

Description and parameters

A

An input (for example, an array of nested arrays) of type [T] or type [T1]. The output that is produced is A' of type [T] or type [T1].

expand

Flattens nested arrays, if no `<expr>` is specified. If you specify an `<expr>`, it binds a default iteration variable, $, that is bound to each element of the input. The type of $ is [T1] and it is often used as input to `<expr>`.

each <var>

Renames the default iteration variable $ to another variable.

<expr>

An expression that returns type [T2]. A common expression that is used with EXPAND is unroll, which repeats the parent of a nested array for each element of the nested array.

Examples

Consider the following nested array of numbers:

```
nestedData = [ [-3,605,9,17],[115,8,-45,56]];
```

To flatten the array, use the following EXPAND operation:

```
nestedData -> expand
```

Which returns:

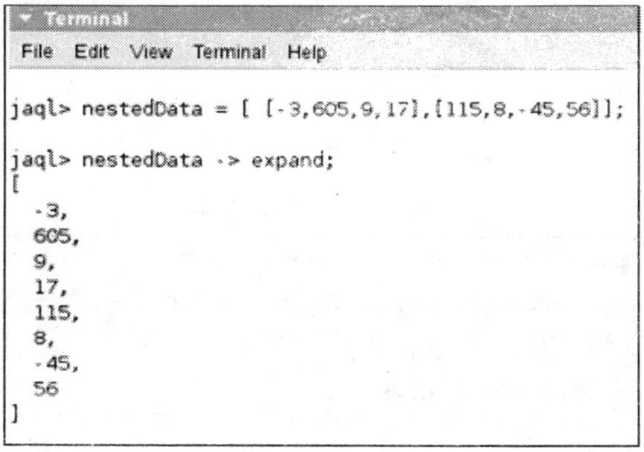

```
Terminal
File Edit View Terminal Help

jaql> nestedData = [ [-3,605,9,17],[115,8,-45,56]];

jaql> nestedData -> expand;
[
  -3,
  605,
  9,
  17,
  115,
  8,
  -45,
  56
]
```

To also perform a TRANSFORM operation on the array (for example, if you wanted to triple each of the numbers), use the following:

```
nestedData -> expand ($ -> transform $ * 3);
```

The following results are returned:

```
Terminal
File Edit View Terminal Help
jaql> nestedData = [ [-3,605,9,17],[115,8,-45,56]];

jaql> nestedData -> expand ($ -> transform $ * 3);
[
  -9,
  1815,
  27,
  51,
  345,
  24,
  -135,
  168
]
```

In this example, the first $ is bound to each nested array and the second $ is bound to each element of each nested array. To perform the same operation with explicitly declared iteration variables, use the following:

```
nestedData -> expand each arr (arr -> transform each n (n * 3));
```

In the next example, consider an array, movies_owned, which contains data about the movie ownership of two individuals:

```
plots_owned = [{name:"Heera Jain", plot_ids:[12,5, 78,72]}, {name:"Ami-
tabh Bajaj", plot_ids:[65,88,12]}];
```

To compile a list of the ids of all the movies that are owned, use the following:

```
plots_owned -> expand $.plot_ids;
```

The following results are returned:

```
jaql> plots_owned = [{name:"Heera Jain", plot_ids:[12,5, 78,72]}, {name:"Amitabh Bajaj", plot_ids:[65,88,12]}];
jaql> plots_owned -> expand $.plot_ids;
[
  12,
  5,
  78,
  72,
  65,
  88,
  12
]
```

To compile a list of all the movies that are owned along with their owner, use EXPAND with unroll. This expression multiplies each parent by the arity of its nested child array.

```
plots_owned -> expand unroll $.plots_ids;
```

The following results are returned:

```
Terminal
File Edit View Terminal Help
plots_owned = [{name:"Heera Jain", plot_ids:[12,5, 78,72]}, {name:"Amitabh Bajaj", plot_ids:[65,88,12]}];

jaql> ;plots_owned -> expand unroll $.plots_ids;

jaql> [
  {
    "name": "Heera Jain",
    "plot_ids": [
      12,
      5,
      78,
      72
    ]
  },
  {
    "name": "Amitabh Bajaj",
    "plot_ids": [
      65,
      88,
      12
    ]
  }
]
```

FILTER function

Use the FILTER operator to remove elements from a specified input array. This operator takes as input an array of elements of type T. It outputs an array of the same type, and retains those elements that a predicate evaluates as true. The FILTER function is the Jaql equivalent of the SQL WHERE clause.

Description and parameters

A

An input (for example, an array) of type [T]. The output that is produced is A' of type [T], count(A') <= count(A).

filter

Binds a default iteration variable, $, that is bound to each element of the input. The type of $ is T and it is often used as input to `<predicate>`.

each *<var>*

Renames the default iteration variable $ to another variable.

`<predicate>`

An expression that returns a Boolean value, meaning that the item is included in the output if the Boolean expression evaluates to true. The following relational and Boolean operators are supported:

==, meaning that the first operand is equal to the second operand

!=, meaning that the first operand is not equal to the second operand

>, meaning that the first operand is greater than the second operand

>=, meaning that the first operand is greater than or equal to the second operand

<, meaning that the first operand is less than the second operand

<=, meaning that the first operand less than or equal to the second operand

```
not
and
or
```

Example

A JSON data set, employees, contains an array with employee details as follows:

```
employees = [
{name: "Vimal Kumar", income: 23500, mgr: false},
{name: "Rajesh Batra", income: 35000, mgr: false},
{name: "Jaspal Arora", income: 72000, mgr: true},
{name: "Amitabh Jain", income: 25000, mgr: false}
];
```

If you want to use the default iteration variable (`$`) to filter the results such that either the employee is a manager or the employee's salary is at a minimum threshold, you would use the following:

```
employees -> filter $.mgr or $.income > 30000;
```

The following results are returned:

```
Terminal
File Edit View Terminal Help
jaql> employees = [
 {name: "Vimal Kumar", income: 23500, mgr: false},
 {name: "Rajesh Batra", income: 35000, mgr: false},
 {name: "Jaspal Arora", income: 72000, mgr: true},
 {name: "Amitabh Jain", income: 25000, mgr: false}
];

jaql> employees -> filter $.mgr or $.income > 30000;
[
  {
    "name": "Rajesh Batra",
    "income": 35000,
    "mgr": false
  },
  {
    "name": "Jaspal Arora",
    "income": 72000,
    "mgr": true
  }
]

jaql>
```

If you wanted to perform the same FILTER operation, but use iteration variable *emp*, you would you use:

```
employees -> filter each emp emp.mgr or emp.income > 30000;
```

To make the syntax easier to read, you can use parentheses to separate the variable declaration as follows:

```
employees -> filter each emp (emp.mgr or emp.income > 30000);
```

Group

Use the GROUP expression to group one or more input arrays on a grouping key and apply an aggregate function per group.

Description and parameters

When evaluated by a MapReduce job, a GROUP expression's grouping key is extracted in the map phase. The per-group aggregate function is evaluated in the reduce phase. If the aggregate function is an algebraic aggregate function, it is evaluated by using the map, combine, and reduce phases. The combine phase computes partial aggregates, which allows more computation to take place in the mapper processes. This potentially reducing network traffic when it transfers intermediate data between mapper and reducer processes. Jaql's GROUP expression is similar to SQL's GROUP BY clause when specified for a single input array. When multiple input arrays are specified, GROUP is similar to PigLatin's co-group operator.

Parameters

A

An input (for example, an array) of type [T1]. The output that is produced is A' of type T2.

stream

A number between 0 and N-1; N is the number of inputs to the grouping expression. This option indicates that the specified input is streamed at the reducer. It can boost performance for large inputs because Jaql can avoid copying the input to temporary storage before it runs the into piece of the grouping. To use this option, the records from the specified input inside of the into cannot be iterated over more than one time.

You can improve performance by streaming an input to GROUP because you avoid making temporary copies of the data from that input. However, doing so implies that within the GROUP's into clause, the input can be iterated only once. For example, the following returns an error because the content of thebig array (the streaming input) is iterated for each element in the non-streaming array:

```
group big_data by k = { $.key } as big,
    small_data by k = { $.key } as small
options { stream: 0 }
into { key: k, val: small -> expand each a ( big -> transform each
b {       a.field1, b.field2 } ) }
;
```

However, if you reverse the two, the option is successful because the big array is iterated one time:

```
group big_data by k = { $.key } as big,
```

```
small_data by k = { $.key } as small
options { stream: 0 }
into { key: k, val: big -> expand each a ( small -> transform each b {
b.field1, a.field2 } ) }
;
```

<aggrExpr>

Produces an output of type T2. <aggrExpr> is invoked for each group. The most common use of <aggrExpr> is to combine value constructors, such as records and array constructors, with aggregate functions.

Examples

A JSON data set, employees, contains an array with employee details as follows:

```
employees = [
 {id:1, dept: 1, income:12000},
 {id:2, dept: 1, income:13000},
 {id:3, dept: 2, income:15000},
 {id:4, dept: 1, income:10000},
 {id:5, dept: 3, income:8000},
 {id:6, dept: 2, income:5000},
 {id:7, dept: 1, income:24000}
];
employees = [
 {id:11, dept: 1, income:22000},
 {id:12, dept: 1, income:23000},
 {id:13, dept: 2, income:25000},
 {id:14, dept: 1, income:20000},
 {id:15, dept: 3, income:18000},
 {id:16, dept: 2, income:15000},
 {id:17, dept: 1, income:34000}
];
```

To compute an aggregate over all employee records, use the following command:

```
employees -> group into count($);
```

The following is returned:

```
File  Edit  View  Terminal  Help
jaql> employees = [
  {id:11, dept: 1, income:22000},
  {id:12, dept: 1, income:23000},
  {id:13, dept: 2, income:25000},
  {id:14, dept: 1, income:20000},
  {id:15, dept: 3, income:18000},
  {id:16, dept: 2, income:15000},
  {id:17, dept: 1, income:34000}
];

jaql> employees -> group into count($);
[
  7
]
```

If you want to group the results by the department number and provide an aggregate total of each department's income, use the following command:

```
employees -> group by d = $.dept into {d, total: sum($[*].income)};
```

The following results are returned:

```
jaql> employees -> group by d = $.dept into {d, total: sum($[*].income)};
[
  {
    "d": 2,
    "total": 40000
  },
  {
    "d": 1,
    "total": 99000
  },
  {
    "d": 3,
    "total": 18000
  }
]

jaql>
```

Note the two uses of $ for both the iteration and group variables. Also, as a shorthand, the first output field (d) has a name that is constructed from the variable name.

To perform the same operation, but renaming iteration and group variables, issue the following command:

```
employees -> group each emp by d = emp.dept as deptEmps
                into {d, total: sum(deptEmps[*].income)};
```

```
Terminal
File Edit View Terminal Help
jaql> employees -> group each emp by d = emp.dept as deptEmps
                  into {d, total: sum(deptEmps[*].income)};
[
  {
    "d": 2,
    "total": 40000
  },
  {
    "d": 1,
    "total": 99000
  },
  {
    "d": 3,
    "total": 18000
  }
]

jaql>
```

There is a data set, depts, which contains the following data:

```
Terminal
File Edit View Terminal Help
jaql> depts = [
  {deptid: 1, name: "hrd"},
  {deptid: 2, name: "marketing"},
  {deptid: 3, name: "salespromotion"}
];

jaql> group employees by g = $.dept as es,
              depts     by g = $.deptid  as ds
      into { dept: g, deptName: ds[0].name, emps: es[*].id, numEmps: count(es) };
```

```
depts = [
  {did: 1, name: "development"},
  {did: 2, name: "marketing"},
  {did: 3, name: "sales"}
];
```

If you wanted to construct a single record per group, providing the department id, department name, the list of matching employee ids, and the count of employees per department, use the following aggregate expression:

```
group employees by g = $.dept as es,
          depts      by g = $.deptid  as ds
        into { dept: g, deptName: ds[0].name, emps: es[*].id, numEmps:
count(es) };
```

The following is returned:

```
[
  {
    "dept": 2,
    "deptName": "marketing",
    "emps": [
      13,
      16
    ],
    "numEmps": 2
  },
  {
    "dept": 1,
    "deptName": "hrd",
    "emps": [
      11,
      12,
      14,
      17
    ],
    "numEmps": 4
  },
  {
    "dept": 3,
    "deptName": "salespromotion",
    "emps": [


      15
    ],
    "numEmps": 1
  }
]
```

8.7 SYNTAX OF CORE OPERATORS

JOIN

Use the JOIN operator to express a join between two or more input arrays. This operator supports multiple types of joins, including natural, left-outer, right-outer, and outer joins.

Syntax

The JOIN condition between two inputs is assumed to be an equijoin. When you join more than two inputs, the JOIN condition is assumed to be a conjunction of equijoins, where any two inputs are connected by a path of multiple equijoins.

Description and parameters

A1, A2, An

An input (for example, an array) of type [T1]. The variables A1, ..., An are in scope for joinExpr and joinOut. The output is TM, where TM is generated by <joinOut>.

preserve

Specifies that on a specific input, all of its values appear, regardless of whether another input has matching values. Using preserve, you can achieve the same semantics as SQL's various OUTER JOIN options. If you do not specify preserve for any of the inputs, then the JOIN is defined to be a natural JOIN.

<var1> in

Renames the default iteration variable $ to another variable. <var1>, ... <varn> are in scope for joinExpr and joinOut.

joinExpr

A conjunction of equality expressions between Ai and Aj, where i != j. In addition, for any i, j, i != j, a path must exist between i and j. For example, consider a graph G where nodes are input variables and edges are specified by conjunctions and equality expressions. For graph G, if x == y and y == z, then there is a path from x to z.

Example

The following JSON data sets contain arrays with information about customers, regions, and nations that are joined by this function:

```
Regions = read(del(location="/demo/mm/jaqlInput/region.tbl",
        delimiter="|",
        schema=schema {r_regionkey:long, r_name:string, r_com-
ment:string}))
        -> filter $.r_name == "AMERICA";
Nations = read(del(location="/demo/mm/jaqlInput/nation.tbl",
        delimiter="|",
        schema=schema {n_nationkey:long, n_name:string, n_region-
key:long,
                 n_comment:string}
                 ));
Customer = read(del(location="/demo/mm/jaqlInput/customer.tbl",
        delimiter="|",
        schema=schema {
                 c_custkey:long, c_name:string, c_address:string,
                 c_nationkey:long, c_phone:string, c_acctbal:double,
                 c_mktsegment:string, c_comment:string
         }));
// Join the "tables"
res = join
      Regions,
      Nations,
      c in Customer
where
```

```
        Regions.r_regionkey == Nations.n_regionkey
        and Nations.n_nationkey == c.c_nationkey
        into {Regions.r_regionkey, Regions.r_name,
                Nations.n_nationkey, Nations.n_name }
        ;
res;
quit;;
```

Streaming Join Input

When you join data together at the reducer, Jaql chooses one of the inputs to the join to "stream" through the reducer. All of the other inputs are temporarily copied into memory (spilling to local disk if necessary) before the into portion of the join is run. For a purely inner join, Jaql always chooses to stream the last input (t3 in this example):

```
join t1, t2, t3 where t1.c1 == t2.c1 and t2.c2 == t3.c2 into { t1.c4 }
```

When you use an outer join, Jaql always chooses the last preserved input. The streaming input is not temporarily copied into memory. As such, you can improve performance by ensuring that the largest input to your join is always the last input (or the last preserved input). For example, in this outer join example, the streaming input is t2:

```
join preserve t1, preserve t2, t3 where t1.c1 == t2.c1 and t2.c2 == t3.c2
into { t1.c4 }
```

To perform input streaming, all records at the reducer are sorted by the reducer before processing. This process ensures that the streaming input is the last set of records processed. As a result, at times the cost of this sorting might outweigh the benefits of streaming input. To disable streaming, the job property jaql.streaming.enable can be set to false. For example:

```
setOptions( { conf: { "jaql.streaming.enable": false } });
```

Join Input Caching

Jaql sorts all non-streaming inputs that come from mappers into memory, spilling to disk as necessary. This activity happens one time for each unique join key value. The largest number or values for a single join key determines the amount of memory (or disk space) is needed. By default, Jaql caches 1000 values (per input) in memory before spilling to disk. However, you can adjust this value by setting the job property jaql.group.input.default to a higher value. For example:

```
setOptions( { conf: { "jaql.group.input.default": 25000 } });
```

SORT

Use the SORT operator to sort an input by one or more fields.

Description and parameters

A

An input (for example, an array) of type [T]. The output is A' of type [T].

each *<var>*

Renames the default iteration variable $ to another variable.

<expr>

Constructs a comparator that is used to sort A.

asc

Specifies that the results are to be in ascending order. This sort order is the default setting.

desc

Specifies that the results are to be in descending order.

Examples

Consider the following array of longs:

```
nums = [ 2, 1, 3 ];
```

To sort them, use the following command:

```
nums -> sort by [ $ ];
```

The following results are returned:

```
[
  1,
  2,
  3
]
```

If you wanted to override the default iteration variable, use the following command:

```
nums -> sort each n by [ n ];
```

If you wanted to sort the array in descending order, use the following command:

```
nums -> sort by [ $ desc ];
```

Next, consider the following array, nums:

```
test = [[2,2,"first"],[1,2,"second"],[2,1,"third"],[1,1,"fourth"]];
```

To sort the data in descending order by using a complex comparator, where each comparator expression projects values from the input, use the following command:

```
test -> sort by [$[0], $[1] desc];
```

The following results are returned:

```
[
 [
   1,
   2,
   "second"
 ],
 [
   1,
   1,
   "fourth"
 ],
 [
   2,
   2,
   "first"
 ],
 [
   2,
   1,
   "third"
 ]
]
```

TOP

The TOP expression selects the first k elements of its input. If a comparator is provided, the output is semantically equivalent to sorting the input, then selecting the first k elements.

Description and parameters

A

An input (for example, an array) of type [T]. The output is an array of type [T] containing the first k elements from A'.

each <*var*>

Renames the default iteration variable $ to another variable.

<expr>

Constructs a comparator that is used to sort A.

asc

Specifies that the results are to be in ascending order. This sort order is the default setting.

desc

Specifies that the results are to be in descending order.

Examples

Consider the following set of numbers:

```
nums = [1,2,3];
```

If you wanted to select the first two elements from nums, regardless of how nums is ordered, use the following command:

```
nums -> top 2;
```

The following results are returned:

```
[
1,
2
]
```

To specify the order of the input from which the elements are selected, use the following command:

```
nums -> top 2 by [ $ desc ];
```

The following results are returned:

```
[
  3,
  2
]
```

TRANSFORM

Use the TRANSFORM operator to realize a projection or to apply a function to all items of an output.

Description and parameters

A

An input (for example, an array) of type [T1]. The output is A' of type [T2], count(A') == count(A)

transform

Binds a default iteration variable, $, that is bound to each element of the input. The type of $ is T1 and it is often used as input to <expr>.

each *<var>*

Renames the default iteration variable $ to another variable.

<expr>

An expression that returns type T2. It is often expressed by using type constructors such as record { ... } and array [...] constructors.

Usage notes

With the TRANSFORM operator, the input is processed item by item. The variable $ is bound to each item in the input, so you can access values from records with the $.key or from arrays with $[n]. When you are copying a value from a record, you can omit the key. It is automatically copied to the result.

Example

A JSON data set, recs, contains an array of numerical values as follows:

```
recs = [
  {a: 1, b: 4},
  {a: 2, b: 5},
  {a: -1, b: 4}
];
```

To combine the values of the numbers in each object, issue the following command:

```
recs -> transform {sum: $.a + $.b};
```

The following results are returned:

```
[
  {
    "sum": 5
  },
  {
    "sum": 7
  }
  {
    "sum": 3
  }
]
```

Using r as the iteration variable to perform the same TRANSFORM operation, issue the following command:

```
recs -> transform each r {sum: r.a + r.b};
```

In this case, a variable, recs, is assigned an array of records. Each record contains numerical values.

EXERCISES 8.2 : ON CORE OPERATORS

1. If you have subsequently rebooted your system since you last started the BigInsights components, or you have stopped Hadoop, you will need to restart it now. Use the icon on the desktop.
2. Start the *Jaql shell.* Open a command window and execute the following:

```
cd $BIGINSIGHTS_HOME/jaql/bin ./jaqlshell
```

3. Located on the lab image is a file of JSON records that contains tweets. First read this file so that you can repeatedly access the data in the file and display the contents of the file.

   The qualified file name is */home/biadmin/SampleData/Twitter Search.json.*

Enter following at the command prompt:

```
tweets   =   read(file("file:///home/biadmin/SampleData/Twitter   Search.
json"));
```

and then enter following at the command prompt:

```
tweets;
```

4. You should have received an error indicating you have an invalid character in the file name.

   It appears that Jaql is not too fond of spaces in file names. Code the following to get around this opportunity. Also, you did not receive the error until you displayed the data in the file. That was due to lazy evaluation. The actual read did not take place until the request to display the data.

```
tweets   =   read(file("file:///home/biadmin/SampleData/Twitter%20Search.
json"));
tweets;
```

5. Retrieve a single field, *from_user,* using the *transform* command.

```
tweets -> transform $.from_user;
```

```
jaql> tweets -> transform $.from_user;
[
  "Petra710",
  "App_BB",
  "benjifletcher",
  "iivans",
  "HerbieBaby2",
  "aNinjaTurtle",
  "MoisesOh",
  "kilroyfsu",
  "miriampomposo",
  "suaven2g",
```

```
  "pitagotica",
  "kamiresources",
  "BIIIITCHplezO_O",
  "blogsoftheworld",
  "splashjosh",
  "JohnQPubliq",
  "BritneyLyrics",
  "intuitivecook",
  "DatBoyMace",
  "AmorEs_IGNANT",
  "dooksofhazard",
  "thenightcabbie",
  "snazmindanielle",
  "MelDubs",
  "theREAL_Tiffany",
  "ArlineCantlow11",
  "smokeypinkalexa",
  "kagranemann",
  "JusYummy1",
  "_AmarettoSour_",
  "BIGZADDYLO",
  "IsaiahPaul",
  "saberfra",
  "AISHA215",
  "JPVanity",
  "TavistockReeves",
  "matiassblog",
  "dennispowers",
  "EatTheezLaays",
  "aJwitaFrO",
  "joint_seminar",
  "luquinhaz",
  "issDatToya",
  "mariacarol",
  "cead22",
  "mobtuts",
  "tutsplus",
  "GreatTwitTips"
]
```

How did this work? When you read the file, you did not provide a schema. So how did Jaql know anything about the *from_user* field? Data in a JSON format has the field name or array name as part of the data. This allows for flexibility. If you had to code a schema for the twitter data and then later on Twitter changed the format of their data, you programs would have a problem. But since Twitter is using a JSON format, adding fields or changing the position of a field in a record has no affect.

6. If you look around the beginning of each record, there is an object called *metadata.* Within that object there is a field called *result_type.* Use the *transform* operator to display the *result_type* field.

```
jaql> tweets -> transform $.metadata.result_type;
[
 "recent",
 "recent",
 "recent",
 "recent",
 "recent",
 "recent",
 "recent",
 "recent",
 "recent",
 "recent",
 "recent",
 "recent",
 "recent",
 "recent",
 "recent",
 "recent",
 "recent",
 "recent",
 "recent",
 "recent",
 "recent",
 "recent",
 "recent",
 "recent",
 "recent",
 "recent",
```

```
  "recent",
  "recent",
  "recent",
  "recent",
  "recent",
  "recent",
  "recent",
  "recent",
  "recent",
  "recent",
  "recent",
  "recent",
  "recent",
  "recent",
  "recent",
  "recent",
  "recent",
  "recent",
  "recent",
  "recent",
  "recent"
]
```

7. Retrieve multiple fields using the *transform* operator. Now you might think that you would just list the fields that you wanted projected. That would not be correct. Multiple fields need to be encapsulated in a record or object.

```
tweets->transform {$.created_at, $.from_user, $.iso_language_code,
$.text};
```

The output list is very long but I have short listed it to show one example of each language.In this list en is English,es Spanish,pt is Portuguese and Zh is Zhuong language (of South China).

```
jaql> tweets->transform {$.created_at, $.from_user, $.iso_language_
code, $.text};
[
  {
    "created_at": "Thu, 13 Jan 2011 05:56:13 +0000",
```

```
   "from_user": "Petra710",
   "iso_language_code": "en",
   "text": "My Twitter account is worth $972! What\'s yours worth?
http://WhatsMyTwitterAccountWorth.com"
 },
 {
   "created_at": "Thu, 13 Jan 2011 05:56:12 +0000",
   "from_user": "App_BB",
   "iso_language_code": "es",
   "text": "Por eso lo digo, también incorpora FaceBook. RT @kuku_ve:
Yo uso mis 2 cuentas Đ twitter, 4sq ÿ fcbk con @socialscope ;)"
 },

 {
   "created_at": "Thu, 13 Jan 2011 06:16:45 +0000",
   "from_user": "kagranemann",
   "iso_language_code": "pt",
   "text": "ALEXANDRE GRAH.. EU SEI QUE VOCÊ ESTÁ NO MEU TWITTER.. VOLTE
PRO MSN QUE TENHO QUE FALAR CONTIGO AGORA! sério"
 },

 {
   "created_at": "Thu, 13 Jan 2011 06:18:18 +0000",
   "from_user": "joint_seminar",
   "iso_language_code": "zh",
   "text": "【拡散希望】 鹿児島県出水市にて、Twitter初心者セミナー開催。 Twitter
の登録から解説しますので、Twitterに興味をお持ちの方にご紹介下さい  詳細⇒http://
bit.ly/dF3bvy 携帯から⇒http://bit.ly/gEmd4b #kagoshima"
 },

]
```


8. Create a new record, *tweetsrecs* and at the same time change the name of one of the fields? Then display the contents of *tweetrecs*.

```
tweetrecs = tweets->transform {$.created_at, $.from_user, language:
$.iso_language_code, $.text};
```

and then enter

```
tweetrecs;
```

9. Use the *filter* operator to see all non-English language records from *tweetrecs*.

```
tweetrecs -> filter $.language != 'en';
```

```
aql> tweetrecs -> filter $.language != 'en';
[
 {
   "created_at": "Thu, 13 Jan 2011 05:56:12 +0000",
   "from_user": "App_BB",
   "language": "es",
   "text": "Por eso lo digo, también incorpora FaceBook. RT @kuku_ve:
Yo uso mis 2 cuentas Ð twitter, 4sq ỹ fcbk con @socialscope ;)"
 },
 {
   "created_at": "Thu, 13 Jan 2011 05:56:10 +0000",
   "from_user": "iivans",
   "language": "es",
   "text": "A falta de iPhone, motorola, i iPad, usar twitter desde el
web mobil pff"
 },
 {
   "created_at": "Thu, 13 Jan 2011 05:56:09 +0000",
   "from_user": "MoisesOh",
   "language": "es",
  "text": "RT @AndresCaamilo: Gente que se crea un Twitter solo por moda
y ni lo utiliza. Lo peor es que tienen como 3,000 o 5,000 seguidores y
todos son fakes."
 },
 {
   "created_at": "Thu, 13 Jan 2011 05:56:09 +0000",
   "from_user": "miriampomposo",
   "language": "es",
    "text": "RT @ciberluis: @alvarez_armando yo los sigo a todos en
#Twitter: @danoga  @blancaleyva @edith_gonzalez @miriampomposo @abulle1
@ylicona ccp @hechos_puebla"
 },
 {
   "created_at": "Thu, 13 Jan 2011 05:56:07 +0000",
j
```

```
    "from_user": "pitagotica",
    "language": "es",
   "text": "@Franzz8 ¬ ¬ no me pases videos por twitter, no tengo tiempo de verlos ahorita, tengo miles que verm dame tantito chance"
 },
 {
   "created_at": "Thu, 13 Jan 2011 05:56:06 +0000",
   "from_user": "kamiresources",
   "language": "es",
   "text": "Filed under:     Selena Gomez,     Justin Bieber,     Foxnews Latino    \n          \n\t          \t Selena Gomez \'s Face - http://bit.ly/dF3N9o"
 },
 {
   "created_at": "Thu, 13 Jan 2011 06:16:45 +0000",
   "from_user": "kagranemann",
   "language": "pt",
   "text": "ALEXANDRE GRAH.. EU SEI QUE VOCÊ ESTÁ NO MEU TWITTER.. VOLTE PRO MSN QUE TENHO QUE FALAR CONTIGO AGORA! sério"
 },
 {
   "created_at": "Thu, 13 Jan 2011 06:18:21 +0000",
   "from_user": "matiassblog",
   "language": "es",
   "text": "@malabanuel jajaja ni me lo recuerdes q ahora estoy en shock con el Twitter... Mi mama..."
 },
 {
   "created_at": "Thu, 13 Jan 2011 06:18:18 +0000",
   "from_user": "joint_seminar",
   "language": "zh",
   "text": "【拡散希望】 鹿児島県出水市にて、Twitter初心者セミナー開催。 Twitterの登録から解説しますので、Twitterに興味をお持ちの方にご紹介下さい  詳細⇒http://bit.ly/dF3bvy 携帯から⇒http://bit.ly/gEmd4b #kagoshima"
 },
 {
   "created_at": "Thu, 13 Jan 2011 06:18:18 +0000",
   "from_user": "luquinhaz",
   "language": "pt",
```

```
  "text": "Concordo RT @Cardoso: Eu acho que o report spam do twitter é um belo de um placebo."
 }
]
```

10. Sort *tweetrecs* so that the records appear in the order in which they were created.

```
tweetrecs -> sort by [$.created_at asc];
```

The list is very long so I have shortlisted it.

```
jaql> tweetrecs -> sort by [$.created_at asc];
[
 {
  "created_at": "Thu, 10 Jun 2010 03:22:33 +0000",
  "from_user": "GreatTwitTips",
  "language": "en",
  "text": "RT @mobtuts: RT @berryizm_feeds: 5 BlackBerry Theme Developer Tips from MMMOOO a BlackBerry theme and app dev comp... http://bit.ly/agf0ND"
 },
 {
  "created_at": "Thu, 10 Jun 2010 03:25:00 +0000",
  "from_user": "tutsplus",
  "language": "en",
  "text": "Subscribe to the @mobtuts weekly podcast now! Choose RSS http://bit.ly/9LMbGX or iTunes http://bit.ly/bq0QMC"
 },
 {
  "created_at": "Thu, 10 Jun 2010 03:45:51 +0000",
  "from_user": "mobtuts",
  "language": "en",
  "text": "Subscribe to the @mobtuts weekly podcast now! Choose RSS http://bit.ly/9LMbGX or iTunes http://bit.ly/bq0QMC"
 },
 {
  "created_at": "Thu, 10 Jun 2010 03:52:28 +0000",
  "from_user": "cead22",
  "language": "en",
  "text": "Quiero un #iPhone4 con #FroYo -- How to Install Android 2.2
```

```
Froyo on iPhone http://bit.ly/c8kBb6 (@mobtuts)"
 },
 {
   "created_at": "Thu, 10 Jun 2010 03:54:22 +0000",
   "from_user": "mariacarol",
   "language": "en",
   "text": "RT @mobtuts: How to Install Android 2.2 Froyo on iPhone
http://bit.ly/c8kBb6"
 },
 {
   "created_at": "Thu, 13 Jan 2011 05:56:06 +0000",
   "from_user": "kamiresources",
   "language": "es",
   "text": "Filed under:     Selena Gomez,     Justin Bieber,     Foxnews
Latino    \n             \n\t          \t Selena Gomez \'s Face - http://
bit.ly/dF3N9o"
 },
 {
   "created_at": "Thu, 13 Jan 2011 05:56:06 +0000",
   "from_user": "BIIIITCHplezO_O",
   "language": "en",
   "text": "Awwwwww dont look on twitter doe lol RT @OhSoSavage Damn i
need an official boo... Im not hip to this \'\'lonely\'\' shidd.. Any
takers?"
 },

jaql>
```

11. If you notice, there are several tweets that occurred at the same time. So not only sort in created sequence but also in descending language sequence.

```
tweetrecs -> sort by [$.create_at asc, $.language desc];
```

12. Aggregate your data and count the number of tweets for each language.

```
tweetrecs -> group by key = $.language into {language: key, num: count($)};
```

```
jaql> tweetrecs -> group by key = $.language into {language:
key, num: count($)};
[
  {
    "language": "zh",
    "num": 1
  },
  {
    "language": "es",
    "num": 7
  },
  {
    "language": "en",
    "num": 38
  },
  {
    "language": "pt",
    "num": 2
  }
]
jaql>
```

13. You are going to write your results to a file in Hadoop but first you must create the target directory in HDFS. You can do this from the *jaqlshell* using the *hdfsShell()*.

    `hdfsShell('-mkdir /user/biadmin/jaql');`

14. Write the results of the previous aggregation to a JSON file in HDFS.

```
tweetrecs->group by key = $.langauage into {language: key, num:
count($)}-
>write(seq("hdfs:/user/biadmin/jaql/twittercount.seq"));
```

15. Verify that your file was created.

    `hdfsShell('-ls /user/biadmin/jaql');`

EXERCISE 8.3 USING JAQL CORE OPERATORS

In this exercises you will use Jaql core operators to manipulate csv data as well as using Jaql's SQL.

Section 1: *Core operators*

1. Located on the lab image is a file of JSON records that contain book titles, the author, theyear published and some reviews. First read this file so that you can repeatedly access the data in the file. Then display the contents of the file.

```
books=read(file("/home/biadmin/SampleData/bookreviews.json"));books;
```

Be case sensitive as the same directory biadmin is having another folder by name sampleData but in that case the name starts with small case letters.

```
[
 {
   "author": "J. K. Rowlings",
   "published": 1997,
   "reviews": [
     {
       "name": "Mary",
       "stars": 5
     },
     {
       "name": "Tom",
       "stars": 5
     }
   ],
   "title": "The Sorcerers Stone"
 },
 {
   "author": "J. K. Rowlings",
   "published": 1998,
   "reviews": [
     {
       "name": "Bill",
       "stars": 5
     },
     {
       "name": "Sue",
       "stars": 4
     },
     {
       "name": "Theo",
       "stars": 5
     }
   ],
   "title": "The Chamber of Secrets"
 },
 {
   "author": "J. K. Rowlings",
```

```
    "published": 1999,
    "reviews": [
      {
        "name": "Mary",
        "stars": 5
      },
      {
        "name": "Cindy",
        "stars": 5
      }
    ],
    "title": "The Prisoner of Azkaban"
  },
  {
    "author": "J. K. Rowlings",
    "published": 2000,
    "reviews": [
      {
        "name": "Andrew",
        "stars": 4
      },
      {
        "name": "Katie",
        "stars": 4
      },
      {
        "name": "Scott",
        "stars": 5
      }
    ],
    "title": "The Goblet of Fire"
  },
  {
    "author": "J. K. Rowlings",
    "published": 2003,
    "reviews": [
      {
```

```
      "name": "Jeff",
      "stars": 3
    },
    {
      "name": "Sara",
      "stars": 4
    },
    {
      "name": "Ryan",
      "stars": 5
    }
  ],
  "title": "The Order of the Phoenix"
},
{
  "author": "J. K. Rowlings",
  "published": 2005,
  "reviews": [
    {
      "name": "Bob",
      "stars": 5
    },
    {
      "name": "Autumn",
      "stars": 4
    }
  ],
  "title": "The Half-Blood Prince"
},
{
  "author": "J. K. Rowlings",
  "published": 2007,
  "reviews": [
    {
      "name": "Betty",
      "stars": 5
    },
```

```
    {
      "name": "Janet",
      "stars": 5
    },
    {
      "name": "Scott",
      "stars": 5
    }
  ],
  "title": "The Deathly Hallows"
},
{
  "author": "David Baldacci",
  "published": 2005,
  "reviews": [
    {
      "name": "Andrew",
      "stars": 4
    },
    {
      "name": "Katie",
      "stars": 4
    },
    {
      "name": "Scott",
      "stars": 5
    }
  ],
  "title": "Camel Club"
},
{
  "author": "David Baldacci",
  "published": 2006,
  "reviews": [
    {
      "name": "Mary",
      "stars": 5
    },
```

```
    {
      "name": "Tom",
      "stars": 5
    }
  ],
  "title": "The Collectors"
},
{
  "author": "David Baldacci",
  "published": 2007,
  "reviews": [
    {
      "name": "Bill",
      "stars": 5
    },
    {
      "name": "Sue",
      "stars": 4
    },
    {
      "name": "Theo",
      "stars": 5
    }
  ],
  "title": "Stone Cold"
},
{
  "author": "David Baldacci",
  "published": 2008,
  "reviews": [
    {
      "name": "Mary",
      "stars": 5
    },
```

```
{
      "name": "Cindy",
      "stars": 5
    }
  ],
  "title": "Divine Justice"
},
{
  "author": "David Baldacci",
  "published": 2010,
  "reviews": [
    {
      "name": "Andrew",
      "stars": 4
    },
    {
      "name": "Katie",
      "stars": 4
    },
    {
      "name": "Scott",
      "stars": 5
    }
  ],
  "title": "Hells Corner"
},
{
  "author": "J. K. Rowlings",
  "published": 2003,
  "reviews": [
    {
      "name": "Jeff",
      "stars": 3
    },
    {
      "name": "Sara",
      "stars": 4
    },
```

```
    {
      "name": "Ryan",
      "stars": 5
    }
  ],
  "title": "Split Second"
},
{
  "author": "David Baldacci",
  "published": 2004,
  "reviews": [
    {
      "name": "Bob",
      "stars": 5
    },
    {
      "name": "Autumn",
      "stars": 4
    }
  ],
  "title": "Hour Game"
},
{
  "author": "David Baldacci",
  "published": 2007,
  "reviews": [
    {
      "name": "Betty",
      "stars": 5
    },
    {
      "name": "Janet",
      "stars": 5
    },
{
      "name": "Scott",
      "stars": 5
    }
```

```
    ],
    "title": "Simple Genius"
  },
  {
    "author": "David Baldacci",
    "published": 2009,
    "reviews": [
      {
        "name": "Andrew",
        "stars": 4
      },
      {
        "name": "Katie",
        "stars": 4
      },
      {
        "name": "Scott",
        "stars": 5
      }
    ],
    "title": "First Family"
  }
]
```

2. What if you were going to be reading several JSON files from the *SampleData* directory?Since none of you gets paid by the keystroke, you can lessen the amount of future typing by incorporating your *read* into a function. Normally the file name is passed to the *read()* function in quotation marks. Here you must concatenate the directory string and the filename parameter.

   (The following is really a single line.)

   ```
   read(file("/home/biadmin/SampleData/"+filename));
   ```

   Next test your function by re-reading the *bookreviews.json* file.

   ```
   readjson("bookreviews.json");
   ```

Note : Same thing can be done by following statements

```
jaql> abhi = fn(filename) read(file("/home/biadmin/SampleData/"+filename));
jaql> abhi('bookreviews.json');
```

3. The *bookreviews* file contains books from two authors, J. K. Rowlings and David Baldacci. List only those books that were written by *David Baldacci.*

```
Books -> filter $.author == 'David Baldacci';
```

```
jaql> books -> filter $.author == 'David Baldacci';
[
 {
   "author": "David Baldacci",
   "published": 2005,
   "reviews": [
     {
       "name": "Andrew",
       "stars": 4
     },
     {
       "name": "Katie",
       "stars": 4
     },
     {
       "name": "Scott",
       "stars": 5
     }
   ],
   "title": "Camel Club"
 },
 {
   "author": "David Baldacci",
   "published": 2006,
   "reviews": [
     {
       "name": "Mary",
       "stars": 5
     },
     {
       "name": "Tom",
       "stars": 5
     }
   ],
   "title": "The Collectors"
```

```
},
{
  "author": "David Baldacci",
  "published": 2007,
  "reviews": [
    {
      "name": "Bill",
      "stars": 5
    },
    {
      "name": "Sue",
      "stars": 4
    },
    {
      "name": "Theo",
      "stars": 5
    }
  ],
  "title": "Stone Cold"
},
{
  "author": "David Baldacci",
  "published": 2008,
  "reviews": [
    {
      "name": "Mary",
      "stars": 5
    },
    {
      "name": "Cindy",
      "stars": 5
    }
  ],
  "title": "Divine Justice"
},
{
  "author": "David Baldacci",
```

```
  "published": 2010,
  "reviews": [
    {
      "name": "Andrew",
      "stars": 4
    },
    {
      "name": "Katie",
      "stars": 4
    },
    {
      "name": "Scott",
      "stars": 5
    }
  ],
  "title": "Hells Corner"
},
{
  "author": "David Baldacci",
  "published": 2004,
  "reviews": [
    {
      "name": "Bob",
      "stars": 5
    },
    {
      "name": "Autumn",
      "stars": 4
    }
  ],
  "title": "Hour Game"
},
{
  "author": "David Baldacci",
  "published": 2007,
  "reviews": [
    {
```

```
        "name": "Betty",
        "stars": 5
      },
      {
        "name": "Janet",
        "stars": 5
      },
      {
        "name": "Scott",
        "stars": 5
      }
    ],
    "title": "Simple Genius"
  },
  {
    "author": "David Baldacci",
    "published": 2009,
    "reviews": [
      {
        "name": "Andrew",
        "stars": 4
      },
      {
        "name": "Katie",
        "stars": 4
      },
      {
        "name": "Scott",
        "stars": 5
      }
    ],
    "title": "First Family"
  }
]
```

3. List all books that were published before 2001.

```
books -> filter $.published < 2001;
```

Following is the result:

```
jaql> books -> filter $.published < 2001;
[
 {
   "author": "J. K. Rowlings",
   "published": 1997,
   "reviews": [
     {
       "name": "Mary",
       "stars": 5
     },
     {
       "name": "Tom",
       "stars": 5
     }
   ],
   "title": "The Sorcerers Stone"
 },
 {
   "author": "J. K. Rowlings",
   "published": 1998,
   "reviews": [
     {
       "name": "Bill",
       "stars": 5
     },
     {
       "name": "Sue",
       "stars": 4
     },
     {
       "name": "Theo",
       "stars": 5
     }
   ],
   "title": "The Chamber of Secrets"
 },
```

```
  {
    "author": "J. K. Rowlings",
    "published": 1999,
    "reviews": [
      {
        "name": "Mary",
        "stars": 5
      },
      {
        "name": "Cindy",
        "stars": 5
      }
    ],
    "title": "The Prisoner of Azkaban"
  },
  {
    "author": "J. K. Rowlings",
    "published": 2000,
    "reviews": [
      {
        "name": "Andrew",
        "stars": 4
      },
      {
        "name": "Katie",
        "stars": 4
      },
      {
        "name": "Scott",
        "stars": 5
      }
    ],
    "title": "The Goblet of Fire"
  }
]
```

5. We can total the number of books by each author and display the name of the author and the book total.

```
books-> group by author = $.author into {author, num_books: count($)};
Following shall be listed on terminal:
```

```
jaql> books -> filter $.published < 2001;
[
 {
   "author": "J. K. Rowlings",
   "published": 1997,
   "reviews": [
     {
       "name": "Mary",
       "stars": 5
     },
     {
       "name": "Tom",
       "stars": 5
     }
   ],
   "title": "The Sorcerers Stone"
 },
 {
   "author": "J. K. Rowlings",
   "published": 1998,
   "reviews": [
     {
       "name": "Bill",
       "stars": 5
     },
     {
       "name": "Sue",
       "stars": 4
     },
     {
       "name": "Theo",
       "stars": 5
     }
```

```
    ],
    "title": "The Chamber of Secrets"
  },
  {
    "author": "J. K. Rowlings",
    "published": 1999,
    "reviews": [
      {
        "name": "Mary",
        "stars": 5
      },
      {
        "name": "Cindy",
        "stars": 5
      }
    ],
    "title": "The Prisoner of Azkaban"
  },
  {
    "author": "J. K. Rowlings",
    "published": 2000,
    "reviews": [
      {
        "name": "Andrew",
        "stars": 4
      },
      {
        "name": "Katie",
        "stars": 4
      },
      {
        "name": "Scott",
        "stars": 5
      }
    ],
    "title": "The Goblet of Fire"
  }
]
```

```
jaql> books-> group by author = $.author into {author, num_books: count($)};
```

```
[
 {
   "author": "David Baldacci",
   "num_books": 8
 },
 {
   "author": "J. K. Rowlings",
   "num_books": 8
 }
]
```

6. Next, for those books published in 2000, write a record that only contains the author and the title.

```
books->filter $.published == 2000 ->transform {$.author, $.title};
```

```
Terminal
File  Edit  View  Terminal  Help
jaql> books->filter $.published == 2000 ->transform {$.author, $.title};
[
  {
    "author": "J. K. Rowlings",
    "title": "The Goblet of Fire"
  }
]

jaql>
```

7. What if you wanted to split your data into multiple files based upon the author? You want only the data for *David Baldacci* to be in one file and all other authors in another.

```
books -> tee( -> filter $.author == 'David Baldacci' ->
write(jsonTextfile("file:///home/biadmin/bd.json"))) -> filter $.author !=
'David Baldacci' -> write(jsonTextFile("file:///home/biadmin/other.
json"));
```

tee command is something like teepoint in a route in which two path emerges.

8. And if you wanted to sort your data on *published?*

```
books -> sort by [$.published asc];
```

WE shall see following listing:

```
jaql> books -> sort by [$.published asc];
[
 {
   "author": "J. K. Rowlings",
   "published": 1997,
   "reviews": [
     {
       "name": "Mary",
       "stars": 5
     },
     {
       "name": "Tom",
       "stars": 5
     }
   ],
   "title": "The Sorcerers Stone"
 },
 {
   "author": "J. K. Rowlings",
   "published": 1998,
   "reviews": [
     {
       "name": "Bill",
       "stars": 5
     },
     {
       "name": "Sue",
       "stars": 4
     },
     {
       "name": "Theo",
       "stars": 5
     }
   ],
   "title": "The Chamber of Secrets"
 },
 {
```

```
"author": "J. K. Rowlings",
   "published": 1999,
   "reviews": [
     {
       "name": "Mary",
       "stars": 5
     },
     {
       "name": "Cindy",
       "stars": 5
     }
   ],
   "title": "The Prisoner of Azkaban"
 },
 {
   "author": "J. K. Rowlings",
   "published": 2000,
   "reviews": [
     {
       "name": "Andrew",
       "stars": 4
     },
     {
       "name": "Katie",
       "stars": 4
     },
     {
       "name": "Scott",
       "stars": 5
     }
   ],
   "title": "The Goblet of Fire"
 },
 {
   "author": "J. K. Rowlings",
   "published": 2003,
   "reviews": [
```

```
      {
        "name": "Jeff",
        "stars": 3
      },
      {
        "name": "Sara",
        "stars": 4
      },
      {
        "name": "Ryan",
        "stars": 5
      }
    ],
    "title": "The Order of the Phoenix"
  },
  {
    "author": "J. K. Rowlings",
    "published": 2003,
    "reviews": [
      {
        "name": "Jeff",
        "stars": 3
      },
      {
        "name": "Sara",
        "stars": 4
      },
      {
        "name": "Ryan",
        "stars": 5
      }
    ],
    "title": "Split Second"
  },
  {
    "author": "David Baldacci",
    "published": 2004,
```

```
    “reviews”: [
      {
        “name”: “Bob”,
        “stars”: 5
      },
      {
        “name”: “Autumn”,
        “stars”: 4
      }
    ],
    “title”: “Hour Game”
  },
  {
    “author”: “J. K. Rowlings”,
    “published”: 2005,
    “reviews”: [
      {
        “name”: “Bob”,
        “stars”: 5
      },
      {
        “name”: “Autumn”,
        “stars”: 4
      }
    ],
    “title”: “The Half-Blood Prince”
  },
  {
    “author”: “David Baldacci”,
    “published”: 2005,
    “reviews”: [
      {
        “name”: “Andrew”,
        “stars”: 4
      },
      {
        “name”: “Katie”,
```

```
            "stars": 4
        },
        {
            "name": "Scott",
            "stars": 5
        }
    ],
    "title": "Camel Club"
},
{
    "author": "David Baldacci",
    "published": 2006,
    "reviews": [
        {
            "name": "Mary",
            "stars": 5
        },
        {
            "name": "Tom",
            "stars": 5
        }
    ],
    "title": "The Collectors"
},
{
    "author": "J. K. Rowlings",
    "published": 2007,
    "reviews": [
        {
            "name": "Betty",
            "stars": 5
        },
        {
            "name": "Janet",
            "stars": 5
        },
        {
            "name": "Scott",
```

```
        "stars": 5
      }
    ],
    "title": "The Deathly Hallows"
  },
  {
    "author": "David Baldacci",
    "published": 2007,
    "reviews": [
      {
        "name": "Bill",
        "stars": 5
      },
      {
        "name": "Sue",
        "stars": 4
      },
      {
        "name": "Theo",
        "stars": 5
      }
    ],
    "title": "Stone Cold"
  },
  {
    "author": "David Baldacci",
    "published": 2007,
    "reviews": [
      {
        "name": "Betty",
        "stars": 5
      },
      {
        "name": "Janet",
        "stars": 5
      },
```

```
      {
        "name": "Scott",
        "stars": 5
      }
    ],
    "title": "Simple Genius"
  },
  {
    "author": "David Baldacci",
    "published": 2008,
    "reviews": [
      {
        "name": "Mary",
        "stars": 5
      },
      {
        "name": "Cindy",
        "stars": 5
      }
    ],
    "title": "Divine Justice"
  },
  {
    "author": "David Baldacci",
    "published": 2009,
    "reviews": [
      {
        "name": "Andrew",
        "stars": 4
      },
      {
        "name": "Katie",
        "stars": 4
      },
      {
        "name": "Scott",
        "stars": 5
      }
```

```
    ],
    "title": "First Family"
  },
  {
    "author": "David Baldacci",
    "published": 2010,
    "reviews": [
      {
        "name": "Andrew",
        "stars": 4
      },
      {
        "name": "Katie",
        "stars": 4
      },
      {
        "name": "Scott",
        "stars": 5
      }
    ],
    "title": "Hells Corner"
  }
]
jaql>
```

9. There is a second file, */home/biadmin/SampleData/books.csv,* that only contains the information about each book. This file is in a csv format. Each record has a book number, the author, the title, and the year published.

CSV (Comma delimited)

This file format (.csv) saves only the text and values as they are displayed in cells of the active worksheet. All rows and all characters in each cell are saved. Columns of data are separated by commas, and each row of data ends in a carriage return. If a cell contains a comma, the cell contents are enclosed in double quotation marks.

If cells display formulas instead of formula values, the formulas are converted as text. All formatting, graphics, objects, and other worksheet contents are lost. The euro symbol will be converted to a question mark.

Note If your workbook contains special font characters such as a copyright symbol (©), and you will be using the converted text file on a computer with a different operating system, save the workbook in the text file format that is appropriate for that system. For example, if you are using Windows and want to use the text file on a Macintosh computer, save the file in the CSV (Macintosh) format. If you are using a Macintosh computer and want to use the text file on a system running Windows or Windows NT, save the file in the CSV (Windows) format.

Read this file but be aware that the *del()* I/O adapter defaults to reading from a Hadoop file system.

```
booksonly=read(del("file:///home/biadmin/SampleData/books.csv"));
booksonly;
Following is the outcome of above action:
jaql> booksonly=read(del("file:///home/biadmin/SampleData/books.csv"));
```

```
jaql> booksonly;
[
 [
   "1",
   "J. K. Rowlings",
   "The Sorcerer\'s Stone",
   "1997"
 ],
 [
   "2",
   "J. K. Rowlings",
   "The Chamber of Secrets",
   "1999"
 ],
 [
   "3",
   "J. K. Rowlings",
   "The Prisoner of Azkaban",
   "1999"
 ],
 [
   "4",
   "J. K. Rowlings",
   "The Goblet of Fire",
   "2000"
 ],
```

```
[
  "5",
  "J. K. Rowlings",
  "The Order of the Phoenix",
  "2003"
],
[
  "6",
  "J. K. Rowlings",
  "The Half-Blood Prince",
  "2005"
],
[
  "7",
  "J. K. Rowlings",
  "The Deathly Hallows",
  "2007"
],
[
  "8",
  "David Baldacci",
  "Camel Club",
  "2005"
],
[
  "9",
  "David Baldacci",
  "The Collectors",
  "2006"
],
[
  "10",
  "David Baldacci",
  "Stone Cold",
  "2007"
],
[
```

```
    "11",
    "David Baldacci",
    "Divine Justice",
    "2008"
  ],
  [
    "12",
    "David Baldacci",
    "Hells Corner",
    "2010"
  ],
  [
    "13",
    "David Baldacci",
    "Split Second",
    "2003"
  ],
  [
    "14",
    "David Baldacci",
    "Hour Game",
    "2004"
  ],
  [
    "15",
    "David Baldacci",
    "Simple Genius",
    "2007"
  ],
  [
    "16",
    "David Baldacci",
    "First Family",
    "2009"
  ]
]
```

10. What if for some reason (and this is a lab exercise so there does not have to be a logical reason to do anything), you wanted the individual arrays in booksonly to be put into a single array? (This takes longer to run.)

```
booksonly -> expand $;
jaql> booksonly -> expand $;
```

```
[
 "1",
 "J. K. Rowlings",
 "The Sorcerer\'s Stone",
 "1997",
 "2",
 "J. K. Rowlings",
 "The Chamber of Secrets",
 "1999",
 "3",
 "J. K. Rowlings",
 "The Prisoner of Azkaban",
 "1999",
 "4",
 "J. K. Rowlings",
 "The Goblet of Fire",
 "2000",
 "5",
 "J. K. Rowlings",
 "The Order of the Phoenix",
 "2003",
 "6",
 "J. K. Rowlings",
 "The Half-Blood Prince",
 "2005",
 "7",
 "J. K. Rowlings",
 "The Deathly Hallows",
 "2007",
 "8",
```

```
  "David Baldacci",
  "Camel Club",
  "2005",
  "9",
  "David Baldacci",
  "The Collectors",
  "2006",
  "10",
  "David Baldacci",
  "Stone Cold",
  "2007",
  "11",
  "David Baldacci",
  "Divine Justice",
  "2008",
  "12",
  "David Baldacci",
  "Hells Corner",
  "2010",
  "13",
  "David Baldacci",
  "Split Second",
  "2003",
  "14",
  "David Baldacci",
  "Hour Game",
  "2004",
  "15",
  "David Baldacci",
  "Simple Genius",
  "2007",
  "16",
  "David Baldacci",
  "First Family",
  "2009"
]
```

11. Because all Jaql had to read was that delimited data, there were no fields assigned and if you notice, the years are read as strings. Reread the file but this time specify a schema to assign fields and to make sure that the data is read correctly.

```
booksonly=read(del("file:///home/biadmin/SampleData/books.csv",schema=schema{booknum:long,author:string,title:string,published:long}));
```

Now enter this command

```
booksonly;
```

and see that the format of data listing has changed:

```
jaql> booksonly;
[
  {
    "booknum": 1,
    "author": "J. K. Rowlings",
    "title": "The Sorcerer\'s Stone",
    "published": 1997
  },
  {
    "booknum": 2,
    "author": "J. K. Rowlings",
    "title": "The Chamber of Secrets",
    "published": 1999
  },
  {
    "booknum": 3,
    "author": "J. K. Rowlings",
    "title": "The Prisoner of Azkaban",
    "published": 1999
  },
  {
    "booknum": 4,
    "author": "J. K. Rowlings",
    "title": "The Goblet of Fire",
    "published": 2000
  },
  {
    "booknum": 5,
```

```
  "author": "J. K. Rowlings",
  "title": "The Order of the Phoenix",
  "published": 2003
},
{
  "booknum": 6,
  "author": "J. K. Rowlings",
  "title": "The Half-Blood Prince",
  "published": 2005
},
{
  "booknum": 7,
  "author": "J. K. Rowlings",
  "title": "The Deathly Hallows",
  "published": 2007
},
{
  "booknum": 8,
  "author": "David Baldacci",
  "title": "Camel Club",
  "published": 2005
},
{
  "booknum": 9,
  "author": "David Baldacci",
  "title": "The Collectors",
  "published": 2006
},
{
  "booknum": 10,
  "author": "David Baldacci",
  "title": "Stone Cold",
  "published": 2007
},
{
  "booknum": 11,
  "author": "David Baldacci",
```

```
    "title": "Divine Justice",
    "published": 2008
  },
  {
    "booknum": 12,
    "author": "David Baldacci",
    "title": "Hells Corner",
    "published": 2010
  },
  {
    "booknum": 13,
    "author": "David Baldacci",
    "title": "Split Second",
    "published": 2003
  },
  {
    "booknum": 14,
    "author": "David Baldacci",
    "title": "Hour Game",
    "published": 2004
  },
  {
    "booknum": 15,
    "author": "David Baldacci",
    "title": "Simple Genius",
    "published": 2007
  },
  {
    "booknum": 16,
    "author": "David Baldacci",
    "title": "First Family",
    "published": 2009
  }
]
```

8. There is another delimited file, called *reviews.csv,* in the same directory. Each record contains a book number, name of the reviewer, and the number of stars. Read it.

```
reviews=read(del("file:///home/biadmin/SampleData/reviews.
csv",schema=schema{booknum:long,name:string,stars:long}));
reviews;
```

The above will cause following listing;

```
jaql>        reviews=read(del("file:///home/biadmin/SampleData/reviews.
csv",schema=schema{booknum:long,name:string,stars:long}));
reviews;
jaql> [
  {
    "booknum": 1,
    "name": "Mary",
    "stars": 5
  },
  {
    "booknum": 1,
    "name": "Tom",
    "stars": 5
  },
  {
    "booknum": 2,
    "name": "Bill",
    "stars": 5
  },
  {
    "booknum": 2,
    "name": "Sue",
    "stars": 4
  },
  {
    "booknum": 2,
    "name": "Theo",
    "stars": 5
  },
  {
    "booknum": 3,
    "name": "Mary",
```

```
    "stars": 5
  },
  {
    "booknum": 3,
    "name": "Cindy",
    "stars": 5
  },
  {
    "booknum": 4,
    "name": "Andrew",
    "stars": 4
  },
  {
    "booknum": 4,
    "name": "Katie",
    "stars": 4
  },
  {
    "booknum": 4,
    "name": "Scott",
    "stars": 5
  },
  {
    "booknum": 5,
    "name": "Jeff",
    "stars": 3
  },
  {
    "booknum": 5,
    "name": "Sara",
    "stars": 4
  },
  {
    "booknum": 5,
    "name": "Ryan",
    "stars": 5
  },
```

```
{
  "booknum": 6,
  "name": "Bob",
  "stars": 5
},
{
  "booknum": 6,
  "name": "Autumn",
  "stars": 4
},
{
  "booknum": 7,
  "name": "Betty",
  "stars": 5
},
{
  "booknum": 7,
  "name": "Janet",
  "stars": 5
},
{
  "booknum": 7,
  "name": "Scott",
  "stars": 5
},
{
  "booknum": 8,
  "name": "Andrew",
  "stars": 4
},
{
  "booknum": 8,
  "name": "Katie",
  "stars": 4
},
{
  "booknum": 8,
```

```
    "name": "Scott",
    "stars": 5
  },
  {
    "booknum": 9,
    "name": "Mary",
    "stars": 5
  },
  {
    "booknum": 9,
    "name": "Tom",
    "stars": 5
  },
  {
    "booknum": 10,
    "name": "Bill",
    "stars": 5
  },
  {
    "booknum": 10,
    "name": "Sue",
    "stars": 4
  },
  {
    "booknum": 10,
    "name": "Theo",
    "stars": 5
  },
  {
    "booknum": 11,
    "name": "Mary",
    "stars": 5
  },
  {
    "booknum": 11,
    "name": "Cindy",
    "stars": 5
  },
```

```
{
  "booknum": 12,
  "name": "Andrew",
  "stars": 4
},
{
  "booknum": 12,
  "name": "Katie",
  "stars": 4
},
{
  "booknum": 12,
  "name": "Scott",
  "stars": 5
},
{
  "booknum": 13,
  "name": "Jeff",
  "stars": 3
},
{
  "booknum": 13,
  "name": "Sara",
  "stars": 4
},
{
  "booknum": 13,
  "name": "Ryan",
  "stars": 5
},
{
  "booknum": 14,
  "name": "Bob",
  "stars": 5
},
```

```
  {
    "booknum": 14,
    "name": "Autumn",
    "stars": 4
  },
  {
    "booknum": 15,
    "name": "Betty",
    "stars": 5
  },
  {
    "booknum": 15,
    "name": "Janet",
    "stars": 5
  },
  {
    "booknum": 15,
    "name": "Scott",
    "stars": 5
  },
  {
    "booknum": 16,
    "name": "Andrew",
    "stars": 4
  },
  {
    "booknum": 16,
    "name": "Katie",
    "stars": 4
  },
  {
    "booknum": 16,
    "name": "Scott",
    "stars": 5
  }
]
```

13. Join the *booksonly* and *reviews* arrays on the *booknum* fields resulting in just the title of the book and the stars associated. This will take some time.

```
booksandstars=join b in booksonly, r in reviews where b.booknum ==
r.booknum into {b.title, r.stars}; booksandstars;
```

14. Now calculate the average number of stars for each book.

```
booksandstars->group by book = $.title into {book, avg_stars: avg($.
stars)};
```

After execution of above command following shall be listed:

```
jaql> booksandstars->group by book = $.title into {book, avg_stars:
avg($.stars)};
[
  {
    "title": "The Sorcerer\'s Stone",
    "stars": 5
  },
  {
    "title": "The Sorcerer\'s Stone",
    "stars": 5
  },
  {
    "title": "The Chamber of Secrets",
    "stars": 5
  },
  {
    "title": "The Chamber of Secrets",
    "stars": 4
  },
  {
    "title": "The Chamber of Secrets",
    "stars": 5
  },
  {
    "title": "The Prisoner of Azkaban",
    "stars": 5
  },
  {
```

```
    "title": "The Prisoner of Azkaban",
    "stars": 5
  },
  {
    "title": "The Goblet of Fire",
    "stars": 4
  },
  {
    "title": "The Goblet of Fire",
    "stars": 4
  },
  {
    "title": "The Goblet of Fire",
    "stars": 5
  },
  {
    "title": "The Order of the Phoenix",
    "stars": 4
  },
  {
    "title": "The Order of the Phoenix",
    "stars": 3
  },
  {
    "title": "The Order of the Phoenix",
    "stars": 5
  },
  {
    "title": "The Half-Blood Prince",
    "stars": 5
  },
  {
    "title": "The Half-Blood Prince",
    "stars": 4
  },
  {
    "title": "The Deathly Hallows",
```

```
  "stars": 5
 },
 {
  "title": "The Deathly Hallows",
  "stars": 5
 },
 {
  "title": "The Deathly Hallows",
  "stars": 5
 },
 {
  "title": "Camel Club",
  "stars": 4
 },
 {
  "title": "Camel Club",
  "stars": 4
 },
 {
  "title": "Camel Club",
  "stars": 5
 },
 {
  "title": "The Collectors",
  "stars": 5
 },
 {
  "title": "The Collectors",
  "stars": 5
 },
 {
  "title": "Stone Cold",
  "stars": 4
 },
 {
  "title": "Stone Cold",
  "stars": 5
```

```
},
{
  "title": "Stone Cold",
  "stars": 5
},
{
  "title": "Divine Justice",
  "stars": 5
},
{
  "title": "Divine Justice",
  "stars": 5
},
{
  "title": "Hells Corner",
  "stars": 4
},
{
  "title": "Hells Corner",
  "stars": 4
},
{
  "title": "Hells Corner",
  "stars": 5
},
{
  "title": "Split Second",
  "stars": 4
},
{
  "title": "Split Second",
  "stars": 3
},
{
  "title": "Split Second",
  "stars": 5
},
{
```

```
},
{
  "title": "Stone Cold",
  "stars": 5
},
{
  "title": "Divine Justice",
  "stars": 5
},
{
  "title": "Divine Justice",
  "stars": 5
},
{
  "title": "Hells Corner",
  "stars": 4
},
{
  "title": "Hells Corner",
  "stars": 4
},
{
  "title": "Hells Corner",
  "stars": 5
},
{
  "title": "Split Second",
  "stars": 4
},
{
  "title": "Split Second",
  "stars": 3
},
{
  "title": "Split Second",
  "stars": 5
},
{
```

```
    "title": "Hour Game",
    "stars": 5
  },
  {
    "title": "Hour Game",
    "stars": 4
  },
  {
    "title": "Simple Genius",
    "stars": 5
  },
  {
    "title": "Simple Genius",
    "stars": 5
  },
  {
    "title": "Simple Genius",
    "stars": 5
  },
  {
    "title": "First Family",
    "stars": 4
  },
  {
    "title": "First Family",
    "stars": 4
  },
  {
    "title": "First Family",
    "stars": 5
  }
]
```

15. You can accomplish the same thing by using co-grouping as you did with the join and the group by statements.

```
group booksonly by g = $.booknum as bs, reviews by g = $.booknum as rs
into {title:bs[0].title, avg_stars: avg(rs.stars)};
```

```
jaql> group booksonly by g = $.booknum as bs, reviews by g = $.booknum
as rs into {title:bs[0].title, avg_stars: avg(rs.stars)};
[
 {
   "book": "Camel Club",
   "avg_stars": 4
 },
 {
   "book": "Divine Justice",
   "avg_stars": 5
 },
 {
   "book": "First Family",
   "avg_stars": 4
 },
 {
   "book": "Hells Corner",
   "avg_stars": 4
 },
 {
   "book": "Hour Game",
   "avg_stars": 4
 },
 {
   "book": "Simple Genius",
   "avg_stars": 5
 },
 {
   "book": "Split Second",
   "avg_stars": 4
 },
 {
   "book": "Stone Cold",
   "avg_stars": 4
 },
 {
   "book": "The Chamber of Secrets",
  "avg_stars": 4
 },
 {
   "book": "The Collectors",
   "avg_stars": 5
```

```
},
{
  "book": "The Deathly Hallows",
  "avg_stars": 5
},
{
  "book": "The Goblet of Fire",
  "avg_stars": 4
},
{
  "book": "The Half-Blood Prince",
  "avg_stars": 4
},
{
  "book": "The Order of the Phoenix",
  "avg_stars": 4
},
{
  "book": "The Prisoner of Azkaban",
  "avg_stars": 5
},
{
  "book": "The Sorcerer\'s Stone",
  "avg_stars": 5
}
]
```

8.8 USE JAQL SQL

1. Earlier you read `/home/biadmin/SampleData/bookreviews.json` into books. This contained both book and review information. Use a select statement to access `author, title,` and `published` from this file.

```
select author, title, published from books;
```

What happened? There are some limitations when using a select statement in Jaql.

The record format needs to be consistent.

2. Use the *transform* operator to get a consistent set of records.

```
sqlbooks = books -> transform {$.author, $.title, $.published};
```

3. Now do your select again.

```
select author, title, published from sqlbooks;
```

```
jaql>
sqlbooks = books -> transform {$.author, $.title, $.published};
jaql> select author, title, published from sqlbooks;
[
 {
   "author": "J. K. Rowlings",
   "title": "The Sorcerers Stone",
   "published": 1997
 },
 {
   "author": "J. K. Rowlings",
   "title": "The Chamber of Secrets",
   "published": 1998
 },
 {
   "author": "J. K. Rowlings",
   "title": "The Prisoner of Azkaban",
   "published": 1999
 },
 {
   "author": "J. K. Rowlings",
   "title": "The Goblet of Fire",
   "published": 2000
 },
 {
   "author": "J. K. Rowlings",
   "title": "The Order of the Phoenix",
   "published": 2003
 },
 {
   "author": "J. K. Rowlings",
   "title": "The Half-Blood Prince",
   "published": 2005
 },
 {
   "author": "J. K. Rowlings",
   "title": "The Deathly Hallows",
   "published": 2007
 },
 {
```

```
    "author": "David Baldacci",
    "title": "Camel Club",
    "published": 2005
  },
  {
    "author": "David Baldacci",
    "title": "The Collectors",
    "published": 2006
  },
  {
    "author": "David Baldacci",
    "title": "Stone Cold",
    "published": 2007
  },
  {
    "author": "David Baldacci",
    "title": "Divine Justice",
    "published": 2008
  },
  {
    "author": "David Baldacci",
    "title": "Hells Corner",
    "published": 2010
  },
  {
    "author": "J. K. Rowlings",
    "title": "Split Second",
    "published": 2003
  },
  {
    "author": "David Baldacci",
    "title": "Hour Game",
    "published": 2004
  },
  {   "author": "David Baldacci",
    "title": "Simple Genius",
    "published": 2007
```

```
  },
  {
    "author": "David Baldacci",
    "title": "First Family",
    "published": 2009
  }
]
```

4. Read in the data from */home/biadmin/SampleData/books.csv* as follows:

   csvbooks=read(del("file:///home/biadmin/SampleData/books.csv"));

5. Select *author, title,* and *published* from this file.

   select author, title, published from csvbooks;

   Once again, not a lot of success.

   Following message is received:

```
jaql> select author, title, published from csvbooks;
parse error: java.lang.RuntimeException: sql requires only records
instead of:schema [ * ]
```

   But why? There is no schema information when just reading a csv file.

6. Earlier you read this file with a schema into *booksonly.* Select *author, title,* and *published* from this file.

```
select author, title, published from booksonly;
jaql> select author, title, published from booksonly;
[
 {
   "author": "J. K. Rowlings",
   "title": "The Sorcerer\'s Stone",
   "published": 1997
 }, {
   "author": "J. K. Rowlings",
   "title": "The Chamber of Secrets",
   "published": 1999
 },
 {
   "author": "J. K. Rowlings",
   "title": "The Prisoner of Azkaban",
   "published": 1999
 },
```

```
{
  "author": "J. K. Rowlings",
  "title": "The Goblet of Fire",
  "published": 2000
},
{
  "author": "J. K. Rowlings",
  "title": "The Order of the Phoenix",
  "published": 2003
},
{
  "author": "J. K. Rowlings",
  "title": "The Half-Blood Prince",
  "published": 2005
},
{
  "author": "J. K. Rowlings",
  "title": "The Deathly Hallows",
  "published": 2007
},
{
  "author": "David Baldacci",
  "title": "Camel Club",
  "published": 2005
},
{
  "author": "David Baldacci",
  "title": "The Collectors",
  "published": 2006
},
{
  "author": "David Baldacci",
  "title": "Stone Cold",
  "published": 2007
},
{
  "author": "David Baldacci",
  "title": "Divine Justice",
  "published": 2008
},
{
```

```
    "author": "David Baldacci",
    "title": "Hells Corner",
    "published": 2010
  },
  {
    "author": "David Baldacci",
    "title": "Split Second",
    "published": 2003
  },
  {
    "author": "David Baldacci",
    "title": "Hour Game",
    "published": 2004
  },
  {
    "author": "David Baldacci",
    "title": "Simple Genius",
    "published": 2007
  },
  {
    "author": "David Baldacci",
    "title": "First Family",
    "published": 2009
  }
]
```

7. Next add a condition to your select. Get only those books published since 2003.

   select author, title, published from booksonly where published > 2003;

```
jaql> select author, title, published from booksonly where published >
2003;
[
  {
    "author": "J. K. Rowlings",
    "title": "The Half-Blood Prince",
    "published": 2005
  },
  {
    "author": "J. K. Rowlings",
    "title": "The Deathly Hallows",
"published": 2007
  },
```

```
  {
    "author": "David Baldacci",
    "title": "Camel Club",
    "published": 2005
  },
  {
    "author": "David Baldacci",
    "title": "The Collectors",
    "published": 2006
  },
  {
    "author": "David Baldacci",
    "title": "Stone Cold",
    "published": 2007
  },
  {
    "author": "David Baldacci",
    "title": "Divine Justice",
    "published": 2008
},
  {
    "author": "David Baldacci",
    "title": "Hells Corner",
    "published": 2010
  },
  {
    "author": "David Baldacci",
    "title": "Hour Game",
    "published": 2004
  },
  {
    "author": "David Baldacci",
    "title": "Simple Genius",
    "published": 2007
  },
  {
    "author": "David Baldacci",
    "title": "First Family",
    "published": 2009
  }
 ]
```

8. Earlier you did a join of two arrays and then a group by to come up with the average number of stars for each book. Then you used co-grouping to accomplish the same task. Now use Jaql SQL in order to do the averaging a third way.

```
select b.title, avg(r.stars) as avg_stars from booksonly b, reviews r
group
by b.title;
```

```
   jaql> select b.title, avg(r.stars) as avg_stars from booksonly b,
reviews r group
   by b.title;
   [
    {
      "title": "Camel Club",
      "avg_stars": 4
    },
    {
      "title": "Divine Justice",
      "avg_stars": 4
    },
    {
      "title": "First Family",
      "avg_stars": 4
    },
    {
      "title": "Hells Corner",
      "avg_stars": 4
    },
    {
      "title": "Hour Game",
      "avg_stars": 4
    },
    {
      "title": "Simple Genius",
      "avg_stars": 4
    },
    {
      "title": "Split Second",
      "avg_stars": 4
```

```
  },
  {
    "title": "Stone Cold",
    "avg_stars": 4
  },
  {
    "title": "The Chamber of Secrets",
    "avg_stars": 4
  },
  {
    "title": "The Collectors",
   "avg_stars": 4
 },
  {
    "title": "The Deathly Hallows",
    "avg_stars": 4
  },
  {
    "title": "The Goblet of Fire",
    "avg_stars": 4
  },
  {
    "title": "The Half-Blood Prince",
    "avg_stars": 4
  },
  {
    "title": "The Order of the Phoenix",
    "avg_stars": 4
  },
  {
    "title": "The Prisoner of Azkaban",
    "avg_stars": 4
  },
  {
    "title": "The Sorcerer\'s Stone",
    "avg_stars": 4
  }
]
```

9. Do an explain on the above *select* and see the code that gets generated. What is interesting is that the explain for the co-grouping distills to a map / reduce whereas the SQL distills to an mrAggregate. If you were to do an explain of your previous join being streamed into your previous group by, it would distill to an mrAggregate as well. Go ahead and try that.

Examples of analyzing data with Jaql

EXAMPLE 2: Computing Word Count

You can compute word count by using the EXPAND operator. In contrast to the TRANSFORM operator, which creates a nested array of strings, EXPAND produces a single array of strings, even if the input is a nested array. Word count requires a single array of strings. To illustrate this example, consider the following input data:

```
example = [
  ["first", "example"],
  ["second", "example"]
];
```

If you perform a TRANSFORM on this input (example -> transform $;), you get the following data:

```
[
  [
    "first",
    "example"
  ],
  [
    "second",
    "example"
  ]
]
```

If you use EXPAND instead (example ->expand;), you get the following data:

```
[
  "first",
  "example",
  "second",
  "example"
]
```

The following code shows how EXPAND is used with a simple tokenizer that is implemented as the user-defined function (UDF) splitArr:

```
splitArr = javaudf("com.acme.extensions.fn.Split1");
splitArr("something simple with five words", " ");
The code returns the following results:
[
```

```
"something",
"simple",
"with",
"five",
"words"
]
```

You can register the UDF by associating a name with its implementing class. Then, you exercise the splitArr function on a sample string by using a simple delimiter. Finally, you implement the word-count by reading the log data, tokenizing each $.msg, expanding the tokens into the output array, grouping on word, computing a count per word, and outputting an object for each word and its associated count:

```
log
-> expand splitArr($.msg, " ")
-> group by word = $
   into { word, num: count($) };
```

Jaql evaluates this query by translating to MapReduce. The read, tokenization, and expansion are performed in the map step. The grouping and count are performed in the reduce step. Because count is an algebraic function, Jaql pushes its computation into the map step and performs a sum in the reduce step. That is, it takes advantage of MapReduce combiners where applicable.

The earlier query returns the following results:

```
[
  {
    "num": 1,
    "word": "Agreed,"
  },
  {
    "num": 1,
    "word": "Ann"
  },
  {
    "num": 2,
    "word": "Hello,"
  },
  {
    "num": 1,
    "word": "Joe,"
  },
  {
    "num": 1,
    "word": "Seinfeld"
  },
  ...
 ]
```

EXAMPLE 3: Using Word-Count For Specific Words

If you want to perform a word-count on specific words, you can add a filter on the words that are returned. To add the filter, use tokenization to produce an array that filters the words according to an in-list of words:

```
inList = ["topic", "Seinfeld"];
```

This array is used as the source of a subpipe, which is a pipe that is nested under another pipe; in this case, the outer pipe.

```
  log
-> expand (splitArr($.msg, " ") -> filter $ in inList )
-> group by word = $
     into { word, num: count($) };
```

The following results are returned:

```
[
  {
    "num": 1,
    "word": "Seinfeld"
  },
  {
    "num": 4,
    "word": "topic"
  }
]
```

8.9 JAQL FUNCTIONS

With Jaql, it is easy to create user-defined functions written entirely in Jaql. Since you have not yet been exposed to most of the features and functions of Jaql, the functions that you will now code will be rather simplistic. In spite of this, you should still be able to get the concept of coding functions in Jaql.

1. Create a function called *myabs* that calls the built-in absolute function.

```
myabs = fn(x) abs(x);
```

2. Test it with both a positive and a negative value.

```
myabs(4);
myabs(-4);
```

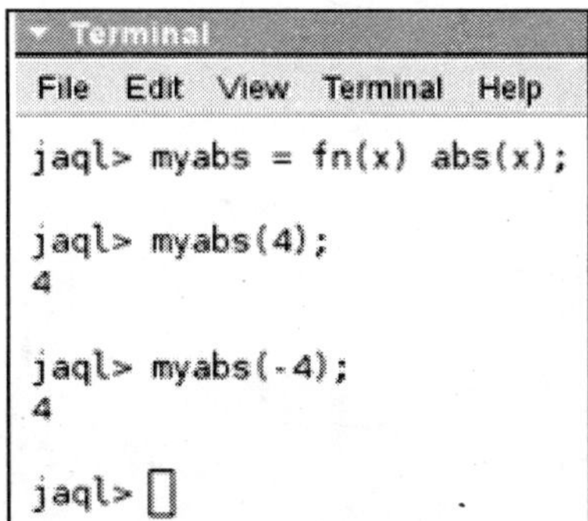

3. Next create a function, *evenodd,* that checks if the input value is even or odd and returns an appropriate string value.

```
evenodd = fn(x) if (mod(x,2) == 0) "even" else "odd";
```

4. Test your function.

```
evenodd(7);
evenodd(8);
evenodd(-7);
```

```
jaql> evenodd = fn(x) if (mod(x,2) == 0) "even" else "odd";

jaql> evenodd(7);
"odd"

jaql> evenodd(8);
"even"

jaql> evenodd(-7);
"odd"

jaql>
```

5. Finally create a function, called *myfunc,* that accepts other functions that support a single value.

```
myfunc = fn(op, val) op(val);
```

6. Test your function.

```
myfunc(myabs, -7);
myfunc(evenodd,7);
```

```
myfunc = fn(op, val) op(val);

jaql> myfunc = fn(op, val) op(val);

jaql>    myfunc(myabs, -7);
7

jaql> myfunc(evenodd,7);
"odd"

jaql>
```

CHAPTER

9

Hive : The Data Ware house of Hadoop

9.1 INTRODUCTION TO HIVE : THE DATA WARE HOUSE OF HADOOP

Hive is an open-source data warehousing solution built on top of Hadoop. Hive supports queries expressed in a SQL-like declarative language - HiveQL, which are compiled into mapreduce jobs that are executed using Hadoop. In addition, HiveQL enables users to plug in custom map-reduce scripts into queries.

Data warehouses offer organizations the ability to gather and store enterprise information in a single conceptual enterprise repository. Basic data modeling techniques are applied to create relationship associations between individual data elements or data element groups. These associations, or "models," often take the form of entity relationship diagrams (ERDs). More advanced techniques include the star schema and snowflake data model concepts. Regardless of the technique chosen, the goal is to build a metadata model that conceptually represents the information usage and relationships within the organization.

The language includes a type system with support for tables containing primitive types, collections like arrays and maps, and nested compositions of the same. The underlying IO libraries can be extended to query data in custom formats. Hive also includes a system catalog - Metastore – that contains schemas and statistics, which are useful in data exploration, query optimization and query compilation. In Facebook, the Hive warehouse contains tens of thousands of tables and stores over

700TB of data and is being used extensively for both reporting and ad-hoc analyses by more than 200 users per month.

9.1.1 Hadoop Revisited

The Hadoop ecosystem contains different sub-projects (tools) such as ***Sqoop, Pig, and Hive*** that are used to help Hadoop modules.

1. Sqoop: It is used to import and export data to and fro between HDFS and RDBMS.
2. Pig: It is a procedural language platform used to develop a script for MapReduce operations.
3. Hive: It is a platform used to develop SQL type scripts to do MapReduce operations.

Note: There are various ways to execute MapReduce operations:

- The traditional approach using Java MapReduce program for structured, semi-structured, and unstructured data.
- The scripting approach for MapReduce to process structured and semi structured data using Pig.
- The Hive Query Language (HiveQL or HQL) for MapReduce to process structured data using Hive.

9.1.2 What is Hive

Hive is a data warehouse infrastructure tool to process structured data in Hadoop. It resides on top of Hadoop to summarize Big Data, and makes querying and analyzing easy.

Initially Hive was developed by Facebook, later the Apache Software Foundation took it up and developed it further as an open source under the name Apache Hive. It is used by different companies. For example, Amazon uses it in Amazon Elastic

9.1.3 Features of Hive

- It stores schema in a database and processed data into HDFS.
- It is designed for OLAP.
- It provides SQL type language for querying called HiveQL or HQL.
- It is familiar, fast, scaExercisele, and extensible.

Hive is not

- A relational database
- A design for OnLine Transaction Processing (OLTP)
- A language for real-time queries and row-level updates

Hive is a data warehouse system for Hadoop that facilitates easy data summarization, ad-hoc queries, and the analysis of large datasets stored in Hadoop compatible file systems. Hive structures data into well-understood database concepts such as tables, rows, columns and partitions. It supports primitive types like Integers, Floats, Doubles, and Strings. Hive also supports Associative Arrays, Lists, Structs, and Serialize and Deserialized API is used to move data in and out of tables.

9.1.4 Architecture of Hive

The following component diagram depicts the architecture of Hive:

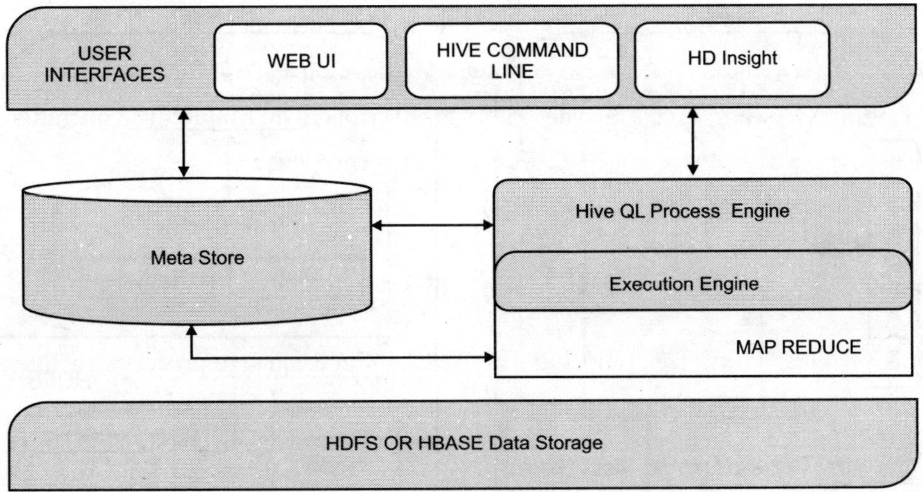

This component diagram contains different units. The following table describes each unit:

Unit Name	Operation
User Interface	Hive is a data warehouse infrastructure software that can create interaction between user and HDFS. The user interfaces that Hive supports are Hive Web UI, Hive command line, and Hive HD Insight (In Windows server).
Meta Store	Hive chooses respective database servers to store the schema or Metadata of tables, databases, columns in a table, their data types, and HDFS mapping.
HiveQL Process Engine	HiveQL is similar to SQL for querying on schema info on the Metastore. It is one of the replacements of traditional approach for MapReduce program. Instead of writing MapReduce program in Java, we can write a query for MapReduce job and process it.
Execution Engine	The conjunction part of HiveQL process Engine and MapReduce is Hive Execution Engine. Execution engine processes the query and generates results as same as MapReduce results. It uses the flavor of MapReduce.
HDFS or HBASE	Hadoop distributed file system or HBASE are the data storage techniques to store data into file system.

9.1.5 Working of Hive

The following diagram depicts the workflow between Hive and Hadoop.

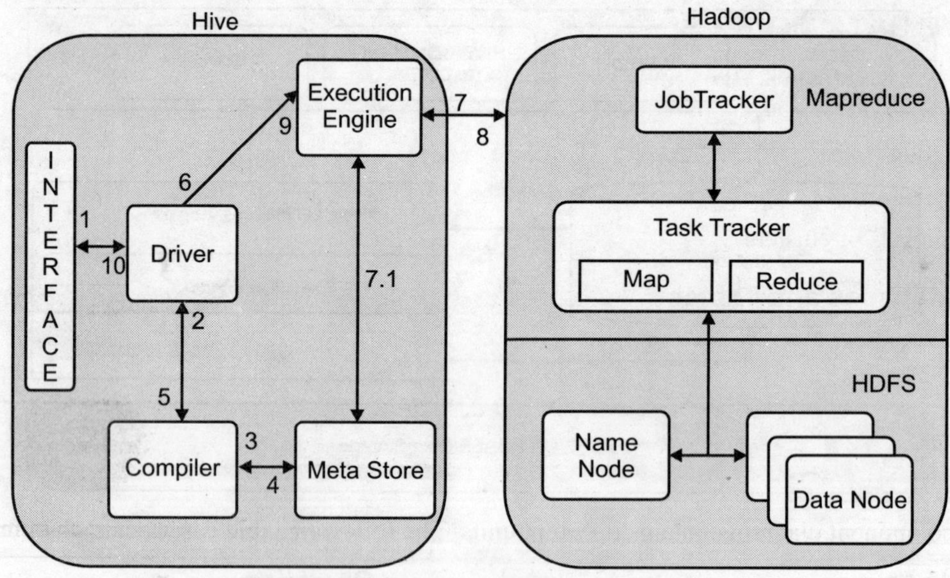

The following table defines how Hive interacts with Hadoop framework:

Step No.	Operation
1	**Execute Query** : The Hive interface such as Command Line or Web UI sends query to Driver (any database driver such as JDBC, ODBC, etc.) to execute.
2	**Get Plan** : The driver takes the help of query compiler that parses the query to check the syntax and query plan or the requirement of query.
3	**Get Metadata** : The compiler sends metadata request to Metastore (any database).
4	**Send Metadata** : Metastore sends metadata as a response to the compiler.
5	**Send Plan** : The compiler checks the requirement and resends the plan to the driver. Up to here, the parsing and compiling of a query is complete.
6	**Execute Plan** : The driver sends the execute plan to the execution engine.
7	**Execute Job** : Internally, the process of execution job is a MapReduce job. The execution engine sends the job to JobTracker, which is in Name node and it assigns this job to TaskTracker, which is in Data node. Here, the query executes MapReduce job.
7.1	**Metadata Ops** : Meanwhile in execution, the execution engine can execute metadata operations with Metastore.
8	**Fetch Result** : The execution engine receives the results from Data nodes.
9	**Send Results** : The execution engine sends those resultant values to the driver.
10	**Send Results** : The driver sends the results to Hive Interfaces.

9.2 HIVE DATA MODELS:

The Hive data models contain the following components:

- Databases
- Tables
- Partitions
- Buckets or clusters

9.2.1 Databases and Tables

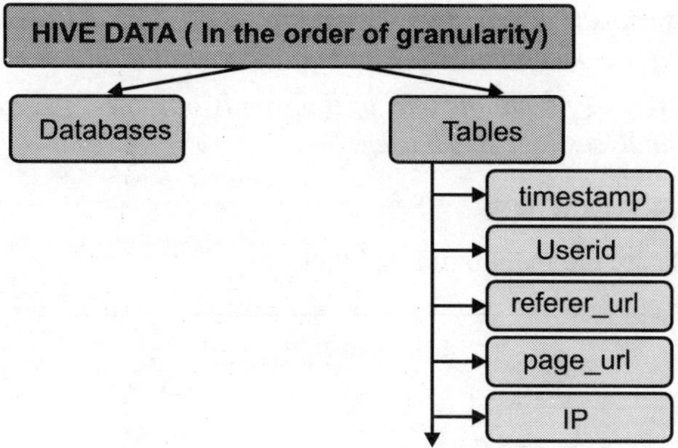

9.2.2 Partitions:

Partition means dividing a table into a coarse grained parts based on the value of a partition column such as 'data'. This makes it faster to do queries on slices of data

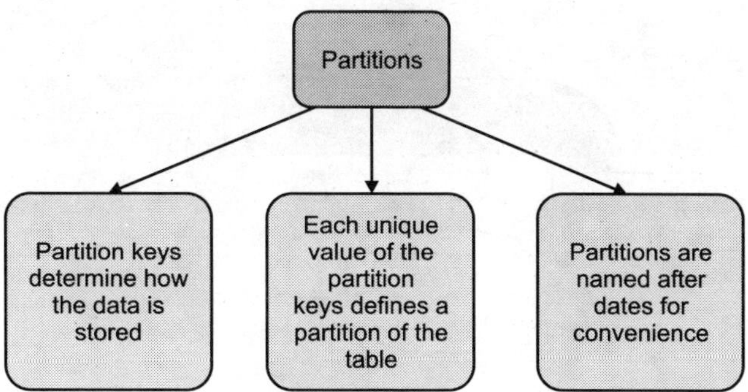

So, what is the function of Partition? The Partition keys determine how data is stored. Here, each unique value of the Partition key defines a Partition of the table. The Partitions are named after dates for convenience. It is similar to 'Block Splitting' in HDFS.

9.2.3 Buckets:

Buckets give extra structure to the data that may be used for efficient queries. A join of two tables that are bucketed on the same columns, including the join column can be implemented as a Map-Side Join.

Bucketing by used ID means we can quickly evaluate a user-based query by running it on a randomized sample of the total set of users.

Yahoo worked on Pig to facilitate application deployment on Hadoop. Their need mainly was focused on unstructured data Simultaneously Facebook started working on deploying warehouse solutions on Hadoop that resulted in Hive.

The size of data being collected and analyzed in industry for business intelligence (BI) is growing rapidly making traditional warehousing solution prohibitively expensive. MR is very low level and requires customers to write custom programs. HIVE supports queries expressed in SQL-like language called HiveQL which are compiled into MR jobs that are executed on Hadoop.

Hive also allows MR scripts. It also includes MetaStore that contains schemas and statistics that are useful for data explorations, query optimization and query compilation.

At Facebook Hive warehouse contains tens of thousands of tables, stores over 700TB and is used for reporting and ad-hoc analyses by 200 Fb users.

9.3 HIVE BUILDING BLOCKS

The following components are the main building blocks in

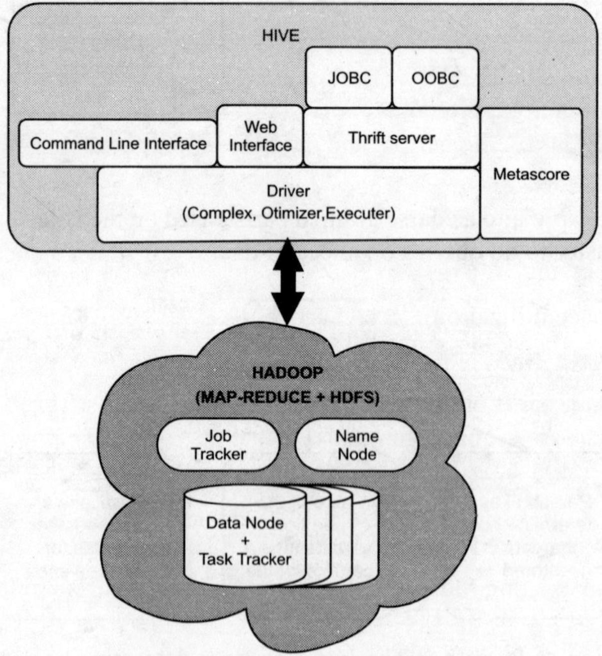

Hive:

1. **Metastore** – The component that stores the system catalog and metadata about tables, columns, partitions etc.

2. **Driver** – The component that manages the lifecycle of a HiveQL statement as it moves through Hive. The driver also maintains a session handle and any session statistics.

3. **Query Compiler** – The component that compiles HiveQL into a directed acyclic graph of map/reduce tasks.
4. **Execution Engine** – The component that executes the tasks produced by the compiler in proper dependency order. The execution engine interacts with the underlying Hadoop instance.
5. **HiveServer n**– The component that provides a thrift interface and a JDBC/ODBC server and provides a way of integrating Hive with other applications.
6. **Clients** components like the Command Line Interface (CLI), the web UI and JDBC/ODBC driver.
7. **Extensibility Interfaces** which include the SerDe and ObjectInspector interfaces already described previously as well as the UDF(User Defined Function) and UDAF(User Defined Aggregate Function) interfaces that enable users to define their own custom functions.

9.4 HIVE DATA FILE FORMATS

For storage specifically, Hadoop provides a few basic file formats which can help to save memory and provide a better way to access relational data. Today, we will be discussing, in detail, how RCFile and ORCFile are used to help store and access relational data in Hadoop.

9.4.1 RCFile

The RCFile (Record Columnar File) is a data storage structure that determines how to minimize the space required for relational data in HDFS (Hadoop Distributed File System). It does this by changing the format of the data using the MapReduce framework. The RCFile combines multiple functions such as data storage formatting, data compression, and data access optimization. It is able to meet all the four requirements of data storage:

(1) Fast data storing,

(2) Improved query processing,

(3) Optimized storage space utilization

(4) Dynamic data access patterns.

The RCFile format can partition the data both horizontally and vertically. This allows it to fetch only the specific fields that are required for analysis, thereby eliminating the standard time needed to analyse the whole table in a database. The overall data size reduction can be as large as 14% of the original data format.

The simplest way to create the RCFile format is using Hive in Hadoop as follows:

(If you do not have an existing file to use, begin by creating one. Example below)

```
CREATE TABLE table_rc (
column1 STRING,
column2 STRING,
column3 INT,
column4 INT
)
STORED AS RCFILE;
```

Enabling Compression for RCFile:

```
SET hive.exec.compress.output=true;
SET mapred.output.compression.type=BLOCK;
SET mapred.output.compression.codec=org.apache.hadoop.io.compress.
SnappyCodec;
  Create a hive table:
CREATE TABLE table_txt (
column1 STRING,
column2 STRING,
column3 INT,
column4 INT
)
ROW FORMAT DELIMITED fields terminated by ' ';
LOCATION '< HDFS FILE PATH >';
```

As we have created a hive table, now we can write this data into "table_rc" table:

```
INSERT OVERWRITE TABLE table_rc SELECT * FROM table_txt;
```

Now you can run a query on an individual column basis. The MapReduce job will begin; however, you must watch the**HDFS_BYTES_READ** parameter to see the difference of the bytes read from the HDFS. You can see that there is a huge difference of the data that is read, as the RCFile is reading only one column and the text format is reading the complete data to execute the query.

9.4.2 ORC File

The ORC File (Optimized Row Columnar) format provides a more efficient way to store relational data than the RC File, reducing the data storage format by up to 75% of the original. The ORC file format performs better than other Hive files formats when Hive is reading, writing, and processing data. Specifically compared to the RC File, ORC takes less time to access data and takes less space to store data. However, the ORC file increases CPU overhead by increasing the time it takes to decompress the relational data. Also, the ORC File format comes with the Hive 0.11 version and cannot be used with previous versions.

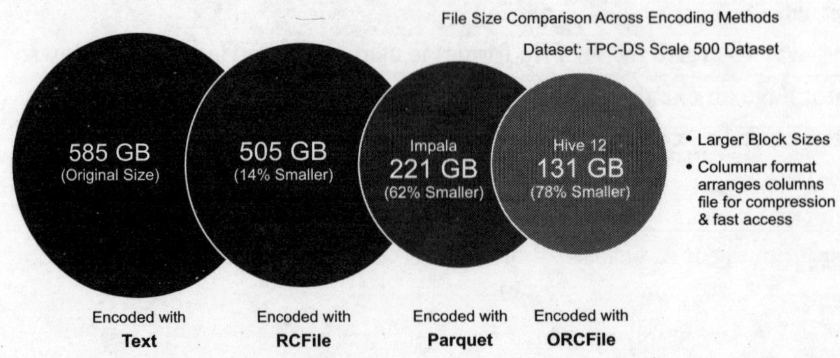

How to create an ORC File using Hive in Hadoop:

If you don't have an existing file to use, begin by creating one:

```
CREATE TABLE table_orc (
column1 STRING,
column2 STRING,
column3 INT,
column4 INT
) STORED AS ORC;
```

Create a hive table:

```
CREATE TABLE table_temp (
name STRING,
address STRING,
age INT,
salary INT
)
ROW FORMAT DELIMITED fields terminated by ' ';
LOCATION '< HDFS FILE PATH >';
```

Write the data into "table_orc" table :

```
INSERT OVERWRITE TABLE table_orc SELECT * FROM table_temp;
```

EXERCISE 9.1 Accessing Hadoop Data Using Hive

Working with Hive DDL

Before we can begin working with and analyzing data in Hive we must first use Hive's data manipulation language. Using Hive DML will enable us to create databases, tables, partitions and more which we can later load with data that can be queried and manipulated.

Throughout this Exercise it is assumed that you will be using the following account login information:

Username	Password
VM image setup screen root	password
Linux biadmin	password

If you are continuing this series of hands on Exercises immediately after completing Accessing Hadoop Data

9.5 ACCESSING THE HIVE BEELINE COMMAND LINE INTERFACE (CLI)

In this section we will navigate to the Hive Beeline CLI and start an interactive CLI session.

1. Open the Linux terminal by double clicking the Terminal icon from within the *BigInsights Shell directory* on the desktop.

Note: You could also directly start the "original Hive CLI shell" by clicking the Hive shell icon within the BigInsights Shell directory. This Exercise however uses the newer Beeline CLI.

9.5.1 What is Beeline

Recently, the Hive community (with Cloudera engineers leading the charge) introduced HiveServer2, an enhanced Hive server designed for multi-client concurrency and improved authentication that also provides better support for clients connecting through JDBC and ODBC. Now HiveServer2, with Beeline as the command-line interface, is the recommended solution; HiveServer1 and Hive CLI are deprecated and the latter won't even work with HiveServer2.

Beeline was developed specifically to interact with the new server. Unlike Hive CLI, which is an Apache Thrift-based client, Beeline is a JDBC client based on the SQLLine CLI — although the JDBC driver used communicates with HiveServer2 using HiveServer2's Thrift APIs.

As Hive development has shifted from the original Hive server (HiveServer1) to the new server (HiveServer2), users and developers accordingly need to switch to the new client tool. However, there's more to this process than simply switching the executable name from "hive" to "beeline". In its original form, Apache Hive was a heavyweight command-line tool that accepted queries and executed them utilizing

2. In the Linux terminal change to the Hive home bin directory

```
~> cd $HIVE_HOME/bin
```

3. Start an interactive Hive shell session.

```
~> ./beeline -u jdbc:hive2://bivm.ibm.com:10000 -n biadmin -p
password
```

```
biadmin@bivm:...ginsights/hive/bin
File Edit View Terminal Help
biadmin@bivm:~> cd $HIVE_HOME/bin
biadmin@bivm:/opt/ibm/biginsights/hive/bin> ./beeline -u jdbc:hive2://bivm.ibm.com:10000 -n biadmin -p password
scan complete in 36ms
Connecting to jdbc:hive2://bivm.ibm.com:10000
Connected to: Hive (version 0.12.0)
Driver: Hive (version 0.12.0)
Transaction isolation: TRANSACTION_REPEATABLE_READ
-hiveconf (No such file or directory)
hive.aux.jars.path=file:/opt/ibm/biginsights/hive/lib/hive-hbase-handler-0.12.0.jar,file:/opt/ibm/biginsights/hive/li
/hive/lib/hbase-client-0.96.0.jar,file:/opt/ibm/biginsights/hive/lib/hbase-common-0.96.0.jar,file:/opt/ibm/biginsight
t/ibm/biginsights/hive/lib/hbase-prefix-tree-0.96.0.jar,file:/opt/ibm/biginsights/hive/lib/hbase-protocol-0.96.0.jar,
6.0.jar,file:/opt/ibm/biginsights/hive/lib/htrace-core-2.01.jar,file:/opt/ibm/biginsights/hive/lib/zookeeper-3.4.5.ja
.jar,file:/opt/ibm/biginsights/sheets/libext/pig-0.11.1.jar,file:/opt/ibm/biginsights/sheets/libext/avro-1.7.4.jar,fi
ar,file:/opt/ibm/biginsights/sheets/libext/json-simple-1.1.jar,file:/opt/ibm/biginsights/sheets/libext/joda-time-1.6.
ts.jar,file:/opt/ibm/biginsights/sheets/libext/bigsheets-serdes-1.0.0.jar,file:/opt/ibm/biginsights/lib/parquet/parqu
ights/lib/parquet/parquet-mr/parquet-common-1.3.2.jar,file:/opt/ibm/biginsights/lib/parquet/parquet-mr/parquet-encodi
parquet-mr/parquet-generator-1.3.2.jar,file:/opt/ibm/biginsights/lib/parquet/parquet-mr/parquet-hadoop-bundle-1.3.2.j
/parquet-hive-bundle-1.3.2.jar,file:/opt/ibm/biginsights/lib/parquet/parquet-mr/parquet-thrift-1.3.2.jar,file:/opt/ib
le or directory)
Beeline version 0.12.0 by Apache Hive
0: jdbc:hive2://bivm.ibm.com:10000>
```

4. Run the SHOW DATABASES statement from within the interactive Hive session.

hive> SHOW DATABASES;

```
biadmin@bivm:...ginsights/hive/bin
File Edit View Terminal Help
0: jdbc:hive2://bivm.ibm.com:10000> SHOW DATABASES;
+----------------+
| database_name  |
+----------------+
| default        |
+----------------+
1 row selected (6.641 seconds)
0: jdbc:hive2://bivm.ibm.com:10000>
```

9.6 WORKING WITH DATABASES IN HIVE

If we neglect to create a new database in Hive, then the "default" database will be used. Let's create a new database and work with it. In this exercise we will create two databases in the Hive system. One of them will be used for future exercises. The other will be deleted.

1. In the Hive shell create a database called *testDB*.

hive> CREATE DATABASE testDB;

```
0: jdbc:hive2://bivm.ibm.com:10000> CREATE DATABASE testDB;
No rows affected (7.362 seconds)
0: jdbc:hive2://bivm.ibm.com:10000>
```

2. Let's confirm that the new database was added to Hive's catalog.

hive> SHOW DATABASES;

```
biadmin@bivm:...ginsights/hive/bin
File Edit View Terminal Help
0: jdbc:hive2://bivm.ibm.com:10000> SHOW DATABASES;
+----------------+
| database_name  |
+----------------+
| default        |
| testdb         |
+----------------+
2 rows selected (2.261 seconds)
0: jdbc:hive2://bivm.ibm.com:10000>
```

Notice that Hive converted "testDB" to lowercase.

3. Now that we have created a new database, let's describe it.

hive> DESCRIBE DATABASE TESTDB;

```
biadmin@bivm:...ginsights/hive/bin
File Edit View Terminal Help
0: jdbc:hive2://bivm.ibm.com:10000> DESCRIBE DATABASE TESTDB;
+----------+----------+-----------------------------------------------------------+-------------+
| db_name  | comment  |                         location                          | parameters  |
+----------+----------+-----------------------------------------------------------+-------------+
| testdb   |          | hdfs://bivm.ibm.com:9000/biginsights/hive/warehouse/testdb.db |          |
+----------+----------+-----------------------------------------------------------+-------------+
1 row selected (1.744 seconds)
0: jdbc:hive2://bivm.ibm.com:10000>
```

The DESCRIBE DATABASE shows us the location of *testdb (Although we entered TESTDB)* on HDFS. Notice that the testdb.db schema is being stored inside HDFS in the /biginsights/hive/warehouse directory.

4. Let's confirm that the new testdb.db directory was in fact created on HDFS. Open a second Linux terminal by double clicking the Terminal icon from within the *BigInsights Shell directory* on the desktop.

5. Check HDFS to confirm our new database directory was created.

~> hadoop fs -ls /biginsights/hive/warehouse

```
biadmin@bivm:~
File Edit View Terminal Help
biadmin@bivm:~> hadoop fs -ls /biginsights/hive/warehouse
Found 1 items
drwxrwxrwt   - biadmin biadmin          0 2016-03-03 06:12 /biginsights/hive/war
ehouse/testdb.db
biadmin@bivm:~>
```

The testdb.db directory WAS created.

Keep this second Linux console open for the rest of this Exercise. We will continue to use it to look at HDFS. You will be going back and forth between the Hive console and this Linux console.

6. Add some information to the DBPROPERTIES metadata for the testdb database. We do this by using the ALTER DATABASE syntax.

hive> ALTER DATABASE testdb SET DBPROPERTIES ('creator' = 'bigdatarockstar');

```
biadmin@bivm:...ginsights/hive/bin
File Edit View Terminal Help
0: jdbc:hive2://bivm.ibm.com:10000> ALTER DATABASE testdb SET DBPROPERTIES ('creator' = 'bigdatarockstar');
No rows affected (1.029 seconds)
0: jdbc:hive2://bivm.ibm.com:10000>
```

7. Let's view the extended details of our *testdb* database.

hive> DESCRIBE DATABASE EXTENDED testdb;

```
File Edit View Terminal Help
0: jdbc:hive2://bivm.ibm.com:10000> DESCRIBE DATABASE EXTENDED testdb;
+----------+---------+------------------------------------------------------------+---------------------------+
| db_name  | comment |                          location                          |         parameters        |
+----------+---------+------------------------------------------------------------+---------------------------+
| testdb   |         | hdfs://bivm.ibm.com:9000/biginsights/hive/warehouse/testdb.db | {creator=bigdatarockstar} |
+----------+---------+------------------------------------------------------------+---------------------------+
1 row selected (1.876 seconds)
0: jdbc:hive2://bivm.ibm.com:10000>
```

Notice the updated database properties.

8. Go ahead and delete the *testdb* database.

hive> DROP DATABASE testdb CASCADE;

Please see the screen shot below:

Notice the CASCADE keyword. That is optional. Using it will cause Hive to delete all the tables in your database (if there are any) before dropping the database. If you try to delete a database that has tables without the CASCADE keyword, Hive won't let you.

9. Confirm that *testdb* is no longer in the Hive metastore catalog.

hive> SHOW DATABASES;

```
biadmin@bivm:...ginsights/hive/bin
File Edit View Terminal Help
0: jdbc:hive2://bivm.ibm.com:10000> DROP DATABASE TESTDB CASCADE;
No rows affected (13.474 seconds)
0: jdbc:hive2://bivm.ibm.com:10000> SHOW DATABASES;
+----------------+
| database_name  |
+----------------+
| default        |
+----------------+
1 row selected (1.65 seconds)
0: jdbc:hive2://bivm.ibm.com:10000>
```

10. Now we are going to create a database that will house the tables we will use for many of the exercises in this course. This database will be called "*computersalesdb*".

hive> CREATE DATABASE computersalesdb;

```
biadmin@bivm:...ginsights/hive/bin
File  Edit  View  Terminal  Help
0: jdbc:hive2://bivm.ibm.com:10000> CREATE DATABASE computersalesdb;
No rows affected (0.435 seconds)
0: jdbc:hive2://bivm.ibm.com:10000>
```

11. Verify the DB was created.

SHOW DATABASES;

```
biadmin@bivm:...ginsights/hive/bin
File  Edit  View  Terminal  Help
0: jdbc:hive2://bivm.ibm.com:10000> SHOW DATABASES;
+------------------+
|  database_name   |
+------------------+
| computersalesdb  |
| default          |
+------------------+
2 rows selected (1.292 seconds)
0: jdbc:hive2://bivm.ibm.com:10000>
```

Note the location of the database directory in HDFS.

hive> DESCRIBE DATABASE computersalesdb;

```
biadmin@bivm:...ginsights/hive/bin
File  Edit  View  Terminal  Help
0: jdbc:hive2://bivm.ibm.com:10000> DESCRIBE DATABASE computersalesdb;
+------------------+----------+---------------------------------------------------------------------+-------------+
|     db_name      | comment  |                              location                               | parameters  |
+------------------+----------+---------------------------------------------------------------------+-------------+
| computersalesdb  |          | hdfs://bivm.ibm.com:9000/biginsights/hive/warehouse/computersalesdb.db |          |
+------------------+----------+---------------------------------------------------------------------+-------------+
1 row selected (1.473 seconds)
0: jdbc:hive2://bivm.ibm.com:10000>
```

We can see that the *computersalesdb* does in fact exist and the new directory was created on HDFS in the /biginsights/hive/warehouse/computersalesdb.db folder.

12. Tell Hive to Use the *computersalesdb* (we will use this database for the rest of this interactive session).

hive> USE computersalesdb;

Keep your Command line Interface (CLI) open – we will be using it in the upcoming exercises.

EXPLORING OUR SAMPLE DATASET

Before we begin creating tables in our new database it is important to understand what data is in our sample files and how that data is structured. Earlier in this course you placed the Exercise data in the /home/biadmin directory. Now we will take a look at the contents of those files.

Finding the Sample Data

1. Click the biadmin's Home shortcut on the desktop

A new window will open that shows us the contents of our /home/biadmin directory.

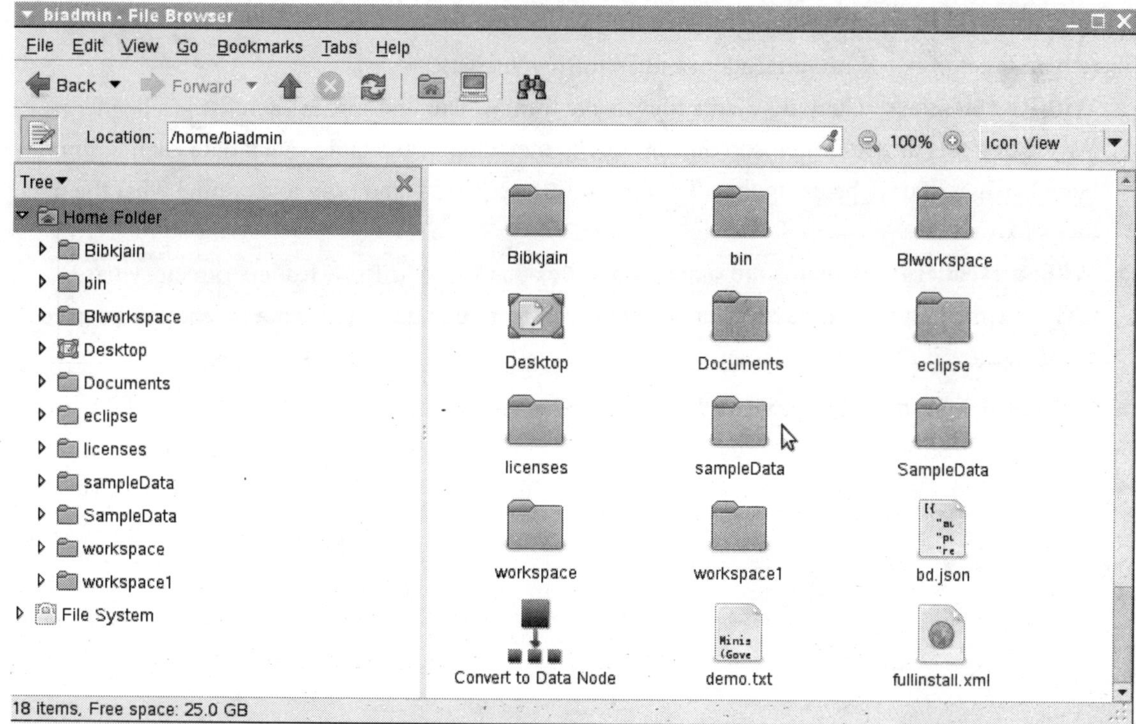

2. Navigate to the following directory sampleData->Computer_Business

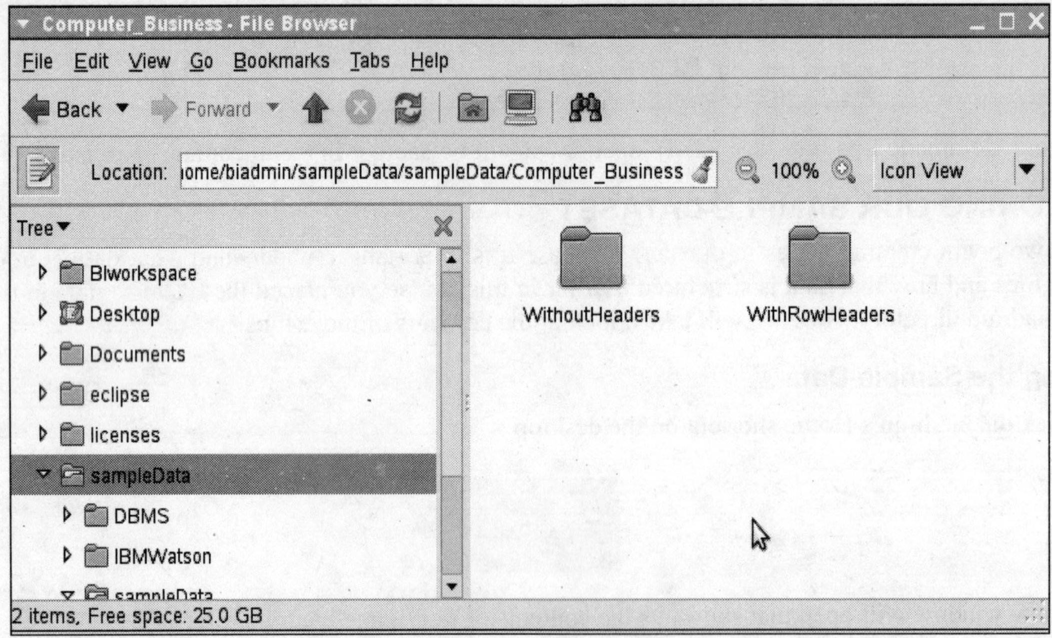

3. In Hive there is not an easy way to remove the header row from a file. To make things easy we have two directories – WithoutHeaders and WithRowHeaders.
   a. **WithRowHeaders** - Contains 3 data files in csv format. The first row in each file is a header row. We created this directory just so you can see the metadata of the table (what data each column holds). You will only be using this directory in this exercise – and only to examine what the data looks like.
   b. **WithoutHeaders** – Contains the same 3 data files that the WithRowHeaders directory has, EXCEPT the first rows (header data) are removed from this data. This data is ready to be used with Hive.
4. Let's check out our data. Navigate to the WithRowHeaders directory.

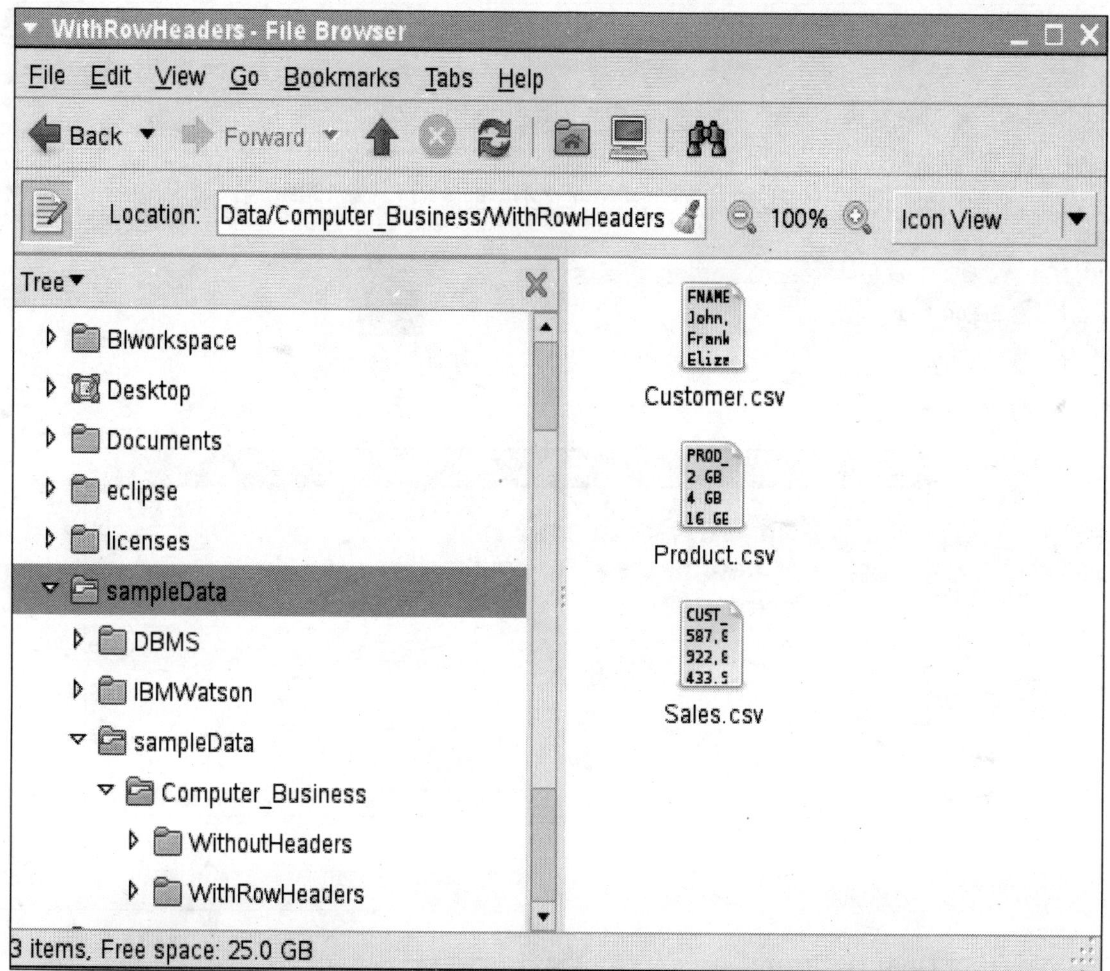

5. To view the contents of one of the files, right-click the file and then click open from the menu. Or double click on one of the files. Then

   click the "Display" button on the pop up box. Examine each of the 3 files.

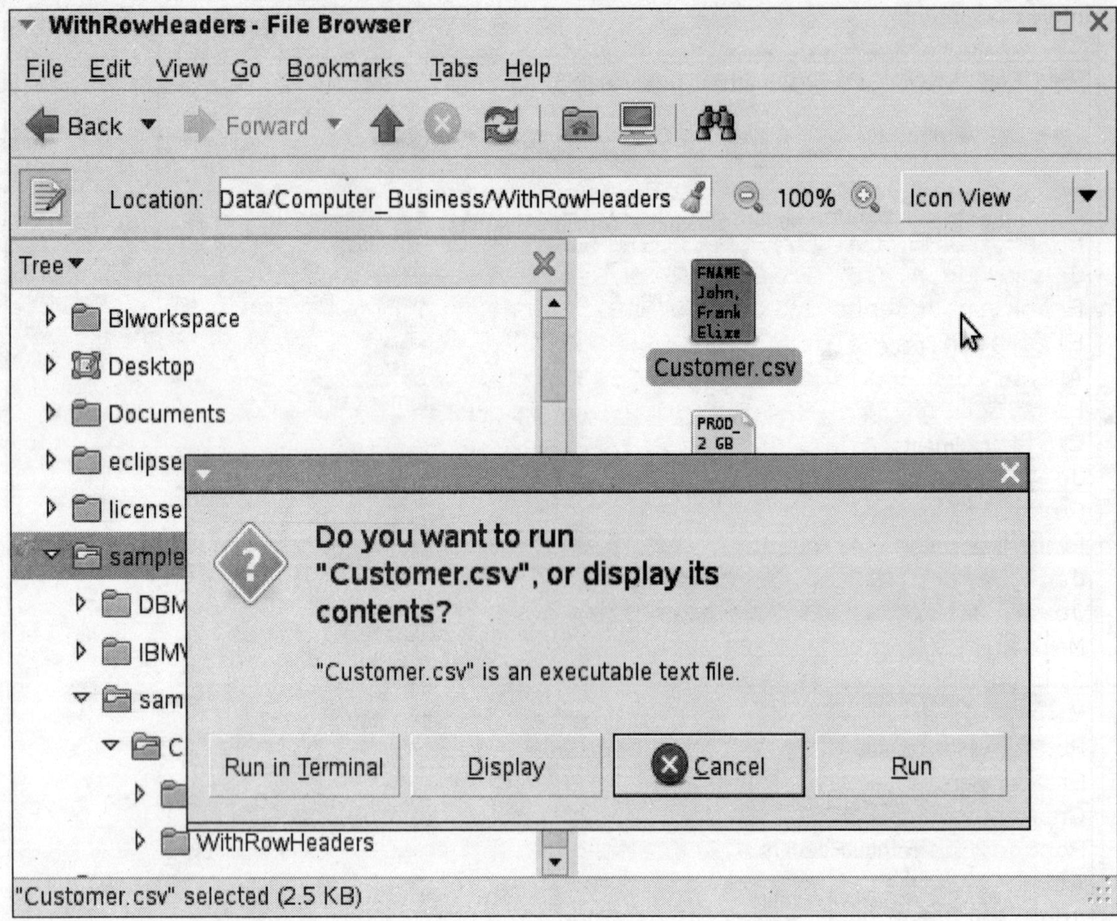

Sample Data Descriptions

Our sample data is from a fictitious computer retailer. The company sells computer parts and generally serves a single State in the country.

Customer.csv:

Purpose: Hold customer records.

Columns:

FNAME	LNAME	STATUS	TELNO	CUSTOMER_ID	CITY|ZIP
Customer's First Name	Customer's Last Name	Active or Inactive status	Telephone #	Customer's unique ID	City and Zip code separated by the "|" character.

Example of Contents

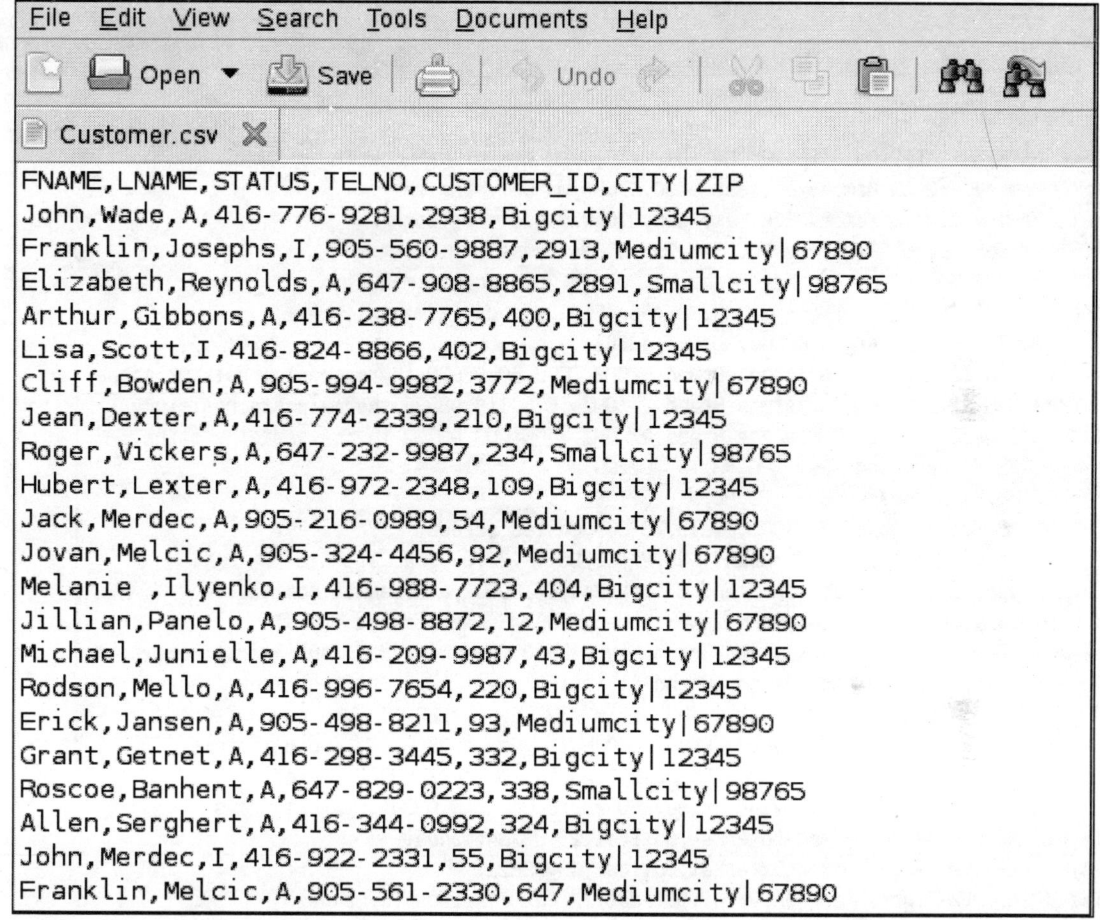

```
FNAME,LNAME,STATUS,TELNO,CUSTOMER_ID,CITY|ZIP
John,Wade,A,416-776-9281,2938,Bigcity|12345
Franklin,Josephs,I,905-560-9887,2913,Mediumcity|67890
Elizabeth,Reynolds,A,647-908-8865,2891,Smallcity|98765
Arthur,Gibbons,A,416-238-7765,400,Bigcity|12345
Lisa,Scott,I,416-824-8866,402,Bigcity|12345
Cliff,Bowden,A,905-994-9982,3772,Mediumcity|67890
Jean,Dexter,A,416-774-2339,210,Bigcity|12345
Roger,Vickers,A,647-232-9987,234,Smallcity|98765
Hubert,Lexter,A,416-972-2348,109,Bigcity|12345
Jack,Merdec,A,905-216-0989,54,Mediumcity|67890
Jovan,Melcic,A,905-324-4456,92,Mediumcity|67890
Melanie ,Ilyenko,I,416-988-7723,404,Bigcity|12345
Jillian,Panelo,A,905-498-8872,12,Mediumcity|67890
Michael,Junielle,A,416-209-9987,43,Bigcity|12345
Rodson,Mello,A,416-996-7654,220,Bigcity|12345
Erick,Jansen,A,905-498-8211,93,Mediumcity|67890
Grant,Getnet,A,416-298-3445,332,Bigcity|12345
Roscoe,Banhent,A,647-829-0223,338,Smallcity|98765
Allen,Serghert,A,416-344-0992,324,Bigcity|12345
John,Merdec,I,416-922-2331,55,Bigcity|12345
Franklin,Melcic,A,905-561-2330,647,Mediumcity|67890
```

Product.csv:

Purpose: Hold product records.

Columns

PROD_ NAME	DESCRIPTION	CATEGORY	QTY_ON_ HAND	PROD_NUM	PACKAGED_ WITH
Name of product	Description of computer product	Category product belongs to	Quantity of product in warehouse	Unique product number	Colon separated list of things that come in package with product

Example of contents:

File Edit View Search Tools Documents Help

Open Save Undo

Product.csv

```
PROD_NAME,DESCRIPTION,CATEGORY,QTY_ON_HAND,PROD_NUM,PACKAGED_WITH
2 GB Memory E,2 GB Memory ECC,Ram,3000,87655,manual:heatsink
4 GB Memory E,4 GB Memory ECC,Ram,1000,87659,manual:heatsink
16 GB Memory E,16 GB Memory ECC,Ram,238,87634,manual
500 GB HD J,500 GB HD Panther Brand,HD,200,45628,atacable:manual
500 GB HD T,500 GB HD Tiger Brand,HD,498,45641,satacable:manual
1 TB HD J,1 TB HD Jargon Brand,HD,231,45691,
4 Core CPU J3,4 Core CPU Jargon Brand 3 GHZ ,CPU,50,98820,thermalpaste:heatsink:manual
2 Core CPU J2,2 Core CPU Jargon Brand 2  GHZ ,CPU,118,98838,thermalpaste:heatsink
1 Core CPU J2,1 Core CPU Jargon Brand 2  GHZ ,CPU,203,98792,thermalpaste:heatsink
94F991 MB,Motherboard F991 CPU,MB,19,282299,
94G822 MB,Motherboard G822 CPU,MB,30,282109,
93H772 MB,Motherboard H772 CPU,MB,15,282009,cables:screws
93G Video,Video Card Jargon Brand 93G,Video,80,99202,dvd:manual:game
84G1 Video,Video Card Jargon Brand 84F1,Video,14,99207,dvd:manual:hdmicable
09K Video,Video Card Tiger Brand 84F1,Video,5,98243,manual:game
J Case 1500,Computer Case Jargon Brand Style 1500,Case,20,77623,fans:manual:screws
J Case 1501,Computer Case Jargon Brand Style 1501,Case,18,77624,fans:manual:screws
T Case 4332,Computer Case Tiger Brand Style 4332,Case,7,88211,fans:manual:screws:watercooler
J Power 300W,Power Supply Jargon Brand 300 Watts,Power,28,92387,cables:screws
J Power 500W,Power Supply Jargon Brand 500 Watts,Power,17,92373,cables:screws
T Power 300W,Power Supply Tiger Brand 300 Watts,Power,8,93347,cables:screws
DVD J INT,DVD Jargon Brand Internal,Optical,23,88734,manual
DVD J EXT,DVD Jargon Brand External,Optical,45,88821,
DVD T INT,DVD Tiger Brand Internal,Optical,19,82331,satacable:manual
DVD T EXT,DVD Tiger Brand External,Optical,17,82337,satacable:manual
```

Sales.csv:

Purpose: Holds all historical sales records. Company updates once a month.

Columns:

CUST_ID	PROD_NUM	QTY	DATE	SALES_ID
ID of customer who made purchase	ID of product that was purchased	QTY purchased	Date of sale	Unique sale ID

Example of contents

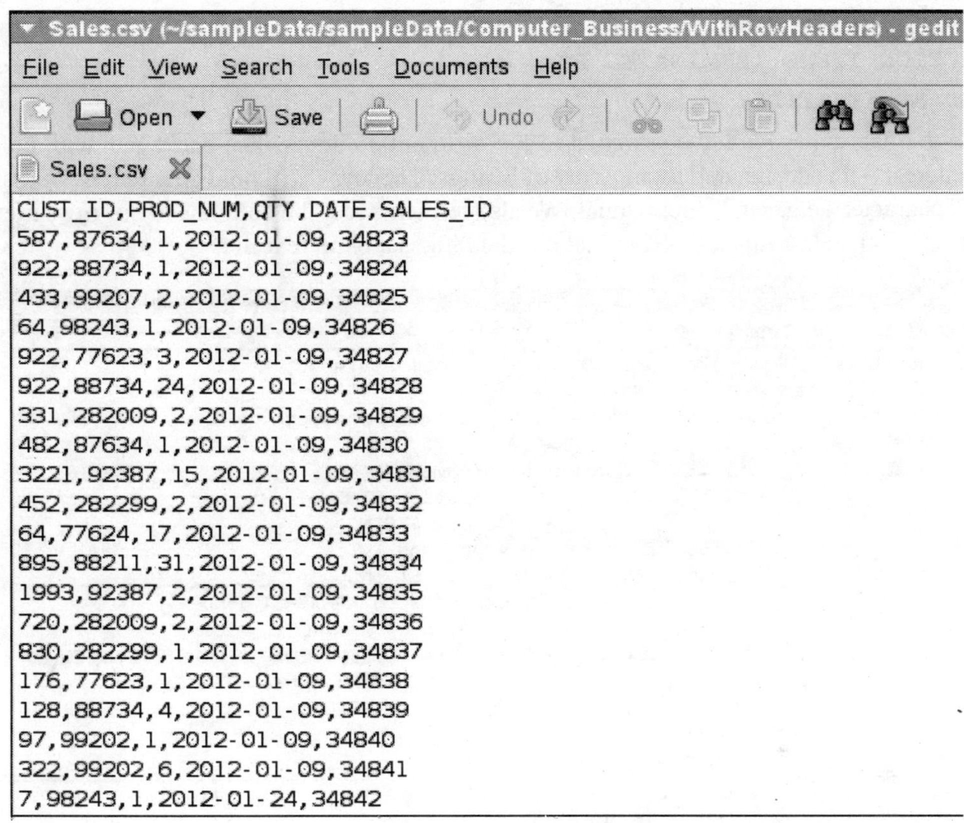

1.4 TABLES IN HIVE

1.4.1 Managed Non-Partitioned Tables

The first table we will create in Hive is the *products* table. This table will be fully managed by Hive and will not contain any partitions.

1. In the CLI, create the new *products* table in Hive.

```
hive> CREATE TABLE products
(
prod_name STRING,
description STRING,
category STRING,
qty_on_hand INT,
prod_num STRING,
packaged_with ARRAY<STRING>
)
ROW FORMAT DELIMITED
```

```
FIELDS TERMINATED BY ','
COLLECTION ITEMS TERMINATED BY ':'
STORED AS TEXTFILE;
```

Note the data types we have assigned to the different columns. The packaged_with column is of special interest – it is designated as an Array of Strings. The array will hold data that is separated by the colon ":" character - e.g. satacable:manual. We also tell Hive that the columns in our rows are delimited by commas ",". The last line tells Hive that our data file is a plain text file.

```
▾ biadmin@bivm:...ginsights/hive/bin
File  Edit  View  Terminal  Help
0: jdbc:hive2://bivm.ibm.com:10000> USE computersalesdb;
No rows affected (0.482 seconds)
0: jdbc:hive2://bivm.ibm.com:10000> CREATE TABLE products
. . . . . . . . . . . . . . . . . > (
. . . . . . . . . . . . . . . . . > prod_name STRING,
. . . . . . . . . . . . . . . . . > description STRING,
. . . . . . . . . . . . . . . . . > cetegory STRING,
. . . . . . . . . . . . . . . . . > qty_on_hand INT,
. . . . . . . . . . . . . . . . . > prod_num STRING,
. . . . . . . . . . . . . . . . . > packaged_with ARRAY<STRING>
. . . . . . . . . . . . . . . . . > )
. . . . . . . . . . . . . . . . . > ROW FORMAT DELIMITED FIELDS TERMINATED BY ','
. . . . . . . . . . . . . . . . . > COLLECTION ITEMS TERMINATED BY ':'
. . . . . . . . . . . . . . . . . > STORED AS TEXTFILE;
No rows affected (3.532 seconds)
0: jdbc:hive2://bivm.ibm.com:10000>
```

2. Ask Hive to show us the tables in our database.

```
hive> SHOW TABLES IN computersalesdb;
```

```
▾ biadmin@bivm:...ginsights/hive/bin
File  Edit  View  Terminal  Help
0: jdbc:hive2://bivm.ibm.com:10000> SHOW TABLES IN computersalesdb;
+-----------+
| tab_name  |
+-----------+
| products  |
+-----------+
1 row selected (1.59 seconds)
0: jdbc:hive2://bivm.ibm.com:10000>
```

We can see that only one table exists in our database and it is the new *products* table we just created.

3. Add a note to the TBLPROPERTIES for our new *products* table.

```
hive> ALTER TABLE products SET TBLPROPERTIES (
'details' = 'This table holds products');
```

```
biadmin@bivm:...ginsights/hive/bin
File  Edit  View  Terminal  Help
0: jdbc:hive2://bivm.ibm.com:10000> ALTER TABLE products SET TBLPROPERTIES ('details' = 'This ta
ble holds products');
No rows affected (2.033 seconds)
0: jdbc:hive2://bivm.ibm.com:10000> DESCRIBE EXTENDED products;
+-----------------------------+-------------------------------------------------+
|          col_name           |                                                 |
+-----------------------------+-------------------------------------------------+
| prod_name                   | string                                          |
| description                 | string                                          |
| cetegory                    | string                                          |
| qty_on_hand                 | int                                             |
| prod_num                    | string                                          |
| packaged_with               | array<string>                                   |
|                             |                                                 |
| Detailed Table Information  | Table(tableName:products, dbName:computersales  |
+-----------------------------+-------------------------------------------------+
8 rows selected (1.728 seconds)
0: jdbc:hive2://bivm.ibm.com:10000>
```

4. List the extended details of the *products* table.

   hive> DESCRIBE EXTENDED products;

Beeline's default settings truncate all the output. Let's adjust Beeline to display data in a different format so we can see all of the output.

Inside of Beeline:

   hive> !set outputformat vertical

```
biadmin@bivm:...ginsights/hive/bin
File  Edit  View  Terminal  Help
0: jdbc:hive2://bivm.ibm.com:10000> !set outputformat vertical
0: jdbc:hive2://bivm.ibm.com:10000> DESCRIBE EXTENDED products;
col_name   prod_name
data_type  string
comment    None

col_name   description
data_type  string
comment    None

col_name   cetegory
data_type  string
comment    None

col_name   qty_on_hand
data_type  int
comment    None

col_name   prod_num
data_type  string
comment    None

col_name   packaged_with
data_type  array<string>
comment    None

col_name
data_type
```

Now, rerun the **DESCRIBE EXTENDED products;** command.

```
biadmin@bivm:...ginsights/hive/bin
File  Edit  View  Terminal  Help

col_name   prod_num
data_type  string
comment    None

col_name   packaged_with
data_type  array<string>
comment    None

col_name
data_type
comment

col_name   Detailed Table Information
data_type  Table(tableName:products, dbName:computersalesdb, owner:biadmin, createTime:145700826
1, lastAccessTime:0, retention:0, sd:StorageDescriptor(cols:[FieldSchema(name:prod_name, type:st
ring, comment:null), FieldSchema(name:description, type:string, comment:null), FieldSchema(name:
cetegory, type:string, comment:null), FieldSchema(name:qty_on_hand, type:int, comment:null), Fie
ldSchema(name:prod_num, type:string, comment:null), FieldSchema(name:packaged_with, type:array<s
tring>, comment:null)], location:hdfs://bivm.ibm.com:9000/biginsights/hive/warehouse/computersal
esdb.db/products, inputFormat:org.apache.hadoop.mapred.TextInputFormat, outputFormat:org.apache.
hadoop.hive.ql.io.HiveIgnoreKeyTextOutputFormat, compressed:false, numBuckets:-1, serdeInfo:SerD
eInfo(name:null, serializationLib:org.apache.hadoop.hive.serde2.lazy.LazySimpleSerDe, parameters
:{colelction.delim=:, serialization.format=,, field.delim=,}), bucketCols:[], sortCols:[], param
eters:{}, skewedInfo:SkewedInfo(skewedColNames:[], skewedColValues:[], skewedColValueLocationMap
s:{}), storedAsSubDirectories:false), partitionKeys:[], parameters:{last_modified_by=biadmin, de
tails=This table holds products, last_modified_time=1457076401, transient_lastDdlTime=1457076401
}, viewOriginalText:null, viewExpandedText:null, tableType:MANAGED_TABLE)
```

That is a lot of details! Notice there is some interesting info including the location of this table within HDFS: /biginsights/hive/warehouse/computersalesdb.db/products

5. Let's verify that the products directory was created on HDFS in the location listed above. Run the HDFS *ls* command from within the Linux console. First list the contents of the database directory, then list the contents of the products table directory.

```
~> hadoop fs -ls /biginsights/hive/warehouse/computersalesdb.db;
~> hadoop fs -ls /biginsights/hive/warehouse/computersalesdb.db/
products;
```

The first command confirms that there is in fact a products table directory on HDFS. The second command shows that there are no files within the products directory yet. This directory will be empty until we load data into the products table in a later exercise.

```
▼ biadmin@bivm:~
File  Edit  View  Terminal  Help
biadmin@bivm:~> hadoop fs -ls /biginsights/hive/warehouse/computersalesdb.db;
Found 1 items
drwxrwxrwt   - biadmin biadmin          0 2016-03-03 07:31 /biginsights/hive/war
ehouse/computersalesdb.db/products
biadmin@bivm:~> hadoop fs -ls /biginsights/hive/warehouse/computersalesdb.db/products;
```

6. Imagine that our fictitious computer company adds sales data to a "*sales_staging*" table at the end of each month. From this *sales_staging* table they then move the data they want to analyze into a partitioned "*sales*" table. The partitioned *sales* table is the one they actual use for their analysis.

   Now that we know how to create tables, we will create one more managed non-partitioned table called "*sales_staging*". This table will hold ALL of the sales data from the sales.csv file. In later exercises we will actually split this *sales_staging* data into a partitioned table called "*sales*".

   In the CLI, create the new *sales_staging* table in Hive.

```
hive> CREATE TABLE sales_staging
(
cust_id STRING,
prod_num STRING,
qty INT,
sale_date STRING,
sales_id STRING
)
COMMENT 'Staging table for sales data'
ROW FORMAT DELIMITED
FIELDS TERMINATED BY ','
STORED AS TEXTFILE;
```

```
▼ biadmin@bivm:...ginsights/hive/bin
File  Edit  View  Terminal  Help
0: jdbc:hive2://bivm.ibm.com:10000> CREATE TABLE sales_staging ( cust_id STRING,
g, sales_id string ) COMMENT 'Staging table for sales data' ROW FORMAT DELIMITED
LE;
No rows affected (0.987 seconds)
0: jdbc:hive2://bivm.ibm.com:10000> SHOW TABLES;
tab_name  products

tab_name  sales_staging

2 rows selected (1.162 seconds)
```

7. We can now assume that the new *sales_staging* table directory is on HDFS in the following folder: /biginsights/hive/warehouse/computersalesdb.db/sales_staging. Let's quickly confirm by entering the following command in the Linux console:

   ~> hadoop fs -ls /biginsights/hive/warehouse/computersalesdb.db;

   Sure enough, the sales_staging directory was created and is now being managed by Hive.

8. Ask Hive to show us the tables in our database. Confirm your new *sales_staging* table is in the Hive catalog.

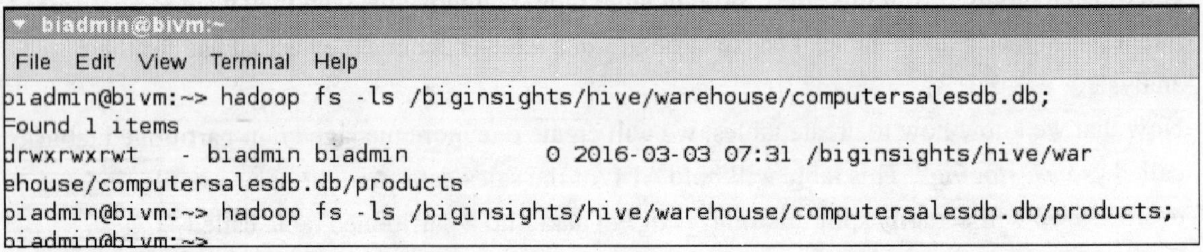

```
biadmin@bivm:~
File  Edit  View  Terminal  Help
biadmin@bivm:~> hadoop fs -ls /biginsights/hive/warehouse/computersalesdb.db;
Found 1 items
drwxrwxrwt   - biadmin biadmin          0 2016-03-03 07:31 /biginsights/hive/war
ehouse/computersalesdb.db/products
biadmin@bivm:~> hadoop fs -ls /biginsights/hive/warehouse/computersalesdb.db/products;
biadmin@bivm:~>
```

   hive> SHOW TABLES;

9. Let's pretend that we have decided we want to update some of our column metadata. We will change the **sale_date** column in the *sales_staging* table from a STRING type to a DATE type.

   hive> ALTER TABLE sales_staging CHANGE sale_date sale_date DATE;

9.7 PARTITIONING CONCEPTS

Partitioning enhances the performance, manageability, and avaiExerciseility of a wide variety of applications and helps reduce the total cost of ownership for storing large amounts of data. Partitioning allows tables, indexes, and index-organized tables to be subdivided into smaller pieces, enabling these database objects to be managed and accessed at a finer level of granularity. Oracle provides a rich variety of partitioning strategies and extensions to address every business requirement. Moreover, since it is entirely transparent, partitioning can be applied to almost any application without the need for potentially expensive and time consuming application changes.

9.7.1 Basics of Partitioning

Partitioning allows a table, index, or index-organized table to be subdivided into smaller pieces, where each piece of such a database object is called a partition. Each partition has its own name, and may optionally have its own storage characteristics.

From the perspective of a database administrator, a partitioned object has multiple pieces that can be managed either collectively or individually. This gives the administrator considerable flexibility in managing partitioned objects. However, from the perspective of the application, a partitioned table is identical to a non-partitioned table; no modifications are necessary when accessing a partitioned table using SQL queries and DML statements.

Figure 9.1 offers a graphical view of how partitioned tables differ from non-partitioned tables.

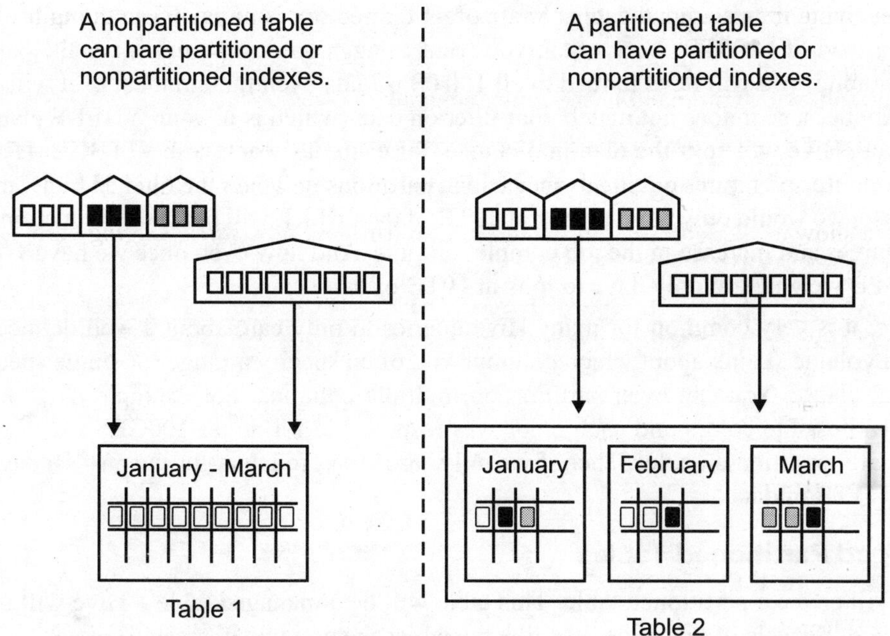

Figure. 9.1: Graphical view showing partitioned and non-partitioned tables

Partitioning Key

Each row in a partitioned table is unambiguously assigned to a single partition. The partitioning key is comprised of one or more columns that determine the partition where each row will be stored. Oracle automatically directs insert, update, and delete operations to the appropriate partition through the use of the partitioning key.

Partitioned Tables

Any table can be partitioned into a million separate partitions except those tables containing columns with LONG or LONG RAW datatypes. You can, however, use tables containing columns with CLOB or BLOB datatypes.

9.7.2 When to Partition a Table

Here are some suggestions for when to partition a table:

- Tables greater than 2 GB should always be considered as candidates for partitioning.
- Tables containing historical data, in which new data is added into the newest partition. A typical example is a historical table where only the current month's data is updatable and the other 11 months are read only.
- When the contents of a table need to be distributed across different types of storage devices. Partitioning allows Hive to access a subset of your data without having to read all of it. Here's a concrete example of why that could be useful.

You are receiving time stamped data at a rate of ~1TB per day. You have data going back 100 days for a total data load of ~100TB. Very often, you want to aggregate some data over the past 10 days. Without partitioning, you will have to read in all 100TB of data even though most of it will be ignored by Hive anyway because it does not match your filter on date (which is in your WHERE clause). If you partition by date, Hive will split the data into chunks for each day, each with ~1TBGB. Hive looks at your WHERE clause and figures out in advance which partitions will pass the filter and only process that data. In this case, we would only have to look at 10TB of data which will be a huge reduction of our use of cluster resources and increase in the job completion time. And now even once we have 1000 days of data totaling 1PB we will still only have to look at 10TB of data.

In practice, it is very common for many Hive queries to only care about a well defined subset of your total data volume. Think about which columns you often specify a range (or single specific value) for in WHERE clause. You can even partition on multiple columns. For example if we had a color column with 10 possible colors and each color was responsible for about 100GB of data per day we might additionally partition on color. Then if we only care about red data for the past 10 days, we only have to process 1TB of data.

9.7.3 Managed Partitioned Tables

1. Now we will create a partitioned table. This table will be a managed table – Hive will manage the metadata and lifecycle of this table, just like the tables we previously created.

   In the CLI create the sales table. This table will be partitioned on the sales date.

```
hive> CREATE TABLE sales
(
cust_id STRING,
prod_num STRING,
qty INT,
sales_id STRING
)
COMMENT 'Table for analysis of sales data'
PARTITIONED BY (sales_date STRING)
ROW FORMAT DELIMITED
FIELDS TERMINATED BY ','
STORED AS TEXTFILE;
```

   Notice that we list the *sales_date* in the PARTITIONED BY clause instead of listing it in the data column metadata. Since we are partitioning on *sales_date*, Hive will keep track of the dates for us outside of the actual data.

```
biadmin@bivm:...ginsights/hive/bin
File  Edit  View  Terminal  Help
0: jdbc:hive2://bivm.ibm.com:10000> CREATE TABLE sales
. . . . . . . . . . . . . . . . . > (
. . . . . . . . . . . . . . . . . >          cust_id  STRING,
. . . . . . . . . . . . . . . . . >           prod_num   STRING,
. . . . . . . . . . . . . . . . . >           qty       INT,
. . . . . . . . . . . . . . . . . >           sales_id  STRING
. . . . . . . . . . . . . . . . . > )
. . . . . . . . . . . . . . . . . > COMMENT 'Table for analysis of sales data'
. . . . . . . . . . . . . . . . . > PARTITIONED BY (sales_date STRING)
. . . . . . . . . . . . . . . . . > ROW FORMAT DELIMITED
. . . . . . . . . . . . . . . . . >           FIELDS TERMINATED BY ','
. . . . . . . . . . . . . . . . . > STORED AS TEXTFILE;
No rows affected (3.416 seconds)
0: jdbc:hive2://bivm.ibm.com:10000>
```

2. Let's view the extended details of our new table.

   hive> DESCRIBE EXTENDED sales;

   We can see a directory was created at /biginsights/hive/warehouse/computersalesdb.db/sales. When we later put data into this table, a new directory will be created inside the sales directory for EACH partition.

```
biadmin@bivm:...ginsights/hive/bin
File  Edit  View  Terminal  Help
0: jdbc:hive2://bivm.ibm.com:10000> DESCRIBE EXTENDED sales;
+-----------------------------+---------------------------------------------------------------
|          col_name           |
+-----------------------------+---------------------------------------------------------------
| cust_id                     | string
| prod_num                    | string
| qty                         | int
| sales_id                    | string
| sales_date                  | string
|                             |
| # Partition Information     |
| # col_name                  | data_type
|                             |
| sales_date                  | string
|                             |
| Detailed Table Information  | Table(tableName:sales, dbName:computersalesdb, owner:biadmin,
+-----------------------------+---------------------------------------------------------------
12 rows selected (2.443 seconds)
0: jdbc:hive2://bivm.ibm.com:10000>
```

The following line in the details shows us how our table is partitioned: partitionKeys: [FieldSchema(name:sales_date, typestring,comment:null)]

9.7.4 External Table

Another department in our fictitious computer company would like to be able to analyze the customer data. It therefore makes sense that we setup the *customer* table as EXTERNAL so they can use their tools on the data and we can use ours (Hive). We will place a copy of the Customer.csv file in HDFS and then create a new table in Hive that points to this data.

1. First we need to create a new directory – let's call it "shared_hive_data" - on HDFS that can house our Customer.csv data file. Let's put this in the /user/biadmin directory. We will run the command to make the new directory from the Linux console.

```
~> hadoop fs -mkdir /user/biadmin/shared_hive_data;
```

```
biadmin@bivm:~
File  Edit  View  Terminal  Help
biadmin@bivm:~> hadoop fs -ls /user/biadmin/shared_hive_data/;
biadmin@bivm:~>
```

2. Now we will move a copy of the Customer.csv file into the /user/biadmin/shared_hive_data directory. We can run the command to do this from within the Linux console.

```
~> hadoop fs -put
/home/biadmin/sampleData/sampleData/Computer_Business/WithoutHeaders/
Customer.csv
/user/biadmin/shared_hive_data/Customer.csv;
```

```
biadmin@bivm:~
File Edit View Terminal Help
biadmin@bivm:~> hadoop fs -put /home/biadmin/sampleData/sampleData/Computer_Business/WithoutHeaders/Customer.csv /user/biadmin/shared_hive_data/Customer.csv
biadmin@bivm:~> hadoop fs -ls /user/biadmin/shared_hive_data/;
Found 1 items
-rw-r--r--   1 biadmin biadmin       2513 2016-03-07 07:21 /user/biadmin/shared_hive_data/Customer.csv
biadmin@bivm:~>
```

3. Confirm that Customer.csv has been copied successfully into HDFS. Enter the following command in the Linux console.

```
~> hadoop fs -ls /user/biadmin/shared_hive_data/;
```

If your output looks similar to the screen capture above, then that is good!

If you'd like, run the "cat" command to verify the data is in the Customer.csv file on HDFS.

```
~> hadoop fs -cat /user/biadmin/shared_hive_data/Customer.csv;
```

```
biadmin@bivm:~
File  Edit  View  Terminal  Help
biadmin@bivm:~> hadoop fs -cat /user/biadmin/shared_hive_data/Customer.csv;
John,Wade,A,416-776-9281,2938,Bigcity|12345
Franklin,Josephs,I,905-560-9887,2913,Mediumcity|67890
Elizabeth,Reynolds,A,647-908-8865,2891,Smallcity|98765
Arthur,Gibbons,A,416-238-7765,400,Bigcity|12345
Lisa,Scott,I,416-824-8866,402,Bigcity|12345
Cliff,Bowden,A,905-994-9982,3772,Mediumcity|67890
Jean,Dexter,A,416-774-2339,210,Bigcity|12345
Roger,Vickers,A,647-232-9987,234,Smallcity|98765
Hubert,Lexter,A,416-972-2348,109,Bigcity|12345
Jack,Merdec,A,905-216-0989,54,Mediumcity|67890
Jovan,Melcic,A,905-324-4456,92,Mediumcity|67890
Melanie ,Ilyenko,I,416-988-7723,404,Bigcity|12345
Jillian,Panelo,A,905-498-8872,12,Mediumcity|67890
Michael,Junielle,A,416-209-9987,43,Bigcity|12345
```

2. Try moving a copy of the Customer1.csv file into the /user/biadmin/shared_hive_data directory. We can run the command to do this from within the Linux console.

```
~> hadoop fs -put
/home/biadmin/sampleData/sampleData/Computer_Business/WithoutHeaders/
Customer1.csv/user/biadmin/shared_hive_data/Customer1.csv;
```

Again If you like, run the "cat" command to verify the data is in the Customer1.csv file on HDFS.

```
~> hadoop fs -cat /user/biadmin/shared_hive_data/Customer.csv;
```

```
biadmin@bivm:~
File  Edit  View  Terminal  Help
biadmin@bivm:~> hadoop fs -put /home/biadmin/sampleData/sampleData/Computer_Business/WithoutHeaders/Customer1.csv /user/biadmin/shared_hive_data/Customer1.csv
biadmin@bivm:~> hadoop fs -cat /user/biadmin/shared_hive_data/Customer1.csv;

Madan,Vadhera,I,011-2345678,162,New Delhi|110011
Megha,Lahiri,A,011-3456789,111,New Delhi|110111
Illias,Mohammed,A,011-4567890,79,New Delhi|123111
Rajnish,Munnabar,A,0120-437097,122,Noida|211312
Harish,Dutta,D,437-987650,71,Itarsi|432567
```

4. Now we just need to define our external *customer* table.

```
hive> CREATE EXTERNAL TABLE customer
(
fname STRING,
lname STRING,
status STRING,
telno STRING,
customer_id STRING,
city_zip STRUCT<city:STRING, zip:STRING>
)
COMMENT 'External table for customer data'
```

```
ROW FORMAT DELIMITED
FIELDS TERMINATED BY ','
COLLECTION ITEMS TERMINATED BY '|'
LOCATION '/user/biadmin/shared_hive_data/';
```

```
biadmin@bivm:...ginsights/hive/bin
File Edit View Terminal Help
0: jdbc:hive2://bivm.ibm.com:10000> CREATE EXTERNAL TABLE customer
. . . . . . . . . . . . . . . . . > ( fname STRING,
. . . . . . . . . . . . . . . . . > lname STRING,
. . . . . . . . . . . . . . . . . > status STRING,
. . . . . . . . . . . . . . . . . > telno STRING,
. . . . . . . . . . . . . . . . . > customer_id STRING,
. . . . . . . . . . . . . . . . . > city_zip STRUCT<city:STRING,zip:STRING>
. . . . . . . . . . . . . . . . . > )
. . . . . . . . . . . . . . . . . > COMMENT 'External table for customer data'
. . . . . . . . . . . . . . . . . > ROW FORMAT DELIMITED
. . . . . . . . . . . . . . . . . > FIELDS TERMINATED BY ','
. . . . . . . . . . . . . . . . . > COLLECTION ITEMS TERMINATED BY '|'
. . . . . . . . . . . . . . . . . > LOCATION '/user/biadmin/shared_hive_data/';
No rows affected (0.844 seconds)
0: jdbc:hive2://bivm.ibm.com:10000>
```

There are a few things to note here. First, we use the EXTERNAL keyword in the CREATE line. We are leaving out the "stored as line" when we are creating this external table since the default format is already set to TEXTFILE. We also add the LOCATION 'location/of/datadirectory' line to the end of the statement.

Hive expects that LOCATION will be a directory, not a file. For our exercises we will only have a single file in the shared_hive_data directory. However, you could put multiple customer data files into the shared_hive_data directory and Hive would use them all for your EXTERNAL table! That is a common scenario.

5. Let's view the extended details of our new table.

```
hive> DESCRIBE EXTENDED customer;
```

```
File  Edit  View  Terminal  Help
0: jdbc:hive2://bivm.ibm.com:10000> DESCRIBE EXTENDED customer;
+----------------------------+-----------------------------------------------------
-------------------------------+
|          col_name          |
                               |
+----------------------------+-----------------------------------------------------
-------------------------------+
| fname                      | string
                               |
| lname                      | string
                               |
| status                     | string
                               |
| telno                      | string
                               |
| customer_id                | string
                               |
| city_zip                   | struct<city:string,zip:string>
                               |
|                            |
                               |
| Detailed Table Information  | Table(tableName:customer, dbName:computersalesdb, owner:biadmin, createTime:1457435155, lastAccessTime
:0, retention:0, sd:StorageDescr |
+----------------------------+-----------------------------------------------------
-------------------------------+
8 rows selected (2.241 seconds)
0: jdbc:hive2://bivm.ibm.com:10000>
```

You can see that the location points to the /user/biadmin/shared_hive_data directory we designated on HDFS. Also notice towards the end of the output that tableType:EXTERNAL_TABLE.

6. Let's set the Beeline output format back to the table style. This will give us cleaner output when we run queries.

   hive> !set outputformat table

7. Since customer is an External table and Hive already knows where the data is sitting, you can already begin to run queries on this table. Reward yourself for completing this Exercise by running a simple select query as proof.

   hive> SELECT * FROM customer LIMIT 5;

```
biadmin@bivm:...ginsights/hive/bin
File  Edit  View  Terminal  Help
0: jdbc:hive2://bivm.ibm.com:10000> !set outputformat table
0: jdbc:hive2://bivm.ibm.com:10000> SELECT * FROM customer LIMIT 5;
+------------+-----------+---------+---------------+--------------+-----------------------------------------+
|   fname    |   lname   | status  |     telno     | customer_id  |                city_zip                 |
+------------+-----------+---------+---------------+--------------+-----------------------------------------+
| John       | Wade      | A       | 416-776-9281  | 2938         | {"city":"Bigcity","zip":"12345"}        |
| Franklin   | Josephs   | I       | 905-560-9887  | 2913         | {"city":"Mediumcity","zip":"67890"}     |
| Elizabeth  | Reynolds  | A       | 647-908-8865  | 2891         | {"city":"Smallcity","zip":"98765"}      |
| Arthur     | Gibbons   | A       | 416-238-7765  | 400          | {"city":"Bigcity","zip":"12345"}        |
| Lisa       | Scott     | I       | 416-824-8866  | 402          | {"city":"Bigcity","zip":"12345"}        |
+------------+-----------+---------+---------------+--------------+-----------------------------------------+
5 rows selected (2.198 seconds)
0: jdbc:hive2://bivm.ibm.com:10000>
```

This Hive query didn't run any MapReduce jobs. Hive is able to read the data file and write the results to the CLI without using MapReduce, since this is a simple SELECT and LIMIT statement.

EXERCISE 9.2 Hive Operators and Functions

1.1 ACCESSING THE HIVE CLI

In this section we will navigate to the Hive Beeline CLI, just as we have done in previous Exercises, and start an interactive CLI session.

1. Open the Linux terminal by double clicking the Terminal icon from within the *BigInsights Shell directory* on the desktop.

2. In the Linux terminal change to the Hive home bin directory

```
~> cd $HIVE_HOME/bin
```

3. Start an interactive Hive shell session.

```
~> ./beeline -u jdbc:hive2://bivm.ibm.com:10000 -n biadmin -p biadmin
```

4. Tell Hive to Use the *computersalesdb* (we will use this database for the rest of this interactive session).

```
hive> USE computersalesdb;
```

1.2 OPERATORS

In this section we will experiment with Relational, Arithmetic, and Logical Operators in the Hive system.

1.2.1 Relational Operators

1. Use the IS NULL operator to find all records in the *products* table that have no item in the zero position of the *packaged_with* array.

```
hive> SELECT * FROM products WHERE packaged_with[0] IS NULL;
```

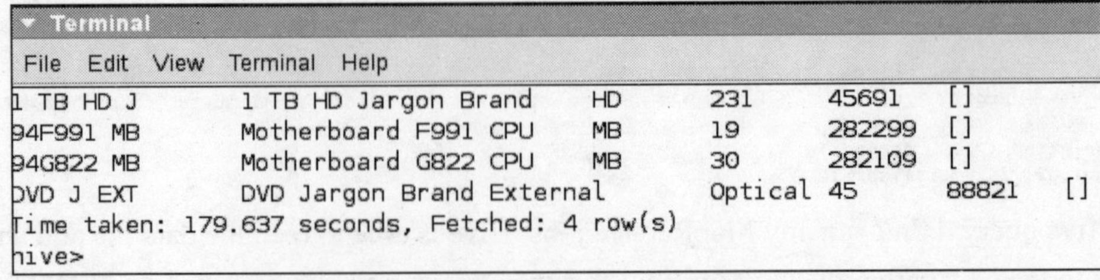

```
Terminal
File  Edit  View  Terminal  Help
1 TB HD J       1 TB HD Jargon Brand       HD       231       45691    []
94F991 MB       Motherboard F991 CPU       MB       19        282299   []
94G822 MB       Motherboard G822 CPU       MB       30        282109   []
DVD J EXT       DVD Jargon Brand External           Optical 45        88821    []
Time taken: 179.637 seconds, Fetched: 4 row(s)
hive>
```

2. Find customers who do not live in the 67890 zipcode. Do this using the != operator to examine the *city_zip* struct column of the *customer* table. Reminder: *city_zip* is described as *struct<city:string,zip:string>* in our table.

```
hive> SELECT * FROM customer WHERE city_zip.zip != '67890';
```

```
hive> SELECT * FROM customer WHERE city_zip.zip != '67890';
John        Wade      A  416-776-9281  2938  {"city":"Bigcity","z
ip":"12345"}
Elizabeth   Reynolds  A  647-908-8865  2891  {"city":"Smallcity","z
ip":"98765"}
Arthur      Gibbons   A  416-238-7765  400   {"city":"Bigcity","z
ip":"12345"}
Lisa        Scott     I  416-824-8866  402   {"city":"Bigcity","z
ip":"12345"}
Jean        Dexter    A  416-774-2339  210   {"city":"Bigcity","z
ip":"12345"}
Roger       Vickers   A  647-232-9987  234   {"city":"Smallcity","z
ip":"98765"}
Hubert      Lexter    A  416-972-2348  109   {"city":"Bigcity","z
ip":"12345"}
MelanieIlyenko I         416-988-7723  404   {"city":"Bigcity","z
ip":"12345"}
Michael     Junielle  A  416-209-9987  43    {"city":"Bigcity","z
ip":"12345"}
Rodson      Mello     A  416-996-7654  220   {"city":"Bigcity","z
ip":"12345"}
Grant       Getnet    A  416-298-3445  332   {"city":"Bigcity","z
ip":"12345"}
Roscoe      Banhent   A  647-829-0223  338   {"city":"Smallcity","z
ip":"98765"}
Allen       Serghert  A  416-344-0992  324   {"city":"Bigcity","z
ip":"12345"}
John        Merdec    I  416-922-2331  55    {"city":"Bigcity","z
ip":"12345"}
Elizabeth   Ilyenko   A  416-354-2778  102   {"city":"Bigcity","z
ip":"12345"}
Lisa        Junielle  A  416-352-9992  323   {"city":"Bigcity","z
ip":"12345"}
```

Cliff	Mello	A	416-210-9997	47	{"city":"Bigcity","zip":"12345"}
Roger	Getnet	I	416-309-9982	24	{"city":"Bigcity","zip":"12345"}
Hubert	Banhent	A	416-526-8888	19	{"city":"Bigcity","zip":"12345"}
Lambert	Givens	A	416-209-8223	587	{"city":"Bigcity","zip":"12345"}
Jansen	Gibbons	A	416-298-3881	895	{"city":"Bigcity","zip":"12345"}
Banhent	Bowden	A	416-989-0223	720	{"city":"Bigcity","zip":"12345"}
Serghert	Dexter	A	416-823-0991	830	{"city":"Bigcity","zip":"12345"}
Merdec	Vickers	I	416-298-0908	176	{"city":"Bigcity","zip":"12345"}
Melcic	Lexter	A	416-823-4443	128	{"city":"Bigcity","zip":"12345"}
Ilyenko	Merdec	A	416-293-8771	97	{"city":"Bigcity","zip":"12345"}
Allen	Jaskobec	A	416-299-0202	7	{"city":"Bigcity","zip":"12345"}
John	Jarkin	A	416-622-0991	11	{"city":"Bigcity","zip":"12345"}
Franklin	Drill	A	647-309-2331	37	{"city":"Smallcity","zip":"98765"}
Elizabeth	Metzer	A	416-322-9001	85	{"city":"Bigcity","zip":"12345"}
Lisa	Hetzer	A	416-980-3229	482	{"city":"Bigcity","zip":"12345"}
Cliff	Brandson	I	416-559-0223	3221	{"city":"Bigcity","zip":"12345"}
Roger	Marjory	A	647-290-6776	557	{"city":"Smallcity","zip":"98765"}
Hubert	Mentz	A	416-577-8233	312	{"city":"Bigcity","zip":"12345"}

```
Madan     Vadhera    I   011-2345678   162   {"city":"New
                                                Delhi","zip":"110011"}
Megha     Lahiri     A   011-3456789   111   {"city":"New
                                                Delhi","zip":"110111"}
Illias    Mohammed   A   011-4567890   79    {"city":"New
                                                Delhi","zip":"123111"}
Rajnish   Munnabar   A   0120-437097   122   {"city":"Noida","zip":"211312"}
Harish    Dutta      D   437-987650    71    {"city":"Itarsi","zip":"432567"}
   Time taken: 152.478 seconds, Fetched: 39 row(s)
   hive>
```

3. Use the LIKE operator to find all product descriptions that contain the word "Tiger".

```
hive> SELECT * FROM products WHERE description LIKE '%Tiger%';
```

```
Terminal
File  Edit  View  Terminal  Help
500 GB HD T     500 GB HD Tiger Brand     HD        498     45641   ["satacable","manual"]
09K Video       Video Card Tiger Brand 84F1        Video   5       98243   ["manual","game"]
T Case 4332     Computer Case Tiger Brand Style 4332   Case    7       88211   ["fans","manual","screws","watercooler"]
T Power 300W    Power Supply Tiger Brand 300 Watts     Power   8       93347   ["cables","screws"]
DVD T INT       DVD Tiger Brand Internal       Optical 19      82331   ["satacable","manual"]
DVD T EXT       DVD Tiger Brand External       Optical 17      82337   ["satacable","manual"]
Time taken: 138.708 seconds, Fetched: 6 row(s)
hive>
```

We can see that 6 records in our table contain the word Tiger in the description column. Hive required a single job to fulfill our request.

1.2.2 Arithmetic Operators

1. Have Hive return the product name, qty, and product number of all the products the company sells. Add 10 to the quantities for each product.

```
hive> SELECT prod_name, qty_on_hand + 10, prod_num FROM products;
```

```
Terminal
File  Edit  View  Terminal  Help
2 GB Memory E      3010      87655
4 GB Memory E      1010      87659
16 GB Memory E     248       87634
500 GB HD J        210       45628
500 GB HD T        508       45641
1 TB HD J          241       45691
4 Core CPU J3      60        98820
2 Core CPU J2      128       98838
1 Core CPU J2      213       98792
94F991 MB          29        282299
94G822 MB          40        282109
93H772 MB          25        282009
93G Video          90        99202
84G1 Video         24        99207
09K Video          15        98243
J Case 1500        30        77623
J Case 1501        28        77624
T Case 4332        17        88211
J Power 300W       38        92387
J Power 500W       27        92373
T Power 300W       18        93347
DVD J INT          33        88734
DVD J EXT          55        88821
DVD T INT          29        82331
DVD T EXT          27        82337
Time taken: 142.77 seconds, Fetched: 25 row(s)
hive>
```

You will notice that each quantity has 10 added to it.

1.2.3 Logical Operators

1. Find all the customers with last names of either "Merdec" OR "Melcic".

   hive> SELECT * FROM customer WHERE lname='Merdec' OR lname='Melcic';

   Using the OR logical operator allowed us to retrieve the 5 records that match either of the last names we queried on.

1.3 FUNCTIONS

In this section we will experiment with built-in Hive functions.

1. Let's find out more about the *upper* function. Run DESCRIBE FUNCTION upper in the Hive CLI.

   hive> DESCRIBE FUNCTION upper;

2. Convert product *category* to upper case and find products with a category equal to "CASE".

   hive> SELECT * FROM products WHERE upper(category) = 'CASE';

The 3 records for computer cases are returned. If we open the BigInsights Web Console we can see that 1 mapper was required and 0 reducers to get us this result set.

Hands-on-Exercise Page 9

3. Let's explode the array for the product with prod_num=98820.

```
hive> SELECT explode(packaged_with) as package_contents FROM products
WHERE prod_num='98820';
```

The array was exploded out and each array element is returned as an individual row.

1.4 EXTENDING HIVE'S FUNCTIONALITY

There are multiple ways to extend Hive's functionality including writing custom User Defined Functions (UDF) and Streaming. In this Exercise we will cover a very simple example of Streaming.

1.4.1 Streaming

1. Let's stream *qty* and *sales_id* columns to the /bin/cat command on the Linux OS.

```
hive> SELECT TRANSFORM (qty, sales_id)
USING '/bin/cat' AS newQty, newSalesID
FROM sales;
```

We can see that the two columns are gathered from the /bin/cat/ process and written out to the Hive console!

EXERCISE 9.3 HIVE DML IN ACTION

1.1 ACCESSING THE HIVE CLI

In this section we will navigate to the Hive Beeline CLI and start an interactive CLI session.

1. Open the Linux terminal by double clicking the Terminal icon from within the *BigInsights Shell directory* on the desktop.

2. In the Linux terminal change to the Hive home bin directory

```
$ cd $HIVE_HOME/bin
```

3. Start an interactive Hive shell session.

```
~> ./beeline -u jdbc:hive2://bivm.ibm.com:10000 -n biadmin -p password
```

```
biadmin@bivm:...ginsights/hive/bin
File  Edit  View  Terminal  Help
biadmin@bivm:/opt/ibm/biginsights/hive/bin> ./beeline -u jdbc:hive2://bivm.ibm.com:10000 -n biadmin -p password
scan complete in 34ms
Connecting to jdbc:hive2://bivm.ibm.com:10000
Connected to: Hive (version 0.12.0)
Driver: Hive (version 0.12.0)
Transaction isolation: TRANSACTION_REPEATABLE_READ
-hiveconf (No such file or directory)
hive.aux.jars.path=file:/opt/ibm/biginsights/hive/lib/hive-hbase-handler-0.12.0.jar,file:/opt/ibm/biginsights/hi
/hive/lib/hbase-client-0.96.0.jar,file:/opt/ibm/biginsights/hive/lib/hbase-common-0.96.0.jar,file:/opt/ibm/bigin
t/ibm/biginsights/hive/lib/hbase-prefix-tree-0.96.0.jar,file:/opt/ibm/biginsights/hive/lib/hbase-protocol-0.96.0
6.0.jar,file:/opt/ibm/biginsights/hive/lib/htrace-core-2.01.jar,file:/opt/ibm/biginsights/hive/lib/zookeeper-3.4
.jar,file:/opt/ibm/biginsights/sheets/libext/pig-0.11.1.jar,file:/opt/ibm/biginsights/sheets/libext/avro-1.7.4.j
ar,file:/opt/ibm/biginsights/sheets/libext/json-simple-1.1.jar,file:/opt/ibm/biginsights/sheets/libext/joda-time
ts.jar,file:/opt/ibm/biginsights/sheets/libext/bigsheets-serdes-1.0.0.jar,file:/opt/ibm/biginsights/lib/parquet/
ights/lib/parquet/parquet-mr/parquet-common-1.3.2.jar,file:/opt/ibm/biginsights/lib/parquet/parquet-mr/parquet-e
parquet-mr/parquet-generator-1.3.2.jar,file:/opt/ibm/biginsights/lib/parquet/parquet-mr/parquet-hadoop-bundle-1.
/parquet-hive-bundle-1.3.2.jar,file:/opt/ibm/biginsights/lib/parquet/parquet-mr/parquet-thrift-1.3.2.jar,file:/o
le or directory)
Beeline version 0.12.0 by Apache Hive
```

4. Tell Hive to Use the computersalesdb (we will use this database for the rest of this interactive session).

```
hive> USE computersalesdb;
```

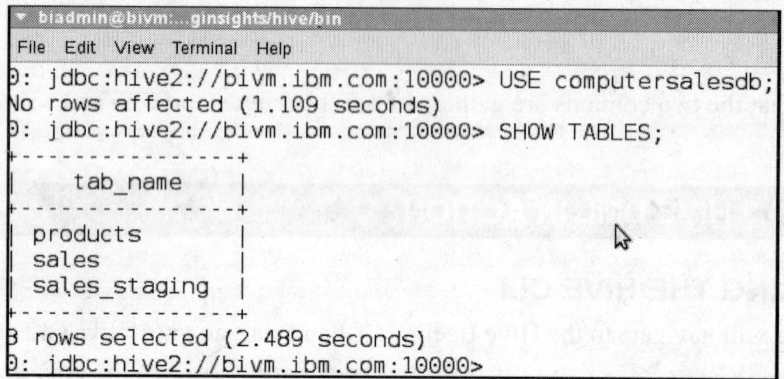

```
biadmin@bivm:...ginsights/hive/bin
File  Edit  View  Terminal  Help
0: jdbc:hive2://bivm.ibm.com:10000> USE computersalesdb;
No rows affected (1.109 seconds)
0: jdbc:hive2://bivm.ibm.com:10000> SHOW TABLES;
+-----------------+
|    tab_name     |
+-----------------+
| products        |
| sales           |
| sales_staging   |
+-----------------+
3 rows selected (2.489 seconds)
0: jdbc:hive2://bivm.ibm.com:10000>
```

1.1.1 Sample Data Descriptions

Before we begin working in Hive, review the data we will be using. It may be useful to print these pages so you can refer to the data when running your queries. Our sample data is from a fictitious computer retailer. The company sells computer parts and generally serves a single State in the country.

We have already seen the contents Customer.csv, Product.csv and Sales.csv

1.2 LOADING DATA

In our previous Exercise, we created 4 new tables. These tables need to have data in them to be useful to us. The table names are *customer, products, sales_staging,* and *sales*. Remember that the customer table is an External table and we already "loaded" data into it.

1.2.1 Viewing Data from BigInsights Web Console

In this Exercise, we will take advantage of the BigInsights Web Console to view our data in HDFS.

1. Open the BigInsights Web Console by clicking the desktop shortcut. Login if required.

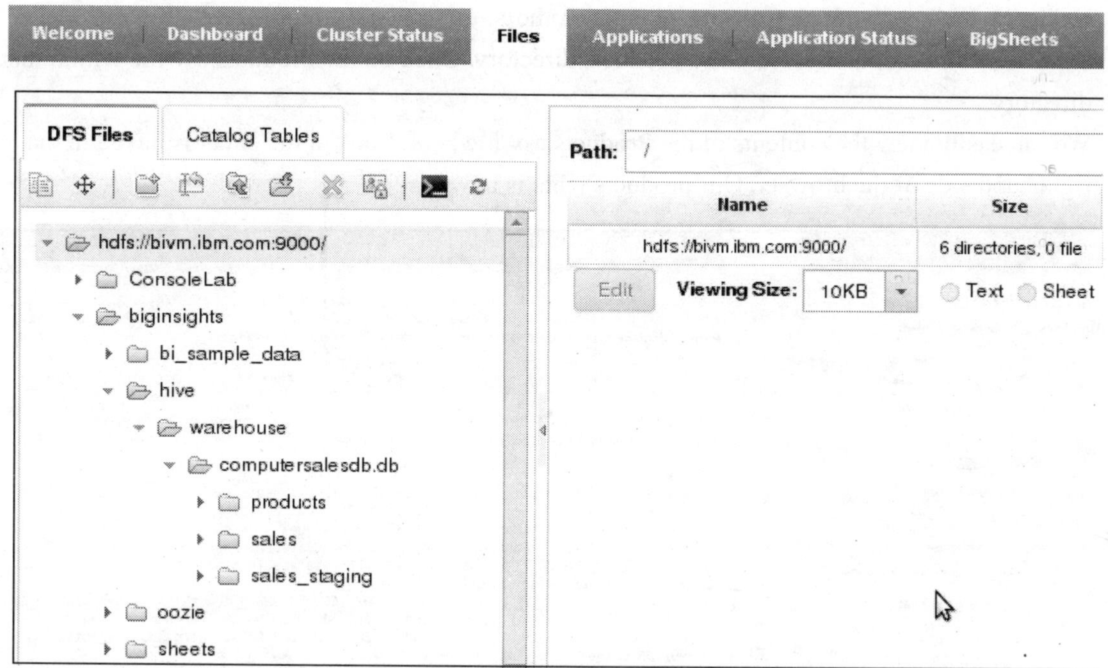

2. Click the Files tab at the top. In the left navigational menu, navigate to hdfs:/bivm:9000/->biginsights->hive->warehouse->computersalesdb.db This is the path that all of our Hive managed tables will be down.

Keep this browser open as you work with the Hive Beeline Command Line Interface. It will allow us to quickly check HDFS and see changes to the files and directories as we work with the Hive DML.

1.2.2 Loading Data into the Managed Non-Partitioned Tables

The first table we created in the previous Exercise was the *products* table. This table is fully managed by Hive and does not contain any partitions. We will now load the *products* table with the data that is stored in the local /home/biadmin/sampleData/Computer_Business/WithoutHeaders/Product.csv file.

1. In the CLI, create the new Products table in Hive.

```
hive> LOAD DATA LOCAL INPATH
'/home/biadmin/sampleData/Computer_Business/WithoutHeaders/Product.csv'
OVERWRITE INTO TABLE products;
```

Hive copies the data from the file. Our products table now has data in it. Let's check it out!

2. Using the BigInsights Web Console, navigate to hdfs:/bivm:9000/->biginsights->hive->warehouse->computersalesdb.db->products directory. Click on the Products.csv file within that directory.
   We can easily view the contents of the Products.csv file here. Look at the data displayed in the right hand side of the browser. Our products table is now loaded!

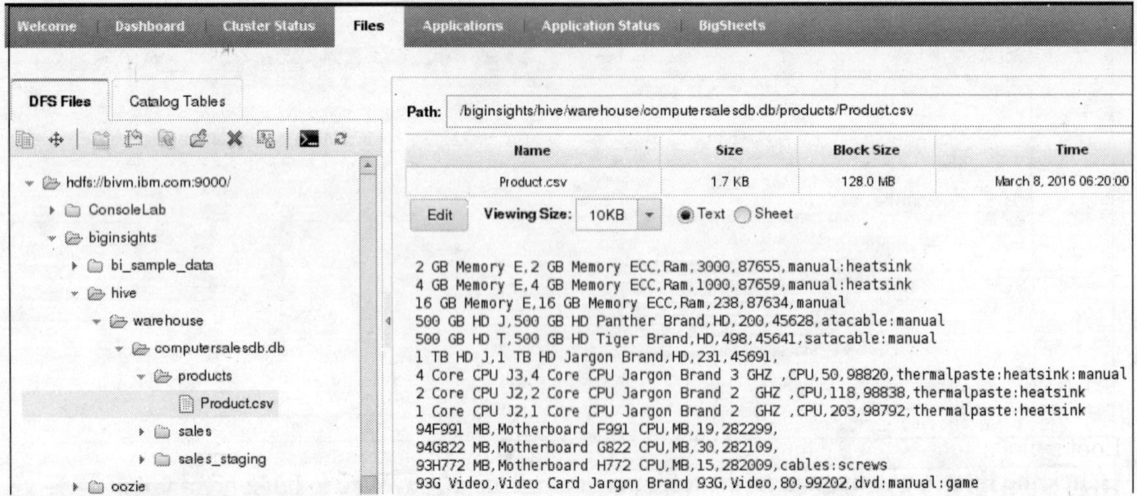

3. Next we will load sales records into the sales_staging table.

```
hive> LOAD DATA LOCAL INPATH
'/home/biadmin/sampleData/
Computer_Business/WithoutHeaders/Sales.csv'
INTO TABLE sales_staging;
```

Notice we left off the OVERWRITE keyword in this statement. This is because we normally would want to add the monthly sales data to our historical list of records already in the sales_staging table. We would not want to overwrite all the records in that table with just this month's data.

4. Again, let's verify that our data is now in HDFS, by checking out the file in the BigInsights Web Console.First click the refresh button to update the navigational tree.
   Now open the sales_staging folder, click on the Sales.csv file and browse the data on the right hand side.

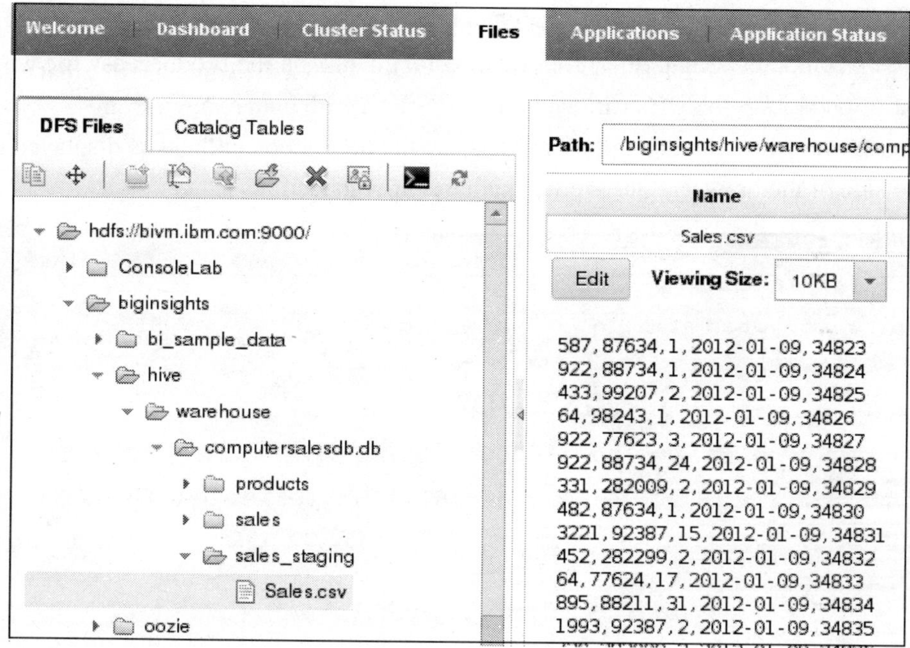

Looks like a success. We can see the presence of tables by issuing following commands: **Hive -> SHOW TABLES; and then describe the contents of SALES table.**

```
biadmin@bivm:...ginsights/hive/bin
File  Edit  View  Terminal  Help
0: jdbc:hive2://bivm.ibm.com:10000> SHOW TABLES;
+----------------+
|    tab_name    |
+----------------+
| customer       |
| products       |
| sales          |
| sales_staging  |
+----------------+
4 rows selected (2.062 seconds)
0: jdbc:hive2://bivm.ibm.com:10000> DESCRIBE SALES;
+--------------------------+----------------------+----------------------+
|         col_name         |      data_type       |       comment        |
+--------------------------+----------------------+----------------------+
| cust_id                  | string               | None                 |
| prod_num                 | string               | None                 |
| qty                      | int                  | None                 |
| sales_id                 | string               | None                 |
| sales_date               | string               | None                 |
|                          |                      |                      |
| # Partition Information  |                      |                      |
| # col_name               | data_type            | comment              |
|                          |                      |                      |
| sales_date               | string               | None                 |
+--------------------------+----------------------+----------------------+
10 rows selected (2.653 seconds)
0: jdbc:hive2://bivm.ibm.com:10000>
```

1.2.3 Loading Data into the Managed Partitioned Table

Now that our *sales_staging* table has data we can work with, let's write some queries that will allow us to load our partitioned *sales* table (partitioned on *sales_date*) with data coming from *sales_staging*.

1. In the CLI, load sales data from '2012-01-09' into a partition of the sales table.

```
hive> INSERT OVERWRITE TABLE sales
PARTITION (sales_date = '2012-01-09')
SELECT cust_id, prod_num, qty, sales_id
FROM sales_staging ss
WHERE ss.sale_date = '2012-01-09';
0: jdbc:hive2://bivm.ibm.com:10000> INSERT OVERWRITE TABLE sales
. . . . . . . . . . . . . . . . . > PARTITION (sales_date = '2012-01-09')
. . . . . . . . . . . . . . . . . . . . > SELECT cust_id, prod_num, qty,
sales_id
. . . . . . . . . . . . . . . . . > FROM sales_staging ss
. . . . . . . . . . . . . . . . . > WHERE ss.sale_date = '2012-01-09';
Error: Error while processing statement: FAILED: SemanticException [Error
10098]: Non-Partition column appears in the partition specification:
sales_data (state=42000,code=10098)
Let us investigate why the INSERT operation failed. Lets describe the
database sale_staging by issuing a command:
0: jdbc:hive2://bivm.ibm.com:10000> describe sales_staging;

0: jdbc:hive2://bivm.ibm.com:10000> describe sales_staging;
```

col_name	data_type	comment
cust_id	string	None
prod_num	string	None
qty	int	None
sales_data	date	None
sales_id	string	None

```
5 rows selected (2.018 seconds)
```

It is seen that the name of sales_date field has been written as sales_data. Another mistake is that in WHERE clause we have written sale_date instead of sales.data. So let us enter :

```
0: jdbc:hive2://bivm.ibm.com:10000> INSERT OVERWRITE TABLE sales
. . . . . . . . . . . . . . . . . > PARTITION (sales_date ='2012-01-09')
```

```
. . . . . . . . . . . . . . . . . . . . . > select cust_id, prod_num, qty, sales_id
. . . . . . . . . . . . . . . . . . . . . > From sales_staging ss
. . . . . . . . . . . . . . . . . . . . . > Where ss.sales_data = '2012-01-09';
```

```
0: jdbc:hive2://bivm.ibm.com:10000> INSERT OVERWRITE TABLE sales
. . . . . . . . . . . . . . . . . . > PARTITION (sales_date ='2012-01-09')
. . . . . . . . . . . . . . . . . . > select cust_id, prod_num, qty, sales_id
. . . . . . . . . . . . . . . . . . > From sales_staging ss
. . . . . . . . . . . . . . . . . . > Where ss.sales_data = '2012-01-09';
No rows affected (198.772 seconds)
0: jdbc:hive2://bivm.ibm.com:10000>
```

Notice it took a while for this to complete. This is because you've invoked a MapReduce job (thanks to the WHERE clause)!

2. In the BigInsights Web Console, refresh the file tree and take a look in the sales folder now. You will see a new subdirectory named sales_date=2012-01-09. Within that directory is a data file named 000000_0. If you select that file you will see in the right hand preview that it only contains the data for our 2012-01-09 sales.

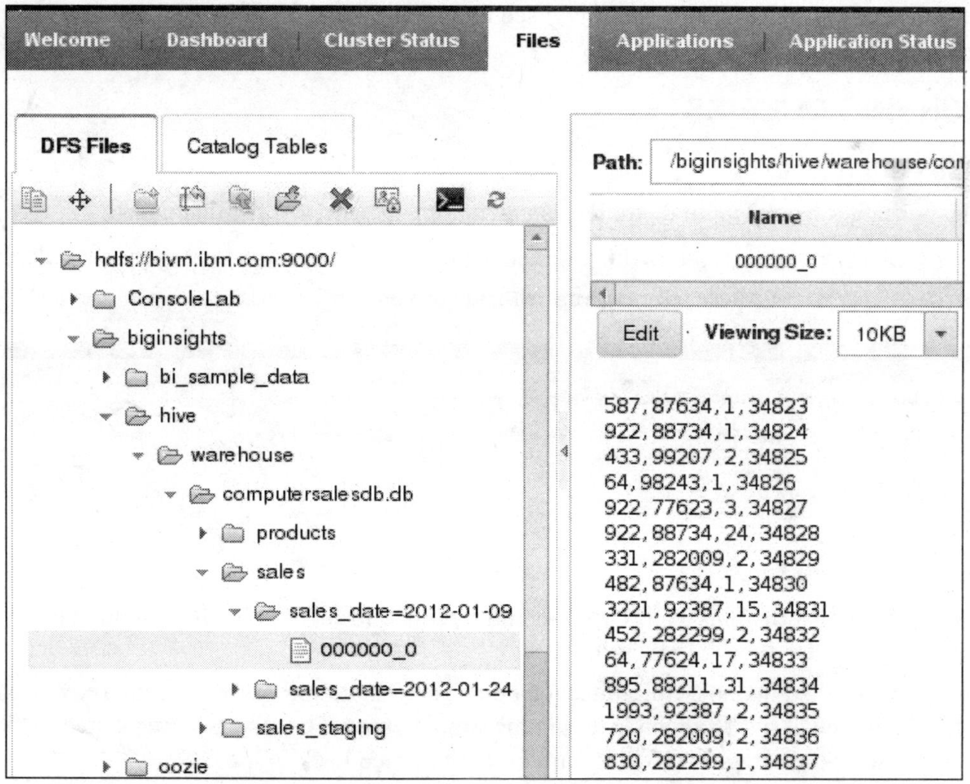

3. Following the same procedures, load sales data from '2012-01-24' into a new partition of the

sales table.

```
hive> INSERT OVERWRITE TABLE sales
PARTITION (sales_date = '2012-01-24')
SELECT cust_id, prod_num, qty, sales_id
FROM sales_staging ss
WHERE ss.sales_data = '2012-01-24';
```

```
biadmin@bivm:...ginsights/hive/bin
File Edit View Terminal Help
0: jdbc:hive2://bivm.ibm.com:10000> INSERT OVERWRITE TABLE sales
. . . . . . . . . . . . . . . . . > PARTITION (sales_date ='2012-01-24')
. . . . . . . . . . . . . . . . . > select cust_id, prod_num, qty, sales_id
. . . . . . . . . . . . . . . . . > From sales_staging ss
. . . . . . . . . . . . . . . . . > Where ss.sales_data = '2012-01-24';
No rows affected (149.864 seconds)
0: jdbc:hive2://bivm.ibm.com:10000>
```

4. In the BigInsights Web Console, refresh the file tree and take a look in the sales folder now. You will see a new subdirectory named sales_date=2012-01-24. Within that directory is a data file named 000000_0. If you select that file you will see in the right hand preview that it only contains the data for our 2012-01-24 sales.

1.3 RUNNING QUERIES

1.3.1 Selecting Data

Now that our tables have data in them, let's start running queries against that data.

1. In the CLI, select all the data in the products table where the product category is 'Video'.

```
hive> SELECT * FROM products WHERE category='Video';
```

```
biadmin@bivm:...ginsights/hive/bin
File Edit View Terminal Help
0: jdbc:hive2://bivm.ibm.com:10000> SELECT * FROM products WHERE cetegory = 'Video';
+------------+------------------------------+-----------+-------------+----------+----------------------------------+
| prod_name  |         description          | cetegory  | qty_on_hand | prod_num |          packaged_with           |
+------------+------------------------------+-----------+-------------+----------+----------------------------------+
| 93G Video  | Video Card Jargon Brand 93G  | Video     | 80          | 99202    | ["dvd","manual","game"]          |
| 84G1 Video | Video Card Jargon Brand 84F1 | Video     | 14          | 99207    | ["dvd","manual","hdmicable"]     |
| 09K Video  | Video Card Tiger Brand 84F1  | Video     | 5           | 98243    | ["manual","game"]                |
+------------+------------------------------+-----------+-------------+----------+----------------------------------+
3 rows selected (155.769 seconds)
0: jdbc:hive2://bivm.ibm.com:10000>
```

Now open the BigInsights Web Console and navigate to the Application Status tab. You will see your query listed under Jobs. Click on it.

This query resulted in one MapReduce job being run. The MapReduce job required one Mapper and zero reducers. It took about 18 seconds to run this simple query. The results were printed to the CLI. The 3 records that have the category="Video" are in fact returned back in the CLI!

2. Now select all the products where category='Video' AND the first element of the PACKAGED_WITH array contains 'dvd'.

```
hive> SELECT * FROM products
WHERE cetegory='Video' AND PACKAGED_WITH[0]='dvd';
```

```
biadmin@bivm:...ginsights/hive/bin
File Edit View Terminal Help
0: jdbc:hive2://bivm.ibm.com:10000> SELECT * FROM products
. . . . . . . . . . . . . . . . . > WHERE cetegory='Video' AND PACKAGED_WITH[0]='dvd';
+-------------+------------------------------+-----------+--------------+------------+------------------------------+
| prod_name   |         description          | cetegory  | qty_on_hand  | prod_num   |        packaged_with         |
+-------------+------------------------------+-----------+--------------+------------+------------------------------+
| 93G Video   | Video Card Jargon Brand 93G  | Video     | 80           | 99202      | ["dvd","manual","game"]      |
| 84G1 Video  | Video Card Jargon Brand 84F1 | Video     | 14           | 99207      | ["dvd","manual","hdmicable"] |
+-------------+------------------------------+-----------+--------------+------------+------------------------------+
2 rows selected (148.379 seconds)
0: jdbc:hive2://bivm.ibm.com:10000>
```

3. Find out how many products we have for each category of item by using the GROUP BY clause.

```
hive> SELECT cetegory, count(*) FROM products
GROUP BY cetegory;
```

We can see our results and they look good.

```
biadmin@bivm:...ginsights/hive/bin
File Edit View Terminal Help
0: jdbc:hive2://bivm.ibm.com:10000> SELECT cetegory, count(*) FROM products
. . . . . . . . . . . . . . . . . > GROUP BY cetegory;
+-----------+------+
| cetegory  | _c1  |
+-----------+------+
| CPU       | 3    |
| Case      | 3    |
| HD        | 3    |
| MB        | 3    |
| Optical   | 4    |
| Power     | 3    |
| Ram       | 3    |
| Video     | 3    |
+-----------+------+
8 rows selected (349.115 seconds)
0: jdbc:hive2://bivm.ibm.com:10000>
```

4. Use a nested select to show the product categories that contain more than 4 products.

```
hive> FROM(
SELECT category, count(*) as count FROM products
GROUP BY category) cats
SELECT * WHERE cats.count > 3;
```

```
▾ biadmin@bivm:...ginsights/hive/bin
File  Edit  View  Terminal  Help
0: jdbc:hive2://bivm.ibm.com:10000> FROM(
. . . . . . . . . . . . . . . . . > SELECT cetegory, count(*) as count FROM products
. . . . . . . . . . . . . . . . . > GROUP BY cetegory) cats
. . . . . . . . . . . . . . . . . > SELECT * WHERE cats.count > 3;
+-----------+--------+
| cetegory  | count  |
+-----------+--------+
| Optical   | 4      |
+-----------+--------+
1 row selected (243.365 seconds)
0: jdbc:hive2://bivm.ibm.com:10000>
```

Your output should like similar to the above screen capture. You will notice that in addition to using a subquery we also used two column aliases ("count" and "cats")

1.3.2 Big SQL Subquery

Imagine that you have been working with this dataset in an RDBMS outside of Hadoop for many years. You've written plenty of queries that worked on your traditional RDBMS and now you'd like to simply copy some of those queries and use them in your Big Data environment. Unfortunately Hive is not fully SQL compliant so you may need to spend time altering your queries to work in HiveQL. A simpler option may be to run your queries using IBM's Big SQL. Big SQL is ANSI SQL compliant and offers many performance benefits and features.

1. In the Hive CLI, run the following subquery. Our goal is to get a list of all of the products that belong to the 'Ram' category and have the number of sales (not quantity sold) that each product was included in. Notice that the subquery is in the SELECT portion of the SQL.

   ```
   hive> SELECT prod_num, (SELECT count(*) FROM sales WHERE
   prod_num=prod.prod_num group by prod_num) as number_of_sales
   FROM products prod WHERE CATEGORY='Ram';
   ```

   ```
   ▾ biadmin@bivm:...ginsights/hive/bin
   File  Edit  View  Terminal  Help
   0: jdbc:hive2://bivm.ibm.com:10000> SELECT prod_num, (SELECT count(*) FROM sales WHERE
   . . . . . . . . . . . . . . . . . > prod_num=prod.prod_num group by prod_num) as number_of_sales
   . . . . . . . . . . . . . . . . . > FROM products prod WHERE CETEGORY='Ram';
   Error: Error while processing statement: FAILED: ParseException line 1:18 cannot recognize input near 'SELECT' 'count' '(
   =40000)
   0: jdbc:hive2://bivm.ibm.com:10000>
   ```

   That doesn't look good! Hive does not allow the subquery to be in that location of the SQL statement.

2. IBM's Big SQL should already be up and running on your Big Insights Virtual Machine. There are many ways to work with Big SQL – for this example we will use the Big SQL JSQSH command line shell. Open the BigInsights Shell folder on the Linux desktop. Then open the BigSQL Shell application.

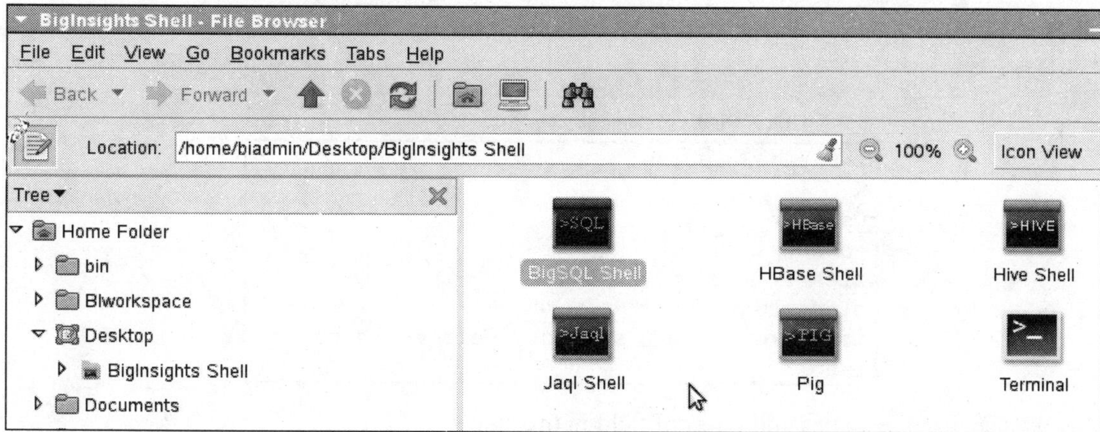

Give the shell a moment to start. Once it is ready, it will look like the following:

3. Ask Big SQL to SHOW DATABASES; You'll notice that Big SQL already knows about our Hive databases!
4. Set the computersalesdb database as our working database for this session.

```
> USE computersalesdb;
```

5. Run the previous SQL query that contains the subquery in the SELECT clause.

```
> SELECT prod_num, (SELECT count(*) FROM sales WHERE
prod_num=prod.prod_num GROUP BY prod_num) as number_of_sales
FROM products prod WHERE category='Ram';
```

Big SQL is able to return our results quickly thanks to its optimization that allows queries on small datasets to be run on the server instead of running a MapReduce job(s).

6. Enter quit; to close the Big SQL shell.

1.3.3 Taking Advantage of Partitioned Data

The *sales* table is partitioned on *sales_date*. In a previous exercise we loaded data into two partitions of this table (2012-01-09 and 2012-01-24 partitions). Let's take advantage of this partitioning to improve latency.

On hive terminal write :

Hive > USE computersalesdb;

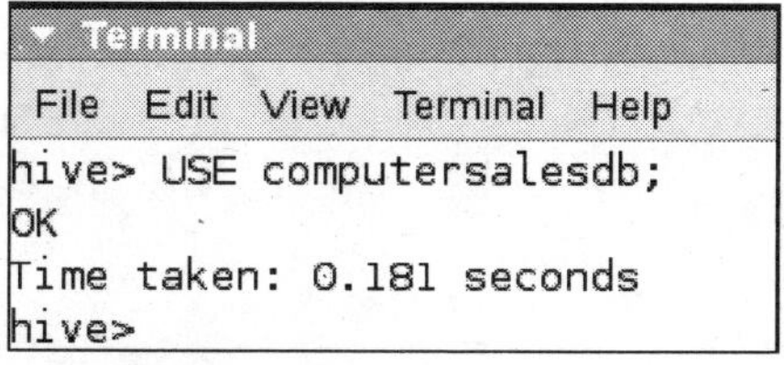

Let us see the tables under this database;

Hive > show tables;

```
Terminal
File  Edit  View  Terminal  Help
hive> show tables;
OK
customer
products
sales
sales_staging
Time taken: 1.275 seconds, Fetched: 4 row(s)
hive>
```

Let us visualise the names and types of field in this table:

Hive> describe sales;

```
Terminal
File  Edit  View  Terminal  Help
hive> describe sales;
OK
cust_id                 string                  None
prod_num                string                  None
qty                     int                     None
sales_id                string                  None
sales_date              string                  None

# Partition Information
# col_name              data_type               comment

sales_date              string                  None
Time taken: 4.031 seconds, Fetched: 10 row(s)
hive>
```

1. In the CLI, run a SELECT query that finds only the sales that occurred on 2012-01-24. Order the results by the sale_id.

```
hive> SELECT * FROM sales
WHERE sales_date = '2012-01-24'
ORDER BY sales_id;
```

```
hive> select * from sales
    > where sales_date = '2012-01-24'
    > order by sales_id;
Total MapReduce jobs = 1
Launching Job 1 out of 1
Number of reduce tasks determined at compile time: 1
In order to change the average load for a reducer (in bytes):
  set hive.exec.reducers.bytes.per.reducer=<number>
In order to limit the maximum number of reducers:
  set hive.exec.reducers.max=<number>
In order to set a constant number of reducers:
  set mapred.reduce.tasks=<number>
Starting Job = job_201603101256_0001, Tracking URL = http://bivm.ibm.com:50030/jobdetails.jsp?jobid=job_201603101256_0001
Kill Command = /opt/ibm/biginsights/IHC/bin/hadoop job  -kill job_201603101256_0001
Hadoop job information for Stage-1: number of mappers: 1; number of reducers: 1
2016-03-11 06:14:30,152 Stage-1 map = 0%,  reduce = 0%
2016-03-11 06:14:42,948 Stage-1 map = 100%,  reduce = 0%, Cumulative CPU 5.27 sec
2016-03-11 06:14:44,002 Stage-1 map = 100%,  reduce = 0%, Cumulative CPU 5.27 sec
2016-03-11 06:14:45,074 Stage-1 map = 100%,  reduce = 0%, Cumulative CPU 5.27 sec
2016-03-11 06:14:46,124 Stage-1 map = 100%,  reduce = 0%, Cumulative CPU 5.27 sec
2016-03-11 06:14:47,196 Stage-1 map = 100%,  reduce = 0%, Cumulative CPU 5.27 sec
2016-03-11 06:14:48,236 Stage-1 map = 100%,  reduce = 0%, Cumulative CPU 5.27 sec
2016-03-11 06:14:49,287 Stage-1 map = 100%,  reduce = 0%, Cumulative CPU 5.27 sec
2016-03-11 06:14:50,314 Stage-1 map = 100%,  reduce = 0%, Cumulative CPU 5.27 sec
2016-03-11 06:14:51,348 Stage-1 map = 100%,  reduce = 0%, Cumulative CPU 5.27 sec
2016-03-11 06:14:52,394 Stage-1 map = 100%,  reduce = 0%, Cumulative CPU 5.27 sec
2016-03-11 06:14:53,430 Stage-1 map = 100%,  reduce = 0%, Cumulative CPU 5.27 sec
2016-03-11 06:14:54,500 Stage-1 map = 100%,  reduce = 0%, Cumulative CPU 5.27 sec
2016-03-11 06:15:04,992 Stage-1 map = 100%,  reduce = 100%, Cumulative CPU 17.86 sec
2016-03-11 06:15:06,057 Stage-1 map = 100%,  reduce = 100%, Cumulative CPU 17.86 sec
2016-03-11 06:15:07,441 Stage-1 map = 100%,  reduce = 100%, Cumulative CPU 17.86 sec
MapReduce Total cumulative CPU time: 17 seconds 860 msec
Ended Job = job_201603101256_0001
MapReduce Jobs Launched:
Job 0: Map: 1  Reduce: 1   Cumulative CPU: 17.86 sec   HDFS Read: 602 HDFS Write: 550 SUCCESS
Total MapReduce CPU Time Spent: 17 seconds 860 msec
OK
7       98243   1       34842   2012-01-24
11      77623   2       34843   2012-01-24
482     88734   1       34844   2012-01-24
3221    282009  1       34845   2012-01-24
452     99202   23      34846   2012-01-24
64      92387   4       34847   2012-01-24
895     282009  7       34848   2012-01-24
1993    92387   3       34849   2012-01-24
720     99207   1       34850   2012-01-24
102     98243   1       34851   2012-01-24
227     77623   1       34852   2012-01-24
323     99207   2       34853   2012-01-24
47      92387   1       34854   2012-01-24
431     87659   1       34855   2012-01-24
24      45641   5       34856   2012-01-24
19      88734   7       34857   2012-01-24
773     45641   4       34858   2012-01-24
647     45628   2       34859   2012-01-24
773     45628   10      34860   2012-01-24
Time taken: 155.36 seconds, Fetched: 19 row(s)
hive>
```

Just the 2012-01-24 sales records were returned.

2. Let's take a look at the job that was run on Hadoop to fulfill our Hive query. We can do this

easily back in the BigInsights Web Console. In the web console, click the Application Status tab, then click on the Jobs link (the proper places to click are highlighted in red in the screen capture below). You will see our job, named after our query – click on that and investigate the job. One MapReduce Job was required to complete this query. This job contained one Map task and one Reduce task. Only the sales_id=2012-01-24 partition file had to be read in to complete this query, saving us some wait time – theoretically a lot of wait time if we had a large number of historical sales data.

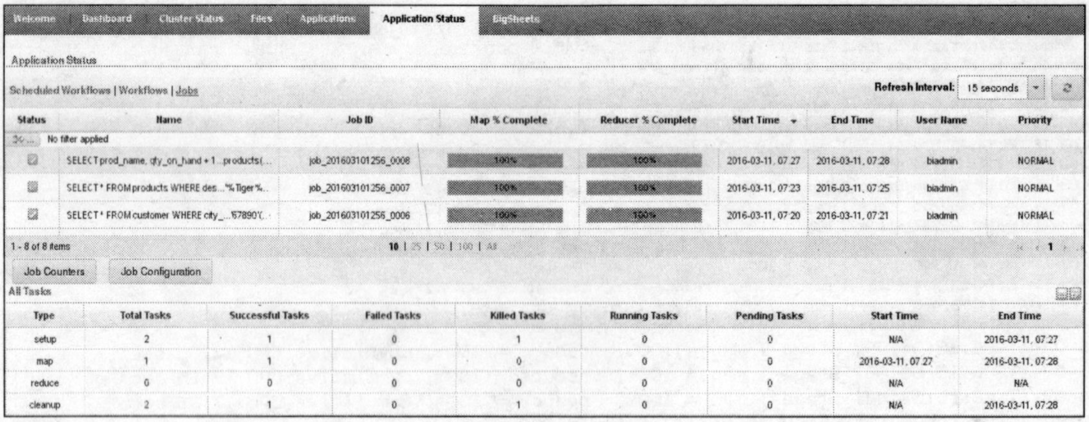

Welcome | Dashboard | Cluster Status | Files | Applications | Application Status | BigSheets

Application Status

Scheduled Workflows | Workflows | Jobs

Refresh Interval: 15 seconds

Status	Name	Job ID	Map % Complete	Reducer % Complete	Start Time	End Time	User Name	Priority
No filter applied								
	SELECT prod_name, qty_on_hand + 1...products(...	job_201603101256_0008	100%	100%	2016-03-11, 07:27	2016-03-11, 07:28	biadmin	NORMAL
	SELECT * FROM products WHERE des...'%Tiger%...	job_201603101256_0007	100%	100%	2016-03-11, 07:23	2016-03-11, 07:25	biadmin	NORMAL
	SELECT * FROM customer WHERE city_...'67890'(...	job_201603101256_0006	100%	100%	2016-03-11, 07:20	2016-03-11, 07:21	biadmin	NORMAL

1 - 8 of 8 items   10 | 25 | 50 | 100 | All   1

Job Counters   Job Configuration

All Tasks

Type	Total Tasks	Successful Tasks	Failed Tasks	Killed Tasks	Running Tasks	Pending Tasks	Start Time	End Time
setup	2	1	0	1	0	0	N/A	2016-03-11, 07:27
map	1	1	0	0	0	0	2016-03-11, 07:27	2016-03-11, 07:28
reduce	0	0	0	0	0	0	N/A	N/A
cleanup	2	1	0	1	0	0	N/A	2016-03-11, 07:28

1.3.4 Joins

1. Let's show all *Optical* category sales that occurred on 2012-01-09. We will need to do an equijoin between the *sales* and *products* tables to gather this information.

```
hive> SELECT s.cust_id, s.prod_num, s.qty, s.sales_id,
p.prod_name, p.category
FROM sales s JOIN products p
ON s.prod_num = p.prod_num
  WHERE s.sales_date = '2012-01-09' AND p.category = 'Optical';
```

```
Terminal
File  Edit  View  Terminal  Help
hive> select s.cust_id, s.prod_num,s.qty,s.sales_id,
    > p.prod_name, p.cetegory FROM sales s JOIN products p ON s.prod_num = p.prod_num
    > WHERE s.sales_date = '2012-01-09' AND p.cetegory = 'Optical';
Total MapReduce jobs = 1
Execution log at: /var/ibm/biginsights/hive/logs/biadmin/.log
2016-03-11 06:33:15     Starting to launch local task to process map join;      maxim
2016-03-11 06:33:18     Dump the side-table into file: file:/tmp/biadmin/hive_2016-03
le00--.hashtable
2016-03-11 06:33:18     Upload 1 File to: file:/tmp/biadmin/hive_2016-03-11_06-32-56_
ble
2016-03-11 06:33:18     End of local task; Time Taken: 3.413 sec.
Execution completed successfully
Mapred Local Task Succeeded . Convert the Join into MapJoin
Mapred Local Task Succeeded . Convert the Join into MapJoin
Launching Job 1 out of 1
Number of reduce tasks is set to 0 since there's no reduce operator
Starting Job = job_201603101256_0002, Tracking URL = http://bivm.ibm.com:50030/jobdet
Kill Command = /opt/ibm/biginsights/IHC/bin/hadoop job  -kill job_201603101256_0002
Hadoop job information for Stage-3: number of mappers: 1; number of reducers: 0
2016-03-11 06:34:19,545 Stage-3 map = 0%,  reduce = 0%
2016-03-11 06:34:30,897 Stage-3 map = 100%,  reduce = 0%, Cumulative CPU 5.09 sec
2016-03-11 06:34:31,927 Stage-3 map = 100%,  reduce = 0%, Cumulative CPU 5.09 sec
2016-03-11 06:34:32,961 Stage-3 map = 100%,  reduce = 0%, Cumulative CPU 5.09 sec
2016-03-11 06:34:33,997 Stage-3 map = 100%,  reduce = 0%, Cumulative CPU 5.09 sec
2016-03-11 06:34:35,032 Stage-3 map = 100%,  reduce = 0%, Cumulative CPU 5.09 sec
2016-03-11 06:34:36,061 Stage-3 map = 100%,  reduce = 0%, Cumulative CPU 5.09 sec
2016-03-11 06:34:37,090 Stage-3 map = 100%,  reduce = 100%, Cumulative CPU 5.09 sec
MapReduce Total cumulative CPU time: 5 seconds 90 msec
```

```
Terminal
File  Edit  View  Terminal  Help
Ended Job = job_201603101256_0002
MapReduce Jobs Launched:
Job 0: Map: 1   Cumulative CPU: 5.09 sec   HDFS Read: 1970 HDFS Write: 109 SUCCESS
Total MapReduce CPU Time Spent: 5 seconds 90 msec
OK
922     88734   1       34824   DVD J INT       Optical
922     88734   24      34828   DVD J INT       Optical
128     88734   4       34839   DVD J INT       Optical
Time taken: 101.328 seconds, Fetched: 3 row(s)
hive>
```

The join was successful. We got the 3 records we were looking for.

1.3.5 Views

1. Now let's create a View that stores a query which returns all the *sales* records (joined with *products* table) where the product category is 'Optical'.

```
hive> CREATE VIEW optical_sales AS
SELECT s.cust_id, s.prod_num, s.qty, s.sales_id,
p.prod_name, p.category
```

```
FROM sales s JOIN products p
ON s.prod_num = p.prod_num
WHERE p.category = 'Optical';
```

```
Terminal
File  Edit  View  Terminal  Help
hive> CREATE VIEW optical_sales AS
    > SELECT s.cust_id, s.prod_num, s.qty, s.sales_id,
    > p.prod_name, p.cetegory
    > FROM sales s JOIN products p
    > ON s.prod_num = p.prod_num
    > WHERE p.cetegory ='Optical';
OK
Time taken: 2.843 seconds
hive>
```

The View was successfully created.

2. Now that we have the optical_sales view, we can use it within other queries, just like it were a table. Notice how short this query is.

```
hive> SELECT * FROM optical_sales
WHERE qty > 1;
```

1.4 EXPORTING DATA

Imagine our management team wants us to extract all sales of Optical devices and give it to them in a format outside of the Hive CLI. We can do this by exporting the data from Hive.

1. Open the BigInsights Web Console and open the Files tab. Navigate to the user->biadmin folder.

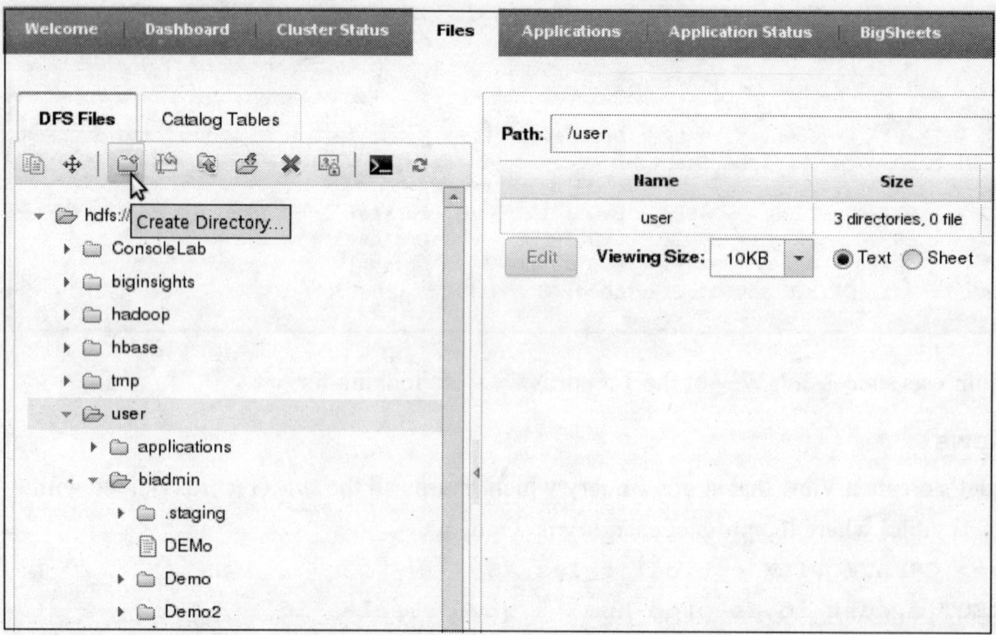

2. Inside of the /user/biadmin directory on HDFS, make a new directory called HiveReport.

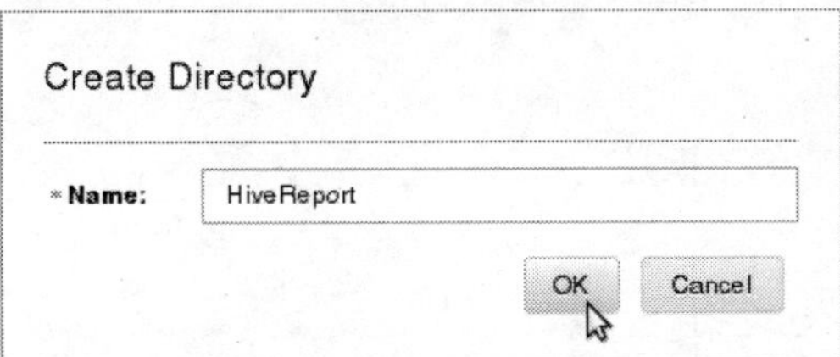

3. Click the permissions box and set this new folder to be writable by all users.

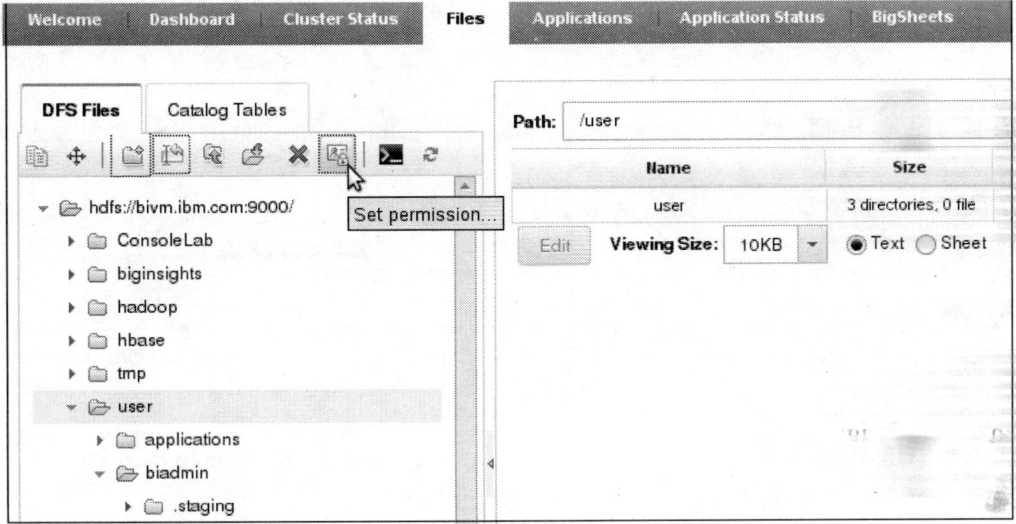

Change permissions

Change permissions for directory: user

Change owner and group recursively

Owner hdfs

Group biadmin

Change permissions recursively

Owner	Group	Others
☑ Read	☑ Read	☑ Read
☑ Write	☐ Write	☐ Write
☑ Execute	☑ Execute	☑ Execute

OK Cancel

Select both the write permissions;

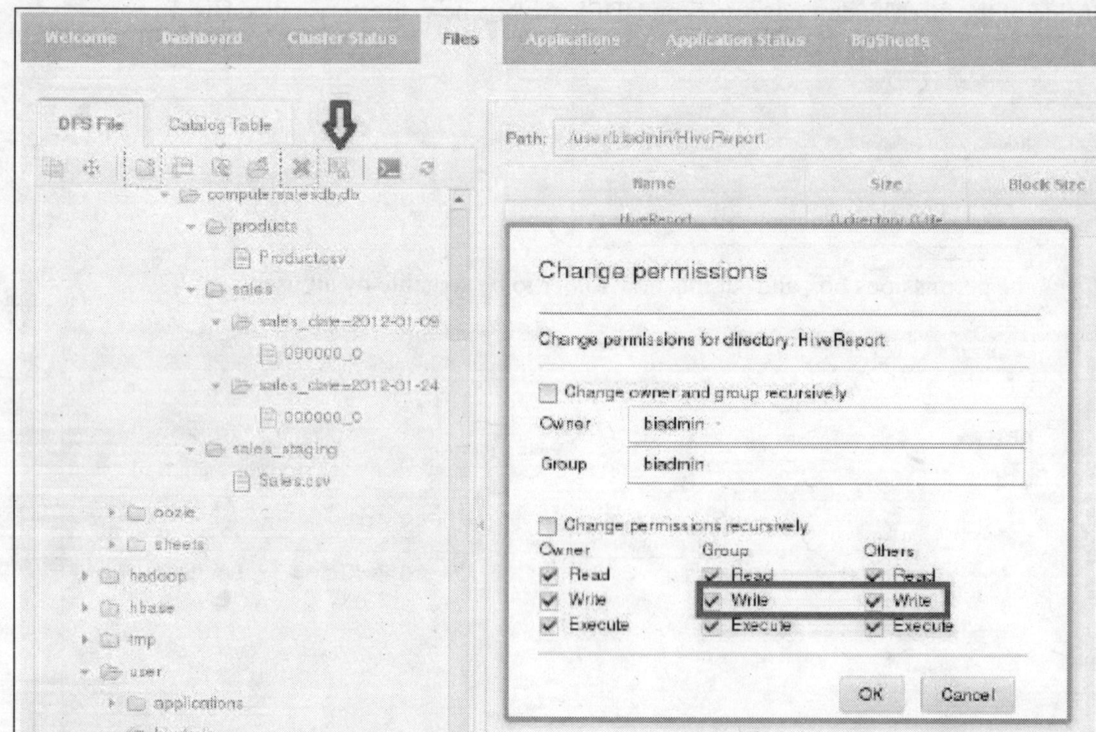

4. Back in the Hive CLI, we will utilize our previous query and write the data to the */user/biadmin/HiveReport* directory on the HDFS file system.

```
hive> INSERT OVERWRITE DIRECTORY '/user/biadmin/HiveReport'
SELECT * FROM optical_sales
WHERE qty > 1;
```

```
hive> INSERT OVERWRITE DIRECTORY '/user/biadmin/HiveReport'
   > SELECT * FROM optical_sales
   > WHERE qty > 1;
Total MapReduce jobs = 1
Execution log at: /var/ibm/biginsights/hive/logs/biadmin/.log
2016-03-11 10:16:17    Starting to launch local task to process map
join;maximum memory = 536870912
2016-03-11 10:16:23    Dump the side-table into file: file:/tmp/biadmin/
hive_2016-03-11_10-15-23_574_4416537697380907579-1/-local-10001/
HashTable-Stage-3/MapJoin-mapfile00--.hashtable
2016-03-11 10:16:23    Upload 1 File to: file:/tmp/biadmin/hive_2016-03-
11_10-15-23_574_4416537697380907579-1/-local-10001/HashTable-Stage-3/
```

```
MapJoin-mapfile00--.hashtable
2016-03-11 10:16:23     End of local task; Time Taken: 6.588 sec.
Execution completed successfully
Mapred Local Task Succeeded . Convert the Join into MapJoin
Mapred Local Task Succeeded . Convert the Join into MapJoin
Launching Job 1 out of 1
Number of reduce tasks is set to 0 since there's no reduce operator
Starting Job = job_201603101256_0009, Tracking URL = http://bivm.ibm.
com:50030/jobdetails.jsp?jobid=job_201603101256_0009
Kill Command = /opt/ibm/biginsights/IHC/bin/hadoop job -kill
job_201603101256_0009
Hadoop job information for Stage-3: number of mappers: 1; number of
reducers: 0
2016-03-11 10:18:40,583 Stage-3 map = 0%,  reduce = 0%
2016-03-11 10:19:13,827 Stage-3 map = 100%,  reduce = 0%, Cumulative
CPU 9.46 sec
2016-03-11 10:19:14,863 Stage-3 map = 100%,  reduce = 0%, Cumulative
CPU 9.46 sec
2016-03-11 10:19:15,899 Stage-3 map = 100%,  reduce = 0%, Cumulative
CPU 9.46 sec
2016-03-11 10:19:16,923 Stage-3 map = 100%,  reduce = 0%, Cumulative
CPU 9.46 sec
2016-03-11 10:19:18,037 Stage-3 map = 100%,  reduce = 0%, Cumulative
CPU 9.46 sec
2016-03-11 10:19:19,064 Stage-3 map = 100%,  reduce = 0%, Cumulative
CPU 9.46 sec
2016-03-11 10:19:20,090 Stage-3 map = 100%,  reduce = 0%, Cumulative
CPU 9.46 sec
2016-03-11 10:19:21,117 Stage-3 map = 100%,  reduce = 0%, Cumulative
CPU 9.46 sec
2016-03-11 10:19:22,138 Stage-3 map = 100%,  reduce = 0%, Cumulative
CPU 9.46 sec
2016-03-11 10:19:23,162 Stage-3 map = 100%,  reduce = 0%, Cumulative
CPU 9.46 sec
2016-03-11 10:19:24,188 Stage-3 map = 100%,  reduce = 0%, Cumulative
CPU 9.46 sec
2016-03-11 10:19:25,213 Stage-3 map = 100%,  reduce = 0%, Cumulative
CPU 9.46 sec
2016-03-11 10:19:26,235 Stage-3 map = 100%,  reduce = 0%, Cumulative
CPU 9.46 sec
```

```
2016-03-11 10:19:27,263 Stage-3 map = 100%,  reduce = 0%, Cumulative
CPU 9.46 sec
2016-03-11 10:19:28,291 Stage-3 map = 100%,  reduce = 0%, Cumulative
CPU 9.46 sec
2016-03-11 10:19:29,319 Stage-3 map = 100%,  reduce = 0%, Cumulative
CPU 9.46 sec
2016-03-11 10:19:30,345 Stage-3 map = 100%,  reduce = 0%, Cumulative
CPU 9.46 sec
2016-03-11 10:19:31,379 Stage-3 map = 100%,  reduce = 0%, Cumulative
CPU 9.46 sec
2016-03-11 10:19:32,411 Stage-3 map = 100%,  reduce = 0%, Cumulative
CPU 9.46 sec
2016-03-11 10:19:33,439 Stage-3 map = 100%,  reduce = 0%, Cumulative
CPU 9.46 sec
2016-03-11 10:19:34,660 Stage-3 map = 100%,  reduce = 100%, Cumulative
CPU 9.46 sec
MapReduce Total cumulative CPU time: 9 seconds 460 msec
Ended Job = job_201603101256_0009
Moving data to: /user/biadmin/HiveReport
MapReduce Jobs Launched:
Job 0: Map: 1   Cumulative CPU: 9.46 sec   HDFS Read: 1970 HDFS Write:
108 SUCCESS
Total MapReduce CPU Time Spent: 9 seconds 460 msec
OK
Time taken: 251.63 seconds
hive>
```

5. Open a new Linux terminal. Enter the following command:

```
~> hadoop fs -ls '/user/biadmin/HiveReport'
```

```
biadmin@bivm:...ginsights/hive/bin
File  Edit  View  Terminal  Help
biadmin@bivm:~> hadoop fs -ls '/user/biadmin/HiveReport'
Found 1 items
-rw-r--r--   1 biadmin biadmin        108 2016-03-11 07:00 /user/biadmin/HiveRep
ort/000000_0
biadmin@bivm:~>
```

Notice we have one new file called 000000_0! This is the data that Hive wrote out.

Now let's cat this file and see what the contents look like:

```
~> hadoop fs -cat '/user/biadmin/HiveReport/000000_0'
```

```
biadmin@bivm:...ginsights/hive/bin
File  Edit  View  Terminal  Help
biadmin@bivm:~> hadoop fs -cat '/user/biaadmin/HiveReport/000000_0'
cat: `/user/biaadmin/HiveReport/000000_0': No such file or directory
biadmin@bivm:~> hadoop fs -cat '/user/biadmin/HiveReport/000000_0'
19␁8734␁␁4857␁VD J INT␁ptical
922␁8734␁4␁4828␁VD J INT␁ptical
128␁8734␁␁4839␁VD J INT␁ptical
biadmin@bivm:~>
```

The odd looking character delimiters are being displayed because Hive's default delimiter is the ^A character. You could copy the new report out of HDFS and work with the results in the tools of your choice.

1.5 Explain

Let's take a brief look at using EXPLAIN in a Hive query.

1. We will have Hive explain the execution plan for a simple query that selects all customer records where the customer status is active.

```
hive> EXPLAIN SELECT * FROM customer;
hive> EXPLAIN SELECT * FROM customer;
OK
ABSTRACT SYNTAX TREE:
 (TOK_QUERY (TOK_FROM (TOK_TABREF (TOK_TABNAME customer))) (TOK_INSERT
(TOK_DESTINATION (TOK_DIR TOK_TMP_FILE)) (TOK_SELECT (TOK_SELEXPR TOK_
ALLCOLREF))))
STAGE DEPENDENCIES:
 Stage-0 is a root stage
STAGE PLANS:
 Stage: Stage-0
   Fetch Operator
     limit: -1
     Processor Tree:
       TableScan
         alias: customer
         Select Operator
           expressions:
                 expr: fname
                 type: string
                 expr: lname
                 type: string
                 expr: status
```

```
                type: string
                expr: telno
                type: string
                expr: customer_id
                type: string
                expr: city_zip
                type: struct<city:string,zip:string>
          outputColumnNames: _col0, _col1, _col2, _col3, _col4, _col5
          ListSink

Time taken: 0.402 seconds, Fetched: 31 row(s)
hive>
```

Can you tell how many MapReduce jobs would be required to run this Hive query? If you guessed none, you would be correct. Hive is able to read the records and dump the output to the console without using MapReduce. Hive is using "local mode" to do this.

9.5 USING HIVE FOR DATA WAREHOUSING

EXERCISE 9.4 Hive Storage Formats

We can use Hive to work with a variety of different file and record formats. Understanding how to work with formats beyond the simple TextFile will empower you to make better decisions when working with Hive and Hadoop. We can also use compression with Hive to reduce the footprint of our data – potentially buying us performance increases and/or storage improvement.

1.1 ACCESSING THE HIVE COMMAND LINE INTERFACE (CLI)

As previously done, in this section also we will start the Hive Beeline Command Line Interface , j, and go through an interactive Hive CLI session.

1. Open the Linux terminal by double clicking the Terminal icon from within the *BigInsights Shell directory* on the desktop.

Terminal

2. In the Linux terminal change to the Hive home bin directory

```
~> cd $HIVE_HOME/bin
```

3. Start an interactive Hive shell session.

```
~> ./beeline -u jdbc:hive2://bivm.ibm.com:10000 -n biadmin -p biadmin
```

1.2 WORKING WITH DIFFERENT FILE AND RECORD FORMATS

4. We will use computersalesdb database for experimenting with different file and record formats in Hive.

```
hive> USE computersalesdb;
```

We have already created multiple tables on our system that are in TEXTFILE format. Let's take advantage of this fact and create some new tables of different formats – then insert data into the new tables by running SELECT queries on the originals.

1.2.1 SequenceFile

Remember that In previous exercise we created the *products* table and described the table with the "STORED AS TEXTFILE" clause. Now we will create a new table called pr*oducts_sequenceformat* that will be stored as a SEQUENCEFILE. Using Hive we will do the conversion from TEXTFILE to SEQUENCEFILE for by simple running an INSERT statement.

1. Create a new table in Hive called *products_sequenceformat.* We will use the exact same DDL we used to create the original products table EXCEPT we will change the STORED AS clause to be SEQUENCEFILE instead of TEXTFILE.

```
hive> CREATE TABLE products_sequenceformat
(
prod_name STRING,
description STRING,
category STRING,
qty_on_hand INT,
prod_num STRING,
packaged_with ARRAY<STRING>
)
ROW FORMAT DELIMITED
FIELDS TERMINATED BY ','
COLLECTION ITEMS TERMINATED BY ':'
STORED AS SEQUENCEFILE;
```

```
biadmin@bivm:...ginsights/hive/bin
File Edit View Terminal Help
0: jdbc:hive2://bivm.ibm.com:10000> CREATE TABLE products_sequenceformat
. . . . . . . . . . . . . . . . . > (
. . . . . . . . . . . . . . . . . > prod_name STRING,
. . . . . . . . . . . . . . . . . > description STRING,
. . . . . . . . . . . . . . . . . > category STRING,
. . . . . . . . . . . . . . . . . > qty_on_hand INT,
. . . . . . . . . . . . . . . . . > prod_num STRING,
. . . . . . . . . . . . . . . . . > packaged_with ARRAY<STRING>
. . . . . . . . . . . . . . . . . > )
. . . . . . . . . . . . . . . . . > ROW FORMAT DELIMITED
. . . . . . . . . . . . . . . . . > FIELDS TERMINATED BY ','
. . . . . . . . . . . . . . . . . > COLLECTION ITEMS TERMINATED BY ':'
. . . . . . . . . . . . . . . . . > STORED AS SEQUENCEFILE;
No rows affected (3.355 seconds)
```

2. Run the SHOW TABLES command to verify the table has been created.

hive> SHOW TABLES;

```
▾ biadmin@bivm:...ginsights/hive/bin
File  Edit  View  Terminal  Help
0: jdbc:hive2://bivm.ibm.com:10000> SHOW TABLES ;
+-------------------------+
|        tab_name         |
+-------------------------+
| customer                |
| optical_sales           |
| products                |
| products_sequenceformat |
| sales                   |
| sales_staging           |
+-------------------------+
6 rows selected (1.541 seconds)
0: jdbc:hive2://bivm.ibm.com:10000>
```

3. Set Hive's outputformat to vertical, then ask Hive to give us the EXTENDED details of our new *products_sequenceformat* table.

hive> !set outputformat vertical

hive> DESCRIBE EXTENDED products_sequenceformat;

```
▾ biadmin@bivm:...ginsights/hive/bin
File  Edit  View  Terminal  Help
0: jdbc:hive2://bivm.ibm.com:10000> !set outputformat vertical
0: jdbc:hive2://bivm.ibm.com:10000> DESCRIBE EXTENDED products_sequenceformat;
col_name   prod_name
data_type  string
comment    None

col_name   description
data_type  string
comment    None

col_name   category
data_type  string
comment    None

col_name   qty_on_hand
data_type  int
comment    None

col_name   prod_num
data_type  string
comment    None

col_name   packaged_with
data_type  array<string>
comment    None

col_name
data_type
```

```
col_name   Detailed Table Information
data_type  Table(tableName:products_sequenceformat, dbName:computersalesdb, owner:biadmin, createTime:1457956938, lastAccessTime:0, retention:0, sd:StorageDescripto
ls:[FieldSchema(name:prod_name, type:string, comment:null), FieldSchema(name:description, type:string, comment:null), FieldSchema(name:category, type:string, commen
ll), FieldSchema(name:qty_on_hand, type:int, comment:null), FieldSchema(name:prod_num, type:string, comment:null), FieldSchema(name:packaged_with, type:array<string
omment:null)], location:hdfs://bivm.ibm.com:9000/biginsights/hive/warehouse/computersalesdb.db/products_sequenceformat, inputFormat:org.apache.hadoop.mapred.Sequenc
eInputFormat, outputFormat:org.apache.hadoop.hive.ql.io.HiveSequenceFileOutputFormat, compressed:false, numBuckets:-1, serdeInfo:SerDeInfo(name:null, serializationL
rg.apache.hadoop.hive.serde2.lazy.LazySimpleSerDe, parameters:{colelction.delim=:, serialization.format=,, field.delim=,}), bucketCols:[], sortCols:[], parameters:{
kewedInfo:SkewedInfo(skewedColNames:[], skewedColValues:[], skewedColValueLocationMaps:{}), storedAsSubDirectories:false), partitionKeys:[], parameters:{transient_l
dlTime=1457956938}, viewOriginalText:null, viewExpandedText:null, tableType:MANAGED_TABLE)
comment

8 rows selected (1.804 seconds)
0: jdbc:hive2://bivm.ibm.com:10000>
```

You'll notice some interesting things listed here:

InputFormat is: **`org.apache.hadoop.mapred.SequenceFileInputFormat`**

OutputFormat is: **`org.apache.hadoop.hive.ql.io.HiveSequenceFileOutputformat`**

SerDe serializationLib is: **`org.apache.hadoop.hive.serde2.lazy.LazySimpleSerDe`**

The HDFS location of the data for this table is:

`/biginsights/hive/warehouse/computersalesdb.db/products_sequenceformat`

It's important to recognize that using the STORED AS SEQUENCEFILE clause in our create table statement set the Input and Output formats behind the scenes appropriately for us. We didn't have to explicitly specify those values when creating the table (though we could have).

4. Time to load our *products_sequenceformat* table with data. We will do this by running an INSERT query.

```
hive> FROM products INSERT OVERWRITE TABLE products_sequenceformat
SELECT *;
```

```
biadmin@bivm:...ginsights/hive/bin
File  Edit  View  Terminal  Help
0: jdbc:hive2://bivm.ibm.com:10000> FROM products INSERT OVERWRITE TABLE products_sequenceformat SELECT *;
No rows affected (146.816 seconds)
```

We can see the tables;

```
File  Edit  View  Terminal  Help
0: jdbc:hive2://bivm.ibm.com:10000> show tables;
tab_name  customer

tab_name  optical_sales

tab_name  products

tab_name  products_sequenceformat

tab_name  sales

tab_name  sales_staging

6 rows selected (1.301 seconds)
0: jdbc:hive2://bivm.ibm.com:10000>
```

Behind the scenes a temp space is being used to store the intermediate data.

5. Let's examine the *products_sequenceformat* table on HDFS and see what Hive did for us. Open the BigInsights Web Console and navigate to the

/biginsights/hive/warehouse/computersalesdb.db/products_sequenceformat

directory. You will find a 000000_0 file. If you click on this file, the data will be displayed in the right hand viewing pane.

That doesn't look like a regular TEXTFILE does it? Some of the characters are displayed oddly. That's a good thing – we are looking at a SEQUENCEFILE here!

6. Let's try something different. Open a new Linux terminal. We can use the –text option in the HDFS fs command to see the data in a human readable format.

```
~> hadoop fs -text
/biginsights/hive/warehouse/computersalesdb.db/products_sequenceformat/
000000_0;
```

That output looks much better!

1.2.2 RCFile

1. Create a new table in Hive called *products_rcfileformat.* We will use similar DDL that we used to create the original products table EXCEPT in this example we will explicitly tell Hive which SerDe and Input/Output formats to use.

```
hive> CREATE TABLE products_rcfileformat
(
prod_name STRING,
description STRING,
```

```
  category STRING,
qty_on_hand INT,
prod_num STRING,
packaged_with ARRAY<STRING>
)
ROW FORMAT SERDE
'org.apache.hadoop.hive.serde2.columnar.ColumnarSerDe'
STORED AS
INPUTFORMAT 'org.apache.hadoop.hive.ql.io.RCFileInputFormat'
OUTPUTFORMAT 'org.apache.hadoop.hive.ql.io.RCFileOutputFormat';
```

2. Ask Hive to give us the EXTENDED details of our new *products_rcfileformat* table.

```
hive> DESCRIBE EXTENDED products_rcfileformat;
```

InputFormat is: **org.apache.hadoop.hive.ql.io.RCFileInputFormat**

OutputFormat is: **org.apache.hadoop.hive.ql.io.RCFileOutputFormat**

SerDe serializationLib is: **org.apache.hadoop.hive.serde2.columnar.ColumnarSerde**

```
File  Edit  View  Terminal  Help
0: jdbc:hive2://bivm.ibm.com:10000> DESCRIBE EXTENDED products_rcfileformat;
+---------------------------+-----------------------------------------------------
---------------------------------------------+
|          col_name         |
                                             |
+---------------------------+-----------------------------------------------------
---------------------------------------------+
| prod_name                 | string
                                             |
| description               | string
                                             |
| category                  | string
                                             |
| qty_on_hand               | int
                                             |
| prod_num                  | string
                                             |
| packaged_with             | array<string>
                                             |
|                           |
                                             |
| Detailed Table Information  | Table(tableName:products_rcfileformat, dbName:co
mputersalesdb, owner:biadmin, createTime:14 |
+---------------------------+-----------------------------------------------------
---------------------------------------------+
8 rows selected (2.215 seconds)
0: jdbc:hive2://bivm.ibm.com:10000>
```

The HDFS location of the data for this table is:

/biginsights/hive/warehouse/computersalesdb.db/products_rcfileformat

Seeing how we explicitly specified the Input/Output formats and the SerDe, these values come as no surprise.

3. Now let's load our *products_rcfileformat* table with data. We will do this by running an INSERT query.

```
hive> FROM products INSERT OVERWRITE TABLE products_rcfileformat
SELECT *;
```

```
biadmin@bivm:...ginsights/hive/bin
File  Edit  View  Terminal  Help
0: jdbc:hive2://bivm.ibm.com:10000>  FROM products INSERT OVERWRITE TABLE products_rcfileformat SELECT *;
No rows affected (153.151 seconds)
0: jdbc:hive2://bivm.ibm.com:10000>
```

4. Set the Beeline outputformat back to table. Then SELECT * from the *products_rcfileformat* table to make sure it was loaded with the product data.

```
hive> !set outputformat table
hive> SELECT * FROM products_rcfileformat;
```

```
biadmin@bivm:...ginsights/hive/bin
File  Edit  View  Terminal  Help
0: jdbc:hive2://bivm.ibm.com:10000> SELECT * FROM products_rcfileformat;
```

prod_name	description	category	qty_on_hand	prod_num	packaged_with
2 GB Memory E	2 GB Memory ECC	Ram	3000	87655	["manual","heatsink"]
4 GB Memory E	4 GB Memory ECC	Ram	1000	87659	["manual","heatsink"]
16 GB Memory E	16 GB Memory ECC	Ram	238	87634	["manual"]
500 GB HD J	500 GB HD Panther Brand	HD	200	45628	["atacable","manual"]
500 GB HD T	500 GB HD Tiger Brand	HD	498	45641	["satacable","manual"]
1 TB HD J	1 TB HD Jargon Brand	HD	231	45691	[]
4 Core CPU J3	4 Core CPU Jargon Brand 3 GHZ	CPU	50	98820	["thermalpaste","heatsink","manual"]
2 Core CPU J2	2 Core CPU Jargon Brand 2 GHZ	CPU	118	98838	["thermalpaste","heatsink"]
1 Core CPU J2	1 Core CPU Jargon Brand 2 GHZ	CPU	203	98792	["thermalpaste","heatsink"]
94F991 MB	Motherboard F991 CPU	MB	19	282299	[]
94G822 MB	Motherboard G822 CPU	MB	30	282109	[]
93H772 MB	Motherboard H772 CPU	MB	15	282009	["cables","screws"]
93G Video	Video Card Jargon Brand 93G	Video	80	99202	["dvd","manual","game"]
84G1 Video	Video Card Jargon Brand 84F1	Video	14	99207	["dvd","manual","hdmicable"]
09K Video	Video Card Tiger Brand 84F1	Video	5	98243	["manual","game"]
J Case 1500	Computer Case Jargon Brand Style 1500	Case	20	77623	["fans","manual","screws"]
J Case 1501	Computer Case Jargon Brand Style 1501	Case	18	77624	["fans","manual","screws"]
T Case 4332	Computer Case Tiger Brand Style 4332	Case	7	88211	["fans","manual","screws","watercooler"]
J Power 300W	Power Supply Jargon Brand 300 Watts	Power	28	92387	["cables","screws"]
J Power 500W	Power Supply Jargon Brand 500 Watts	Power	17	92373	["cables","screws"]
T Power 300W	Power Supply Tiger Brand 300 Watts	Power	8	93347	["cables","screws"]
DVD J INT	DVD Jargon Brand Internal	Optical	23	88734	["manual"]
DVD J EXT	DVD Jargon Brand External	Optical	45	88821	[]
DVD T INT	DVD Tiger Brand Internal	Optical	19	82331	["satacable","manual"]
DVD T EXT	DVD Tiger Brand External	Optical	17	82337	["satacable","manual"]

```
25 rows selected (2.449 seconds)
0: jdbc:hive2://bivm.ibm.com:10000>
```

All the data should be there.

5. We can assume that Hive created a 000000_0 file in the products_rcfileformat directory on HDFS. Let's examine this file on HDFS and see exactly what Hive did for us. Open a Linux terminal and run the hadoop fs -cat command.

```
~> hadoop fs -cat
/biginsights/hive/warehouse/computersalesdb.db/products_rcfileformat/00
0000_0;
```

The file in RCFile format looks a bit wacky to the human eye. We need to view it using a tool that displays the contents in more human friendly format. The hadoop fs –text tool also performs the same, so we will need to use a different tool.

6. In the Linux terminal change to the Hive home bin directory. From the bin directory we will pass a statement to hive that will allow us to view the RCFile.

```
~> cd $HIVE_HOME/bin
./hive --service rcfilecat
/biginsights/hive/warehouse/computersalesdb.db/products_rcfileformat/00
0000_0
```

That output looks quite a bit better!

1.2.3 ORC File

1. Create a new table in Hive called *products_orcformat.* We will use the exact same DDL we used to create the original products table EXCEPT we will change the STORED AS clause to be ORC instead of TEXTFILE.

```
hive> CREATE TABLE products_orcformat
(
prod_name STRING,
description STRING,
category STRING,
qty_on_hand INT,
prod_num STRING,
packaged_with ARRAY<STRING>
)
ROW FORMAT DELIMITED
FIELDS TERMINATED BY ','
COLLECTION ITEMS TERMINATED BY ':'
STORED AS ORC;
```

2. Load data into the new ORC table.

```
hive> FROM products INSERT OVERWRITE TABLE products_orcformat
SELECT *;
```

```
File  Edit  View  Terminal  Help
0: jdbc:hive2://bivm.ibm.com:10000> FROM products INSERT OVERWRITE TABLE products_orcformat          SELECT *;
No rows affected (225.856 seconds)
0: jdbc:hive2://bivm.ibm.com:10000> SELECT * FROM products_orcformat;
```

prod_name	description	category	qty_on_hand	prod_num	packaged_with
2 GB Memory E	2 GB Memory ECC	Ram	3000	87655	["manual","heatsink"]
4 GB Memory E	4 GB Memory ECC	Ram	1000	87659	["manual","heatsink"]
16 GB Memory E	16 GB Memory ECC	Ram	238	87634	["manual"]
500 GB HD J	500 GB HD Panther Brand	HD	200	45628	["atacable","manual"]
500 GB HD T	500 GB HD Tiger Brand	HD	498	45641	["satacable","manual"]
1 TB HD J	1 TB HD Jargon Brand	HD	231	45691	[]
4 Core CPU J3	4 Core CPU Jargon Brand 3 GHZ	CPU	50	98820	["thermalpaste","heatsink","manual"]
2 Core CPU J2	2 Core CPU Jargon Brand 2 GHZ	CPU	118	98838	["thermalpaste","heatsink"]
1 Core CPU J2	1 Core CPU Jargon Brand 2 GHZ	CPU	203	98792	["thermalpaste","heatsink"]
94F991 MB	Motherboard F991 CPU	MB	19	282299	[]
94G822 MB	Motherboard G822 CPU	MB	30	282109	[]
93H772 MB	Motherboard H772 CPU	MB	15	282009	["cables","screws"]
93G Video	Video Card Jargon Brand 93G	Video	80	99202	["dvd","manual","game"]
84G1 Video	Video Card Jargon Brand 84F1	Video	14	99207	["dvd","manual","hdmicable"]
09K Video	Video Card Tiger Brand 84F1	Video	5	98243	["manual","game"]
J Case 1500	Computer Case Jargon Brand Style 1500	Case	20	77623	["fans","manual","screws"]
J Case 1501	Computer Case Jargon Brand Style 1501	Case	18	77624	["fans","manual","screws"]
T Case 4332	Computer Case Tiger Brand Style 4332	Case	7	88211	["fans","manual","screws","watercooler"]
J Power 300W	Power Supply Jargon Brand 300 Watts	Power	28	92387	["cables","screws"]
J Power 500W	Power Supply Jargon Brand 500 Watts	Power	17	92373	["cables","screws"]
T Power 300W	Power Supply Tiger Brand 300 Watts	Power	8	93347	["cables","screws"]
DVD J INT	DVD Jargon Brand Internal	Optical	23	88734	["manual"]
DVD J EXT	DVD Jargon Brand External	Optical	45	88821	[]
DVD T INT	DVD Tiger Brand Internal	Optical	19	82331	["satacable","manual"]
DVD T EXT	DVD Tiger Brand External	Optical	17	82337	["satacable","manual"]

```
25 rows selected (2.284 seconds)
0: jdbc:hive2://bivm.ibm.com:10000>
```

3. SELECT * from the *products_orcformat* table to make sure it was loaded with the product data.

   hive> SELECT * FROM products_orcformat;

4. Let's examine the *products_orcformat* table on HDFS and see what Hive did for us. Open the BigInsights Web Console and navigate to the

   /biginsights/hive/warehouse/computersalesdb.db/products_orcformat

   directory. You will find a 000000_0 file. If you click on this file, the data will be displayed in the right hand viewing pane.

   Analyze the details of the file, including file size.

1.3 COMPRESSION

In this section we will take a peak at using compression with Hive.

1. From within the Hive CLI, enter the following set commands. These changes will only last this one session.

   hive> set hive.exec.compress.output=true;

   hive> set mapred.output.compression.code=org.apache.hadoop.io.compress.GzipCodec;

   We are telling Hive to compress the output (not intermediate compression) into Gzip format.

2. Open the BigInsights Web Console and navigate to the **/biginsights/hive/warehouse/computersalesdb.db/products_rcfileformat/000000_0 file**

   On the right you can see the file is 1.7KB.

3. Now let's reload our *products_rcfileformat* table with data from the *products* table.

   hive> FROM products INSERT OVERWRITE TABLE products_rcfileformat SELECT *;

4. Back in the BigInsights Web Console refresh the file view and navigate to the **/biginsights/hive/warehouse/computersalesdb.db/products_rcfileformat/000000_0 file again.**

   You can see the file has now been compressed and is certainly smaller than before!

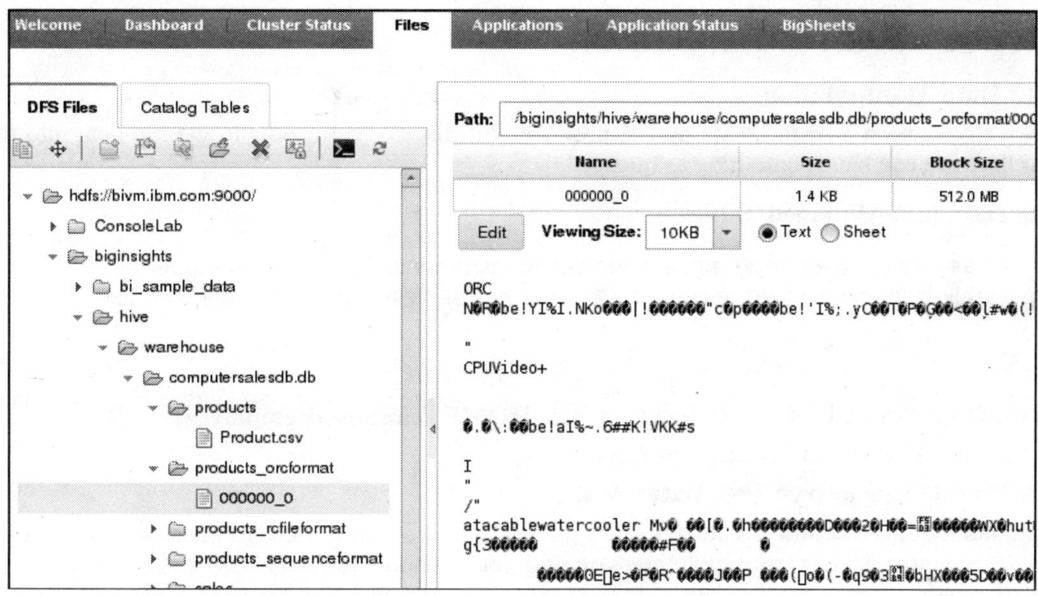

5. For good measure, run a SELECT query from the *products_rcfileformat* table to make sure you are still able to query this compressed data.

hive> SELECT prod_name FROM products_rcfileformat LIMIT 5;

```
biadmin@bivm:...ginsights/hive/bin
File  Edit  View  Terminal  Help
0: jdbc:hive2://bivm.ibm.com:10000> set hive.exec.compress.output=true;
No rows affected (0.217 seconds)
0: jdbc:hive2://bivm.ibm.com:10000> set mapred.output.compression.code=org.apache.hadoop.io.compress.GzipCodec;
No rows affected (0.245 seconds)
0: jdbc:hive2://bivm.ibm.com:10000> FROM products INSERT OVERWRITE TABLE products_rcfileformat SELECT *;
No rows affected (149.763 seconds)
0: jdbc:hive2://bivm.ibm.com:10000>  SELECT prod_name FROM products_rcfileformat LIMIT 5;
+-----------------+
|    prod_name    |
+-----------------+
| 2 GB Memory E   |
| 4 GB Memory E   |
| 16 GB Memory E  |
| 500 GB HD J     |
| 500 GB HD T     |
+-----------------+
5 rows selected (139.817 seconds)
0: jdbc:hive2://bivm.ibm.com:10000>
```

6. From within the Hive CLI, enter the following set command to turn compression off for this session.

hive> set hive.exec.compress.output=false;

1.4 SUMMARY

Congratulations! You now know how to work with different file formats include SequenceFiles, RCFiles and ORC Files. You explicitly stated Input and Output formats and SerDe in a CREATE TABLE statement. You've also turned output compression on in Hive and saw a size reduction with your own eyes. You may move on to the next Unit.

9.6 HIVEQL – DATA MANIPULATION

HiveQL: Data Manipulation

Till now we have seen how to create tables, now we will discuss about how to get the data into these tables so that you can have something to query!

Loading Data into Managed Tables

Since Hive has no row-level insert, update and delete operations, the only way to put data into a table is to use the load operation. Or you can just write the file into the correct directory.

Ex.

```
hive>LOAD DATA LOCAL INPATH '${env:HOME}/californai-employees'
>OVERWRITE INTO TABLE employees
>PARTITION (country='US', state='CA');
```

This command will create the directory for the partition, if it doesn't already exists and then copy the data to it. If the table is not partitioned, then you will not be using the PARTITIO clause.

If the LOCAL keyword is used, the path is assumed to be in the local file system. The data is copied into the final location. If LOCAL is omitted, the path is assumed to be in distributed file system. In this case, the data is moved from a path to the final location.

If you use the OVERWRITE keyword, any data already present in the directory will be deleted first. Without the keyword, the new files are simply added to the target directory.

The PARTITION clause is required if the table is partitioned and you must specify a value for each partition.

There is one limitation while using the INPATH – it cannot contain any directories.

Inserting data into Table from Queries

The INSERT statement let you load data into a table from a query. For example, let's assume there is a staging table staged_employees from where we will load the data into our main table employees. This can be achieved using the following statement.

```
hive> INSERT OVERWRITE TABLE employees
>PARTITION(country='US', state='OR')
>SELECT * FROM staged_employees a
>where a.count='US' and a.stat='OR';
```

With OVERWRITE, any previous content in the table/partition will be replaced. If you want to append the new data to the already existing data, then use INTO in place of OVERWRITE.

Assuming, if staged_employees is very huge table and it is having say data for 50 different states. So in order to cover all the states, you would have to execute the statement like above for 50 times and this means, hive have to scan staged_employees 50 times. In order to achieve this requirement, hive offers an alternative INSERT syntax that allows you to scan the input data once and split it multiple ways as shown below:

hive> FROM staged_employees a

>INSERT OVERWRITE TABLE employees

>PARTITION(country='US',state='OR')

>SELECT * WHERE a.count='US' and a.stat='OR'

>INSERT OVERWRITE TABLE employees

>PARTITION(country='US', state='IL')

>SELECT * WHERE a.count='US',state='IL')

>INSERT OVERWRITE TABLE employees

>PARTITION(country='US',state='CA')

>SELECT * WHERE a.count='US' and a.stat='CA';

We have taken the example to insert records for 3 different states into the table employees.

By using, this construct, some records from the source table can be written to the multiple partitions of the destination table or none of them.

If a record satisfied a given SELECT…WHERE… clause, it gets written to the specified table and partition. Each INSERT clause can insert into different table. Some of these tables can be partitioned while others are not.

You can also mix INSERT OVERWRITE and INSERT INTO clauses.

Dynamic Partition Inserts

There is one drawback with the syntax of PARTITION, which we were using till now (Static Partitions): If you have a lot of partitions to create, you have to write a LOT of SQL. However, to overcome this, Hive supports Dynamic Partition feature, where it can infer the partitions to create based on query partitions.

hive> **INSERT OVERWRITE TABLE employees**

>PARTITION(country, state)

>SELECT ….., a.count, a.stat

>FROM staged_employees a;

Hive determines the values of partition keys, country and state based on the last two columns in the SELECT clause. Suppose that the staged_employees has data for 100 country and state pairs, after running this query, employees table will have 100 partitions.

You can also mix the dynamic and static partitions, as shown in the example below:

hive> INSERT OVERWRITE TABLE employees

>PARTITION(country='US', state)

>SELECT ….., a.count, a.stat

>FROM staged_employees a where a.count = 'US';

Note: The Static Partition must come before the dynamic partition keys.

Dynamic partition is not enabled by default and when it is enabled it works in "strict" mode by default. Below is the table describing the properties associated with Dynamic Partition:

Table 9.1 describing the properties associated with Dynamic Partition

Name	Default Value	Description
hive.exec.dynamic.partition	FALSE	Set to true to enable dynamic partition
hive.exec.dynamic.partition.mode	strict	Set to **nonstrict** to enable all partition to be determined dynamically.
hive.exec.max.dynamic.partitions.pernode	100	The maximum number of partitions that can be created by each mapper or reducer. Raises fatal error if one mapper or reducer tries to create more than the threshold.
hive.exec.max.dynamic.partitions	1000	The total number of partitions that can be created by one statement with dynamic partitioning. Raises a fatal error if the limit is exceeded.
hive.exec.max.created.files	100000	The maximum number of files that can be created globally. A Hadoop counter is used to track the number of files created. Raises a fatal error if the limit is exceeded.

So for example shown above will actually look like this:

hive> set hive.exec.dynamic.partition=true;
>set hive.exec.dynamic.partition.mode=nonstrict;
>set hive.exec.max.dynamic.partitions.pernode=1000;
hive> INSERT OVERWRITE TABLE employees
>PARTITIONS(country, state)
>SELECT ….., a.count, a.stat
>FROM staged_employees a;

Creating and Loading Tables in one Query

You can also create a table and insert query results in a single statement:

hive> **CREATE TABLE ca_employees**
>AS SELECT name, salary, address FROM employees
>WHERE state = 'CA';

The new table ca_employees will contain only name, salary and address from the employees table record for employees in state "CA". The schema for the new table is taken from the SELECT clause.

A use for this feature is to extract a convenient subset of data from a larger and more unwieldy dataset.

Note: This feature cannot be used with External tables. "Populating" the partition for external table is done with an ALTER TABLE statement, where we aren't "loading" data but just pointing metadata to a location where the data can be found.

Exporting Data

If the data files are already formatted the way you want, then it is simple to copy the directories of files using

hadoop fs –cp source_path target_path;

Otherwise, you can use INSERT…DIRECTORY as shown in example below:

hive> INSERT OVERWRITE LOCAL DIRECTORY ***'/tmp/ca/employees'***

>SELECT name, salary, address FROM employees

>WHERE state='CA';

One or more file will be written to the directory /tmp/ca/employees based on the number of reducers invoked.

Just like inserting data to tables, you can specify multiple inserts to directories:

hive> FROM staged_employees a

>INSERT OVERWRITE LOCAL DIRECTORY '/tmp/ca/employees'

>SELECT * WHERE a.state='CA' and a.country ='US'

>INSERT OVERWRITE LOCAL DIRECTORY '/tmp/is/employees'

>SELECT * WHERE a.state='IL' and a.country='US'

>INSERT OVERWRITE LOCAL DIRECTORY '/tmp/or/employees'

>SELECT * WHERE a.state='OR' and a.country='US';

9.7 QUERRIES

To reference a STRUCT, you can use the "dot" notation, similar to table_alias.column as shown below:

hive> **SELECT name, address.city FROM employees;**

John Doe	**Chicago**
Mary Smith	**Chicago**
Todd Jones	**Oak Park**
Bill King	**Obscuria**

When Hive can avoid MapReduce

Hive implements some kind of queries without using MapReduce, in local mode For example:

hive> Select * from employees;

In this case, Hive will read all the records from employees and dump the formatted output to the console and hence no MapReduce jobs will be started.

This works for where clauses that only filter on entire partition keys, with or without LIMIT clause.

Hive will attempt to run other operations in local mode if the property hive.exec.mode.local.auto is set to true. Otherwise, hive will use MapReduce to run other queries.

Join Optimization

Hive assumes that the last table in the query is the largest. It attempts to buffer the other tables first and then stream the last table through, while performing joins on individual records. Therefore, you should structure your join such that the largest table is the last.

Example: Consider the following query

```
hive> SELECT s.ymd, s.symbol, s.price_close, d.dividend
>FROM stocks s JOIN dividends d ON s.ymd = d.ymd AND s.symbol = d.symbol
>WHERE s.symbol = 'AAPL';
```

Assuming, that the dividends table is smaller table, we can optimize the query by making stocks as the last table in the query.

```
hive> SELECT s.ymd, s.symbol, s.price_close, d.dividend
>FROM dividends d JOIN stocks s ON s.ymd = d.ymd AND s.symbol = d.symbol
>WHERE s.symbol = 'AAPL';
```

You don't have to put the largest table at the last always, instead Hive provides you with the "hint" mechanism to tell the query optimized which table should be streamed:

```
hive> SELECT /*+ STREAMTABLE(s) */ s.ymd, s.symbol, s.price_close, d.dividend
FROM stocks s JOIN dividends d ON s.ymd = d.ymd AND s.symbol = d.symbol
WHERE s.symbol = 'AAPL';
```

Now Hive will stream the table stocks though it is not the last table in the query.

Map-side joins

If all but one table is small, the largest table can be streamed through the mappers while the small table is cached in memory. Hive can do all the joining map-side, since it can look up all the possible match against the small tables in memory, thereby eliminating the reduce step required in the more common scenarios. This will also reduce the number of map steps required.

Before Hive v0.7, it was necessary to add the hints to the query to enable the optimization. The hint still works but is now deprecated as of Hive v0.7

Now you can set the property **hive.auto.convert.join** to **true** before Hive attempts the optimization. By default it is set as false.

```
hive> hive.auto.convert.join = true;
hive> Select s.ymd, s.symbol, s.price_close, d.dividend
> FROM stocks s JOIN dividends d ON s.ymd = d.ymd AND s.symbol = d.symbol
> WHERE s.symbol = 'AAPL';
```

Note that you can also configure the threshold size for table files considered small enough to use this optimization. The default definition of the property is bytes is:

```
hive.mapjoin.smalltable.filesize=25000000
```

Note: Hive does not support the optimization for right- and full-outer joins

Order By and Sort By

The Order By performs a total ordering of the query result set. This means that all the data is passed through a single reducer, which may take a very long time to execute for larger data sets.

The Sort By orders the data within each reducer thereby performing a local ordering, where each reducer output will be sorted. Better performance is traded for total ordering.

Here is an example using **ORDER BY:**

```
hive> SELECT s.ymd, s.symbol, s.price_close
> FROM stocks s
> ORDER BY s.ymd ASC, s.symbol DESC;
```

Here is the same example using SORT BY:

```
hive> SELECT s.ymd, s.symbol, s.price_close
> FROM stocks s
> SORT BY s.ymd ASC, s.symbol DESC;
```

The two queries looks identical, but if more than one reducer is invoked, the output will be sorted differently. While each reducer's output file will be sorted, the data will probably overlap with the output of other reducers.

As Order By can result in excessively long run times, Hive will require the Limit clause by Order By if the property hive.mapred.mode is set to strict, by default it is set to nonstrict.

Example

Let us assume the **employee** table is composed of fields named Id, Name, Salary, Designation, and Dept as shown below. Generate a query to retrieve the employee details whose Id is 1205.

```
+-----+--------------+--------+---------------------------+------+
| Id  | Name         | Salary | Designation               | Dept |
+-----+--------------+------------------------------------+------+
|1201 | Gopal        | 45000  | Technical manager         | TP   |
|1202 | Manisha      | 45000  | Proofreader               | PR   |
|1203 | Masthanvali  | 40000  | Technical writer          | TP   |
|1204 | Krian        | 40000  | Hr Admin                  | HR   |
|1205 | Kranthi      | 30000  | Op Admin                  | Admin|
+-----+--------------+--------+---------------------------+------+
```

The following query is executed to retrieve the employee details using the above table:

```
hive> SELECT * FROM employee WHERE Id=1205;
```

On successful execution of query, you get to see the following response:

```
+-----+-----------+-----------+----------------------------------+------+
| ID  | Name      | Salary    | Designation                      | Dept |
+-----+-----------+-----------+----------------------------------+------+
|1205 | Kranthi   | 30000     | Op Admin                         | Admin |
+-----+-----------+-----------+----------------------------------+------+
```

The following query is executed to retrieve the employee details whose salary is more than or equal to Rs 40000.

```
hive> SELECT * FROM employee WHERE Salary>=40000;
```

On successful execution of query, you get to see the following response:

```
+-----+------------+--------+-----------------------------+------+
| ID  | Name       | Salary | Designation                 | Dept |
+-----+------------+--------+-----------------------------+------+
|1201 | Gopal      | 45000  | Technical manager           | TP   |
|1202 | Manisha    | 45000  | Proofreader                 | PR   |
|1203 | Masthanvali| 40000  | Technical writer            | TP   |
|1204 | Krian      | 40000  | Hr Admin                    | HR   |
+-----+------------+--------+-----------------------------+------+
```

Arithmetic Operators

These operators support various common arithmetic operations on the operands. All of them return number types. The following table describes the arithmetic operators avaiExercisele in Hive:

Operators	Operand	Description
A + B	all number types	Gives the result of adding A and B.
A - B	all number types	Gives the result of subtracting B from A.
A * B	all number types	Gives the result of multiplying A and B.
A / B	all number types	Gives the result of dividing B from A.
A % B	all number types	Gives the reminder resulting from dividing A by B.
A & B	all number types	Gives the result of bitwise AND of A and B.
A | B	all number types	Gives the result of bitwise OR of A and B.
A ^ B	all number types	Gives the result of bitwise XOR of A and B.
~A	all number types	Gives the result of bitwise NOT of A.

Example

The following query adds two numbers, 20 and 30.

```
hive> SELECT 20+30 ADD FROM temp;
```

On successful execution of the query, you get to see the following response:

```
+--------+
|   ADD  |
+--------+
|   50   |
+--------+
```

Logical Operators

The operators are logical expressions. All of them return either TRUE or FALSE.

Operators	Operands	Description
A AND B	boolean	TRUE if both A and B are TRUE, otherwise FALSE.
A && B	boolean	Same as A AND B.
A OR B	boolean	TRUE if either A or B or both are TRUE, otherwise FALSE.
A || B	boolean	Same as A OR B.
NOT A	boolean	TRUE if A is FALSE, otherwise FALSE.
!A	boolean	Same as NOT A.

Example

The following query is used to retrieve employee details whose Department is TP and Salary is more than Rs 40000.

```
hive> SELECT * FROM employee WHERE Salary>40000 && Dept=TP;
```

On successful execution of the query, you get to see the following response:

```
+------+--------------+-------------+-------------------+--------+
| ID   | Name         | Salary      | Designation       | Dept   |
+------+--------------+-------------+-------------------+--------+
|1201  | Gopal        | 45000       | Technical manager | TP     |
+------+--------------+-------------+-------------------+--------+
```

Complex Operators

These operators provide an expression to access the elements of Complex Types.

Operator	Operand	Description
A[n]	A is an Array and n is an int	It returns the nth element in the array A. The first element has index 0.
M[key]	M is a Map<K, V> and key has type K	It returns the value corresponding to the key in the map.
S.x	S is a struct	It returns the x field of S.

9.8 HIVE - BUILT-IN FUNCTIONS

This section explains the built-in functions avaiExercisele in Hive. The functions look quite similar to SQL functions, except for their usage.

Hive supports the following built-in functions:

Return Type	Signature	Description
BIGINT	round(double a)	It returns the rounded BIGINT value of the double.
BIGINT	floor(double a)	It returns the maximum BIGINT value that is equal or less than the double.
BIGINT	ceil(double a)	It returns the minimum BIGINT value that is equal or greater than the double.
double	rand(), rand(int seed)	It returns a random number that changes from row to row.
string	concat(string A, string B,...)	It returns the string resulting from concatenating B after A.
string	substr(string A, int start)	It returns the substring of A starting from start position till the end of string A.
string	substr(string A, int start, int length)	It returns the substring of A starting from start position with the given length.
string	upper(string A)	It returns the string resulting from converting all characters of A to upper case.
string	ucase(string A)	Same as above.
string	lower(string A)	It returns the string resulting from converting all characters of B to lower case.
string	lcase(string A)	Same as above.
string	trim(string A)	It returns the string resulting from trimming spaces from both ends of A.
string	ltrim(string A)	It returns the string resulting from trimming spaces from the beginning (left hand side) of A.
string	rtrim(string A)	rtrim(string A) It returns the string resulting from trimming spaces from the end (right hand side) of A.
string	regexp_replace(string A, string B, string C)	It returns the string resulting from replacing all substrings in B that match the Java regular expression syntax with C.

Return Type	Signature	Description
int	size(Map<K.V>)	It returns the number of elements in the map type.
int	size(Array<T>)	It returns the number of elements in the array type.
value of <type>	cast(<expr> as <type>)	It converts the results of the expression expr to <type> e.g. cast('1' as BIGINT) converts the string '1' to it integral representation. A NULL is returned if the conversion does not succeed.
string	from_unixtime(int unixtime)	convert the number of seconds from Unix epoch (1970-01-01 00:00:00 UTC) to a string representing the timestamp of that moment in the current system time zone in the format of "1970-01-01 00:00:00"
string	to_date(string timestamp)	It returns the date part of a timestamp string: to_date("1970-01-01 00:00:00") = "1970-01-01"
int	year(string date)	It returns the year part of a date or a timestamp string: year("1970-01-01 00:00:00") = 1970, year("1970-01-01") = 1970
int	month(string date)	It returns the month part of a date or a timestamp string: month("1970-11-01 00:00:00") = 11, month("1970-11-01") = 11
int	day(string date)	It returns the day part of a date or a timestamp string: day("1970-11-01 00:00:00") = 1, day("1970-11-01") = 1
string	get_json_object(string json_string, string path)	It extracts json object from a json string based on json path specified, and returns json string of the extracted json object. It returns NULL if the input json string is invalid.

Aggregate Functions

Hive supports the following built-in **aggregate functions**. The usage of these functions is as same as the SQL aggregate functions.

Return Type	Signature	Description
BIGINT	count(*), count(expr),	count(*) - Returns the total number of retrieved rows.
DOUBLE	sum(col), sum(DISTINCT col)	It returns the sum of the elements in the group or the sum of the distinct values of the column in the group.
DOUBLE	avg(col), avg(DISTINCT col)	It returns the average of the elements in the group or the average of the distinct values of the column in the group.
DOUBLE	min(col)	It returns the minimum value of the column in the group.
DOUBLE	max(col)	It returns the maximum value of the column in the group.

CHAPTER

10

PIG : The Higher Level Programming Environment

10.1 INTRODUCTION TO PIG

In Map Reduce framework, programs need to be translated into a series of Map and Reduce stages. However, this is not a programming model which data analysts are familiar with. So, in order to bridge this gap, an abstraction called Pig was built on top of Hadoop.

Pig is a high level programming language useful for analyzing large data sets. Pig was a result of development effort at Yahoo!

Although programming Map and Reduce applications is not overly complex, doing so does require some experience with software development. Apache Pig changes this by creating a simpler procedural language abstraction over MapReduce to expose a more Structured Query Language (SQL)-like interface for Hadoop applications. So instead of writing a separate MapReduce application, you can write a single script in Pig Latin that is automatically parallelized and distributed across a cluster.

Pig enables people to focus more on **analyzing bulk data sets and to spend less time in writing Map-Reduce programs.**

Similar to Pigs, who eat anything, the Pig programming language is designed to work upon any kind of data. That's why the name, Pig!

10.2 COMPONENTS OF PIG

Pig consists of two components:

1. Pig Latin, which is a language
2. Runtime environment, for running PigLatin programs.

A Pig Latin program consist of a series of operations or transformations which are applied to the input data to produce output. These operations describe a data flow which is translated into an executable representation, by Pig execution environment. Underneath, results of these transformations are series of MapReduce jobs which a programmer is unaware of. So, in a way, Pig allows programmer to focus on data rather than the nature of execution.

PigLatin is a relatively stiffened language which uses familiar keywords from data processing e.g., Join, Group and Filter.

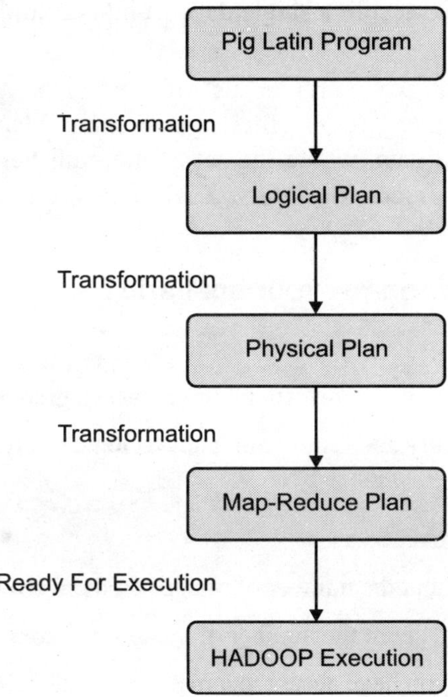

10.3 PIG PROGRAM EXECUTION MODES:

Pig has two execution modes:

1. Local mode : In this mode, Pig runs in a single JVM and makes use of local file system. This mode is suitable only for analysis of small data sets using Pig
2. Map Reduce mode: In this mode, queries written in Pig Latin are translated into MapReduce jobs and are run on a Hadoop cluster (cluster may be pseudo or fully distributed). MapReduce mode with fully distributed cluster is useful of running Pig on large data sets.

10.4 DATA FORMATS AND MODELS

Pig can process data of any format. (Pigs eat anything!) A few common formats such as tab delimited text files, are supported via built-in capabilities. A user can add support for a file format by writing a function that parses the bytes of a file into objects in Pig's data model, and vice versa.

Pig's data model is similar to the relational data model, except that tuples (a.k.a. records or rows) can be nested. For example, you can have a table of tuples, where the third field of each tuple contains a table. In Pig, tables are called bags. Pig also has a "map" data type, which is useful in representing semi-structured data, e.g. JSON or XML.

10.5 OTHER CAPABILITIES

- **Combining multiple data sets:** Pig can combine multiple data sets, via operations such as join, union or cogroup.
- **Splitting data sets:** Pig can split a single data set into multiple ones, using an operation called split.
- **Semistructured data:** Pig supports "maps" of (key, value) pairs, where retrieving the value associated with a given key is an efficient operation. Maps provide a convenient way to represent semistructured data, where the set of non-null fields varies from record to record. Maps are helpful when processing JSON, XML, and sparse relational data (i.e., tables with a lot of null values).

10.5.1 Is Pig the right platform for your scenario?

Pig is right for you if you:

1. Need to analyze data that is small (*kilobytes*), tall (*megabytes*), grande (*gigabytes*), or venti (*terabytes*).
2. Want to be able to create, modify and reuse your analysis logic easily.
3. Process one data set at a time
4. ... or need to combine multiple data sets.
5. Do simple processing (e.g., count the number of images on the web)
6. ... or complex processing (e.g., count the number of images that contain faces).
7. It's especially right for you if you have access to a many-computer cluster already running hadoop.

Pig is not right for you if you:

1. Need to retrieve individual records, or small ranges of records, from a very large data set (e.g., lookup Jayesh Smith's customer profile).
2. Have real-time data serving requirements (e.g., assemble a web page for Jayesh in under 100ms).
3. Need to be able to do random writes to specific data records.
4. Don't like barnyard animals.

Pig is a high-level platform for creating MapReduce programs used with Hadoop. The language for this platform is called Pig Latin. Pig Latin abstracts the programming from the Java MapReduce idiom into a notation which makes MapReduce programming high level, similar to that of SQL for RDBMS systems. Pig Latin can be extended using UDF (User Defined Functions) which the user can write in Java, Python, JavaScript, Ruby or Groovy and then call directly from the language.

Pig was originally developed at Yahoo Research around 2006 for researchers to have an ad-hoc way of creating and executing map-reduce jobs on very large data sets. In 2007, it was moved into the Apache Software Foundation.

10.5.2 Pig vs SQL

In comparison to SQL, Pig

1. uses lazy evaluation,
2. uses extract, transform, load (ETL),
3. is able to store data at any point during a pipeline,
4. declares execution plans,
5. supports pipeline splits, thus allowing workflows to proceed along DAGs instead of strictly sequential pipelines.

On the other hand, it has been argued DBMSs are substantially faster than the MapReduce system once the data is loaded, but that loading the data takes considerably longer in the database systems. It has also been argued RDBMSs offer out of the box support for column-storage, working with compressed data, indexes for efficient random data access, and transaction-level fault tolerance.

Pig Latin is procedural and fits very naturally in the pipeline paradigm while SQL is instead declarative. In SQL users can specify that data from two tables must be joined, but not what join implementation to use (You can specify the implementation of JOIN in SQL, thus "... for many SQL applications the query writer may not have enough knowledge of the data or enough expertise to specify an appropriate join algorithm."). Pig Latin allows users to specify an implementation or aspects of an implementation to be used in executing a script in several ways.[7] In effect, Pig Latin programming is similar to specifying a query execution plan, making it easier for programmers to explicitly control the flow of their data processing task.

SQL is oriented around queries that produce a single result. SQL handles trees naturally, but has no built in mechanism for splitting a data processing stream and applying different operators to each sub-stream. Pig Latin script describes a directed acyclic graph (DAG) rather than a pipeline.

Pig Latin's ability to include user code at any point in the pipeline is useful for pipeline development. If SQL is used, data must first be imported into the database, and then the cleansing and transformation process can begin.

10.6 PIG V/S MAPREDUCE

- There are several higher-level programming interfaces such as Pig and Hive to program parallel applications built on top of MapReduce. The comparison Pig and MapReduce is given in tabular format.

Mapreduce	Pig
It is too low-level and rigid, and leads to a great deal of custom user code that is hard to maintain and reuse	High level Programming
Development cycle is very long Writing mappers and reducers, compiling and packaging the code, submitting jobs, and retrieving the results is a time Consuming process	In pig, no need of compiling or packaging of code. Pig operators will be converted into map or reduce tasks internally.
To extract small portion of data from large datasets using Mapreduce is preferable	Pig is not suitable small portions of data in a large dataset, since it is set up to scan the whole dataset, or at least large portions of it
Not Easily Extendable. We need to write functions starting from scratch.	UDFs tend to be more reusable than the libraries developed for writing MapReduce programs
We need MapReduce when we need very deep level and fine grained control on the way we want to process our data	Sometimes, it is not very convenient to express what we need exactly in terms of Pig and Hive queries.
Performing Data set joins is very difficult	Joins are simple to achieve in Pig.

10.7 DIFFRENCE BETWEEN HIVE AND PIG

Pig is described as a data flow language, rather than a query language. In Pig, you write a series of declarative statements that define relations from other relations, where each new relation performs some new data transformation. Pig looks at these declarations and then builds up a sequence of MapReduce jobs to perform the transformations until the final results are computed the way that you want. This step-by-step "flow" of data can be more intuitive than a complex set of queries. For this reason, Pig is often used as part of ETL (Extract, Transform, and Load) processes used to ingest external data into a Hadoop cluster and transform it into a more desirable form.

A drawback of Pig is that it uses a custom language not based on SQL. This is appropriate, since it is not designed as a query language, but it also means that Pig is less suitable for porting over SQL applications and experienced SQL users will have a larger learning curve with Pig. Nevertheless, it's common for Hadoop teams to use a combination of Hive and Pig, selecting the appropriate tool for particular jobs.

Hive can be treated as competitor for Pig in some cases and Hive also operates on HDFS similar to Pig but there are some significant differences. HiveQL is query language based on SQL but Pig Latin is not a query language. It is data flow scripting language.

Since Pig Latin is procedural, it fits very naturally in the pipeline paradigm. HiveQL on the other hand is declarative.

10.8 APACHE PIG HISTORY

The word "Pig" is named after a domestic animal, it is not any acronym. This entertaining nomenclature lead to some silly names in Pig project like Pig Latin for its language and Grunt for its Interactive shell

Apache Pig is top level project in Apache Software foundation, prior to this it was started by Yahoo researchers and later contributed it to Apache Open source community in 2010.

10.8.1 Using Pig programming language

Unzip Pig distribution by running the following command. We will call it PIG_HOME.

```
> tar xvf pig-0.10.0.tar.gz
```

To run Pig commands, change the directory to PIG_HOME and run the pig command. It starts the grunt shell.

```
>cd PIG_HOME
>bin/pig --help
>bin/pig-x local
grunt>
```

Above is called grunt shell. (Remember grunt the name of soung produced by the animal pig)You can issue the Pig commands from the grunt shell.

Let's first look at the programming language itself so you can see how it's significantly easier than having to write mapper and reducer programs.

1. The first step in a Pig program is to LOAD the data you want to manipulate from HDFS.
2. Then you run the data through a set of transformations (which, under the covers, are translated into a set of mapper and reducer tasks).
3. Finally, you DUMP the data to the screen or you STORE the results in a file somewhere.

(a) **Load**

As is the case with all the Hadoop features, the objects that are being worked on by Hadoop are stored in HDFS. In order for a Pig program to access this data, the program must first tell Pig what file (or files) it will use, and that's done through the LOAD 'data_file' command (where 'data_file' specifies either an HDFS file or directory). If a directory is specified, all the files in that directory will be loaded into the program. If the data is stored in a file format that is not natively accessible to Pig, you can optionally add the USING function to the LOAD statement to specify a user-defined function that can read in and interpret the data.

(b) **Transform**

The transformation logic is where all the data manipulation happens. Here you can FILTER out rows that are not of interest, JOIN two sets of data files, GROUP data to build aggregations, ORDER results, and much more.

(c) **Dump And Store**

If you don't specify the DUMP or STORE command, the results of a Pig pro¬gram are not generated. You would typically use the DUMP command, which sends the output to the screen, when you are debugging your Pig programs. When you go into production, you simply change the DUMP call to a STORE call so that any results from running your programs are stored in a file for further processing or analysis. Note that you can use the DUMP command anywhere in your program to dump intermediate result sets to the screen, which is very useful for debugging purposes.

10.8.2 Pig Latin programs:

Pig Latin has built-in relational-style operations such as filter, project, group, join. Pig Latin also has a map operation that applies a custom user function to every member of a set. In Pig Latin, the map operation is called "foreach".

Additionally, users can incorporate their own custom code into essentially any Pig Latin operation. For example, if a user has a function that determines whether a given image contains a human face, the user can ask Pig to filter images according to this function. Pig will then evaluate this function on the user's behalf, over the images. If the evaluation mechanism incorporates parallelism, as is the case with the Hadoop evaluation mechanism, then the user's function will be executed in a parallel fashion.

10.8.3 Pig statements

Pig Latin is a relatively simple language that executes statements. A statement is an operation that takes input (such as a bag, which represents a set of tuples) and emits another bag as its output. A bag is a relation, similar to table, that you'll find in a relational database (where tuples represent the rows, and individual tuples are made up of fields).

For example log_sample is a **bag** of **tuples**, two of the basic Pig Latin data types. Put concisely:

- 1227714 is a **field**
- (1227714,2012-09-30:22:56:03,6,,39451,6,) is a **tuple**, an ordered collection of fields
- {(1227714,2012-09-30:22:56:03,6,,39451,6,), (1070227,2012-09-30:19:09:32,8,,,,)} is a **bag**, a collection of tuples

Case Sensitivity in pig statements

The names (aliases) of relations and fields are case sensitive. The names of Pig Latin functions are case sensitive. The names of parameters (see Parameter Substitution) and all other Pig Latin keywords (see Reserved Keywords) are case insensitive.

In the example below, note the following:

1. The names (aliases) of relations A, B, and C are case sensitive.
2. The names (aliases) of fields f1, f2, and f3 are case sensitive.
3. Function names PigStorage and COUNT are case sensitive.
4. Keywords LOAD, USING, AS, GROUP, BY, FOREACH, GENERATE, and DUMP are case insensitive. They can also be written as load, using, as, group, by, etc.
5. In the FOREACH statement, the field in relation B is referred to by positional notation ($0).

10.8.4 Data Types and More

(1) Identifiers

Identifiers include the names of relations (aliases), fields, variables, and so on. In Pig, identifiers start with a letter and can be followed by any number of letters, digits, or underscores.

Valid identifiers:

```
A
A123
abc_123_BeX_
```

Invalid identifiers:

```
_A123
abc_$
A!B
```

(2) Relations, Bags, Tuples, Fields

Pig Latin statements work with relations. A relation can be defined as follows:

- A relation is a bag (more specifically, an outer bag).
- A bag is a collection of tuples.
- A tuple is an ordered set of fields.
- A field is a piece of data.

A Pig relation is a bag of tuples. A Pig relation is similar to a table in a relational database, where the tuples in the bag correspond to the rows in a table. Unlike a relational table, however, Pig relations don't require that every tuple contain the same number of fields or that the fields in the same position (column) have the same type.

Also note that relations are unordered which means there is no guarantee that tuples are processed in any particular order. Furthermore, processing may be parallelized in which case tuples are not processed according to any total ordering.

(3) Referencing Relations

Relations are referred to by name (or alias). Names are assigned by you as part of the Pig Latin statement. In this example the name (alias) of the relation is A.

```
A = LOAD 'student' USING PigStorage() AS (name:chararray, age:int,
gpa:float);
DUMP A;
(Jay,18,4.0F)
(Mary,19,3.8F)
(Amit,20,3.9F)
(Jayesh,18,3.8F)
```

```
A = LOAD 'student' USING PigStorage() AS (name:chararray, age:int,
gpa:float);
B = A;
DUMP B;
```

You an assign an alias to another alias. The new alias can be used in the place of the original alias to refer the original relation.

(4) Referencing Fields

Fields are referred to by positional notation or by name (alias).

- Positional notation is generated by the system. Positional notation is indicated with the dollar sign ($) and begins with zero (0); for example, $0, $1, $2.
- Names are assigned by you using schemas (or, in the case of the GROUP operator and some functions, by the system). You can use any name that is not a Pig keyword (see Identifiers for valid name examples).

Given relation A above, the three fields are separated out in this table.

	First Field	Second Field	Third Field
Data type	chararray	int	float
Positional notation (generated by system)	$0	$1	$2
Possible name (assigned by you using a schema)	name	age	gpa
Field value (for the first tuple)	Jay	18	4.0

As shown in this example when you assign names to fields (using the AS schema clause) you can still refer to the fields using positional notation. However, for debugging purposes and ease of comprehension, it is better to use field names.

```
A = LOAD 'student' USING PigStorage() AS (name:chararray, age:int,
gpa:float);
X = FOREACH A GENERATE name,$2;
DUMP X;
(Jay,4.0F)
(Mary,3.8F)
(Amit,3.9F)
(Jayesh,3.8F)
```

In this example an error is generated because the requested column ($3) is outside of the declared schema (positional notation begins with $0). Note that the error is caught before the statements are executed.

```
A = LOAD 'data' AS (f1:int,f2:int,f3:int);
B = FOREACH A GENERATE $3;
DUMP B;
2009-01-21  23:03:46,715  [main]  ERROR  org.apache.pig.tools.grunt.
GruntParser - java.io.IOException:
Out of bound access. Trying to access non-existent  : 3. Schema {f1:
bytearray,f2: bytearray,f3: bytearray} has 3 column(s).
etc ...
```

As noted, the fields in a tuple can be any data type, including the complex data types *Referencing Fields that are Complex Data Types*: bags, tuples, and maps.

- Use the schemas for complex data types to name fields that are complex data types.
- Use the dereference operators to reference and work with fields that are complex data types.

In this example the data file contains tuples. A schema for complex data types (in this case, tuples) is used to load the data. Then, dereference operators (the dot in t1.t1a and t2.$0) are used to access the fields in the tuples. Note that when you assign names to fields you can still refer to these fields using positional notation.

```
cat data;
(3,8,9) (4,5,6)
(1,4,7) (3,7,5)
(2,5,8) (9,5,8)
A = LOAD 'data' AS (t1:tuple(t1a:int,
t1b:int,t1c:int),t2:tuple(t2a:int,t2b:int,t2c:int));
DUMP A;
((3,8,9),(4,5,6))
((1,4,7),(3,7,5))
((2,5,8),(9,5,8))
X = FOREACH A GENERATE t1.t1a,t2.$0;
DUMP X;
(3,4)
(1,3)
(2,9)
```

10.9 DATA TYPES

(a) *Simple and Complex*

Simple Types	Description	Example
int	Signed 32-bit integer	10

Simple Types	Description	Example
long	Signed 64-bit integer	Data: 10L or 10l Display: 10L
float	32-bit floating point	Data: 10.5F or 10.5f or 10.5e2f or 10.5E2F Display: 10.5F or 1050.0F
double	64-bit floating point	Data: 10.5 or 10.5e2 or 10.5E2 Display: 10.5 or 1050.0
chararray	Character array (string) in Unicode UTF-8 format	hello world
bytearray	Byte array (blob)	
boolean	boolean	true/false (case insensitive)
Complex Types		
tuple	An ordered set of fields.	(19,2)
bag	An collection of tuples.	{(19,2), (18,1)}
map	A set of key value pairs.	[open#apache]

Note the following general observations about data types:

Use schemas to assign types to fields. If you don't assign types, fields default to type bytearray and implicit conversions are applied to the data depending on the context in which that data is used. For example, in relation B, f1 is converted to integer because 5 is integer. In relation C, f1 and f2 are converted to double because we don't know the type of either f1 or f2.

```
A = LOAD 'data' AS (f1,f2,f3);
B = FOREACH A GENERATE f1 + 5;
C = FOREACH A generate f1 + f2;
```

If a schema is defined as part of a load statement, the load function will attempt to enforce the schema. If the data does not conform to the schema, the loader will generate a null value or an error.

```
A = LOAD 'data' AS (name:chararray, age:int, gpa:float);
```

If an explicit cast is not supported, an error will occur. For example, you cannot cast a chararray to int.

```
A = LOAD 'data' AS (name:chararray, age:int, gpa:float);
B = FOREACH A GENERATE (int)name;
This will cause an error …
```

If Pig cannot resolve incompatible types through implicit casts, an error will occur. For example, you cannot add chararray and float (see the Types Table for addition and subtraction).

```
A = LOAD 'data' AS (name:chararray, age:int, gpa:float);
B = FOREACH A GENERATE name + gpa;
This will cause an error …
```

All data types have corresponding schemas.

(b) Tuple

A tuple is an ordered set of fields.

Syntax

```
( field [, field …] )
```

Terms

( )	A tuple is enclosed in parentheses ( ).
field	A piece of data. A field can be any data type (including tuple and bag).

Usage

You can think of a tuple as a row with one or more fields, where each field can be any data type and any field may or may not have data. If a field has no data, then the following happens:

- In a load statement, the loader will inject null into the tuple. The actual value that is substituted for null is loader specific; for example, PigStorage substitutes an empty field for null.
- In a non-load statement, if a requested field is missing from a tuple, Pig will inject null.

Example

In this example the tuple contains three fields.

```
(Jay,18,4.0F)
```

Bag

A bag is a collection of tuples.

Syntax: Inner bag

```
{ tuple [, tuple …] }
```

Terms

{ }	An inner bag is enclosed in curly brackets { }.
tuple	A tuple.

Usage

Note the following about bags:

- A bag can have duplicate tuples.
- A bag can have tuples with differing numbers of fields. However, if Pig tries to access a field that does not exist, a null value is substituted.
- A bag can have tuples with fields that have different data types. However, for Pig to effectively process bags, the schemas of the tuples within those bags should be the same. For example, if half of the tuples include chararray fields and while the other half include float fields, only half of the tuples will participate in any kind of computation because the chararray fields will be converted to null.

Bags have two forms: outer bag (or relation) and inner bag.

Example: Outer Bag

In this example A is a relation or bag of tuples. You can think of this bag as an outer bag.

```
A = LOAD 'data' as (f1:int, f2:int, f3;int);
DUMP A;
(1,2,3)
(4,2,1)
(8,3,4)
(4,3,3)
```

Example: Inner Bag

Now, suppose we group relation A by the first field to form relation X.

In this example X is a relation or bag of tuples. The tuples in relation X have two fields. The first field is type int. The second field is type bag; you can think of this bag as an inner bag.

```
X = GROUP A BY f1;
DUMP X;
(1,{(1,2,3)})
(4,{(4,2,1),(4,3,3)})
(8,{(8,3,4)})
```

EXERCISE 10.1: Working With Pig

After completing this hands-on lab, you'll be able to:

1. Execute Pig statements from the Grunt shell
2. Execute a Pig script
3. Pass parameters to a Pig script
4. Load data for using within Pig

1.1 PIG BASICS

1. If Hadoop is not running, start it and its components using the icon on the desktop.
2. Open a command line. Right-click the desktop and select **Open in Terminal**.
3. Next start the *Grunt shell.* Change to the *Pig bin* directory and start the shell running in local mode.

```
cd $PIG_HOME/bin
./pig -x local
```

```
biadmin@bivm:...iginsights/pig/bin
File  Edit  View  Terminal  Help
biadmin@bivm:~> cd $PIG_HOME/bin
biadmin@bivm:/opt/ibm/biginsights/pig/bin> ./pig -x local
grunt>
```

4. Read the data from a comma separated values file,

/home/biadmin/SampleData/books.csv into a relation called *data* using the default *PigStorage()* loader.

```
data = load '/home/biadmin/SampleData/books.csv';
```

5. Next access the first field in each tuple and then write the results out to the console. You will have to use the *foreach* operator to accomplish this. I understand that we have not covered that operator yet. Just bare with me.

```
b = foreach data generate $0;
dump b;
```

```
File  Edit  View  Terminal  Help
grunt> data = load '/home/biadmin/SampleData/books.csv';
grunt> b = foreach data generate $0;
grunt> dump b;
WARN  [JobControl]    org.apache.hadoop.mapred.JobClient      - No job jar file s
et.  User classes may not be found. See JobConf(Class) or JobConf#setJar(String)
.
WARN  [JobControl] org.apache.hadoop.mapred.LocalJobRunner      - LocalJobRunner
does not support symlinking into current working dir.
WARN  [main] org.apache.pig.tools.pigstats.PigStatsUtil     - Failed to get Runn
ingJob for job job_local_0001
WARN  [main] org.apache.pig.data.SchemaTupleBackend     - SchemaTupleBackend has
 already been initialized
(1,J. K. Rowlings,The Sorcerer's Stone,1997)
(2,J. K. Rowlings,The Chamber of Secrets,1999)
(3,J. K. Rowlings,The Prisoner of Azkaban,1999)
(4,J. K. Rowlings,The Goblet of Fire,2000)
(5,J. K. Rowlings,The Order of the Phoenix,2003)
(6,J. K. Rowlings,The Half-Blood Prince,2005)
(7,J. K. Rowlings,The Deathly Hallows,2007)
(8,David Baldacci,Camel Club,2005)
(9,David Baldacci,The Collectors,2006)
(10,David Baldacci,Stone Cold,2007)
(11,David Baldacci,Divine Justice,2008)
(12,David Baldacci,Hells Corner,2010)
(13,David Baldacci,Split Second,2003)
(14,David Baldacci,Hour Game,2004)
(15,David Baldacci,Simple Genius,2007)
(16,David Baldacci,First Family,2009)
grunt>
```

First of all, let me explain what you just did. For each tuple in the *data* bag (or relation), you accessed the first field ($0 remember, positions begin with zero) and projected it to a field called *f1* that is in the relation called *b*.

The data listed shows a tuple on each line and each tuple contains a single character string that contains all of the data. This may not be what you expected, since each line contained several fields separated by commas.

6. The problem in the previous step was that the default field separator is the tab character (\t); Reread the data but this time specify a comma as being the separating character.

Then project the first field in each tuple into a field in a new relation. Then dump the new relation. (You can use the up and down cursor keys to recall previous command.)

```
data = load '/home/biadmin/SampleData/books.csv'using PigStorage(',');
b = foreach data generate $0;
dump b;
```

```
biadmin@bivm:...iginsights/pig/bin
File  Edit  View  Terminal  Help
grunt> datal = load '/home/biadmin/SampleData/books.csv'using PigStorage(',');
grunt> b= foreach data generate $0;
grunt> dump b;
WARN  [JobControl]    org.apache.hadoop.mapred.JobClient      - No job jar file set.  User classes may not be found. See JobCo
ERROR [JobControl] org.apache.hadoop.security.UserGroupInformation      - PriviledgedActionException as:biadmin (auth:SIMPLE)
e.ExecException: ERROR 2118: Input path does not exist: file:/home/biadmin/SamplData/books.csv
WARN  [main] org.apache.pig.backend.hadoop.executionengine.mapReduceLayer.MapReduceLauncher      - Ooops! Some job has failed!
o stop immediately on failure.
ERROR [main] org.apache.pig.tools.pigstats.SimplePigStats      - ERROR 2997: Unable to recreate exception from backend error:
Exception: ERROR 2118: Input path does not exist: file:/home/biadmin/SamplData/books.csv
        at org.apache.pig.backend.hadoop.executionengine.mapReduceLayer.PigInputFormat.getSplits(PigInputFormat.java:288)
```

Note that now comma separated fields became individual fields in the tuple. And the first field appears to be a number.

7. What if you wanted to be able to access the fields in the tuple by name instead of only by position? You have to using the *LOAD* operator and specify a schema.

```
data = load '/home/biadmin/SampleData/books.csv' using PigStorage(',')
as
(booknum:int, author:chararray, title:chararray, published:int);
b = foreach data generate author, title;
dump b;
```

```
biadmin@bivm:...iginsights/pig/bin
File  Edit  View  Terminal  Help
grunt> data = load '/home/biadmin/SampleData/books.csv'using PigStorage(',') as (booknum:int, author:chararray, title:chararray, pubblished:int);
grunt> b =foreach data generate author, title;
grunt> dump b;
WARN  [JobControl]    org.apache.hadoop.mapred.JobClient      - No job jar file set.  User classes may not be found. See JobConf(Class) or JobConf
WARN  [JobControl] org.apache.hadoop.mapred.LocalJobRunner      - LocalJobRunner does not support symlinking into current working dir.
WARN  [main] org.apache.pig.tools.pigstats.PigStatsUtil      - Failed to get RunningJob for job job_local_0005
WARN  [main] org.apache.pig.data.SchemaTupleBackend      - SchemaTupleBackend has already been initialized
(J. K. Rowlings,The Sorcerer's Stone)
(J. K. Rowlings,The Chamber of Secrets)
(J. K. Rowlings,The Prisoner of Azkaban)
(J. K. Rowlings,The Goblet of Fire)
(J. K. Rowlings,The Order of the Phoenix)
(J. K. Rowlings,The Half-Blood Prince)
(J. K. Rowlings,The Deathly Hallows)
(David Baldacci,Camel Club)
(David Baldacci,The Collectors)
(David Baldacci,Stone Cold)
(David Baldacci,Divine Justice)
(David Baldacci,Hells Corner)
(David Baldacci,Split Second)
(David Baldacci,Hour Game)
(David Baldacci,Simple Genius)
(David Baldacci,First Family)
grunt>
```

8. The presentation indicated that both relations and fields were case sensitive. Verify this. Reread the book information with the following schema.

```
data = load '/home/biadmin/SampleData/books.csv' using PigStorage(',')
as
(f1:int, F1:chararray, f2:chararray, F2:int);
```

```
biadmin@bivm:...iginsights/pig/bin
File  Edit  View  Terminal  Help
grunt> data = load '/home/biadmin/SampleData/books.csv'using PigStorage(',') as (f1:int, F1:chararray,f2:chararray, F2:int);
grunt>
```

Surprise, that actually worked.

9. Now dump your data file the following command.

```
dump DATA;
```

```
biadmin@bivm:...iginsights/pig/bin
File  Edit  View  Terminal  Help
grunt> dump DATA;
ERROR [main]      org.apache.pig.tools.grunt.Grunt     - ERROR 1003: Unable to find an operator for alias DATA
Details at logfile: /opt/ibm/biginsights/pig/bin/pig_1458676310310.log
grunt>
```

You will get error message an error.

10. This time dump the data but capitalize the *dump* command.

```
DUMP data;
```

```
biadmin@bivm:...iginsights/pig/bin
File  Edit  View  Terminal  Help
grunt> DUMP data;
WARN  [JobControl]    org.apache.hadoop.mapred.JobClient  - No job jar file set.  User classes may not be foun
WARN  [JobControl] org.apache.hadoop.mapred.LocalJobRunner     - LocalJobRunner does not support symlinking i
WARN  [main] org.apache.pig.tools.pigstats.PigStatsUtil     - Failed to get RunningJob for job job_local_0006
WARN  [main] org.apache.pig.data.SchemaTupleBackend     - SchemaTupleBackend has already been initialized
(1,J. K. Rowlings,The Sorcerer's Stone,1997)
(2,J. K. Rowlings,The Chamber of Secrets,1999)
(3,J. K. Rowlings,The Prisoner of Azkaban,1999)
(4,J. K. Rowlings,The Goblet of Fire,2000)
(5,J. K. Rowlings,The Order of the Phoenix,2003)
(6,J. K. Rowlings,The Half-Blood Prince,2005)
(7,J. K. Rowlings,The Deathly Hallows,2007)
(8,David Baldacci,Camel Club,2005)
(9,David Baldacci,The Collectors,2006)
(10,David Baldacci,Stone Cold,2007)
(11,David Baldacci,Divine Justice,2008)
(12,David Baldacci,Hells Corner,2010)
(13,David Baldacci,Split Second,2003)
(14,David Baldacci,Hour Game,2004)
(15,David Baldacci,Simple Genius,2007)
(16,David Baldacci,First Family,2009)
grunt>
```

11. Terminate your *Grunt shell.*

```
quit;
```

Although the up and down cursors recall previous commands, I have found that when a recalled command spans two lines, I was not able to move the cursor to the first line.Also, I like using a script because I can copy and pasted previous commands.

12. Create a script that contains Pig commands. Open another command line and execute *gedit.*

```
gedit &
```

13. You can pass parameters to a Pig script. Create a parameter that passes the directory structure for your data. In the *gedit* edit area, type the following:

```
dir = /home/biadmin/SampleData
```

```
Unsaved Document 1 - gedit
biadmin@bivm:~
File  Edit  View  Terminal  Help
biadmin@bivm:~> gedit &
[1] 58922
biadmin@bivm:~> dir = /home/biadmin/SampleData
ls: cannot access =: No such file or directory
/home/biadmin/SampleData:
total 52
-rwxrw-rw- 1 biadmin biadmin  2415 Jan 12  2012 bookreviews.json
-rwxrw-rw- 1 biadmin biadmin   628 Oct  7  2013 books.csv
-rwxrw-rw- 1 biadmin biadmin  2709 Oct  9  2013 pig_bookreviews.json
-rwxrw-rw- 1 biadmin biadmin   419 Jan 12  2012 reviews.csv
-rwxrw-rw- 1 biadmin biadmin 33157 Feb 19 06:35 Twitter Search.json
[1]+  Done                    gedit
biadmin@bivm:~> 
```

14. Save your file as **/home/biadmin/myparams**.

15. Next, in *gedit,* open a new edit window. Type the *LOAD* command that will read data from a field called */home/biadmin/SampleData/pig_bookreviews.json.*

As the file extension indicates, this is a JSON file. This requires your using the JsonLoader().

16. Type the following. Note *$dir* references your parameter.

```
data = load '$dir/pig_bookreviews.json' using JsonLoader();
dump data;
```

17. Save your work to */home/biadmin/pig.script.*

18. From the command line, invoke your Pig script and pass in your parameter file.

```
./pig -x local -param_file ~/myparams ~/pig.script
```

You should have an error. It says that it could not find a schema file. The *JsonLoader()* requires a schema. There are no defaults. If you do not code the schema in the *LOAD* statement, then the function is expecting to find a schema file in the same directory as your data.

19. It probably would be more informative if you were to look at the format of the data in the *pig_bookreviews.json* file so that you can see how the schema matches. For those of you who are not really motivated, here is a partial look at the data. The important thing to note is that each JSON record is on a single line.

```
[{"author": "J. K. Rowlings", "title": "The Sorcerers Stone", "published":
1997,
"reviews": [{"name": "Mary", "stars": 5},{"name": "Tom", "stars": 5}]},
...
{"author": "David Baldacci", "title": "First Family", "published": 2009,
"reviews": [{"name": "Andrew", "stars": 4},{"name": "Katie", "stars":
4},{"name": "Scott", "stars": 5}]}]
```

20. In your Pig script, modify it so that the JsonLoader() has a schema.

```
data = load '$dir/pig_bookreviews.json' using
   JsonLoader('author:chararray,title:chararray,year:int,reviews:{review:(name:c
   hararray,stars:int)}');
   dump data;
```

21. This should have solved your problem and this ends this exercise

EXERCISE 10.2 Pig Relational Operators

1.1 CORE OPERATORS

1. If Hadoop is not running, start it and its components using the icon on the desktop.
2. Bring up a command line. Right click your desktop and select **Open in Terminal.**.
3. You have the option of running your Pig commands from either the *Grunt shell* or from your Pig script. In either case you need to change to the *Pig bin* directory and start the shell running in local mode.

```
cd $PIG_HOME/bin
```

4. If you are going to run from the *Grunt shell* locally, then execute;

```
./pig -x local
```

If your are going to use your *pig.script,* then you will execute the script and pass in your directory parameter by doing the following:

```
./pig -x local -param_file ~/myparams ~/pig.script
```

You can edit your *pig.script* by using *gedit.* Also remember that in your script, you can comment out any commands by coding two dashes (--) before the command.

5. Read the */home/labfiles/SampleData/books.csv* file. Filter the resulting relation so that you only have those books published prior to 2002. In the *LOAD* operator below, it is referencing a parameter for the directory structure. If you are running the command from the *Grunt shell,* then you will replace *$dir* with the qualified directory path.

```
grunt> a = load '/home/biadmin/SampleData/books.csv' using PigStorage(',')
as (bkun: int, author:chararray, title:chararray, pubyear:int);
grunt> dump a;
```

```
biadmin@bivm:...iginsights/pig/bin
File Edit View Terminal Help
grunt> a = load '/home/biadmin/SampleData/books.csv' using PigStorage(',') as (b
kun: int, author:chararray, title:chararray, pubyear:int);
grunt> dump a;
WARN  [JobControl]    org.apache.hadoop.mapred.JobClient        - No job jar file s
et.  User classes may not be found. See JobConf(Class) or JobConf#setJar(String)

WARN  [JobControl] org.apache.hadoop.mapred.LocalJobRunner        - LocalJobRunner
does not support symlinking into current working dir.
WARN  [main] org.apache.pig.tools.pigstats.PigStatsUtil        - Failed to get Runn
ingJob for job job_local_0002
WARN  [main] org.apache.pig.data.SchemaTupleBackend        - SchemaTupleBackend has
 already been initialized
(1,J. K. Rowlings,The Sorcerer's Stone,1997)
(2,J. K. Rowlings,The Chamber of Secrets,1999)
(3,J. K. Rowlings,The Prisoner of Azkaban,1999)
(4,J. K. Rowlings,The Goblet of Fire,2000)
(5,J. K. Rowlings,The Order of the Phoenix,2003)
(6,J. K. Rowlings,The Half-Blood Prince,2005)
(7,J. K. Rowlings,The Deathly Hallows,2007)
(8,David Baldacci,Camel Club,2005)
(9,David Baldacci,The Collectors,2006)
(10,David Baldacci,Stone Cold,2007)
(11,David Baldacci,Divine Justice,2008)
(12,David Baldacci,Hells Corner,2010)
(13,David Baldacci,Split Second,2003)
(14,David Baldacci,Hour Game,2004)
(15,David Baldacci,Simple Genius,2007)
(16,David Baldacci,First Family,2009)
grunt>
```

Enter following code and press **Enter** to get the result as shown in window below

```
b = filter a by pubyear < 2002;
dump b;
```

```
biadmin@bivm:...iginsights/pig/bin
File Edit View Terminal Help
grunt> b = filter a by pubyear <2002;
grunt> dump b;
(1,J. K. Rowlings,The Sorcerer's Stone,1997)
(2,J. K. Rowlings,The Chamber of Secrets,1999)
(3,J. K. Rowlings,The Prisoner of Azkaban,1999)
(4,J. K. Rowlings,The Goblet of Fire,2000)
grunt>
```

If at any time you want to see the data from any relation, just code a *dump* statement for that relation.

6. Next take the results of the *FILTER* and sort the records in descending order by *pubyear.* Dump the resulting relation.

c = order b by pubyear desc;

desc will list the result in decreasing order.

```
biadmin@bivm:...iginsights/pig/bin
File Edit View Terminal Help
grunt> c = order b by pubyear desc;
grunt> dump c ;
(4,J. K. Rowlings,The Goblet of Fire,2000)
(2,J. K. Rowlings,The Chamber of Secrets,1999)
(3,J. K. Rowlings,The Prisoner of Azkaban,1999)
(1,J. K. Rowlings,The Sorcerer's Stone,1997)
grunt> d = group c by pubyear;
```

7. Next take the sorted relation and group it by *pubyear.*

d = group c by pubyear;

and see the resulting list.

dump d;

```
biadmin@bivm:...iginsights/pig/bin
File Edit View Terminal Help
grunt> d = group c by pubyear;
grunt> dump d;
(1997,{(1,J. K. Rowlings,The Sorcerer's Stone,1997)})
(1999,{(2,J. K. Rowlings,The Chamber of Secrets,1999),(3,J. K. Rowlings,The Prisoner of Azkaban,1999)})
(2000,{(4,J. K. Rowlings,The Goblet of Fire,2000)})
grunt>
```

For those years where there were two published, note that the inner bag contains two tuples.

8. Do some projection. Take the relation that was the result of the *LOAD* operator and create tuples that only have the author and the book.

e = foreach a generate author, title;

and see the dumping result.

dump e;

```
biadmin@bivm:...iginsights/pig/bin
File Edit View Terminal Help
grunt> e = foreach a generate author, title;
grunt> dump e;
(J. K. Rowlings,The Sorcerer's Stone)
(J. K. Rowlings,The Chamber of Secrets)
(J. K. Rowlings,The Prisoner of Azkaban)
(J. K. Rowlings,The Goblet of Fire)
(J. K. Rowlings,The Order of the Phoenix)
(J. K. Rowlings,The Half-Blood Prince)
(J. K. Rowlings,The Deathly Hallows)
(David Baldacci,Camel Club)
(David Baldacci,The Collectors)
(David Baldacci,Stone Cold)
(David Baldacci,Divine Justice)
(David Baldacci,Hells Corner)
(David Baldacci,Split Second)
(David Baldacci,Hour Game)
(David Baldacci,Simple Genius)
(David Baldacci,First Family)
grunt> f = foreach d generate group, c.author, c.title;
```

9. Now do the same with the resulting relation from the *GROUP* operator, except add to the project the grouping value. In this case you will have to dereference your field names.

```
f = foreach d generate group, c.author, c.title;
```

and see the result by dumping the contents as below:

dump f:

```
biadmin@bivm:...iginsights/pig/bin
File Edit View Terminal Help
grunt> f = foreach d generate group, c.author, c.title;
grunt> dump f;
(1997,{(J. K. Rowlings)},{(The Sorcerer's Stone)})
(1999,{(J. K. Rowlings),(J. K. Rowlings)},{(The Chamber of Secrets),(The Prisoner of Azkaba
n)})
(2000,{(J. K. Rowlings)},{(The Goblet of Fire)})
grunt>
```

10. Flatten the inner bag for the above relation so that only the author is returned.

```
g = foreach f generate flatten($1);
```

see the result by dumping the contents:

```
dump g;
```

```
biadmin@bivm:...iginsights/pig/bin
File Edit View Terminal Help
grunt> g = foreach f generate flatten($1);
grunt> dump g;
(J. K. Rowlings)
(J. K. Rowlings)
(J. K. Rowlings)
(J. K. Rowlings)
```

11. Take the relation created by the original *LOAD* operator and split the file so that the books for David Baldacci are in one relation and the books of all other authors are in a second relation. Dump both newly created relations

```
split a into h if author == 'David Baldacci', i if author != 'David
Baldacci';
dump h;
dump i;
```

12. Finally, read in a second file. This file has the name of people who reviewed the books and the number of stars that they gave each book. Then join the relations for the books file and the reviews file on bknum.

```
j = load '$dir/reviews.csv' using PigStorage(',') as (bknum:int,
reviewer:chararray, stars:int);
k = join a by bknum, j by bknum;
dump k;
```

EXERCISE 10.3 Pig Evaluation Functions

This exercise gives you the opportunity work with some of the Pig relational operators in order to use some Pig evaluation functions.

1.1 EVALUATION FUNCTIONS

1. If Hadoop is not running, start it and its components using the icon on the desktop.
2. Bring up a command line. Right click your desktop and select **Open in Terminal**.
3. You have the option of running your Pig commands from either the *Grunt shell* or from your Pig script. In either case you need to change to the *Pig bin* directory and start the shell running in local mode.

```
cd $PIG_HOME/bin
```

```
biadmin@bivm:...iginsights/pig/bin
File Edit View Terminal Help
biadmin@bivm:~> cd $PIG_HOME/bin
biadmin@bivm:/opt/ibm/biginsights/pig/bin>
```

4. If you are going to run from the *Grunt shell* locally, then execute;

```
./pig -x local
```

```
biadmin@bivm:...iginsights/pig/bin
File Edit View Terminal Help
biadmin@bivm:/opt/ibm/biginsights/pig/bin> ./pig -x local
grunt>
```

directory parameter by doing the following:

```
./pig -x local -param_file ~/myparams ~/pig.script
```

You can edit your *pig.script* by using *gedit.* Also remember that in your script, you can comment out any commands by coding two dashes (--) before the command.

In the directions, the *DUMP* operator will only be specified for the final output. But that does not stop you from adding intermediate *DUMP* operators in order to see the affects of each operator.

5. Read the */home/biadmin/SampleData/books.csv* file.

```
books = load '/home/biadmin/SampleData/books.csv' using PigStorage(',')
as (bknum: int,author:chararray, book:chararray, pubyear:int);
```

6. Read the */home/biadmin/SampleData/reviews.csv* file.

```
reviews = load '/home/biadmin/reviews.csv' using PigStorage(',') as
(bknum:int, reviewer:chararray, stars:int);
```

7. Group the *books* relations by *pubyear.*

```
booksInYear = group books by pubyear;
```

```
File  Edit  View  Terminal  Help
grunt> books = load '/home/biadmin/SampleData/books.csv' using PigStorage(',') as (bknum: int, author:chararray, book:chararray, pubyear:int);
grunt> reviews = load '/home/biadmin/SampleData/reviews.csv' using PigStorage(',') as (bknum:int, reviewer:chararray, stars:int);
grunt> booksInYear = group books by pubyear;
grunt> dump booksInYear;
```

You can see the listing by dump command:

```
grunt> dump booksInYear;
WARN  [JobControl]     org.apache.hadoop.mapred.JobClient      - No job jar file set.  User classes may not be found. See JobConf(
WARN  [JobControl] org.apache.hadoop.mapred.LocalJobRunner      - LocalJobRunner does not support symlinking into current working
WARN  [Thread-12] org.apache.pig.data.SchemaTupleBackend      - SchemaTupleBackend has already been initialized
WARN  [main] org.apache.pig.tools.pigstats.PigStatsUtil       - Failed to get RunningJob for job job_local_0001
WARN  [main] org.apache.pig.data.SchemaTupleBackend       - SchemaTupleBackend has already been initialized
(1997,{(1,J. K. Rowlings,The Sorcerer's Stone,1997)})
(1999,{(2,J. K. Rowlings,The Chamber of Secrets,1999),(3,J. K. Rowlings,The Prisoner of Azkaban,1999)})
(2000,{(4,J. K. Rowlings,The Goblet of Fire,2000)})
(2003,{(13,David Baldacci,Split Second,2003),(5,J. K. Rowlings,The Order of the Phoenix,2003)})
(2004,{(14,David Baldacci,Hour Game,2004)})
(2005,{(6,J. K. Rowlings,The Half-Blood Prince,2005),(8,David Baldacci,Camel Club,2005)})
(2006,{(9,David Baldacci,The Collectors,2006)})
(2007,{(10,David Baldacci,Stone Cold,2007),(7,J. K. Rowlings,The Deathly Hallows,2007),(15,David Baldacci,Simple Genius,2007)})
(2008,{(11,David Baldacci,Divine Justice,2008)})
(2009,{(16,David Baldacci,First Family,2009)})
(2010,{(12,David Baldacci,Hells Corner,2010)})
```

8. Calculate the number of books published in each year.

```
booksPerYear = foreach booksInYear generate group, COUNT($1);
dump booksPerYear;
```

```
biadmin@bivm:...iginsights/pig/bin
File  Edit  View  Terminal  Help
grunt> booksPerYear = foreach booksInYear generate group, COUNT ($1); dump booksPerYear;
(1997,1)
(1999,2)
(2000,1)
(2003,2)
(2004,1)
(2005,2)
(2006,1)
(2007,3)
(2008,1)
(2009,1)
(2010,1)
grunt>
```

9. This is going to be a bit more interesting. Calculate the average number of stars for each book. Start by joining the *books* relation and the *reviews* relation on *bknum*.

```
booksAndReviews = join books by bknum, reviews by bknum;
```

and list the same by dump command:

```
dump booksAndReviews
```

```
biadmin@bivm:...iginsights/pig/bin
File  Edit  View  Terminal  Help
grunt> booksAndReviews = join books by bknum, reviews by bknum;
grunt> dump booksAndReviews;
(1,J. K. Rowlings,The Sorcerer's Stone,1997,1,Mary,5)
(1,J. K. Rowlings,The Sorcerer's Stone,1997,1,Tom,5)
(2,J. K. Rowlings,The Chamber of Secrets,1999,2,Bill,5)
(2,J. K. Rowlings,The Chamber of Secrets,1999,2,Sue,4)
(2,J. K. Rowlings,The Chamber of Secrets,1999,2,Theo,5)
(3,J. K. Rowlings,The Prisoner of Azkaban,1999,3,Mary,5)
(3,J. K. Rowlings,The Prisoner of Azkaban,1999,3,Cindy,5)
(4,J. K. Rowlings,The Goblet of Fire,2000,4,Andrew,4)
(4,J. K. Rowlings,The Goblet of Fire,2000,4,Katie,4)
(4,J. K. Rowlings,The Goblet of Fire,2000,4,Scott,5)
(5,J. K. Rowlings,The Order of the Phoenix,2003,5,Jeff,3)
(5,J. K. Rowlings,The Order of the Phoenix,2003,5,Sara,4)
(5,J. K. Rowlings,The Order of the Phoenix,2003,5,Ryan,5)
(6,J. K. Rowlings,The Half-Blood Prince,2005,6,Bob,5)
(6,J. K. Rowlings,The Half-Blood Prince,2005,6,Autumn,4)
(7,J. K. Rowlings,The Deathly Hallows,2007,7,Betty,5)
(7,J. K. Rowlings,The Deathly Hallows,2007,7,Janet,5)
(7,J. K. Rowlings,The Deathly Hallows,2007,7,Scott,5)
(8,David Baldacci,Camel Club,2005,8,Andrew,4)
(8,David Baldacci,Camel Club,2005,8,Katie,4)
(8,David Baldacci,Camel Club,2005,8,Scott,5)
(9,David Baldacci,The Collectors,2006,9,Mary,5)
(9,David Baldacci,The Collectors,2006,9,Tom,5)
(9,David Baldacci,The Collectors,2006,9,Tom,5)
(10,David Baldacci,Stone Cold,2007,10,Sue,4)
(10,David Baldacci,Stone Cold,2007,10,Bill,5)
(10,David Baldacci,Stone Cold,2007,10,Theo,5)
(11,David Baldacci,Divine Justice,2008,11,Mary,5)
(11,David Baldacci,Divine Justice,2008,11,Cindy,5)
(12,David Baldacci,Hells Corner,2010,12,Andrew,4)
(12,David Baldacci,Hells Corner,2010,12,Katie,4)
(12,David Baldacci,Hells Corner,2010,12,Scott,5)
(13,David Baldacci,Split Second,2003,13,Sara,4)
(13,David Baldacci,Split Second,2003,13,Jeff,3)
(13,David Baldacci,Split Second,2003,13,Ryan,5)
(14,David Baldacci,Hour Game,2004,14,Bob,5)
(14,David Baldacci,Hour Game,2004,14,Autumn,4)
(15,David Baldacci,Simple Genius,2007,15,Betty,5)
(15,David Baldacci,Simple Genius,2007,15,Janet,5)
(15,David Baldacci,Simple Genius,2007,15,Scott,5)
(16,David Baldacci,First Family,2009,16,Andrew,4)
(16,David Baldacci,First Family,2009,16,Katie,4)
(16,David Baldacci,First Family,2009,16,Scott,5)
grunt>
```

10. Next project a new relation so that you only are working with the title of the book and the number of stars for each reviewer.

```
booksAndStars = foreach booksAndReviews generate book, stars;
```

```
biadmin@bivm:...iginsights/pig/bin
File Edit View Terminal Help
grunt> booksAndStars = foreach booksAndReviews generate book, stars;
grunt> dump booksAndStars;
(The Sorcerer's Stone,5)
(The Sorcerer's Stone,5)
(The Chamber of Secrets,5)
(The Chamber of Secrets,4)
(The Chamber of Secrets,5)
(The Prisoner of Azkaban,5)
(The Prisoner of Azkaban,5)
(The Goblet of Fire,4)
(The Goblet of Fire,4)
(The Goblet of Fire,5)
(The Order of the Phoenix,3)
(The Order of the Phoenix,4)
(The Order of the Phoenix,5)
(The Half-Blood Prince,5)
(The Half-Blood Prince,4)
(The Deathly Hallows,5)
(The Deathly Hallows,5)
(The Deathly Hallows,5)
(Camel Club,4)
(Camel Club,4)
(Camel Club,5)
(The Collectors,5)
(The Collectors,5)
(Stone Cold,4)
(Stone Cold,5)
(Stone Cold,5)
(Divine Justice,5)
(Divine Justice,5)
(Hells Corner,4)
(Hells Corner,4)
(Hells Corner,5)
(Split Second,4)
(Split Second,3)
(Split Second,5)
(Hour Game,5)
(Hour Game,4)
(Simple Genius,5)
(Simple Genius,5)
(Simple Genius,5)
(First Family,4)
(First Family,4)
(First Family,5)
grunt>
```

11. Group the *booksAndStars* relation by book title.

```
starsInBooks = group booksAndStars by book;
```

12. Now it might be a good idea to look at the schema for *starsInBooks*. Enter following code:

```
describe starsInBooks;
```

```
biadmin@bivm:...iginsights/pig/bin
File  Edit  View  Terminal  Help
grunt> starsInBooks = group booksAndStars by book;
grunt> describe starsInBooks;
starsInBooks: {group: chararray,booksAndStars: {(books::book: chararray,reviews::stars: int)}}
grunt>
```

13. Next you are going to have to use the *FOREACH* operator. Getting access to the book title is easy since that how the records are grouped. But what about the number of stars? Which relation was used in the first grouping? it was *booksAndStars*. So you will have to dereference *stars* using *booksAndStars*.

```
avgStars = foreach starsInBooks generate group, AVG(booksAndStars.
stars);
dump avgStars;
```

14. Having the value for *stars* as a double may not be what you want. You cannot give a half of a star or a third of a star so when calculating the average, you might want it to stay as an integer. To do this, cast the average value to *int*.

```
avgStars = foreach starsInBooks generate group,
(int)AVG(booksAndStars.stars);
dump avgStars;
```

15. What if you wanted to eliminate any ratings that were less than four stars. (I know that is may not make sense, but who says that a learning opportunity has to make sense?) You could use a *FOREACH* operator with a nested block.

```
bogusAvgStars = foreach starsInBooks {filteredStars = filter
booksAndStars by stars > 3;
numStars = filteredStars.stars;
generate group, (int)AVG(numStars);}
dump bogusAvgStars;
```

16. Using the *EXPLAIN* operator, it is possible to get and understanding as to how Pig is going to attack a particular MapReduce problem.

```
explain bogusAvgStars;
```

17. A quick look at running hdfs commands from the *Grunt shell*. If you do not have the *Grunt shell* open in local mode, execute the following:

```
./pig -x local
```

18. Next list the current directory using the *FSShell* command from the *Grunt shell*.

```
fs -ls
```

What is listed? It is the $PIG_HOME/bin directory. Interesting. Why did it not list the directories and files in hdfs? You are running in local mode.

19. Exit from Pig local mode.

```
quit;
```

20. Invoke the *Grunt shell* in MapReduce mode. Remember it is the default mode.

```
./pig
```

21. Again execute the *FSShell* and do a directory listing.

```
fs -ls
```

This time it listed the data in hdfs.

22. You can quit from pig. You can stop Hadoop. This is the end of the exercise

10.9 FORMAT OF SCRIPTING IN PIG

A script in Pig Latin often follows a specific format in which data is read from the file system, a number operations are performed on the data (transforming it in one or more ways), and then the resulting relation is written back to the file system. You can see this pattern in its simplest form (with one transformation) in Listing 1.

Listing 1 shows the simplicity of this process in Pig. Given the three lines shown, only one is the actual search. The first line simply reads the test data set (the messages log) into a bag that represents a collection of tuples. You filter this data (the only entry in the tuple, represented as $0, or field 1) with a regular expression, looking for the character sequence WARN. Finally, you store this bag, which now represents all of those tuples from messages that contain WARN into a new file called warnings in the host file system.

Listing 1. A simple Pig Latin script

```
messages = LOAD 'messages';
warns = FILTER messages BY $0 MATCHES '.*WARN+.*';
STORE warns INTO 'warnings';
```

Pig has a rich set of data types, supporting not only high-level concepts like bags, tuples, and maps, but also simple data types such as ints,longs, floats, doubles, chararrays, and bytearrays. With the simple types, you'll find a range of arithmetic operators (such as add,subtract, multiply, divide, and module) in addition to a conditional operator called bincond that operates similar to the C ternaryoperator. And as you'd expect, a full suite of comparison operators, including rich pattern matching using regular expressions.

All Pig Latin statements operate on relations (and are called relational operators). As you saw in Listing 1, there's an operator for loading data from and storing data in the file system. There's a means to FILTER data by iterating the rows of a relation. This functionality is commonly used to remove data from the relation that is not needed for subsequent operations. Alternatively, if you need to iterate the columns of a relation instead of the rows, you can use the FOREACH operator. FOREACH permits nested operations such as FILTER and ORDER to transform the data during the iteration.

The ORDER operator provides the ability to sort a relation based on one or more fields. The JOIN operator performs an inner or outer join of two or more relations based on common fields. The SPLIT operator provides the ability to split a relation into two or more relations based on a user-defined expression. Finally, the GROUP operator groups the data in one or more relations based on some expression. 10.1 provides a partial list of relational operators in Pig.

Table 10.1. Incomplete list of Pig Latin Relational Operators

Operator	Description
FILTER	Select a set of tuples from a relation based on a condition.
FOREACH	Iterate the tuples of a relation, generating a data transformation.
GROUP	Group the data in one or more relations.
JOIN	Join two or more relations (inner or outer join).
LOAD	Load data from the file system.
ORDER	Sort a relation based on one or more fields.
SPLIT	Partition a relation into two or more relations.
STORE	Store data in the file system.

Although this isn't an exhaustive list of operators within Pig Latin, this table provides an extremely useful set of operations to process large data sets. You can learn about the complete Pig Latin language through Resources, as Pig has a nice set of online documentation. Now try your hand at writing some Pig Latin scripts to understand how these operators work in practice.

10.10 Pig in Local mode

For Local mode, simply start Pig and specify Local mode with the exectype option. Doing so brings you to the Grunt shell, which allows you to interactively enter Pig statements:

```
$ pig -x local
...
grunt>
```

From here, you can interactively code your Pig Latin script, seeing the result after each operator. Return to Listing 1 and try this script out (seeListing 2). Note in this case that instead of storing your data to a file, you simply dump it as a set of relations. You'll note in the modified output that each log line (that matches the search criteria defined by the FILTER) is itself a relation (bounded by parentheses [()]).

Examples:

Example 10.1: Hello Pig

Suppose you have a function, makeThumbnail(), that converts an image into a small thumbnail representation. You want to convert a set of images into thumbnails. A Pig Latin program to do this is:

```
images = load '/myimages' using myImageStorageFunc();
thumbnails = foreach images generate makeThumbnail(*);
store thumbnails into '/mythumbnails' using myImageStorageFunc();
```

The first line tells Pig: (1) what is the input to your computation (in this case, the content of the directory '/myimages'), and (2) how can Pig interpret the file and delineate individual images (in this case, by invoking myImageStorageFunc). (#2 is optional; if omitted, Pig will attempt to parse the file using its default parser.)

The second line instructs Pig to convert every image into a thumbnail, by running the user's makeThumbnail function on each image.

The third line instructs Pig to store the result into the directory '/mythumbnails', and encode the data into the file according to the myImageStorageFunc() function.

Most Pig Latin commands consist of an assignment to a variable (e.g., images, thumbnails). These variables denote tables, but these tables are not necessarily materialized on disk or in the memory of any one machine. The final "store" command causes Pig to compile the preceeding commands into an execution plan, e.g., one or more Map-Reduce jobs to execute on Hadoop. In the above example, the program will get compiled into a single Map-Reduce job where the Reduce phase is disabled, i.e., the output of the Map is the final output.

Example 10.2: Using the relational-style operations

Suppose you have a log of users visiting web pages, which has entries of the form (user, url, time). Say you want to compute the average number of page visits done by a user (e.g., if the answer is 4, that means that, on average, each user generated four page visit events in the log). Here's a Pig Latin program that computes this number:

```
VISITS = load '/visits' as (user, url, time);
USER_VISITS = group VISITS by user;
USER_COUNTS = foreach USER_VISITS generate group as user, COUNT(VISITS)
as numvisits;
ALL_COUNTS = group USER_COUNTS all;
AVG_COUNT = foreach ALL_COUNTS generate AVG(USER_COUNTS.numvisits);
dump AVG_COUNT;
```

The first line loads the data and specifies the schema. The "using" clause has been omitted because here we assuming the data is in a tab-delimited text format that Pig can parse by default. Since this data is multifaceted, we use the "as" clause to assign names to the data fields: user, url, time. The "as" clause is optional; if it is not used you can refer to the fields by position (e.g., $0 for user, $1 for url, $2 for time).

The second line forms groups of tuples, one group for each unique user. The third line computes the size of each group, i.e., the number of log events associated with each user.

The fourth line places all tuples output from the previous step into a single group, and the fifth line computes the average of these values, i.e., the average of the per-user counts. If you wanted, say, standard deviation instead of average, which at present is not a built-in Pig function, you could write your own function and referenced it in the "generate" clause in place of AVG.

Since the output is small (a single number), the user decided to use "dump" instead of "store" to produce the output. Dump causes the output to be printed to the screen, instead of written to a file. In general, we recommend that you use this command with caution 😐

Example 10.3: Combining multiple data sets

One of the key features of Pig is that you can combine multiple data sets using operations like join, union, cogroup. (These operations are explained in detail in our documentation.)

Suppose we have our web page visit log from Example 2, and we also have a file that records the pagerank of each URL in the known universe, including all URLs in the visit log. If you aren't familiar with pagerank, just think of it as a numeric quality score of each web page. (In this example we assume the pagerank values have been computed in advance; although the iterative pagerank computation can be expressed in Pig Latin with an outer Java function controlling the looping.) Say you want to identify users who tend visit "good" pages, defined in terms of average pagerank exceeding some threshold. Here it is in Pig Latin:

```
VISITS = load '/visits' as (user, url, time);
PAGES = load '/pages' as (url, pagerank);
VISITS_PAGES = join VISITS by url, PAGES by url;
USER_VISITS = group VISITS_PAGES by user;
USER_AVGPR = foreach USER_VISITS generate group, AVG(VISITS_PAGES.
pagerank) as avgpr;
GOOD_USERS = filter USER_AVGPR by avgpr > '0.5';
store GOOD_USERS into '/goodusers';
```

The first two lines load our two data sets (visits and pages). The third line specifies a join over the two sets -- it finds visits tuples that have the same URL as pages tuples, and glues them together. Hence the VISITS_PAGES table gives us the pagerank of the URL in each visit tuple.

The fourth line groups tuples by user, and the fifth line computes the average pagerank of each user's visited URLs.

The fifth line filters out users whose pagerank is not greater than 0.5.

After invoking the Grunt shell, you can run your Pig scripts in the shell. In addition to that, there are certain useful shell and utility commands provided by the Grunt shell. This chapter explains the shell and utility commands provided by the Grunt shell.

Note – In some portions of this chapter, the commands like Load and Store are used. Refer the respective chapters to get in-detail information on them.

10.11 GRUNT SHELL COMMANDS

The Grunt shell of Apache Pig is mainly used to write Pig Latin scripts. Prior to that, we can invoke any shell commands using **sh** and **fs**.

sh Command

Using **sh** command, we can invoke any shell commands from the Grunt shell. Using **sh**command from the Grunt shell, we cannot execute the commands that are a part of the shell environment (**ex** – cd).

Syntax

Given below is the syntax of **sh** command.

```
grunt> sh shell command parameters
```

Example

We can invoke the **ls** command of Linux shell from the Grunt shell using the **sh** option as shown below. In this example, it lists out the files in the **/pig/bin/** directory.

```
grunt> sh ls

pig
pig_1444799121955.log
pig.cmd
pig.py
```

fs Command

Using the **fs** command, we can invoke any FsShell commands from the Grunt shell.

Syntax

Given below is the syntax of **fs** command.

```
grunt> sh File System command parameters
```

Example 10.4 Invoking is command (HDFS) from Grunt shell

We can invoke the ls command of HDFS from the Grunt Shell using fs command. In the following example, it lists the files in the HDFS root directory.

```
Terminal
File  Edit  View  Terminal  Help
grunt> fs -ls
Found 15 items
drwx------    - biadmin biadmin          0 2016-03-21 08:25 .staging
-rw-r--r--    1 biadmin biadmin      21555 2016-03-04 09:16 DEMo
drwxr-xr-x    - biadmin biadmin          0 2016-02-12 06:36 Demo
drwx--x--x    - biadmin biadmin          0 2016-02-12 06:56 Demo2
drwxr-xr-x    - biadmin biadmin          0 2016-02-15 07:31 Dummy1
drwxrwxrwx    - biadmin biadmin          0 2016-03-11 06:55 HIveReport
drwxr-xr-x    - biadmin biadmin          0 2016-03-11 10:19 HiveReport
drwxr-xr-x    - biadmin biadmin          0 2014-07-24 20:38 WordCount
drwxr-xr-x    - biadmin biadmin          0 2014-07-24 20:36 credstore
drwx--x--x    - biadmin biadmin          0 2016-02-15 07:44 dummy1Out
drwx--x--x    - biadmin biadmin          0 2016-02-15 07:44 oozie-oozi
drwxr-xr-x    - biadmin biadmin          0 2016-03-07 10:38 shared_hive_data
-rw-r--r--    1 biadmin biadmin         10 2016-02-22 12:56 test.csv
drwxr-xr-x    - biadmin biadmin          0 2016-03-03 13:44 test2
drwxr-xr-x    - biadmin biadmin          0 2016-03-03 02:05 testing
grunt>
```

In the same way, we can invoke all the other file system shell commands from the Grunt shell using the **fs** command.

10.3.2 Utility Commands

The Grunt shell provides a set of utility commands. These include utility commands such as**clear, help, history, quit,** and **set**; and commands such as **exec, kill,** and **run** to control Pig from the Grunt shell. Given below is the description of the utility commands provided by the Grunt shell.

clear Command

The **clear** command is used to clear the screen of the Grunt shell.

Syntax

You can clear the screen of the grunt shell using the **clear** command as shown below.

```
grunt> clear
```

help Command

The **help** command gives you a list of Pig commands or Pig properties.

Usage

You can get a list of Pig commands using the **help** command as shown below.

```
grunt> help
Commands: <pig latin statement>; - See the PigLatin manual for details:
http://hadoop.apache.org/pig

File system commands:fs <fs arguments> - Equivalent to Hadoop dfs
command:
http://hadoop.apache.org/common/docs/current/hdfs_shell.html

Diagnostic Commands:describe <alias>[::<alias] - Show the schema for
the alias.
Inner aliases can be described as A::B.
    explain [-script <pigscript>] [-out <path>] [-brief] [-dot|-xml]
        [-param <param_name>=<pCram_value>]
        [-param_file <file_name>] [<alias>] -
       Show the execution plan to compute the alias or for entire script.
        -script - Explain the entire script.
       -out - Store the output into directory rather than print to stdout.
        -brief - Don't expand nested plans (presenting a smaller graph for
overview).
```

```
    -dot - Generate the output in .dot format. Default is text format.
    -xml - Generate the output in .xml format. Default is text format.
    -param <param_name - See parameter substitution for details.
    -param_file <file_name> - See parameter substitution for details.
    alias - Alias to explain.
   dump <alias> - Compute the alias and writes the results to stdout.
Utility Commands: exec [-param <param_name>=param_value] [-param_file
<file_name>] <script> -
     Execute the script with access to grunt environment including
aliases.
    -param <param_name - See parameter substitution for details.
    -param_file <file_name> - See parameter substitution for details.
    script - Script to be executed.
   run [-param <param_name>=param_value] [-param_file <file_name>]
<script> -
    Execute the script with access to grunt environment.
          -param <param_name - See parameter substitution for details.
    -param_file <file_name> - See parameter substitution for details.
    script - Script to be executed.
  sh  <shell command> - Invoke a shell command.
  kill <job_id> - Kill the hadoop job specified by the hadoop job id.
  set <key> <value> - Provide execution parameters to Pig. Keys and
values are case sensitive.
    The following keys are supported:
    default_parallel - Script-level reduce parallelism. Basic input
size heuristics used
    by default.
    debug - Set debug on or off. Default is off.
   job.name - Single-quoted name for jobs. Default is PigLatin:<script
name>
    job.priority - Priority for jobs. Values: very_low, low, normal,
high, very_high.
   Default is normal stream.skippath - String that contains the path.
    This is used by streaming any hadoop property.
  help - Display this message.
  history [-n] - Display the list statements in cache.
    -n Hide line numbers.
  quit - Quit the grunt shell.
```

history Command

This command displays a list of statements executed / used so far since the Grunt sell is invoked.

Usage

Assume we have executed three statements since opening the Grunt shell.

```
grunt> customers = LOAD 'hdfs://localhost:9000/pig_data/customers.txt'
USING PigStorage(',');

grunt> orders = LOAD 'hdfs://localhost:9000/pig_data/orders.txt' USING
PigStorage(',');

grunt>  student  =  LOAD  'hdfs://localhost:9000/pig_data/student.txt'
USING PigStorage(',');
```

```
grunt> customers = LOAD 'hdfs://localhost:9000/pig_data/customers.txt' USING PigStorage(',');
grunt> orders = LOAD 'hdfs://localhost:9000/pig_data/orders.txt' USING PigStorage(',');
grunt> student = LOAD 'hdfs://localhost:9000/pig_data/student.txt' USING PigStorage(',');
```

Then, using the **history** command will produce the following output.

```
grunt> history
1   customers = LOAD 'hdfs://localhost:9000/pig_data/customers.txt' USING PigStorage(',');
2   orders = LOAD 'hdfs://localhost:9000/pig_data/orders.txt' USING PigStorage(',');
3   student = LOAD 'hdfs://localhost:9000/pig_data/student.txt' USING PigStorage(',');
grunt>
```

set Command

The **set** command is used to show/assign values to keys used in Pig.

Usage

Using this command, you can set values to the following keys.

Key	Description and values
default_parallel	You can set the number of reducers for a map job by passing any whole number as a value to this key.
debug	You can turn off or turn on the debugging freature in Pig by passing on/off to this key.
job.name	You can set the Job name to the required job by passing a string value to this key.

job.priority	You can set the job priority to a job by passing one of the following values to this key – very_low low normal high very_high
stream.skippath	For streaming, you can set the path from where the data is not to be transferred, by passing the desired path in the form of a string to this key.

quit Command

You can quit from the Grunt shell using this command.

Usage

Quit from the Grunt shell as shown below.

```
grunt> quit
```

Let us now take a look at the commands using which you can control Apache Pig from the Grunt shell.

exec Command

Using the **exec** command, we can execute Pig scripts from the Grunt shell.

Syntax

Given below is the syntax of the utility command **exec**.

```
grunt> exec [-param param_name = param_value] [-param_file file_name]
[script]
```

Example

Let us assume there is a file named **student.txt** in the **/pig_data/** directory of HDFS with the following content.

Student.txt

```
001,Rajiv,Hyderabad
002,siddarth,Kolkata
003,Rajesh,Delhi
```

And, assume we have a script file named **sample_script.pig** in the **/pig_data/** directory of HDFS with the following content.

Sample_script.pig

```
student = LOAD 'hdfs://localhost:9000/pig_data/student.txt' USING
PigStorage(',')
  as (id:int,name:chararray,city:chararray);
 Dump student;
```

Now, let us execute the above script from the Grunt shell using the **exec** command as shown below.

```
grunt> exec /sample_script.pig
```

Output

The **exec** command executes the script in the **sample_script.pig**. As directed in the script, it loads the **student.txt** file into Pig and gives you the result of the Dump operator displaying the following content.

```
(1,Rajiv,Hyderabad)
(2,siddarth,Kolkata)
(3,Rajesh,Delhi)
```

kill Command

You can kill a job from the Grunt shell using this command.

Syntax

Given below is the syntax of the **kill** command.

```
grunt> kill JobId
```

Example

Suppose there is a running Pig job having id **Id_0055**, you can kill it from the Grunt shell using the **kill** command, as shown below.

```
grunt> kill Id_0055
```

run Command

You can run a Pig script from the Grunt shell using the **run** command

Syntax

Given below is the syntax of the **run** command.

```
grunt> run [-param param_name = param_value] [-param_file file_name]
script
```

Example

Let us assume there is a file named **student.txt** in the **/pig_data/** directory of HDFS with the following content.

Student.txt

```
001,Rajiv,Hyderabad
002,siddarth,Kolkata
003,Rajesh,Delhi
```

And, assume we have a script file named **sample_script.pig** in the local filesystem with the following content.

Sample_script.pig

```
student = LOAD 'hdfs://localhost:9000/pig_data/student.txt' USING
 PigStorage(',') as (id:int,name:chararray,city:chararray);
```

Now, let us run the above script from the Grunt shell using the run command as shown below.

```
grunt> run /sample_script.pig
```

You can see the output of the script using the **Dump operator** as shown below.

```
grunt> Dump;
(1,Rajiv,Hyderabad)
(2,siddarth,Kolkata)
(3,Rajesh,Delhi)
```

Note – The difference between **exec** and the **run** command is that if we use **run**, the statements from the script are available in the command history.

BigSheets : Spreadsheet like Environment

BigSheets uses a spreadsheet-like interface that can model, filter, combine, and chart data collected from multiple sources, such as an application that collects social media data by crawling the Internet.

Data is categorized and formatted by creating *master workbooks*, read-only representations of your complete original data set. From these master workbooks, you can derive *child workbooks*, editable versions of the master workbooks in which you can create specific sheets to manipulate and analyze your data.

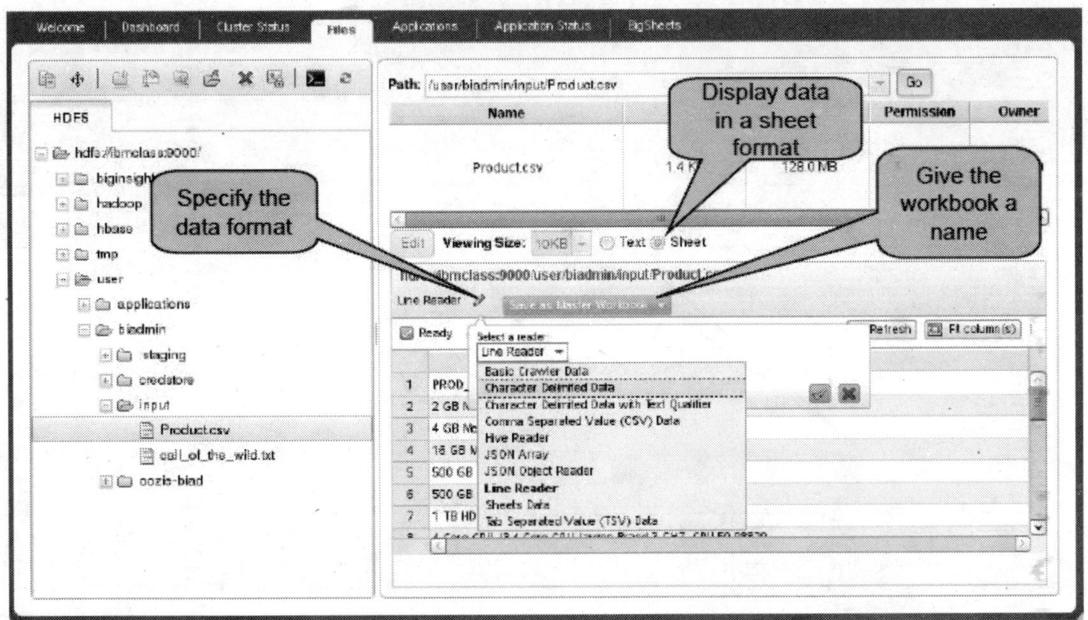

BigSheets workbooks

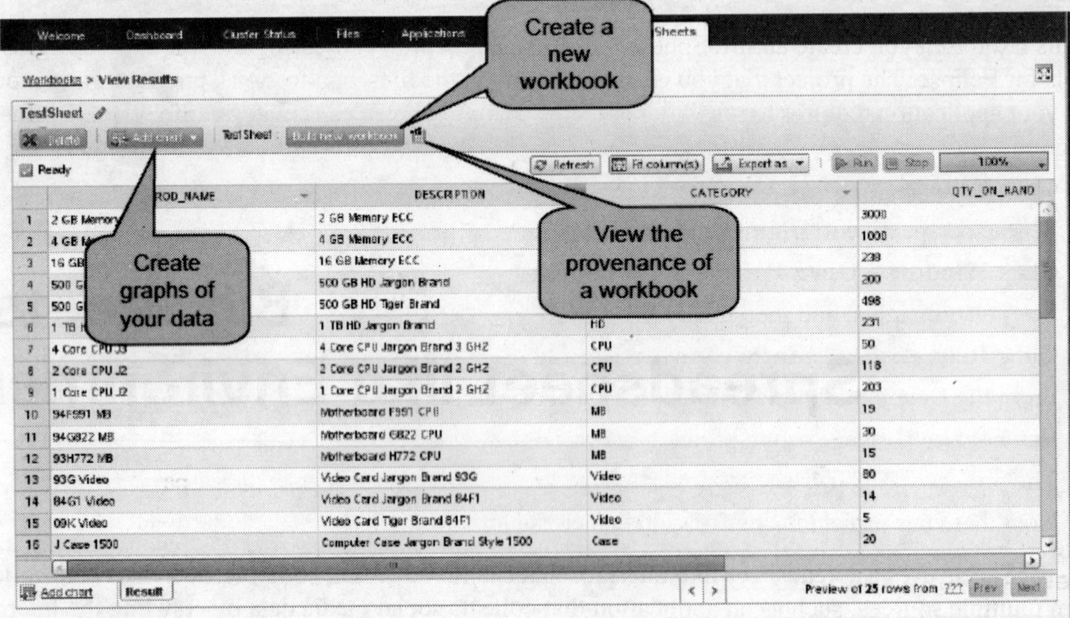

Manipulation of data in BigSheets

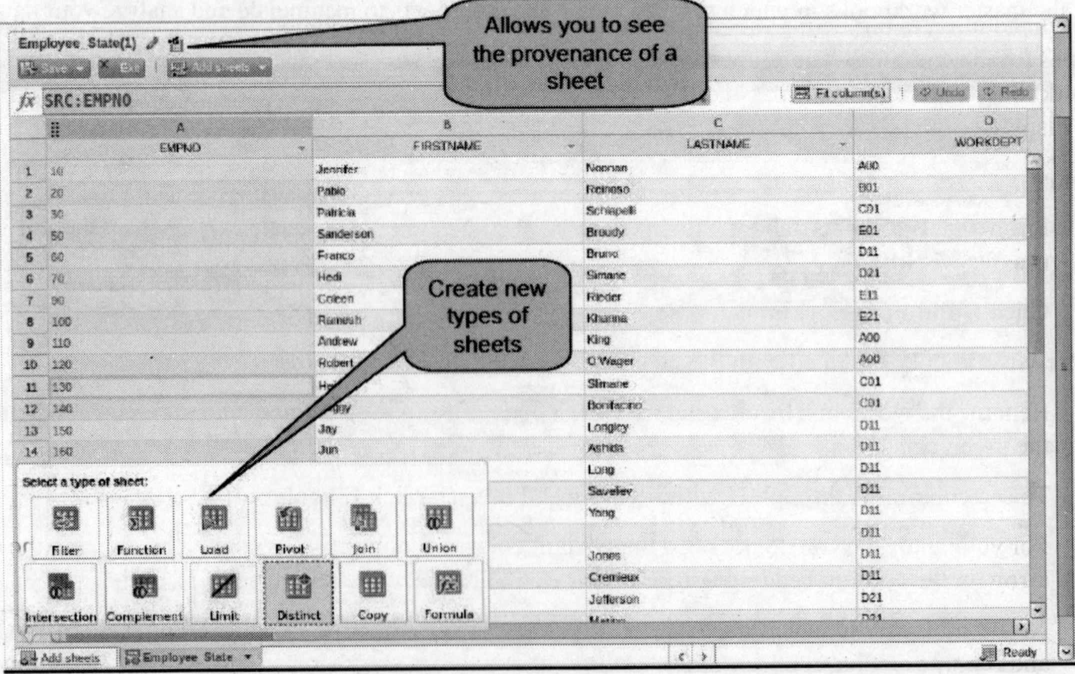

EXERCISE 11.1: Creating An InfoSphere BigInsights Project

In this Exercise , you create an InfoSphere® BigInsights™ project by using the InfoSphere BigInsights Tools for Eclipse. The project that you create will contain the files, applications, programs, and modules that your application requires to run. After you create a project, you can create an InfoSphere BigInsights program.

Open **Eclipse**.

Set the perspective to BigInsights.

Click **Window > Open Perspective > Other.**

Select BigInsights, and then click OK.

Click **Help > Task Launcher for Big Data to open the Task Launcher for Big Data.**

From the Develop tab, under Quick Links, click **Create a new BigInsights project.**

Enter **WriteMessage** as the project name, and then click **Finish**.

The project that you created, WriteMessage, displays in the Project Explorer pane.

Now that your project is created, you can create a program.

Exercise 20.2: Tailoring Your Data By Creating Child Workbooks

Typically, before you analyze and explore data, you must tailor its format and content. In this Exercise , you create child workbooks from each master workbook and remove unwanted columns to refine the amount and type of your data.

In addition to protecting the original data, master workbooks set the data format (including the data types for the columns). Therefore, you must create child workbooks in which to modify your data. Child workbooks inherit their format and data from their master workbooks, but you can tailor their attributes to display only necessary data.

Start

1. From the **BigSheets** tab of the InfoSphere® BigInsights™ Console, select the **Watson_News master workbook**.

2. Click **Build new workbook.**

A new workbook is created with the name: Watson_News(1).

3. Rename the workbook by clicking the **Edit** icon ( ), entering **Watson News Revised**, and clicking the green check mark ( ).

4. To see columns A through H within your web browser, click **Fit column(s)**.

5. For your analysis, you do not need the IsAdult column (column E). Remove it by clicking the down arrow in the column heading and selecting Remove.

   Notice all the column actions that are available to you in the drop-down list. You can rename, hide, and remove a column; insert a new column; sort the data in a column; and organize the columns.

When you remove columns from a child workbook, you delete only the data from the child workbook. The master workbook on which this child workbook is based always contains the original data as it was loaded. If you decide later that you want the IsAdult data in your analysis, you can create another child workbook from the Watson_News master workbook.

When you hide a column, the data in that column is still included when you run the workbook or create a chart. The only way to remove the data from the analysis or chart is to remove the column.

6. As you review the data in this Watson News Revised child workbook, you decide that you do not need several other columns. You can use the same method, as in the previous step, to remove them one at a time or remove multiple columns at once:

   a) Click the down arrow in any column heading, and select Organize Columns.

   b) Click the red X (✖) next to the following columns to mark them for removal:

   - Crawled
   - Inserted
   - MoveoverUrl
   - PostSize

   c) Click the green check mark (✔) to remove the columns.

   Tip: If you accidentally remove more columns than you intend, you can click Undo to undo your last action.

7. Click **Fit column(s) to resize the remaining columns**. You now see columns A through

A	B	C	D	E	F	G	H
Country	FeedInfo	Language	Published	SubjectHtml	Tags	Type	Url

8. Save and exit the workbook by clicking Save and selecting Save & Exit. If you are prompted with a Save workbook window, you can save the workbook with or without entering a description.

9. You are prompted with the message "`This workbook has never been run. Press Run to run it or Close to dismiss this message`". Click **Run**. You see a progress indicator in the upper right corner of the window.

   Until now, you have been working with a subset of the Watson and internal IBM data. BigSheets keeps only a limited number of rows in memory. The lower right corner displays a message that indicates you are seeing only a simulated sample of 50 rows of data. When you run the data, you apply all changes that you made since the last time you saved the workbook to the full data set.

   The progress bar monitors the progress of the job. Behind the scenes, Pig scripts initiate MapReduce jobs. The runtime performance depends upon the volume of data that is associated with your data collection and the system resources that are available.

10. Now, create a child workbook from the Watson_Blogs master workbook, and remove the columns that are not needed for your analysis:

a) To return to the page that displays all your workbooks, click the Workbooks link.

b) Select the **Watson_Blogs master workbook**, and click Build new workbook. A new workbook is created with the name: Watson_blogs(1).

Notice that the Watson News Revised workbook has a child workbook icon ( ) that looks like a mini spreadsheet next to it, whereas the Watson_Blogs and Watson_News master workbooks have a different icon ( ) that looks like a lock that requires a key over the spreadsheet image, indicating that the master workbook is read-only. You can quickly distinguish master workbook from child workbooks by these icons.

(c) Rename the new child workbook by clicking the Edit icon ( ), typing `Watson Blogs` Revised, and clicking the green check mark ( ).

(d) Use the Organize Columns function to remove the following columns:

- Crawled
- Inserted
- IsAdult
- PostSize

Remember to select the green check mark in the Organize Columns window. Now, the `Watson News Revised` and `Watson Blogs Revised` workbooks contain the same columns. To merge workbooks, each workbook must contain the same data types and columns, or *schema*.

(e) Save and exit the workbook.

(f) When prompted, click Run to apply the changes that you made to the child workbook.

Outcome

Because both new child workbooks have the same schema, you can merge them into a new workbook, where you can explore and analyze your data.

EXERCISE 11.2: Combining The Data From Two Workbooks

In this Exercise , you combine the data from the two child workbooks into a single data collection. By merging the data, you have a central place to explore, analyze, and chart the coverage of the IBM Watson™ data.

To merge the data, create a new workbook from an existing workbook, then load the data from the second workbook into the new workbook.

Start

1. In the InfoSphere® BigInsights™ Console, click the **BigSheets** tab, and select the **Watson News Revised workbook.**
2. Click **Build new workbook.** The name of the workbook is Watson News Revised(1), indicating that it is a child workbook of Watson News Revised. You change the name of this workbook later when you save and exit the workbook.

3. Click **Add sheets**, and select **Load**.

   Each type of sheet provides different predefined logic for analyzing data. Use the Load sheet to include the data of another workbook as a sheet in the current workbook.

4. In the Load window, select the **Watson Blogs Revised** workbook link from the list of existing workbooks.
5. In the **Sheet Name** field, enter `Watson Blogs Revised`. In the Load window, you see details of the columns and the first few rows of data in that workbook.
6. Click the green check mark ( ). At the bottom of your workbook, you see two tabs, Watson News Revised and Watson Blogs Revised.
7. Click **Add sheets, and select Union**.
8. In the Sheet Name field of the New sheet: Union dialog, enter `News and Blogs` to indicate that this sheet contains the merged data.
9. From the **Select sheet drop-down** list, select the Watson News Revised sheet, click the green plus sign ( ) to add the sheet (you see the sheet move to the bottom of the dialog). From the **Select sheet drop-down** list, select the Watson Blogs Revised sheet, click the green plus sign ( ) to add the sheet (you see the sheet move to the bottom of the dialog). Then click the green check mark ( ) to add both sheets. Your workbook now displays the new tab, News and Blogs, at the bottom of your screen.
10. Click **Save.** When prompted for a name and description, enter `Watson News Blogs` in the Name field and `Combined news and blogs data` in the Description text box, and click Save.

EXERCISE 11.3: Creating Columns By Grouping Data

In this Exercise , you learn how to create columns by grouping similar information. You want to discover how many news articles and blog posts are written in each language. You accomplish this goal by using the Group sheet and its functions to combine, calculate, and sort the language data.

First, use the Calculate function to count the number of articles and posts by language. Then, sort the column by language to display the most popular languages first.

1. Make sure that the Watson News Blogs workbook is open. If the workbook is not open, from the BigSheets tab, click the **Edit link next to Watson News Blogs**. Clicking the Edit link opens the selected workbook in edit mode, so you do not have to click the Edit icon ( ).
2. Click **Add Sheets**, and select **Group**.
3. In the **New sheet: Group window,** complete the required information:

   a. In the Sheet name field, enter `Group by language.`

   b. From the Group by columns drop-down list, select Language, and click the green plus sign ( ) to add the column. The Language column name displays in the bottom of the dialog.

   c. At the bottom of the window, click the Calculate tab.

d. In the Create columns based on groups text box, enter `NumberArticlesandPosts`, and click the green plus sign ( ).

e. From the NumberArticlesandPosts drop-down list, select **COUNT**.

f. From the Column drop-down list, **select Language**, then click the green check mark ( ).

On the Group by language sheet, you see two columns, Language and NumberArticlesandPosts. The Language column displays all the languages from the News and Blogs sheet. The NumberArticlesandPosts column counts the number of posts in each language.

4. To see the most common languages for posts about IBM Watson™, sort the Group sheet by the number of posts. Click the drop-down arrow to the right of the NumberArticlesandPosts column, select **Sort**, and select **Descending**. You see that English is the most popular language with 3169 posts, followed by Russian, Spanish, and Chinese - Simple. But notice that Chinese (spelling) and Chinese - Traditional are also near the top of the list. You combine these values into one Chinese language value later when you create a chart.

5. Click **Save > Save & Exit** to save and close the workbook.

6. Click **Run** to save, sort, and process the entire data set for the workbook. You see a progress indicator in the upper right corner of the window. After you run the workbook, you see different Outcomes for the number of English posts in the NumberArticlesandPosts column, `5464`.

EXERCISE 11.4: Viewing Data In Bigsheets Diagrams

In this Exercise , you view diagrams in BigSheets to understand the relationships between workbooks and sheets and the process of modifying data in a workbook.

The Workbook Diagram ( ) beside a child workbook shows the sheets and processes that created the selected workbook, the relationships between workbooks, and on which master or child workbook the current workbook is based.

The Workflow Diagram ( ) shows how you used the Watson Blogs Revised and Watson News Revised child workbooks to create the Watson News Blogs workbook. You can also see the source (master workbook) for each child workbook.

Start

1. From the **Watson News Blogs workbook**, click the **Workflow Diagram** icon ( ).
2. When you are finished looking at the diagram, click the red X ( ) in the upper right corner.
3. Click the **Workbook Diagram** icon ( ). In the diagram, you can see the types of sheets and history of the current workbook.
4. When you are finished looking at the diagram, click the red in the upper right corner.

Outcome

You now know how the two diagrams in BigSheets can help you visualize the relationships between workbooks and sheets and the process of creating a workbook. Now you are ready to explore and analyze the data in the Watson News and Blogs workbook.

EXERCISE 11.5 : Visualizing And Refining The Outcomes In Charts

In this Exercise , you visualize the Outcomes of the sorted and combined Watson blogs and news data in the Watson News Blogs workbook by creating a simple horizontal bar chart. Then, you refine your chart to improve your data.

BigSheets provides various charts and maps. A *chart* plots data points in a grid, such as a typical pie or bar chart. A *cloud* shows the importance of values by displaying the size of the words relative to their importance. A *map* contains charts that represent geographic data, such as a heat map that shows the concentration of data points geographically.

Start

1. Open the Watson News Blogs workbook, click Add chart, and then select **chart > Horizontal Bar.**
2. In the New chart: Horizontal Bar window, enter or select the following values:
   a. In the Chart Name field, enter `Language Coverage`. The chart name is the name that displays on the tab at the bottom of the worksheet.
   b. In the Title field, enter `IBM Watson Coverage by Language`. The title of the chart displays at the top of the chart.
   c. From the X Axis drop-down list, select NumArticlesandPosts.
   d. In the X Axis Label, enter `Number of posts`.
   e. From the Y Axis drop-down list, select `Language`.
   f. In the Y Axis Label, enter `Language of post`.
   g. From the Sort By drop-down list, select X Axis. You want to sort by the number of posts.
   h. From the Occurrence Order drop-down list, select Descending. You want to see the language with the highest number of posts first.
   i. In the Limit field, enter 12. You want to see only the top 12 languages by the number of posts.
   j. Leave the Template and Style default values.
   k. Click the green check mark (✓) to preview the chart with sample data.
3. Click Run to generate the chart from the full set of workbook data. Even though you see the preview chart immediately, the actual chart is not displayed until you see 100% on the progress bar. It might take some time to generate the chart from the full set of data. Use the progress bar to monitor the status of the completed chart.

After the bar chart is generated, you can see that Russian is the second most popular language for posts. You also see that the fifth and sixth most popular languages are variations on the Chinese language. By combining these values, Chinese is actually the second most popular language for posts. This situation is common, especially when you combine data from various sources such as different social media sites.

4. To clean up the data, combine the Chinese languages and post numbers:
   a. Click **Edit**. You return to the Group by language sheet.

b. Select the **News and Blogs sheet** by clicking the tab name at the bottom of the window.

c. Insert a new column by clicking the down arrow next to the Language column and selecting Insert **Right > New Column**.

d. Enter `Language_Revised` for the name of the new column, and then click the green check mark (✓) to create the column. Your cursor moves to the fx (or function) area, where you provide the function to generate the contents of the new column.

e. Enter the following formula as the function `IF(SEARCH('Chin*', #Language) >0, 'Chinese', #Language)`, and click the green check mark (✓) to apply the formula and generate the values for the new Language Revised column.

   This formuia searches the Language column (indicated by *`#column_name`*) for any value that starts with Chin and combines those values into one value in the Language Revised column. The wildcard asterisk character ensures that all variations of the Chinese language, regardless of spelling or words that follow the word *Chinese* (such as Chinese Simple), are included. If the value does not start with `Chin`, then the formula copies the value, as is, into the Language Revised column.

   To understand how to use the BigSheets functions, and to see some examples of using formulas, see Formulas.

f. Change the settings for the Group by language sheet to use the new column by clicking the down arrow next to the Group by language sheet and selecting Sheet Settings.

g. In the **Group** window, from the **Group by Columns** drop-down list, select **Language_Revised,** and click the green plus sign (+) to add the column.

h. Click the **red X** (✗) next to the Language column to remove it. You want to group and calculate the number of posts by the Language_Revised column instead of the Language column.

i. Click the **Calculate** tab. In the Column drop-down list, select **Language_Revised**.

j. Click the green check mark (✓) to apply your changes.

   The new Language_Revised column replaces the Language column to the right of the NumArticlesandPosts column. Click the B at the top of the Language_Revised column and drag it to the left of the NumArticlesandPosts column.

5. Click **Save > Save & Exit**, then click **Run to update the entire data set for the workbook**.

6. Click the **Language Coverage** sheet, and you see a message that `An error occurred while sampling the chart`. You updated the Group by language chart to use the Language_Revised column, but the current Language Coverage chart is based on the Language column.

7. Click **OK** to close the error message.

8. Delete the previous Language Coverage chart by clicking the triangle to the right of the Language Coverage sheet, and selecting **Delete chart**.

9. Click Add chart, and select chart > Horizontal Bar to create another chart that is based on the updated data.

10. In the New chart: **Horizontal Bar** window, enter or select the following values:
    a. In the Chart Name field, enter `Language Coverage`. The chart name is the name that displays on the tab at the bottom of the worksheet.
    b. In the Title field, enter `IBM Watson Coverage by Language`. The title of the chart displays at the top of the chart.
    c. From the X Axis drop-down list, select NumArticlesandPosts.
    d. In the X Axis Label, enter `Number of posts`.
    e. From the Y Axis drop-down list, select `Language_Revised`.
    f. In the Y Axis Label, enter `Language of post`.
    g. From the Sort By drop-down list, select X Axis. You want to sort by the number of posts.
    h. From the Occurrence Order drop-down list, select Descending. You want to see the language with the highest number of posts first.
    i. In the Limit field, enter `12`.
    j. Click the green check mark ( ) to preview the chart with sample data.
11. Click Run to generate a new chart. After the chart completes, all Chinese languages are combined into one bar in the bar chart, which shows Chinese as the second most popular language for posts and Russian as the third. If you hover over the bars in the chart, you can see the actual numbers of posts.

Outcome

You used BigSheets to generate a simple horizontal bar chart from your social media data collections. You also analyzed the bar chart and refined the data to determine the 12 most commonly used languages to generate posts about IBM Watson™.

EXERCISE 11.6: Exporting Data From Your Workbooks

In this Exercise , you export the data from the Watson News and Blogs workbook into a web browser tab and a CSV file.

You might want to share the Outcomes of your BigSheets analysis with colleagues who do not have direct access to IBM® InfoSphere® BigInsights™. You can export your analysis Outcomes in various data formats, including CSV (comma-separated values), JSON Array, and TSV (tab-separated values).

You can also export the data to a new web browser tab or to the Hadoop Distributed File System (HDFS). Or you can save the data, if your privileges include saving files to the cluster.

Start

1. If the Watson News Blogs workbook is not open, open it. From the **BigSheets** tab, select **Watson News Blogs**. Do not click Edit to open the workbook in Edit mode. You cannot export workbooks from Edit mode. If you do open the workbook in Edit mode, you see Add sheets instead of Export data.

2. Export your data to a browser tab:
   a. Click **Export data**. The Export to option is set by default to Browser Tab.
   b. Click **OK** to export the Outcome sheet data into a new tab on your web browser.
3. Click the **IBM InfoSphere BigInsights** tab in your web browser to return to the InfoSphere BigInsights Console and the Watson News Blogs workbook.
4. Export your data to a CSV file:
   a. Click Export data again.
   b. In the Format Type drop-down list, select CSV, which produces a comma-separated value file.
   c. In the Export data option, select File.
   d. Click Browse and enter or select the following parameters:
      i. Set the path by opening the main hdfs:// folder and selecting the tmp folder.
      ii. In the file name text box at the bottom of the window, enter watson_news_blogs as the file name, then click OK. File names can contain spaces. Avoid entering special characters in the file name.
   e. Select the Include Headers check box to include column names in the file. This option is available only if you selected either CSV or TSV format.
   f. Click **OK**. You receive a message that the `Workbook has been successfully exported`. Click OK to close the message. You can check your Outcomes by clicking the Files tab and opening the main hdfs:// folder and then the tmp folder. You see the watson_news_blogs.csv file listed.

Outcome

You just exported the Outcomes of the Watson News Blogs workbook into both a web browser tab and a CSV file on your distributed file system (DFS) cluster.

CHAPTER

12

Big SQL : The IBM's NoSql

12.1 REFRESHING SQL

SQL is Structured Query Language, which is a computer language for storing, manipulating and retrieving data stored in relational database. SQL is the standard language for Relation Database Management System (RDBMS). All relational database management systems like MySQL, MS Access, Oracle, Sybase, Informix, postgres and SQL Server use SQL as standard database language. RDBMS stands for **R**elational **D**atabase **M**anagement **S**ystem. RDBMS is the basis for SQL and for all modern database systems like MS SQL Server, IBM DB2, Oracle, MySQL, and Microsoft Access.

12.2 THE BIG PICTURE ABOUT BIG SQL

Big SQL is a software layer that enables IT professionals to create tables and query data in InfoSphere BigInsights using familiar SQL statements. To do so, programmers use standard SQL syntax and, in some cases, SQL extensions created by IBM to make it easy to exploit certain Hadoop-based technologies.

To give you an idea of what Big SQL is all about, Figure 12.1 illustrates its architecture and how it fits into the InfoSphere BigInsights Enterprise Edition V2.1 platform.

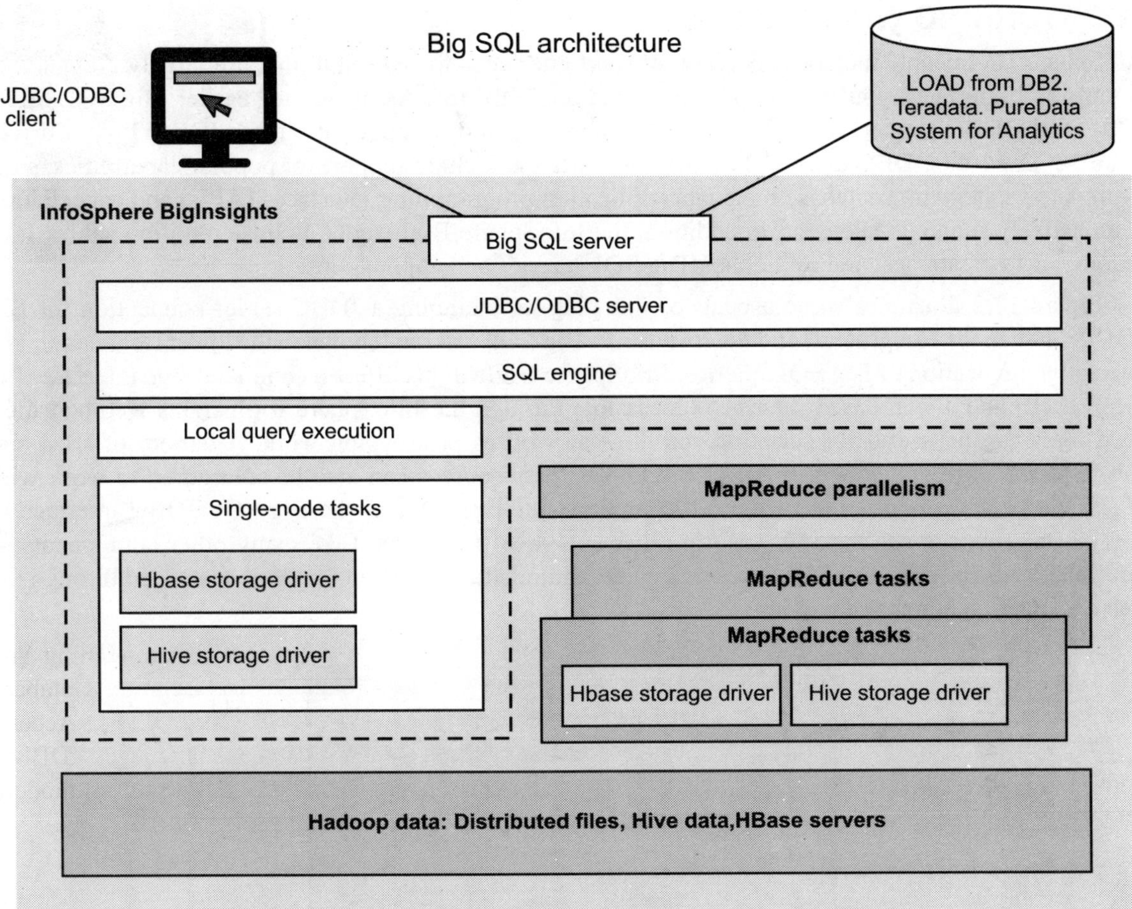

Figure. 12.1: Relationship between BigSQL and BigInsight

In such situations and others, Big SQL can play an important role. However, it's inappropriate to think of Big SQL as a replacement for relational DBMS technology. Big SQL was designed to complement and leverage the Hadoop-based infra-structure in InfoSphere BigInsights. Certain features common in relational DBMSs aren't present in Big SQL, and certain Big SQL features aren't present in most relational DBMSs. For example, Big SQL supports querying data but does not support SQL UPDATE or DELETE statements. INSERT statements are supported only for HBase tables. Big SQL tables may contain columns of complex data types such as struct and array, rather than simply "flat" rows. Furthermore, several underlying storage mechanisms are supported, including:

1. Delimited files, such as comma-separated files, stored in HDFS or GPFS-FPO
2. Hive tables in sequence file format, RCFile format and so on; Hive is Hadoop's data warehouse implementation
3. HBase tables; HBase is Hadoop's key-value or column-based data store

Let's explore Big SQL in greater detail so you can get a better idea of its capabilities.

12.3 WORKING WITH BIG SQL

InfoSphere BigInsights includes several tools and interfaces for Big SQL that are largely comparable to tools and interfaces you'll find with most relational DBMSs. As mentioned earlier, Big SQL offers JDBC and ODBC support to Java, C and C++ application developers through a JDBC Type 4 driver and a 32- or 64-bit ODBC driver. These Big SQL drivers include support for popular capabilities, such as prepared statements, database metadata application programming interfaces (APIs) and cancellation of an actively running statement. In addition, the InfoSphere BigInsights Eclipse plug-in enables Java developers to create, test and refine their Big SQL queries and applications.

Figure 12.2 illustrates some aspects of this plug-in, including a JDBC server connection for Big SQL (shown in the foreground) and the results of a Big SQL test run (shown in the lower right pane). For interactive invocation of Big SQL queries, InfoSphere BigInsights offers a command-line interface (the JSqsh shell) and a web-based interface (accessible through the InfoSphere BigInsights web console). Such tools can be useful for scripting activities as well as prototyping work. A variety of IBM and non-IBM software that supports JDBC and ODBC data sources can also be configured to work with Big SQL. As an example, IBM Cognos® Business Intelligence uses the Big SQL JDBC interface to query data, generate reports and perform other analytical functions. Like many other components of InfoSphere BigInsights, Big SQL is a service that administrators launch (or stop) as needed through the web console or a command window.

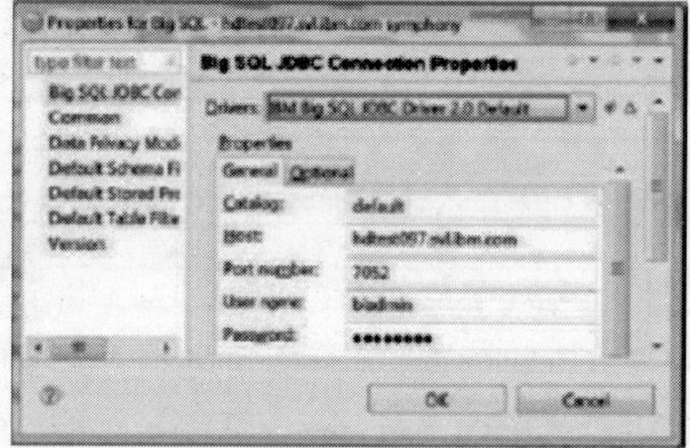

Results of a Big SQL test run are shown in the lower right pane.

12.4 BIG SQL ON HADOOP

Big SQL, a component of InfoSphere BigInsights, IBM's big data platform based on Apache Hadoop. In particular, you'll use Big SQL to query traditional structured data as well as data derived from social media sites.

Big SQL enables IT professionals to create tables and query data in BigInsights using familiar SQL statements. To do so, programmers use standard SQL syntax and, in some cases, SQL extensions created by IBM to make it easy to exploit certain Hadoop-based technologies. Big SQL shares query compiler technology with DB2 (a relational DBMS) and, as such, offers a wide breadth of SQL capabilities.

Organizations interested in Big SQL often have considerable SQL skills in-house, as well as a suite of SQL-based business intelligence applications and query/reporting tools. The idea of being able to leverage existing skills and tools — and perhaps reuse portions of existing applications — can be quite appealing to organizations new to Hadoop. Indeed, some companies with large data warehouses built on relational DBMS systems are looking to Hadoop-based platforms as a potential target for offloading "cold" or infrequently used data in a manner that still allows for query access. In other cases, organizations turn to Hadoop to analyze and filter non-traditional data (such as logs, sensor data, social media posts, etc.), ultimately feeding subsets or aggregations of this information to their relational warehouses to extend their view of products, customers, or services.

12.4.1. Pre-requisites

Before beginning this Exercise, you should have a working BigInsights environment launched with a Big SQL 3.0 server active. You must be able to log into your system with an account that has administrative privileges. Prior knowledge of industry-standard SQL is useful.

This Exercise was developed for the InfoSphere BigInsights 3.0 Quick Start Edition VMware image. As such, its Exercise exercises are based on the following information:

	User	Password
VM Image root account	root	password
VM Image Exercise user account	biadmin	biadmin
BigInsights Administrator	biadmin	biadmin
Big SQL Administrator	bigsql	bigsql
Exercise user	biadmin	password

Property	Value
Host name	bivm.ibm.com
BigInsights Web Console URL	http://bivm.ibm.com:8080
Big SQL database name	bigsql
Big SQL port number	51000

12.4.2 Launching VMware image

1. Launch the VMware image. When logging in for the first time, use the root ID (with a password of password). Follow the instructions to configure your environment, accept the licensing agreement, and enter the passwords for the root and biadmin IDs (root/password and biadmin/biadmin) when prompted. This is a one-time only requirement.

2. When the one-time configuration process is completed, you will be presented with a SUSE Linux log in screen. By default Hadoop uses this Linux environment. Log in as below:

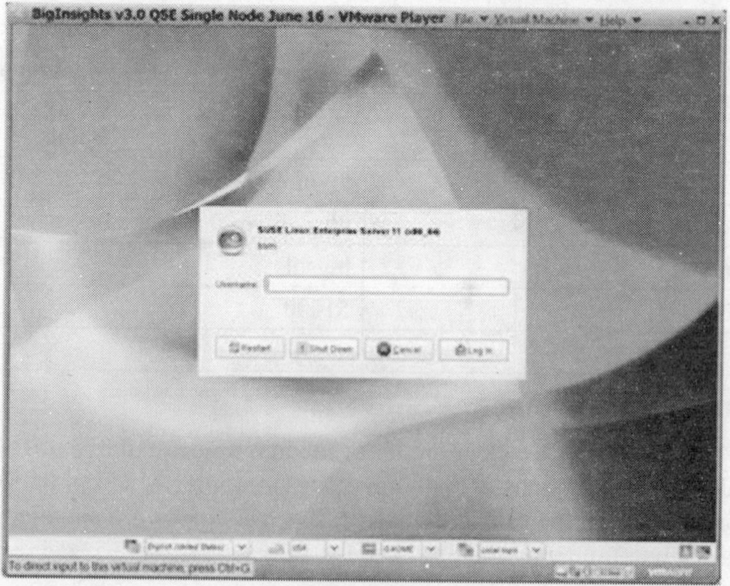

3. Enter username as **biadmin** to get another screen prompting you to enter the password.
4. Enter the password as **password**.

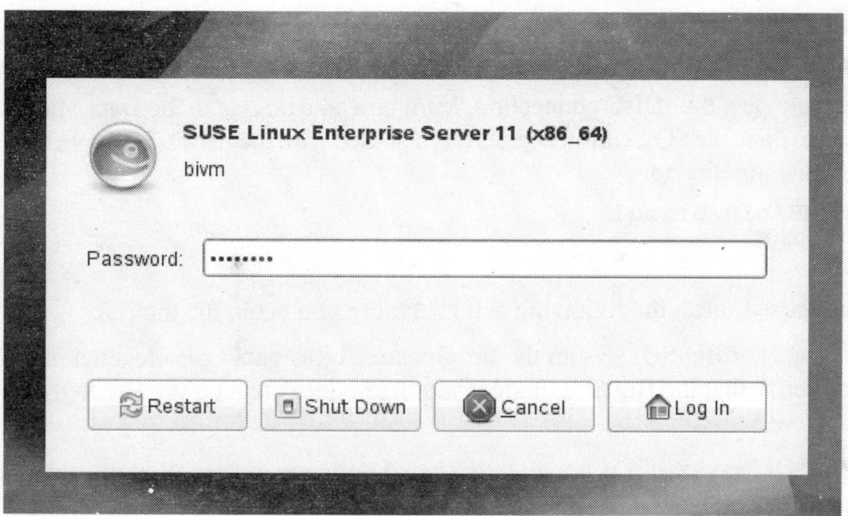

5. Verify that your screen appears similar to this:

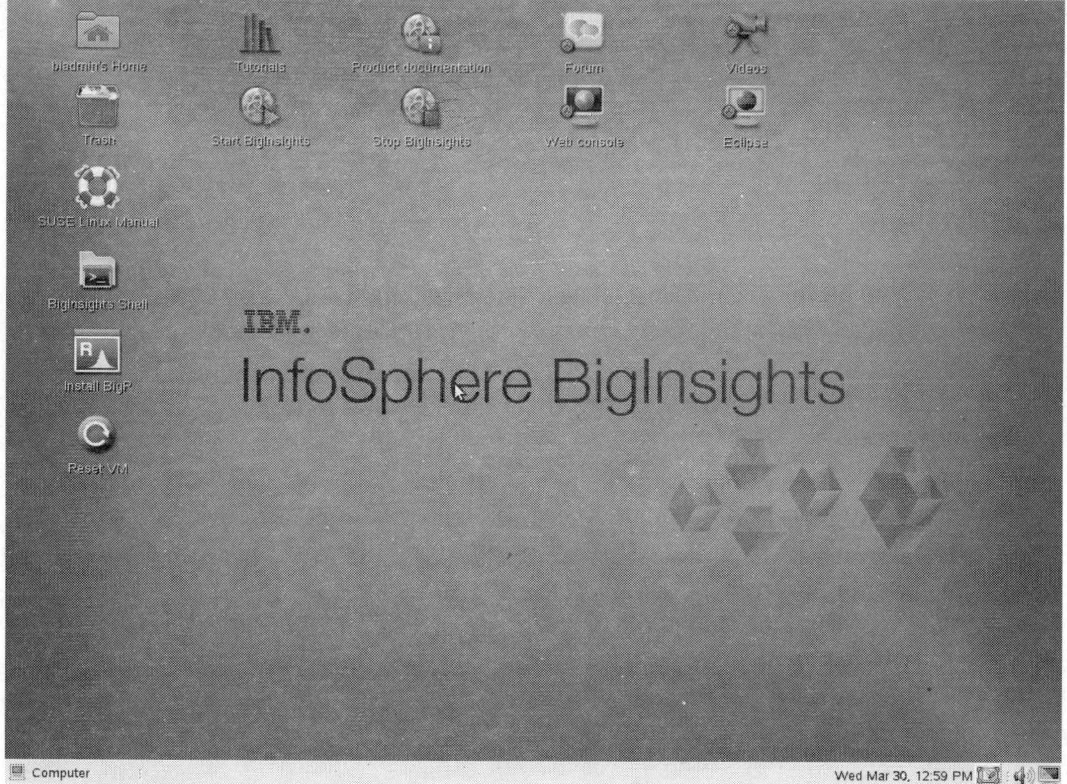

Your VMware image is now ready to use for this Excercise.

EXERCISE 12.1 : CONNECTING TO THE IBM BIG SQL SERVER

In this exercise, you view the JDBC connection, learn how to navigate to the Data Management view in Eclipse, and how to open the SQL editor. Big SQL is installed with the IBM® InfoSphere® BigInsights™ product in the following directory :

```
$BIGSQL_HOME/bin/bigsql.
```

Prerequisites

Ensure that you complete the following actions before you begin the tutorial:

1. Review the status of Big SQL. From the InfoSphere BigInsights Console, click the **Cluster Status** page. Then, verify that the Big SQL node is in a `Running` state on the Big SQL Server Summary page.
2. Start the Big SQL service if it is not already started with one of the following actions:

   From the command-line type the following command:

```
<$BIGSQL_HOME>/bin/bigsql start
```

Tip: $BIGSQL_HOME usually refers to **/opt/ibm/biginsights/bigsql.**

From the InfoSphere BigInsights Console

1. Click the **Cluster Status** page.
2. Select Big SQL Server and click **Start** in the Big SQL Server Summary page if the Big SQL server is not started.
3. From the InfoSphere BigInsights Console **Welcome** page, find the Quick Links section, and click **Enable your Eclipse development environment for BigInsights application development**.
4. Choose one of the options to install the InfoSphere BigInsights Tools for Eclipse based on whether you want to install from the web server directly or download an archive with the plug-ins to your computer first.
5. Start **Eclipse**, and complete the instructions in Installing the InfoSphere BigInsights Tools for Eclipse to add theInfoSphere BigInsights Tools for Eclipse.
6. Ensure that a JDBC driver definition exists. Generally, either a JDBC or an ODBC driver definition must exist before you can create a connection to a Big SQL server. For the purposes of this tutorial, only a JDBC driver definition is required.

If you created an InfoSphere BigInsights server connection to a particular InfoSphere BigInsights server, the Big SQLJDBC driver connection and the Big SQL JDBC connection profile were both created for you automatically.

Procedures

1. From the IBM InfoSphere BigInsights Eclipse environment, click **Window** > **Open Perspective** > **Other** > **Database Development**. Ensure that the **Data Source Explorer** view is open.

2. From the **Data Source Explorer** view, expand the `Database Connections` folder.
3. Right-click the **Big SQL** connection, and select **Properties**. Verify the host name and other connection information.
4. Click **Test Connection** to make sure that you have a valid connection to the Big SQL server. If you do not have a connection, follow these steps:
   a. From the **Data Source Explorer** view, right-click the **Database Connections** directory and click **Add Repository**.
   b. In the New Connection Profile window, select `Big SQL JDBC` in the **Connection Profile Types** list.
   c. Optional: Edit the text in the **Name** field or the **Description** field, and click **Next**.
   d. Optional: In the Specify a Driver and Connection Details window, select a Big SQL Driver from the Drivers list. You can add or modify a driver by clicking the **New Driver Definition** icon or the **Edit Driver Definition** icon.
   e. On the **General** page, complete the connection properties:

Schema

Use the default name, which is `default`, or specify a valid schema or database name. The catalog (`syscat`) stores the valid schema and database names.

Host : The name of the host where the Big SQL server is running, such as **my.server.com**

Port number : The port number that is used by the Big SQL server. The default port number is 7052.

User name : The name of the user ID that is used to connect to the Big SQL server.

Password : The password that is associated with the user name.

Note: If the InfoSphere BigInsights server is installed with security, you must provide a valid InfoSphere BigInsights user ID and password to connect when you use the Big SQL JDBC driver. Otherwise, enter any user ID and password in the **User name** and **Password** fields to enable the **Finish** or **Next** and **Test Connection** buttons. For example, you can type the following information:

User name : user

Password : user

1. Specify the **Save password** check box to save the password for the Big SQL server login.
2. The **Connection URL** field displays the URL that is generated. For example,

   ```
   jdbc:bigsql://<host_name>:7052/default
   ```

3. If the Big SQL server is configured with SSL authentication, open the **Optional** page to view or add an SSL property according to the `$BIGSQL_HOME/bigsql/conf/bigsql-conf.xml` configuration file from the target Big SQL server.
4. Specify the **Connect when the wizard completes** check box to connect to the Big SQL server after you finish defining this connection profile.
5. Specify the **Connect every time the workbench is started** to connect to the Big SQL server automatically by using this connection profile when you launch this Eclipse workspace.

6. Click **Test Connection** to ping the server and to verify that the connection profile is working.
7. Click **Finish** to create the connection profile. For information about how to create a simple JDBC application that opens a database connection, and runs a Big SQL query.

EXERCISE 12.2 : Using The Big SQL Command Line Interface (JSqsh)

BigInsights supports a command-line interface for Big SQL through the Java SQL Shell (JSqsh, pronounced "jay-skwish"). JSqsh is an open source project for querying JDBC databases. You may find it handy to become familiar with basic JSqsh capabilities, particularly if you don't expect to have access to an Eclipse environment at all times for your work.

In this exercise, you will learn how to

1. Verify that the Biginsights services are running from the Web Console.
2. Launch JSqsh.
3. Issue Big SQL queries.
4. Issue popular JSqsh commands to get help, retrieve your query history, and perform other functions.

12.2.1. Launching the Web Console to verify BigInsights services are up and running

1. Select the **Start BigInsights** icon to start all services. (Alternatively, you can open a terminal window and issue this command:

```
$BIGINSIGHTS_HOME/bin/start-all.sh)
```

Wait until the operation completes. This may take several minutes, depending on your machine's resources.

2. Verify that all required BigInsights services are up and running, including Big SQL.

   (a)Launch the BigInsights Web console.(Direct your browser to http://bivm.ibm.com:8080 or select the Web Console icon on your desktop.)

   (b) Log in with your user name and password.

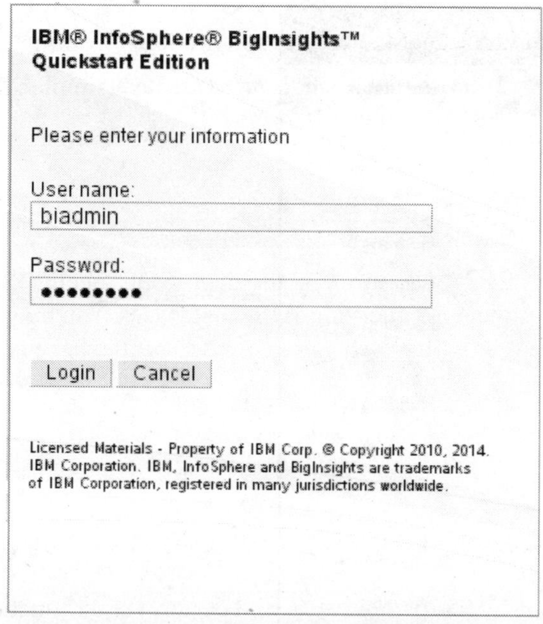

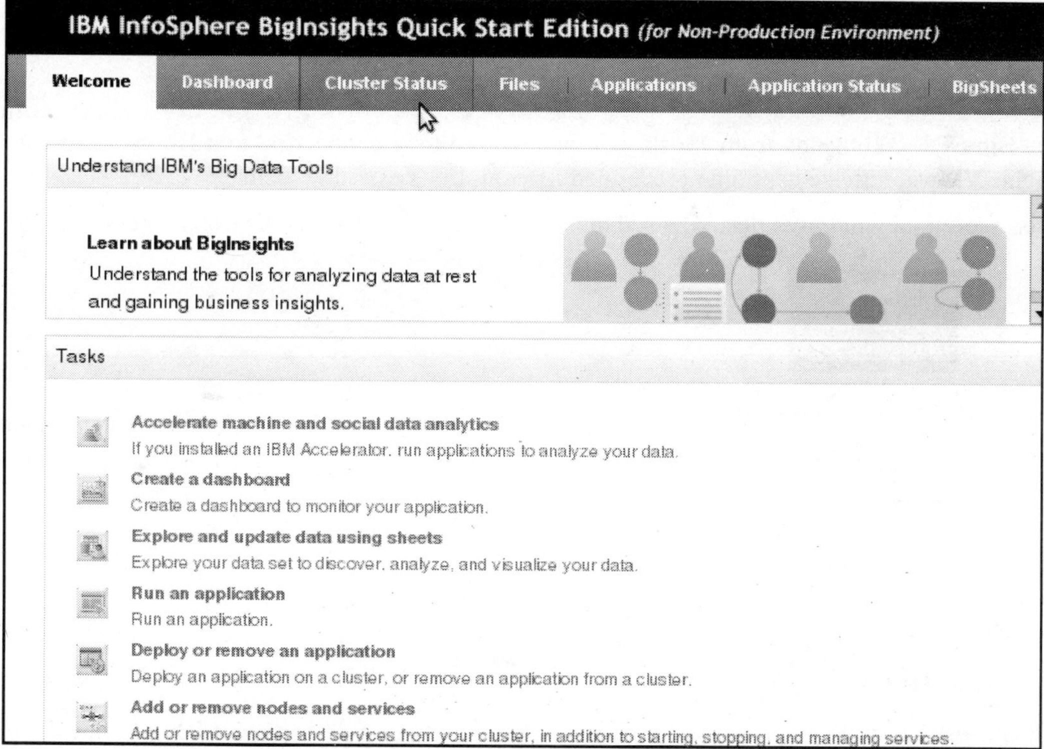

(c) Click on the Cluster Status tab to inspect the running services. Monitoring and Alert services do not need to be active for this Exercise.

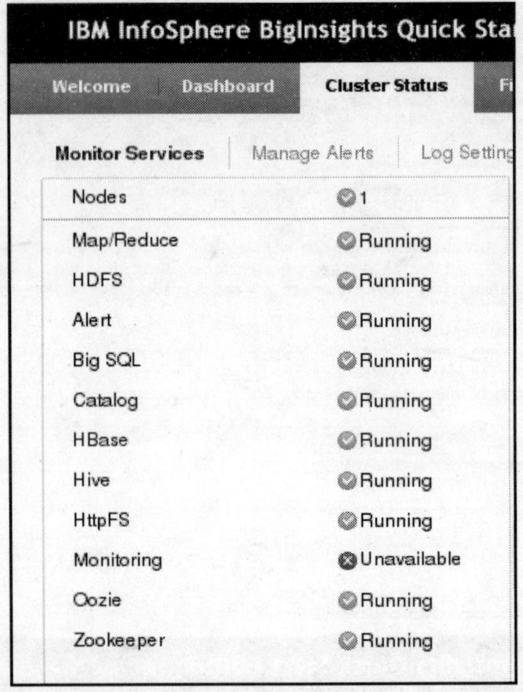

12.2.2. Understanding JSqsh connections

To issue Big SQL commands from JSqsh, you need to define a connection to a Big SQL server. The BigInsights VMware image has some predefined for you. Let's examine them.

1. Open a terminal window.If desired, used the desktop icons.First, open the **BigInsights Shell** folder.

Then, click on **Terminal** icon.

2. Launch the JSqsh shell.

$JSQSH_HOME/bin/jsqsh

3. If this is the first time you launched JSqsh, a welcome screen will display. When prompted, enter c to launch the connection wizard.

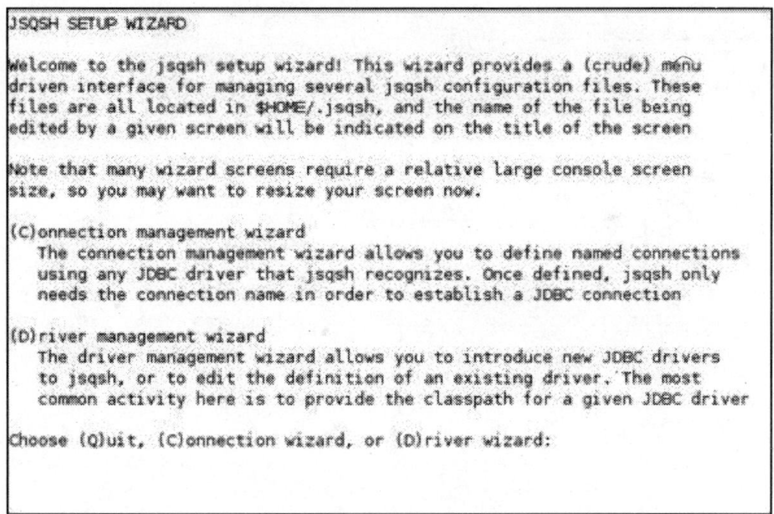

In the future, you can enter 'setup connections in the JSqsh shell to invoke this wizard.

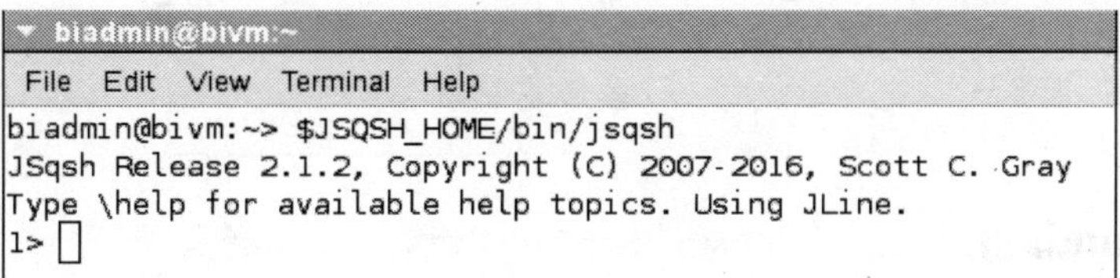

4. Inspect any existing connections in your environment.

\setup connections

Remember that in above command we have used reverse slash.

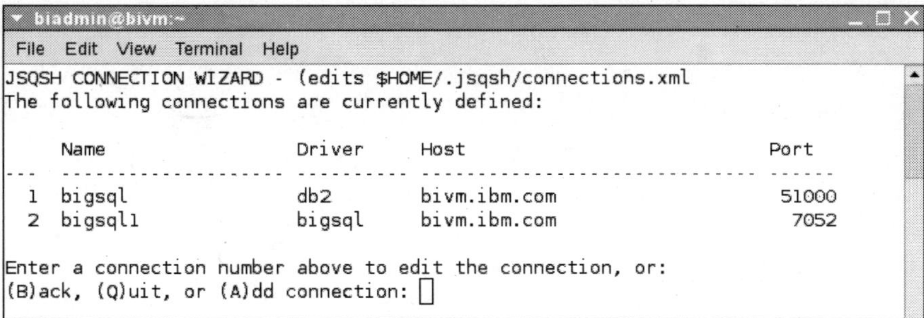

Throughout this exercise, you will work with the bigsql database at port 51000, which is accessible through the DB2 JDBC driver provided with BigInsights.

5. Examine the connection details for bigsql. Provide the connection number displayed by the wizard (in this case, 1) and press **Enter**.

```
biadmin@bivm:~
File  Edit  View  Terminal  Help
JSQSH CONNECTION WIZARD - (edits $HOME/.jsqsh/connections.xml)

The following configuration properties are supported by this driver.

    Connection name : bigsql
             Driver : IBM Data Server (DB2, Informix, Big SQL)
           JDBC URL : jdbc:db2://${server}:${port}/${db}

Connection URL Variables
------------------------
1                db : BIGSQL
2              port : 51000
3            server : bivm.ibm.com
4              user : biadmin
5          password :
6       Autoconnect : false

JDBC Driver Properties
------------------------
None

Enter a number to change a given configuration property, or
(T)est, (D)elete, (B)ack, (Q)uit, Add (P)roperty, or (S)ave:
```

Note: that the Big SQL database name is a constant; it was defined during the installation of BigInsights.

6. Enter t to test your configuration.

```
Enter a number to change a given configuration property, or
(T)est, (D)elete, (B)ack, (Q)uit, Add (P)roperty, or (S)ave: t

Attempting connection...
Password: ********
```

You will be prompted to enter the password. Enter passwors as password.

7. You will be prompted to enter the password. Enter **passwors** as password.
8. Verify that the test succeeded, and press **Enter**.

```
Enter a number to change a given configuration property, or
(T)est, (D)elete, (B)ack, (Q)uit, Add (P)roperty, or (S)ave: t

Attempting connection...
Password: ********
WARN [State:      ][Code: 0]: Statement processing was successful.. SQLCODE=0,
QLSTATE=     , DRIVER=3.67.33
Succeeded!

Hit enter to continue:
```

9. Exit this current session. Enter **q** and then quit.

```
Enter a number to change a given configuration property, or
(T)est, (D)elete, (B)ack, (Q)uit, Add (P)roperty, or (S)ave: Q
1>
```

12.2.3. Optional: Creating your own database connection

The BigInsights Quick Start Edition VMware image is pre-configured with a connection to your Big SQL server with access for the biadmin account. However, you can also create your own JSqsh connections to Big SQL. This can be handy if you want to test capabilities available to different user accounts on your platform.

In this portion of exercise, you'll learn how to create a Big SQL database connection in JSqsh.

1. If necessary, open a terminal window and launch the JSqsh shell.

   $JSQSH_HOME/bin/jsqsh

2. Invoke the setup wizard by entering the 'setup connections command.

   \setup connections

3. When prompted, enter a to add a connection.

```
biadmin@bivm:~
File  Edit  View  Terminal  Help
JSQSH CONNECTION WIZARD - (edits $HOME/.jsqsh/connections.xml
The following connections are currently defined:

      Name                  Driver      Host                            Port
---  --------------------  ----------  ------------------------------  ------
  1  bigsql                db2         bivm.ibm.com                     51000
  2  bigsql1               bigsql      bivm.ibm.com                      7052

Enter a connection number above to edit the connection, or:
(B)ack, (Q)uit, or (A)dd connection:
```

4. Inspect the list of drivers displayed by the wizard by pressing A (for Add connection), and note the number for the db2 driver (not the db2zos driver).Depending on the size of your command window, you may need to scroll up to see the full list of drivers. In the screen capture below, the correct DB2 driver is 2. The order of your drivers may differ, as pre-installed drivers are listed first.

```
biadmin@bivm:~
File  Edit  View  Terminal  Help

JSQSH CONNECTION WIZARD - (edits $HOME/.jsqsh/connections.xml)

Choose a driver for use by your new connection

    Name             Target                Class
--- ---------------- --------------------- --------------------------------------
-------------
  1 *bigsql          IBM Big SQL v1        com.ibm.biginsights.bigsql.jdbc.BigSQL
Driver
  2 *db2             IBM Data Server (DB2 com.ibm.db2.jcc.DB2Driver

  3 *db2zos          IBM DB2 z/OS          com.ibm.db2.jcc.DB2Driver

  4 *hive            Apache Hive           org.apache.hadoop.hive.jdbc.HiveDriver

  5 *hive2           Apache Hive           org.apache.hive.jdbc.HiveDriver

  6 *jdbcodbc        JDBC ODBC Bridge      sun.jdbc.odbc.JdbcOdbcDriver

  7  derby           Apache Derby Server  org.apache.derby.jdbc.ClientDriver

  8  derbyembed      Apache Derby Embedde org.apache.derby.jdbc.EmbeddedDriver
```

NOTE

Note : You may be wondering why we have used the DB2 driver rather than the Big SQL driver. In 2014, IBM released a common SQL query engine as part of its DB2 and BigInsights offerings. Doing so provides for greater SQL commonality across its relational DBMS and Hadoop-based offerings. It also brings a greater breadth of SQL function to Hadoop (BigInsights) users. This common query engine is accessible through the "DB2" driver listed. The Big SQL driver remains operational and offers connectivity to an earlier, BigInsights-specific SQL query engine. This Exercise focuses on using the common SQL query engine.

5. At the prompt line, enter the number of the DB2 driver.
6. The connection wizard displays some default values for the connection properties and prompts you to change them.(Your default values may differ from those shown below.)

```
biadmin@bivm:~
File  Edit  View  Terminal  Help
JSQSH CONNECTION WIZARD - (edits $HOME/.jsqsh/connections.xml)

The following configuration properties are supported by this driver.

    Connection name : _temp_
             Driver : IBM Data Server (DB2, Informix, Big SQL)
           JDBC URL : jdbc:db2://${server}:${port}/${db}

Connection URL Variables
------------------------
1                 db : changeme
2               port : 50000
3             server : localhost
4               user : biadmin
5           password :
6        Autoconnect : false

JDBC Driver Properties
------------------------
None

Enter a number to change a given configuration property, or
(T)est, (B)ack, (Q)uit, Add (P)roperty, or (S)ave:
```

7. Change each variable as needed, one at a time.To do so, enter the variable number and specify a new value when prompted.For example, to change the value of the password variable (which is null by default)

1. Specify variable number 5 and press **Enter**.
2. Enter the password value and press **Enter.**

```
Enter a number to change a given configuration property, or
(T)est, (B)ack, (Q)uit, Add (P)roperty, or (S)ave: 5

Please enter a new value:
password: ****
```

3. You may like to change the user instead of biadmin to say your name (in this case) vkjain Enter.

```
Enter a number to change a given configuration property, or
(T)est, (B)ack, (Q)uit, Add (P)roperty, or (S)ave: 4

Please enter a new value:
user: vkjain
```

4. Change the port number from 50000 to 51000 by entering the variable as 2 for port value.

```
File  Edit  View  Terminal  Help
The following configuration properties are supported by this driver.

    Connection name : _temp_
             Driver : IBM Data Server (DB2, Informix, Big SQL)
           JDBC URL : jdbc:db2://${server}:${port}/${db}

Connection URL Variables
------------------------
1                db : changeme
2              port : 50000
3            server : localhost
4              user : vkjain
5          password : ****
6       Autoconnect : false

JDBC Driver Properties
------------------------
None

Enter a number to change a given configuration property, or
(T)est, (B)ack, (Q)uit, Add (P)roperty, or (S)ave: 2

Please enter a new value:
port: 51000
```

From above snapshot of the screen you can see that user name is already changed as vkjain and password is also might have changed but you cannot see the same as against password **** is mentioned but you can guess something that only four stars are shown as you changed the password as hina that contains only for letters. Press Enter Key.

5. Now you may like to change the db name from **changeme** to **bigsql.** Enter 1 to make the change.

```
File  Edit  View  Terminal  Help
JSQSH CONNECTION WIZARD - (edits $HOME/.jsqsh/connections.xml)

The following configuration properties are supported by this driver.

    Connection name : _temp_
             Driver : IBM Data Server (DB2, Informix, Big SQL)
           JDBC URL : jdbc:db2://${server}:${port}/${db}

Connection URL Variables
------------------------
1                db : changeme
2              port : 51000
3            server : localhost
4              user : vkjain
5          password : ****
6       Autoconnect : false

JDBC Driver Properties
------------------------
None

Enter a number to change a given configuration property, or
(T)est, (B)ack, (Q)uit, Add (P)roperty, or (S)ave: 1
```

```
Enter a number to change a given configuration property, or
(T)est, (B)ack, (Q)uit, Add (P)roperty, or (S)ave: 1

Please enter a new value:
db: bigsql
```

6. Inspect the variable settings that are displayed again to verify your change.

Repeat this process as needed for each variable that needs to be changed. In particular, you may need to change the values for the db (database), port, and server variables.

After making all necessary changes, the variables should reflect values that are accurate for your environment. Here is an example of a connection created for the bigsql user account (password hina) that will connect to the database named "bigsql" at port 51000 on the localhost server.

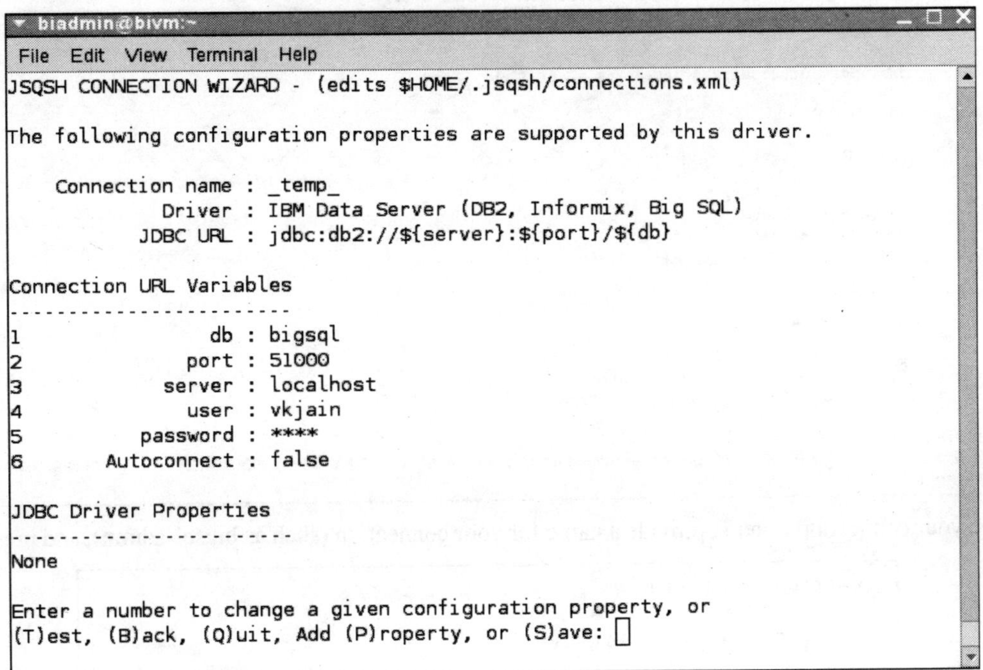

7. Enter t to test your configuration.

```
Enter a number to change a given configuration property, or
(T)est, (B)ack, (Q)uit, Add (P)roperty, or (S)ave: t

Attempting connection...
Failed!
SQL Exception(s) Encountered:
[State: 28000][Code: -4214]: Unable to connect via JDBC url 'jdbc:db2://localhost:51000/bigsql'
ed.  Reason: User ID or Password invalid. ERRORCODE=-4214, SQLSTATE=28000

Hit enter to continue:
```

The failure is due to our changing the username as explained below:

NOTE

Note : The Big SQL database is defined during the installation of BigInsights. The default is bigsql. In addition, a Big SQL database administrator account is also defined at installation. This account has SECADM (security administration) authority for Big SQL. By default, that user account is bigsql.

8. Enter **t** to test your configuration.So once again change the username to bigsql.
9. Verify that the test succeeded, and hit **Enter**.

```
File  Edit  View  Terminal  Help
JSQSH CONNECTION WIZARD - (edits $HOME/.jsqsh/connections.xml)

The following configuration properties are supported by this driver.

    Connection name : _temp_
             Driver : IBM Data Server (DB2, Informix, Big SQL)
           JDBC URL : jdbc:db2://${server}:${port}/${db}

Connection URL Variables
-------------------------
1                db : bigsql
2              port : 51000
3            server : localhost
4              user : bigsql
5          password : ******
6       Autoconnect : false

JDBC Driver Properties
-------------------------
None

Enter a number to change a given configuration property, or
(T)est, (B)ack, (Q)uit, Add (P)roperty, or (S)ave: t

Attempting connection...
WARN [State:      ][Code: 0]: Statement processing was successful.. SQLCODE=0, SQLSTATE=      , DRIVER=3.67.33
Succeeded!
```

10. Save your connection.Enter s, provide a name for your connection (such as bigsql-admin), and press **Enter**.

```
Connection URL Variables
-------------------------
1                db : bigsql
2              port : 51000
3            server : localhost
4              user : bigsql
5          password : ******
6       Autoconnect : false

JDBC Driver Properties
-------------------------
None

Enter a number to change a given configuration property, or
(T)est, (B)ack, (Q)uit, Add (P)roperty, or (S)ave: s

Please provide a connection name: bigsql_admin
```

11. Finally, quit the connection wizard when prompted.(Enter q.)

```
File   Edit   View   Terminal   Help
JSQSH CONNECTION WIZARD - (edits $HOME/.jsqsh/connections.xml
The following connections are currently defined:

     Name                 Driver     Host                              Port
---  -------------------- ---------- --------------------------------- ------
  1  bigsql               db2        bivm.ibm.com                       51000
  2  bigsql1              bigsql     bivm.ibm.com                        7052
  3  bigsql_admin         db2        localhost                          51000

Enter a connection number above to edit the connection, or:
(B)ack, (Q)uit, or (A)dd connection:
```

12.2.4. Getting Help for JSqsh

Now since you're familiar with JSqsh connections, you're ready to work further with the shell.

1. Launch the JSqsh shell from a terminal without any parameters

   $JSQSH_HOME/bin/jsqsh

2. Verify that the JSqsh command prompt of 1> appears.

3. Type **\help** to display a list of available help categories.

```
4> $JSQSH_HOME/bin/jsqsh
5> \help
Available help categories. Use "\help <category>" to display topics within that category
+----------+------------------------------------------+
| Category | Description                              |
+----------+------------------------------------------+
| commands | Help on all avaiable commands            |
| vars     | Help on all avaiable configuration variables |
| topics   | General help topics for jsqsh            |
+----------+------------------------------------------+
5>
```

4. Optionally, type **\help commands** to display help for supported commands. A partial list of supported commands is displayed on the initial screen.

```
1> \help commands
Available commands. Use "\help <command>" to display detailed help for a given c
ommand
+-----------+----------------------------------------------------------------+
| Command   | Description                                                    |
+-----------+----------------------------------------------------------------+
| \alias    | Creates an alias                                               |
| \buf-appen | Appends the contents of one SQL buffer into another           |
| d         |                                                                |
| \buf-copy | Copies the contents of one SQL buffer into another             |
| \buf-edit | Edits a SQL buffer                                             |
| \buf-load | Loads an external file into a SQL buffer                       |
| \call     | Call a prepared statement                                      |
| \connect  | Establishes a connection to a database.                        |
| \create   | Generates a CREATE TABLE using table definitions               |
| \databases | Displays set of available databases (catalogs)                |
| \debug    | (Internal) Used to enable debugging                            |
| \describe | Displays a description of a database object                    |
| \diff     | Compares results from multiple sessions                        |
| \drivers  | Displays a list of JDBC drivers known by jsqsh.                |
| \echo     | Displays a line of text.                                       |
| \end      | Ends the current session                                       |
| \eval     | Read and execute an input file full of SQL                     |
| \globals  | Displays all global variables                                  |
--More--
```

Press the space bar to display the next page or **q** to quit the display of help information.

5. Enter quit to exit the JSqsh shell.

EXERCISE 12.3: Issuing JSqsh Commands and Big SQL Queries

In this Exercise, you will execute some simple JSqsh commands and Big SQL queries so that you can become familiar with the JSqsh shell.

1. Launch the JSqsh shell and connect to your Big SQL server by specifying the connection name on the command line. When prompted, enter your password.

   $JSQSH_HOME/bin/jsqsh bigsql

```
biadmin@bivm:~> $JSQSH_HOME/bin/jsqsh bigsql
Password:*********
WARN [State:      ][Code: 0]: Statement processing was successful.. SQLCODE=0,
QLSTATE=      , DRIVER=3.67.33
JSqsh Release 2.1.2, Copyright (C) 2007-2016, Scott C. Gray
Type \help for available help topics. Using JLine.
[bivm.ibm.com][biadmin] 1>
```

2. Type **\show tables -e | more** to display essential information about all available tables one page at a time. The structure of your output will be similar to the results shown below, although the specific information will vary depending on the tables available in your environment. Press **space bar** to continue scrolling or **q** to stop scrolling.

```
biadmin@bivm:~
File  Edit  View  Terminal  Help
+------------+-------------+-----------------------------------+-------------+
| TABLE_CAT  | TABLE_SCHEM | TABLE_NAME                        | TABLE_TYPE  |
+------------+-------------+-----------------------------------+-------------+
| [NULL]     | SYSPUBLIC   | DUAL                              | ALIAS       |
| [NULL]     | SYSIBM      | SYSATTRIBUTES                     | SYSTEM TABLE |
| [NULL]     | SYSIBM      | SYSAUDITEXCEPTIONS                | SYSTEM TABLE |
| [NULL]     | SYSIBM      | SYSAUDITPOLICIES                  | SYSTEM TABLE |
| [NULL]     | SYSIBM      | SYSAUDITUSE                       | SYSTEM TABLE |
| [NULL]     | SYSIBM      | SYSBUFFERPOOLNODES                | SYSTEM TABLE |
| [NULL]     | SYSIBM      | SYSBUFFERPOOLS                    | SYSTEM TABLE |
| [NULL]     | SYSIBM      | SYSCHECKS                         | SYSTEM TABLE |
| [NULL]     | SYSIBM      | SYSCODEPROPERTIES                 | SYSTEM TABLE |
| [NULL]     | SYSIBM      | SYSCOLAUTH                        | SYSTEM TABLE |
| [NULL]     | SYSIBM      | SYSCOLCHECKS                      | SYSTEM TABLE |
| [NULL]     | SYSIBM      | SYSCOLDEPENDENCIES                | SYSTEM TABLE |
| [NULL]     | SYSIBM      | SYSCOLDIST                        | SYSTEM TABLE |
| [NULL]     | SYSIBM      | SYSCOLGROUPDIST                   | SYSTEM TABLE |
| [NULL]     | SYSIBM      | SYSCOLGROUPDISTCOUNTS             | SYSTEM TABLE |
| [NULL]     | SYSIBM      | SYSCOLGROUPS                      | SYSTEM TABLE |
| [NULL]     | SYSIBM      | SYSCOLGROUPSCOLS                  | SYSTEM TABLE |
| [NULL]     | SYSIBM      | SYSCOLLATIONS                     | SYSTEM TABLE |
| [NULL]     | SYSIBM      | SYSCOLOPTIONS                     | SYSTEM TABLE |
| [NULL]     | SYSIBM      | SYSCOLPROPERTIES                  | SYSTEM TABLE |
--More--
```

3. Next, cut and paste the following command into JSqsh to create a simple Hadoop table:

```
Create hadoop table test1 (col1 int, col2 varchar(5));
```

```
[bivm.ibm.com][biadmin] 1> create hadoop table test1 (col1 int, col2 varchar(5));
0 rows affected (total: 1m41.55s)
[bivm.ibm.com][biadmin] 1>
```

Because you didn't specify a schema name for the table it was created in your default schema, which is your user name. This is equivalent to

```
Create hadoop table yourID.test1 (col1 int, col2 varchar(5));
```

where *yourID* is your user name.

NOTE

Note 1. We've intentionally created a very simple Hadoop table for this exercise so that you can concentrate on working with JSqsh. In later modules, you'll learn more about CREATE TABLE options supported by Big SQL. For example, you'll learn about the LOCATION clause of CREATE TABLE. In these examples, where LOCATION is omitted, the default Hadoop directory path for these tables are at /biginsights/hive/warehouse/<schema>.db/<table>.

Note 2. Big SQL 3.0 enables users with appropriate authority to create their own schemas by issuing a command such as create schema if not exists testschema;

Note 3. Authorized users can then create tables in that schema as desired. Furthermore, users can also create a table in a different schema, and if it doesn't already exist it will be implicitly created.

4. Display all user tables (avoiding views and system tables) with the \tables user command. Note that with this command you may also see tables defined by other users, but you won't have the privileges to query them.

\tables user

```
[bivm.ibm.com][biadmin] 2> \tables user
+-------------+-------------------+------------+
| TABLE_SCHEM | TABLE_NAME        | TABLE_TYPE |
+-------------+-------------------+------------+
| BIADMIN     | TEST1             | TABLE      |
| SYSTOOLS    | HMON_ATM_INFO     | TABLE      |
| SYSTOOLS    | HMON_COLLECTION   | TABLE      |
| SYSTOOLS    | POLICY            | TABLE      |
+-------------+-------------------+------------+
[bivm.ibm.com][biadmin] 2>
```

5. If your output contains too many user tables from other users, you can narrow your results by specifying a schema with the command \tables –s BIADMIN. The schema name should be provided in upper case since it will be used directly to filter the list of tables.

\tables -s BIADMIN

```
[bivm.ibm.com][biadmin] 2>     \tables -s BIADMIN
+-------------+------------+------------+
| TABLE_SCHEM | TABLE_NAME | TABLE_TYPE |
+-------------+------------+------------+
| BIADMIN     | TEST1      | TABLE      |
+-------------+------------+------------+
[bivm.ibm.com][biadmin] 2>
```

6. Try inserting a row into your table.

Insert into test1 values(1, 'one');

```
[bivm.ibm.com][biadmin] 1> insert into test1 values(1, 'one');
1 row affected (total: 47.35s)
[bivm.ibm.com][biadmin] 1>
```

This form of the INSERT statement (INSERT INTO … VALUES ….) should be used for test purposes only because the operation will not be parallelized on your cluster. To populate a table with data in a manner that exploits parallel processing, use the Big SQL LOAD command, INSERT INTO … SELECT FROM statement, or CREATE TABLE AS … SELECT statement.

7. To view the meta data about a table, use the \describe command with the fully qualified table name in upper case.

\describe BIADMIN.TEST1

```
[bivm.ibm.com][biadmin] 1>   \describe BIADMIN.TEST1
+-------------+-------------+-----------+-------------+----------------+-------------+
| TABLE_SCHEM | COLUMN_NAME | TYPE_NAME | COLUMN_SIZE | DECIMAL_DIGITS | IS_NULLABLE |
+-------------+-------------+-----------+-------------+----------------+-------------+
| BIADMIN     | COL1        | INTEGER   |          10 |              0 | YES         |
| BIADMIN     | COL2        | VARCHAR   |           5 |         [NULL] | YES         |
+-------------+-------------+-----------+-------------+----------------+-------------+
[bivm.ibm.com][biadmin] 1>
```

8. Optionally, you can query the system for metadata about this table:

```
select tabschema, colname, colno, typename, length
from syscat.columns
where tabschema = USER and tabname= 'TEST1';
```

You can split the query across multiple lines in the JSqsh shell if you'd like.Whenever you press Enter, the shell will provide another line for you to continue your command or SQL statement. A semi-colon or go command causes your SQL statement to execute.

```
[bivm.ibm.com][biadmin] 1> select tabschema, colname, colno, typename, length
[bivm.ibm.com][biadmin] 2> from syscat.columns
[bivm.ibm.com][biadmin] 3> where tabschema = USER and tabname= 'TEST1';
+-----------+---------+-------+----------+--------+
| TABSCHEMA | COLNAME | COLNO | TYPENAME | LENGTH |
+-----------+---------+-------+----------+--------+
| BIADMIN   | COL1    |     0 | INTEGER  |      4 |
| BIADMIN   | COL2    |     1 | VARCHAR  |      5 |
+-----------+---------+-------+----------+--------+
2 rows in results(first row: 0.8s; total: 0.8s)
[bivm.ibm.com][biadmin] 1>
```

In case you're wondering, syscat.columns is one of a number of views supplied over system catalog data automatically maintained for you by the Big SQL service.

Note : Once again, notice that we used the table name in upper case in these queries and 'describe command.This is because table and column names are folded to upper case in the system catalog tables.

9. Issue a query that restricts the number of rows returned to 5. For example, select the first 5 rows from syscat.tables:

Select tabschema, tabname from **syscat.tables** fetch **first 5 rows only;**

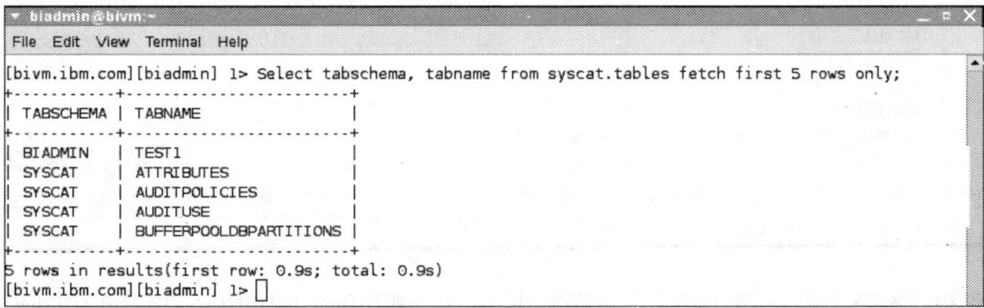

```
biadmin@bivm:~
File  Edit  View  Terminal  Help
[bivm.ibm.com][biadmin] 1> Select tabschema, tabname from syscat.tables fetch first 5 rows only;
+-----------+-----------------------+
| TABSCHEMA | TABNAME               |
+-----------+-----------------------+
| BIADMIN   | TEST1                 |
| SYSCAT    | ATTRIBUTES            |
| SYSCAT    | AUDITPOLICIES         |
| SYSCAT    | AUDITUSE              |
| SYSCAT    | BUFFERPOOLDBPARTITIONS |
+-----------+-----------------------+
5 rows in results(first row: 0.9s; total: 0.9s)
[bivm.ibm.com][biadmin] 1>
```

Restricting the number of rows returned by a query is a useful development technique when working with large volumes of data.

10. Review the history of commands you recently executed in the JSqsh shell. Type \history

And press Enter. Note that previously run statements are prefixed with a number in parentheses. You can reference this number in the JSqsh shell to recall that query.

11. Enter **\history**

```
[bivm.ibm.com][biadmin] 1> \history
(1) setup connections
    Q
(2) $JSQSH_HOME/bin/jsqsh
    $HOME/.jsqsh/connections.xml
    describe
    $JSQSH_HOME/bin/jsqsh
(3) createhadoop tabletest1 (col1 int, col2 varchar(5))
(4) createhadoop tableyourID.test1 (col1 int, col2 varchar(5))
(5) Create hadoop tabletest1 (col1 int, col2 varchar(5))
(6) create hadoop table test1 (col1 int, col2 varchar(5))
(7) insertinto test1 values(1, 'one')
(8) insert into test1 values(1, 'one')
(9) select tabschema, colname, colno, typename, length
    from syscat.columns
    where tabschema = USER and tabname= 'TEST1'
(10) select tabschema, colname, colno, typename, length
     from syscat.columns
     where tabschema = USER and tabname= 'TEST1'
(11) Select tabschema, tabname from syscat.tables fetch first 5 rows only
[bivm.ibm.com][biadmin] 1>
```

Enter **!!** (two exclamation points, without spaces) to recall the previously run statement. In the example below, the previous statement selects the first 5 rows from syscat. tables. To run the statement, type a semi-colon on the following line.

```
[bivm.ibm.com][biadmin] 1> !!
[bivm.ibm.com][biadmin] 1> Select tabschema, tabname from syscat.tables fetch first 5 rows only
[bivm.ibm.com][biadmin] 2> ;
+-----------+----------------------+
| TABSCHEMA | TABNAME              |
+-----------+----------------------+
| BIADMIN   | TEST1                |
| SYSCAT    | ATTRIBUTES           |
| SYSCAT    | AUDITPOLICIES        |
| SYSCAT    | AUDITUSE             |
| SYSCAT    | BUFFERPOOLDBPARTITIONS |
+-----------+----------------------+
5 rows in results(first row: 0.9s; total: 0.9s)
[bivm.ibm.com][biadmin] 1>
```

12. Recall a previous SQL statement by referencing the number reported via the \history command.

For example, if you wanted to recall the 4th statement, you would enter !4. After the statement is recalled, add a semi-column to the final line to run the statement.

```
[bivm.ibm.com][biadmin] 1> !4
[bivm.ibm.com][biadmin] 1> createhadoop tableyourID.test1 (col1 int, col2 varchar(5))
[bivm.ibm.com][biadmin] 2> 
```

13. Experiment with JSqsh's ability to support piping of output to an external program. Enter the following two lines on the command shell:

select tabschema, tabname from **syscat.tables**

go | more

The go statement in the second line causes the query on the first line to be executed.(Note that there is no semi-colon at the end of the SQL query on the first line. The semi-colon is a Big SQL short cut for the JSqsh go command. The | more clause causes the output that results from running the query to be piped through the Unix/Linux more command to display one screen of content at a time. Your results should look similar to this:

```
File  Edit  View  Terminal  Help
[bivm.ibm.com][biadmin] 1> select tabschema, tabname from syscat.tables
[bivm.ibm.com][biadmin] 2> go | more
+-----------+-----------------------------------+
| TABSCHEMA | TABNAME                           |
+-----------+-----------------------------------+
| BIADMIN   | TEST1                             |
| SYSCAT    | ATTRIBUTES                        |
| SYSCAT    | AUDITPOLICIES                     |
| SYSCAT    | AUDITUSE                          |
| SYSCAT    | BUFFERPOOLDBPARTITIONS            |
| SYSCAT    | BUFFERPOOLEXCEPTIONS              |
| SYSCAT    | BUFFERPOOLNODES                   |
| SYSCAT    | BUFFERPOOLS                       |
| SYSCAT    | CASTFUNCTIONS                     |
| SYSCAT    | CHECKS                            |
| SYSCAT    | COLAUTH                           |
| SYSCAT    | COLCHECKS                         |
| SYSCAT    | COLDIST                           |
| SYSCAT    | COLGROUPCOLS                      |
| SYSCAT    | COLGROUPDIST                      |
| SYSCAT    | COLGROUPDISTCOUNTS                |
| SYSCAT    | COLGROUPS                         |
| SYSCAT    | COLIDENTATTRIBUTES                |
| SYSCAT    | COLLATIONS                        |
| SYSCAT    | COLOPTIONS                        |
| SYSCAT    | COLUMNS                           |
| SYSCAT    | COLUSE                            |
| SYSCAT    | CONDITIONS                        |
| SYSCAT    | CONSTDEP                          |
| SYSCAT    | CONTEXTATTRIBUTES                 |
| SYSCAT    | CONTEXTS                          |
| SYSCAT    | CONTROLDEP                        |
| SYSCAT    | CONTROLS                          |
--More--438 rows in results(first row: 0.8s; total: 0.17s)
```

Since there are more than 400 rows to display in this example, enter q to quit displaying further results and return to the JSqsh shell.

14. Experiment with JSqsh's ability to redirect output to a local file rather than the console display. Enter the following two lines on the command shell, adjusting the path information on the second line as needed for your environment:

```
1   Select tabschema, colname, colno, typename, length
2   From syscat.columns
3   Where tabschema = USER and tabname= 'TEST1'
4   go > $HOME/test1.out
```

This example directs the output of the query shown on the first line to the output file test1.out in your user's home directory.

```
[bivm.ibm.com][biadmin] 1> Select tabschema, colname, colno, typename, length
[bivm.ibm.com][biadmin] 2> From syscat.columns
[bivm.ibm.com][biadmin] 3> Where tabschema = USER and tabname= 'TEST1'
[bivm.ibm.com][biadmin] 4> go > $HOME/test1.out
2 rows in results(first row: 0.65s; total: 0.65s)
[bivm.ibm.com][biadmin] 1>
```

15. Exit the shell and view the output file:

cat $HOME/test1.out

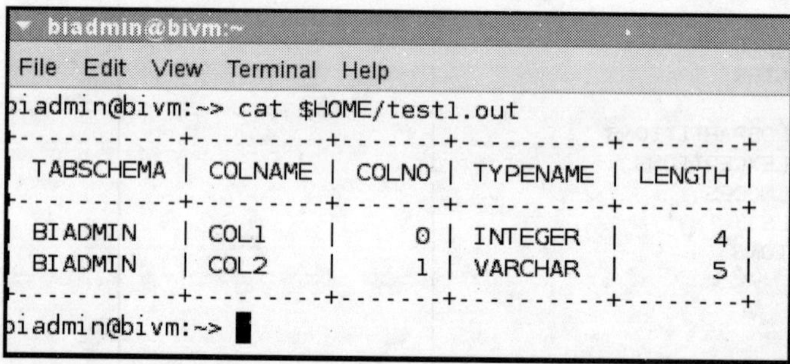

16. Invoke JSqsh using an input file containing Big SQL commands to be executed. Maintaining SQL script files can be quite handy for repeatedly executing various queries.

    a. From the Unix/Linux command line, use any available editor to create a new file in your local directory named test.sql. For example, type

    `vi test.sql`

    or in case of suse linux type :

    `gedit test.sql`

    b. Add the following 2 queries into your file

```
select tabschema, tabname from syscat.tables fetch first 5 rows only;
select tabschema, colname, colno, typename, length
from syscat.columns
fetch first 10 rows only;
```

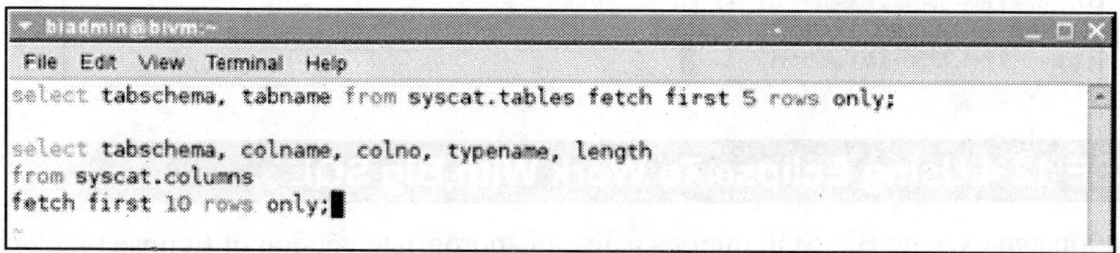

c.. Save your file (hit 'esc' to exit INSERT mode then type :wq) and return to the command line.

d. Invoke JSQSH, instructing it to connect to your bigsql database and execute the contents of the script you just created:

```
$JSQSH_HOME/bin/jsqsh bigsql -P biadmin < test.sql
```

e. Inspect the output. As you will see, JSQSH executes each instruction and displays its output. (Partial results are shown below.)

```
biadmin@bivm:~
File Edit View Terminal Help
biadmin@bivm:~> $JSQSH_HOME/bin/jsqsh bigsql -P biadmin < test.sql
WARN [State:      ][Code: 0]: Statement processing was successful.. SQLCODE=0, SQLST
ATE=      , DRIVER=3.67.33
JSqsh Release 2.1.0-SNAPSHOT, Copyright (C) 2007-2014, Scott C. Gray
Type \help for available help topics. Using JLine.
[bivm.ibm.com][biadmin] 1> select tabschema, tabname from syscat.tables fetch first
5 rows only;
+-----------+----------------------+
| TABSCHEMA | TABNAME              |
+-----------+----------------------+
| BIADMIN   | TEST1                |
| SYSCAT    | ATTRIBUTES           |
| SYSCAT    | AUDITPOLICIES        |
| SYSCAT    | AUDITUSE             |
| SYSCAT    | BUFFERPOOLDBPARTITIONS |
+-----------+----------------------+
5 rows in results(first row: 0.3s; total: 0.3s)
[bivm.ibm.com][biadmin] 1>
[bivm.ibm.com][biadmin] 2> select tabschema, colname, colno, typename, length
[bivm.ibm.com][biadmin] 3> from syscat.columns
[bivm.ibm.com][biadmin] 4> fetch first 10 rows only;
+-----------+-------------+-------+-----------+-----------+
| TABSCHEMA | COLNAME     | COLNO | TYPENAME  |    LENGTH |
+-----------+-------------+-------+-----------+-----------+
| SYSIBM    | NAME        |     0 | VARCHAR   |       128 |
| SYSIBM    | CREATOR     |     1 | VARCHAR   |       128 |
| SYSIBM    | TYPE        |     2 | CHARACTER |         1 |
| SYSIBM    | CTIME       |     3 | TIMESTAMP |        10 |
| SYSIBM    | REMARKS     |     4 | VARCHAR   |       254 |
| SYSIBM    | PACKED_DESC |     5 | BLOB      | 133169152 |
```

17. Finally, clean up the your database:

    $JSQSH_HOME/bin/jsqsh bigsql

    drop table test1;

```
[bivm.ibm.com][biadmin] 1> drop table test1;
0 rows affected (total: 3.19s)
[bivm.ibm.com][biadmin] 1>
```

EXERCISE 12.4 Using Eclipse To Work With Big SQL

You can develop and execute Big SQL queries using an appropriate version of Eclipse (4.2.2) and some additional software. Some people prefer to use Eclipse over JSqsh, as query result sets are formatted in an easy-to-read fashion and queries are typically organized in scripts within projects.

In this exercise , you will learn how to:

1. Configure Eclipse to work with Big SQL.
2. Create a connection to your Big SQL 3.0 server.
3. Create projects and Big SQL scripts.
4. Issue Big SQL queries.

If you prefer to only use JSqsh to develop and execute your Big SQL queries, you can skip this section and continue to the next Exercise.

12.4.1. Launching the Web Console to verify BigInsights services are up and running

You have to launch all required BigInsights services and use the Web console to verify that all required BigInsights services are up and running.You can skip this section if you have already completed this work as part of an earlier Exercise or if your instructor tells you that this work has been done for you.

1. Select the **Start BigInsights** icon to start all services. (Alternatively, you can open a terminal window and issue this command:

   $BIGINSIGHTS_HOME/bin/start-all.sh)

Wait until the operation completes. This make take several minutes, depending on your machine resources.

2. Verify that all required BigInsights services are up and running, including Big SQL.
   a. Launch the **BigInsights Web** console.(Direct your browser tohttp://bivm.ibm.com:8080 or select the Web Console icon on your desktop.)

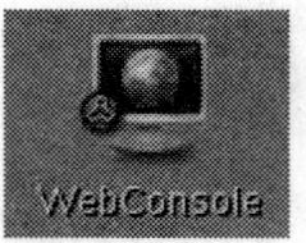

b. Log in with your user name and password.

IBM® InfoSphere® BigInsights™
Quickstart Edition

Please enter your information

User name:
biadmin

Password:
●●●●●●●●●

Login Cancel

Licensed Materials - Property of IBM Corp. © Copyright 2010, 2014.
IBM Corporation. IBM, InfoSphere and BigInsights are trademarks
of IBM Corporation, registered in many jurisdictions worldwide.

c. Click on the **Cluster Status** tab to inspect the running services. Monitoring and Alert services do not need to be active for this Exercise.

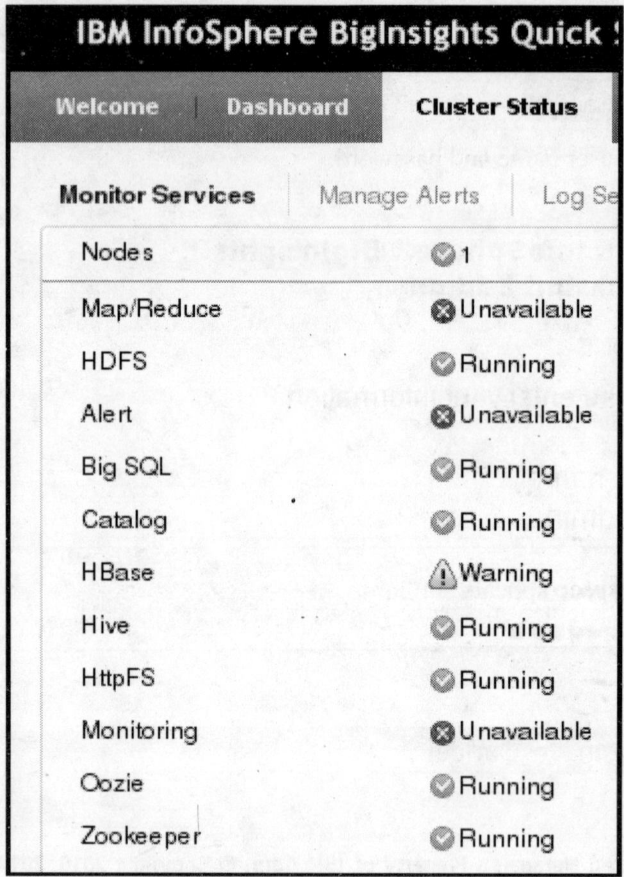

12.4.2. Creating a Big SQL Connection in Eclipse

Certain tasks require a live connection to a Big SQL server within the BigInsights cluster. This section explains how you can define a JDBC connection to your Big SQL server.

If you're working with the Quick Start Edition VMware image, this section is optional. (The image is pre-configured with a Big SQL connection.)

1. Launch Eclipse using this icon on your Desktop.

2. Accept the default workspace name when prompted.

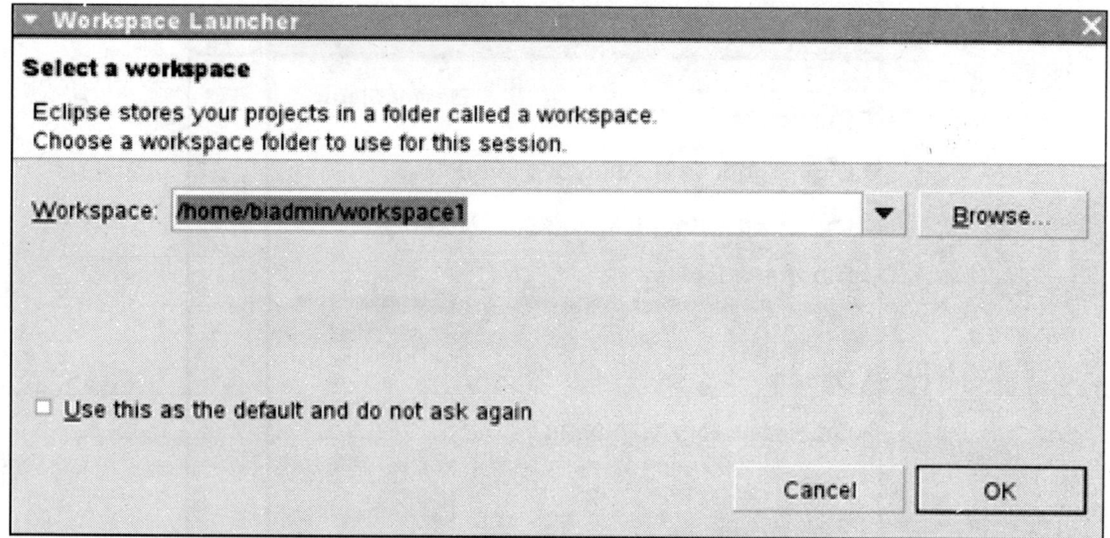

3. Verify that your workspace appears similar to this:

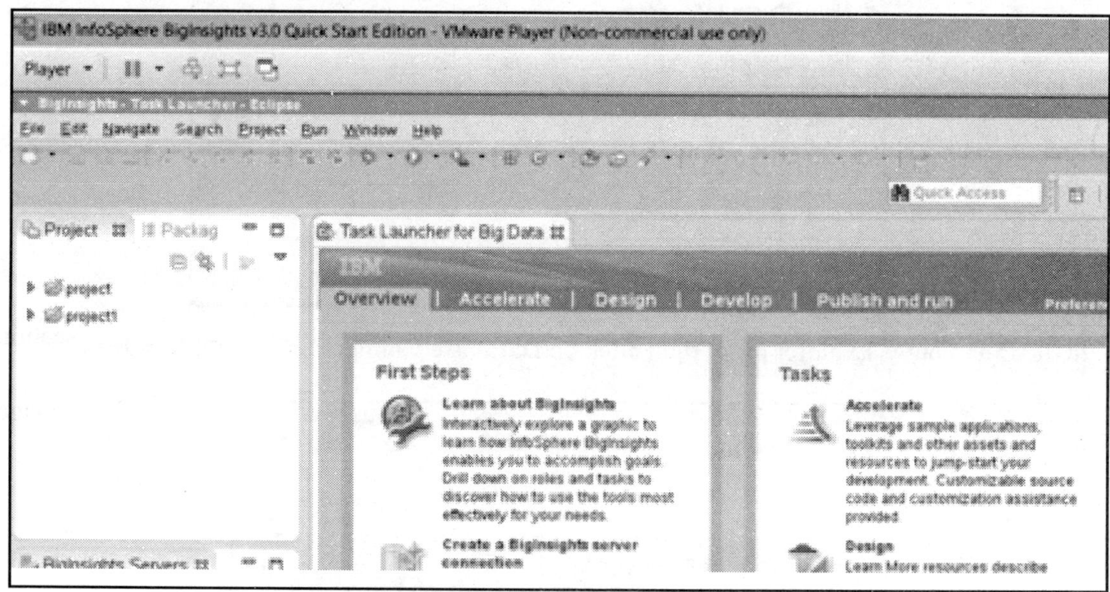

4. Open the Database Development perspective. **Window > Open Perspective > Other > Database Development.**

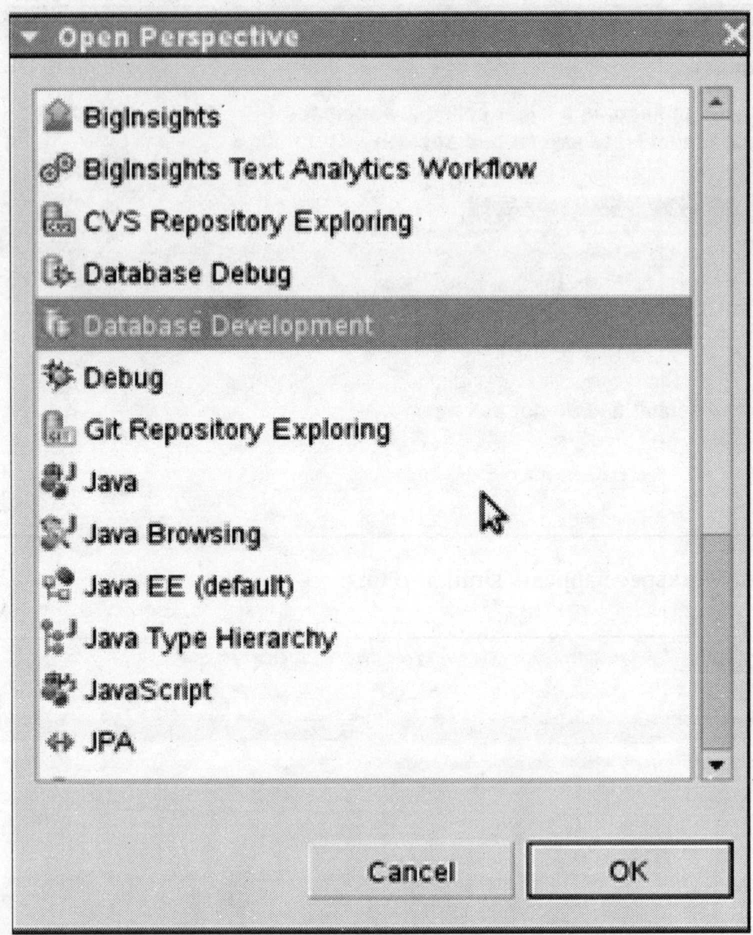

5. In the Data Source Explorer pane, right click on **Database Connections > Add Repository**

In the New Connection Profile menu, select Big SQL JDBC Driver. Enter the appropriate connection information for your environment, including the host name, port number (51000, by default) user ID, and password. Verify that you have selected the correct JDBC driver at the top.

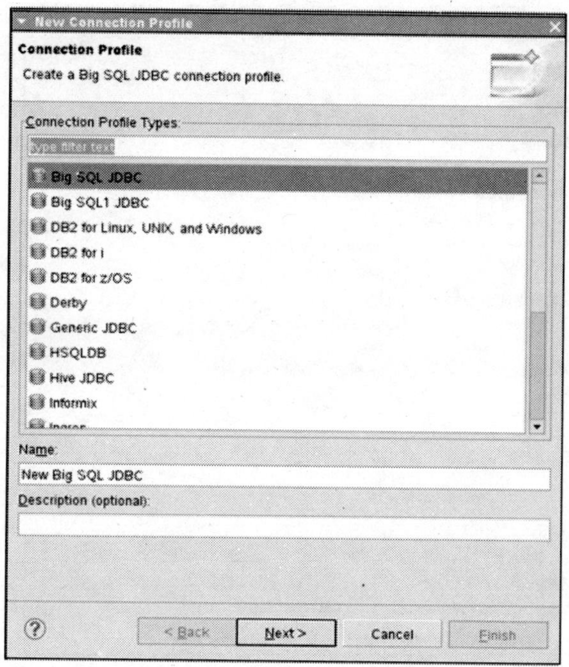

6. Click **Next.**

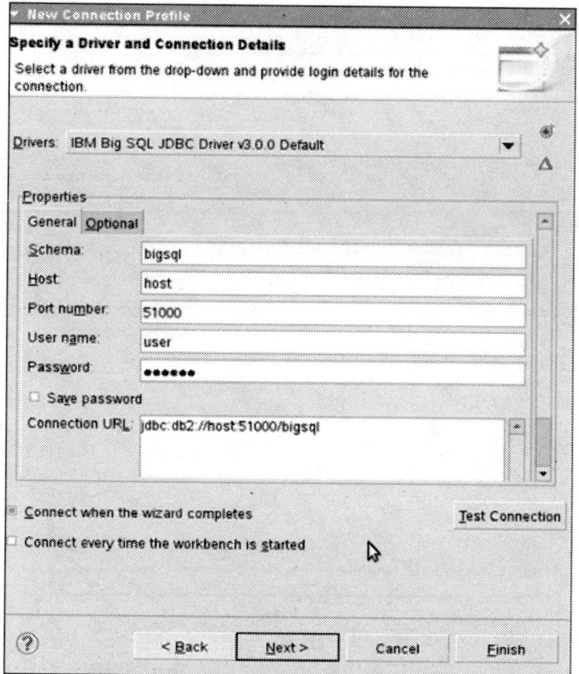

You will be presented with a Summary sheet.

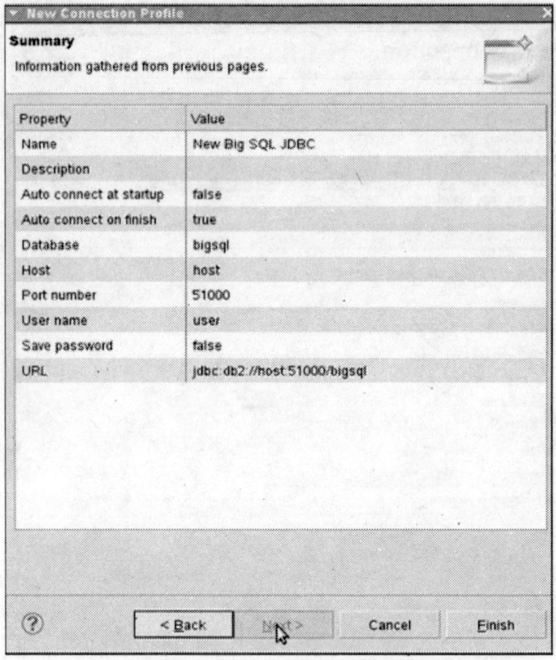

7. The information shown below contains information for the BigInsights Quick Start Edition VMware image (V3.0).

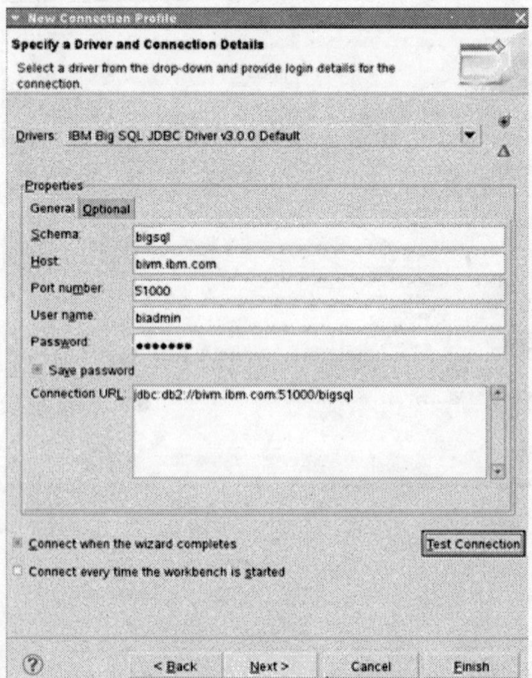

8. Click the **Optional tab** under the **Properties** heading to expose another menu that allows you to add more properties to the connection.
9. In the **Property** field, enter retrieveMessagesFromServerOnGetMessage, In the **Value** field, enter true.
10. Click **Add**. Verify that your screen appears similar to this:

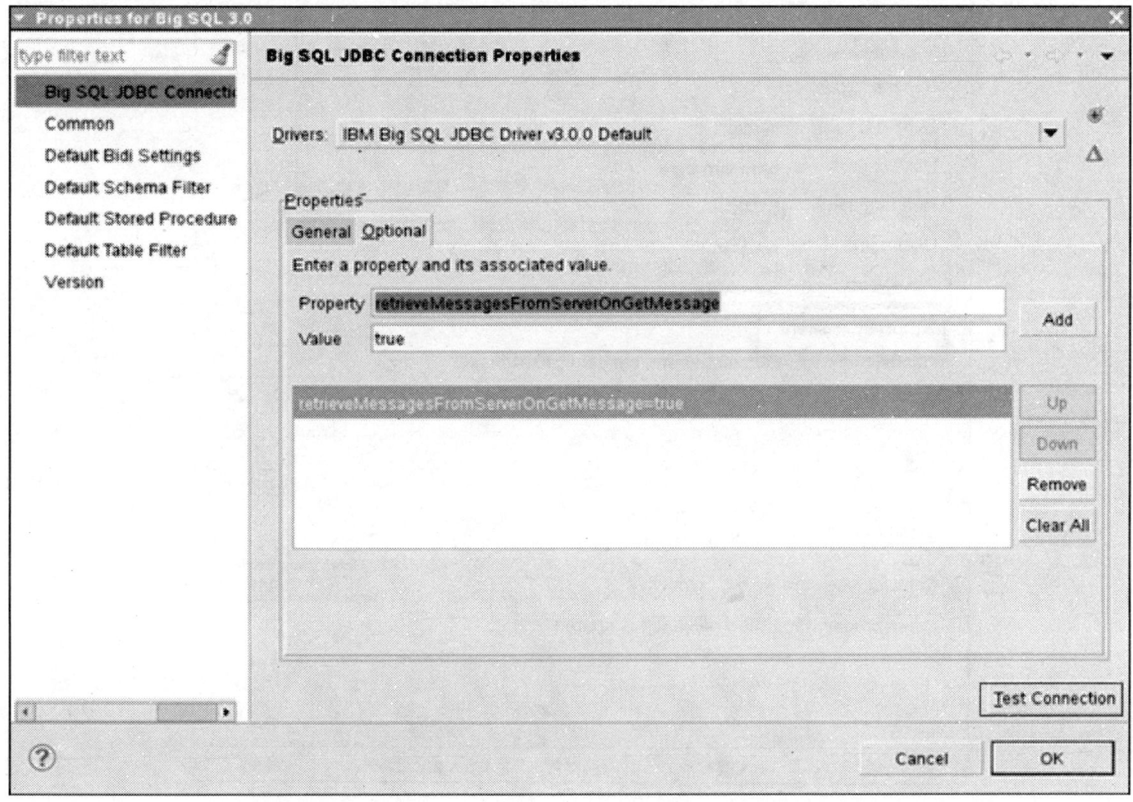

11. Click the **General** tab again.
12. Click the Test connection button and verify that you can successfully connect to your target Big SQL server.
13. Click the **Save password** box and **Finish**.

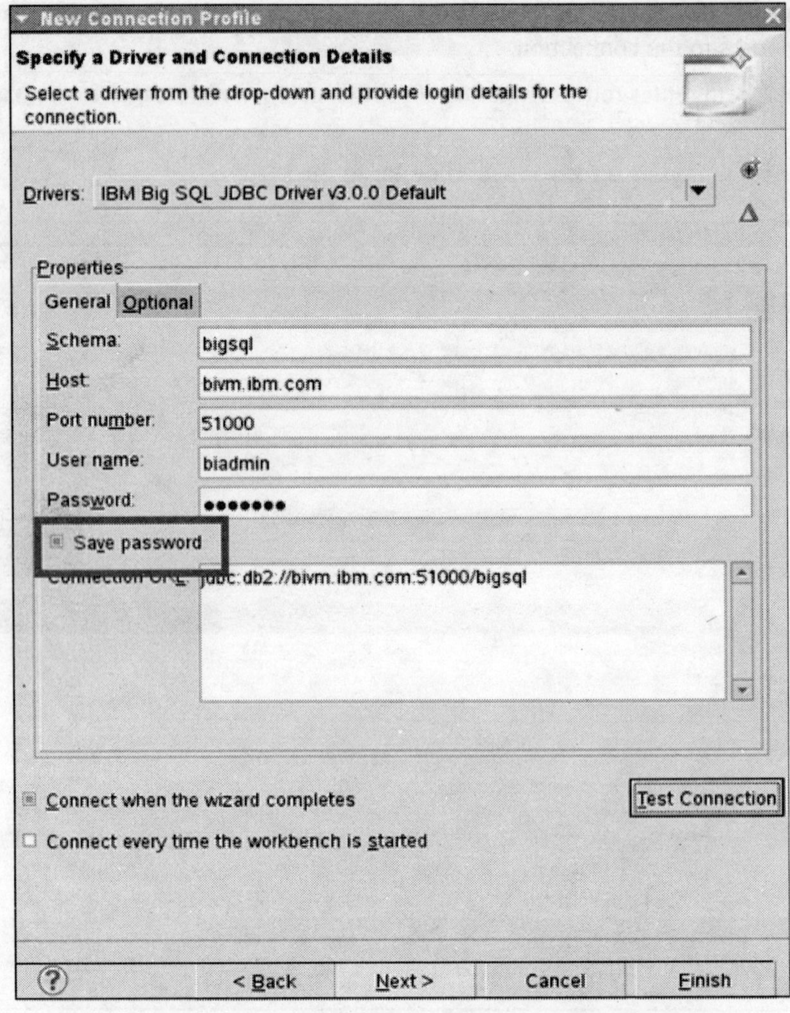

14. In the Data Source Explorer, expand the list of data sources and verify that your Big SQL connection appears.

15. Return to the BigInsights perspective.

EXERCISE 12.5: Creating A Project And An SQL Acript File

You can create Big SQL scripts and run them from the InfoSphere® BigInsights™ Eclipse environment.

Procedures

1. Create an InfoSphere BigInsights project in Eclipse.
   a. From the Eclipse menu bar, click **File > New > Other**

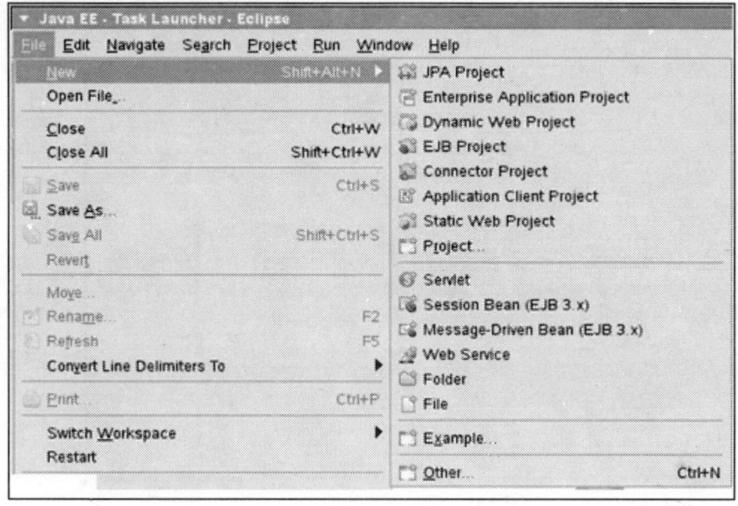

2. In the **Select a wizard window**, expand the BigInsights folder, select **BigInsights Project**, and then click **Next.**

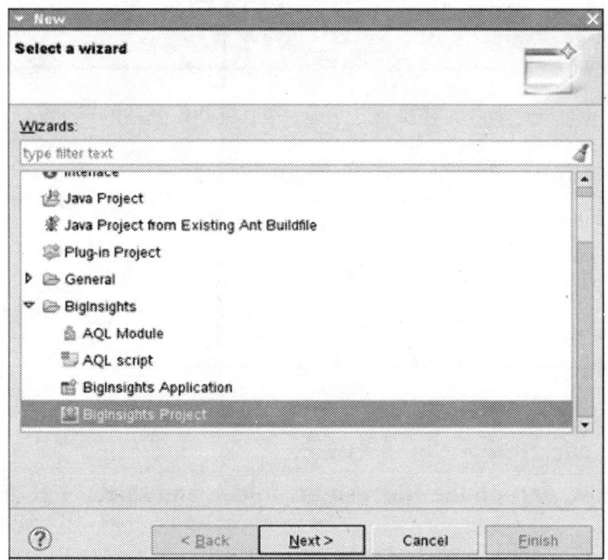

a. Type **myBigSQL** in the **Project name field**, and then click **Finish**.

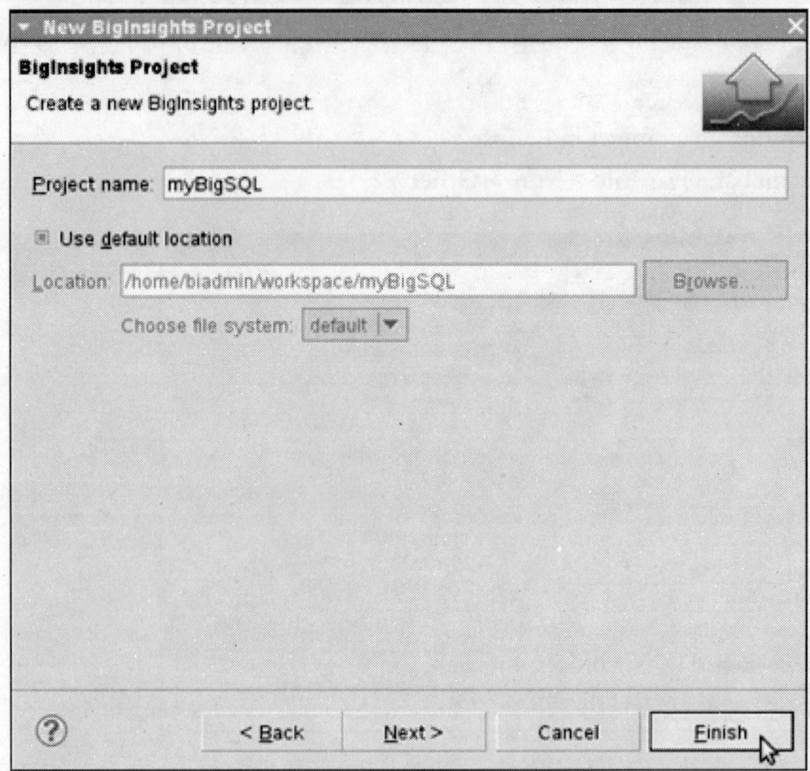

b. If you are not already in the BigInsights perspective, a Switch to the BigInsights perspective window opens. Click **Yes** to switch to the BigInsights perspective.

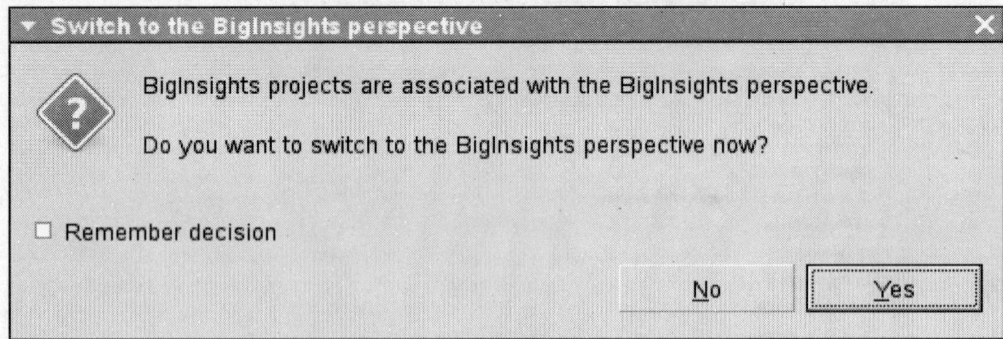

3. Create an SQL script file.

   a. From the **Eclipse** menu bar, click **File > New > Other.**

   b. In the Select a wizard window, expand the **BigInsights** folder, and select **SQL Script**, and then click **Next**.

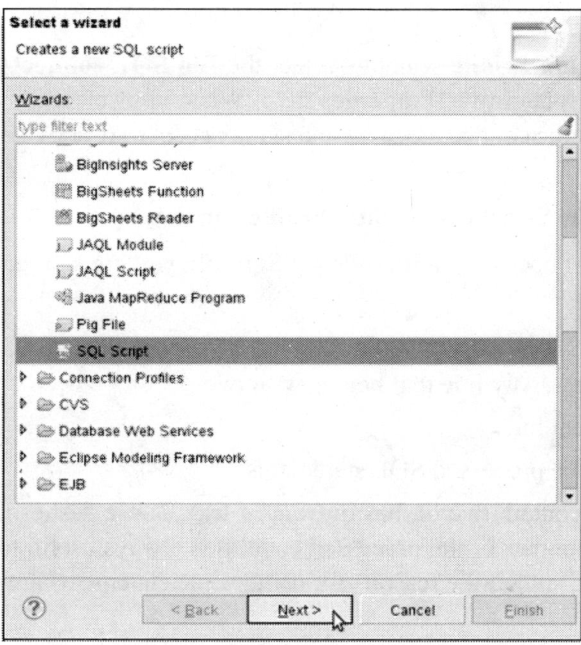

c. In the New SQL File window, in the Enter or select the **parent folder** field, select **myBigSQL**. Your new SQL file is stored in this project folder.

d. In the File name field, type **aFirstFile**. The **.sql** file extension is added automatically.

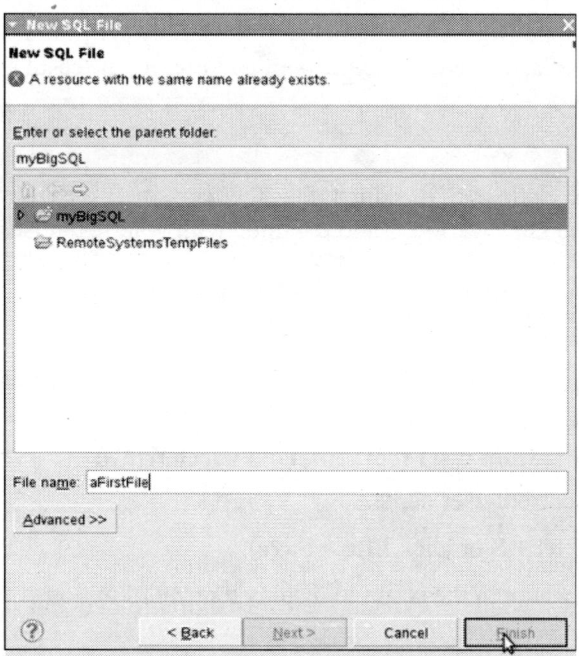

e. Click **Finish**.

4. In the **Select Connection Profile** window, select the **Big SQL connection**. The properties of the selected connection display in the Properties field. When you select the Big SQL connection, the Big SQL database-specific context assistant and syntax checks are activated in the editor that is used to edit your SQL file.
5. Click Finish to close the Select **Connection Profile** window.
6. In the **SQL Editor** that opens the aFirstFile.sql SQL file you created, add the following Big SQL comments:
   - This is a beginning SQL script
   - These are comments. Any line that begins with two
   - dashes is a comment line,
   - and is not part of the processed SQL statements.

   Some lines in the file contain two dashes in front of text. Those dashes mark the text as comment lines. Comment lines are not part of the processed code. It is always useful to comment your Big SQL code as you write the code, so that the reasons for using some statements are clear to all who must use the file.

   You will be using this file in later lessons.
7. Save **aFirstFile.sql** by using the keyboard short, CTRL-S.

EXERCISE 12.6: Creating and Issuing Queries

Now you're ready to add some Big SQL statements to the empty script file that you just created. Once you've added some statements, you will execute them and inspect the results.

Note: In some cases, the Eclipse SQL editor may flag certain Big SQL statements as containing syntax errors. Ignore these false warnings and continue with your exercises.

1. Copy the following statement into the SQL script you created earlier:

   Create hadoop table **test1 (col1 int, col2 varchar(5));**

   Because you didn't specify a schema name for the table it was created in your default schema, which is your user name. This is equivalent to:

   Create hadoop table **biadmin.test1 (col1 int, col2 varchar(5));**

   where **biadmin** is the current user name.
2. **Save** your file (press **Ctrl + S** or click **File > Save**).
3. Right mouse click anywhere in the script to display a menu of options.

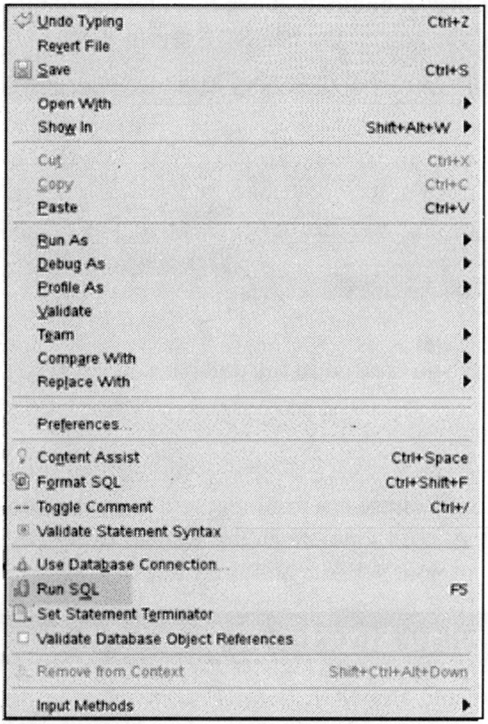

4. Select **Run SQL** or press **F5**. This causes all statements in your script to be executed.
5. Inspect the SQL Results pane that appears towards the bottom of your display. (If desired, double click on the SQL Results tab to enlarge this pane. Then double click on the tab again to return the pane to its normal size.) Verify that the statement executed successfully. Your Big SQL database now contains a new table named BIADMIN.TEST1 where BIADMIN is the name of the current user. Note that your schema and table name were folded into upper case.

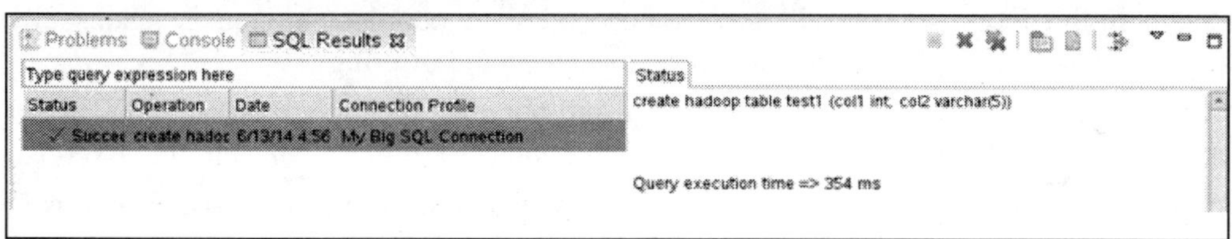

For the remainder of this Exercise, to execute each SQL statement individually highlight the statement and press F5.When you're developing a SQL script with multiple statements, it's generally a good idea to test each statement one at a time to verify that each is working as expected.

6. From your Eclipse project, query the system for meta data about your test1 table:

```
select tabschema, colname, colno, typename, length
from syscat.columns where tabschema = USER and tabname= 'TEST1';
```

In case you're wondering, syscat.columns is one of a number of views supplied over system catalog data automatically maintained for you by the Big SQL service.

7. Inspect the SQL Results to verify that the query executed successfully, and click on the Result1 tab to view its output.

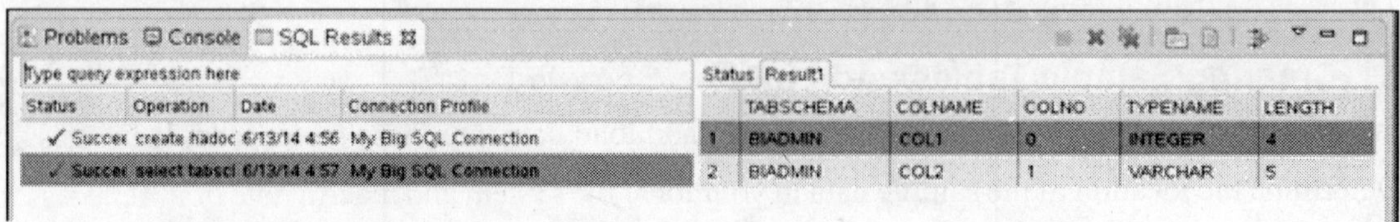

8. Finally, clean up the object you created in the database.

```
Drop table test1;
```

9. Save your file. If desired, leave it open to execute statements for subsequent exercises.

Now that you've set up your Eclipse environment and know how to create SQL scripts and execute queries, you're ready to develop more sophisticated scenarios using Big SQL. In the next Exercise, you will create a number of tables in your schema and use Eclipse to query them.

EXERCISE 12.7 Querying Structured Data With Big SQL

In this Exercise, you will execute Big SQL queries to investigate data stored in Hadoop. Big SQL provides broad SQL support based on the ISO SQL standard.You can issue queries using JDBC or ODBC drivers to access data that is stored in InfoSphere BigInsights in the same way that you access relational databases from your enterprise applications. Multiple queries can be executed concurrently.The SQL query engine supports joins, unions, grouping, common table expressions, windowing functions, and other familiar SQL expressions.

In this exercise we shall use sales data from a fictional company that sells and distributes outdoor products to third-party retailer stores as well as directly to consumers through its online store. It maintains its data in a series of FACT and DIMENSION tables, as is common in relational data warehouse environments.In this Exercise, you will explore how to create, populate, and query a subset of the star schema database to investigate the company's performance and offerings.

Note that BigInsights provides scripts to create and populate the more than 60 tables that comprise the sample GOSALESDW database. You will use fewer than 10 of these tables in this Exercise.

Prior to starting this Exercise, you must have completed at least one of the two previous Exercises on JSqsh or Eclipse. In particular, you must be familiar with how to execute queries in your target development platform (JSqsh or Eclipse), and you must have established a connection to your Big SQL 3.0 database. Screen captures shown in this Exercise are based on Eclipse, as query result sets are generally easier to read.

After you complete the lessons in this module, you will understand how to:

- Create Big SQL tables that use Hadoop text file and Parquet file formats.
- Populate Big SQL tables from local files and from the results of queries.

- Query Big SQL tables using projections, restrictions, joins, aggregations, and other popular expressions.
- Create and query a view based on multiple Big SQL tables.
- Create and run a JDBC client application for Big SQL using Eclipse.

This exercise will require 1.5 hours to complete.

12.7.1 Creating Sample Tables and Loading Sample Data

In this section, you will create several sample tables and load data into these tables from local files.

1. Determine the location of the sample data in your local file system and make a note of it. If necessary, ask your instructor for the location of the sample GOSALESDW data used in this Exercise. You will need to use this path specification when issuing LOAD commands later in this Exercise.

   Note : Subsequent examples in this section presume your sample data is in the /opt/ibm/biginsights/bigsql/samples/data directory. This is the location of the data on the BigInsights VMware image, and it is the default location in typical BigInsights installations.

   Furthermore, the /opt/ibm/biginsights/bigsql/samples/queriesdirectory contains SQL scripts that include the CREATE TABLE, LOAD, and SELECT statements used in this Exercise, as well as other statements.

2. Create several tables in this schema. Issue each of the following CREATE TABLE statements one at a time, and verify that each completed successfully:
3. We shall create several tables in this schema. Issue each of the following CREATE TABLE statements one at a time, and verify that each completed successfully:

Study the following code and Enter following code lines

1. Dimension table for region info

```
CREATE HADOOP TABLE IF NOT EXISTS go_region_dim ( country_key INT
NOT NULL , country_code INT NOT NULL , flag_image VARCHAR(45) , iso_
three_letter_code VARCHAR(9) NOT NULL , iso_two_letter_code VARCHAR(6)
NOT NULL , iso_three_digit_code VARCHAR(9) NOT NULL , region_key INT
NOT NULL , region_code INT NOT NULL , region_en VARCHAR(90) NOT NULL
, country_en VARCHAR(90) NOT NULL , region_de VARCHAR(90), country_de
VARCHAR(90), region_fr VARCHAR(90) , country_fr VARCHAR(90), region_ja
VARCHAR(90), country_ja VARCHAR(90) , region_cs VARCHAR(90), country_cs
VARCHAR(90), region_da VARCHAR(90) , country_da VARCHAR(90), region_el
VARCHAR(90), country_el VARCHAR(90) , region_es VARCHAR(90), country_es
VARCHAR(90), region_fi VARCHAR(90) , country_fi VARCHAR(90), region_hu
VARCHAR(90), country_hu VARCHAR(90) , region_id VARCHAR(90), country_id
VARCHAR(90), region_it VARCHAR(90) , country_it VARCHAR(90), region_ko
VARCHAR(90), country_ko VARCHAR(90) , region_ms VARCHAR(90), country_ms
VARCHAR(90), region_nl VARCHAR(90) , country_nl VARCHAR(90), region_no
VARCHAR(90), country_no VARCHAR(90) , region_pl VARCHAR(90), country_pl
VARCHAR(90), region_pt VARCHAR(90) , country_pt VARCHAR(90), region_ru
VARCHAR(90), country_ru VARCHAR(90) , region_sc VARCHAR(90), country_sc
VARCHAR(90), region_sv VARCHAR(90) , country_sv VARCHAR(90), region_tc
```

```
VARCHAR(90), country_tc VARCHAR(90) , region_th VARCHAR(90), country_th
VARCHAR(90) ) ROW FORMAT DELIMITED FIELDS TERMINATED BY '\t' LINES
TERMINATED BY '\n' STORED AS TEXTFILE ;
```

```
biadmin@bivm:~
File Edit View Terminal Help
[bivm.ibm.com][biadmin] 1> CREATE HADOOP TABLE IF NOT EXISTS go_region_dim ( country_key INT
NULL , flag_image VARCHAR(45) , iso_three_letter_code VARCHAR(9) NOT NULL , iso_two_letter_co
_digit_code VARCHAR(9) NOT NULL , region_key INT NOT NULL , region_code INT NOT NULL , regi
y_en VARCHAR(90) NOT NULL , region_de VARCHAR(90), country_de VARCHAR(90), region_fr VARCHAR(
n_ja VARCHAR(90), country_ja VARCHAR(90) , region_cs VARCHAR(90), country_cs VARCHAR(90), reg
CHAR(90), region_el VARCHAR(90), country_el VARCHAR(90) , region_es VARCHAR(90), country_es V
, country_fi VARCHAR(90), region_hu VARCHAR(90), country_hu VARCHAR(90) , region_id VARCHAR(90
t VARCHAR(90) , country_it VARCHAR(90), region_ko VARCHAR(90), country_ko VARCHAR(90) , regio
R(90), region_nl VARCHAR(90) , country_nl VARCHAR(90), region_no VARCHAR(90), country_no VARC
untry_pl VARCHAR(90), region_pt VARCHAR(90) , country_pt VARCHAR(90), region_ru VARCHAR(90),
 VARCHAR(90), country_sc VARCHAR(90), region_sv VARCHAR(90) , country_sv VARCHAR(90), region_t
90) , region_th VARCHAR(90), country_th VARCHAR(90) ) ROW FORMAT DELIMITED FIELDS TERMINATED
 STORED AS TEXTFILE ;
 rows affected (total: 14.12s)
[bivm.ibm.com][biadmin] 1>
```

Enter following and see the table structure:

```
\describe go_region_dim
```

```
[bivm.ibm.com][biadmin] 2> \describe go_region_dim
+-----------------+-------------+-----------+-----------+--------+-------+
| PROCEDURE_SCHEM | COLUMN_NAME | TYPE_NAME | PRECISION | LENGTH | SCALE |
+-----------------+-------------+-----------+-----------+--------+-------+
+-----------------+-------------+-----------+-----------+--------+-------+
[bivm.ibm.com][biadmin] 2>
```

2. Dimension table tracking method of order for the sale (e.g., Web, fax)

```
CREATE HADOOP TABLE IF NOT EXISTS sls_order_method_dim ( order_method_
key INT NOT NULL , order_method_code INT NOT NULL , order_method_
en VARCHAR(90) NOT NULL , order_method_de VARCHAR(90), order_method_fr
VARCHAR(90) , order_method_ja VARCHAR(90), order_method_cs VARCHAR(90) ,
order_method_da VARCHAR(90), order_method_el VARCHAR(90) , order_method_
es VARCHAR(90), order_method_fi VARCHAR(90) , order_method_hu VARCHAR(90),
order_method_id VARCHAR(90) , order_method_it VARCHAR(90), order_method_
ko VARCHAR(90) , order_method_ms VARCHAR(90), order_method_nl VARCHAR(90)
, order_method_no VARCHAR(90), order_method_pl VARCHAR(90) , order_
method_pt VARCHAR(90), order_method_ru VARCHAR(90) , order_method_sc
VARCHAR(90), order_method_sv VARCHAR(90) , order_method_tc VARCHAR(90),
order_method_th VARCHAR(90)
) ROW FORMAT DELIMITED FIELDS TERMINATED BY '\t' LINES TERMINATED BY
'\n' STORED AS TEXTFILE ;
```

```
File  Edit  View  Terminal  Help
[bivm.ibm.com][biadmin] 2> CREATE HADOOP TABLE IF NOT EXISTS sls_order_method_dim  ( order_method_key  INT NOT NULL , order_meth
od_code  INT NOT NULL , order_method_en VARCHAR(90) NOT NULL , order_method_de VARCHAR(90), order_method_fr VARCHAR(90) , order_
method_ja VARCHAR(90), order_method_cs VARCHAR(90) , order_method_da VARCHAR(90), order_method_el VARCHAR(90) , order_method_es
VARCHAR(90), order_method_fi VARCHAR(90) , order_method_hu VARCHAR(90), order_method_id VARCHAR(90) , order_method_it VARCHAR(9C
), order_method_ko VARCHAR(90) , order_method_ms VARCHAR(90), order_method_nl VARCHAR(90) , order_method_no VARCHAR(90), order_m
ethod_pl VARCHAR(90) , order_method_pt VARCHAR(90), order_method_ru VARCHAR(90) , order_method_sc VARCHAR(90), order_method_sv V
ARCHAR(90) , order_method_tc VARCHAR(90), order_method_th VARCHAR(90)
[bivm.ibm.com][biadmin] 3> ) ROW FORMAT DELIMITED  FIELDS TERMINATED BY '\t'  LINES TERMINATED BY '\n' STORED AS TEXTFILE ;
0 rows affected (total: 3.66s)
[bivm.ibm.com][biadmin] 1>
```

3. Look Up Table with Product Brand Info in Various Languages

```
CREATE HADOOP TABLE IF NOT EXISTS sls_product_brand_lookup  ( product_
brand_code  INT NOT NULL , product_brand_en VARCHAR(90) NOT NULL ,
product_brand_de VARCHAR(90), product_brand_fr VARCHAR(90) , product_
brand_ja VARCHAR(90), product_brand_cs VARCHAR(90) , product_brand_da
VARCHAR(90), product_brand_el VARCHAR(90) , product_brand_es VARCHAR(90),
product_brand_fi VARCHAR(90) , product_brand_hu VARCHAR(90), product_
brand_id VARCHAR(90) , product_brand_it VARCHAR(90), product_brand_ko
VARCHAR(90) , product_brand_ms VARCHAR(90), product_brand_nl VARCHAR(90)
, product_brand_no VARCHAR(90), product_brand_pl VARCHAR(90) , product_
brand_pt VARCHAR(90), product_brand_ru VARCHAR(90) , product_brand_sc
VARCHAR(90), product_brand_sv VARCHAR(90) , product_brand_tc VARCHAR(90),
product_brand_th VARCHAR(90)  ) ROW FORMAT DELIMITED  FIELDS TERMINATED
BY '\t'  LINES TERMINATED BY '\n' STORED AS TEXTFILE ;
```

```
▾ biadmin@bivm:~
File  Edit  View  Terminal  Help
[bivm.ibm.com][biadmin] 2> CREATE HADOOP TABLE IF NOT EXISTS sls_product_brand_lookup  (
uct_brand_en VARCHAR(90) NOT NULL , product_brand_de VARCHAR(90), product_brand_fr VARCHA
roduct_brand_cs VARCHAR(90) , product_brand_da VARCHAR(90), product_brand_el VARCHAR(90)
_brand_fi VARCHAR(90) , product_brand_hu VARCHAR(90), product_brand_id VARCHAR(90) , proc
_ko VARCHAR(90) , product_brand_ms VARCHAR(90), product_brand_nl VARCHAR(90) , product_br
RCHAR(90) , product_brand_pt VARCHAR(90), product_brand_ru VARCHAR(90) , product_brand_sc
90) , product_brand_tc VARCHAR(90), product_brand_th VARCHAR(90)  ) ROW FORMAT DELIMITED
NATED BY '\n' STORED AS TEXTFILE ;
0 rows affected (total: 4.5s)
[bivm.ibm.com][biadmin] 1>
```

4. Product Dimension Table

```
CREATE HADOOP TABLE IF NOT EXISTS sls_product_dim  ( product_key  INT
NOT NULL , product_line_code  INT NOT NULL , product_type_key  INT NOT
NULL , product_type_code  INT NOT NULL , product_number  INT NOT NULL
, base_product_key  INT NOT NULL , base_product_number  INT NOT NULL ,
product_color_code  INT , product_size_code  INT , product_brand_key  INT
NOT NULL , product_brand_code  INT NOT NULL , product_image  VARCHAR(60)
, introduction_date  TIMESTAMP , discontinued_date  TIMESTAMP  ) ROW
FORMAT DELIMITED  FIELDS TERMINATED BY '\t'  LINES TERMINATED BY '\n'
STORED AS TEXTFILE ;
```

```
biadmin@bivm:~
File  Edit  View  Terminal  Help
[bivm.ibm.com][biadmin] 1> CREATE HADOOP TABLE IF NOT EXISTS sls_product_dim  ( product_key
INT NOT NULL , product_type_key  INT NOT NULL , product_type_code  INT NOT NULL , product_num
y  INT NOT NULL , base_product_number  INT NOT NULL , product_color_code  INT , product_size_
NOT NULL , product_brand_code  INT NOT NULL , product_image  VARCHAR(60) , introduction_date
ESTAMP  ) ROW FORMAT DELIMITED  FIELDS TERMINATED BY '\t'  LINES TERMINATED BY '\n' STORED AS
0 rows affected (total: 1.86s)
```

5. Look Up Table with Product Line Info in Various Languages

```
CREATE HADOOP TABLE IF NOT EXISTS sls_product_line_lookup  ( product_line_code  INT NOT NULL , product_line_en VARCHAR(90) NOT NULL , product_line_de  VARCHAR(90),  product_line_fr  VARCHAR(90)  , product_line_ja VARCHAR(90), product_line_cs VARCHAR(90) , product_line_da VARCHAR(90), product_line_el VARCHAR(90) , product_line_es VARCHAR(90), product_line_fi VARCHAR(90) , product_line_hu VARCHAR(90), product_line_id VARCHAR(90) , product_line_it VARCHAR(90), product_line_ko VARCHAR(90) , product_line_ms  VARCHAR(90),  product_line_nl  VARCHAR(90)  ,  product_line_no VARCHAR(90), product_line_pl VARCHAR(90) , product_line_pt VARCHAR(90), product_line_ru VARCHAR(90) , product_line_sc VARCHAR(90), product_line_sv VARCHAR(90) , product_line_tc VARCHAR(90), product_line_th VARCHAR(90) ) ROW FORMAT DELIMITED  FIELDS TERMINATED BY '\t'  LINES TERMINATED BY '\n' STORED AS TEXTFILE;
```

```
biadmin@bivm:~
File  Edit  View  Terminal  Help
[bivm.ibm.com][biadmin] 2>  CREATE HADOOP TABLE IF NOT EXISTS sls_product_line_lookup  (
ct_line_en VARCHAR(90) NOT NULL , product_line_de VARCHAR(90), product_line_fr VARCHAR(90
t_line_cs VARCHAR(90)  , product_line_da VARCHAR(90), product_line_el VARCHAR(90) , produc
VARCHAR(90) , product_line_hu VARCHAR(90), product_line_id VARCHAR(90) , product_line_it
) , product_line_ms VARCHAR(90), product_line_nl VARCHAR(90) , product_line_no VARCHAR(90
t_line_pt VARCHAR(90), product_line_ru VARCHAR(90) , product_line_sc VARCHAR(90), product
VARCHAR(90), product_line_th VARCHAR(90)  ) ROW FORMAT DELIMITED  FIELDS TERMINATED BY '\
TEXTFILE;
0 rows affected (total: 1.95s)
[bivm.ibm.com][biadmin] 3>
```

6. Look Up Table for Products

```
CREATE HADOOP TABLE IF NOT EXISTS sls_product_lookup  ( product_number INT NOT NULL , product_language VARCHAR(30) NOT NULL , product_name VARCHAR(150) NOT NULL , product_description VARCHAR(765)  ) ROW FORMAT DELIMITED  FIELDS TERMINATED BY '\t'  LINES TERMINATED BY '\n' STORED AS TEXTFILE;
```

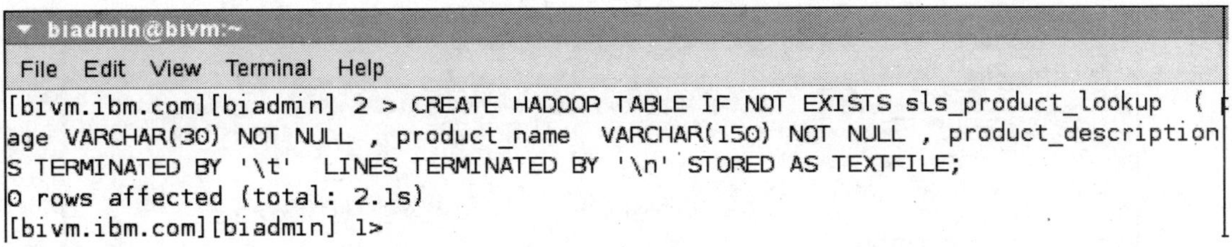

```
biadmin@bivm:~
File  Edit  View  Terminal  Help
[bivm.ibm.com][biadmin] 2 > CREATE HADOOP TABLE IF NOT EXISTS sls_product_lookup  ( p
age VARCHAR(30) NOT NULL , product_name  VARCHAR(150) NOT NULL , product_description
S TERMINATED BY '\t'  LINES TERMINATED BY '\n' STORED AS TEXTFILE;
0 rows affected (total: 2.1s)
[bivm.ibm.com][biadmin] 1>
```

7. Fact Table For Sales

```
CREATE HADOOP TABLE IF NOT EXISTS sls_sales_fact  ( order_day_key  INT
NOT NULL , organization_key  INT NOT NULL , employee_key  INT NOT NULL ,
retailer_key  INT NOT NULL , retailer_site_key  INT NOT NULL , product_
key  INT NOT NULL , promotion_key  INT NOT NULL , order_method_key  INT
NOT NULL , sales_order_key  INT NOT NULL , ship_day_key  INT NOT NULL
, close_day_key  INT NOT NULL , quantity  INT , unit_cost  DOUBLE ,
unit_price  DOUBLE , unit_sale_price  DOUBLE , gross_margin  DOUBLE ,
sale_total  DOUBLE , gross_profit  DOUBLE  )
ROW FORMAT DELIMITED  FIELDS TERMINATED BY '\t'  LINES TERMINATED BY '\n'
STORED AS TEXTFILE ;
```

```
biadmin@bivm:~
File  Edit  View  Terminal  Help
[bivm.ibm.com][biadmin] 1> CREATE HADOOP TABLE IF NOT EXISTS sls_sales_fact  ( o
NT NOT NULL , employee_key  INT NOT NULL , retailer_key  INT NOT NULL , retai
T NULL , promotion_key  INT NOT NULL , order_method_key  INT NOT NULL , sales_o
ULL , close_day_key  INT NOT NULL , quantity  INT , unit_cost  DOUBLE , unit_p
margin  DOUBLE , sale_total  DOUBLE , gross_profit  DOUBLE  )
[bivm.ibm.com][biadmin] 2> ROW FORMAT DELIMITED  FIELDS TERMINATED BY '\t'  LINE
0 rows affected (total: 2.51s)
[bivm.ibm.com][biadmin] 1>
```

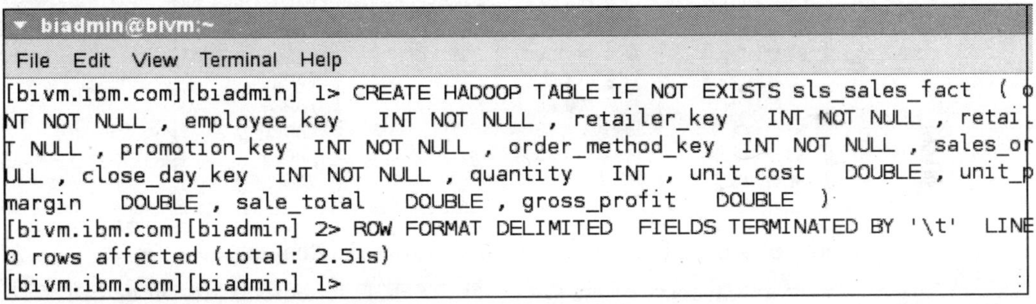

8. Fact Table For Marketing Promotions

```
CREATE HADOOP TABLE IF NOT EXISTS mrk_promotion_fact  ( organization_key
INT NOT NULL , order_day_key  INT NOT NULL , rtl_country_key  INT NOT NULL
, employee_key  INT NOT NULL , retailer_key  INT NOT NULL , product_key
INT NOT NULL , promotion_key  INT NOT NULL , sales_order_key  INT NOT
NULL , quantity  SMALLINT , unit_cost  DOUBLE , unit_price  DOUBLE ,
unit_sale_price  DOUBLE , gross_margin  DOUBLE , sale_total  DOUBLE ,
gross_profit  DOUBLE  ) ROW FORMAT DELIMITED  FIELDS TERMINATED BY '\t'
LINES TERMINATED BY '\n' STORED AS TEXTFILE;
```

```
biadmin@bivm:~
File  Edit  View  Terminal  Help
[bivm.ibm.com][biadmin] 1> CREATE HADOOP TABLE IF NOT EXISTS mrk_promotion_fact  (
y  INT NOT NULL , rtl_country_key  INT NOT NULL , employee_key   INT NOT NULL , re
NOT NULL , promotion_key  INT NOT NULL , sales_order_key  INT NOT NULL , quantity
 DOUBLE , unit_sale_price  DOUBLE , gross_margin   DOUBLE , sale_total   DOUBLE ,
 FIELDS TERMINATED BY '\t'  LINES TERMINATED BY '\n' STORED AS TEXTFILE;
0 rows affected (total: 0.75s)
[bivm.ibm.com][biadmin] 1>
```

Verify that all tables have been created by issuing following command:

\tables user

```
biadmin@bivm:~
File  Edit  View  Terminal  Help
[bivm.ibm.com][biadmin] 2> \tables user
+-------------+---------------------------+------------+
| TABLE_SCHEM | TABLE_NAME                | TABLE_TYPE |
+-------------+---------------------------+------------+
| BIADMIN     | GO_REGION_DIM             | TABLE      |
| BIADMIN     | MRK_PROMOTION_FACT        | TABLE      |
| BIADMIN     | SLS_ORDER_METHOD_DIM      | TABLE      |
| BIADMIN     | SLS_PRODUCT_BRAND_LOOKUP  | TABLE      |
| BIADMIN     | SLS_PRODUCT_DIM           | TABLE      |
| BIADMIN     | SLS_PRODUCT_LINE_LOOKUP   | TABLE      |
| BIADMIN     | SLS_PRODUCT_LOOKUP        | TABLE      |
| BIADMIN     | SLS_SALES_FACT            | TABLE      |
| SYSTOOLS    | HMON_ATM_INFO             | TABLE      |
| SYSTOOLS    | HMON_COLLECTION           | TABLE      |
| SYSTOOLS    | POLICY                    | TABLE      |
+-------------+---------------------------+------------+
```

Eight newly created tables have been listed alongwith some system tables.

Let's briefly explore some aspects of the CREATE TABLE statements shown here. If you have a SQL background, the majority of these statements should be familiar to you. However, after the column specification, there are some additional clauses unique to Big SQL – clauses that enable it to exploit Hadoop storage mechanisms (in this case, Hive).The ROW FORMAT clause specifies that fields are to be terminated by tabs ("'t") and lines are to be terminated by new line characters ("'n").The table will be stored in a TEXTFILE format, making it easy for a wide range of applications to work with.For details on these clauses, refer to the Apache Hive documentation.

4. Load data into each of these tables using sample data provided in files. One at a time, issue each of the following LOAD statements and verify that each completed successfully. Remember to change the SFTP and file path specifications (if needed) to match your environment. The statements will return a warning message providing details on the number of rows loaded, etc

```
load hadoop using file url
'sftp://biadmin:password@bivm:22/opt/ibm/biginsights/bigsql/samples/
data/GOSALESDW.GO_REGION_ DIM.txt' with SOURCE PROPERTIES ('field.
delimiter'='\t') INTO TABLE GO_REGION_DIM overwrite;
```

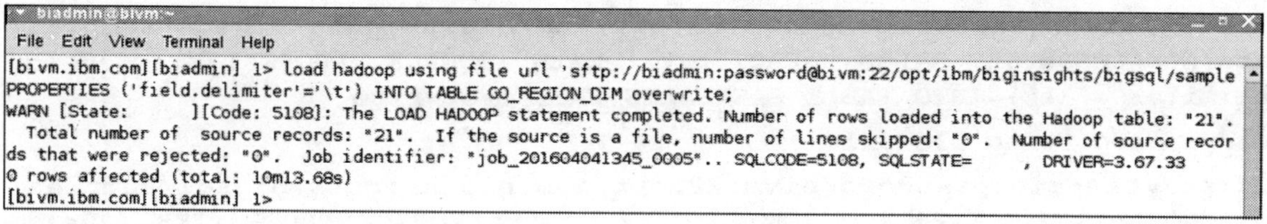

```
biadmin@bivm:~
File Edit View Terminal Help
[bivm.ibm.com][biadmin] 1> load hadoop using file url 'sftp://biadmin:password@bivm:22/opt/ibm/biginsights/bigsql/sample
PROPERTIES ('field.delimiter'='\t') INTO TABLE GO_REGION_DIM overwrite;
WARN [State:      ][Code: 5108]: The LOAD HADOOP statement completed. Number of rows loaded into the Hadoop table: "21".
 Total number of  source records: "21".  If the source is a file, number of lines skipped: "0".  Number of source recor
ds that were rejected: "0".  Job identifier: "job_201604041345_0005".. SQLCODE=5108, SQLSTATE=     , DRIVER=3.67.33
0 rows affected (total: 10m13.68s)
[bivm.ibm.com][biadmin] 1>
```

load hadoop using file url 'sftp://biadmin:password@bivm:22/opt/ibm/biginsights/bigsql/samples/data/GOSALESDW.SLS_ORDER_ METHOD_DIM.txt' with SOURCE PROPERTIES ('field. delimiter'='\t') INTO TABLE SLS_ORDER_METHOD_DIM overwrite;

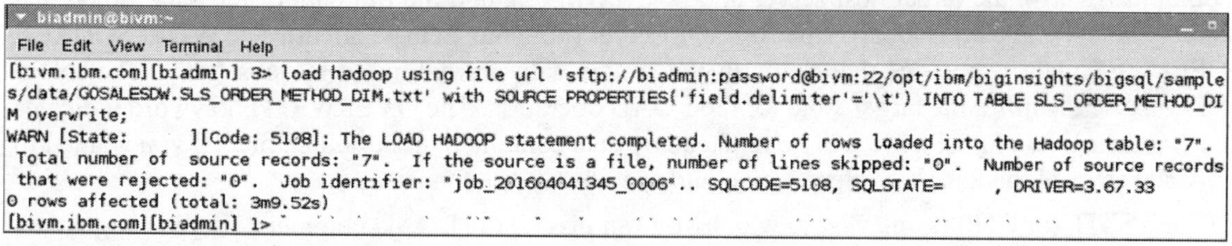

```
biadmin@bivm:~
File Edit View Terminal Help
[bivm.ibm.com][biadmin] 3> load hadoop using file url 'sftp://biadmin:password@bivm:22/opt/ibm/biginsights/bigsql/sample
s/data/GOSALESDW.SLS_ORDER_METHOD_DIM.txt' with SOURCE PROPERTIES('field.delimiter'='\t') INTO TABLE SLS_ORDER_METHOD_DI
M overwrite;
WARN [State:      ][Code: 5108]: The LOAD HADOOP statement completed. Number of rows loaded into the Hadoop table: "7".
 Total number of  source records: "7".  If the source is a file, number of lines skipped: "0".  Number of source records
 that were rejected: "0".  Job identifier: "job_201604041345_0006".. SQLCODE=5108, SQLSTATE=     , DRIVER=3.67.33
0 rows affected (total: 3m9.52s)
[bivm.ibm.com][biadmin] 1>
```

load hadoop using file url 'sftp://biadmin:password@bivm:22/opt/ibm/biginsights/bigsql/samples/data/GOSALESDW.SLS_PRODUC T_BRAND_LOOKUP.txt' with SOURCE PROPERTIES ('field.delimiter'='\t') INTO TABLE SLS_PRODUCT_BRAND_LOOKUP overwrite;

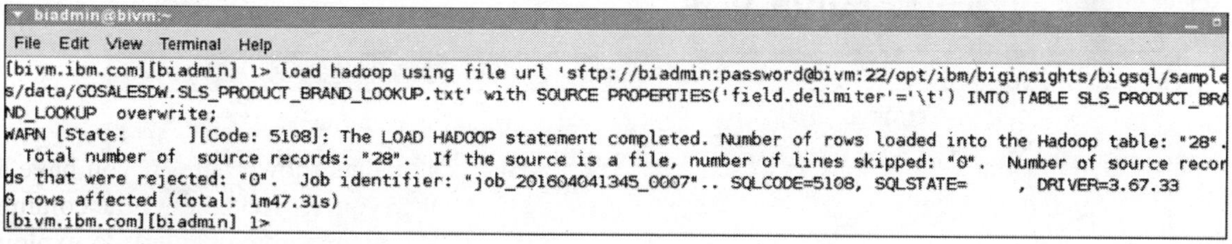

```
biadmin@bivm:~
File Edit View Terminal Help
[bivm.ibm.com][biadmin] 1> load hadoop using file url 'sftp://biadmin:password@bivm:22/opt/ibm/biginsights/bigsql/sample
s/data/GOSALESDW.SLS_PRODUCT_BRAND_LOOKUP.txt' with SOURCE PROPERTIES('field.delimiter'='\t') INTO TABLE SLS_PRODUCT_BRA
ND_LOOKUP  overwrite;
WARN [State:      ][Code: 5108]: The LOAD HADOOP statement completed. Number of rows loaded into the Hadoop table: "28".
 Total number of  source records: "28".  If the source is a file, number of lines skipped: "0".  Number of source recor
ds that were rejected: "0".  Job identifier: "job_201604041345_0007".. SQLCODE=5108, SQLSTATE=     , DRIVER=3.67.33
0 rows affected (total: 1m47.31s)
[bivm.ibm.com][biadmin] 1>
```

load hadoop using file url 'sftp://biadmin:password@bivm:22/opt/ibm/biginsights/bigsql/samples/data/GOSALESDW.SLS_PRODUC T_DIM.txt' with SOURCE PROPERTIES ('field. delimiter'='\t') INTO TABLE SLS_PRODUCT_DIM overwrite;

load hadoop using file url 'sftp://biadmin:password@bivm:22/opt/ibm/biginsights/bigsql/samples/data/GOSALESDW.SLS_PRODUC T_LINE_LOOKUP.txt' with SOURCE PROPERTIES ('field.delimiter'='\t') INTO TABLE SLS_PRODUCT_LINE_LOOKUP overwrite;

load hadoop using file url 'sftp://biadmin:password@bivm:22/opt/ibm/biginsights/bigsql/samples/data/GOSALESDW.SLS_PRODUC T_LOOKUP.txt' with SOURCE PROPERTIES ('field. delimiter'='\t') INTO TABLE SLS_PRODUCT_LOOKUP overwrite;

load hadoop using file url

```
'sftp://biadmin:password@bivm:22/opt/ibm/biginsights/bigsql/samples/data/GOSALESDW.SLS_SALES_ FACT.txt' with SOURCE PROPERTIES ('field.delimiter'='\t') INTO TABLE SLS_SALES_FACT overwrite;
load hadoop using file url
'sftp://biadmin:password@bivm:22/opt/ibm/biginsights/bigsql/samples/data/GOSALESDW.MRK_PROMOT ION_FACT.txt' with SOURCE PROPERTIES ('field.delimiter'='\t') INTO TABLE MRK_PROMOTION_FACT overwrite;
```

Let's explore the LOAD syntax shown in these examples briefly. Each example loads data into a table using a file URL specification that relies on SFTP to locate the source file (in this case, in a file on your local VM). In particular, the SFTP specification includes a valid user ID and password (biadmin/password), the target host server and port (bivm:22), and the full path of the data file on that system. Note that the path is local to the Big SQL server (not your Eclispe client). The WITH SOURCE PROPERTIES clause specifies that fields in the source data are delimited by tabs ("\t"). The INTO TABLE clause identifies the target table for the LOAD operation. The OVERWRITE keyword indicates that any existing data in the table will be replaced by data contained in the source file. (If you wanted to simply add rows to the table's content, you could specify APPEND instead.)

Using SFTP (or FTP) is one way in which you can invoke the LOAD command. If your target data already resides in your distributed file system, you can provide the DFS directory information in your file URL specification. Indeed, for optimal runtime performance, you may prefer to take that approach. In addition, you can load data directly from a remote relational DBMS via a JDBC connection.

1. Finding total rows in GO_REGION_DIM = 21

   select count(*) from GO_REGION_DIM;

```
biadmin@bivm:~
File  Edit  View  Terminal  Help
[bivm.ibm.com][biadmin] 1> select count(*) from GO_REGION_DIM;
+----+
|  1 |
+----+
| 21 |
+----+
1 row in results(first row: 1m15.67s; total: 1m15.68s)
[bivm.ibm.com][biadmin] 1>
```

2. To find total rows in sls_order_method_dim = 7

   Select count(*) from sls_order_method_dim;

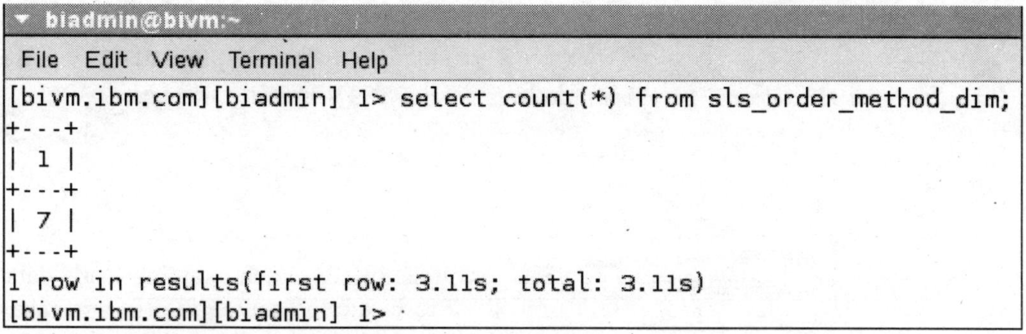

```
biadmin@bivm:~
File Edit View Terminal Help
[bivm.ibm.com][biadmin] 1> select count(*) from sls_order_method_dim;
+---+
| 1 |
+---+
| 7 |
+---+
1 row in results(first row: 3.11s; total: 3.11s)
[bivm.ibm.com][biadmin] 1>
```

3. To find total rows in SLS_PRODUCT_BRAND_LOOKUP = 28

   select count(*) from SLS_PRODUCT_BRAND_LOOKUP;

```
biadmin@bivm:~
File Edit View Terminal Help
[bivm.ibm.com][biadmin] 17> select count(*) from SLS_PRODUCT_BRAND_LOOKUP;
+----+
|  1 |
+----+
| 28 |
+----+
1 row in results(first row: 1.33s; total: 1.33s)
[bivm.ibm.com][biadmin] 1>
```

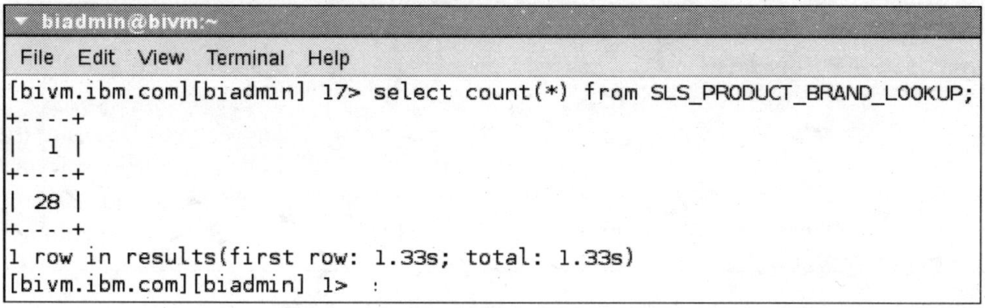

4. To find total rows in SLS_PRODUCT_DIM = 274

   select count(*) from SLS_PRODUCT_DIM;

```
biadmin@bivm:~
File Edit View Terminal Help
[bivm.ibm.com][biadmin] 1>      select count(*) from SLS_PRODUCT_DIM;
+-----+
|   1 |
+-----+
| 274 |
+-----+
1 row in results(first row: 0.10s; total: 0.10s)
[bivm.ibm.com][biadmin] 1> select count(*) from SLS_PRODUCT_LINE_LOOKUP;
```

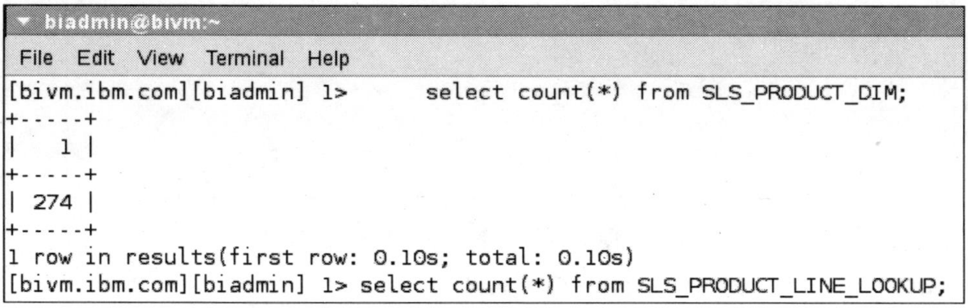

5. To find total rows in SLS_PRODUCT_LINE_LOOKUP = 5

   select count(*) from SLS_PRODUCT_LINE_LOOKUP;

```
biadmin@bivm:~
File  Edit  View  Terminal  Help
[bivm.ibm.com][biadmin] 1> select count(*) from SLS_PRODUCT_LINE_LOOKUP;
+---+
| 1 |
+---+
| 5 |
+---+
1 row in results(first row: 0.13s; total: 0.13s)
[bivm.ibm.com][biadmin] 1>
```

6. To find total rows in SLS_PRODUCT_LOOKUP = 6302

select count(*) from SLS_PRODUCT_LOOKUP;

```
biadmin@bivm:~
File  Edit  View  Terminal  Help
[bivm.ibm.com][biadmin] 2>     select count(*) from SLS_PRODUCT_LOOKUP;
+------+
|    1 |
+------+
| 6302 |
+------+
1 row in results(first row: 0.11s; total: 0.11s)
[bivm.ibm.com][biadmin] 1>
```

7. To find total rows in SLS_SALES_FACT = 446023

select count(*) from SLS_SALES_FACT;

```
[bivm.ibm.com][biadmin] 2>     select count(*) from SLS_SALES_FACT;
+--------+
|      1 |
+--------+
| 446023 |
+--------+
1 row in results(first row: 0.26s; total: 0.26s)
[bivm.ibm.com][biadmin] 1>
```

8. To find total rows gosalesdw.MRK_PROMOTION_FACT = 11034

select count(*) from MRK_PROMOTION_FACT;

```
[bivm.ibm.com][biadmin] 2>  select count(*) from MRK_PROMOTION_FACT;
+-------+
|     1 |
+-------+
| 11034 |
+-------+
1 row in results(first row: 0.15s; total: 0.15s)
```

EXERCISE 12.8: Querying The Data With Big SQL

Now we have created sufficient base to query above tables. Based on earlier exercises, you've already seen that you can perform basic SQL operations, including projections (to extract specific columns from your tables) and restrictions (to extract specific rows meeting certain conditions you specified).Let's explore a few examples that are a bit more sophisticated.

In this lesson, you will create and run Big SQL queries that join data from multiple tables as well as perform aggregations and other SQL operations. Note that the queries included in this section are based on queries shipped with BigInsights as samples.

You may find it easiest to use Eclipse to issue the following Big SQL statements. You can also execute them from the JSqsh shell, but some return hundreds of thousands of rows. The Eclipse SQL Results page limits output to only 500 rows. (You can change that value in the Data Management preferences.)

1. Join data from multiple tables to return the product name, quantity and order method of goods that have been sold. To do so, execute the following query.

```
-- Fetch the product name, quantity, and order method
-- of products sold.
-- Query 1
SELECT pnumb.product_name, sales.quantity, meth.order_method_en
FROM
sls_sales_fact sales,
sls_product_dim prod,
sls_product_lookup pnumb,
sls_order_method_dim meth
WHERE
pnumb.product_language='EN'
AND sales.product_key=prod.product_key
AND prod.product_number=pnumb.product_number
AND meth.order_method_key=sales.order_method_key
AND order_method_en='Sales visit';
```

We have asked pnumb.product_name, sales.quantity, meth.order_method from the table MRK_PROMOTION_FACT

Let's review a few aspects of this query briefly:

- Data from four tables will be used to drive the results of this query (see the tables referenced in the FROM clause).Relationships between these tables are resolved through 3 join predicates specified as part of the WHERE clause.The query relies on 3 equi-joins to filter data from the referenced tables.(Predicates such as prod.product_number=pnumb.product_number help to narrow the results to product numbers that match in two tables.)

- For improved readability, this query uses aliases in the SELECT and FROM clauses when referencing tables.For example, pnumb.product_name refers to "pnumb," which is the alias for the gosalesdw.sls_product_lookup table. Once defined in the FROM clause, an alias can be used in the WHERE clause so that you do not need to repeat the complete table name.
- The use of the predicate and pnumb.product_language='EN' helps to further narrow the result to only English output. This database contains thousands of rows of data in various languages, so restricting the language provides some optimization.

We have asked for listing the details under following heads (columns) of the table:

PRODUCT_NAME	QUANTITY	ORDER_METHOD_EN

```
biadmin@bivm:~
File  Edit  View  Terminal  Help
| Legend                                        |         5 | Web              |
| Zone                                          |        52 | Web              |
| Kodiak                                        |        13 | Web              |
| Venue                                         |         5 | Web              |
| Fairway                                       |        20 | Web              |
| Inferno                                       |        29 | Web              |
| Lux                                           |        12 | Web              |
| Lux                                           |        15 | Web              |
| Maximus                                       |        22 | Web              |
| TX                                            |        11 | Web              |
| Lux                                           |        38 | Web              |
| Lux                                           |        39 | Web              |
| TX                                            |        34 | Web              |
| Legend                                        |        25 | Web              |
| Zone                                          |       179 | Web              |
| Infinity                                      |        31 | Web              |
| Ranger Vision                                 |        48 | Web              |
| TX                                            |        42 | Web              |
| Zone                                          |       244 | Web              |
| Zone                                          |       210 | Web              |
| Retro                                         |       125 | Web              |
| Cat Eye                                       |        56 | Web              |
| Dante                                         |        40 | Web              |
| Inferno                                       |        32 | Web              |
| Inferno                                       |        23 | Web              |
| Inferno                                       |        30 | Web              |
| Max Gizmo                                     |         6 | Web              |
+-----------------------------------------------+-----------+------------------+
446023 rows in results(first row: 1.60s; total: 1m1.50s)
[bivm.ibm.com][biadmin] 1>
```

The table is so big, it is not possible to show it here. Although it shoes only web as Order-Method, it has listed so many other methods like Sales Visit, Fxx, Telephone,E-mail, Mail and Specialetc.

2. Modify the query to restrict the order method to one type – those involving a Sales visit. To do so, add the following query predicate just before the semi-colon:

   --Query 2

   AND order_method_en='Sales visit'

3. Inspect the results, a subset of which is shown below:

```
| Granite Climbing Helmet              |   808 | Sales visit   |
| TrailChef Water Bag                  |  4363 | Sales visit   |
| TrailChef Cook Set                   |   937 | Sales visit   |
| TrailChef Utensils                   |  1962 | Sales visit   |
| Star Gazer 6                         |    43 | Sales visit   |
| Firefly Lite                         |   718 | Sales visit   |
| Firefly Mapreader                    |   925 | Sales visit   |
| Firefly 4                            |   390 | Sales visit   |
| Firefly Extreme                      |   204 | Sales visit   |
| EverGlow Single                      |   716 | Sales visit   |
| EverGlow Butane                      |   170 | Sales visit   |
| Husky Rope 60                        |   171 | Sales visit   |
| Firefly Climbing Lamp                |   191 | Sales visit   |
| Firefly Charger                      |   236 | Sales visit   |
| Granite Axe                          |  1470 | Sales visit   |
| Granite Extreme                      |  1176 | Sales visit   |
| Husky Harness Extreme                |   990 | Sales visit   |
| Granite Signal Mirror                |   535 | Sales visit   |
| Firefly Climbing Lamp                |   536 | Sales visit   |
| Firefly Charger                      |   536 | Sales visit   |
| Firefly Rechargeable Battery         |   536 | Sales visit   |
| Granite Ice                          |   734 | Sales visit   |
| Granite Hammer                       |   479 | Sales visit   |
| Granite Shovel                       |   377 | Sales visit   |
| Granite Grip                         |  1006 | Sales visit   |
| Sun Shield                           |   382 | Sales visit   |
+--------------------------------------+-------+---------------+
15842 rows in results(first row: 1.2s; total: 3.13s)
[bivm.ibm.com][biadmin] 1>
```

4. To find out which sales method of all the methods has the greatest quantity of orders, add a GROUP BY clause (group by pll.product_line_en, md.order_method_en). In addition, invoke the SUM aggregate function (sum(sf.quantity)) to total the orders by product and method. Finally, this query cleans up the output a bit by using aliases (e.g., as Product) to substitute a more readable column header.

```
        -- Query 3
SELECT pll.product_line_en AS Product,
md.order_method_en AS Order_method,
sum(sf.QUANTITY) AS total
FROM
sls_order_method_dim AS md,
```

```
sls_product_dim AS pd,
sls_product_line_lookup AS pll,
sls_product_brand_lookup AS pbl,
sls_sales_fact AS sf
WHERE
pd.product_key = sf.product_key
AND md.order_method_key = sf.order_method_key
AND pll.product_line_code = pd.product_line_code
AND pbl.product_brand_code = pd.product_brand_code
GROUP BY pll.product_line_en, md.order_method_en;
```

5. Inspect the results, which should contain 35 rows. A portion is shown below.

```
biadmin@bivm:~
File Edit View Terminal Help
[bivm.ibm.com][biadmin] 1> SELECT pll.product_line_en AS Product,
[bivm.ibm.com][biadmin] 2> md.order_method_en AS Order_method,
[bivm.ibm.com][biadmin] 3> sum(sf.QUANTITY) AS total
[bivm.ibm.com][biadmin] 4> FROM
[bivm.ibm.com][biadmin] 5> sls_order_method_dim AS md,
[bivm.ibm.com][biadmin] 6> sls_product_dim AS pd,
[bivm.ibm.com][biadmin] 7> sls_product_line_lookup AS pll,
[bivm.ibm.com][biadmin] 8> sls_product_brand_lookup AS pbl,
[bivm.ibm.com][biadmin] 9> sls_sales_fact AS sf
[bivm.ibm.com][biadmin] 10> WHERE
[bivm.ibm.com][biadmin] 11> pd.product_key = sf.product_key
[bivm.ibm.com][biadmin] 12> AND md.order_method_key = sf.order_method_key
[bivm.ibm.com][biadmin] 13> AND pll.product_line_code = pd.product_line_code
[bivm.ibm.com][biadmin] 14> AND pbl.product_brand_code = pd.product_brand_code
[bivm.ibm.com][biadmin] 15> GROUP BY pll.product_line_en, md.order_method_en;
+----------------------------+---------------+----------+
| PRODUCT                    | ORDER_METHOD  |    TOTAL |
+----------------------------+---------------+----------+
| Camping Equipment          | E-mail        |  1413084 |
| Camping Equipment          | Fax           |   413958 |
| Camping Equipment          | Mail          |   348058 |
| Camping Equipment          | Sales visit   |  2899754 |
| Camping Equipment          | Special       |   203528 |
| Camping Equipment          | Telephone     |  2792588 |
| Camping Equipment          | Web           | 19230179 |
| Golf Equipment             | E-mail        |   333300 |
```

12.13.4. Optional: Using Big SQL to work with data exported from BigSheets

In some cases, you may want to share data from BigSheets workbooks with a variety of applications, including Big SQL applications. Rather than creating a Big SQL table directly (as you did in a previous exercise), you may find it convenient to work directly with an exported file, such as the TSV file you created earlier.This optional section explores how you can do so.

As a reminder, the BigSheets workbook that you exported earlier into a TSV file with these fields:

1. Country – a two-letter country identifier.
2. FeedInfo – information from web feeds, with varying lengths.
3. Language – string that identifies the language of the feed.
4. Published – date and time of publication.
5. SubjectHtml – a string-based subject of varying length.
6. Tags – a string of varying length that provides categories.
7. Type – a string identifying the source of the web feed, e.g., blog or news feed.
8. URL – the web address of the feed, with varying length.

In this section, you will create a Big SQL table for this data that points to the DFS directory where you exported your workbook. In effect, you will be layering a Big SQL schema definition over all files in the directory and creating a table that is managed externally from the Hive warehouse.Later, if you were to drop the Big SQL table, this directory and its contents would remain.

1. Issue the following CREATE TABLE statement:

```
        -- Create an external table based on BigSheets data exported to your
DFS.
-- Before running this statement,

-- update the location info as needed for your system
createhadoop tablesheetsOut
(country varchar(2),
FeedInfo varchar(300),
Country Lang varchar(25),
published varchar(25),
subject varchar(300),
mediatype varchar(20),
tags varchar(100),
url varchar(100))
row format delimited fields terminated by'\t'
location '/user/biadmin/sampleData/SheetsExport'
```

2. Query the table 1

   Select countrylang, subject, url from sheets Out fetch first5 rows only;

3. Inspect the results.

Status Result1

	COUNTRYLANG	SUBJECT	URL
1	English	Are you ready for <Keyword>IBM Wats	http://fbhalper.wordpress.com/2012/02/13/are-you-ready-for-i
2	English	<Keyword>IBM Watson</Keyword> – v	http://andvijaysays.wordpress.com/2012/03/22/ibm-watson-what
3	English	<Keyword>IBM Watson</Keyword> Gc	http://ducknetweb.blogspot.com/2012/03/ibm-watson-going-to-w
4	English	<Keyword>IBM Watson</Keyword>, dc	http://likeabanana.wordpress.com/2012/02/02/ibm-watson-does-
5	Portuguese	Processamento de linguagem natural u	http://imasters.com.br.feedsportal.com/c/33212/f/546640/s/1b

EXERCISE 12.9: Working With Non-Traditional Data

While data structured in CSV and TSV columns are often stored in BigInsights and loaded into Big SQL tables, you may also need to work with other types of data – data that might require the use of a serializer / deserializer (SerDe). SerDes are common in the Hadoop environment. You'll find a number of SerDes available in the public domain, or you can write your own following typical Hadoop practices.

Using a SerDe with Big SQL is pretty straightforward. Once you develop or locate the SerDe you need, just add its JAR file to the appropriate BigInsights subdirectories. Then stop and restart the Big SQL service, and specify the SerDe class name when you create your table. (Note: If needed, look in your JAR file to determine the class name of the SerDe you'll be using. The CREATE TABLE statement requires the class name, not the JAR file name.)

In this exercise, you will use a SerDe to define a table for blog data collected in a JSON (JavaScript Object Notation) format. JSON files have a nested, varied structure defined by the user or application that created them. The JSON-based blog file for this exercise is the same blog file you used as input to BigSheets in a prior Exercise. As you'll recall, this data was generated by a BigInsights sample application that collects social media data from various public Web sites. The sample data is available for free download as part of a developer Works article on Analyzing Social Media and Structured Data with InfoSphere Biginsights.

After you complete the lessons in this module, you will understand how to:

- Register a SerDe with Big SQL and Hive
- Create a Big SQL table that uses a SerDe for processing JSON data
- Populate a Big SQL table with JSON data
- Query this Big SQL table

12.14.1 Registering a SerDe

In this exercise, you will provide a JSON-based SerDe to Big SQL and Hive so that you can later create a table that relies on this SerDe.

1. Download the hive-json-serde-0.2.jar into a directory of your choice on your local file system, such as/home/biadmin/sampleData. (As of this writing, the full URL for this SerDe ishttps://code.google.com/p/hive-json-serde/downloads/detail?name=hive-json-serde-0.2.jar)
2. Register the SerDe with BigInsights.
   a) Stop the Big SQL server.(You can do this from a terminal window with the command$BIGINSIGHTS_HOME/bin/stop.sh bigsql or you can use the Cluster Status tab of the BigInsights Web console.)

b) Copy the SerDe .jar file to the $BIGSQL_HOME/userlib and $HIVE_HOME/lib directories.

c) Restart the Big SQL server.(You can do this from a terminal window with the command$BIGINSIGHTS_HOME/bin/start.sh bigsql or you can use the Cluster Status tab of the Web console.)

12.14.2 Creating, populating, and querying a table that uses a SerDe

Now that you've registered your SerDe, you're ready to use it. In this section, you will create a table that relies on the SerDe you just registered. For simplicity, this will be an externally managed table – i.e., a table created over a user directory that resides outside of the Hive warehouse. This user directory will contain all the table's data in files.As part of this exercise, you will upload the sample blogs-data.txt file into the target DFS directory.

Creating a Big SQL table over an existing DFS directory has the effect of populating this table with all the data in the directory. To satisfy queries, Big SQL will look in the user directory specified when you created the table and consider all files in that directory to be the table's contents. This is consistent with the Hive concept of an externally managed table.

Once the table is created, you'll query that table.In doing so, you'll note that the presence of a SerDe is transparent to your queries.

1. If necessary, download the .zip file containing the sample data from the bottom half of the articlereferenced in the introduction.Unzip the file into a directory on your local file system, such as/home/biadmin. You will be working with the blogs-data.txt file.

From the Files tab of the Web console, navigate to the /user/biadmin/sampleData directory of your distributed file system. Use the create directory button to create a subdirectory named SerDe-Test.

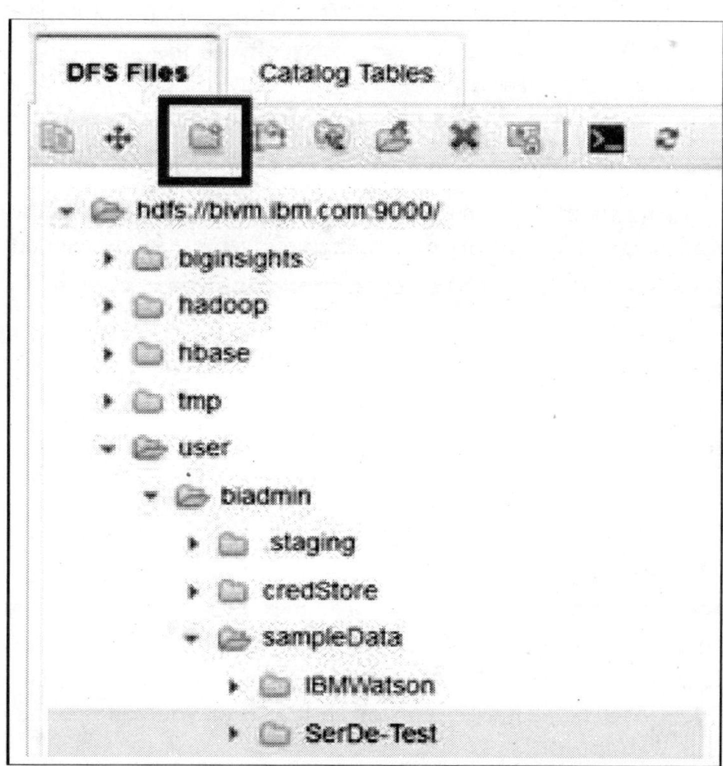

2. Upload the blogs-data.txt file into /user/biadmin/sampleData/SerDe-Test.

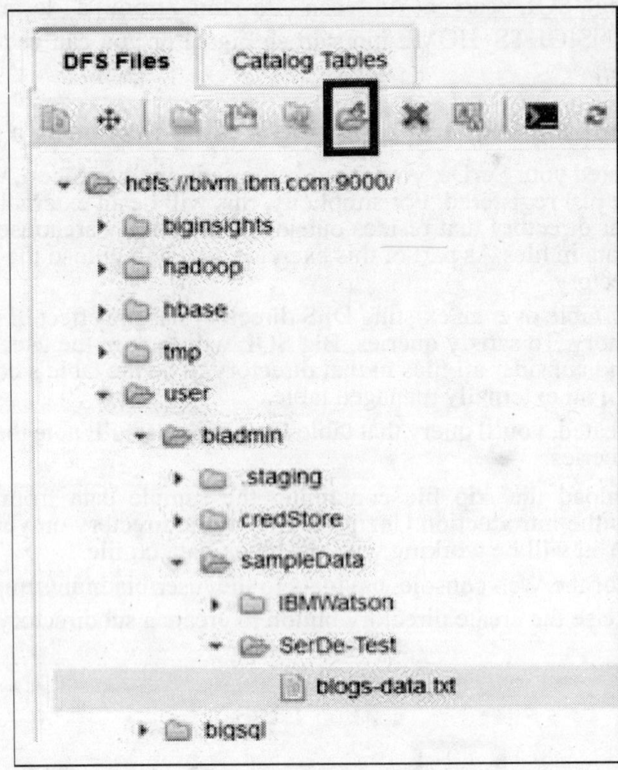

3. Return to the Big SQL execution environment of your choice (JSqsh or Eclipse).
4. Execute the following statement, which creates a TESTBLOGS table that includes a LOCATION clause that specifies the DFS directory containing your sample blogs-data.txt file:

```
Create hadoop table if notexists testblogs (
Country String,
Crawled String,
FeedInfo String,
Inserted String,
IsAdult int,
Language String,
Postsize int,
Published String,
SubjectHtml String,
Tags String,
Type String,
Url String )
```

```
row format serde 'org.apache.hadoop.hive.contrib.serde2.JsonSerde'
location '/user/biadmin/sampleData/SerDe-Test'
```

5. Finally, query the table using the following statement.

```
select* fromtestblogs</pre>
<pre>wheresubjecthtml isnotnull</pre>
<pre>fetchfirst5 rowsonly;
```

Note that the SELECT syntax does not reference the SerDe in any way.

6. Inspect the results.

	COUNTRY	CRAWLED	FEEDINFO	INSERTED	ISADULT	LANGUAGE	POSTSIZE	PUBLISHED	SUBJECTHTML	TAGS	TYPE	URL
1		2012-03-24	{"Title":"",[illegible]	2012-03-24	0	English	10628	2012-03-22 1	<Keyword>IBM		blog	http://andejaysays.wordpress.co
2		2012-03-07	{"Title":"Me	2012-03-07	0	English	15625	2012-03-07 C	<Keyword>IBM		blog	http://ducknetweb.blogspot.com/2
3		2012-02-02	{"Title":"Fly	2012-02-02	0	English	3227	2012-02-02 2	<Keyword>IBM		blog	http://likeabanana.wordpress.com
4		2012-01-18	{"Title":"iMa	2012-01-18	0	Portuguese	9892	2012-01-18 1	Processamento		blog	http://imasters.com.br.feedsportal
5	DE	2012-03-06	{"Title":"Ru	2012-03-06	0	German	3036	2012-03-06 1	Citi Bank prüft E		blog	http://www.ruk-publishing.com/info

CHAPTER

13

Sqoop : Importing Data from Heterogeneous Sources

13.1 INTRODUCTION TO SQOOP

Big data systems are popular for processing huge amounts of unstructured data from multiple data sources. The complexity of the big data system increases with each data source. Most of the business domains have different data types like marketing genes in healthcare, audio and video systems, telecom CDR, and social media. All these have diverse data sources and data from these sources is consistently produced on large scale.

Getting data into the Hadoop cluster plays a critical role in any big data deployment. Data ingestion is important in any big data project because the volume of data is generally in petabytes or exabytes. Sqoop and Hadoop Flume are the two tools in Hadoop which is used to gather data from different sources and load them into HDFS. Sqoop in Hadoop is mostly used to extract structured data from databases like Teradata, Oracle, etc., and Flume in Hadoop is used to sources data which is stored in various sources like and deals mostly with unstructured data.

The challenge is to leverage the resources available and manage the consistency of data. Data ingestion is complex in hadoop because processing is done in batch, stream or in real time which increases the management and complexity of data. Some of the common challenges with data ingestion in Hadoop are parallel processing, data quality, machine data on a higher scale of several gigabytes per minute, multiple source ingestion, real-time ingestion and scalability. Apache Sqoop and Apache Flume help organizations overcome the challenges encountered in data ingestion.

Apache Sqoop (SQL-to-Hadoop) is designed to support bulk import of data into HDFS from structured data stores such as relational databases, enterprise data warehouses, and NoSQL systems. Sqoop is based upon a connector architecture which supports plugins to provide connectivity to new external systems.

An example use case of Sqoop, is an enterprise that runs a nightly Sqoop import to load the day's data from a production transactional RDBMS into a Hive data warehouse for further analysis.

13.2 SQOOP CONNECTORS

Data transfer between Sqoop and external storage system is made possible with the help of Sqoop's connectors. All the existing Database Management Systems are designed with SQL standard in mind. However, each DBMS differs with respect to dialect to some extent. So, this difference poses challenges when it comes to data transfers across the systems. Sqoop Connectors are components which help overcome these challenges.

Sqoop has connectors for working with a range of popular relational databases, including MySQL, PostgreSQL, Oracle, SQL Server, and DB2. Each of these connectors knows how to interact with its associated DBMS. There is also a generic JDBC connector for connecting to any database that supports Java's JDBC protocol. In addition, Sqoop provides optimized MySQL and PostgreSQL connectors that use database-specific APIs to perform bulk transfers efficiently.

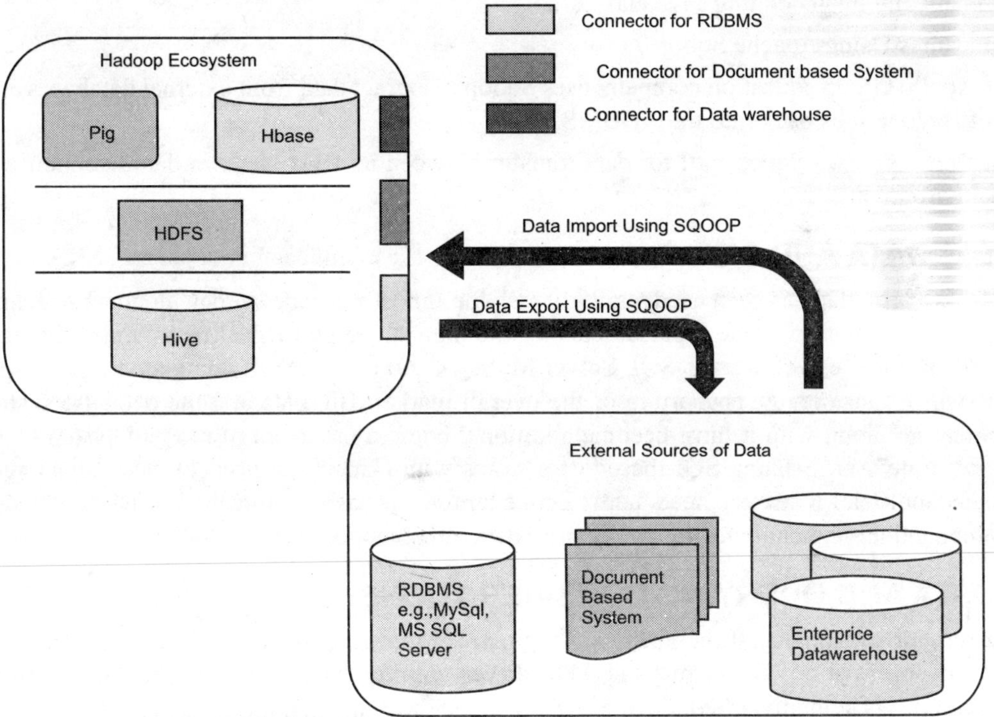

Figure. 13.1: Data Connectors in SQOOP

In addition to this, Sqoop has various third party connectors for data stores, ranging from enterprise data warehouses (including Netezza, Teradata, and Oracle) to NoSQL stores (such as Couchbase). However, these connectors do not come with Sqoop bundle; those need to be downloaded separately and can be added easily to an existing Sqoop installation.

13.3 HOW APACHE SQOOP WORKS?

Sqoop is an effective hadoop tool for non-programmers which functions by looking at the databases that need to be imported and choosing a relevant import function for the source data. Once the input is recognized by Sqoop hadoop, the metadata for the table is read and a class definition is created for the input requirements. Hadoop Sqoop can be forced to function selectively by just getting the columns needed before input instead of importing the entire input and looking for the data in it. This saves considerable amount of time. In reality, the import from the database to HDFS is accomplished by a MapReduce job that is created in the background by Apache Sqoop.

Apache Sqoop supports bulk import i.e. it can import the complete database or individual tables into HDFS. The files will be stored in the HDFS file system and the data in built-in directories.Sqoop parallelizes data transfer for optimal system utilization and fast performance.

Apache Sqoop provides direct input i.e. it can map relational databases and import directly into HBase and Hive.Sqoop makes data analysis efficient.

Sqoop helps in mitigating the excessive loads to external systems.Sqoop provides data interaction programmatically by generating Java classes.

Companies Using Apache Sqoop

The Apollo Group education company uses Sqoop to extract data from external databases and inject results of Hadoop jobs back into the RDBMS's.

Coupons.com uses Sqoop tool for data transfer between its IBM Netezza data warehouse and the hadoop environment.

13.4 BIG DATA AND SQL

"Big data" is a term that has been used regularly now for almost a decade. And it, along with technologies such as NoSQL, are seen as the replacements for the long successful RDBMS solutions that use SQL. Today, DB2®, Oracle, Microsoft® SQL Server MySQL, and PostgreSQL dominate the SQL space and still make up a considerable proportion of the overall market. Big data and the database systems and services that go along with it have become additional cogs in the gears of modern systems. But how do you integrate your existing SQL-based data stores with Hadoop so you can take advantage of the different technologies when you need them? Let's examine the basic architectural aspects of exchanging information and basic techniques for performing data interchange.

13.5 DATA AND QUERYING CONSIDERATIONS

The most important consideration when exchanging information between SQL and Hadoop is the data format of the information. The format should be driven entirely from the perspective of the information and the reason it is being exported.

Simply exporting your data and then importing it into Hadoop doesn't solve any problems. You need to know exactly what you are importing, why you are importing it, and what you expect to get out of the process.

Before we look at the specifics of why you are exchanging the data to begin with, first consider the nature of the data exchange. Is it one-way? Or is it two-way?

One-way data exchange — from SQL to Hadoop, or Hadoop to SQL — is practical in situations where the data is being transported to take advantage of the query functionality, and the source is not the companion database solution. For example, pure-textual data, or the raw results of a computational or analysis program, might be stored in Hadoop, processed with MapReduce, and stored in SQL (see Figure 13.2).

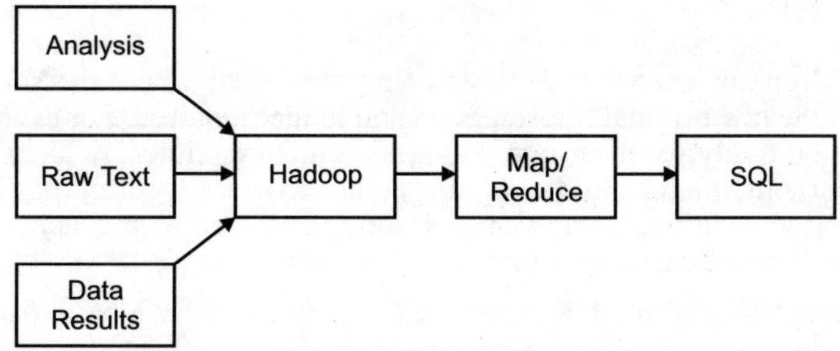

Figure. 13.2: Hadoop to SQL translations

The reverse is less common, where information is extracted from SQL into Hadoop, but it can be used to process SQL-based content that provides a lot of textual content, such as blogs, forums, CRM and other systems (see Figure 13.3).

Figure. 13.3: SQL to Hadoop translations

Two-way data exchange is more common and provides the best of both worlds in terms of the data exchange and data processing (see Figure 13.4).

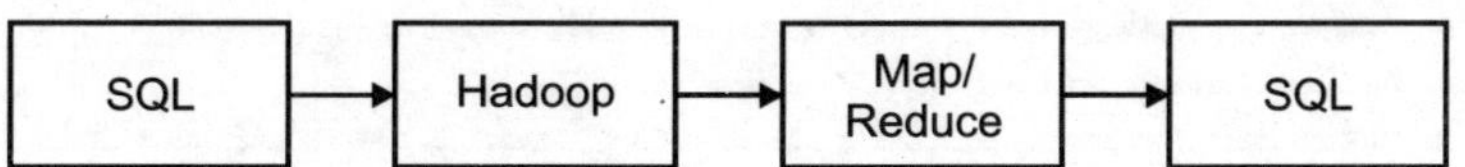

Figure. 13.4: Bidirectional translations

Although there are many examples, the most common one is to take large, linear datasets and text datasets from the SQL and convert that into summarized information that can be processed by a Hadoop cluster. The summarized information can then be imported back into your SQL store. This is particularly useful where the large dataset would take too long to process within an SQL query. An example would be a large corpus of review scores or word/term counts.

As a rule, there are three primary reasons for interfacing between SQL and Hadoop:

1. **Exporting for storage**— Hadoop provides a practical solution for storing large amounts of infrequently used data in a format that can be queried, processed, and extracted. For example: Usage logs, access logs, and error information are all practical for insertion into a Hadoop cluster to take advantage of the HDFS architecture. A secondary feature of this type of export is that the information can later be processed or parsed and converted into a format that can be used again.

2. **Exporting for analysis**— Two common cases are exporting for reimport to SQL and exporting the analysis output to be used directly in your application (analyzing and storing the result in JSON, for example). Hadoop provides the advantage here by allowing for distributed large-scale processing of information rather than the single-table host processing provided in SQL. With the analysis route, the original information is generally kept, but the analysis process is used to provide summary or statistical bases that work alongside the original data.
3. **Exporting for processing**— Processing-based exports are designed to take the original raw source information, process and reduce or simplify it, then store that information back to replace the original data. This type of exchange is most commonly used where the source information has been captured, but the raw original information is no longer required. For example, logging data of various forms can be easily resolved into a simpler structure, either by looking for specific event types or by summarizing the data to counts of specific errors or occurrences. The raw data is often not required here. Reducing that data through Hadoop and loading the summary stats back, saves time and makes the content easier to query.
4. With these basic principles in mind, let's look at the techniques for a basic data exchange between SQL and Hadoop.

13.6 IMPORTING A TABLE

Sqoop tool 'import' is used to import table data from the table to the Hadoop file system as a text file or a binary file. The following command is used to import the **emp** table from MySQL database server to HDFS.

```
$ sqoop import \
--connect jdbc:mysql://localhost/userdb \
--username root \
--table emp --m 1
```

If it is executed successfully, then you get the following output.

```
14/12/22 15:24:54 INFO sqoop.Sqoop: Running Sqoop version: 1.4.5
14/12/22 15:24:56 INFO manager.MySQLManager: Preparing to use a MySQL streaming resultset.
14/12/22 15:24:56 INFO tool.CodeGenTool: Beginning code generation
14/12/22 15:24:58 INFO manager.SqlManager: Executing SQL statement: SELECT t.* FROM `emp` AS t LIMIT 1
14/12/22 15:24:58 INFO manager.SqlManager: Executing SQL statement: SELECT t.* FROM `emp` AS t LIMIT 1
14/12/22 15:24:58 INFO orm.CompilationManager: HADOOP_MAPRED_HOME is /usr/local/hadoop
14/12/22 15:25:11 INFO orm.CompilationManager: Writing jar file: /tmp/sqoop-
hadoop/compile/cebe706d23ebb1fd99c1f063ad51ebd7/emp.jar
-----------------------------------------------------
-----------------------------------------------------
14/12/22 15:25:40 INFO mapreduce.Job: The url to track the job:
http://localhost:8088/proxy/application_1419242001831_0001/
14/12/22 15:26:45 INFO mapreduce.Job: Job job_1419242001831_0001 running in uber mode : false
14/12/22 15:26:45 INFO mapreduce.Job: map 0% reduce 0%
14/12/22 15:28:08 INFO mapreduce.Job: map 100% reduce 0%
14/12/22 15:28:16 INFO mapreduce.Job: Job job_1419242001831_0001 completed successfully
-----------------------------------------------------
-----------------------------------------------------
14/12/22 15:28:17 INFO mapreduce.ImportJobBase: Transferred 145 bytes in 177.5849 seconds (0.8165 bytes/sec)
14/12/22 15:28:17 INFO mapreduce.ImportJobBase: Retrieved 5 records.
```

To verify the imported data in HDFS, use the following command.

```
$ $HADOOP_HOME/bin/hadoop fs -cat /emp/part-m-*
```

It shows you the **emp** table data and fields are separated with comma (,).

```
1201, gopal,    manager, 50000, TP
1202, manisha,  preader, 50000, TP
1203, kalil,    php dev, 30000, AC
1204, prasanth, php dev, 30000, AC
1205, kranthi,  admin,   20000, TP
```

13.6.1 Importing into Target Directory

We can specify the target directory while importing table data into HDFS using the Sqoop import tool.

Following is the syntax to specify the target directory as option to the Sqoop import command.

```
--target-dir <new or exist directory in HDFS>
```

The following command is used to import **emp_add** table data into '/queryresult' directory.

```
$ sqoop import \
--connect jdbc:mysql://localhost/userdb \
--username root \
--table emp_add \
--m 1 \
--target-dir /queryresult
```

The following command is used to verify the imported data in /queryresult directory form **emp_add** table.

```
$ $HADOOP_HOME/bin/hadoop fs -cat /queryresult/part-m-*
```

It will show you the emp_add table data with comma (,) separated fields.

```
1201, 288A, vgiri,   jublee
1202, 108I, aoc,     sec-bad
1203, 144Z, pgutta,  hyd
1204, 78B,  oldcity, sec-bad
1205, 720C, hitech,  sec-bad
```

13.6.2 Import Subset of Table Data

We can import a subset of a table using the 'where' clause in Sqoop import tool. It executes the corresponding SQL query in the respective **database** server and stores the result in a target directory in HDFS.

The syntax for where clause is as follows.

```
--Where <condition>
```

The following command is used to import a subset of **emp_add** table data. The subset query is to retrieve the employee id and address, who lives in Secunderabad city.

```
$ sqoop import \
--connect jdbc:mysql://localhost/userdb \
--username root \
--table emp_add \
--m 1 \
--where "city ='sec-bad'" \
--target-dir /wherequery
```

The following command is used to verify the imported data in /wherequery directory from the **emp_add** table.

```
$ $HADOOP_HOME/bin/hadoop fs -cat /wherequery/part-m-*
```

It will show you the **emp_add** table data with comma (,) separated fields.

```
1202, 108I, aoc,      sec-bad
1204, 78B,  oldcity, sec-bad
1205, 720C, hitech,   sec-bad
```

13.6.3 Incremental Import

Incremental import is a technique that imports only the newly added rows in a table. It is required to add 'incremental', 'check-column', and 'last-value' options to perform the incremental import.

The following syntax is used for the incremental option in Sqoop import command.

```
--incremental <mode>
--check-column <column name>
--last value <last check column value>
```

Let us assume the newly added data into emp table is as follows:

```
1206, satish p, grp des, 20000, GR
```

The following command is used to perform the incremental import in the **emp**table.

```
$ sqoop import \
--connect jdbc:mysql://localhost/userdb \
--username root \
--table emp \
--m 1 \
--incremental append \
--check-column id \
-last value 1205
```

The following command is used to verify the imported data from emp table to HDFS emp/ directory.

```
$ $HADOOP_HOME/bin/hadoop fs -cat /emp/part-m-*
```

It shows you the **emp** table data with comma (,) separated fields.

```
1201, gopal,    manager, 50000, TP
1202, manisha,  preader, 50000, TP
1203, kalil,    php dev, 30000, AC
1204, prasanth, php dev, 30000, AC
1205, kranthi,  admin,   20000, TP
1206, satish p, grp des, 20000, GR
```

The following command is used to see the modified or newly added rows from the **emp** table.

```
$ $HADOOP_HOME/bin/hadoop fs -cat /emp/part-m-*1
```

It shows you the newly added rows to the **emp** table with comma (,) separated fields.

```
20000, GR 1206, satish p, grp des,
```

13.7 SQOOP - IMPORT ALL TABLES

This section describes how to import all the tables from the RDBMS database server to the HDFS. Each table data is stored in a separate directory and the directory name is same as the table name.

Syntax

The following syntax is used to import all tables.

```
$ sqoop import-all-tables (generic-args) (import-args)
$ sqoop-import-all-tables (generic-args) (import-args)
```

Example

Let us take an example of importing all tables from the **userdb** database. The list of tables that the database **userdb** contains is as follows.

```
+-------------------+
|      Tables       |
+-------------------+
|      emp          |
|      emp_add      |
|      emp_contact  |
+-------------------+
```

The following command is used to import all the tables from the **userdb**database.

```
$ sqoop import-all-tables \
--connect jdbc:mysql://localhost/userdb \
--username root
```

Note: If you are using the import-all-tables, it is mandatory that every table in that database must have a primary key field.

The following command is used to verify all the table data to the userdb **database in HDFS**

```
$ $HADOOP_HOME/bin/hadoop fs -ls
```

It will show you the list of table names in userdb database as directories.

Output

```
drwxr-xr-x - hadoop supergroup 0 2014-12-22 22:50 _sqoop
drwxr-xr-x - hadoop supergroup 0 2014-12-23 01:46 emp
drwxr-xr-x - hadoop supergroup 0 2014-12-23 01:50 emp_add
drwxr-xr-x - hadoop supergroup 0 2014-12-23 01:52 emp_contact
```

13.8 EXPORTING

This section describes how to export data back from the HDFS to the RDBMS database. The target table must exist in the target database. The files which are given as input to the Sqoop contain records, which are called rows in table. Those are read and parsed into a set of records and delimited with user-specified delimiter.

The default operation is to insert all the record from the input files to the database table using the INSERT statement. In update mode, Sqoop generates the UPDATE statement that replaces the existing record into the database.

Syntax

The following is the syntax for the export command.

```
$ sqoop export (generic-args) (export-args)
$ sqoop-export (generic-args) (export-args)
```

Example

Let us take an example of the employee data in file, in HDFS. The employee data is available in **emp_data** file in 'emp/' directory in HDFS. The **emp_data**is as follows.

```
1201, gopal,     manager, 50000, TP
1202, manisha,   preader, 50000, TP
1203, kalil,     php dev, 30000, AC
1204, prasanth,  php dev, 30000, AC
1205, kranthi,   admin,   20000, TP
1206, satish p,  grp des, 20000, GR
```

It is mandatory that the table to be exported is created manually and is present in the database from where it has to be exported.

The following query is used to create the table 'employee' in mysql command line.

```
$ mysql
mysql> USE db;
mysql> CREATE TABLE employee (
  id INT NOT NULL PRIMARY KEY,
  name VARCHAR(20),
  deg VARCHAR(20),
  salary INT,
  dept VARCHAR(10));
```

The following command is used to export the table data (which is in **emp_data**file on HDFS) to the employee table in db database of Mysql database server.

```
$ sqoop export \
--connect jdbc:mysql://localhost/db \
--username root \
--table employee \
--export-dir /emp/emp_data
```

The following command is used to verify the table in mysql command line.

```
mysql>select * from employee;
```

If the given data is stored successfully, then you can find the following table of given employee data.

```
+------+-------------+------------+-----------------+--------+
| Id   | Name        | Designation | Salary         | Dept   |
+------+-------------+------------+-----------------+--------+
| 1201 | gopal       | manager    | 50000           | TP     |
| 1202 | manisha     | preader    | 50000           | TP     |
| 1203 | kalil       | php dev    | 30000           | AC     |
| 1204 | prasanth    | php dev    | 30000           | AC     |
| 1205 | kranthi     | admin      | 20000           | TP     |
| 1206 | satish p    | grp des    | 20000           | GR     |
+------+-------------+------------+-----------------+--------+
```

13.9 CREATING AND MAINTAINING THE SQOOP JOBS

This section describes how to create and maintain the Sqoop jobs. Sqoop job creates and saves the import and export commands. It specifies parameters to identify and recall the saved job. This re-calling or re-executing is used in the incremental import, which can import the updated rows from RDBMS table to HDFS.

Syntax

The following is the syntax for creating a Sqoop job.

```
$ sqoop job (generic-args) (job-args)
  [-- [subtool-name] (subtool-args)]
$ sqoop-job (generic-args) (job-args)
  [-- [subtool-name] (subtool-args)]
```

Create Job (--create)

Here we are creating a job with the name **myjob**, which can import the table data from RDBMS table to HDFS. The following command is used to create a job that is importing data from the **employee** table in the **db** database to the HDFS file.

```
$ sqoop job --create myjob \
--import \
--connect jdbc:mysql://localhost/db \
--username root \
--table employee --m 1
```

Verify Job (--list)

'**--list**' argument is used to verify the saved jobs. The following command is used to verify the list of saved Sqoop jobs.

```
$ sqoop job --list
```

It shows the list of saved jobs.

```
Available jobs:
  myjob
```

Inspect Job (–show)

'**--show**' argument is used to inspect or verify particular jobs and their details. The following command and sample output is used to verify a job called **myjob**.

```
$ sqoop job --show myjob
```

It shows the tools and their options, which are used in **myjob**.

```
Job: myjob
Tool: import Options:
----------------------------
direct.import = true
codegen.input.delimiters.record = 0
hdfs.append.dir = false
db.table = employee
...
incremental.last.value = 1206
```

Execute Job (--exec)

'**--exec**' option is used to execute a saved job. The following command is used to execute a saved job called **myjob**.

```
$ sqoop job --exec myjob
```

It shows you the following output.

```
10/08/19 13:08:45 INFO tool.CodeGenTool: Beginning code generation
```

13.10 SQOOP – CODEGEN TOOL

This section describes the importance of 'codegen' tool. From the viewpoint of object-oriented application, every database table has one DAO class that contains 'getter' and 'setter' methods to initialize objects. This tool (-codegen) generates the DAO class automatically.

It generates DAO class in Java, based on the Table Schema structure. The Java definition is instantiated as a part of the import process. The main usage of this tool is to check if Java lost the Java code. If so, it will create a new version of Java with the default delimiter between fields.

Syntax

The following is the syntax for Sqoop codegen command.

```
$ sqoop codegen (generic-args) (codegen-args)
$ sqoop-codegen (generic-args) (codegen-args)
```

Example

Let us take an example that generates Java code for the **emp** table in the**userdb** database.

The following command is used to execute the given example.

```
$ sqoop codegen \
--connect jdbc:mysql://localhost/userdb \
--username root \
--table emp
```

If the command executes successfully, then it will produce the following output on the terminal.

```
14/12/23 02:34:40 INFO sqoop.Sqoop: Running Sqoop version: 1.4.5
14/12/23 02:34:41 INFO tool.CodeGenTool: Beginning code generation
................
14/12/23 02:34:42 INFO orm.CompilationManager: HADOOP_MAPRED_HOME is /
usr/local/hadoop
Note:  /tmp/sqoop-hadoop/compile/9a300a1f94899df4a9b10f9935ed9f91/emp.
java uses or overrides a deprecated API.
Note: Recompile with -Xlint:deprecation for details.
14/12/23 02:34:47 INFO orm.CompilationManager: Writing jar file: /tmp/
sqoop-hadoop/compile/9a300a1f94899df4a9b10f9935ed9f91/emp.jar
```

Verification

Let us take a look at the output. The path, which is in bold, is the location that the Java code of the **emp** table generates and stores. Let us verify the files in that location using the following commands.

```
$ cd /tmp/sqoop-hadoop/compile/9a300a1f94899df4a9b10f9935ed9f91/
$ ls
emp.class
emp.jar
emp.java
```

If you want to verify in depth, compare the **emp** table in the **userdb** database and emp.java in the following directory

/tmp/sqoop-hadoop/compile/9a300a1f94899df4a9b10f9935ed9f91/.

13.11 SQOOP – EVAL

This section describes how to use the Sqoop 'eval' tool. It allows users to execute user-defined queries against respective database servers and preview the result in the console. So, the user can expect the resultant table data to import. Using eval, we can evaluate any type of SQL query that can be either DDL or DML statement.

Syntax

The following syntax is used for Sqoop eval command.

```
$ sqoop eval (generic-args) (eval-args)
$ sqoop-eval (generic-args) (eval-args)
```

Select Query Evaluation

Using eval tool, we can evaluate any type of SQL query. Let us take an example of selecting limited rows in the **employee** table of **db** database. The following command is used to evaluate the given example using SQL query.

```
$ sqoop eval \
--connect jdbc:mysql://localhost/db \
--username root \
--query "SELECT * FROM employee LIMIT 3"
```

If the command executes successfully, then it will produce the following output on the terminal.

```
+------+--------------+-------------+-------------------+--------+
| Id   | Name         | Designation | Salary            | Dept   |
+------+--------------+-------------+-------------------+--------+
| 1201 | gopal        | manager     | 50000             | TP     |
| 1202 | manisha      | preader     | 50000             | TP     |
| 1203 | khalil       | php dev     | 30000             | AC     |
+------+--------------+-------------+-------------------+--------+
```

Insert Query Evaluation

Sqoop eval tool can be applicable for both modeling and defining the SQL statements. That means, we can use eval for insert statements too. The following command is used to insert a new row in the **employee** table of **db**database.

```
$ sqoop eval \
--connect jdbc:mysql://localhost/db \
--username root \
-e "INSERT INTO employee VALUES(1207,'Raju','UI dev',15000,'TP')"
```

If the command executes successfully, then it will display the status of the updated rows on the console.

Or else, you can verify the employee table on MySQL console. The following command is used to verify the rows of **employee** table of **db** database using select' query.

```
mysql>
mysql> use db;
mysql> SELECT * FROM employee;
+------+--------------+-------------+-------------------+--------+
| Id   | Name         | Designation | Salary            | Dept   |
+------+--------------+-------------+-------------------+--------+
| 1201 | gopal        | manager     | 50000             | TP     |
| 1202 | manisha      | preader     | 50000             | TP     |
| 1203 | khalil       | php dev     | 30000             | AC     |
| 1204 | prasanth     | php dev     | 30000             | AC     |
| 1205 | kranthi      | admin       | 20000             | TP     |
| 1206 | satish p     | grp des     | 20000             | GR     |
| 1207 | Raju         | UI dev      | 15000             | TP     |
+------+--------------+-------------+-------------------+--------+
```

13.12 SQOOP - LIST DATABASE

This section describes how to list out the databases using Sqoop. Sqoop list-databases tool parses and executes the 'SHOW DATABASES' query against the database server. Thereafter, it lists out the present databases on the server.

Syntax

The following syntax is used for Sqoop list-databases command.

```
$ sqoop list-databases (generic-args) (list-databases-args)
$ sqoop-list-databases (generic-args) (list-databases-args)
```

Sample Query

The following command is used to list all the databases in the MySQL database server.

```
$ sqoop list-databases \
--connect jdbc:mysql://localhost/ \
--username root
```

If the command executes successfully, then it will display the list of databases in your MySQL database server as follows.

```
...
13/05/31 16:45:58 INFO manager.MySQLManager: Preparing to use a MySQL
streaming resultset.
mysql
test
userdb
db
```

13.13 SQOOP - LIST TABLES

This section describes how to list out the tables of a particular database in MySQL database server using Sqoop. Sqoop list-tables tool parses and executes the 'SHOW TABLES' query against a particular database. Thereafter, it lists out the present tables in a database.

Syntax

The following syntax is used for Sqoop list-tables command.

```
$ sqoop list-tables (generic-args) (list-tables-args)
$ sqoop-list-tables (generic-args) (list-tables-args)
```

Sample Query

The following command is used to list all the tables in the **userdb** database of MySQL database server.

```
$ sqoop list-tables \
--connect jdbc:mysql://localhost/userdb \
--username root
```

If the command is executes successfully, then it will display the list of tables in the **userdb** database as follows.

```
...
13/05/31 16:45:58 INFO manager.MySQLManager: Preparing to use a MySQL
streaming resultset.
emp
emp_add
emp_contact
```

13.14 SOME IMPORTANT SQOOP COMMANDS OTHER THAN IMPORT AND EXPORT.

Create Job (--create)

Here we are creating a job with the name my job, which can import the table data from RDBMS table to HDFS. The following command is used to create a job that is importing data from the employee table in the db database to the HDFS file.

```
$ Sqoop job --create myjob \
--import \
--connect jdbc:mysql://localhost/db \
--username root \
--table employee --m 1
```

Verify Job (--list)

'--list' argument is used to verify the saved jobs. The following command is used to verify the list of saved Sqoop jobs.

```
$ Sqoop job --list
```

Inspect Job (--show)

'--show' argument is used to inspect or verify particular jobs and their details. The following command and sample output is used to verify a job called myjob.

```
$ Sqoop job --show myjob
```

Execute Job (--exec)

'--exec' option is used to execute a saved job. The following command is used to execute a saved job called myjob.

```
$ Sqoop job --exec myjob
```

CHAPTER 14

Data Streamming and Mining

14.1 DATA STREAMMING AND MINING

Data Stream Mining is the process of extracting knowledge structures from continuous, rapid data records. A data stream is an ordered sequence of instances that in many applications of data stream mining can be read only once or a small number of times using limited computing and storage capabilities. Examples of data streams include computer network traffic, phone conversations, ATM transactions, web searches, and sensor data. Data stream mining can be considered a subfield of data mining, machine learning, and knowledge discovery.

14.2 THE STREAM DATA MODEL

Let us begin by discussing the elements of streams and stream processing. We explain the difference between streams and databases and the special problems that arise when dealing with streams. Some typical applications where the stream model applies will be examined.

In analogy to a database-management system, we can view a stream processor as a kind of data-management system, the high-level organization of which is suggested in Fig. 14.1. Any number of streams can enter the system. Each stream can provide elements at its own schedule; they need not have the same data rates or data types, and the time between elements of one stream need not be uniform. The fact that the rate of arrival of stream elements is not under the control of the system distinguishes stream processing from the processing of data that goes on within a database-management system. The latter system controls the rate at which data is read from the disk, and therefore never has to worry about data getting lost as it attempts to execute queries. Streams may be archived in a large archival store, but we assume it is not possible to answer queries from the archival store. It could be examined only under special circumstances using time-consuming retrieval processes. There is also a working store, into which summaries or parts of streams may be placed, and which can be used for answering queries. The working store might be disk, or it might be main memory, depending on how fast we need to process queries. But either way, it is of sufficiently limited capacity that it cannot store all the data from all the streams. The unique characteristics of data streams and continuous queries dictate the following requirements of data stream management systems: The data model and query semantics must allow order-based and time-based operations (e.g. queries over a five-minute moving window).

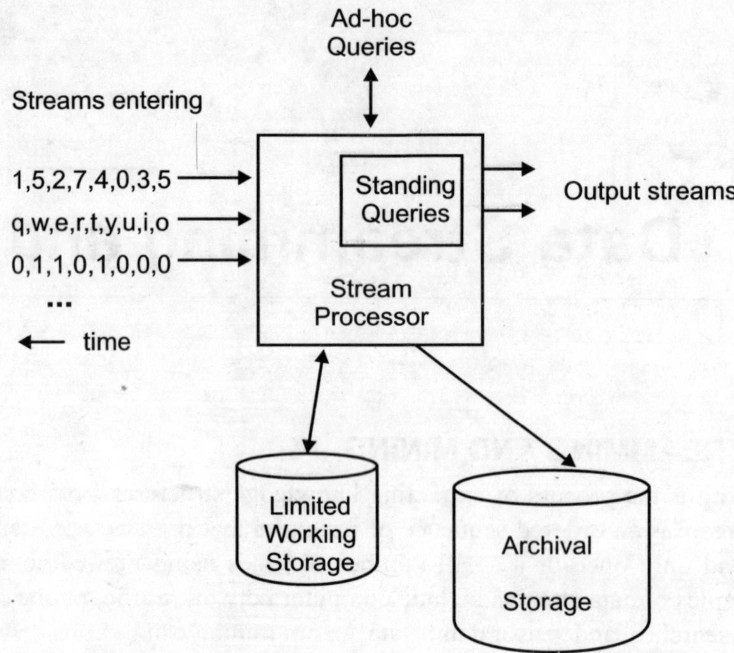

Figure. 14.1: Data Stream management System

The inability to store a complete stream suggests the use of approximate summary structures, referred to in the literature as synopses or digests . As a result, queries over the summaries may not return exact answers. Streaming query plans may not use blocking operators that must consume the entire input before any results are produced. Due to performance and storage constraints, backtracking over a data stream is not feasible. On-line stream algorithms are restricted to making only one pass over the data. Applications that monitor streams in real-time must react quickly to unusual data values. Long-running queries may encounter changes in system conditions throughout their execution lifetimes (e.g. variable stream rates). Shared execution of many continuous queries is needed to ensure scalability.

Proposed data stream systems resemble the abstract architecture shown in Figure 4.2. An input monitor may regulate the input rates, perhaps by dropping packets. Data are typically stored in three partitions:

1. temporary working storage (e.g. for window queries),
2. summary storage for stream synopses, and
3. static storage for meta-data (e.g. physical location of each source).

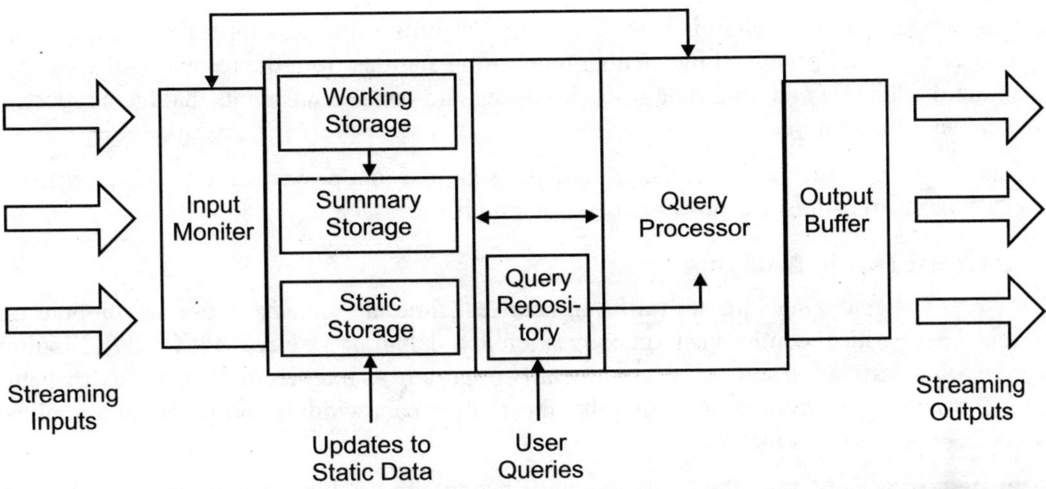

Figure. 14.2: Architecture of Data Stream management System

Long-running queries are registered in the query repository and placed into groups for shared processing, though one-time queries over the current state of the stream may also be posed. The query processor communicates with the input monitor and may re-optimize the query plans in response to changing input rates. Results are streamed to the users or temporarily buffered.

14.3 STREAMING APPLICATIONS

We begin by reviewing a collection of data stream applications in order to define a set of query types that a data stream management system should support.

14.3.1 Sensor Networks

Imagine a temperature sensor bobbing about in the ocean, sending back to a base station a reading of the surface temperature each hour. The data produced by this sensor is a stream of real numbers. It is not a very interesting stream, since the data rate is so low. It would not stress modern technology, and the entire stream could be kept in main memory, essentially forever. Now, give the sensor a GPS unit, and let it report surface height instead of temperature. The surface height varies quite rapidly compared with tempera- ture, so we might have the sensor send back a reading every tenth of a second. If it sends a 4-byte real number each time, then it produces 3.5 megabytes per day. It will still take some time to fill up main memory, let alone a single disk. But one sensor might not be that interesting. To learn something about ocean behavior, we might want to deploy a million sensors, each sending back a stream, at the rate of ten per second. A million sensors isn't very many; there would be one for every 150 square miles of ocean. Now we have 3.5 terabytes arriving every day, and we definitely need to think about what can be kept in working storage and what can only be archived. Sensor networks may be used in various monitoring applications that involve complex filtering and activation of an alarm in response to unusual conditions. Aggregation and joins over multiple streams are required to analyze data from many sources, while aggregation over a single stream may be needed to compensate for individual sensor failures. Representative queries include the following:

1. Drawing temperature contours on a weather map: Perform a join of temperature streams (on the temperature attribute) produced by weather monitoring stations. Join the results with a static table containing the latitude and longitude of each station, and connect all points that have reported the same temperature with lines.
2. Analyze a stream of recent power usage statistics reported to a power station (group by location, e.g. city block), and adjust the power generation rate if necessary .

14.3.2 Network Traffic Analysis

Ad-hoc systems for analyzing Internet traffic in near-real time are already in use to compute traffic statistics and detect critical conditions (e.g. congestion and denial of service) (14, 16, 29). Monitoring popular source and destination addresses is particularly important as Internet traffic patterns are believed to obey the Power Law distribution, meaning that most of the bandwidth is consumed by a small set of heavy users. Example queries include:

1. **Traffic matrices**: Determine the total amount of bandwidth used by each source-destination pair, and group by protocol type or subnet mask.
2. Compare the number of distinct source destination pairs in the (logical) streams containing the second and third steps, respectively, of the three-way TCP handshake. If the counts differ by a large margin, then a denial-of-service attack may be taking place.

14.3.3 Internet and Web Traffic

A switching node in the middle of the Internet receives streams of IP packets from many inputs and routes them to its outputs. Normally, the job of the switch is to transmit data and not to retain it or query it. But there is a tendency to put more capability into the switch, e.g., the ability to detect denial-of-service attacks or the ability to reroute packets based on information about congestion in the network.

Web sites receive streams of various types. For example, Google receives sev-eral hundred million search queries per day. Yahoo! accepts billions of "clicks" per day on its various sites. Many interesting things can be learned from these streams. For example, an increase in queries like "sore throat" enables us to track the spread of viruses.

14.3.4 Financial Tickers

On-line analysis of stock prices involves discovering correlations, identifying trends and arbitrage opportunities, and forecasting future values. The following are typical queries :

(a) High Volatility with Recent Volume Surge: Find all stocks priced between $20 and $200, where the spread between the high tick and the low tick over the past 30 minutes is greater than 3% of the last price, and where in the last 5 minutes the average volume has surged by more than 300%.

(b) NASDAQ Large Cap Gainers: Find all NASDAQ stocks trading above their 200-day moving average with a market cap greater than $5 Billion that have gained in price today by at least 2%, and are within 2% of today's high.

14.3.5 Transaction Log Analysis

On-line mining of Web usage logs, telephone call records, and Automated Bank Machine transactions also conform to the data stream model. The goal is to find interesting customer behaviour patterns, identify suspicious spending behaviour that could indicate fraud, and forecast future data values. The following are some examples:

(a) Examine Web server logs in real-time and reroute users to backup servers if the primary servers are overloaded.

(b) Roaming diameter: Mine cellular phone records and for each customer, determine the greatest number of distinct base stations used during one telephone call.

14.3.6 Analysis of Requirements

The preceding examples show significant similarities in data models and basic operations across applications (and some differences related to workload characteristics, such as stream arrival rates or the amount of historical data needed). A set of fundamental continuous query operations is listed below over streaming data, keeping in mind that new streaming applications, possibly with additional requirements, will likely be proposed in the future.

- **Selection**: All streaming applications require support for complex filtering.
- **Nested aggregation**: Complex aggregates, including nested aggregates (e.g. comparing a minimum with a running average) are needed to compute trends in the data.
- **Multiplexing and demultiplexing**: These are similar to group-by and union, respectively, and are used to decompose and merge logical streams.
- **Frequent item queries**: These are also known as top-k or threshold queries, depending on the cuto _ condition.
- **Stream mining**: Operations such as pattern matching, similarity searching, and forecastingare needed for on-line mining of streaming data.
- **Joins**: Support should be included for multistream joins and joins of streams with static meta-data.
- **Windowed queries**: All of the above query types may be constrained to return results inside a
- window (e.g. the last 24 hours or the last one hundred packets).
- **Image Data** Satellites often send down to earth streams consisting of many terabytes of images per day. Surveillance cameras produce images with lower resolution than satellites, but there can be many of them, each producing a stream of images at intervals like one second. London is said to have six million such cameras, each producing a stream.

14.4 DATA MODELS AND QUERY LANGUAGES FOR STREAMS

The above requirements demand specific features to be included in the data models and query languages for data streams. In this section, we survey the proposed models and languages.

14.4.1 Data Models

A real-time data stream is a sequence of data items that arrive in some order and may be seen only once. Since items may arrive in bursts, a data stream may instead be modeled as a sequence of lists of elements. Individual stream items may take the form of relational tuples or instantiations of objects. In relation-based models (e.g. STREAm), items are transient tuples stored in virtual relations, possibly horizontally partitioned across remote nodes. In object-based models (e.g. COUGAR and Tribeca), sources and item types are modeled as hierarchical data types with associated methods. In many cases, only an excerpt of a stream is of interest at any given time, giving rise to window models, which may be classi_ed according the the following three criteria:

1. **Direction of movement of the endpoints**: Two fixed endpoints define a fixed window, two sliding endpoints (either forward or backward, replacing old items as new items arrive) define a sliding window, while one fixed endpoint and one moving endpoint (forward or backward) define a landmark window.
2. **Physical vs. logical:** Physical, or time-based windows are de_ned in terms of a time interval, while logical, (also known as count-based) windows are de_ned in terms of the number of tuples.
3. **Update interval**: Eager re-evaluation updates the window upon arrival of each new tuple, while batch processing (lazy re-evaluation) induces a jumping window". If the update interval is larger than the window size, the result is a series of non-overlapping tumbling windows.

14.5 CONTINUOUS QUERY PROCESSING AND OPTIMIZATION

We now discuss problems related to processing and optimizing continuous queries. In what follows, we outline emerging research in cost metrics, query plans, quality-of-service guarantees, and distributed optimization of streaming queries.

14.5.1 Cost Metrics and Statistics

Traditional cost metrics do not apply to (possibly approximate) continuous queries over infinite streams, where processing cost per-unit-time is more appropriate. Below, we list possible cost metrics for streaming queries along with necessary statistics that must be maintained.

1. **Accuracy and reporting delay vs. memory usage:** Sampling and load shedding may be used to decrease memory usage by increasing the error. It is necessary to know the accuracy of each operator as a function of the available memory, and how to combine such functions to obtain the overall accuracy of a plan. Furthermore, batch processing may be done instead of reevaluating a query whenever a new item arrives.
2. **Output rate:** If the stream arrival rates and output rates of query operators are known, it is possible to optimize for the highest output rate or to find a plan that takes the least time to output a given number of tuples .
3. **Power usage**: In a wireless network of batteryoperated sensors, energy consumption may be minimized if each sensor's power consumption characteristics (when transmitting and receiving) are known.

14.5.2 Continuous Query Plans

In relational DBMSs, all operators are pull-based: an operator requests data from one of its children in the plan tree only when needed. In contrast, stream operators consume data pushed to the system by the sources. One approach to reconcile these differences, as considered in Fjords and STREAM , is to connect operators with queues, allowing sources to push data into a queue and operators to retrieve data as needed. Since queues may overflow, operators should be scheduled so as to minimize queue sizes and queuing delays. Another challenge in continuous query plans deals with supporting historical queries. Designing disk-based data structures and indices to exploit access patterns of stream archives is an open problem .

14.5.3 Processing Multiple Queries

Two approaches have been proposed to execute similar continuous queries together: sharing query plans and indexing query predicates . In the former, queries belonging to the same group share a plan, which produces the union of the results needed by each query in the group. A final selection is then applied to the shared result set. Problems include dynamic re-grouping as new queries are added to the system, and shared evaluation of windowed joins with various window sizes . In the indexing approach, query predicates are stored in a table. When a new tuple arrives for processing, its attribute values are extracted and looked up in the query table to see which queries are satisfied by this tuple. Data and queries are treated as duals, reducing query processing to a multi-way join of the predicate table with the data tables. The indexing approach works well for queries with simple boolean predicates, but is currently not applicable to, e.g. windowed aggregates .

14.5.4 QUERY OPTIMIZATION

14.5.4.1 Query Rewriting

A useful rewriting technique in relational databases deals with re-ordering a sequence of binary joins in order to minimize a particular cost metric. There has been some preliminary work in join ordering for data streams in the context of the rate-based model and in main-memory window joins.

14.5.4.2 Adaptivity

The cost of a query plan may change for three reasons: change in processing time of an operator, change in selectivity of a predicate, and change in the arrival rate of a stream . Consequently, instead of maintaining a rigid tree-structured query plan, the Eddies approach (introduced in , extended to multi-way joins in , and applied to continuous queries in performs scheduling of each tuple separately by routing it through the operators that make up the query plan. In effect, the query plan is dynamically re-ordered to match current system conditions. This is accomplished by tuple routing policies that attempt to discover which operators are fast and selective, and those operators are scheduled first. There is, however, an important trade-of between the resulting adaptivity and the overhead required to route each tuple separately.

14.6 Distributed Query Processing

In sensor networks, Internet traffic analysis, and Web usage logs, multiple data streams arrive from remote sources. Distributed optimization strategies aim at decreasing communication costs by re-ordering query operators across sites and performing simple query functions (e.g. filtering or aggregation) locally at a sensor or a network router. For example, if each node pre-aggregates its results by sending to the central node the sum and count of its values, the co-ordinator may then take the cumulative sum and cumulative count, and compute the overall average. A similar technique involves sending updates to the central node only if new data values differ significantly from previously reported values .

Some optimization techniques have been designed specifically for ad-hoc wireless sensor networks in order to decrease communication costs, extend battery life, and deal with poor wireless connectivity .

These techniques make use of the fact that query dissemination and result collection in a wireless sensor network proceed along a routing tree (or a DAG) via a shared wireless channel. For example, if a sensor reports its maximum local value x in response to a MAX query, a neighbouring sensor that overhears this transmission need not respond if its local maximum is smaller than x. Moreover, a sensor could broadcast redundant copies of its maximum value to all of its neighbours in order to minimize the chances of packet loss (at a cost of increased bandwidth and battery usage). However, this does not work for other aggregates such as SUM and COUNT, as duplicate values would contaminate the result. In these cases, a sensor may \split" its local sum and send partial sums to each of its neighbours. Even if one packet is lost, the remainder of the sum should still reach the root.

Designing an effective data stream management system requires extensive modifications of nearly every part of a traditional database, creating many interesting database problems such as adding time, order, and windowing to data models and query languages, implementing approximate operators, combining push-based and pull-based operators in query plans, adaptive query re-optimization, and distributed query processing. Recent interest in these problems has generated a number of academic projects. There exist at least the following systems:

1. **Aurora** is a workflow-oriented system that allows users to build query plans by arranging boxes (operators) and arrows (data flow among operators).
2. **COUGAR** is a sensor database that models sensors as ADTs and their output as time series.
3. **Gigascope** is a distributed network monitoring architecture that proposes pushing some query operators to the sources (e.g. routers).
4. **NiagaraCQ** (is a continuous query system that allows continuous XML-QL queries to be posed over dynamic Web content.
5. **OpenCQ** is another continuous query system for monitoring streaming Web content. Its focus is on scalable event-driven query processing.
6. **StatStream** is a stream monitoring system designed to compute online statistics across many streams.
7. **STREAM** is an all-purpose relation-based system with an emphasis on memory management and approximate query answering.
8. **TelegraphCQ** is a continuous query processing system that focuses on shared query evaluation and adaptive query processing
9. **Tribeca** is an early on-line Internet traffic monitoring tool.

14.7 DATA STREAM V/S CONVENTIONAL STORED RELATION MODEL

Data streams differ from the conventional stored relation model in several ways:

1. The data elements in the stream arrive online.
2. The system has no control over the order in which data elements arrive to be processed, either within a data stream or across data streams.
3. Data streams are potentially unbounded in size.
4. Once an element from a data stream has been processed it is discarded or archived — it cannot be retrieved easily unless it is explicitly stored in memory, which typically is small relative to the size of the data streams.

14.8 QUERIES

Queries over continuous data streams have much in common with queries in a traditional database management system. However, there are two important distinctions peculiar to the data stream model. The first distinction is between *one-time queries* and *continuous queries* . One-time queries (a class that includes traditional DBMS queries) are queries that are evaluated once over a point-in-time snapshot of the data set, with the answer returned to the user. Continuous queries, on the other hand, are evaluated continuously as data streams continue to arrive. Continuous queries are the more interesting class of data stream queries, and it is to them that we will devote most of our attention. The answer to a continuous query is produced over time, always reflecting the stream data seen so far. Continuous query answers may be stored and updated as new data arrives, or they may be produced as data streams themselves. Sometimes one or the other mode is preferred. For example, aggregation queries may involve frequent changes to answer tuples, dictating the stored approach, while join queries are monotonic and may produce rapid, unbounded answers, dictating the stream approach.

The second distinction is between *predefined queries* and *ad hoc queries*. A predefined query is one that is supplied to the data stream management system before any relevant data has arrived. Predefined queries are generally continuous queries, although scheduled one-time queries can also be predefined. Adhoc queries, on the other hand, are issued online after the data streams have already begun. Ad hoc queries can be either one-time queries or continuous queries. Ad hoc queries complicate the design of a data stream management system, both because they are not known in advance for the purposes of query optimization, identification of common sub expressions across queries, etc., and more importantly because the correct answer to an ad hoc query may require referencing data elements that have already arrived on the data streams (and potentially have already been discarded).

14.9 IBM'S INFOSPHERE STREAMS 3.0

In the recently released InfoSphere Streams 3.0, IBM has taken its stream computing functionality to the next level of scale and sophistication. Whether deployed on its own or in conjunction with other platforms, InfoSphere Streams now accomplishes the following:

- Handles simple and extremely complex analytics with agility
- Scales for computational intensity
- Supports a wide range of relational and non-relational data types
- Analyzes continuous, massive volumes of data at rates up to petabytes per day
- Performs complex analytics of heterogeneous data types including text, images, audio, voice, VoIP, video, web traffic, email, GPS data, financial transaction data, satellite data, sensors, and any other type of digital information that is relevant to your business
- Leverages sub-millisecond latencies to react to events and trends as they are unfolding, while it is still possible to improve business outcomes
- Adapts to rapidly changing data forms and types
- Seamlessly deploys applications on any size computer cluster
- Meets current reaction time and scalability requirements with the flexibility to evolve with future changes in data volumes and business rules
- Supports development of new applications rapidly that can be mapped to a variety of hardware configurations and adapted with shifting priorities
- Provides security and information confidentiality for shared information
- Provides a new IBM Netezza loader to improve performance when loading data into the data warehouse platform

- Integrates out of the box with IBM Information Server for improved exchange of information with IBM InfoSphere DataStage and tighter interoperability with Extract, Transform and Load (ETL) jobs in DataStage
- Integrates out of the box with the latest release of BigInsights (version 2.0)

In addition to all these new features, InfoSphere Streams supports several optional IBM solution accelerators to support custom application development of several key real-time big data applications. Accelerators supported in this release include the Time Series Accelerator, Geospatial Accelerator, IBM Accelerator for Telecommunications Event Data Analytics, IBM Accelerator for Social Data Analytics, and IBM Accelerator for Machine Data Analytics. InfoSphere Streams 3.0 also comes standard with several toolkits—financial, mining, complex event processing, and advanced text analytics—to help provide rapid successful outcomes on low-latency big data projects in any of these areas.

In many ways, stream computing—as implemented in InfoSphere Streams—is a full-fledged, enterprise-grade runtime engine and development platform for the vast range of real-time big data applications. But stream computing can also be deployed outside of big data environments as a low-latency data integration technology for operational business intelligence, business event monitoring, and other applications that don't require large volumes or wide varieties of data types.

In other words, stream computing can also play a central role in otherwise small data applications.

Application streaming is a form of on-demand software distribution. In these scenarios, only essential portions of an application's code need to be installed on the computer: while the end user performs actions in the application, the necessary code and files are delivered over the network as and when they are required.

Application streaming is a related concept to application virtualization, where applications are run directly from a virtual machine on a central server that is completely separate from the local system. By contrast, application streaming runs the program locally, but still involves the centralized storage of application code.

Stream server An application is packaged and stored on a streaming server. Packaging or sequencing produces an image of the application in a way that orders delivery or predicatively optimizes delivery to the client.

Launch and streaming of application The initial launch of an application would be important for the end user and the Packaging process might be optimized to achieve this. Once launched, common functions would be followed. As these functions are requested by the end user, these may be streamed in a similar manner. In this case the client is pulling the application from the stream server. Otherwise, the full application might be delivered from the server to the client in the background. In this case, the server pushes the application to the client.

AdvantagesThe concept of application streaming carries several major advantages over traditional software distribution: given the complexity of modern applications, many functions are never or seldom used, and pulling the application on demand is more efficient in terms of server, client and network usage; streaming also allows for applications to be cached on the local system and still run in a traditional manner; updates can also be deployed automatically to the cached application files.

CHAPTER

15

Flume: Big Data Realtime Streaming

15.1 FLUME : INTRODUCTION

Apache Flume is a tool/service/data ingestion mechanism for collecting aggregating and transporting large amounts of streaming data such as log files, events (etc...) from various sources to a centralized data store.

Apache Flume is service designed for streaming logs into Hadoop environment. Flume is a distributed and reliable service for collecting and aggregating huge amounts of log data. With a simple and easy to use architecture based on streaming data flows, it also has tunable reliability mechanisms and several recovery and failover mechanisms.

Flume is a highly reliable, distributed, and configurable tool.

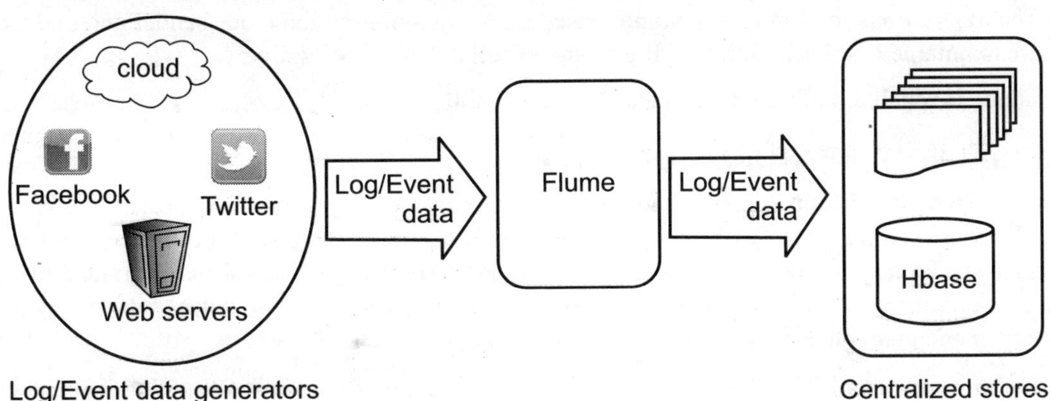

Figure. 15.1: Flume service designed for streaming logs into Hadoop environment

15.2 NEED FOR FLUME

Logs are usually a source of stress and argument in most of the big data companies. Logs are one of the most painful resources to manage for the operations team as they take up huge amount of space. Logs are rarely present at places on the disk where someone in the company can make effective use of them or hadoop developers can access them. Many big data companies wind up building tools and processes to collect logs from application servers, transfer them to some repository so that they can control the lifecycle without consuming unnecessary disk space.

This frustrates developers as the logs are often not present at the location where they can view them easily, they have limited number of tools available for processing logs and have confined capabilities in intelligently managing the lifecycle. Apache Flume is designed to address the difficulties of both operations group and developers by providing them an easy to use tool that can push logs from bunch of applications servers to various repositories via a highly configurable agent. CLICK HERE

15.3 APPLICATIONS OF FLUME

Assume an e-commerce web application wants to analyze the customer behavior from a particular region. To do so, they would need to move the available log data in to Hadoop for analysis. Here, Apache Flume comes to our rescue.Flume is used to move the log data generated by application servers into HDFS at a higher speed.

15.4 ADVANTAGES OF FLUME

Here are some of the advantages of using Flume Application in Hadoop Environment:

1. Using Apache Flume we can store the data in to any of the centralized stores (HBase, HDFS).
2. When the rate of incoming data exceeds the rate at which data can be written to the destination, Flume acts as a mediator between data producers and the centralized stores and provides a steady flow of data between them.
3. Flume provides the feature of contextual routing.
4. The transactions in Flume are channel-based where two transactions (one sender and one receiver) are maintained for each message. It guarantees reliable message delivery.
5. Flume is reliable, fault tolerant, scalable, manageable, and customizable.

15.5 SALIENT FEATURES OF FLUME

Flume in Hadoop is fault tolerant, linearly scalable and stream oriented. Flume has flexible design based upon streaming data flows. It is fault tolerant and robust with multiple failover and recovery mechanisms. Flume has different levels of reliability to offer which includes 'best-effort delivery' and an 'end-to-end delivery'. Best-effort delivery does not tolerate any Flume node failure whereas 'end-to-end delivery' mode guarantees delivery even in the event of multiple node failures.

Flume carries data between sources and sinks. This gathering of data can either be scheduled or event driven. Flume has its own query processing engine which makes it easy to transform each new batch of data before it is moved to the intended sink.

Possible Flume sinks include HDFS and Hbase. Flume can also be used to transport event data including but not limited to network traffic data, data generated by social-media websites and email messages.

Some of the notable features of Flume are as follows :

1. Flume ingests log data from multiple web servers into a centralized store (HDFS, HBase) efficiently.
2. Using Flume, we can get the data from multiple servers immediately into Hadoop.
3. Along with the log files, Flume is also used to import huge volumes of event data produced by social networking sites like Facebook and Twitter, and e-commerce websites like Amazon and Flipkart.
4. Flume supports a large set of sources and destinations types.
5. Flume supports multi-hop flows, fan-in fan-out flows, contextual routing, etc.
6. Flume can be scaled horizontally.
7. Flume is a flexible tool as it allows to scale in environments with as low as five machines to as high as several thousands of machines.
8. Apache Flume provides high throughput and low latency.
9. Apache Flume has a declarative configuration but provides ease of extensibility.
10. Since July 2012, Flume is being released as Flume NG (New Generation), as it differs significantly from its original release, as known as Flume OG (Original Generation).

15.6 HOW APACHE FLUME WORKS?

Apache Flume is a system used for moving massive quantities of streaming data into HDFS. Collecting log data present in log files from web servers and aggregating it in HDFS for analysis, is one common example use case of Flume.

Flume supports multiple sources like –

1. 'tail' (which pipes data from local file and write into HDFS via Flume, similar to Unix command 'tail')
2. System logs
3. Apache log4j (enable Java applications to write events to files in HDFS via Flume).

   Flume has a simple event driven pipeline architecture with 3 important roles-Source, Channel and Sink.

   a) Source defines where the data is coming from, for instance a message queue or a file.

   b) Sinks defined the destination of the data pipelined from various sources.

   c) Channels are pipes which establish connect between sources and sinks.

Apache flume works on two important concepts-

4. The master acts like a reliable configuration service which is used by nodes for retrieving their configuration.
5. If the configuration for a particular node changes on the master then it will dynamically be updated by the master.

6. Node is generally an event pipe in Hadoop Flume which reads from the source and writes to the Sink. The characteristics and role of a flume node is determine by the behaviour of source and sinks. Apache Flume is built with several source and sink options but if none of them fits in your requirements then developers can write their own. A flume node can also be configured with the help of a sink decorator which can interpret the event and transforms it as it passes through. With all these basic primitives, developers can create different topologies to collect data on any application server and direct it to any log repository.

15.6.1 Data Flow in Flume

A Flume agent is a JVM process which has 3 components -Flume Source, Flume Channel and Flume Sink- through which events propagate after initiated at an external source .

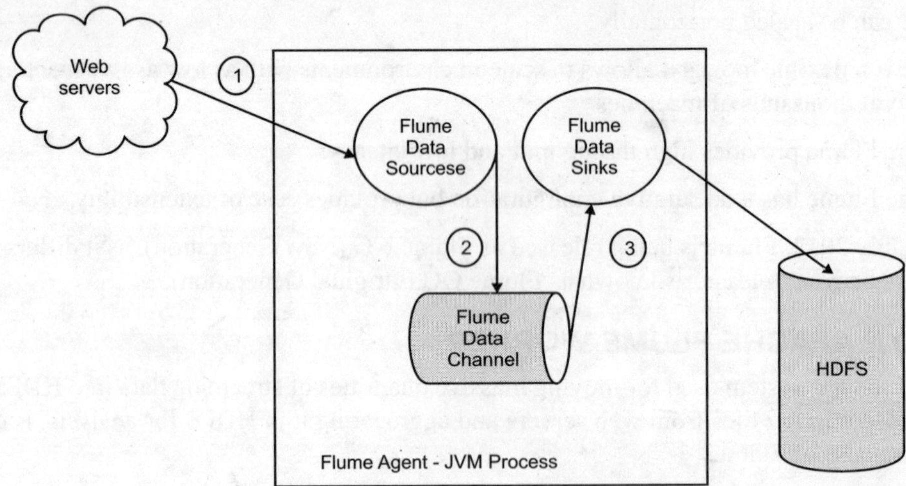

1. In above diagram, the events generated by external source (WebServer) are consumed by Flume Data Source. The external source sends events to Flume source in a format that is recognized by the target source.
2. Flume Source receives an event and stores it into one or more channels. The channel acts as a store which keeps the event until it is consumed by the flume sink. This channel may use local file system in order to store these events.
3. Flume sink removes the event from channel and stores it into an external repository like e.g., HDFS. There could be multiple flume agents, in which case flume sink forwards the event to the flume source of next flume agent in the flow.

15.6.2 Streaming / Log Data

Generally, most of the data that is to be analyzed will be produced by various data sources like applications servers, social networking sites, cloud servers, and enterprise servers. This data will be in the form of log files and events.

Log file − In general, a log file is a file that lists events/actions that occur in an operating system. For example, web servers list every request made to the server in the log files.

On harvesting such log data, we can get information about –

1. the application performance and locate various software and hardware failures.
2. the user behavior and derive better business insights.

15.7 BASIC ARCHITECTURE OF FLUME

Apache Flume is a tool/service/data ingestion mechanism for collecting aggregating and transporting large amounts of streaming data such as log data, events (etc...) from various webserves to a centralized data store.

It is a highly reliable, distributed, and configurable tool that is principally designed to transfer streaming data from various sources to HDFS.

The following illustration depicts the basic architecture of Flume. As shown in the illustration, data generators (such as Facebook, Twitter) generate data which gets collected by individual Flume agents running on them. Thereafter, a data collector (which is also an agent) collects the data from the agents which is aggregated and pushed into a centralized store such as HDFS or HBase.

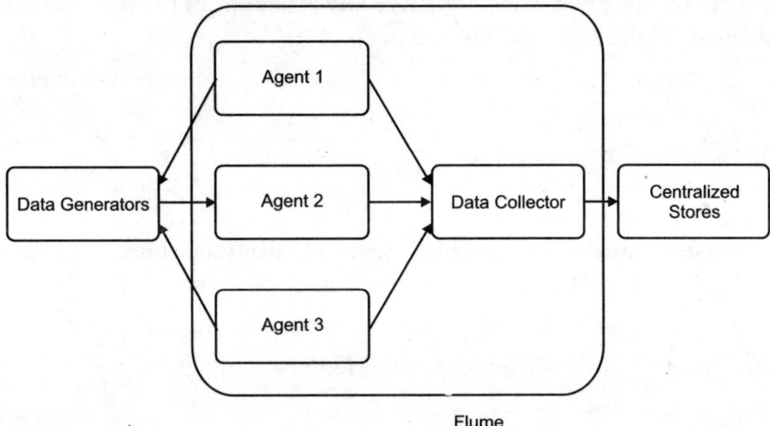

Flume

(1) Flume Event

An **event** is the basic unit of the data transported inside **Flume**. It contains a payload of byte array that is to be transported from the source to the destination accompanied by optional headers. A typical Flume event would have the following structure –

Flume event

(2) Flume Agent

An **agent** is an independent daemon process (JVM) in Flume. It receives the data (events) from clients or other agents and forwards it to its next destination (sink or agent). Flume may have more than one agent. Following diagram represents a **Flume Agent**

As shown in the diagram a Flume Agent contains three main components namely, **source**, **channel**, and **sink**.

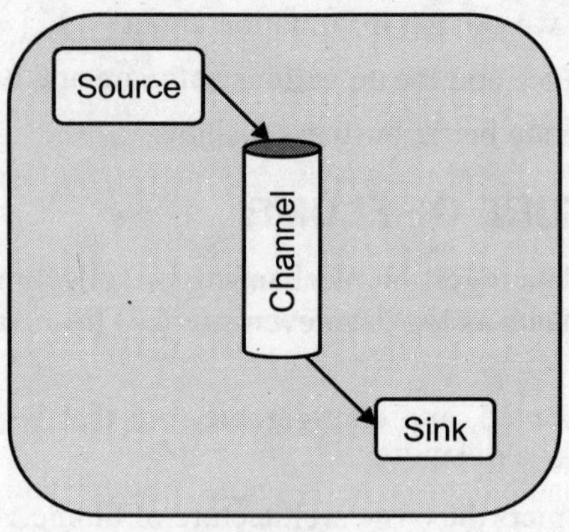

Flume Agent

(3) Source

A **source** is the component of an Agent which receives data from the data generators and transfers it to one or more channels in the form of Flume events.

Apache Flume supports several types of sources and each source receives events from a specified data generator.

Example – Avro source, Thrift source, twitter 1% source etc.

(3) Channel

A **channel** is a transient store which receives the events from the source and buffers them till they are consumed by sinks. It acts as a bridge between the sources and the sinks.

These channels are fully transactional and they can work with any number of sources and sinks.

Example – JDBC channel, File system channel, Memory channel, etc.

(3) Sink

A **sink** stores the data into centralized stores like HBase and HDFS. It consumes the data (events) from the channels and delivers it to the destination. The destination of the sink might be another agent or the central stores.

Example – HDFS sink

Note – A flume agent can have multiple sources, sinks and channels. We have listed all the supported sources, sinks, channels in the Flume configuration chapter of this tutorial.

15.6.3 Additional Components of Flume Agent

What we have discussed above are the primitive components of the agent. In addition to this, we have a few more components that play a vital role in transferring the events from the data generator to the centralized stores.

(1) Interceptors

Interceptors are used to alter/inspect flume events which are transferred between source and channel.

(2) Channel Selectors

These are used to determine which channel is to be opted to transfer the data in case of multiple channels. There are two types of channel selectors –

- Default channel selectors – These are also known as replicating channel selectors they replicates all the events in each channel.
- Multiplexing channel selectors – These decides the channel to send an event based on the address in the header of that event.

(3) Sink Processors

These are used to invoke a particular sink from the selected group of sinks. These are used to create failover paths for your sinks or load balance events across multiple sinks from a channel.

Flume is a framework which is used to move log data into HDFS. Generally events and log data are generated by the log servers and these servers have Flume agents running on them. These agents receive the data from the data generators.

The data in these agents will be collected by an intermediate node known as **Collector**. Just like agents, there can be multiple collectors in Flume.

Finally, the data from all these collectors will be aggregated and pushed to a centralized store such as HBase or HDFS. The following diagram explains the data flow in Flume.

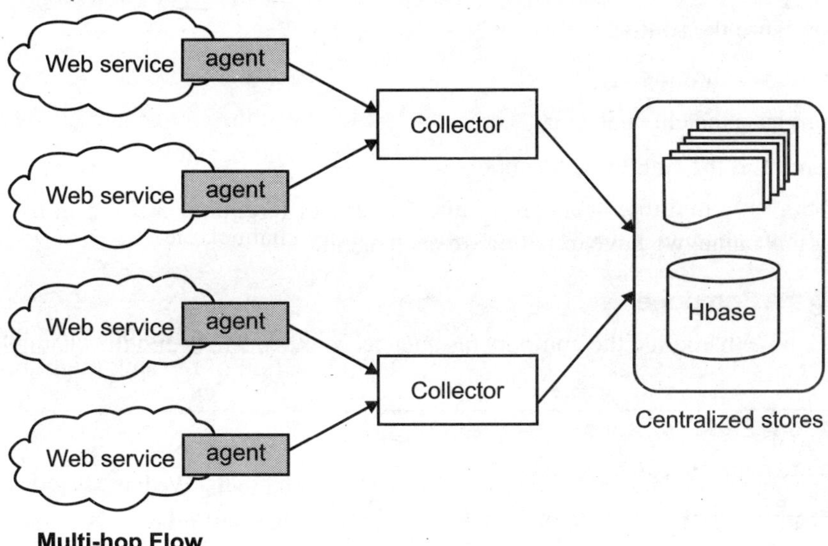

Multi-hop Flow

(4) Multi-hop Flow

Within Flume, there can be multiple agents and before reaching the final destination, an event may travel through more than one agent. This is known as multi-hop flow.

(5) Fan-out Flow

The dataflow from one source to multiple channels is known as **fan-out flow**. It is of two types –

1. Replicating – The data flow where the data will be replicated in all the configured channels.
2. Multiplexing – The data flow where the data will be sent to a selected channel which is mentioned in the header of the event.

(6) Fan-in Flow

The data flow in which the data will be transferred from many sources to one channel is known as **fan-in flow**.

(7) Failure Handling

In Flume, for each event, two transactions take place: one at the sender and one at the receiver. The sender sends events to the receiver. Soon after receiving the data, the receiver commits its own transaction and sends a "received" signal to the sender. After receiving the signal, the sender commits its transaction. (Sender will not commit its transaction till it receives a signal from the receiver.)

15.8 APACHE FLUME – ENVIRONMENT

After installing Flume, we need to configure it using the configuration file which is a Java property file having **key-value pairs**. We need to pass values to the keys in the file.

In the Flume configuration file, we need to :

1. Name the components of the current agent.
2. Describe/Configure the source.
3. Describe/Configure the sink.
4. Describe/Configure the channel.
5. Bind the source and the sink to the channel.

Usually we can have multiple agents in Flume. We can differentiate each agent by using a unique name. And using this name, we have to configure each agent.

15.8.1 Naming the Components

First of all, you need to name/list the components such as sources, sinks, and the channels of the agent, as shown below.

```
agent_name.sources = source_name
agent_name.sinks = sink_name
agent_name.channels = channel_name
```

Flume supports various sources, sinks, and channels. They are listed in the table given below.

Sources	Channels	Sinks
• Avro Source • Thrift Source • Exec Source • JMS Source • Spooling Directory Source • Twitter 1% firehose Source • Kafka Source • NetCat Source • Sequence Generator Source • Syslog Sources • Syslog TCP Source • Multiport Syslog TCP Source • Syslog UDP Source • HTTP Source • Stress Source • Legacy Sources • Thrift Legacy Source • Custom Source • Scribe Source	• Memory Channel • JDBC Channel • Kafka Channel • File Channel • Spillable Memory Channel • Pseudo Transaction Channel	• HDFS Sink • Hive Sink • Logger Sink • Avro Sink • Thrift Sink • IRC Sink • File Roll Sink • Null Sink • HBaseSink • AsyncHBaseSink • MorphlineSolrSink • ElasticSearchSink • Kite Dataset Sink • Kafka Sink

You can use any of them. For example, if you are transferring Twitter data using Twitter source through a memory channel to an HDFS sink, and the agent name id **TwitterAgent**, then

```
TwitterAgent.sources = Twitter
TwitterAgent.channels = MemChannel
TwitterAgent.sinks = HDFS
```

After listing the components of the agent, you have to describe the source(s), sink(s), and channel(s) by providing values to their properties.

15.8.2 Describing the Source

Each source will have a separate list of properties. The property named "type" is common to every source, and it is used to specify the type of the source we are using.

Along with the property "type", it is needed to provide the values of all the **required** properties of a particular source to configure it, as shown below.

```
agent_name.sources. source_name.type = value
agent_name.sources. source_name.property2 = value
agent_name.sources. source_name.property3 = value
```

For example, if we consider the **twitter source**, following are the properties to which we *must* provide values to configure it.

```
TwitterAgent.sources.Twitter.type = Twitter (type name)
TwitterAgent.sources.Twitter.consumerKey =
TwitterAgent.sources.Twitter.consumerSecret =
TwitterAgent.sources.Twitter.accessToken =
TwitterAgent.sources.Twitter.accessTokenSecret =
```

Describing the Sink

Just like the source, each sink will have a separate list of properties. The property named "type" is common to every sink, and it is used to specify the type of the sink we are using. Along with the property "type", it is needed to provide values to all the **required** properties of a particular sink to configure it, as shown below.

```
agent_name.sinks. sink_name.type = value
agent_name.sinks. sink_name.property2 = value
agent_name.sinks. sink_name.property3 = value
```

For example, if we consider **HDFS sink**, following are the properties to which we *must* provide values to configure it.

```
TwitterAgent.sinks.HDFS.type = hdfs (type name)
TwitterAgent.sinks.HDFS.hdfs.path = HDFS directory's Path to store the
data
```

Describing the Channel

Flume provides various channels to transfer data between sources and sinks. Therefore, along with the sources and the channels, it is needed to describe the channel used in the agent. To describe each channel, you need to set the required properties, as shown below.

```
agent_name.channels.channel_name.type = value
agent_name.channels.channel_name. property2 = value
agent_name.channels.channel_name. property3 = value
```

For example, if we consider **memory channel**, following are the properties to which we *must* provide values to configure it.

```
TwitterAgent.channels.MemChannel.type = memory (type name)
```

Binding the Source and the Sink to the Channel

Since the channels connect the sources and sinks, it is required to bind both of them to the channel, as shown below.

```
agent_name.sources.source_name.channels = channel_name
agent_name.sinks.sink_name.channels = channel_name
```

The following example shows how to bind the sources and the sinks to a channel. Here, we consider **twitter source, memory channel,** and **HDFS sink**.

```
TwitterAgent.sources.Twitter.channels = MemChannel
TwitterAgent.sinks.HDFS.channels = MemChannel
```

Starting a Flume Agent

After configuration, we have to start the Flume agent. It is done as follows –

```
$ bin/flume-ng agent --conf ./conf/ -f conf/twitter.conf
Dflume.root.logger=DEBUG,console -n TwitterAgent
```

where –

- **agent** – Command to start the Flume agent
- **--conf ,-c<conf>** – Use configuration file in the conf directory
- **-f<file>** – Specifies a config file path, if missing
- **--name, -n <name>** – Name of the twitter agent
- **-D property =value** – Sets a Java system property value

EXERCISE 15.1: Moving Data To HDFS Using Flume

After completing this exercise, you'll be able to:

1. Move data from your local file system to HDFS using Flume
2. Setup and configure Flume agents
3. Start the agents to collect data.

1. Setting up Flume configurations

Before we can start to collect data, we must first configure our Flume agents

Open a terminal and navigate to $BIGINSIGHTS_HOME/flume/conf

cd $BIGINSIGHTS_HOME/flume/conf

```
biadmin@bivm:...nsights/flume/conf
File  Edit  View  Terminal  Help
biadmin@bivm:~> cd $BIGINSIGHTS_HOME/flume/conf
biadmin@bivm:/opt/ibm/biginsights/flume/conf>
```

2. Execute an ls command to list all the files in this directory

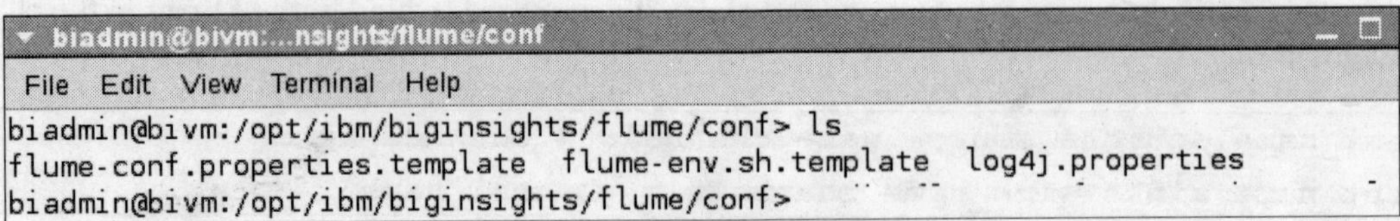

The file we will edit is called flume-conf.properties.template. This is the file in which you configure the Flume agents. You can add configurations for more than one agent as will be shown in later steps.

3. To edit this file enter the following:

   gedit flume-conf.properties.template

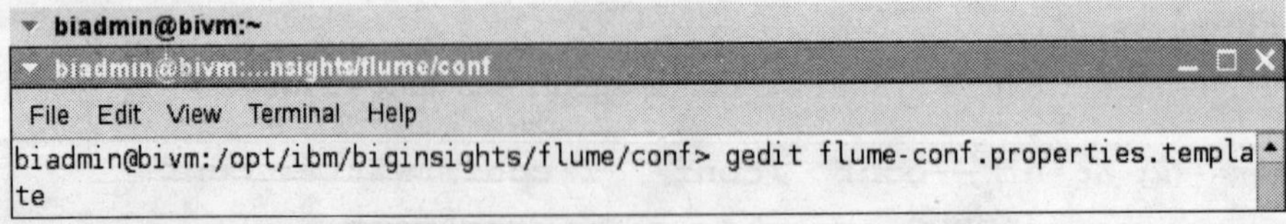

You do not need to use gedit, you may use vi or any editor you wish.

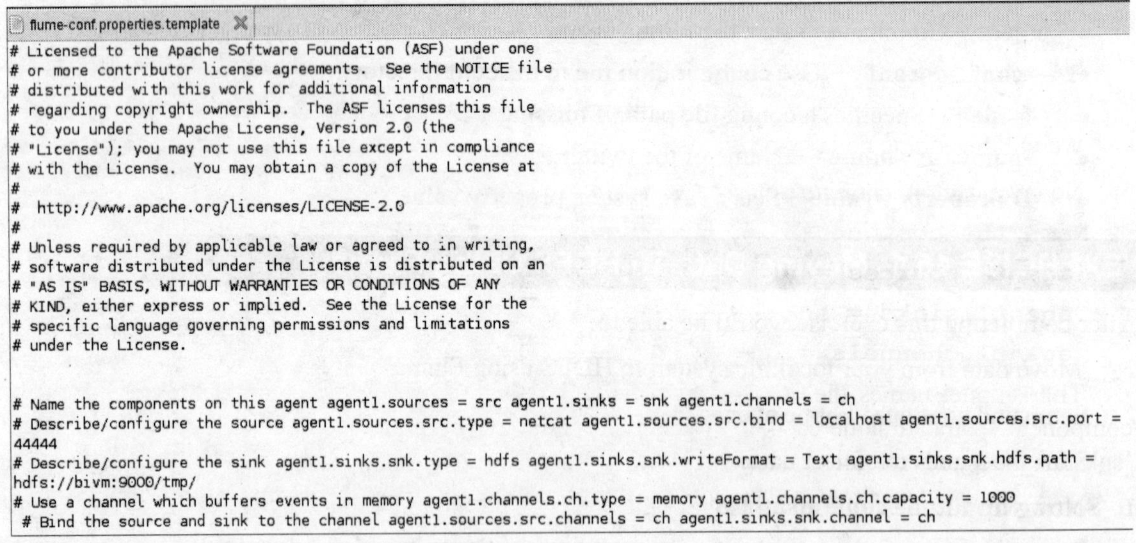

flume-conf.properties.template

```
# Licensed to the Apache Software Foundation (ASF) under one
# or more contributor license agreements.  See the NOTICE file
# distributed with this work for additional information
# regarding copyright ownership.  The ASF licenses this file
# to you under the Apache License, Version 2.0 (the
# "License"); you may not use this file except in compliance
# with the License.  You may obtain a copy of the License at
#
#  http://www.apache.org/licenses/LICENSE-2.0
#
# Unless required by applicable law or agreed to in writing,
# software distributed under the License is distributed on an
# "AS IS" BASIS, WITHOUT WARRANTIES OR CONDITIONS OF ANY
# KIND, either express or implied.  See the License for the
# specific language governing permissions and limitations
# under the License.

# Name the components on this agent agent1.sources = src agent1.sinks = snk agent1.channels = ch
# Describe/configure the source agent1.sources.src.type = netcat agent1.sources.src.bind = localhost agent1.sources.src.port =
44444
# Describe/configure the sink agent1.sinks.snk.type = hdfs agent1.sinks.snk.writeFormat = Text agent1.sinks.snk.hdfs.path =
hdfs://bivm:9000/tmp/
# Use a channel which buffers events in memory agent1.channels.ch.type = memory agent1.channels.ch.capacity = 1000
 # Bind the source and sink to the channel agent1.sources.src.channels = ch agent1.sinks.snk.channel = ch
```

4. Erase all the code except for what is shown in the image below:

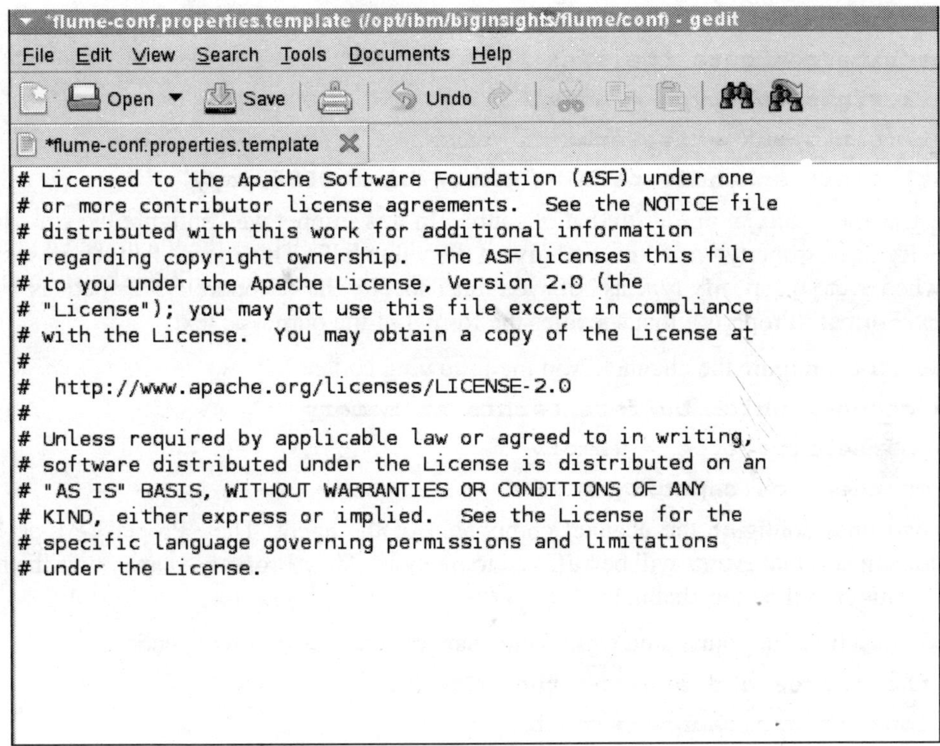

We will be adding code snippets to this file and explaining them as we go

5. Now we want to configure our source agent. Add the following code:

```
# Name the components on this agent
   agent1.sources = src
   agent1.sinks = snk
   agent1.channels = ch
```

This snippet names the components of agent1. Each agent needs a source, sinks, and channels component. You can name each component anything you wish; in this case we used ‘src’ for sources, ‘snk’ for sinks and ‘ch’ for channels.

6. Now we must describe and configure the source. Add the following code:

```
# Describe/configure the source
agent1.sources.src.type = netcat
agent1.sources.src.bind = localhost
agent1.sources.src.port = 44444
```

Notice the syntax: `<Agent>.sources.<SourceName>.<Property> = value.`

For the first line we specify the <Property> as type and the value as netcat. Each source must have the ‘type’ property. On the next line we have bind with value localhost, this the hostname or ip address to listen on. The last line is the port number to bind to.

7. Now we must describe and configure the sink. Add the following code:

```
# Describe/configure the sink
agent1.sinks.snk.type = hdfs
agent1.sinks.snk.writeFormat = Text
agent1.sinks.snk.hdfs.path = hdfs://bivm:9000/tmp/
```

Notice how the syntax is similar to that of source. In this snippet we configure the sink. In the first line we specify the <Property> as 'type' and give it the value hdfs. This means that it will write the file to HDFS, when ever you specify type as hdfs you must specify the <Property> hdfs.path as well. There is also a writeFormat <Property> that specifies the format of the output as text.

8. Now we must configure the channel. Add the following code:

```
# Use a channel which buffers events in memory
agent1.channels.ch.type = memory
agent1.channels.ch.capacity = 1000
```

These two lines configure the channel component of the agent. The <Property> type has value memory which means that events will be buffered to memory. The <Property> capacity is the maximum number of events stored on the channel.

9. Now we must bind the source and sink to the channel. Add the following code:

```
# Bind the source and sink to the channel
agent1.sources.src.channels = ch
agent1.sinks.snk.channel = ch
```

These two lines simply bind the source and the sink to the channel.

Your file should now look like the image below.

10. We do not want to overwrite the previous file. Save As sampleconf.properties. and close the window.

1. Clear the terminal and execute the `ls` command to make sure your file is in the directory.

```
clear ls
```

2.1 Running the flume agent

Now that we have setup the flume agent configuration file we can now run the agent.

To run this agent execute the following:

```
$BIGINSIGHTS_HOME/flume/bin/flume-ng agent -f sampleconf.properties -n agent1 -Dflume.root.logger=INFO,console
```

If executed correctly your terminal will look similar to the image below

```
SinkProcessor@44484448 counterGroup:{ name:null counters:{} } }} channels:{ch=org.apache.flume.channel.MemoryChannel{name: ch}} }
13/06/04 17:24:43 INFO nodemanager.DefaultLogicalNodeManager: Starting Channel ch
13/06/04 17:24:43 INFO nodemanager.DefaultLogicalNodeManager: Waiting for channel: ch to start. Sleeping for 500 ms
13/06/04 17:24:43 INFO instrumentation.MonitoredCounterGroup: Monitoried counter group for type: CHANNEL, name: ch, registered successfu
lly.
13/06/04 17:24:43 INFO instrumentation.MonitoredCounterGroup: Component type: CHANNEL, name: ch started
13/06/04 17:24:43 INFO nodemanager.DefaultLogicalNodeManager: Starting Sink snk
13/06/04 17:24:43 INFO nodemanager.DefaultLogicalNodeManager: Starting Source src
13/06/04 17:24:43 INFO source.NetcatSource: Source starting
13/06/04 17:24:43 INFO instrumentation.MonitoredCounterGroup: Monitoried counter group for type: SINK, name: snk, registered successfull
y.
13/06/04 17:24:43 INFO instrumentation.MonitoredCounterGroup: Component type: SINK, name: snk started
13/06/04 17:24:43 INFO source.NetcatSource: Created serverSocket:sun.nio.ch.ServerSocketChannelImpl[/127.0.0.1:44444]
```

2. The agent is now listening on port 44444 on your localhost. To see that the agent is listening open a new terminal and do the following:

```
telnet localhost 44444
type anything you wish
```

```
biadmin@bivm:/opt/ibm/biginsights/flume/conf
File Edit View Terminal Tabs Help
[biadmin@bivm conf]$ telnet localhost 44444
Trying 127.0.0.1...
Connected to localhost.localdomain (127.0.0.1).
Escape character is '^]'.
Testing 1 2 3 testing...
OK
```

You may exit telnet by pressing ^ +] then <Enter> then type quit. Do not close the terminal window as you will need it in the next few steps.

The terminal in which your Flume agent was running should be updated and look similar to the image below.

You can now open the Web Console and navigate to the tmp folder and find that the output is inside.

3. To end this flume agent process you must manually kill it. On the terminal where you used telnet, issue the following command:

```
ps -ef | grep flume | awk '{print $2}'
```

This command lists all the flume processes.

Now manually kill all the flume processes by issuing the following command:

```
kill -9 <pid> <pid>..
```

HDFS put Command

Flume is a distributed service for efficiently moving the large amounts of data. The primary use case of Flume is to gather a set of log files on every machine in a cluster and aggregate them to a centralized persistent store such as Hadoop Distributed File System (HDFS).

The traditional method of transferring data into the HDFS system is to use the put command. Let us see how to use the put command. The diagram below shows a deployment of Flume that collects log data from a set of application servers. The follow demonstrates it in three tiers. The first tier is the agent tier. Agent nodes are typically installed on the machines that generate the logs and are the initial point of contact with Flume. The second tier is the collector tier which is typically installed where the Flume master is. The third tier is the final destination of the file which can be either GPFS, HDFS or the local file system.

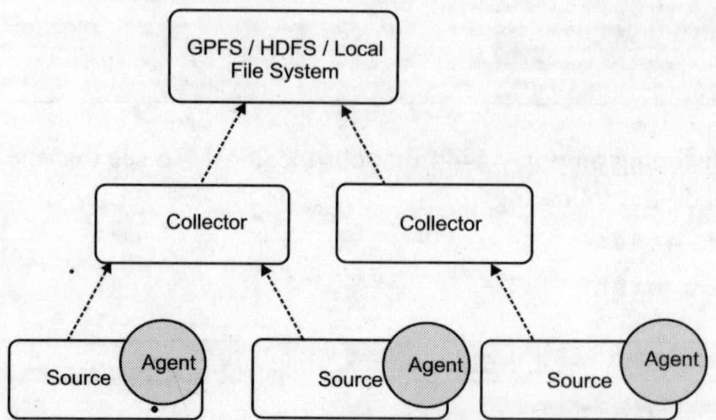

Figure. 15.2: Three Tiers of Data Collection

The main challenge in handling the log data is in moving these logs produced by multiple servers to the Hadoop environment.

Hadoop **File System Shell** provides commands to insert data into Hadoop and read from it. You can insert data into Hadoop using the **put** command as shown below.

```
$ Hadoop fs -put /path of the required file  /path in HDFS where to save
the file
```

roblem with put Command

We can use the **put** command of Hadoop to transfer data from these sources to HDFS. But, it suffers from the following drawbacks –

- Using put command, we can transfer only one file at a time while the data generators generate data at a much higher rate. Since the analysis made on older data is less accurate, we need to have a solution to transfer data in real time.
- If we use put command, the data is needed to be packaged and should be ready for the upload. Since the webservers generate data continuously, it is a very difficult task.

What we need here is a solutions that can overcome the drawbacks of **put** command and transfer the "streaming data" from data generators to centralized stores (especially HDFS) with less delay.

15.9 PROBLEM WITH HDFS

In HDFS, the file exists as a directory entry and the length of the file will be considered as zero till it is closed. For example, if a source is writing data into HDFS and the network was interrupted in the middle of the operation (without closing the file), then the data written in the file will be lost.

Therefore we need a reliable, configurable, and maintainable system to transfer the log data into HDFS.

Note – In POSIX file system, whenever we are accessing a file (say performing write operation), other programs can still read this file (at least the saved portion of the file). This is because the file exists on the disc before it is closed.

(1) Available Solutions

To send streaming data (log files, events etc..,) from various sources to HDFS, we have the following tools available at our disposal –

(2) Facebook's Scribe

Scribe is an immensely popular tool that is used to aggregate and stream log data. It is designed to scale to a very large number of nodes and be robust to network and node failures.

(3) Apache Kafka

Kafka has been developed by Apache Software Foundation. It is an open-source message broker. Using Kafka, we can handle feeds with high-throughput and low-latency.

EXERCISE 15.2: Fetching Twitter Data

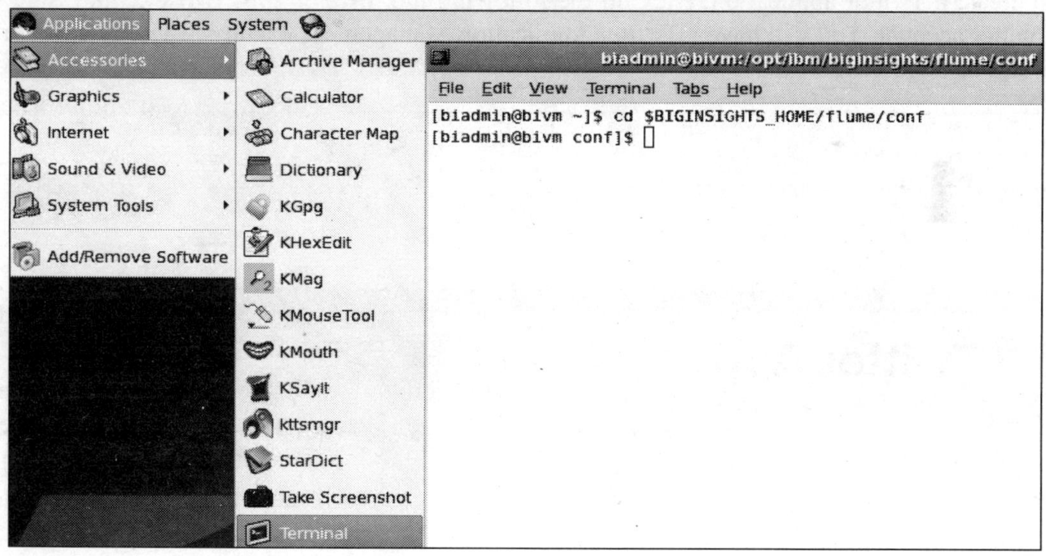

Using Flume, we can fetch data from various services and transport it to centralized stores (HDFS and HBase). This chapter explains how to fetch data from Twitter service and store it in HDFS using Apache Flume.

As discussed in Flume Architecture, a webserver generates log data and this data is collected by an agent in Flume. The channel buffers this data to a sink, which finally pushes it to centralized stores.

In the example provided in this chapter, we will create an application and get the tweets from it using the experimental twitter source provided by Apache Flume. We will use the memory channel to buffer these tweets and HDFS sink to push these tweets into the HDFS.

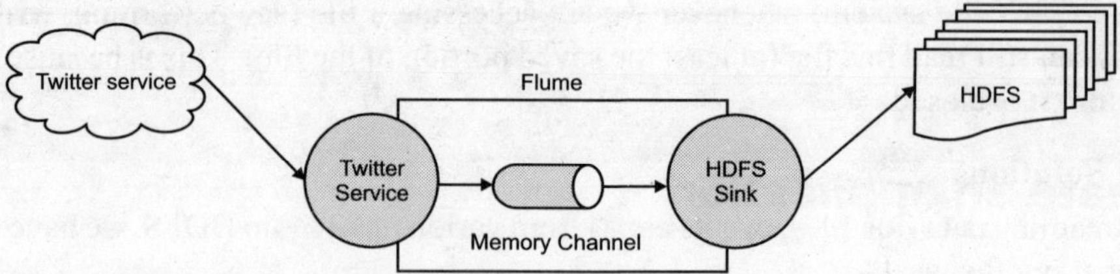

To fetch Twitter data, we will have to follow the steps given below –

- Create a twitter Application
- Install / Start HDFS
- Configure Flume

Creating a Twitter Application

In order to get the tweets from Twitter, it is needed to create a Twitter application. Follow the steps given below to create a Twitter application.

Step 1

To create a Twitter application, click on the following link **https://apps.twitter.com/.** Sign in to your Twitter account. You will have a Twitter Application Management window where you can create, delete, and manage Twitter Apps.

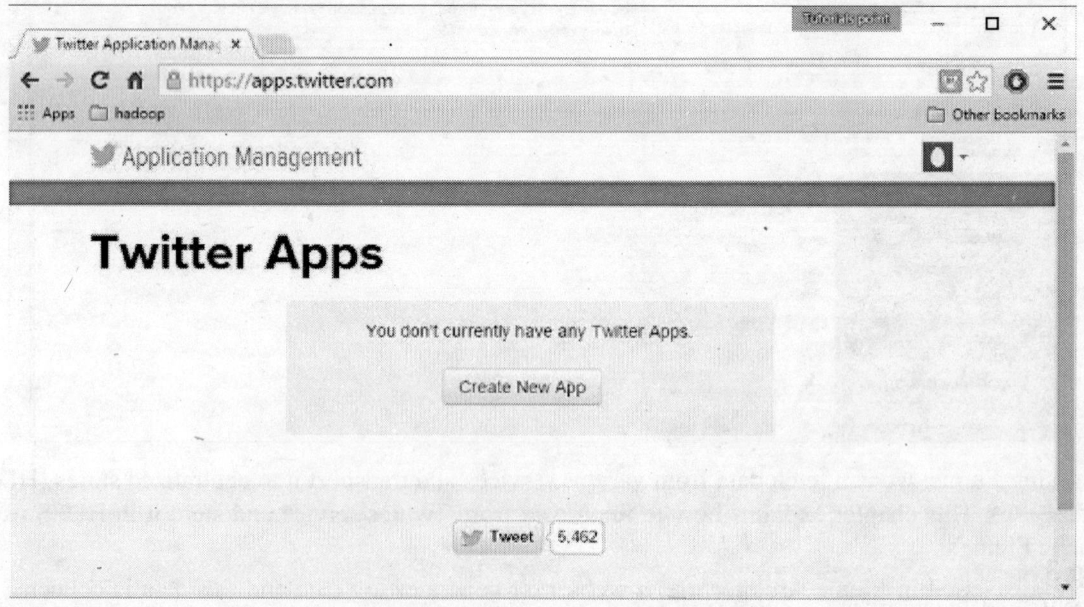

Step 2

Click on the **Create New App** button. You will be redirected to a window where you will get an application form in which you have to fill in your details in order to create the App. While filling the website address, give the complete URL pattern, for example, http://example.com.

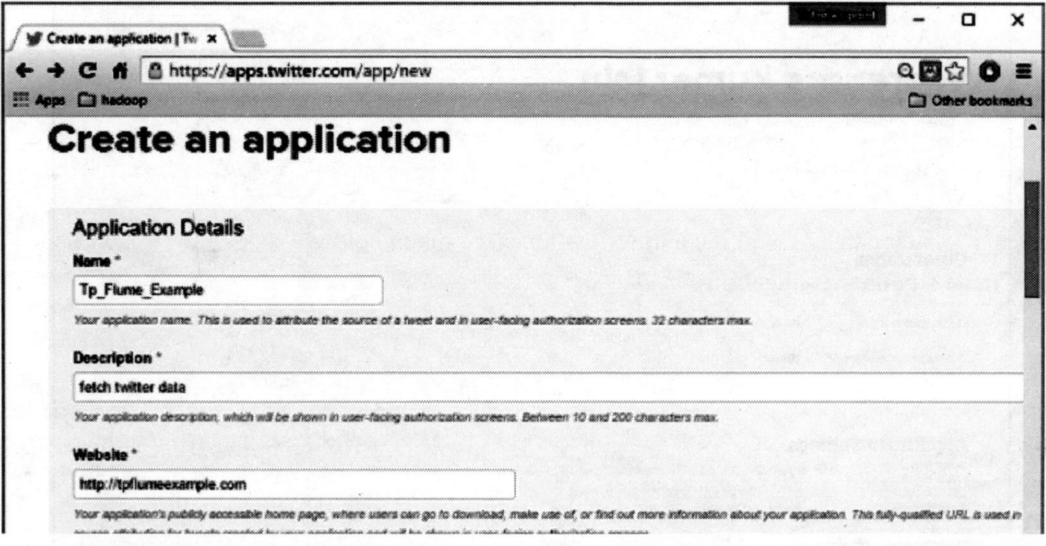

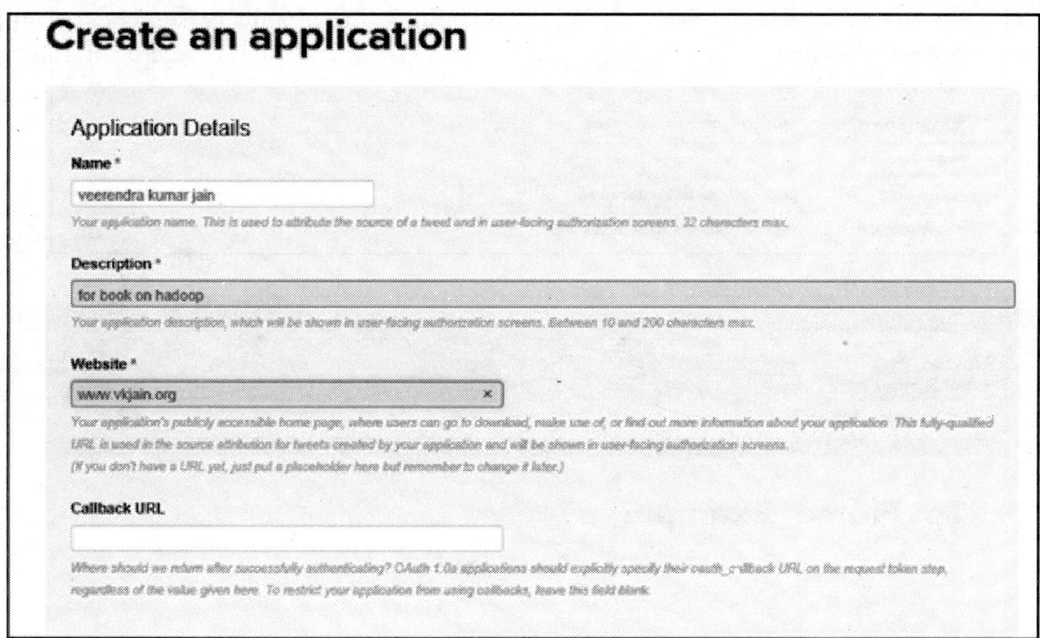

Step 3

Fill in the details, accept the **Developer Agreement** when finished, click on the **Create your Twitter application button** which is at the bottom of the page. If everything goes fine, an App will be created with the given details as shown below.

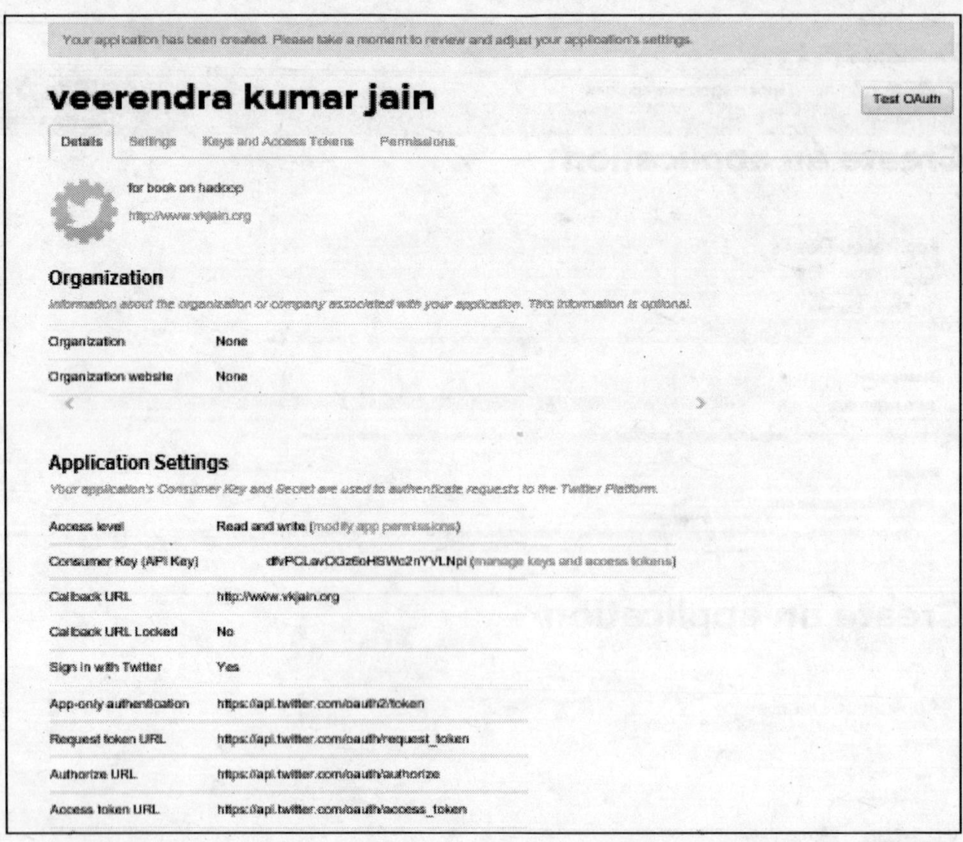
Your application has been created. Please take a moment to review and adjust your application's settings.
veerendra kumar jain
Test OAuth
Details
Settings
Keys and Access Tokens
Permissions
for book on hadoop
http://www.vkjain.org
Organization
Information about the organization or company associated with your application. This information is optional.
Organization None
Organization website None
Application Settings
Your application's Consumer Key and Secret are used to authenticate requests to the Twitter Platform.
Access level Read and write (modify app permissions)
Consumer Key (API Key) dfvPCLavOGz6oHSWc2nYVLNpi (manage keys and access tokens)
Callback URL http://www.vkjain.org
Callback URL Locked No
Sign in with Twitter Yes
App-only authentication https://api.twitter.com/oauth2/token
Request token URL https://api.twitter.com/oauth/request_token
Authorize URL https://api.twitter.com/oauth/authorize
Access token URL https://api.twitter.com/oauth/access_token

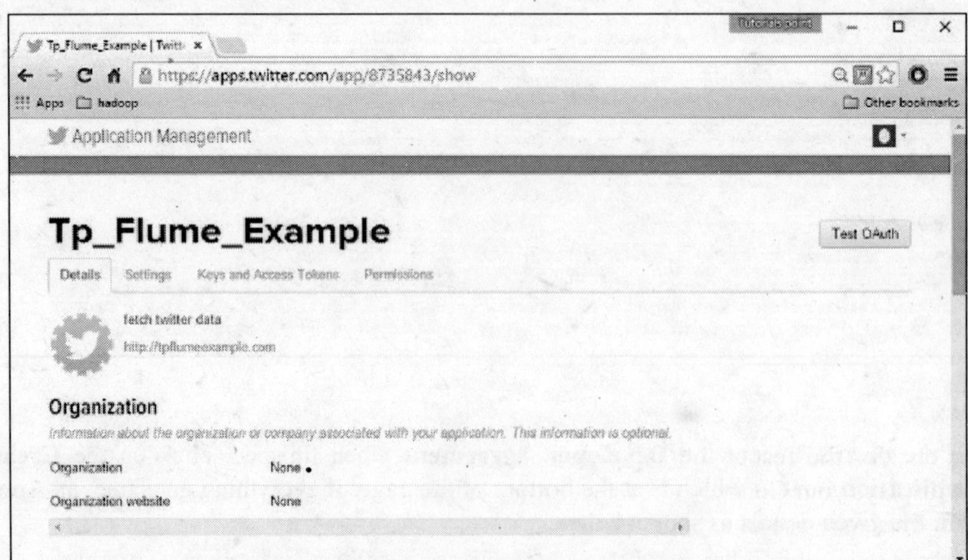
https://apps.twitter.com/app/8735843/show
Apps
hadoop
Other bookmarks
Application Management
Tp_Flume_Example
Test OAuth
Details
Settings
Keys and Access Tokens
Permissions
fetch twitter data
http://tpflumeexample.com
Organization
Information about the organization or company associated with your application. This information is optional.
Organization None
Organization website None

Step 4

Under keys and Access Tokens tab at the bottom of the page, you can observe a button named Create my access token. Click on it to generate the access token.

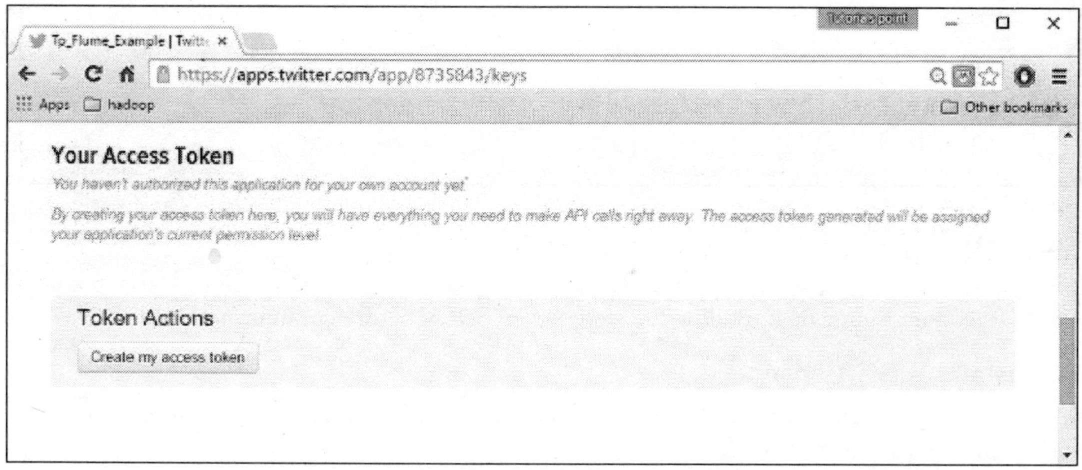

Step 5

Finally, click on the Test OAuth button which is on the right side top of the page. This will lead to a page which displays your Consumer key, Consumer secret, Access token, and Access token secret. Copy these details. These are useful to configure the agent in Flume.

OAuth Tool

OAuth Settings

Consumer key: *

dfvPCLavOGz6oHSWc2nYVLNgl

Consumer secret: *

bigSebz9X4HsBOYAg7FzTgtStbnlwsE0eVKCmulErQNsoh7EzR

Remember this should not be shared.

Access token:

Access token secret:

Request Settings

Request type: *

◉ GET ○ POST ○ DELETE ○ PUT ○ HEAD

Request URI: *

https://api.twitter.com/1.1/

The full URL, without parameters. For example: https://api.twitter.com/1.1/statuses/home_timeline.json

Request query:

The parameters for your request. For example: include_entities=true&page=2. Note these parameters will be sent on the querystring for GET requests, and in the request body for POST requests.

Starting HDFS

Since we are storing the data in HDFS, we need to install / verify Hadoop. Start Hadoop and create a folder in it to store Flume data. Follow the steps given below before configuring Flume.

Step 1: Install / Verify Hadoop

Install Hadoop. If Hadoop is already installed in your system, verify the installation using Hadoop version command, as shown below.

```
$ hadoop version
```

If your system contains Hadoop, and if you have set the path variable, then you will get the following output –

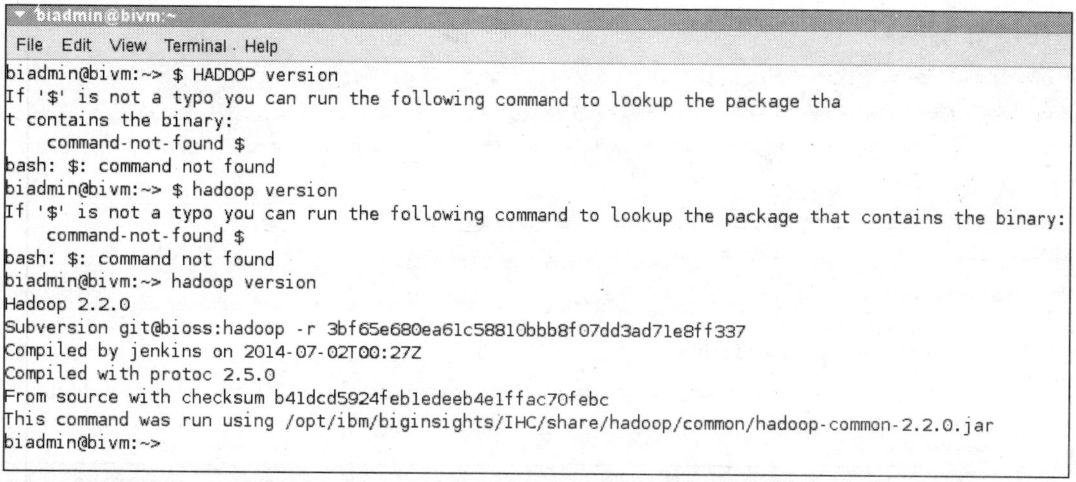

```
biadmin@bivm:~
File  Edit  View  Terminal  Help
biadmin@bivm:~> $ HADDOP version
If '$' is not a typo you can run the following command to lookup the package tha
t contains the binary:
    command-not-found $
bash: $: command not found
biadmin@bivm:~> $ hadoop version
If '$' is not a typo you can run the following command to lookup the package that contains the binary:
    command-not-found $
bash: $: command not found
biadmin@bivm:~> hadoop version
Hadoop 2.2.0
Subversion git@bioss:hadoop -r 3bf65e680ea61c58810bbb8f07dd3ad71e8ff337
Compiled by jenkins on 2014-07-02T00:27Z
Compiled with protoc 2.5.0
From source with checksum b41dcd5924feb1edeeb4e1ffac70febc
This command was run using /opt/ibm/biginsights/IHC/share/hadoop/common/hadoop-common-2.2.0.jar
biadmin@bivm:~>
```

```
Hadoop 2.6.0
Subversion https://git-wip-us.apache.org/repos/asf/hadoop.git -r
e3496499ecb8d220fba99dc5ed4c99c8f9e33bb1
Compiled by jenkins on 2014-11-13T21:10Z
Compiled with protoc 2.5.0
From source with checksum 18e43357c8f927c0695f1e9522859d6a
This command was run using /home/Hadoop/hadoop/share/hadoop/common/
hadoop-common-2.6.0.jar
```

Step 2: Starting Hadoop

Browse through the **sbin** directory of Hadoop and start yarn and Hadoop dfs (distributed file system) as shown below.

```
cd /$Hadoop_Home/sbin/
$ start-dfs.sh
localhost: starting namenode, logging to
          /home/Hadoop/hadoop/logs/hadoop-Hadoop-namenode-localhost.
localdomain.out
localhost: starting datanode, logging to
          /home/Hadoop/hadoop/logs/hadoop-Hadoop-datanode-localhost.
localdomain.out
Starting secondary namenodes [0.0.0.0]
starting secondarynamenode, logging to
   /home/Hadoop/hadoop/logs/hadoop-Hadoop-secondarynamenode-localhost.
localdomain.out
```

```
$ start-yarn.sh
starting yarn daemons
starting resourcemanager, logging to
      /home/Hadoop/hadoop/logs/yarn-Hadoop-resourcemanager-localhost.
localdomain.out
localhost: starting nodemanager, logging to
          /home/Hadoop/hadoop/logs/yarn-Hadoop-nodemanager-localhost.
localdomain.out
```

Step 3: Create a Directory in HDFS

In Hadoop DFS, you can create directories using the command **mkdir**. Browse through it and create a directory with the name **twitter_data** in the required path as shown below.

```
$cd /$Hadoop_Home/bin/
$ hdfs dfs -mkdir hdfs://localhost:9000/user/Hadoop/twitter_data
```

Configuring Flume

We have to configure the source, the channel, and the sink using the configuration file in the **conf** folder. The example given in this chapter uses an experimental source provided by Apache Flume named **Twitter 1% Firehose** Memory channel and HDFS sink.

Twitter 1% Firehose Source

This source is highly experimental. It connects to the 1% sample Twitter Firehose using streaming API and continuously downloads tweets, converts them to Avro format, and sends Avro events to a downstream Flume sink.

We will get this source by default along with the installation of Flume. The **jar** files corresponding to this source can be located in the **lib** folder as shown below.

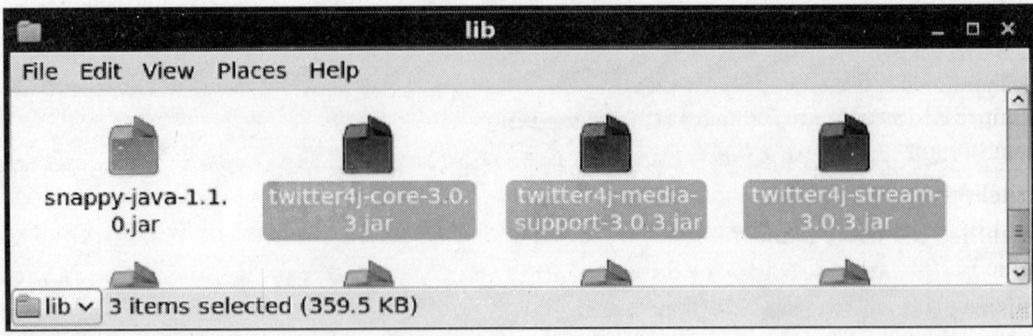

Setting the classpath

Set the **classpath** variable to the **lib** folder of Flume in **Flume-env.sh** file as shown below.

```
export CLASSPATH=$CLASSPATH:/FLUME_HOME/lib/*
```

This source needs the details such as **Consumer key, Consumer secret, Access token,** and **Access token secret** of a Twitter application. While configuring this source, you have to provide values to the following properties –

1. Channels
2. Source type : org.apache.flume.source.twitter.TwitterSource
3. consumerKey – The OAuth consumer key
4. consumerSecret – OAuth consumer secret
5. accessToken – OAuth access token
6. accessTokenSecret – OAuth token secret
7. maxBatchSize – Maximum number of twitter messages that should be in a twitter batch. The default value is 1000 (optional).
8. maxBatchDurationMillis – Maximum number of milliseconds to wait before closing a batch. The default value is 1000 (optional).

Channel

We are using the memory channel. To configure the memory channel, you *must* provide value to the type of the channel.

1. type – It holds the type of the channel. In our example, the type is MemChannel.
2. Capacity – It is the maximum number of events stored in the channel. Its default value is 100 (optional).
3. TransactionCapacity – It is the maximum number of events the channel accepts or sends. Its default value is 100 (optional).

HDFS Sink

4. This sink writes data into the HDFS. To configure this sink, you must provide the following details.
5. Channel
6. type – hdfs
7. hdfs.path – the path of the directory in HDFS where data is to be stored.

And we can provide some optional values based on the scenario. Given below are the optional properties of the HDFS sink that we are configuring in our application.

8. fileType – This is the required file format of our HDFS file. SequenceFile, DataStream and CompressedStream are the three types available with this stream. In our example, we are using the DataStream.
9. writeFormat – Could be either text or writable.
10. batchSize – It is the number of events written to a file before it is flushed into the HDFS. Its default value is 100.
11. rollsize – It is the file size to trigger a roll. It default value is 100.
12. rollCount – It is the number of events written into the file before it is rolled. Its default value is 10.

Example – Configuration File

Given below is an example of the configuration file. Copy this content and save as **twitter.conf** in the conf folder of Flume.

```
# Naming the components on the current agent.
TwitterAgent.sources = Twitter
TwitterAgent.channels = MemChannel
TwitterAgent.sinks = HDFS

# Describing/Configuring the source
TwitterAgent.sources.Twitter.type = org.apache.flume.source.twitter.
TwitterSource
TwitterAgent.sources.Twitter.consumerKey = Your OAuth consumer key
TwitterAgent.sources.Twitter.consumerSecret = Your OAuth consumer
secret
TwitterAgent.sources.Twitter.accessToken = Your OAuth consumer key
access token
TwitterAgent.sources.Twitter.accessTokenSecret = Your OAuth consumer
key access token secret
TwitterAgent.sources.Twitter.keywords = tutorials point,java, bigdata,
mapreduce, mahout, hbase, nosql

# Describing/Configuring the sink
TwitterAgent.sinks.HDFS.type = hdfs
TwitterAgent.sinks.HDFS.hdfs.path = hdfs://localhost:9000/user/Hadoop/
twitter_data/
TwitterAgent.sinks.HDFS.hdfs.fileType = DataStream
TwitterAgent.sinks.HDFS.hdfs.writeFormat = Text
TwitterAgent.sinks.HDFS.hdfs.batchSize = 1000
TwitterAgent.sinks.HDFS.hdfs.rollSize = 0
TwitterAgent.sinks.HDFS.hdfs.rollCount = 10000

# Describing/Configuring the channel TwitterAgent.channels.MemChannel.
type = memory
TwitterAgent.channels.MemChannel.capacity = 10000
TwitterAgent.channels.MemChannel.transactionCapacity = 100

# Binding the source and sink to the channel
TwitterAgent.sources.Twitter.channels = MemChannel
TwitterAgent.sinks.HDFS.channel = MemChannel
```

Execution

Browse through the Flume home directory and execute the application as shown below.

```
$ cd $FLUME_HOME
$ bin/flume-ng agent --conf ./conf/ -f conf/twitter.conf
Dflume.root.logger=DEBUG,console -n TwitterAgent
```

If everything goes fine, the streaming of tweets into HDFS will start. Given below is the snapshot of the command prompt window while fetching tweets.

Verifying HDFS

You can access the Hadoop Administration Web UI using the URL given below.

```
http://localhost:50070/
```

Click on the dropdown named **Utilities** on the right-hand side of the page. You can see two options as shown in the snapshot given below.

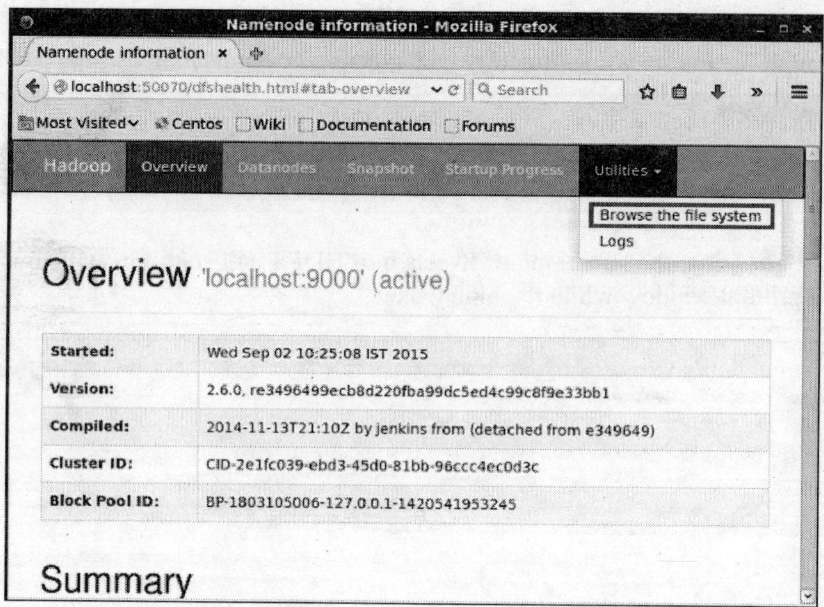

Click on **Browse the file system** and enter the path of the HDFS directory where you have stored the tweets. In our example, the path will be **/user/Hadoop/twitter_data/**. Then, you can see the list of twitter log files stored in HDFS as given below.

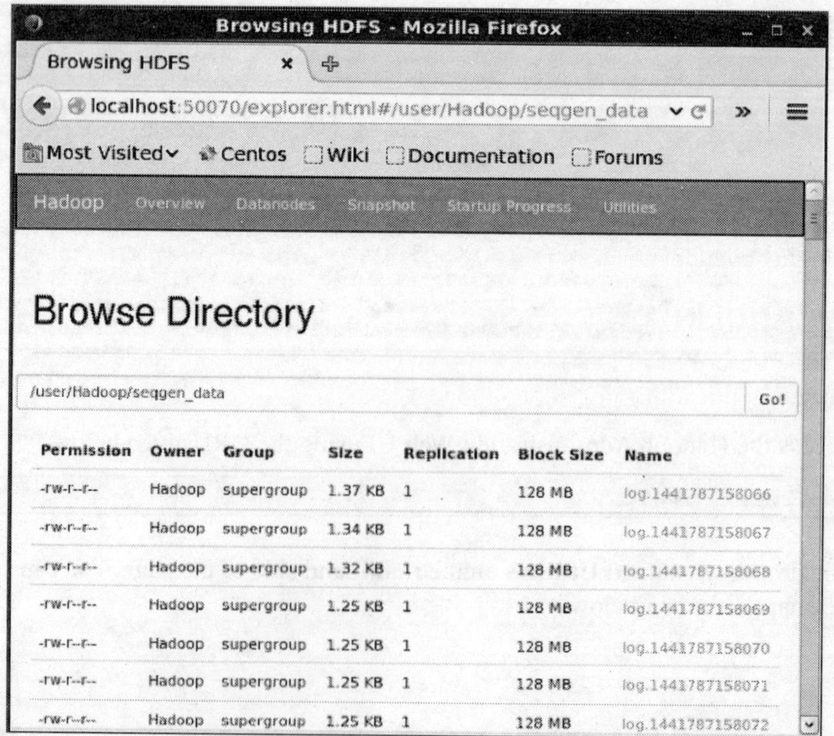

15.10 DIFFERENCE BETWEEN SQOOP AND FLUME

The following points describes the difference between these two applications of Hadoop.

1. Apache Sqoop and Apache Flume work with various kinds of data sources. Flume functions well in streaming data sources which are generated continuously in hadoop environment such as log files from multiple servers whereas Apache Sqoop is designed to work well with any kind of relational database system that has JDBC connectivity. Sqoop can also import data from NoSQL databases like MongoDB or Cassandra and also allows direct data transfer or Hive or HDFS. For transferring data to Hive using Apache Sqoop tool, a table has to be created for which the schema is taken from the database itself.
2. In Apache Flume data loading is event driven whereas in Apache Sqoop data load is not driven by events.
3. Flume is a better choice when moving bulk streaming data from various sources like JMS or Spooling directory whereas Sqoop is an ideal fit if the data is sitting in databases like Teradata, Oracle, MySQL Server, Postgres or any other JDBC compatible database then it is best to use Apache Sqoop.
4. In Apache Flume, data flows to HDFS through multiple channels whereas in Apache Sqoop HDFS is the destination for importing data.
5. Apache Flume has agent based architecture i.e. the code written in flume is known as agent which is responsible for fetching data whereas in Apache Sqoop the architecture is based on connectors. The connectors in Sqoop know how to connect with the various data sources and fetch data accordingly.
6. Lastly, Sqoop and Flume cannot be used to achieve the same tasks as they are developed specifically to serve different purposes. Apache Flume agents are designed to fetch streaming data like tweets from Twitter or log file from the web server whereas Sqoop connectors are designed to work only with structured data sources and fetch data from them.
7. Apache Sqoop is mainly used for parallel data transfers, for data imports as it copies data quickly where Apache Flume is used for collecting and aggregating data because of its distributed, reliable nature and highly available backup routes.

15.11 DATA HANDLING IN SQOOP , FLUME AND HDFS

The following table describes the three methods of deployment of big data i.e Squoop , Flume and HDFS under various applications in Hadoop Framework.

Sqoop	Flume	HDFS
Sqoop is used importing data from structured data sources such as RSBMS.	Flume is used for moving bulk streaming data into HDFS	HDFS is a distributed file system used by Hadoop ecosystem to store data.
Sqoop has a connector based architec ture. Connectors know how to connect to the respective data source and fetch the data.	Flume has an agent based architecture. Here, code is written (which is called as agent)which takes care of fetching data.	HDFS has a distributed architecture where data is distributed across multiple data nodes.
HDFS is a destination for data import using Sqoop.	Data flows to HDFS through zero or more channels.	HDFS is an ultima te destination for data storage.
Sqoop data load is not event driven.	Flume data load can be driven by event.	HDFS just stores data provided to it by what soever means.
In order to import data from structured data sources,one has to use Sqoop only, because its connectors know how to interact with structured data sources nd fetch data from them.	In order to load streaming data such as tweets generated on Twitter or log files of a web server, Flume should be used Flume agents are built for fetching streaming data.	HDFS has its own built-in shell commands to store data into it. HDFS can not import streaming data

Companies Using Apache Flume

1. Goibibo uses Hadoop flume to transfer logs from the production systems into HDFS.
2. Mozilla uses flume Hadoop for the BuildBot project along with Elastic Search.
3. Capillary technologies uses Flume for aggregating logs from 25 machines in production.

CHAPTER

16

R Programming : A Strong Visualization and Graphics Tool

16.1 R PROGRAMMING AND COOL GRAPHICS USING R LANGUAGE

A picture may be worth 1000 words, however only 10 words are required to create remarkably expressive pictures or charts in R programming language. The growth and maturity of R programming language has led to its widespread adoption and several learning resources. R might just be the 18th letter of English alphabet to someone but R is the lingua franca of many data scientists and analysts in academia and organizations across various industries. Why R programming language has quickly found a following among engineers, statisticians and scientists? Why now is the right time to learn R programming?

The ability to create pleasing graphics because of its parallel processing functionality makes R a strong visualization and graphics tool. R data science language allows data scientists to create navigational graphics from the data analysis results. The graphics can be used gain meaningful insights from the large datasets or can also be exported in a presentation report.

16.2 THE POWER OF R PROGRAMMING LANGUAGE

With petabytes of data, every organization is trying to find out the best tools and techniques to gain customer knowledge. However, merely using pivot tables in Microsoft Excel to analyse huge amounts of data is illogical and thus many organizations are doing data science using R programming language to cull the voluminosity of business analytics.

For people who are not yet familiar with R language- it is a fascinating statistical programming language that has become an appealing IT skill in a programmers' resume. According to the statistics of download site log files, R language has more than 3 million users in US alone. R language is used by statisticians or mostly by data scientists in various professions like business analytics, scientific research, business intelligence, software development and statistical reporting.

1. **R Language is more than a Statistics Application**

   Most of the new developments in statistics are in the form of R packages before they make way as commercial solutions. R is not just a statistical tool but a complete package of what an object oriented programming language can do. Programmers can enjoy the benefits of an interactive language whilst capitalizing on the speed of compiled code because R language supports embedding compiled code in other languages like FORTRAN or C.

2. **R Language has Endless Possibilities**

   The online community and distribution system of R language beats anything out there and R language also has unrivalled resources for learning. The quantity and quality of help from the vibrant online community for R programmers is relevant when they already have grasped the basics of R language and are trying to learn new statistical techniques.

   The most favourite feature of R programmers is that any code that they write for an analysis task can be saved and reused at a later point of time. R programmers can also share their code with others to expand the knowledge base among R users. If the programmers notice that changes need to be made during analysis - it is rather simple as they need not reanalyse the entire data.

3. **R Language has great presence in the Research Community**

   R language has great presence in the research community and anybody who develops a new visualization or predictive model using R language shares the code as an open source and not just publish it in the research journals so that others can share and reuse the code.

4. **R is a Fun to Learn Language**

   Programmers are usually attracted to learn R programming because of its extraordinary capabilities to generate plots and charts with just few lines of code which would otherwise require several 100's of lines of code in any other language. R language does have a steep learning curve but when programmers start learning R they really enjoy the powerful features it provides which are geared towards complex data analysis.

With the growing popularity and functionality of R language, it is going stay for long as organizations like Google, Pfizer, Bank of America, Merck, Oracle widely adopt its usage for complex business analytics. A powerful community, strong partners and a promise of providing easy-to-integrate solutions, R language is capitalizing big data analytics revolution.

16.3 R PROGRAMMING FOR DATA SCIENCE

R data science language is the magic wand for 21st century data scientists to handle and analyse huge amounts of complex and unstructured data productively. The popular saying "Patience is the mother of all virtues" holds good for R language because to learn R programming is definitely a challenge. The commands that work theoretically might not work practically and being a beginner it would be difficult to know what is exactly is going wrong with the code. Thus, students or professionals who want to make a career progression in data science should learn through a comprehensive training that offers hands-on working experience on various projects.

Persistence and Patience are the key to beginning data science with R programming language, but considering the wonders R language can do, it is worth learning R language now. R language has a teaching package called Swirl that helps beginners learn commands and also provides immediate user feedback.

The longevity of R language twigs from its awesome perks – the average salary for R programmers is better than NoSQL or MapReduce programmers.

Let's return to the question at hand –why should professionals put in efforts to learn R language? Other than the popularly known fact that it's free - we bring you the most convincing reasons to learn R programming language now.

R language is at the core of Facebook's data science team as it gives them the best overview on the kind of data they are dealing with. The data can be anything like the correlations with the number of Facebook friends a user has or the news feed numbers.

According to Solomon Messing, Data Scientist at Facebook- "Generally, we use R language to move fast when we get a new data set. With R language, we don't need to develop custom tools or write a bunch of code. Instead, we can just go about cleaning and exploring the data."

"One of the things we like about commercial R is that it can create beautiful graphics compared to, for example, SAS, which has very ugly, horribly ugly graphics."- said Tess Nesbitt, director of analytics at DataSong

16.4 R IS A PLATFORM INDEPENDENT LANGUAGE

If you are student or professional who lives in windows environment all day this reason might not appeal to you but for others who use Mac or Linux and share work with colleagues who use windows, this feature of R language comes as a boon. All thanks to the core development team of R language, it also runs on few operating systems of Mainframes.

There is a possibility that the system might run out of memory when handling huge amount of data but there are several commercial versions of R language which ease the process of handling tons of business data without any hassle. Revolution analytics provides a commercial library of analytics algorithms known as ScaleR that helps organizations to tackle petabytes of business data by scaling it to work effectively on parallel processors. The data is processed in chunks on different servers simultaneously.

DataSong, a San Francisco based company that is transforming marketing analytics technology uses commercial R packages provided by Revolution Analytics. Their aim is to create a quantitative model based on different variables for a retail customer. The commercial R packages have helped them process 30 million rows of data for 60 variables in just 10 minutes.

16.5 DATA SCIENCE USING BIG R FOR IN-HADOOP ANALYTICS

Big R provides an end-to-end integration of R within IBM InfoSphere BigInsights. This makes it easy to write and execute R programs that operate on data stored in a Hadoop cluster.

Using Big R, an R user can explore, transform, and analyze big data hosted in a BigInsights cluster using familiar R syntax and paradigm. All of these capabilities are accessible from a standard R client.

Big R provides the following capabilities:

1. Enable the use of R as a query language for big data: Big R hides many of the complexities pertaining to the underlying Hadoop / MapReduce framework. Using classes such as bigr.frame, bigr.vector and bigr.list, a user is presented with an API that is heavily inspired by R's foundâtional API on data. frames, vectors and frames.

2. Enable the pushdown of R functions such that they run right on the data: Via mechanisms such as groupApply, rowApply and tableApply, user-written functions composed in R can be shipped to the cluster. BigInsights transparently parallelizes execution of these functions and provides consolidated results back to the user. Almost any R code, including most packages available on open-source repositories such as CRAN (Comprehensive R Archive Network), can be run using this mechanism.

EXAMPLE 16.1: Getting Started With Big R

The following exercises are also available in a file named "BigRLab4.R" in the "/home/biadmin/labs-bigr/" directory. You can open this file in RStudio and follow along. When practical, it is suggested that you type in the code in the "Console" to see how Big R operates. For longer batches of statements, you can certainly copy-and-paste the statements into the RStudio console and execute them.

1. Start BigInsights

   From the Desktop, click on the **"Start BigInsights"** icon.

This action will start up various BigInsights components, including HDFS and Map/Reduce, on your machine. A Terminal window will pop up that will indicate progress. Eventually, the Terminal window will disappear. Once done, return to RStudio.

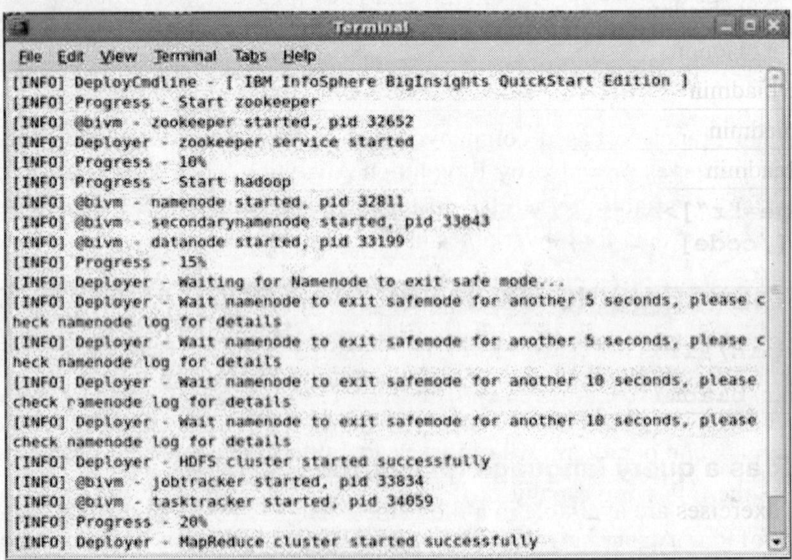

2. Back to RStudio

   Return to RStudio session in the browser.

```
[code language="r"]>setwd("~/labs-bigr")      # change directory[/code]
[code language="r"]>rm(list = ls())           # clear workspace[/code]
Load Big R Load the Big R package into your R session.
[code language="r"]>library(bigr) [/code]
```

3. Connect to BigInsights

   Note how one needs to specify the right credentials for this call.

```
[code language="r"]>bigr.connect(host="localhost", port=7052,[/code]
[code language="r"]>user="biadmin", password="biadmin") [/code]
Verify that the connection was successful.
[code language="r"]>is.bigr.connected() [/code]
```

If you ever lose your connection during these exercises, run the following line to reconnect. You can also invoke bigr.connect() as we did above.

[code language="r"]>bigr.reconnect()[/code]

4. Browse files on HDFS

   Once connected, you will be able to browse the HDFS file system and examine datasets that have already been loaded onto the cluster.

```
[code language="r"]>bigr.listfs()             # List files under root "/"[/
code]
```

Path	Owner length	BlockSize	Permission
1	/biginsights biadmin	0	0 rwxr-xr-x
2	/hadoop biadmin	0	0 rwxr-xr-x
3	/hbase biadmin	0	0 rwxr-xr-x
4	/tmp biadmin	0	0 rwxrwxrwx
5	/user biadmin	0	0 rwxrwxrwx

```
[code language="r"]>bigr.listfs("/user/biadmin")      # List files under /
user/biadmin[/code]
```

```
path   owner   length blockSize permission
1 /user/biadmin/airline_lab.csv biadmin 12055574 134217728 rw-r--r--
2         /user/biadmin/credstore biadmin       0         0 rwx--x-x
```

Part 2 – Using R as a query language for Big Data

The following exercises are available in a filę named "BigRLab5.R" in the "/home/biadmin/labs-bigr/" directory.

1. Connect to a big data set

   "/user/biadmin/airline_lab.csv" is one of the datasets that you will see on HDFS. This is a comma-delimited file (type = “DEL”). Let’s connect to it and explore it a bit. This is done by creating a bigr.frame over the dataset. A bigr.frame is an R object that mimics R’s own data.frame. However, unlike R, a bigr.frame does not load that data in memory as that would be impractical. The data stays in HDFS. However, you will still be able to explore this data using the Big R API.

[code language=”r”]>air <- bigr.frame(dataSource="DEL",

>dataPath="/user/biadmin/airline_lab.csv")[/code]

Check that “air” is an object of “bigr.frame”

[code language=”r”]>class(air)[/code]

```
[1] "bigr.frame"
```

[code language=”r”]>attr(,"package")[/code]

```
[1] "bigr"
```

Basic exploration

2. Exploring table metadata

Examine the structure of the dataset. Note that the output looks very similar to R’s data.frames. The dataset has 29 variables (i.e. columns). The first few values of each column are also shown. Examine the columns and see what they may possibly represent.

```
[code language="r"]>str(air)[/code]
'bigr.frame': 29 variables:
$ Year             : chr "2004" "2004" "2004" "2004" "2004" "2004"
$ Month            : chr "2" "2" "2" "2" "2" "2"
$ DayofMonth       : chr "12" "16" "18" "19" "21" "24"
$ DayOfWeek        : chr "4" "1" "3" "4" "6" "2"
$ DepTime          : chr "633" "2115" "700" "1140" "936" "1117"
$ CRSDepTime       : chr "635" "2120" "700" "1145" "935" "1120"
$ ArrTime          : chr "935" "2340" "817" "1427" "1036" "1922"
$ CRSArrTime       : chr "930" "2350" "820" "1420" "1035" "1930"
$ UniqueCarrier    : chr "B6" "B6" "B6" "B6" "B6" "B6"
$ FlightNum        : chr "165" "199" "2" "67" "68" "206"
$ TailNum          : chr "N553JB" "N570JB" "N544JB" "N570JB" "N544JB"
                         "N548JB"
$ ActualElapsedTime: chr "182" "325" "77" "167" "60" "305"
$ CRSElapsedTime   : chr "175" "330" "80" "155" "60" "310"
```

```
$ AirTime          : chr "162" "114" "49" "141" "41" "468"
$ ArrDelay         : chr "5" "-10" "-3" "7" "1" "-8"
$ DepDelay         : chr "-2" "-5" "0" "-5" "1" "-3"
$ Origin           : chr "JFK" "JFK" "JFK" "RSW" "JFK" "LGB"
$ Dest             : chr "TPA" "LAS" "BUF" "JFK" "SYR" "JFK"
$ Distance         : chr "1005" "2248" "301" "1074" "209" "2465"
$ TaxiIn           : chr "3" "8" "2" "7" "3" "7"
$ TaxiOut          : chr "17" "23" "26" "19" "16" "10"
$ Cancelled        : chr "0" "0" "0" "0" "0" "0"
$ CancellationCode : chr "NA" "NA" "NA" "NA" "NA" "NA"
$ Diverted         : chr "0" "0" "0" "0" "0" "0"
$ CarrierDelay     : chr "0" "0" "0" "0" "0" "0"
$ WeatherDelay     : chr "0" "0" "0" "0" "0" "0"
$ NASDelay         : chr "0" "0" "0" "0" "0" "0"
$ SecurityDelay    : chr "0" "0" "0" "0" "0" "0"
$ LateAircraftDelay: chr "0" "0" "0" "0" "0" "0"
```

3. Assign column types

Notice that the column types are all "character" (abbreviated as "chr"). Unless specified otherwise, Big R automatically assumes all data to be strings. However, we know that only columns Year (1), Month (2), UniqueCarrier (9), TailNum (11), Origin (17), Dest (18), CancellationCode (23) are strings, while the rest are numbers. Let us assign the correct column types.

First, we build a vector that holds the column types for all columns

```
[code language="r"]>ct <- ifelse(1:29 %in% c(1,2,9,11,17,18,23),
>"character", "integer")
>print(ct) [/code]
[1]  "character" "character" "integer"  "integer"  "integer"  "integer"
[7]  "integer"  "integer"  "character" "integer"  "character" "integer"
[13] "integer"  "integer"  "integer"  "integer"  "character"
     "character"
[19] "integer"  "integer"  "integer"  "integer"  "character" "integer"
[25] "integer"  "integer"  "integer"  "integer"  "integer"
```

Assign the column types

```
[code language="r"]>coltypes(air) <- ct[/code]
```

4. Data dimensions

This data originally comes from US Department of Transportation (http://www.rita.dot.gov), and it provides us information on every US flight over the past couple of decades. The original data has approximately 125+ million rows. For this lab, we're only using a small sample. Let us examine the dimensions of the dataset.

```
[code language="r"]>nrow(air)        # Number of rows (i.e. flights) in the data[/code]
```

```
[1] 128790
```

[code language="r"]>ncol(air) # Number of attributes recorded for each flight[/code]

```
[1] 29
```

Data summarization

5. Summarizing frames

Let us summarize some key columns to gain further understanding of this data. You'll see that the years range from 1987-2008.

```
[code language="r"]>summary(air[, c("Year", "Month", "UniqueCarrier")])
[/code]
```

```
Year        Month    UniqueCarrier
A Min.  :1987 Min.  :1 Min.  :9E
B Max.  :2008 Max.  :9 Max.  :YV
```

6. Summarizing vectors and basic visualization

Summarizing columns one by one will give us additional information. In some cases, we will also visualize the information.

The following statement shows us the distribution of flights by year. Again, we have 22 years worth of data. What you will see is a vector that has the "year" for the name, and the flight count for the values.

[code language="r"]>summary(air$Year)[/code]

1987 1988 1989 1990 1991 1992 1993 1994 1995 1996 1997 1998 1999 2000 2001 2002

1364 5408 5282 5518 5279 5300 5325 5394 5532 5560 5635 5614 5748 5915 6165 5475

2003 2004 2005 2006 2007 2008

6810 7455 7463 7469 7753 7326

Let us glue Big R's summary() with R's visualization capabilities to see the same data distribution graphically. Before you do this, make sure the "Plots" window (lower right hand pane of RStudio) is in view, and that it is sized big enough to display the plot. We see that the flight volume has gradually increased over the years. Feel free to "Zoom" the plot to pop up a separate window. To close the popped-up window, press "Ctrl F4".

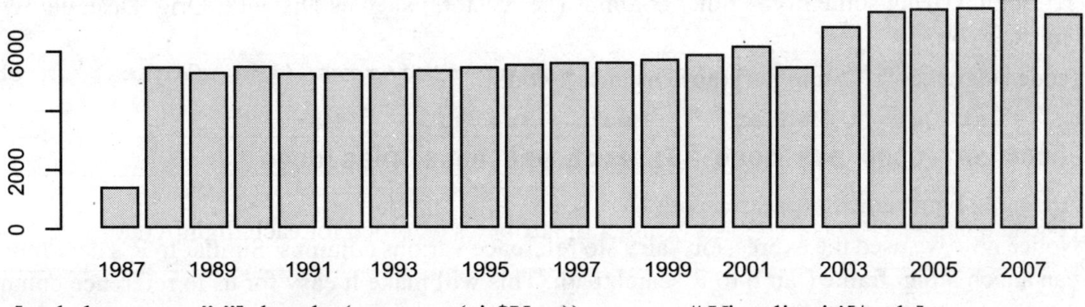

[code language="r"]>barplot(summary(air$Year)) # Visualize it![/code]

Similarly, we can also examine the distribution of flights by airline (UniqueCarrier). We have 29 airlines in this dataset, including United (UA), Delta (DL), and many others.

[code language="r"]>summary(air$UniqueCarrier)[/code]

9E AA AQ AS B6 CO DH DL EA
526 15641 146 2981 877 8394 710 17397 952
EV F9 FL HA HP ML (1) MQ NW OH
1778 371 1289 269 3839 76 4040 10630 1547
OO PA (1) PI PS TW TZ UA US WN
3270 346 900 92 4019 240 13872 14751 16464
XE YV
2474 899

Again, visualizing the data will give us a better perspective. We will use Big R to aggregate the data, sort it, and then plot it. Can you tell which airlines have the most # of flights? Which ones have the least? Does this resonate with your own experience? Again, you can "Zoom" the plot window for a better view, and close it when done.

[code language="r"]>barplot(sort(summary(air$UniqueCarrier)))[/code]

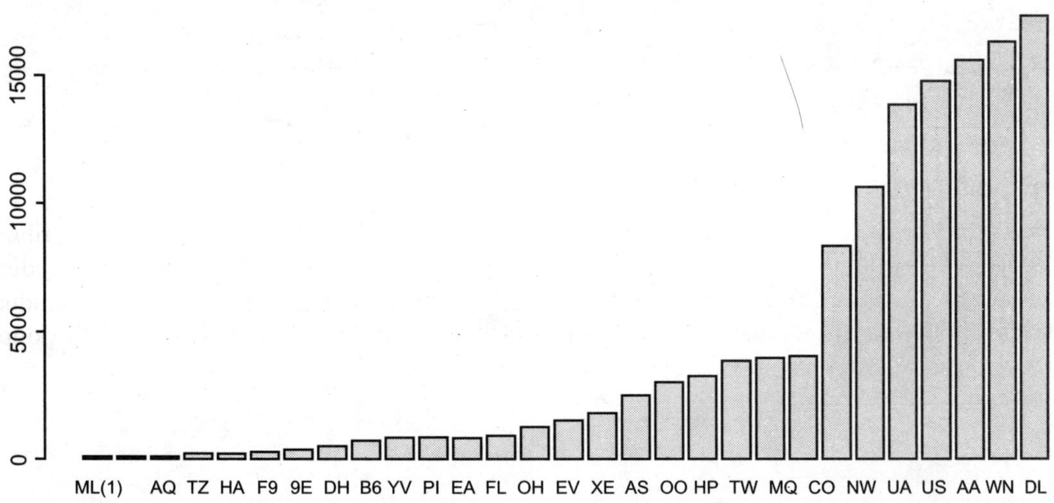

Try summarizing some of the other columns (i.e. vectors) such as Distance, Orig, Dest, etc. What does this tell you?

[code language="r"]>summary(air$Distance)[/code]

```
 Min.    1st Qu.    Median     Mean   3rd Qu.      Max.
11.0000 307.0000 545.0000 701.9441 936.0000 4983.0000
```

7. Attaching bigr.frame to R search path

Notice how we used the expression "air$" to reference various columns. Similar to R's data.frames, you can attach a bigr.frame ('air') to R search path. This will make it easy for us to reference columns without requiring a prefix.

```
[code language="r"]>attach(air)[/code]
```

Slicing and dicing big data

CHAPTER

17

Other Components of Hadoop : Ozzie,Zookeeper and Mahout

17.1 INTRODUCTION TO OOZIE WORKFLOW SCHEDULER FOR HADOOP

Apache Oozie is a workflow scheduler for Hadoop. It is a system which runs workflow of dependent jobs. Here, users are permitted to create Directed Acyclic Graphs of workflows, which can be run in parallel and sequentially in Hadoop.

It consists of two parts:

1. Workflow engine : Responsibility of a workflow engine is to store and run workflows composed of Hadoop jobs e.g., MapReduce, Pig, Hive.
2. Coordinator engine: It runs workflow jobs based on predefined schedules and availability of data.

Oozie is scalable and can manage timely execution of thousands of workflows (each consisting of dozens of jobs) in a Hadoop cluster.

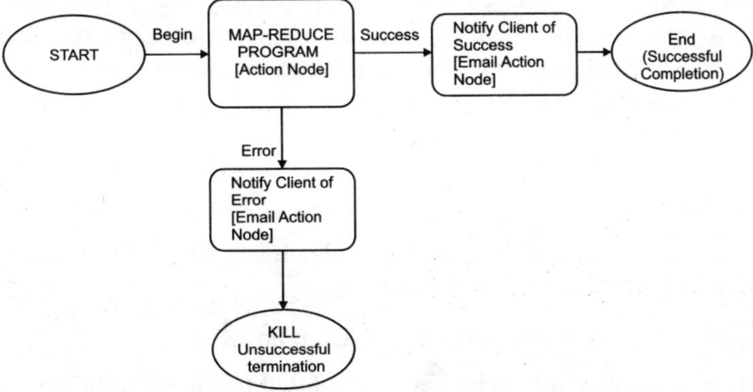

Figure. 17.1: Oozie is a workflow scheduler for Hadoop

Oozie is very much flexible, as well. One can easily start, stop, suspend and rerun jobs. Oozie makes it very easy to rerun failed workflows. One can easily understand how difficult it can be to catch up missed or failed jobs due to downtime or failure. It is even possible to skip a specific failed node.

Oozie v1 is a server based Workflow Engine specialized in running workflow jobs with actions that execute Hadoop Map/Reduce and Pig jobs. Oozie v2 is a server based Coordinator Engine specialized in running workflows based on time and data triggers. It can continuously run

workflows based on time (e.g. run it every hour), and data availability (e.g. wait for my input data to exist before running my workflow).

Oozie v3 is a server based Bundle Engine that provides a higher-level oozie abstraction that will batch a set of coordinator applications. The user will be able to start/stop/suspend/resume/rerun a set coordinator jobs in the bundle level resulting a better and easy operational control.

17.1.1 How does OOZIE work?

Oozie runs as a service in the cluster and clients submit workflow definitions for immediate or later processing. Oozie workflow consists of action nodes and control-flow nodes.

An action node represents a workflow task, e.g., moving files into HDFS, running a MapReduce, Pig or Hive jobs, importing data using Sqoop or running a shell script of a program written in Java

Oozie is very much flexible, as well. One can easily start, stop, suspend and rerun jobs. Oozie makes it very easy to rerun failed workflows. One can easily understand how difficult it can be to catch up missed or failed jobs due to downtime or failure. It is even possible to skip a specific failed node.

A control-flow node controls the workflow execution between actions by allowing constructs like conditional logic wherein different branches may be followed depending on the result of earlier action node. Start Node, End Node and Error Node fall under this category of nodes.

Start Node, designates start of the workflow job.End Node, signals end of the job. Error Node, designates an occurrence of error and corresponding error message to be printed.

At the end of execution of workflow, HTTP callback is used by Oozie to update client with the workflow status. Entry-to or exit-from an action node may also trigger callback.

17.1.2 Why use Oozie?

Main purpose of using Oozie is to manage different type of jobs being processed in Hadoop system. Dependencies between jobs are specified by user in the form of Directed Acyclic Graphs. Oozie consumes this information and takes care of their execution in correct order as specified in a workflow. That way user's time to manage complete workflow is saved. In addition, Oozie has a provision to specify frequency of execution of a particular job.

17.1.3 Features of Oozie

1. Oozie has client API and command line interface which can be used to launch, control and monitor job from Java application.
2. Using its Web Service APIs one can control jobs from anywhere.
3. Oozie has provision to execute jobs which are scheduled to run periodically.
4. Oozie has provision to send email notifications upon completion of jobs.

5. Oozie is a server based Workflow Engine specialized in running workflow jobs with actions that run Hadoop Map/Reduce and Pig jobs.
6. Oozie is a Java Web-Application that runs in a Java servlet-container.
7. For the purposes of Oozie, a workflow is a collection of actions (i.e. Hadoop Map/Reduce jobs, Pig jobs) arranged in a control dependency DAG (Direct Acyclic Graph). "control dependency" from one action to another means that the second action can't run until the first action has completed.
8. Oozie workflows definitions are written in hPDL (a XML Process Definition Language similar to JBOSS JBPM jPDL).
9. Oozie workflow actions start jobs in remote systems (i.e. Hadoop, Pig). Upon action completion, the remote systems callback Oozie to notify the action completion, at this point Oozie proceeds to the next action in the workflow.
10. Oozie workflows contain control flow nodes and action nodes.
11. Control flow nodes define the beginning and the end of a workflow (start , end and fail nodes) and provide a mechanism to control the workflow execution path (decision , fork andjoin nodes).
12. Action nodes are the mechanism by which a workflow triggers the execution of a computation/ processing task. Oozie provides support for different types of actions: Hadoop map-reduce, Hadoop file system, Pig, SSH, HTTP, eMail and Oozie sub-workflow. Oozie can be extended to support additional type of actions.

17.1.4 Setting Up the Examples

Oozie examples are bundled within the Oozie distribution in the oozie-examples.tar.gz file. Expanding this file will create an examples/ directory in the local file system.

The examples/ directory must be copied to the user HOME directory in HDFS:

$ hadoop fs -put examples examples

Note: If an examples directory already exists in HDFS, it must be deleted before copying it again. Otherwise files may not be copied.

17.2 ZOOKEEPER : SYNCHRONIZATION ACROSS A CLUSTER

17.2.1 Introduction to Apache ZooKeeper

ZooKeeper is an open source Apache™ project that provides a centralized infrastructure and services that enable synchronization across a cluster. ZooKeeper maintains common objects needed in large cluster environments. Examples of these objects include configuration information, hierarchical naming space, and so on. Applications can leverage these services to coordinate distributed processing across large clusters.

The formal definition of Apache Zookeeper says that it is a distributed, open-source configuration, synchronization service along with naming registry for distributed applications. Apache Zookeeper is used to manage and coordinate large cluster of machines. For example Apache Storm which is used by Twitter for storing machine state data has Apache Zookeeper as the coordinator between machines.

The ZooKeeper framework was originally built at "Yahoo!" for accessing their applications in an easy and robust manner. Later, Apache ZooKeeper became a standard for organized service used by Hadoop, HBase, and other distributed frameworks. For example, Apache HBase uses ZooKeeper to track the status of distributed data.

17.2.2 Need of Zookeeper in the Hadoop

Distributed applications are difficult to coordinate and work with as they are much more error prone due to huge number of machines attached to network. As many machines are involved, race condition and deadlocks are common problems when implementing distributed applications. Race condition occurs when a machine tries to perform two or more operations at a time and this can be taken care by serialization property of ZooKeeper. Deadlocks are when two or more machines try to access same shared resource at the same time. More precisely they try to access each other's resources which leads to lock of system as none of the system is releasing the resource but waiting for other system to release it. Synchronization in Zookeeper helps to solve the deadlock. Another major issue with distributed application can be partial failure of process, which can lead to inconsistency of data. Zookeeper handles this through atomicity, which means either whole of the process will finish or nothing will persist after failure. Thus Zookeeper is an important part of Hadoop that take care of these small but important issues so that developer can focus more on functionality of the application.

17.2.3 Challenges of Distributed Applications

1. Race condition – Two or more machines trying to perform a particular task, which actually needs to be done only by a single machine at any given time. For example, shared resources should only be modified by a single machine at any given time.
2. Deadlock – Two or more operations waiting for each other to complete indefinitely.
3. Inconsistency – Partial failure of data.

The common services provided by ZooKeeper are as follows –

1. Naming service – Identifying the nodes in a cluster by name. It is similar to DNS, but for nodes.
2. Configuration management – Latest and up-to-date configuration information of the system for a joining node.
3. Cluster management – Joining / leaving of a node in a cluster and node status at real time.
4. Leader election – Electing a node as leader for coordination purpose.
5. Locking and synchronization service – Locking the data while modifying it. This mechanism helps you in automatic fail recovery while connecting other distributed applications like Apache HBase.
6. Highly reliable data registry – Availability of data even when one or a few nodes are down.

Distributed applications offer a lot of benefits, but they throw a few complex and hard-to-crack challenges as well. ZooKeeper framework provides a complete mechanism to overcome all the challenges. Race condition and deadlock are handled using **fail-safe synchronization approach**. Another main drawback is inconsistency of data, which ZooKeeper resolves with **atomicity**.

17.2.4 Working of Zookeeper

Imagine a Hadoop® cluster spanning 500 or more commodity servers. If you've ever managed a database cluster with just 10 servers, you know there's a need for centralized management of the entire cluster in terms of name services, group services, synchronization services, configuration management, and more.

In addition, many other open source projects that leverage Hadoop clusters require these types of cross-cluster services, and having them available in ZooKeeper means that each of these projects can embed ZooKeeper without having to build synchronization services from scratch into each project. Interaction with ZooKeeper occurs via Java or C interfaces time.

ZooKeeper provides an infrastructure for cross-node synchronization and can be used by applications to ensure that tasks across the cluster are serialized or synchronized. It does this by maintaining status type information in memory on ZooKeeper servers. A ZooKeeper server is a machine that keeps a copy of the state of the entire system and persists this information in local log files. A very large Hadoop cluster can be supported by multiple ZooKeeper servers (in this case, a master server synchronizes the top-level servers). Each client machine communicates with one of the ZooKeeper servers to retrieve and update its synchronization information.

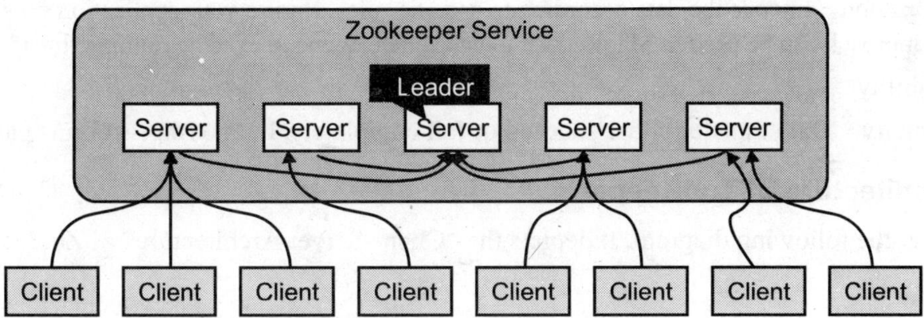

Figure. 17.2: Working of Zookeeper

Zookeeper is a coordination service for distributed application that enables synchronization across a cluster. Zookeeper can be viewed as centralized repository where distributed applications can put data and get data out of it. It is used to keep the distributed system function together as a single unit using its synchronization, serialization and coordination goals. For simplicity sake Zookeeper can be thought of as a file system where we have znodes that store data instead of files or directories storing data.

Multiple server nodes are collectively called ZooKeeper ensemble. At any given time, one ZooKeeper client is connected to at least one ZooKeeper server. A master node is dynamically chosen by consensus within the ensemble, thus usually ensemble of Zookeeper is an odd number so that there is a majority of vote. If the master node fails, another master is chosen in no time and it takes over the previous master. Other than master and slaves there are also observers in Zookeeper. Observers were brought in to address the issue of scaling. With the addition of slaves the write performance is going to be affected as voting process is expensive. So observers are slaves that do not take part into voting process but have similar duties as other slaves.

(a) **Writes in Zookeeper:** All the writes in Zookeeper go through the Master node, thus it is guaranteed that all writes will be sequential. On performing write operation to the Zookeeper, each server attached to that client persists the data along with master. Thus, this makes all the servers updated about the data. However this also means that concurrent writes cannot be made. Linear writes guarantee can be problematic if Zookeeper is used for write dominant workload. Zookeeper is ideally used for coordinating message exchanges between clients, which involves less writes and more reads. Zookeeper is helpful till the time the data is shared but if application has concurrent data writing then Zookeeper can come in way of the application and impose strict ordering of operations.

(b) **Reads in Zookeeper:** Zookeeper is best at reads as reads can be concurrent. Concurrent reads are done as each client is attached to different server and all clients can read from the servers simultaneously. Although having concurrent reads leads to eventual consistency as master is not involved. There can be cases where client may have an outdated view, which gets updated with a little delay.

17.2.5 Benefits of ZooKeeper

Here are the benefits of using ZooKeeper :

1. Simple distributed coordination process
2. Synchronization – Mutual exclusion and co-operation between server processes. This process helps in Apache HBase for configuration management.
3. Ordered Messages
4. Serialization – Encode the data according to specific rules. Ensure your application runs consistently. This approach can be used in MapReduce to coordinate queue to execute running threads.
5. Reliability
6. Atomicity – Data transfer either succeed or fail completely, but no transaction is partial.

17.2.6 Architecture of ZooKeeper

Take a look at the following diagram. It depicts the "Client-Server Architecture" of ZooKeeper.

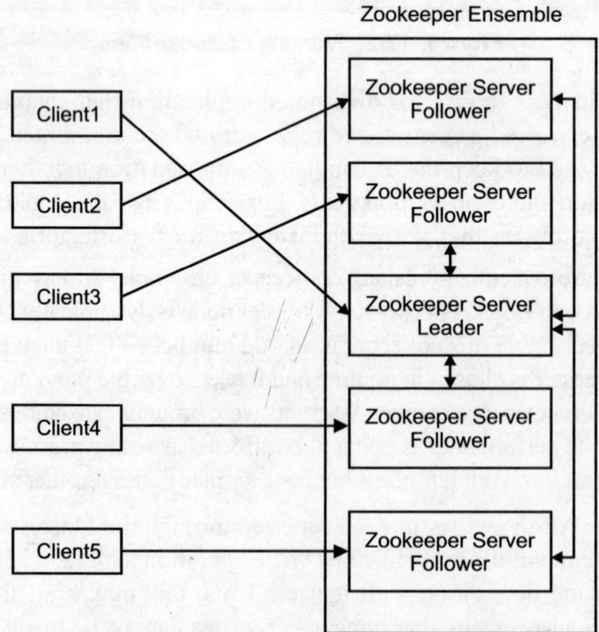

Figure. 17.3: Architecture of ZooKeeper

Each one of the components that is a part of the ZooKeeper architecture has been explained in the following table.

Part	Description
Client	Clients, one of the nodes in our distributed application cluster, access information from the server. For a particular time interval, every client sends a message to the server to let the sever know that the client is alive. Similarly, the server sends an acknowledgement when a client connects. If there is no response from the connected server, the client automatically redirects the message to another server.
Server	Server, one of the nodes in our ZooKeeper ensemble, provides all the services to clients. Gives acknowledgement to client to inform that the server is alive.
Ensemble	Group of ZooKeeper servers. The minimum number of nodes that is required to form an ensemble is 3.
Leader	Server node which performs automatic recovery if any of the connected node failed. Leaders are elected on service startup.
Follower	Server node which follows leader instruction.

17.2.7 Hierarchical Namespace

The following diagram depicts the tree structure of ZooKeeper file system used for memory representation. ZooKeeper node is referred as **znode**. Every znode is identified by a name and separated by a sequence of path (/).

- In the diagram, first you have a root znode separated by "/". Under root, you have two logical namespaces config and workers.
- The config namespace is used for centralized configuration management and the workers namespace is used for naming.
- Under config namespace, each znode can store upto 1MB of data. This is similar to UNIX file system except that the parent znode can store data as well. The main purpose of this structure is to store synchronized data and describe the metadata of the znode. This structure is called as ZooKeeper Data Model.

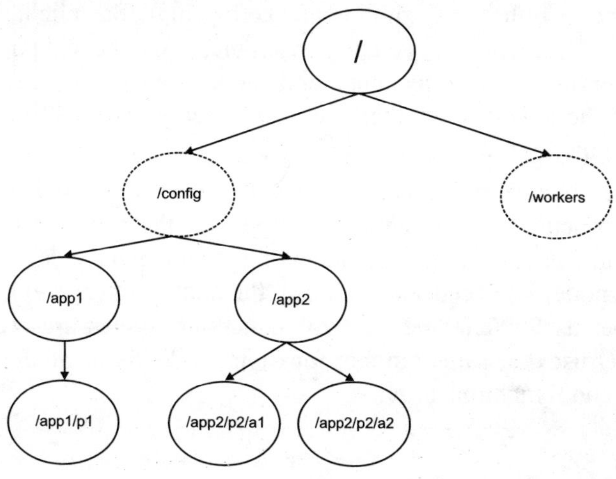

Every znode in the ZooKeeper data model maintains a **stat** structure. A stat simply provides the **metadata** of a znode. It consists of *Version number, Action control list (ACL), Timestamp, and Data length.*

- Version number – Every znode has a version number, which means every time the data associated with the znode changes, its corresponding version number would also increased. The use of version number is important when multiple zookeeper clients are trying to perform operations over the same znode.
- Action Control List (ACL) – ACL is basically an authentication mechanism for accessing the znode. It governs all the znode read and write operations.
- Timestamp – Timestamp represents time elapsed from znode creation and modification. It is usually represented in milliseconds. ZooKeeper identifies every change to the znodes from "Transaction ID" (zxid). Zxid is unique and maintains time for each transaction so that you can easily identify the time elapsed from one request to another request.
- Data length – Total amount of the data stored in a znode is the data length. You can store a maximum of 1MB of data.

As compared earlier user can use Zookeeper like a file system where directories can be created and data can be stored inside it. The directories made above can also have children and grandchildren like any other file system. This file system is stored centrally thus giving access from any spot. Example of Zookeeper can be a data model. Each directory in our example is called znode in Zookeeper. They are containers for data and other nodes. It stores statistical data like version details and user data up to 1Mb. This tiny space available to store information makes it clear that Zookeeper is not used for data storage like database but instead it is used for storing small amount of data like configuration data that needs to be shared.

17.2.8 Types of Znodes

Znodes are categorized as persistence, sequential, and ephemeral.

- Persistence znode – Persistence znode is alive even after the client, which created that particular znode, is disconnected. By default, all znodes are persistent unless otherwise specified.
- Ephemeral znode – Ephemeral znodes are active until the client is alive. When a client gets disconnected from the ZooKeeper ensemble, then the ephemeral znodes get deleted automatically. For this reason, only ephemeral znodes are not allowed to have a children further. If an ephemeral znode is deleted, then the next suitable node will fill its position. Ephemeral znodes play an important role in Leader election.
- Sequential znode – Sequential znodes can be either persistent or ephemeral. When a new znode is created as a sequential znode, then ZooKeeper sets the path of the znode by attaching a 10 digit sequence number to the original name. For example, if a znode with path /myapp is created as a sequential znode, ZooKeeper will change the path to /myapp0000000001 and set the next sequence number as 0000000002. If two sequential znodes are created concurrently, then ZooKeeper never uses the same number for each znode. Sequential znodes play an important role in Locking and Synchronization.

17.2.9 Sessions

Sessions are very important for the operation of ZooKeeper. Requests in a session are executed in FIFO order. Once a client connects to a server, the session will be established and a **session id** is assigned to the client.

The client sends **heartbeats** at a particular time interval to keep the session valid. If the ZooKeeper ensemble does not receive heartbeats from a client for more than the period (session timeout) specified at the starting of the service, it decides that the client died.

Session timeouts are usually represented in milliseconds. When a session ends for any reason, the ephemeral znodes created during that session also get deleted.

17.2.10 Watches

Watches are a simple mechanism for the client to get notifications about the changes in the ZooKeeper ensemble. Clients can set watches while reading a particular znode. Watches send a notification to the registered client for any of the znode (on which client registers) changes.

Znode changes are modification of data associated with the znode or changes in the znode's children. Watches are triggered only once. If a client wants a notification again, it must be done through another read operation. When a connection session is expired, the client will be disconnected from the server and the associated watches are also removed.

17.3 MAHOUT : MACHINE LEARNING FOR HADOOP

17.3.1 Introducing Apache Mahout

A mahout (in Hindi) is a person who keeps and drives an elephant. The name Mahout comes from the project's (sometime) use of Apache Hadoop — which has a yellow elephant as its logo — for scalability and fault tolerance.

Once the exclusive domain of academics and corporations with large research budgets, intelligent applications that learn from data and user input are becoming more common. The need for machine-learning techniques like clustering, collaborative filtering, and categorization has never been greater, be it for finding commonalities among large groups of people or automatically tagging large volumes of Web content. The Apache Mahout project aims to make building intelligent applications easier and faster

Apache Mahout is a project of the Apache Software Foundation to produce free implementations of distributed or otherwise scalable machine learning algorithms focused primarily in the areas of collaborative filtering, clustering and classification. Many of the implementations use the Apache Hadoop platform.

We are living in a day and age where information is available in abundance. The information overload has scaled to such heights that sometimes it becomes difficult to manage our little mailboxes! Imagine the volume of data and records some of the popular websites (the likes of Facebook, Twitter, and Youtube) have to collect and manage on a daily basis. It is not uncommon even for lesser known websites to receive huge amounts of information in bulk.

Normally we fall back on data mining algorithms to analyze bulk data to identify trends and draw conclusions. However, no data mining algorithm can be efficient enough to process very large datasets and provide outcomes in quick time, unless the computational tasks are run on multiple machines distributed over the cloud.

We now have new frameworks that allow us to break down a computation task into multiple segments and run each segment on a different machine. Mahoutis such a data mining framework that normally runs coupled with the Hadoop infrastructure at its background to manage huge volumes of data.

Apache Mahout is an open source project that is primarily used for creating scalable machine learning algorithms. It implements popular machine learning techniques such as:

- Recommendation
- Classification
- Clustering

Apache Mahout started as a sub-project of Apache's Lucene in 2008. In 2010, Mahout became a top level project of Apache.

17.3.2 Features of Mahout

The primitive features of Apache Mahout are listed below.

1. The algorithms of Mahout are written on top of Hadoop, so it works well in distributed environment. Mahout uses the Apache Hadoop library to scale effectively in the cloud.
2. Mahout offers the coder a ready-to-use framework for doing data mining tasks on large volumes of data.
3. Mahout lets applications to analyze large sets of data effectively and in quick time.
4. Includes several MapReduce enabled clustering implementations such as k-means, fuzzy k-means, Canopy, Dirichlet, and Mean-Shift.
5. Supports Distributed Naive Bayes and Complementary Naive Bayes classification implementations.
6. Comes with distributed fitness function capabilities for evolutionary programming.
7. Includes matrix and vector libraries.

17.3.3 Applications of Mahout

1. Companies such as Adobe, Facebook, LinkedIn, Foursquare, Twitter, and Yahoo use Mahout internally.
2. Foursquare helps you in finding out places, food, and entertainment available in a particular area. It uses the recommender engine of Mahout.
3. Twitter uses Mahout for user interest modelling.
4. Yahoo! uses Mahout for pattern mining

Apache Mahout introduces a new math environment we call Samsara, for its theme of universal renewal. It reflects a fundamental rethinking of how scalable machine learning algorithms are built and customized. Mahout-Samsara is here to help people create their own math while providing some off-the-shelf algorithm implementations. At its core are general linear algebra and statistical operations along with the data structures to support them. You can use is as a library or customize it in Scala with Mahout-specific extensions that look something like R. Mahout-Samsara comes with an interactive shell that runs distributed operations on a Spark cluster. This make prototyping or task submission much easier and allows users to customize algorithms with a whole new degree of freedom.

17.3.4 Machine Learning Task in Mahout

What is Machine Learning?

Machine learning is a branch of science that deals with programming the systems in such a way that they automatically learn and improve with experience. Here, learning means recognizing and understanding the input data and making wise decisions based on the supplied data.

It is very difficult to cater to all the decisions based on all possible inputs. To tackle this problem, algorithms are developed. These algorithms build knowledge from specific data and past experience with the principles of statistics, probability theory, logic, combinatorial optimization, search, reinforcement learning, and control theory.

The developed algorithms form the basis of various applications such as:

1. Vision processing
2. Language processing
3. Forecasting (e.g., stock market trends)
4. Pattern recognition
5. Games
6. Data mining
7. Expert systems
8. Robotics

Machine learning is a vast area and it is quite beyond the scope of this tutorial to cover all its features. There are several ways to implement machine learning techniques, however the most commonly used ones are

- supervised and
- unsupervised learning.

Supervised Learning

Supervised learning deals with learning a function from available training data. A supervised learning algorithm analyzes the training data and produces an inferred function, which can be used for mapping new examples. Common examples of supervised learning include:

- classifying e-mails as spam,
- labeling webpages based on their content, and
- voice recognition.

There are many supervised learning algorithms such as neural networks, Support Vector Machines (SVMs), and Naive Bayes classifiers. Mahout implements Naive Bayes classifier.

Unsupervised Learning

Unsupervised learning makes sense of unlabeled data without having any predefined dataset for its training. Unsupervised learning is an extremely powerful tool for analyzing available data and look for patterns and trends. It is most commonly used for clustering similar input into logical groups. Common approaches to unsupervised learning include:

- k-means
- self-organizing maps, and
- hierarchical clustering

Following are three specific machine-learning tasks that Mahout currently implements. They also happen to be three areas that are quite commonly used in real applications:

1. Collaborative filtering
2. Clustering
3. Categorization

(1) **Collaborative filtering:** *Collaborative filtering* (CF) is a technique, popularized by Amazon and others, that uses user information such as ratings, clicks, and purchases to provide recommendations to other site users. CF is often used to recommend consumer items such as books, music, and movies, but it is also used in other applications where multiple actors need to collaborate to narrow down data. Chances are you've seen CF in action on Amazon, as shown in Figure 17.4:

Figure. 17.4: Example of collaborative filter on Amazon

Given a set of users and items, CF applications provide recommendations to the current user of the system. Four ways of generating recommendations are typical:

1. **User-based**: Recommend items by finding similar users. This is often harder to scale because of the dynamic nature of users.
2. **Item-based**: Calculate similarity between items and make recommendations. Items usually don't change much, so this often can be computed offline.
3. **Slope-One**: A very fast and simple item-based recommendation approach applicable when users have given ratings (and not just boolean preferences).
4. **Model-based**: Provide recommendations based on developing a model of users and their ratings.

All CF approaches end up calculating a notion of similarity between users and their rated items. There are many ways to compute similarity, and most CF systems allow you to plug in different measures so that you can determine which one works best for your data.

(2) **Clustering:** Given large data sets, whether they are text or numeric, it is often useful to group together, or *cluster*, similar items automatically. For instance, given all of the news for the day from all of the newspapers in the United States, you might want to group all of the articles about the same story together automatically; you can then choose to focus on specific clusters and stories without needing to wade through a lot of unrelated ones. Another example: Given the output from sensors on a machine over time, you could cluster the outputs to determine normal versus problematic operation, because normal operations would all cluster together and abnormal operations would be in outlying clusters.

Like CF, clustering calculates the similarity between items in the collection, but its only job is to group together similar items. In many implementations of clustering, items in the collection are represented as vectors in an *n*-dimensional space. Given the vectors, one can calculate the distance between two items using measures such as the Manhattan Distance, Euclidean distance, or cosine similarity. Then, the actual clusters can be calculated by grouping together the items that are close in distance.

There are many approaches to calculating the clusters, each with its own trade-offs. Some approaches work from the bottom up, building up larger clusters from smaller ones, whereas others break a single large cluster into smaller and smaller clusters. Both have criteria for exiting the process at some point before they break down into a trivial cluster representation (all items in one cluster or all items in their own cluster). Popular approaches include k-Means and hierarchical clustering.

(3) **Categorization:** The goal of *categorization* (often also called *classification*) is to label unseen documents, thus grouping them together. Many classification approaches in machine learning calculate a variety of statistics that associate the features of a document with the specified label, thus creating a model that can be used later to classify unseen documents. For example, a simple approach to classification might keep track of the words associated with a label, as well as the number of times those words are seen for a given label. Then, when a new document is classified, the words in the document are looked up in the model, probabilities are calculated, and the best result is output, usually along with a score indicating the confidence the result is correct.

Features for classification might include words, weights for those words (based on frequency, for instance), parts of speech, and so on. Of course, features really can be anything that helps associate a document with a label and can be incorporated into the algorithm.

Mahout also provides Java libraries for common maths operations (focused on linear algebra and statistics) and primitive Java collections. Mahout is a work in progress; the number of implemented algorithms has grown quickly,[3] but various algorithms are still missing.

While Mahout's core algorithms for clustering, classification and batch based collaborative filtering are implemented on top of Apache Hadoop using the map/reduce paradigm, it does not restrict contributions to Hadoop-based implementations. Contributions that run on a single node or on a non-Hadoop cluster are also welcomed. For example, the 'Taste' collaborative-filtering recommender component of Mahout was originally a separate project and can run stand-alone without Hadoop.

Apache Mahout is a highly scalable machine learning library that enables developers to use optimized algorithms. Mahout implements popular machine learning techniques such as recommendation, classification, and clustering. Therefore, it is prudent to have a brief section on machine learning before we move further.

Recommendation

Recommendation is a popular technique that provides close recommendations based on user information such as previous purchases, clicks, and ratings.

- Amazon uses this technique to display a list of recommended items that you might be interested in, drawing information from your past actions. There are recommender engines that work behind Amazon to capture user behavior and recommend selected items based on your earlier actions.
- Facebook uses the recommender technique to identify and recommend the "people you may know list".

Classification

Classification, also known as categorization, is a machine learning technique that uses known data to determine how the new data should be classified into a set of existing categories. Classification is a form of supervised learning.

Mail service providers such as Yahoo! and Gmail use this technique to decide whether a new mail should be classified as a spam. The categorization algorithm trains itself by analyzing user habits of marking certain mails as spams. Based on that, the classifier decides whether a future mail should be deposited in your inbox or in the spams folder.

- iTunes application uses classification to prepare playlists.

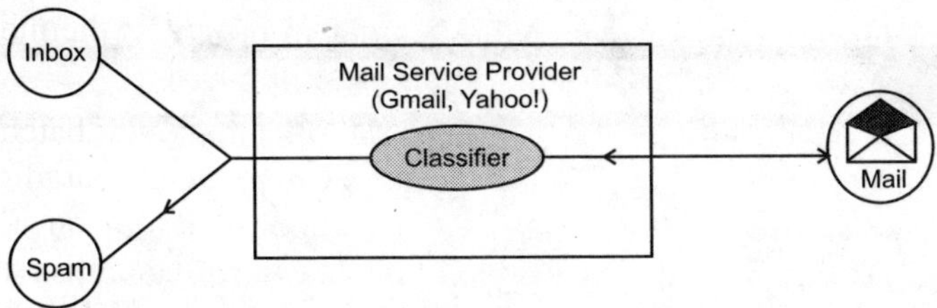

Clustering

Clustering is used to form groups or clusters of similar data based on common characteristics. Clustering is a form of unsupervised learning.

- Search engines such as Google and Yahoo! use clustering techniques to group data with similar characteristics.
- Newsgroups use clustering techniques to group various articles based on related topics.

The clustering engine goes through the input data completely and based on the characteristics of the data, it will decide under which cluster it should be grouped. Take a look at the following example.

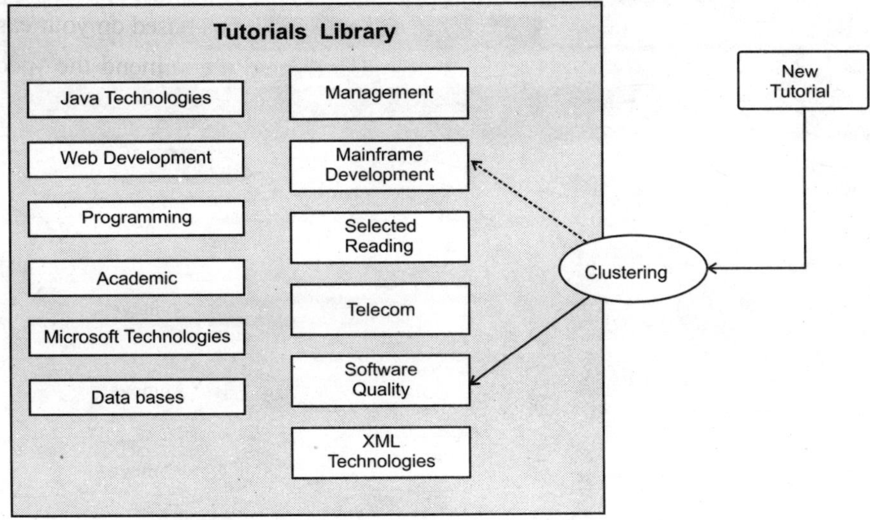

Mahauot Recommendations

This section covers the popular machine learning technique calledrecommendation, its mechanisms, and how to write an application implementing Mahout recommendation.

Recommendation

Ever wondered how Amazon comes up with a list of recommended items to draw your attention to a particular product that you might be interested in!

Suppose you want to purchase the bookswritten by VK jain from Amazon:

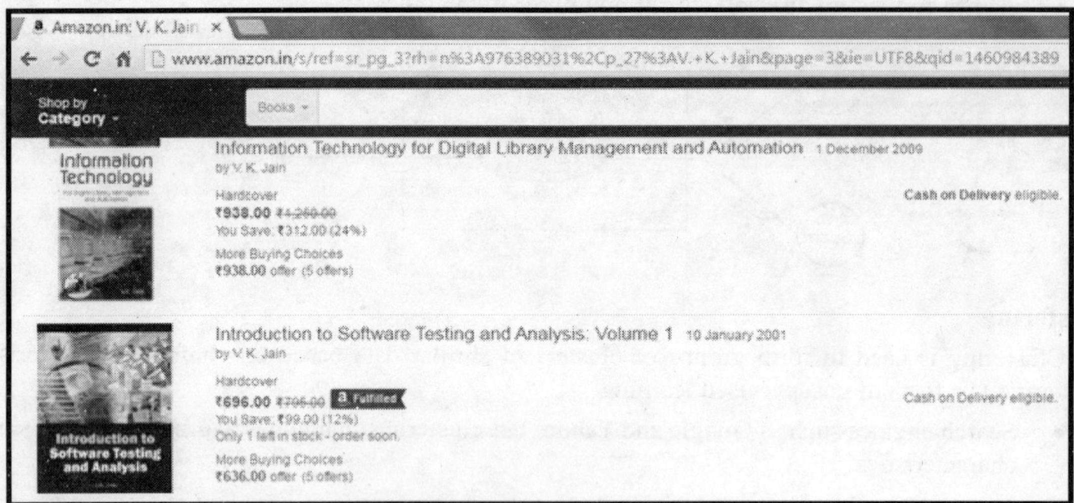

Similarly from Flikart.

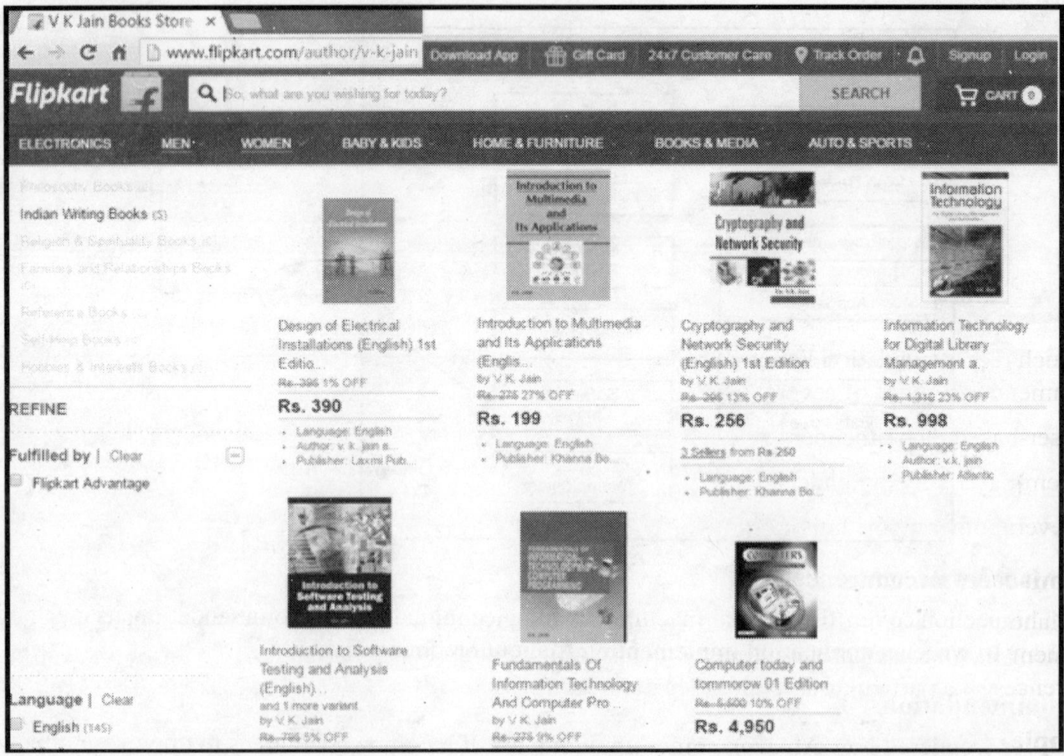

Along with the selected product, Amazon also displays a list of related recommended items, as shown below.

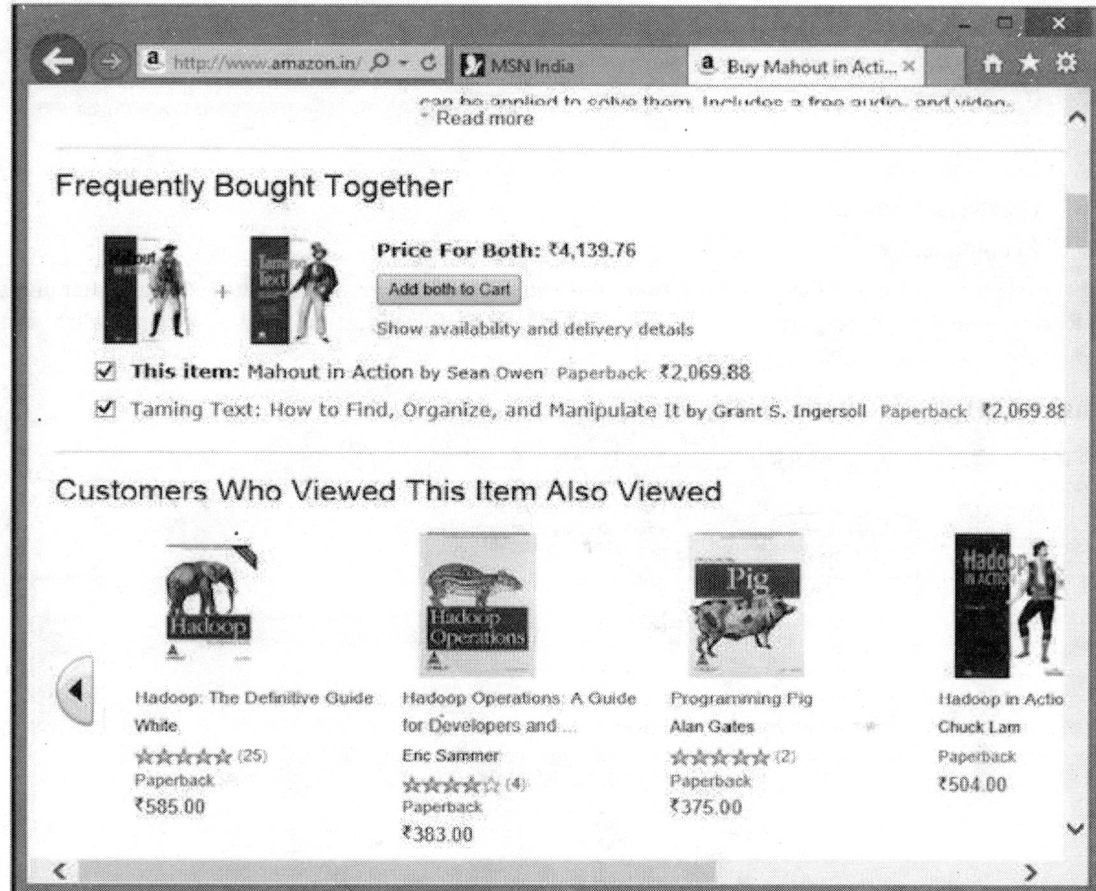

Such recommendation lists are produced with the help of **recommender engines**. Mahout provides recommender engines of several types such as:

1. user-based recommenders,
2. item-based recommenders, and
3. several other algorithms.

Mahout Recommender Engine

Mahout has a non-distributed, non-Hadoop-based recommender engine. You should pass a text document having user preferences for items. And the output of this engine would be the estimated preferences of a particular user for other items.

Example

Consider a website that sells consumer goods such as mobiles, gadgets, and their accessories. If we want to implement the features of Mahout in such a site, then we can build a recommender engine. This engine analyzes past purchase data of the users and recommends new products based on that.

The components provided by Mahout to build a recommender engine are as follows:

- DataModel
- UserSimilarity
- ItemSimilarity
- UserNeighborhood
- Recommender

From the data store, the data model is prepared and is passed as an input to the recommender engine. The Recommender engine generates the recommendations for a particular user. Given below is the architecture of recommender engine.

Architecture of Recommender Engine

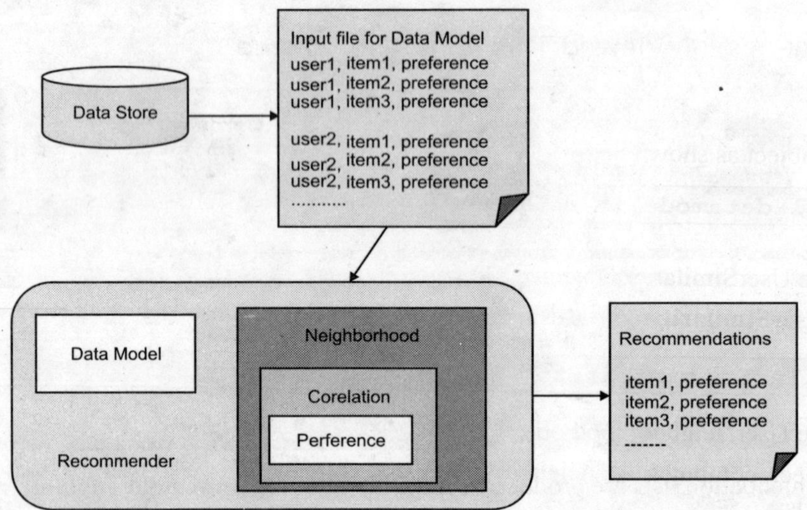

Building a Recommender using Mahout

Here are the steps to develop a simple recommender:

Step1: Create DataModel Object

The constructor of PearsonCorrelationSimilarity class requires a data model object, which holds a file that contains the Users, Items, and Preferences details of a product. Here is the sample data model file:

1,00,1.0

1,01,2.0

1,02,5.0

1,03,5.0

1,04,5.0

2,00,1.0

2,01,2.0

2,05,5.0

2,06,4.5

2,02,5.0

3,01,2.5

3,02,5.0

3,03,4.0

3,04,3.0

4,00,5.0

4,01,5.0

4,02,5.0

4,03,0.0

The **DataModel** object requires the file object, which contains the path of the input file. Create the **DataModel** object as shown below.

```
DataModel datamodel = new FileDataModel(new File("input file"));
```

Step2: Create UserSimilarity Object

Create **UserSimilarity** object using **PearsonCorrelationSimilarity** class as shown below:

```
UserSimilarity similarity = new PearsonCorrelationSimilarity(datamodel);
```

Step3: Create UserNeighborhood object

This object computes a "neighborhood" of users like a given user. There are two types of neighborhoods:

- NearestNUserNeighborhood - This class computes a neighborhood consisting of the nearest n users to a given user. "Nearest" is defined by the given UserSimilarity.
- ThresholdUserNeighborhood - This class computes a neighborhood consisting of all the users whose similarity to the given user meets or exceeds a certain threshold. Similarity is defined by the given UserSimilarity.

Here we are using **ThresholdUserNeighborhood** and set the limit of preference to 3.0.

```
UserNeighborhood neighborhood = new ThresholdUserNeighborhood(3.0, similarity, model);
```

Step 4: Create Recommender Object

Create **UserbasedRecomender** object. Pass all the above created objects to its constructor as shown below.

```
UserBasedRecommender recommender = new GenericUserBasedRecommender(model,
neighborhood, similarity);
```

Step5: Recommend Items to a User

Recommend products to a user using the recommend() method of**Recommender** interface. This method requires two parameters. The first represents the user id of the user to whom we need to send the recommendations, and the second represents the number of recommendations to be sent. Here is the usage of **recommender()** method:

```
List<RecommendedItem> recommendations = recommender.recommend(2, 3);
for (RecommendedItem recommendation : recommendations) {
  System.out.println(recommendation);
}
```

Example Program

Given below is an example program to set recommendation. Prepare the recommendations for the user with user id 2.

```
import java.io.File;
import java.util.List;
import org.apache.mahout.cf.taste.impl.model.file.FileDataModel;
import                    org.apache.mahout.cf.taste.impl.neighborhood.
ThresholdUserNeighborhood;
import                     org.apache.mahout.cf.taste.impl.recommender.
GenericUserBasedRecommender;
import                      org.apache.mahout.cf.taste.impl.similarity.
PearsonCorrelationSimilarity;
import org.apache.mahout.cf.taste.model.DataModel;
import org.apache.mahout.cf.taste.neighborhood.UserNeighborhood;
import org.apache.mahout.cf.taste.recommender.RecommendedItem;
import org.apache.mahout.cf.taste.recommender.UserBasedRecommender;
import org.apache.mahout.cf.taste.similarity.UserSimilarity;
public class Recommender {
  public static void main(String args[]){
     try{
        //Creating data model
       DataModel datamodel = new FileDataModel(new File("data")); //data

        //Creating UserSimilarity object.
```

```
                    UserSimilarity    usersimilarity    =    new
PearsonCorrelationSimilarity(datamodel);

        //Creating UserNeighbourHHood object.
    UserNeighborhood userneighborhood = new ThresholdUserNeighborhood(3.0,
usersimilarity, datamodel);

        //Create UserRecomender
                    UserBasedRecommender    recommender    =    new
GenericUserBasedRecommender(datamodel,               userneighborhood,
usersimilarity);

      List<RecommendedItem> recommendations = recommender.recommend(2,
3);

        for (RecommendedItem recommendation : recommendations) {
           System.out.println(recommendation);
        }

     }catch(Exception e){}

   }
 }
```

Compile the program using the following commands:

```
javac Recommender.java
java Recommender
```

It should produce the following output:

```
RecommendedItem [item:3, value:4.5]
RecommendedItem [item:4, value:4.0]
```

CHAPTER

18

Spark, Scala and Amazon Web Services

18.1 INTRODUCTION OF SPARK : A FAST AND GENERAL COMPUTE ENGINE FOR HADOOP DATA

Spark is a general-purpose distributed processing system used for big data workloads. It has been deployed in every type of big data use case to detect patterns, and provide real-time insight.

Apache Spark is designed as an interface for large-scale processing, while Apache Hadoop provides a broader software framework for the distributed storage and processing of big data. Both can be used either together or as standalone services. Spark provides a simple and expressive programming model that supports a wide range of applications, including ETL, machine learning, stream processing, and graph computation.

Spark is a formally defined computer programming language based on the Ada programming language, intended for the development of high integrity software used in systems where predictable and highly reliable operation is essential.

Hadoop is not a database, but rather an open-source software framework specifically built to handle large volumes of structured and semi-structured data.

Hadoop and Spark, both developed by the Apache Software Foundation, are widely used open-source frameworks for big data architectures. Each framework contains an extensive ecosystem of open-source technologies that prepare, process, manage and analyze big data sets. Spark and Hadoop are better together. *Hadoop is not essential* to run Spark. If you go by Spark documentation, it is mentioned that there is no need for Hadoop if you run Spark in a standalone mode. In this case, you need resource managers like *CanN or Mesos* only.

18.2 APACHE SPARK

Apache Spark is a Java virtual machine (JVM)-based cluster framework that runs on top of platforms like *Hadoop or Mesos*. It can also run on its own and in the cloud. Spark provides programmers with a resilient distributed dataset (RDD). The RDD is a read-only multiset of data items that is distributed throughout the cluster.

Apache Spark is one of the most popular framework choices among data engineers for analysing big data and deploying machine learning algorithms. Spark has APIs for *Python, Scala, Java and R, but Python* and Scala have emerged as the most popularly used languages for Spark in the data science industry.

Apache Spark is a multi-language framework for data engineering and machine learning on single-node machines or clusters. It unifies data processing into batches and real-time streaming and can perform Exploratory Data Analysis (EDA) on petabyte-scale data without down sampling. Engineers can execute SQL queries for dashboarding quite fast in this framework. They can also train machine learning algorithms on the laptop and use that code itself to scale up manifolds.

18.2.1 Characteristic Features of Apache Spark

1. Spark Core provides the basic distributed task dispatching system.
2. It supports JVM-based languages like Scala, Java, and R.
3. The Core supports Spark SQL.
4. It is a domain-specific language for manipulating DataFrames, a data abstraction for structured and semi-structured data. Of course, it provides SQL semantics.
5. The Spark Streaming system moves data from Spark data sources and processes the information. Internally it does this in small batches.
6. The other two major pieces to Spark are the MLlib machine learning library and GraphX. The latter is a graph processing framework.
7. SPARK is a common term adopted by a number of applications, platforms, etc. SPARK 2014 and Apache SPARK are just two; most are as different as these two systems. For example, the Particle Spark Core is a Wi-Fi development kit based on Texas Instruments' CC3000 chip.

18.3 SPARK DATA PROCESSING ENGINE : APACHE SCALA

Apache Spark — which is also open source — is a data processing engine for big data sets. The Spark engine itself is written in **Scala**. Any code written in Scala runs natively on Java Virtual Machine (JVM). Like Hadoop, Spark splits up large tasks across different nodes. However, it tends to perform faster than Hadoop and it uses random access memory (RAM) to cache and process data instead of a file system.

Scala is faster than Python due to its static type language. If faster performance is a requirement, Scala is a good bet. Spark is native in Scala, hence making writing Spark jobs in Scala the native way.

18.3.1 Why Scala Outperforms

Scala, pushes data engineers to build a software engineering mindset that can have a long term impact on their careers. It supports *functional and object-oriented programming*. In addition, its Java Virtual Machine (JVM) and JavaScript runtimes create high-performance systems. Java and Scala stacks can be mixed for seamless integration as Scala runs on JVM.

We can mix multiple traits into a class in Scala to combine their interface and behaviour. Structural data types are represented through case classes in Scala. Scala supports generic classes, variance annotations, abstract type members, compound types and more.

It comes with a simple structure which makes it suitable for big data processors.

The Scala Library Index (Scaladex) is a representation of a map of all published Scala libraries. A developer can query more than 175,000 releases of Scala libraries.

18.3.2 Choosing between Scala and Python for Apache Spark

If one has to choose between Scala and Python for Apache Spark, the choice should be completely based on the project they are working on. Usually, Python is suitable for smaller projects, and Scala works best for large-scale ones. Companies like Netflix and Airbnb, which deal with huge amounts of data, use Scala and write many pipelines. Both of them have their own pros and cons, and proper evaluation of needs must be done before choosing one over the other.

Scala is faster than Python due to its static type language. If faster performance is a requirement, Scala is a good bet. Spark is native in Scala, hence making writing Spark jobs in Scala the native way.

18.4 WORKING OF APACHE SPARK

Hadoop MapReduce is a programming model for processing big data sets with a parallel, distributed algorithm. Developers can write massively parallelized operators, without having to worry about work distribution, and fault tolerance. However, a challenge to MapReduce is the sequential multi-step process it takes to run a job. With each step, MapReduce reads data from the cluster, performs operations, and writes the results back to HDFS. Because each step requires a disk read, and write, MapReduce jobs are slower due to the latency of disk I/O.

Spark was created to address the limitations to MapReduce, by doing processing in-memory, reducing the number of steps in a job, and by reusing data across multiple parallel operations. With Spark, only one-step is needed where data is read into memory, operations performed, and the results written back—resulting in a much faster execution. Spark also reuses data by using an in-memory cache to greatly speed up machine learning algorithms that repeatedly call a function on the same dataset. Data re-use is accomplished through the creation of DataFrames, an abstraction over Resilient Distributed Dataset (RDD), which is a collection of objects that is cached in memory, and reused in multiple Spark operations. This dramatically lowers the latency making Spark multiple times faster than MapReduce, especially when doing machine learning, and interactive analytics.

18.4.1 Resilient Distributed Datasets

Resilient Distributed Datasets (RDD) is a fundamental data structure of Spark. [1] It is an immutable distributed collection of objects. Each dataset in RDD is divided into logical partitions, which may be computed on different nodes of the cluster. RDDs can contain any type of Python, Java, or Scala objects, including user-defined classes.

Formally, an RDD is a read-only, partitioned collection of records. RDDs can be created through deterministic operations on either data on stable storage or other RDDs. RDD is a fault-tolerant collection of elements that can be operated on in parallel.

There are two ways to create RDDs – parallelizing an existing collection in your driver program, or referencing a dataset in an external storage system, such as a shared file system, HDFS, HBase, or any data source offering a Hadoop Input Format.

Spark makes use of the concept of RDD to achieve faster and efficient MapReduce operations. Let us first discuss how MapReduce operations take place and why they are not so efficient.

(1) Data Sharing is Slow in MapReduce

MapReduce is widely adopted for processing and generating large datasets with a parallel, distributed algorithm on a cluster. It allows users to write parallel computations, using a set of high-level operators, without having to worry about work distribution and fault tolerance.

Unfortunately, in most current frameworks, the only way to reuse data between computations (Ex – between two MapReduce jobs) is to write it to an external stable storage system (Ex – HDFS). Although this framework provides numerous abstractions for accessing a cluster's computational resources, users still want more.

Both Iterative and Interactive applications require faster data sharing across parallel jobs. Data sharing is slow in MapReduce due to replication, serialization, and disk IO. Regarding storage system, most of the Hadoop applications, they spend more than 90% of the time doing HDFS read-write operations.

(2) Iterative Operations on MapReduce

Reuse intermediate results across multiple computations in multi-stage applications. The following illustration explains how the current framework works, while doing the iterative operations on MapReduce. This incurs substantial overheads due to data replication, disk I/O, and serialization, which makes the system slow.

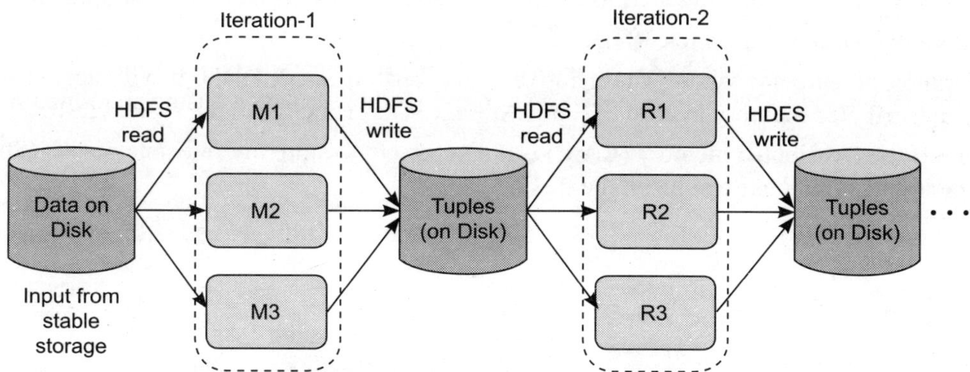

Figure. 18.1 : Iterative operations on MapReduce makes the system slow.

Note : *A tuple (as far as Java is concerned) is a generic data structure that treats each element as an object, and these objects stores in a separate byte array. In other words, we can also say that tuple is an ordered collection of objects of different types.*

(3) Interactive Operations on MapReduce

User runs ad-hoc queries on the same subset of data. Each query will do the disk I/O on the stable storage, which can dominate application execution time. The following illustration explains how the current framework works while doing the interactive queries on MapReduce.

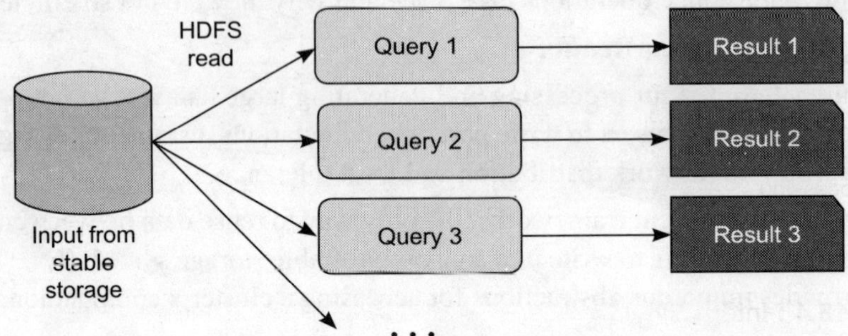

Figure. 18.2 : Interactive Queries on MapReduce

(3) Data Sharing using Spark RDD

Data sharing is slow in MapReduce due to *replication, serialization, and disk IO*. Most of the Hadoop applications, they spend more than 90% of the time doing HDFS read-write operations.

Recognizing this problem, researchers developed a specialized framework called Apache Spark. The key idea of spark is Resilient Distributed Datasets (RDD); it supports in-memory processing computation. This means, it stores the state of memory as an object across the jobs and the object is sharable between those jobs. Data sharing in memory is 10 to 100 times faster than network and Disk.

Let us now try to find out how iterative and interactive operations take place in Spark RDD.

(4) Iterative Operations on Spark RDD

The illustration given below shows the iterative operations on Spark RDD. It will store intermediate results in a distributed memory instead of Stable storage (Disk) and make the system faster.

Note – If the Distributed memory (RAM) is not sufficient to store intermediate results (State of the JOB), then it will store those results on the disk.

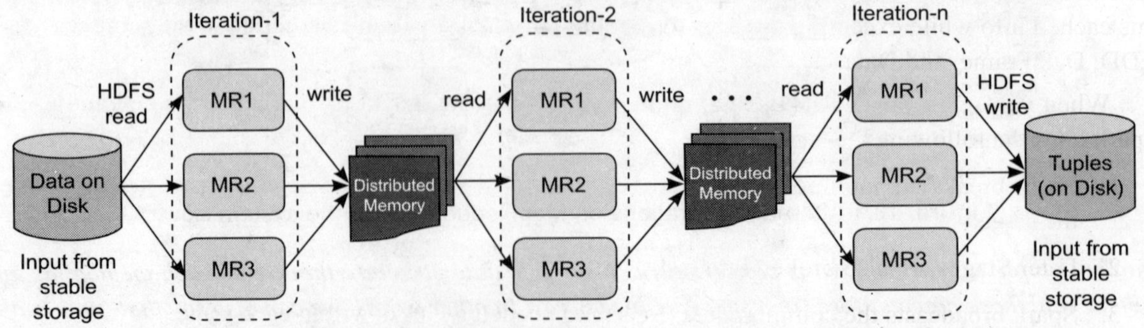

Figure. 18.3 : Iterative Operations on Spark Resilient Distributed Datasets (RDD)

(5) Interactive Operations on Spark RDD

The Figure 18.4 shows interactive operations on Spark RDD. If different queries are run on the same set of data repeatedly, this particular data can be kept in memory for better execution times.

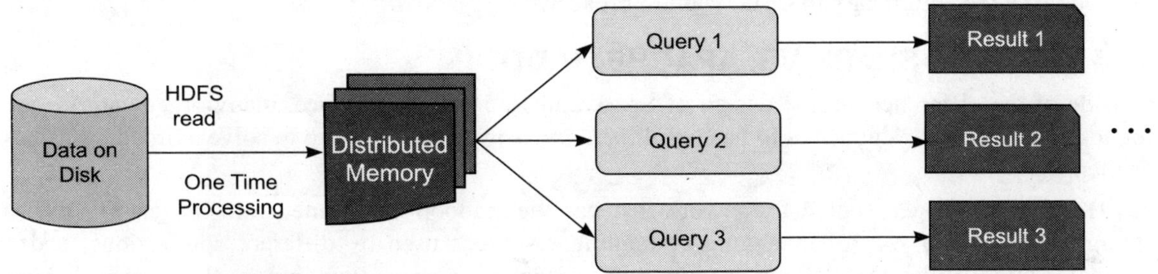

Figure. 18.4 : Interactive operations on Spark Resilient Distributed Datasets (RDD)

By default, each transformed RDD may be recomputed each time you run an action on it. However, you may also persist an RDD in memory, in which case Spark will keep the elements around on the cluster for much faster access, the next time you query it. There is also support for persisting RDDs on disk, or replicated across multiple nodes.

(6) Spark Broadcast Variables

In Spark RDD and DataFrame, Broadcast variables are read-only shared variables that are cached and available on all nodes in a cluster in-order to access or use by the tasks. Instead of sending this data along with every task, spark distributes broadcast variables to the machine using efficient broadcast algorithms to reduce communication costs.

Let us take an example, assume you are getting a two-letter country state code in a file and you wanted to transform it to full state name, (for example CA to California, NY to New York etc.) by doing a lookup to reference mapping. In some instances, this data could be large and you may have many such lookups (like zip code).

Instead of distributing this information along with each task over the network (overhead and time consuming), we can use the broadcast variable to cache this lookup info on each machine and tasks use this cached info while executing the transformations. Broadcast variables are used in the same way for RDD, DataFrame, and Dataset.

When you run a Spark RDD, DataFrame jobs that has the Broadcast variables defined and used, Spark does the following :

1. Spark breaks the job into stages that have distributed shuffling and actions are executed with in the stage.
2. Later Stages are also broken into tasks
3. Spark broadcasts the common data (reusable) needed by tasks within each stage.

The broadcasted data is cache in serialized format and deserialized before executing each task. You should be creating and using broadcast variables for data that shared across multiple stages and tasks. Note that the broadcast variables are not sent to executors with `sc.broadcast(variable)` call instead, they will be sent to executors when they are first used.

The Spark Broadcast is created using the broadcast(v) method of the SparkContext class. This method takes the argument v that you want to broadcast.

18.5 APACHE SPARK VS. APACHE HADOOP

Outside of the differences in the design of Spark and Hadoop MapReduce, many organizations have found these big data frameworks to be complimentary, using them together to solve a broader business challenge.

Hadoop is an open source framework that has the Hadoop Distributed File System (HDFS) as storage, YARN as a way of managing computing resources used by different applications, and an implementation of the MapReduce programming model as an execution engine. In a typical Hadoop implementation, different execution engines are also deployed such as Spark, Tez, and Presto.

Spark is an open source framework focused on interactive query, machine learning, and real-time workloads. It does not have its own storage system, but runs analytics on other storage systems like HDFS, or other popular stores like Amazon Redshift, Amazon S3, Couchbase, Cassandra, and others. Spark on Hadoop leverages YARN to share a common cluster and dataset as other Hadoop engines, ensuring consistent levels of service, and response.

Apache Spark requires a cluster manager and a distributed storage system. For cluster management, Spark supports standalone (native Spark cluster, where you can launch a cluster either manually or use the launch scripts provided by the install package. It is also possible to run these daemons on a single machine for testing), Hadoop YARN, Apache Mesos or Kubernetes. For distributed storage, Spark can interface with a wide variety, including Alluxio, Hadoop Distributed File System (HDFS), MapR File System (MapR-FS), Cassandra, OpenStack Swift, Amazon S3, Kudu, Lustre file system, or a custom solution can be implemented. Spark also supports a pseudo-distributed local mode, usually used only for development or testing purposes, where distributed storage is not required and the local file system can be used instead; in such a scenario, Spark is run on a single machine with one executor per CPU core.

Apache Spark Workloads (Components)

The Spark framework includes:

1. Spark Core as the foundation for the platform
2. Spark SQL for interactive queries
3. Spark Streaming for real-time analytics
4. Spark MLlib for machine learning
5. Spark GraphX for graph processing

18.5.1 Spark Core

Spark Core is the foundation of the platform. It is responsible for memory management, fault recovery, scheduling, distributing & monitoring jobs, and interacting with storage systems. Spark Core is exposed through an *application programming interface* (APIs) built for *Java, Scala, Python and R*. These APIs hide the complexity of distributed processing behind simple, high-level operators.

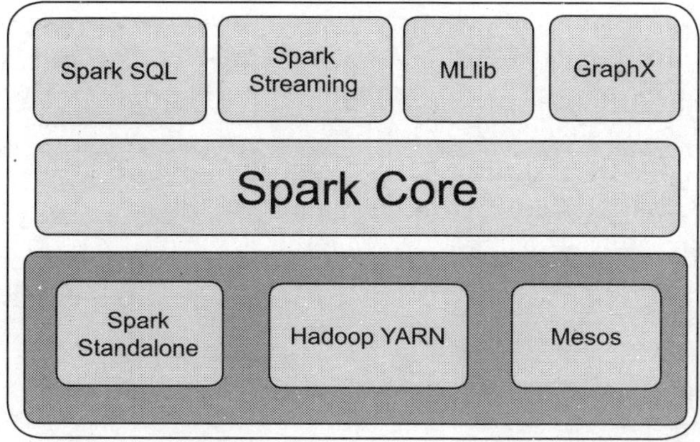

Figure. 18.5(a) : Components of Spark Core

Spark Core is also the foundation of the overall project. It provides distributed task dispatching, scheduling, and basic I/O functionalities, exposed through an application programming interface (for *Java, Python, Scala, .NET and R*) centered on the RDD abstraction (the Java API is available for other JVM languages, but is also usable for some other non-JVM languages that can connect to the JVM, such as **Julia.** This interface mirrors a functional/higher-order model of programming: a "driver" program invokes parallel operations such as map, filter or reduce on an RDD by passing a function to Spark, which then schedules the function's execution in parallel on the cluster. These operations, and additional ones such as joins, take RDDs as input and produce new RDDs. RDDs are immutable and their operations are lazy; fault-tolerance is achieved by keeping track of the "lineage" of each RDD (the sequence of operations that produced it) so that it can be reconstructed in the case of data loss. RDDs can contain any type of *Python, .NET, Java, or Scala* objects.

Besides the RDD-oriented functional style of programming, Spark provides two restricted forms of shared variables: broadcast variables reference read-only data that needs to be available on all nodes, while accumulators can be used to program reductions in an imperative style. [2]

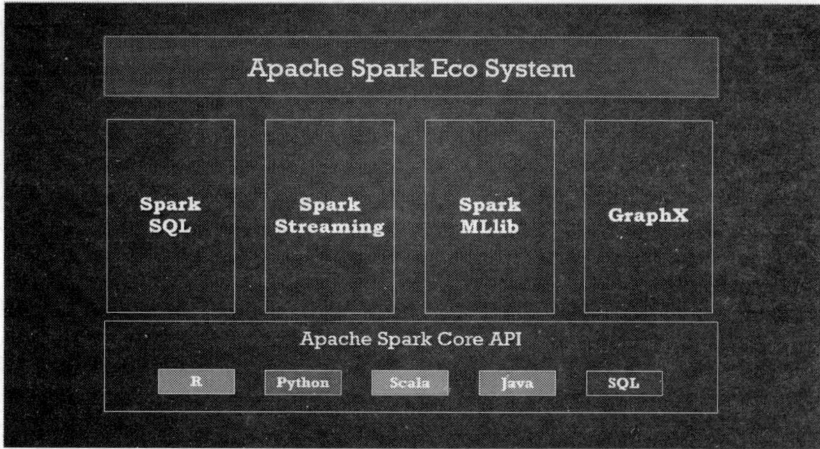

Figure. 18.5(b) : Components of Spark Core foundation of the platform

Apache Spark is an open-source unified analytics engine for large-scale data processing. Spark provides an interface for programming clusters with implicit data parallelism and fault tolerance. Originally developed at the University of California, Berkeley's AMPLab, the Spark codebase was later donated to the Apache Software Foundation, which has maintained it since.

Spark and its RDDs were developed in 2012 in response to limitations in the MapReduce cluster computing paradigm, which forces a particular linear dataflow structure on distributed programs: MapReduce programs read input data from disk, map a function across the data, reduce the results of the map, and store reduction results on disk. Spark's RDDs function as a working set for distributed programs that offers a (deliberately) restricted form of distributed shared memory.

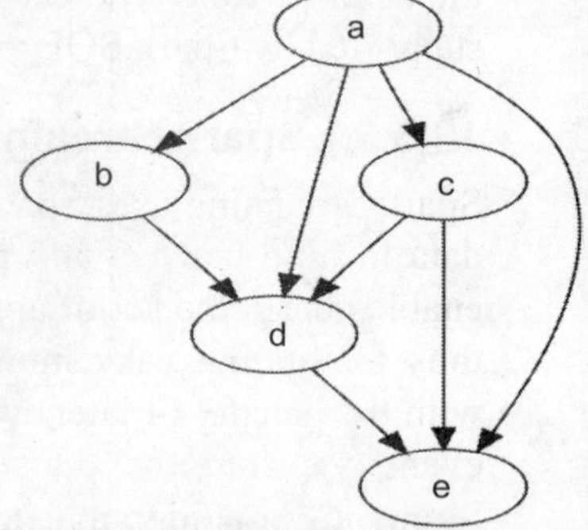

Figure. 18.6 : Example of a Directed Acyclic Graph (DAG)

In mathematics, particularly graph theory, and computer science, a directed acyclic graph (DAG) is a directed graph with no directed cycles. (vide Figure 18.6.) That is, it consists of vertices and edges (also called arcs), with each edge directed from one vertex to another, such that following those directions will never form a closed loop. A directed graph is a DAG if and only if it can be topologically ordered, by arranging the vertices as a linear ordering that is consistent with all edge directions. DAGs have numerous scientific and computational applications, ranging from biology (evolution, family trees, epidemiology) to information science (citation networks) to computation (scheduling).

Directed acyclic graphs are sometimes instead called acyclic directed graphs [2] or acyclic digraphs.

18.5.2 Spark SQL

Many data scientists, analysts, and general business intelligence users rely on interactive SQL queries for exploring data. Spark SQL is a Spark module for structured data processing. It provides a programming abstraction called DataFrames and can also act as a distributed SQL query engine. It enables unmodified Hadoop Hive queries to run up to 100x faster on existing deployments and data. It also provides powerful integration with the rest of the Spark ecosystem (e.g., integrating SQL query processing with machine learning).

Spark SQL brings native support for SQL to Spark and streamlines the process of querying data stored both in RDDs (Spark's distributed datasets) and in external sources. Spark SQL conveniently blurs the lines between RDDs and relational tables. Unifying these powerful abstractions makes it easy for developers to intermix SQL commands querying external data with complex analytics, all within in a single application. Concretely, Spark SQL will allow developers to:

1. Import relational data from Parquet files and Hive tables
2. Run SQL queries over imported data and existing RDDs
3. Easily write RDDs out to Hive tables or Parquet files

Spark SQL also includes a cost-based optimizer, columnar storage, and code generation to make queries fast. At the same time, it scales to thousands of nodes and multi-hour queries using the Spark engine, which provides full mid-query fault tolerance, without having to worry about using a different engine for historical data.

Spark SQL is a component on top of Spark Core that introduced a data abstraction called DataFrames, which provides support for structured and semi-structured data. Spark SQL provides a domain-specific language (DSL) to manipulate **DataFrames** in *Scala, Java, Python or .NET*. It also provides SQL language support, with command-line interfaces and ODBC/JDBC server. Although DataFrames lack the compile-time type-checking afforded by RDDs, as of Spark 2.0, the strongly typed DataSet is fully supported by Spark SQL as well.

18.5.3 Spark Streaming

Spark Streaming uses Spark Core's fast scheduling capability to perform *streaming analytics*. It ingests data in mini-batches and performs RDD transformations on those mini-batches of data. This design enables the same set of application code written for batch analytics to be used in streaming analytics, thus facilitating easy implementation of lambda architecture. [5] However, this convenience comes with the penalty of latency equal to the mini-batch duration. Other streaming data engines that process event by event rather than in mini-batches include **Storm** and the streaming component of **Flink.** Spark Streaming has support built-in to consume from *Kafka, Flume, Twitter, ZeroMQ, Kinesis, and TCP/IP sockets*. We have already discussed Flume in chapter 15 of this book. We will learn about Storm (discussed in section 18.11. Kafka (discussed in section 18.12) and Flink (discussed in section 18.13).

In Spark 2.x, a separate technology based on Datasets, called **Structured Streaming**, that has a higher-level interface is also provided to support streaming. Spark can be deployed in a traditional on-premises data center as well as in the cloud.

Spark Streaming is a scalable, high-throughput, fault-tolerant streaming processing system that supports both batch and streaming workloads. The processed data can be pushed to databases, Kafka, live dashboards etc.

Figure. 18.7: Spark Streaming Supports

18.5.4 MLlib Machine Learning Library

Spark MLlib is a distributed machine-learning framework on top of Spark Core that, due in large part to the distributed memory-based Spark architecture, is as much as **nine times** as fast as the disk-based implementation used by Apache Mahout (according to benchmarks done by the MLlib developers against the alternating least squares (ALS) implementations, and before Mahout itself gained a Spark interface), and scales better than Vowpal Wabbit.[2] Vowpal Wabbit (VW) is an open-source fast online interactive machine learning system library and program developed originally at Yahoo! Research, and currently at Microsoft Research.

MLlib goal is to make practical machine learning scalable and easy. At a high level, it provides tools such as:

1. ML Algorithms: common learning algorithms such as classification, regression, clustering, and collaborative filtering
2. Featurization: feature extraction, transformation, dimensionality reduction, and selection
3. Pipelines: tools for constructing, evaluating, and tuning ML Pipelines
4. Persistence: saving and load algorithms, models, and Pipelines
5. Utilities: linear algebra, statistics, data handling, etc.

Many common machine learning and statistical algorithms have been implemented and are shipped with MLlib which simplifies large scale machine learning pipelines, including: summary statistics, correlations, stratified sampling, hypothesis testing, random data generation[6] classification and regression: support vector machines, logistic regression, linear regression, naive Bayes classification, Decision Tree, Random Forest, Gradient-Boosted Tree collaborative filtering techniques including alternating least squares (ALS) cluster analysis methods including k-means, and latent Dirichlet allocation (LDA) dimensionality reduction techniques such as singular value decomposition (SVD), and principal component analysis (PCA) feature extraction and transformation functions optimization algorithms such as stochastic gradient descent, limited-memory BFGS (L-BFGS)

18.5.5 GraphX

GraphX is a distributed graph-processing framework on top of Apache Spark. GraphX is a new component in Spark for graphs and graph-parallel computation. At a high level, GraphX extends the Spark RDD by introducing a new Graph abstraction: a directed multigraph with properties attached to each vertex and edge. It provides an API to implement and express graph computation that has the ability to model user-defined graphs with the use of the Pregel abstraction API. This API also boosts and implements better and optimized runtimes for the Pregel abstraction. Because it is based on RDDs, which are immutable, graphs are immutable and thus GraphX is unsuitable for graphs that need to be updated, let alone in a transactional manner like a graph database. GraphX provides two separate APIs for implementation of massively parallel algorithms (such as PageRank): a Pregel abstraction, and a more general MapReduce-style API. [7] Unlike its predecessor Bagel, which was formally deprecated in Spark 1.6, GraphX has full support for property graphs (graphs where properties can be attached to edges and vertices).

Like Apache Spark, GraphX initially started as a research project at UC Berkeley's AMPLab and Databricks, and was later donated to the Apache Software Foundation and the Spark project. [3]

18.6 APACHE SPARK ARCHITECTURE

Apache Spark works in a master-slave architecture where the master is called "Driver" and slaves are called "Workers". When you run a Spark application, Spark Driver creates a context that is an entry point to your application, and all operations (transformations and actions) are executed on worker nodes, and the resources are managed by Cluster Manager.

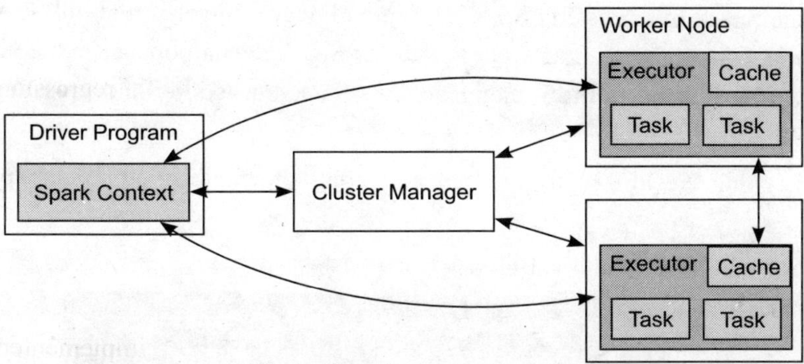

Figure. 18.8: Master-Slave Architecture of Apache Spark

Cluster Manager Types

As of writing this Apache Spark Tutorial, Spark supports below cluster managers:

1. **Standalone** – a simple cluster manager included with Spark that makes it easy to set up a cluster.
2. **Apache Mesos** – Mesons is a Cluster manager that can also run Hadoop MapReduce and Spark applications.
3. **Hadoop YARN** – the resource manager in Hadoop 2. This is mostly used, cluster manager.
4. **Kubernetes** – an open-source system for automating deployment, scaling, and management of containerized applications.

Local – which is not really a cluster manager but still I wanted to mention as we use "local" for master() in order to run Spark on your laptop/computer.

18.7 SPARK INSTALLATION

In order to run Apache Spark examples mentioned in this tutorial, you need to have Spark and it's needed tools to be installed on your computer. Since most developers use Windows for development, I will explain how to install Spark on windows in this tutorial. you can also Install Spark on Linux server if needed.

Download Apache Spark™

1. Choose a Spark release: 3.0.0 (Jun 18 2020)
2. Choose a package type: Pre-built for Apache Hadoop 2.7
3. Download Spark: spark-3.0.0-bin-hadoop2.7.tgz
4. Verify this release using the 3.0.0 signatures, checksums and project release KEYS.

Figure. 18.9: Downloading Guide

Download Apache Spark by accessing Spark Download page and select the link from "Download Spark (point 3)". If you wanted to use a different version of Spark & Hadoop, select the one you wanted from drop downs and the link on point 3 changes to the selected version and provides you with an updated link to download.

After download, untar the binary using 7zip and copy the underlying folder spark-3.0.0-bin-hadoop2.7 to c:\apps

Now set the following environment variables.

```
SPARK_HOME  = C:\apps\spark-3.0.0-bin-hadoop2.7
HADOOP_HOME = C:\apps\spark-3.0.0-bin-hadoop2.7
PATH=%PATH%;C:\apps\spark-3.0.0-bin-hadoop2.7\bin
```

Setup winutils.exe : Download wunutils.exe file from winutils, and copy it to %SPARK_HOME%\bin folder. Winutils are different for each Hadoop version hence download the right version from https://github.com/steveloughran/winutils

Spark-shell : Spark binary comes with an interactive spark-shell. In order to start a shell, go to your SPARK_HOME/bin directory and type "spark-shell2". This command loads the Spark and displays what version of Spark you are using.

```
C:\apps\opt\spark-3.0.0-bin-hadoop2.7\bin>spark-shell2
20/08/22 22:59:56 WARN NativeCodeLoader: Unable to load native-hadoop library fo
r your platform... using builtin-java classes where applicable
Using Spark's default log4j profile: org/apache/spark/log4j-defaults.properties
Setting default log level to "WARN".
To adjust logging level use sc.setLogLevel(newLevel). For SparkR, use setLogLeve
l(newLevel).
20/08/22 23:00:04 WARN Utils: Service 'SparkUI' could not bind on port 4040. Att
empting port 4041.
Spark context Web UI available at http://DELL-ESUHAO2KAJ:4041
Spark context available as 'sc' (master = local[*], app id = local-1598162404202
).
Spark session available as 'spark'.
Welcome to
      ____              __
     / __/__  ___ _____/ /__
    _\ \/ _ \/ _ `/ __/  '_/
   /___/ .__/\_,_/_/ /_/\_\   version 3.0.0
      /_/

Using Scala version 2.12.10 (Java HotSpot(TM) 64-Bit Server VM, Java 1.8.0_191)
Type in expressions to have them evaluated.
Type :help for more information.

scala> spark
res0: org.apache.spark.sql.SparkSession = org.apache.spark.sql.SparkSession@c82f
6bd
```

Figure. 18.10 : Spark Interface downloads Scala Automatically.

By default, spark-shell provides with spark (SparkSession) and sc (SparkContext) object's to use. Let's see some examples:

```
scala> spark
res0: org.apache.spark.sql.SparkSession = org.apache.spark.sql.SparkSession@c82f
6bd

scala> sc
res1: org.apache.spark.SparkContext = org.apache.spark.SparkContext@1fdc2d45

scala> 20/08/22 23:00:17 WARN ProcfsMetricsGetter: Exception when trying to comp
ute pagesize, as a result reporting of ProcessTree metrics is stopped

scala> val rdd = spark.sparkContext.parallelize(Seq(1,2,3))
rdd: org.apache.spark.rdd.RDD[Int] = ParallelCollectionRDD[0] at parallelize at
<console>:23

scala> rdd.count
[Stage 0:>                                                          (0 + 4) / 4]

res2: Long = 3

scala> rdd.foreach(println)
1
2
3

scala>
```

Figure. 18.11: Utilization of Scala : Examples

Apache Spark is a framework that is supported in Scala, Python, R Programming, and Java. Below are different implementations of Spark.

18.7.1 Scala

Scala is a modern multi-paradigm programming language designed to express common programming patterns in a concise, elegant, and type-safe way. Scala has been created by Martin Odersky and he released the first version in 2003. Scala smoothly integrates the features of object-oriented and functional languages. This tutorial explains the basics of Scala in a simple and reader-friendly way.

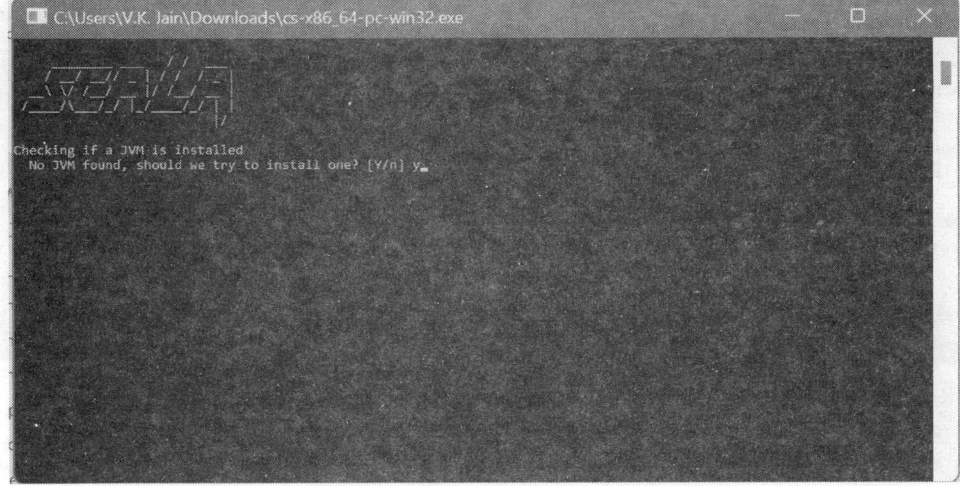

Figure. 18.12 : SCALA Interface

18.7.2 Use cases of Apache Spark

As of 2016, surveys show that more than 1,000 organizations are using Spark in production. Some of them are listed on the Powered By Spark page. Apache Spark has become one of the most popular big data distributed processing framework with 365,000 meetup members in 2017.

Examples of various customers include:

1. Act Now : Spark powers NOW APPS, a big data, real-time, predictive analytics platform. We use Spark SQL, MLlib and GraphX components for both batch ETL and analytics applied to telecommunication data, providing faster and more meaningful insights and actionable data to the operators.
2. Agile Lab
3. Alibaba Taobao
4. Alluxio : Alluxio, formerly Tachyon, is the world's first system that unifies disparate storage systems at memory speed.
5. Amazon
6. Autodesk
7. Baidu
8. Spark SQL, MLlib : Using Spark for travel and expenses analytics and personalization<
9. eBay Inc.: Using Spark core for log transaction aggregation and analytics
10. Elsevier Labs : Building Machine Reading Pipeline, Knowledge Graphs, Content as a Service, Content and Event Analytics, Content/Event based Predictive Models and Big Data Processing.
11. We use Scala and Python over Databricks Notebooks for most of our work.
12. NASA JPL - Deep Space Network
13. Nokia Solutions and Networks
14. Radius Intelligence : Using Scala, Spark and MLLib for Radius Marketing and Sales intelligence platform including data aggregation, data processing, data clustering, data analysis and predictive modeling of all US businesses.
15. TripAdvisor
16. Yahoo!
17. UC Berkeley AMPLab - Big data research lab that initially launched Spark

18.8 AMAZON WEB SERVICES (APACHE SPARK CLUSTER IN THE CLOUD)

Amazon EMR is the best place to deploy Apache Spark in the cloud, because it combines the integration and testing rigor of commercial Hadoop & Spark distributions with the scale, simplicity, and cost effectiveness of the cloud. It allows you to launch Spark clusters in minutes without needing to do node provisioning, cluster setup, Spark configuration, or cluster tuning. EMR enables you to provision one, hundreds, or thousands of compute instances in minutes. You can use Auto Scaling to have EMR automatically scale up your Spark clusters to process data of any size, and back down when your job is complete to avoid paying for unused capacity. You can lower your bill by committing to a set term, and saving up to 75% using Amazon EC2 Reserved Instances, or running your clusters on spare AWS compute capacity and saving up to 90% using EC2 Spot.

Amazon EMR is the best place to run Apache Spark. You can quickly and easily create managed Spark clusters from the AWS Management Console, AWS CLI, or the Amazon EMR API. Additionally, you can leverage additional Amazon EMR features, including fast Amazon S3 connectivity using the Amazon EMR File System (EMRFS), integration with the Amazon EC2 Spot market and the AWS Glue Data Catalog, and EMR Managed Scaling to add or remove instances from your cluster. AWS Lake Formation brings fine-grained access control, while integration with AWS Step Functions helps with orchestrating your data pipelines. EMR Studio (preview) is an integrated development environment (IDE) that makes it easy for data scientists and data engineers to develop, visualize, and debug data engineering and data science applications written in *R, Python, Scala, and PySpark.* EMR Studio provides fully managed Jupyter Notebooks, and tools like Spark UI and YARN Timeline Service to simplify debugging. EMR Notebooks make it easy for you to experiment and build applications with Spark. If you prefer, you can use Apache Zeppelin to create interactive and collaborative notebooks for data exploration using Spark.

18.8.1 Use cases of Amazon EMR

(1) **Stream processing** : Consume and process real-time data from Amazon Kinesis, Apache Kafka, or other data streams with Spark Streaming on EMR. Perform streaming analytics in a fault-tolerant way and write results to S3 or on-cluster HDFS.

(2) **Machine learning :** Apache Spark on EMR includes **MLlib** for a variety of scalable machine learning algorithms, or you can use your own libraries. By storing datasets in-memory during a job, Spark has great performance for iterative queries common in machine learning workloads. You can enhance Amazon SageMaker capabilities by connecting the notebook instance to an Apache Spark cluster running on *Amazon EMR*, with **Amazon SageMaker Spark** for easily training models and hosting models.

(3) **Interactive SQL :** Use Spark SQL for low-latency, interactive queries with SQL or HiveQL. Spark on EMR can leverage EMRFS, so you can have ad hoc access to your datasets in S3. Also, you can utilize EMR Studio, EMR Notebooks, Zeppelin notebooks, or BI tools via ODBC and JDBC connections.

18.8.2 Versions of Spark Language

Originally, there were three versions of the SPARK language (SPARK83, SPARK95, SPARK2005) based on Ada 83, Ada 95 and Ada 2005 respectively.

SPARK 2014 is the latest incarnation of the SPARK programming environment. The language is a subset of the Ada 2012 programming language that includes features like contract programming.

SPARK 2014 consists of a programming language that is a subset of Ada, a design methodology and a verification toolset. The language subset is chosen so that applications written in SPARK 2014 and be proven to match the specification that is part of the program. It is designed for low defect software that is necessary for programming in general, as well as safety- and security-related applications such as avionics. The matching toolset utilizes the information within application code to statically analyze the program and verify that it matches the specification.

SPARK 2014 is a **programming environment** based on the Ada programming language. Apache's open-source SPARK project is an advanced, **Directed Acyclic Graph** (DAG) execution engine.

Both are used for applications, albeit of much different types. SPARK 2014 is used for embedded applications, while Apache SPARK is designed for very large clusters.

18.9 USES OF SPARK

Apache Spark is a great tool to handle and process Big Data. It is a much-valued skill, and as the software industry marches towards better apps, the demand for these developers will keep growing.

Spark executes much faster by caching data in memory across multiple parallel operations, whereas MapReduce involves more reading and writing from disk. Spark runs multi-threaded tasks inside of JVM processes, whereas MapReduce runs as heavier weight JVM processes. The speciality of Spark lies in:

(1) **Data Integration**: The data generated by systems are not consistent enough to combine for analysis. To fetch consistent data from systems we can use processes like Extract, transform, and load (ETL). Spark is used to reduce the cost and time required for this ETL process.

(2) **Stream Processing**: It is always difficult to handle the real-time generated data such as log files. Spark is capable enough to operate streams of data and refuses potentially fraudulent operations.

Machine learning: Machine learning approaches become more feasible and increasingly accurate due to enhancement in the volume of data. As spark is capable of storing data in memory and can run repeated queries quickly, it makes it easy to work on machine learning algorithms.

Interactive analytics: Spark is able to generate the respond rapidly. So, instead of running pre-defined queries, we can handle the data interactively. In fact, you can apply Spark's machine learning and graph processing algorithms on data streams. Internally, it works as follows. Spark Streaming receives live input data streams and divides the data into batches, which are then processed by the Spark engine to generate the final stream of results in batches.

(3) Apache Spark and Flink both are next generations Big Data tool grabbing industry attention. Both provide native connectivity with Hadoop and NoSQL Databases and can process HDFS data. Both are the nice solution to several Big Data problems. But Flink is faster than Spark, due to its underlying architecture.

(4) **Industry Specific Uses of Spark**

(a) Currently [2021], Spark is one of the primary SQL engines at **Facebook** in addition to being the primary system for writing custom batch applications.

(b) Apache Spark is a foundational piece of **Uber's Big Data infrastructure** that powers many critical aspects of our business. We currently run more than one hundred thousand Spark applications per day, across multiple different compute environments.

(c) Apache Spark is a parallel processing framework that supports in-memory processing to boost the performance of big-data analytic applications. Apache Spark in **Azure HDInsight** is the Microsoft implementation of Apache Spark in the cloud, and is one of several Spark offerings in Azure.

In general, Spark can run well with anywhere from 8 GB to hundreds of gigabytes of memory per machine. In all cases, we recommend allocating only at most 75% of the memory for Spark; leave the rest for the operating system and buffer cache.

Is it worth learning Apache Spark in 2021?

The definitive answer is yes. But again, you have to have a project with a concrete problem that needs solving and that can be solved in a divide-and-conquer kind of way and a large amount of data for it to make sense to use spark

18.10 LIMITATIONS OF APACHE SPARK PROGRAMMING

1. **No Support for Real-time Processing** : Basically, Spark is near real-time processing of live data. In other words, Micro-batch processing takes place in Spark Streaming. Hence we can not say Spark is completely Real-time Processing engine.
2. **Problem with Small File :** In RDD, each file is a small partition. It means, there is the large amount of tiny partition within an RDD. Hence, if we want efficiency in our processing, the RDDs should be repartitioned into some manageable format. Basically, that demands extensive shuffling over the network.
3. **No File Management System :** A major issue is Spark does not have its own file management system. Basically, it relies on some other platform like Hadoop or another cloud-based platform.
4. **Expensive :** While we desire cost-efficient processing of big data, Spark turns out to be very expensive. Since keeping data in memory is quite expensive. However the memory consumption is very high, and it is not handled in a user-friendly manner. Moreover, we require lots of RAM to run in-memory, thus the cost of spark is much higher. The consumption problem doesn't make it much user-friendly. The additional memory needed to run Spark costs very high which makes Spark **expensive**. *Hadoop, Splunk, Cassandra, Apache Beam, and Apache Flume* are the most popular alternatives and competitors to Apache Spark.
5. **Availability of number of Algorithms :** Spark MLlib have very less number of available algorithms. For example, Tanimoto distance.
6. **Manual Optimization :** It is must that Spark job is manually optimized and is adequate to specific datasets. Moreover, to partition and cache in spark to be correct, it is must to control it manually.
7. **Iterative Processing :** Basically, here data iterates in batches. Also, each iteration is scheduled and executed separately.
8. **Latency :** On comparing with Flink, Apache Spark has higher latency.
9. **Window Criteria :**Spark only support time-based window criteria not record based window criteria.

Due to these limitations of Apache Spark, industries have started shifting to Apache Flink– 4G of Big Data. Kafka analyses the events as they unfold. As a result, it employs a continuous (event-at-a-time) processing model. Spark, on the other hand, uses a micro-batch processing approach, which divides incoming streams into small batches for processing.

There are many limitations of Apache Spark. Let's learn all one by one:

Note: To overcome these limitations of Spark, we can use Apache Flink – 4G of Big Data.

18.11 APACHE STORM

Apache Storm is the stream processing engine for processing real-time streaming data. While Apache Spark is general purpose computing engine. It provides Spark Streaming to handle streaming data. It process data in near real-time. Let's understand which is better in the battle of Spark vs storm.

Storm: We can create Storm applications in Java, Clojure, and Scala.

Spark Streaming: We can create Spark applications in Java, Scala, Python, and R.

Apache Storm vs Spark Streaming

Parameter	Apache Storm	Spark Streaming
Processing Model	It supports true stream processing model through core storm layer.	Apache Spark Streaming is a wrapper over Spark batch processing.
Primitives	It provides a very rich set of primitives to perform tuple level process at intervals of a stream (filters, functions). Aggregations over messages in a stream are possible through group by semantics. It supports left join, right join, inner join (default) across the stream.	It provides 2 wide varieties of operators. First is Stream transformation operators that transform one DStream into another DStream. Second is output operators that write information to external systems. The previous includes stateless operators (filter, map, mapPartitions, union, distinct than on) still as stateful window operators (countByWindow, reduceByWindow then on).
State Management	Core Storm by default doesn't offer any framework level support to store any intermediate bolt output (the result of user operation) as a state. Hence, any application has to create/update its own state as and once required.	The underlying Spark by default treats the output of every RDD operation(Transformations and Actions) as an intermediate state. It stores it as RDD. Spark Streaming permits maintaining and changing state via updateStateByKey API. A pluggable method couldn't be found to implement state within the external system.

Parameter	Apache Storm	Spark Streaming
Message Delivery Guarantees (Handling message level failures)	It supports 3 message processing guarantees: at least once, at-most-once and exactly once. Storm's reliability mechanisms are distributed, scalable, and fault-tolerant.	Apache Spark Streaming defines its fault tolerance semantics, the guarantees provided by the recipient and output operators. As per the Apache Spark architecture, the incoming data is read and replicated in different Spark executor's nodes. This generates failure scenarios data received but may not be reflected. It handles fault tolerance differently in the case of worker failure and driver failure.
Debuggability and Monitoring	Apache Storm UI support image of every topology; with the entire break-up of internal spouts and bolts. UI additionally contributes information having any errors coming in tasks and fine-grained stats on the throughput and latency of every part of the running topology. It helps in debugging problems at a high level. Metric based monitoring: Storm's inbuilt metrics feature supports framework level for applications to emit any metrics, which can simply integrate with external metrics/monitoring systems.	Spark web UI displays an extra Streaming tab that shows statistics of running receivers (whether receivers are active, the variety of records received, receiver error, and so on.) and completed batches (batch process times, queuing delays, and so on). It is useful to observe the execution of the application. The following 2 info in Spark web UI are significantly necessary for standardization of batch size: Processing Time – The time to process every batch of data.
Ease of development	It provides extremely easy, rich and intuitive APIs that simply describe the DAG nature of process flow (topology). The Storm tuples, which give the abstraction of data flowing between nodes within the DAG, are dynamically written. The motivation there's to change the APIs for simple use. Any new custom tuple can be plugged in once registering its Kryo serializer. Developers will begin with writing topologies and run them in native cluster mode. In local mode, threads are used to simulate worker nodes, permitting the developer to set breakpoints, halt the execution, examine variables, and profile before deploying it to a distributed cluster wherever all this is often way tougher.	It offers Scala and Java APIs that have a lot of a practical programming (transformation of data). As a result, the topology code is way a lot of elliptic. There's an upscale set of API documentation and illustrative samples on the market for the developer.

18.12 APACHE KAFKA STREAMS

Apache Kafka is a popular open-source event store and streaming platform developed by the Apache Software Foundation in Java and Scala. The platform is used by thousands of organizations for streaming analytics, high-performance data pipelines, data integration, and mission-critical applications. It is a fault-tolerant messaging system based on a publish-subscriber model that can handle massive data volumes. For real-time streaming data analysis, Apache Kafka can be integrated seamlessly with Apache Storm and Apache Spark. Basically, Kafka is a system for collecting, storing, reading, and analyzing streaming data at scale.

The easiest way to write mission-critical real-time applications and microservices

Kafka Streams is a client library for building applications and microservices, where the input and output data are stored in Kafka clusters. It combines the simplicity of writing and deploying standard Java and Scala applications on the client side with the benefits of Kafka's server-side cluster technology.

Kafka Streams is a library for building streaming applications, specifically applications that transform input Kafka topics into output Kafka topics (or calls to external services, or updates to databases, or whatever). It lets you do this with concise code in a way that is distributed and fault-tolerant. Stream processing is a computer programming paradigm, equivalent to data-flow programming, event stream processing, and reactive programming, that allows some applications to more easily exploit a limited form of parallel processing. The real-time processing of data continuously, concurrently, and in a record-by-record fashion is what we call Kafka Stream processing.

Real-time processing in Kafka is one of the applications of Kafka. Basically, Kafka Real-time processing includes a continuous stream of data. Hence, after the analysis of that data, we get some useful data out of it.

Now, while it comes to Kafka, real-time processing typically involves reading data from a topic (source), doing some analysis or transformation work, and then writing the results back to another topic (sink). To do this type of work, there are several options.

Either we can write our own custom code with a Kafka Consumer to read the data and write that data via a Kafka Producer. Or we use a full-fledged stream processing framework like Spark Streaming, Flink, Storm, etc.

18.12.1 Uses of Kafka Streams

Kafka Streams, a client library, we use it to process and analyze data stored in Kafka.It relied on important streams processing concepts like properly distinguishing between event time and processing time, windowing support, and simple yet efficient management and real-time querying of application state.

In addition, Kafka Streams has a low barrier to entry that means we can quickly write and run a small-scale proof-of-concept on a single machine. For that, we only need to run additional instances of our application on multiple machines to scale up to high-volume production workloads. oreover, by leveraging Kafka's parallelism model, it transparently handles the load balancing of multiple instances of the same application.

Some key points related to Kafka Streams:

1. Kafka Stream can be easily embedded in any Java application and integrated with any existing packaging, deployment and operational tools that users have for their streaming applications because it is a simple and lightweight client library.
2. There are no external dependencies on systems other than Apache Kafka itself as the internal messaging layer.
3. In order to enable very fast and efficient stateful operations (windowed joins and aggregations), it supports the fault-tolerant local state.
4. To guarantee that each record will be processed once and only once even when there is a failure on either Streams clients or Kafka brokers in the middle of processing, it offers exactly-once processing semantics.

In order to achieve millisecond processing latency, employs one-record-at-a-time processing. Also, with the late arrival of records, it supports event-time based windowing operations.

Along with a high-level Streams DSL and a low-level Processor API, it offers necessary stream processing primitives.

Many Fortune 100 brands such as Twitter, LinkedIn, Airbnb, and several others have been using Apache Kafka for multiple projects and communications. This sudden credibility shift to Kafka sure makes one question the reason for this growth.

Developed in 2010, Kafka was rendered by a LinkedIn team, originally to solve latency issues for the website and its infrastructure. It proved to be a credible solution for offline systems and had an effective use for the problem at hand. In 2011, Kafka was used as an Enterprise Messaging Solution for fetching data reliably and moving it in real-time in a batch-based approach.

Since then Kafka Streams have been used increasingly, each passing day to follow a robust mechanism for data relay. Read along to know more about Apache Kafka and access a detailed guide for working with Kafka Streams.

Kafka can handle huge volumes of data and remains responsive, this makes Kafka the preferred platform when the volume of the data involved is big to huge. Hence, Kafka Big Data can be used for real-time analysis as well as to process real-time streams to collect Big Data.

18.12.2 Need of Kafka Streams

Ideally, Stream Processing platforms are required to provide integration with Data Storage platforms, both for stream persistence, and static table/data stream joins.

However, the fault-tolerance and scalability factors are staunchly limited in most frameworks. The deployment, configuration, and network specifics can not be controlled completely.

You can overcome the challenges of Stream Processing by using Kafka Streams which offer more robust options to accommodate these requirements. Kafka Streams come with the below-mentioned advantages.

1. Kafka Streams comes with a fault-tolerant cluster architecture that is highly scalable, making it suitable for handling hundreds of thousands of messages every second.

2. Kafka Streams can be connected to Kafka directly and is also readily deployable on the cloud.
3. Kafka Streams can be accessed on Linux, Mac, and Windows Operating Systems, and by writing standard Java or Scala scripts.
4. Kafka Streams handles sensitive data in a very secure and trusted way as it is fully integrated with Kafka Security.

18.12.3. Kafka Streams Architecture

Here is the anatomy of an application that leverages the Streams API. This provides a logical view of Kafka Streams application that can contain multiple stream threads, which can in turn contain multiple stream tasks. [8]

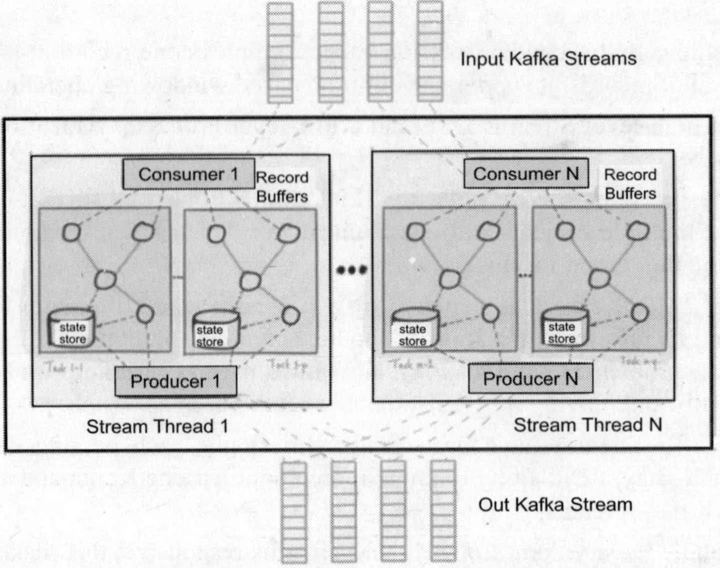

Figure. 18.14: Kafka Streams application containing multiple stream threads having multiple streaming tasks.

A Processor topology (or topology in simple terms) is used to define the Stream Processing Computational logic for your application. It refers to the way in which input data is transformed to output data. A topology is a graph of nodes or stream processors that are connected by edges (streams) or shared state stores. In this topology, you can access the following two special processors:

Sink Processor: A Sink Processor is a kind of stream processor that does not include downstream processors. Sink Processors send any received records from their upstream processors to a particular Kafka topic.

Source Processor: A Source Processor is a kind of stream processor that does not leverage any upstream processors. Instead, it produces an input stream to its topology from one or multiple Kafka topics by extracting records from these topics and forwarding them to its downstream processors.

A Stream Processing Application can be used to define one or more such topologies, although it is generally used to define one specific topology. Developers can define topologies either through the low-level processor API or through the Kafka Streams DSL, which incrementally builds on top of the former.

Therefore, you can define processor topology as a logical abstraction for your Stream Processing code. The logical topology gets instantiated at runtime and is replicated within the application for parallel processing.

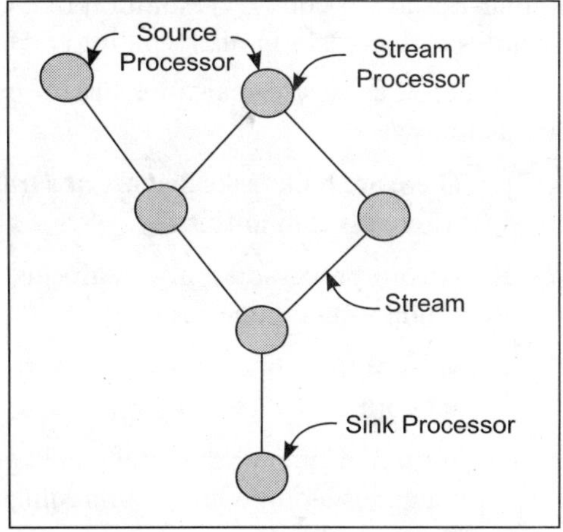

Figure. 18.15: Processor Topology

18.12.4 Kafka Streams API: Use Cases

Here are a few handy Kafka Streams examples that leverage Kafka Streams API to simplify operations [8] :

Finance Industry can build applications to accumulate data sources for real-time views of potential exposures. It can also be leveraged for minimizing and detecting fraudulent transactions.

Travel companies can build applications with the API to help them make real-time decisions to find the best suitable pricing for individual customers. This allows them to cross-sell additional services and process reservations and bookings.

Retailers can leverage this API to decide in real-time on the next best offers, pricing, personalized promotions, and inventory management.

It can also be used by logistics companies to build applications to track their shipments reliably, quickly, and in real-time.

Manufacturing and automotive companies can easily build applications to ensure their production lines offer optimum performance while extracting meaningful real-time insights into their supply chains. The API can also be leveraged to monitor the telemetry data from linked cars to make a decision as to the need for a thorough inspection.

18.12.5 Benefits of Using Kafka

Kafka offers some distinct benefits over standard messaging brokers.

1. It allows de-bulking of the load as no indexes are required to be kept for the message.
2. It enhances stream efficiency and gives a no-buffering experience to end-users.
3. All data logs are kept with a punched time without any data deletion taking place. Thus, it reduces the risk of data loss.
4. Due to these performance characteristics and scalability factors, Kafka has become an effective big data solution for big companies, looking to channelize their data fast and efficiently. It eventually brought in video stream services, such as Netflix, to use Kafka as a primary source of ingestion.

18.12.6 Limitations of Kafka Stream Processing

However, extracting data from Kafka and integrating it with data from all your sources can be a time-consuming & resource-intensive job. Alternatively, you can opt for a more economical & effortless Cloud-Based No-code ETL solution like Hevo Data that supports Kafka and 100+ other data sources to seamlessly load data in real-time into a Data Warehouse or a destination of your choice.

When it comes to real-time stream processing, some typical challenges during stream processing are as follows:

1. There are bulk tasks that are at a transient stage over different machines and need to be scheduled efficiently and uniformly.
2. Stream processors only retain just the adequate amount of data to fulfill the criteria of all the window-based queries active in the system, resulting in not-so-efficient memory management.
3. Most frameworks have to resort to code serializations and consequent transmission over a network.
4. For a real-time or dynamic package transfer, the code has to be sent and deployed at individual machines along with the prerequisites needed to execute the same.
5. Real-time BI visualization requires data to be stored first in a table, which introduces latency and table management issues, particularly with data streams.

18.13 APACHE FLINK

Apache Flink is an open-source, unified stream-processing and batch-processing framework developed by the Apache Software Foundation. The core of Apache Flink is a distributed streaming data-flow engine written in *Java and Scala*. Flink executes arbitrary dataflow programs in a data-parallel and pipelined manner.[9]

Apache Flink is a framework and distributed processing engine for stateful computations over unbounded and bounded data streams. Flink has been designed to run in all common cluster environments, perform computations at in-memory speed and at any scale.

Following are the important aspects of Flink's architecture:

1. **Process Unbounded and Bounded Data :** Any kind of data is produced as a stream of events. Credit card transactions, sensor measurements, machine logs, or user interactions on a website or mobile application, all of these data are generated as a stream.
2. Data can be processed as unbounded or bounded streams.
3. Unbounded streams have a start but no defined end. They do not terminate and provide data as it is generated. Unbounded streams must be continuously processed, i.e., events must be promptly handled after they have been ingested. It is not possible to wait for all input data to arrive because the input is unbounded and will not be complete at any point in time. Processing unbounded data often requires that events are ingested in a specific order, such as the order in which events occurred, to be able to reason about result completeness.
4. Bounded streams have a defined start and end. Bounded streams can be processed by ingesting all data before performing any computations. Ordered ingestion is not required to process bounded

streams because a bounded data set can always be sorted. Processing of bounded streams is also known as batch processing.

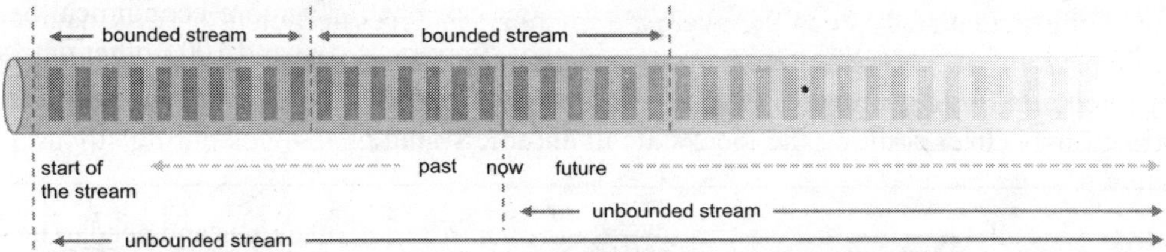

Figure. 18.16 : Batch Processing of Bounded Streams

Apache Flink excels at processing unbounded and bounded data sets. Precise control of time and state enable Flink's runtime to run any kind of application on unbounded streams. Bounded streams are internally processed by algorithms and data structures that are specifically designed for fixed sized data sets, yielding excellent performance.[9]

18.13.1 Deployability of Flink Applications Anywhere

Apache Flink is a distributed system and requires compute resources in order to execute applications. Flink integrates with all common cluster resource managers such as Hadoop YARN and Kubernetes, but can also be setup to run as a stand-alone cluster.

Flink is designed to work well each of the previously listed resource managers. This is achieved by resource-manager-specific deployment modes that allow Flink to interact with each resource manager in its idiomatic way.

When deploying a Flink application, Flink automatically identifies the required resources based on the application's configured parallelism and requests them from the resource manager. In case of a failure, Flink replaces the failed container by requesting new resources. All communication to submit or control an application happens via REST calls. This eases the integration of Flink in many environments.

18.13.2 Run Applications at any Scale

Flink is designed to run stateful streaming applications at any scale. Applications are parallelized into possibly thousands of tasks that are distributed and concurrently executed in a cluster. Therefore, an application can leverage virtually unlimited amounts of CPUs, main memory, disk and network IO. Moreover, Flink easily maintains very large application state. Its asynchronous and incremental checkpointing algorithm ensures minimal impact on processing latencies while guaranteeing exactly-once state consistency.

Users reported impressive scalability numbers for Flink applications running in their production environments, such as:

1. Applications processing multiple trillions of events per day,
2. Applications maintaining multiple terabytes of state, and
3. Applications running on thousands of cores.

18.13.3 Leverage In-Memory Performance

Stateful Flink applications are optimized for local state access. Task state is always maintained in memory or, if the state size exceeds the available memory, in access-efficient on-disk data structures. Hence, tasks perform all computations by accessing local, often in-memory, state yielding very low processing latencies. Flink guarantees exactly-once state consistency in case of failures by periodically and asynchronously checkpointing the local state to durable storage.

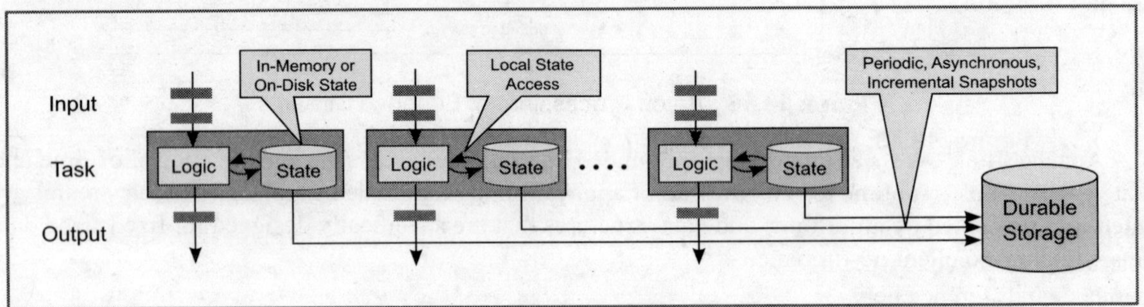

Figure. 18.17: Maintaining state consistency in case of failures

18.13.4 Use Cases of Flink

Apache Flink is an excellent choice to develop and run many different types of applications due to its extensive features set. Flink's features include support for stream and batch processing, sophisticated state management, event-time processing semantics, and exactly-once consistency guarantees for state. Moreover, Flink can be deployed on various resource providers such as YARN and Kubernetes, but also as stand-alone cluster on bare-metal hardware. Configured for high availability, Flink does not have a single point of failure. Flink has been proven to scale to thousands of cores and terabytes of application state, delivers high throughput and low latency, and powers some of the world's most demanding stream processing applications.

Below, we explore the most common types of applications that are powered by Flink and give pointers to real-world examples.

1. Event-driven Applications
2. Data Analytics Applications
3. Data Pipeline Applications
4. Event-driven Applications

18.13.5 Event-driven Applications

An event-driven application is a stateful application that ingest events from one or more event streams and reacts to incoming events by triggering computations, state updates, or external actions.

Event-driven applications are an evolution of the traditional application design with separated compute and data storage tiers. In this architecture, applications read data from and persist data to a remote transactional database.

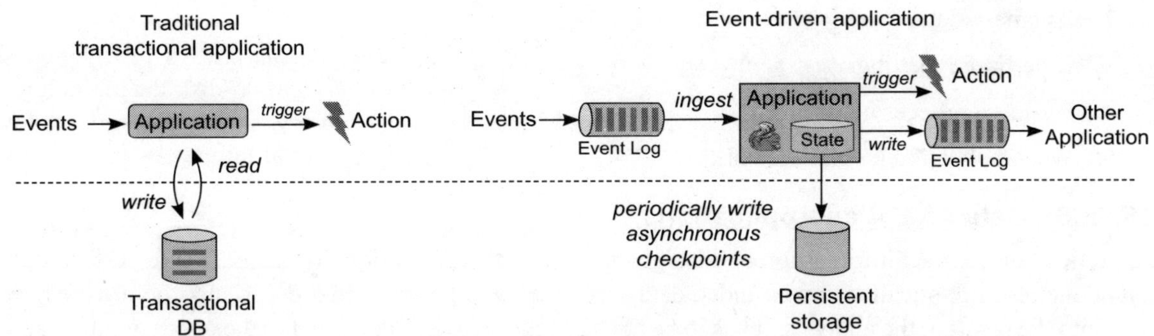

Figure. 18.18: Comparison of traditional transactional v/s event driven application

In contrast, event-driven applications are based on stateful stream processing applications. In this design, data and computation are co-located, which yields local (in-memory or disk) data access. Fault-tolerance is achieved by periodically writing checkpoints to a remote persistent storage. The figure below depicts the difference between the traditional application architecture and event-driven applications.

18.13.5.1 Advantages of event-driven Applications

Instead of querying a remote database, event-driven applications access their data locally which yields better performance, both in terms of throughput and latency. The periodic checkpoints to a remote persistent storage can be asynchronously and incrementally done. Hence, the impact of checkpointing on the regular event processing is very small. However, the event-driven application design provides more benefits than just local data access. In the tiered architecture, it is common that multiple applications share the same database. Hence, any change of the database, such as changing the data layout due to an application update or scaling the service, needs to be coordinated. Since each event-driven application is responsible for its own data, changes to the data representation or scaling the application requires less coordination.

18.13.5.2 How does Flink support event-driven Applications?

The limits of event-driven applications are defined by how well a stream processor can handle time and state. Many of Flink's outstanding features are centered around these concepts. Flink provides a rich set of state primitives that can manage very large data volumes (up to several terabytes) with exactly-once consistency guarantees. Moreover, Flink's support for event-time, highly customizable window logic, and fine-grained control of time as provided by the Process Function enable the implementation of advanced business logic. Moreover, Flink features a library for Complex Event Processing (CEP) to detect patterns in data streams.

However, Flink's outstanding feature for event-driven applications is savepoint. A savepoint is a consistent state image that can be used as a starting point for compatible applications. Given a savepoint, an application can be updated or adapt its scale, or multiple versions of an application can be started for A/B testing.

What are typical event-driven applications?

1. Fraud detection

2. Anomaly detection
3. Rule-based alerting
4. Business process monitoring
5. Web application (social network)

18.13.6 Data Analytics Applications

Analytical jobs extract information and insight from raw data. Traditionally, analytics are performed as batch queries or applications on bounded data sets of recorded events. In order to incorporate the latest data into the result of the analysis, it has to be added to the analyzed data set and the query or application is rerun. The results are written to a storage system or emitted as reports.

With a sophisticated stream processing engine, analytics can also be performed in a real-time fashion. Instead of reading finite data sets, streaming queries or applications ingest real-time event streams and continuously produce and update results as events are consumed. The results are either written to an external database or maintained as internal state. Dashboard application can read the latest results from the external database or directly query the internal state of the application.

Apache Flink supports streaming as well as batch analytical applications as shown in the Figure 18.19.

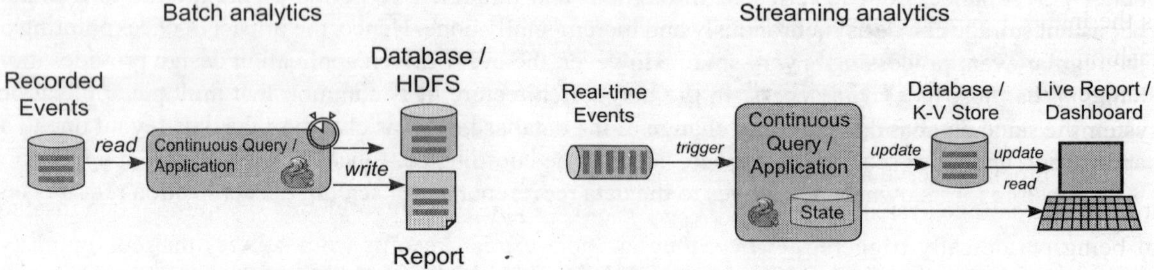

Figure. 18.19: Difference between streaming analytic and batch analytic processes

18.13.6.1. Advantages of Streaming Analytics Applications

The advantages of continuous streaming analytics compared to batch analytics are not limited to a much lower latency from events to insight due to elimination of periodic import and query execution. In contrast to batch queries, streaming queries do not have to deal with artificial boundaries in the input data which are caused by periodic imports and the bounded nature of the input.

Another aspect is a simpler application architecture. A batch analytics pipeline consist of several independent components to periodically schedule data ingestion and query execution. Reliably operating such a pipeline is non-trivial because failures of one component affect the following steps of the pipeline. In contrast, a streaming analytics application which runs on a sophisticated stream processor like Flink incorporates all steps from data ingestions to continuous result computation. Therefore, it can rely on the engine's failure recovery mechanism.

18.13.6.2 How does Flink support data analytics applications?

Flink provides very good support for continuous streaming as well as batch analytics. Specifically, it features an ANSI-compliant SQL interface with unified semantics for batch and streaming queries. SQL queries compute the same result regardless whether they are run on a static data set of recorded events or on a real-time event stream. Rich support for user-defined functions ensures that custom code can be executed in SQL queries. If even more custom logic is required, Flink's DataStream API or DataSet API provide more low-level control. Moreover, Flink's Gelly library provides algorithms and building blocks for large-scale and high-performance graph analytics on batch data sets.

What are typical data analytics applications?

1. Quality monitoring of Telco networks
2. Analysis of product updates & experiment evaluation in mobile applications
3. Ad-hoc analysis of live data in consumer technology
4. Large-scale graph analysis

18.13.7 Data Pipeline Applications

Data pipeline, is a set of data processing elements connected in series, where the output of one element is the input of the next one. The elements of a pipeline are often executed in parallel or in time-sliced fashion. **Extract-transform-load** (ETL) is a common approach to convert and move data between storage systems. Often ETL jobs are periodically triggered to copy data from transactional database systems to an analytical database or a data warehouse.

Data pipelines serve a similar purpose as ETL jobs. They transform and enrich data and can move it from one storage system to another. However, they operate in a continuous streaming mode instead of being periodically triggered. Hence, they are able to read records from sources that continuously produce data and move it with low latency to their destination. For example a data pipeline might monitor a file system directory for new files and write their data into an event log. Another application might materialize an event stream to a database or incrementally build and refine a search index.

The figure 18.20 depicts the difference between periodic ETL jobs and continuous data pipelines.

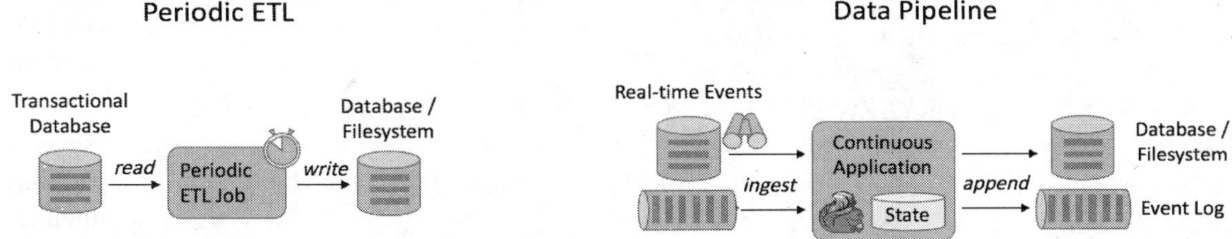

Figure. 18.20: Difference between periodic ETL jobs and continuous data pipelines

18.13.8 Advantages of Data Pipelines

The obvious advantage of continuous data pipelines over periodic ETL jobs is the reduced latency of moving data to its destination. Moreover, data pipelines are more versatile and can be employed for more use cases because they are able to continuously consume and emit data.

18.13.9 How does Flink support data pipelines?

Many common data transformation or enrichment tasks can be addressed by Flink's SQL interface (or Table API) and its support for user-defined functions. Data pipelines with more advanced requirements can be realized by using the Data Stream API which is more generic. Flink provides a rich set of connectors to various storage systems such as Kafka, Kinesis, Elastic search, and JDBC database systems. It also features continuous sources for file systems that monitor directories and sinks that write files in a time-bucketed fashion.

18.14 BIRD EYE VIEW OF BIG DATA TOOLS

Big data comes from myriad sources -- some examples are transaction processing systems, customer databases, documents, emails, medical records, internet clickstream logs, mobile apps and social networks.

"Big data" is a term relative to the available computing and storage power on the market — so in 1999, one gigabyte (1 GB) was considered big data. Today, it may consist of petabytes (1,024 terabytes) or exabytes (1,024 petabytes) of information, including billions or even trillions of records from millions of people. The largest hard drive being manufactured has 15 terabytes, and the largest SSD reaches 100 terabytes. The term Big Data refers to a dataset which is too large or too complex for ordinary computing devices to process.

18.14.1 Data Storage

Typically, this type of big data technology includes infrastructure that allows data to be fetched, stored, and managed, and is designed to handle massive amounts of data. Various software programs are able to access, use, and process the collected data easily and quickly. Among the most widely used big data technologies for this purpose are:

(1) Apache Hadoop

We have already studied in chapter 2 and 4 othis book. Apache Hadoop is an open-source, Java-based framework for storing and processing big data, developed by the Apache Software Foundation. In essence, it provides a distributed storage platform and processes big data using the MapReduce programming model. The Hadoop framework is designed to automatically handle hardware failures since they are common occurrences. Hadoop framework consists of five modules, namely Hadoop Distributed File System (HDFS), Hadoop YARN (Yet Another Resource Negotiator), Hadoop MapReduce, Hadoop Common, and Hadoop Ozone.

Companies using Hadoop: *LinkedIn, Intel, IBM, MapR, Facebook, Microsoft, Hortonworks, Cloudera, etc.*

Characteristic features:

1. A distributed file system, called HDFS (Hadoop Distributed File System), enables fast data transfer between nodes.

2. HDFS is a fundamentally resilient file system. In Hadoop, data that is stored on one node is also replicated on other nodes of the cluster to prevent data loss in case of hardware or software failure.
3. Hadoop is an inexpensive, fault-tolerant, and extremely flexible framework capable of storing and processing data in any format (structured, semi-structured, or unstructured).
4. MapReduce is a built-in batch processing engine in Hadoop that splits large computations across multiple nodes to ensure optimum performance and load balancing.

(2) MongoDB

We have already studied MongoDB in chapter 5 of this book. MongoDB is an open-source, cross-platform, document-oriented database designed to store and handle large amounts of data while providing high availability, performance, and scalability. Since MongoDB does not store or retrieve data in the form of tables, it is considered a NoSQL database. A new entrant to the data storage field, MongoDB is very popular due to its document-oriented NoSQL features, distributed key-value store, and Map Reduce calculation capabilities. This was named "Database Management System of the Year," by DB-Engines, which isn't surprising since NoSQL databases are more adept at handling Big Data than traditional RDBMS.

Companies using MongoDB: *MySQL, Facebook, eBay, MetLife, Google, Shutterfly, Aadhar,* etc.

Characteristic features :

1. It seamlessly integrates with languages like Ruby, Python, and JavaScript ; this seamless integration facilitates high coding velocity.
2. A MongoDB database stores data in JSON documents, which provide a rich data model that maps effortlessly to native programming languages.
3. MongoDB has several features that are unavailable in a traditional RDBMS, such as dynamic queries, secondary indexes, rich updates, sorting, and easy aggregation.
4. In document-based database systems, related data is stored in a single document, making it possible to run queries faster than with a traditional relational database where related data is stored in multiple tables and later joined using joins.

(3) Rain Stor

Rain Stor is a database management system that manages and analyzes big data and is developed by the Rain Stor company. A de-duplication technique is used in order to streamline the storage of large amounts of data for reference. Due to its ability to sort and store large volumes of information for reference, it eliminates duplicate files. Additionally, it supports cloud storage and multi-tenancy. The Rain Stor database product is available in two editions: Big Data Retention and Big Data Analytics on Hadoop, which enable highly efficient data management and accelerate data analysis and queries.

Companies using Rain Stor: *Barclays, Reimagine Strategy, Credit Suisse*, etc.

Characteristic features :

1. With Rain Stor, large enterprises can manage and analyze Big Data at the lowest total cost.
2. The enterprise database is built on Hadoop to support faster analytics.

3. It allows you to run faster queries and analyses using both SQL queries and MapReduce, leading to 10-100x faster results.
4. RainStor provides the highest compression level. Data is compressed up to 40x (97.5 percent) or more compared to raw data and has no re-inflation required when accessed.

(4) Cassandra

We have already studied this in chapter 6 of this book Cassandra is an open-source, distributed NoSQL database that enables the in-depth analysis of multiple sets of real-time data. It enables high scalability and availability without compromises in performance. To interact with the database, it uses CQL (Cassandra Structure Language). With scalability and fault tolerance on cloud infrastructure or commodity hardware, this is the ideal platform for mission-critical data processing. As a major Big Data tool, it accommodates all types of data formats, including structured, semi-structured, and unstructured.

Companies using Cassandra: *Facebook, GoDaddy, Netflix, GitHub, Rackspace, Cisco, Hulu, eBay*, etc.

Characteristic features :

1. Cassandra's decentralized architecture prevents single points of failure within a cluster.
2. Data sensitivity makes Cassandra suitable for enterprise applications that cannot afford data loss, even when the entire data center fails.
3. ACID (Atomicity, Consistency, Isolation, and Durability) are all supported by Cassandra.
4. It allows Hadoop integration with Map Reduce. It also supports Apache Hive & Apache Pig.
5. Due to its scalability, Cassandra can be scaled up to accommodate more customers and more data as required.

18.14.2 Data Mining Based Big Data Tools

Data mining is the process of extracting useful information from raw data and analyzing it. In many cases, raw data is very large, highly variable, and constantly streaming at speeds that make data extraction nearly impossible without a special technique. Among the most widely used big data technologies for data mining are:

(1) Elastic Search

Written in Java, it is a common search engine tool used by a number of companies (such as Accenture, Stack Overflow, Netflix, etc.) It provides a full-text search engine that is based on the Lucene library and provides an HTTP Web Interface and Schema-free JSON documents.

Built on Apache Lucene, Elastic search is an open-source, distributed, modern search and analytics engine that allows you to search, index, and analyze data of all types. Some of its most common use cases include log analytics, security intelligence, operational intelligence, full-text search, and business analytics. Unstructured data from various sources is retrieved and stored in a format that is highly optimized for language-based searches. Users can easily search and explore a large volume of data at a very fast speed. DB-Engines ranks Elastic search as the top enterprise search engine.

Companies using Elastic Search: *Netflix, Facebook, Uber, Shopify, Linkedln, Stack Overflow, GitHub, Instacart, etc.*

Characteristic features :

1. Using Elastic Search, you can store and analyze structured and unstructured data up to petabytes.
2. By providing simple restful APIs and schema-free JSON documents, Elasticsearch makes it easy to search, index, and query data.
3. Moreover, it provides near real-time search, scalable search, and multitenancy capabilities.
4. Elasticsearch is written in Java, which makes it compatible with nearly every platform.
5. As a language-agnostic open-source application, Elasticsearch makes it easy to extend its functionality with plugins and integrations.
6. Several management tools, UIs (User Interfaces), and APIs (Application Programming Interfaces) are provided for full control over data, cluster operations, users, etc.

(2) Rapid Miner

It can perform a range of functions from ETL to data mining and even predictive modeling and machine learning. RapidMiner is a useful tool as it helps in solving problems faced in business analytics, supports multiple languages, and provides the users with a simple user interactive interface. It is open-source which is one of its biggest advantages as even while being open-sourced it is still generally considered secure.

RapidMiner is an advanced open-source data mining tool for predictive analytics. It's a powerful data science platform that lets data scientists and big data analysts analyze their data quickly. In addition to data mining, it enables model deployment and model operation. With this solution, you will have access to all the machine learning and data preparation capabilities you need to make an impact on your business operations. By providing a unified environment for data preparation, machine learning, deep learning, text mining, and predictive analytics, it aims to enhance productivity for enterprise users of every skill level.

Companies using RapidMiner: *Domino's Pizza, McKinley Marketing Partners, Windstream Communications, George Mason University*, etc.

Characteristic features:

1. There is an integrated platform for processing data, building machine learning models, and deploying them.
2. Further, it integrates the Hadoop framework with its inbuilt RapidMiner Radoop.
3. RapidMiner Studio provides access, loading, and analysis of any type of data, whether it is structured data or unstructured data such as text, images, and media.
4. Automated predictive modeling is available in RapidMiner.

(3) Presto

Developed by Facebook, Presto is an open-source SQL query engine that enables interactive query analyses on massive amounts of data. This distributed search engine supports fast analytics queries on data sources of various sizes, from gigabytes to petabytes. With this technology, it is possible to query data right where it lives, without moving the data into separate analytics systems. It is possible even to query data from multiple sources within a single query. It supports both relational data sources (such as

PostgreSQL, MySQL, Microsoft SQL Server, Amazon Redshift, Teradata, etc.) and non-relational data sources (such as HDFS (Hadoop Distributed File System), MongoDB, Cassandra, HBase, Amazon S3, etc.).

Companies using Presto: *Repro, Netflix, Facebook, Airbnb, GrubHub, Nordstrom, Nasdaq, Atlassian*, etc.

Characteristic features :

1. With Presto, you can query data wherever it resides, whether it is in Cassandra, Hive, Relational databases, or even proprietary data stores.
2. With Presto, multiple data sources can be queried at once. This allows you to reference data from multiple databases in one query.
3. It does not rely on MapReduce techniques and is capable of retrieving data very quickly within seconds to minutes. Query responses are typically returned within a few seconds.
4. Presto supports standard ANSI SQL, making it easy to use. The ability to query your data without learning a dedicated language is always a big plus, whether you're a developer or a data analyst. Additionally, it connects easily to the most common BI (Business Intelligence) tools with JDBC (Java Database Connectivity) connectors.

(4) MapReduce

We have already studied this technology in chapter 7 of this book. It is because of MapReduce that it is possible to deal with the volume aspect of Big Data as it employs parallel and distributed algorithms to apply logic to the huge data. Thus MapReduce that plays a crucial role in transforming the otherwise unmanageable data into a manageable structure. The word MapReduce is a portmanteau, as the word represents a combination of two methodologies – Map and Reduce. While Map is responsible for sorting and filtering data, Reduce is pivotal for summarizing and aggregating data.

(5) Apache PIG

We have already studied PIG in chapter 10 of this book. Developed by Yahoo, PIG works on a query-based language known as Pig Latin which is similar to SQL and is used for structuring, processing, and analyzing big data. It provides ease of programming as it allows the user to create their own custom functions while translating them into MapReduce program in the background.

(6) RapidMiner

It can perform a range of functions from ETL to data mining and even predictive modeling and machine learning. RapidMiner is a useful tool as it helps in solving problems faced in business analytics, supports multiple languages, and provides the users with a simple user interactive interface. It is open-source which is one of its biggest advantages as even while being open-sourced it is still generally considered secure.

(7) Apache Storm : Storm is an open-source, scalable distributed real-time computational framework. Based on Clojure and Java, it helps in dealing with processing unbounded streams of data. See also 18……

(8) Flink : We have already studied about Flink in section 18.13. of this chapter. Apache Flink is designed to deal with both unbounded and bounded streams of data. While bounded data has a definite start and end, its processing is also equated to batch processing. As a result, Flink is a highly scalable distributed processing engine. You can use Flink with data pipelines and data analytics applications. See also 18.13

18.14.3 Data Visualization Based Big Data Tools

Data visualization is a way of visualizing data through a graphic representation. Data visualization techniques utilize visual elements such as graphs, charts, and maps to provide an easy way of viewing and interpreting trends, patterns, and outliers in data. Data is processed to create graphic illustrations that enable people to grasp large amounts of information in seconds. Below are a few top technologies for data visualization.

(1) Tableau

A powerful data visualization tool, Tableau can now be integrated with spreadsheets and even with big data platforms, cloud, relational databases, etc., providing quick insights from raw data. As it is a secure proprietary tool that even allows sharing of dashboards in real-time, the popularity of this tool is ever increasing.

In the business intelligence and analytics industry, Tableau is the fastest growing tool for Data Visualization. It makes it easy for users to create graphs, charts, maps, and dashboards, for visualizing and analyzing data, thus aiding them in driving the business forward. Using this platform, data is rapidly analyzed, resulting in interactive dashboards and worksheets that display the results. With Tableau, users are able to work on live datasets, obtaining valuable insights and enhancing decision-making. You don't need any programming knowledge to get started; even those without relevant experience can create visualizations with Tableau right away.

Companies using Tableau: Accenture, Myntra, Nike, Skype, Coca-Cola, Wells Fargo, Citigroup, Qlik, etc

Characteristic features :

1. In Tableau, a user can easily create visualizations in the form of Bar charts, Pie charts, Histograms, Treemaps, Box plots, Gantt charts, Bullet charts, and other tools.
2. Tableau supports a wide array of data sources, including on-premise files, CSV, Text files, Excel, spreadsheets, relational and non-relational databases, cloud data, and big data.\
3. Some of Tableau's significant features include data blending and real-time analytics.
4. It allows real-time sharing of data in the form of dashboards, sheets, etc.

(2) Plotly

Plotly is a library that allows the user to create interactive dashboards. It provides API libraries for all the common languages including Python, R MATLAB, and Julia. For example, Plotly Dash is something that helps in creating interactive graphs easily using python.

Plotly is a Python library that facilitates interactive visualizations of big data. This tool makes it possible to create superior graphs more quickly and efficiently. Plotly has many advantages, including user-friendliness, scalability, reduced costs, cutting-edge analytics, and flexibility. It offers a much richer set of libraries and APIs, including Python, R, MATLAB, Arduino, Julia, etc. It can be used interactively within Jupyter notebooks and Pycharm in order to create interactive graphs. With Plotly, we can include interactive features such as buttons, sliders, and dropdowns to display different perspectives on a graph.

Companies using Plotly: *Paladins, Bitbank,* etc.

Characteristic features :

1. A unique feature of Plotly is its interactivity. Users can interact with graphs on display, providing an enhanced storytelling experience.
2. It's like drawing on paper, you can draw anything you want. When compared with other visualization tools like Tableau, Plotly enables full control over what is being plotted.
3. Additionally to Seaborn and Matplotlib charts, Plotly also offers a wide range of graphs, and charts, such as Statistical Charts, Scientific Charts, Financial Charts, geographical maps, and so forth.
4. Furthermore, Plotly offers a broad range of AI and ML charts, which allow you to step up your machine learning game.

18.14.4 Emerging Big Data Technologies and Tools

There are a number of latest big data technologies that are going to be in high demand. This makes it highly important for data science aspirants, especially those who want to build a career in big data, to understand these latest big data technologies and know at least the basics of them. Previously, we covered 16 important big data analytics tools in our blog. Along with those, here are a few more that need your attention.

(1) **Docker :** Docker allows the users to build, test, deploy and run their applications. It uses the concept of containers which is a mechanism for dividing the software into standardized units. It helps the user to package their application such that all aspects of the application such as dependent libraries, system tools, etc are all in one place. Docker helps to standardize the application operations, cut costs and increase the reliability of the whole deployment process.

(2) **TensorFlow :** The use of AI is trending in Big Data and one of the leading tools in this race is TensorFlow, an ecosystem of recourses, modules, and tools in itself. TensorFlow can be used to create Machine Learning and Deep Learning models that can be applied to Big Data.

(3) **Apache Beam :** It is used for creating Parallel data processing pipelines. This helps in simplifying large-scale data processing. The user has to build a program defining the pipeline, and these programs can be written in Java, Python, Go, etc.

(4) **Kubernetes :** This big data tool helps the user to automate, deploy and scale containerized applications across clusters of hosts. Container applications deployed in the cloud can easily be tracked by using Kubernetes.

(5) **Blockchain :** This Big Data technology helps in creating encrypted blocks of data and chains them together making the transaction of digit currency such as bitcoin extremely secure. Blockchain's potential application in the world of big data is huge – so much that the BFSI domain is all set to encompass the benefits of implementing it.

(6) **Airflow :** Apache Airflow is a scheduling and pipeline tool. It helps in scheduling and managing complex data pipelines stemming from various sources. In this tool Directed Acyclic Graphs (DAG) are used to represent these workflows. Airflow helps make and handle the data pipelines, which makes ML models become more accurate and efficient.

18.14.5 Miscellaneous Big Data Tools

1. KNIME :

KNIME (Short for Konstanz Information Miner) is a free, open-source platform for analytics, reporting, and integration of large sets of data. In addition to being intuitive and open, KNIME actively incorporates new ideas and developments to make understanding data and developing data science workflows and reusable components as easy and accessible as possiBased on Java, this big data tool helps the user in workflow and data analytics by using sophisticated data mining techniques, data extraction using SQL style queries, predictive analytics, etc. It also has the capability to connect to the common Hadoop distributions and use machine learning algorithms via MLlib integration.ble. KNIME allows users to visually create and design data flows (or pipelines), execute analysis steps selectively, and analyze the results and models later using interactive views and widgets. As part of the core version, there are hundreds of modules for integration, data transformations (such as filters, converters, splitters, combiners, and joiners), as well as methods used for analytics, statistics, data mining, and text analytics.

Companies using KNIME: *Fiserv, Opplane, Procter & Gamble, Eaton Corporation*, etc.

Characteristic features :

1. Additional Plugins are added via its Extension mechanism in order to extend functionality.
2. Furthermore, additional plugins provide integration of methods for image mining, text mining, time-series analysis, and network analysis.
3. The KNIME workflows can serve as data sets for creating report templates that can be exported to a variety of file formats, including doc, pdf, ppt, xls, etc.
4. Additionally, KNIME integrates a variety of open-source projects such as machine learning algorithms from Spark, Weka, Keras, LIBSVM, and R projects; as well as ImageJ, JFreeChart, and the Chemistry Development Kit.
5. You can perform simple ETL operations with it.

(2) Splunk

This big data tool is used to provide quick insights into the data. The user can access Hadoop clusters from virtual indexes, and connect to tools such as Tableau and different databases including Oracle, MYSQL, etc. It helps in dealing with real-time streaming data by helping the user in indexing, capturing, and correlating such data. Additionally, the users can easily gain insights by generating reports, graphs dashboards, etc.

Splunk is a scalable, advanced software platform that searches, analyzes, and visualizes machine-generated data from websites, applications, sensors, devices, etc., in order to provide metrics, diagnose problems, and gain insight into business operations. In Splunk, real-time data is captured, indexed, and correlated into a searchable repository, which can be used to generate Reports, Alerts, Graphs, Dashboards, and Visualizations. In addition to application management, security, and compliance, Splunk also provides web analytics and business intelligence. The advent of big data makes Splunk capable of ingesting big data from a variety of sources, which may or may not include machine data, and performing analytics on it.

Companies using Splunk: *JPMorgan Chase, Lenovo, Wells Fargo, Verizon, BookMyShow, John Lewis, Domino's, Porsche, etc.*

Characteristic features :

1. Improve the performance of your business with automated operations, advanced analytics, and end-to-end integrations.
2. In addition to structured data formats like JSON and XML, Splunk can ingest unstructured machine data like web and application logs.
3. Splunk indexes the ingested data to enable faster search and querying based on different conditions.
4. Splunk provides analytical reports including interactive graphs, charts, and tables, as well as allows sharing them with other people.

3. **Apache Sqoop :** This tool is used to move big data to structured data stores such as MYSQL, Oracle from Apache Hadoop, and vice-a-versa. It provides connectors for all the major RDBMS.
4. **QlikView :** A highly powerful BI tool, QlikView helps in generating quick and detailed insights from big data. It has a simple, straightforward user interface helping the user to simply click on data points and perform unrestricted data analytics. It helps in identifying the relationship between features in datasets or among datasets and uses associative data modeling.
5. **Qlik Sense :** Similar to QlikView, Qlik Sense has a drag and drop User Interface that helps users to create story-based reports quickly.
6. **Hunk :** Hunk is a Big Data tool that helps explore, analyze, and visualize data in the Hadoop Ecosystem. It allows for drag and Drops analytics, a rich developer environment, customer dashboards, integrated analytics, and fast deployment. In order to analyze the data, it uses the Splunk Search Processing Language.
7. **Platfora :** It is a subscription-based big data tool that helps in Big Data Analytics. It is an interactive tool that helps the user with raw data and early identification of patterns.

References

[1] Apache Spark - RDD,https://www.tutorialspoint.com/apache_spark/apache_spark_rdd.htm

[2] Thulasiraman, K.; Swamy, M. N. S. (1992), "5.7 Acyclic Directed Graphs", Graphs: Theory and Algorithms, John Wiley and Son, p. 118, ISBN 978-0-471-51356-8

[3] Wikipedia, Apache Spark, https://en.wikipedia.org/wiki/Apache_Spark

[4] "Spark 2.2.0 Quick Start". apache.org. 2017-07-11. Retrieved 2017-10-19.

[5] "Applying the Lambda Architecture with Spark, Kafka, and Cassandra | Pluralsight". www.pluralsight.com.

[6] "MLlib | Apache Spark". spark.apache.org. Retrieved 2016-01-18.

[7] Malak, Michael (1 July 2016). Spark GraphX in Action. Manning. p. 89. ISBN 9781617292521.

[8] What is Kafka Streams: A Comprehensive Guide 101, Aman Sharma on ETL

[9] What is Apache Flink? — Architecture,https://flink.apache.org/flink-architecture.html

CHAPTER

19

Apache and Cloudera Impala

19.1 HADOOP AND IMPALA

Hadoop has continued to grow and develop ever since it was introduced in the market 10 years ago. Every new release and abstraction on Hadoop is used to improve one or the other drawback in data processing, storage and analysis. Apache Hive was introduced by Facebook to manage and process the large datasets in the distributed storage in Hadoop. Apache Hive is an abstraction on Hadoop Map Reduce and has its own SQL like language HiveQL. Cloudera Impala was developed to resolve the limitations posed by the low interaction of Hadoop Sql. Cloudera Impala provides low latency high-performance SQL-like queries to process and analyze data with only one condition that the data be stored on Hadoop clusters.

Data explosion in the past decade has not disappointed big data enthusiasts one bit. It has thrown up a number of challenges and created new industries which require continuous improvements and innovations in the way we leverage technology.

There two prominent Impala type:

1. Apache Impala
2. Cloudera Impala

19.2 APCHE IMPALA

Apache Impala is a query engine that runs on Apache Hadoop. Apache Impala is an open source massively parallel processing (MPP) SQL query engine for data stored in a computer cluster running Apache Hadoop.[1]

Impala brings scalable parallel database technology to Hadoop, enabling users to issue low-latency SQL queries to data stored in HDFS and Apache HBase without requiring data movement or transformation. Impala is integrated with Hadoop to use the same file and data formats, metadata, security and resource management frameworks used by MapReduce, Apache Hive, Apache Pig and other Hadoop software.

Impala is promoted for analysts and data scientists to perform analytics on data stored in Hadoop via SQL or business intelligence tools. The result is that large-scale data processing (via MapReduce) and interactive queries can be done on the same system using the same data and metadata – removing the need to migrate data sets into specialized systems and/or proprietary formats simply to perform analysis.

19.2.1 Architecture

To avoid latency, Impala circumvents MapReduce to directly access the data through a specialized distributed query engine that is very similar to those found in commercial parallel RDBMSs. The result is order-of-magnitude faster performance than Hive, depending on the type of query and configuration.

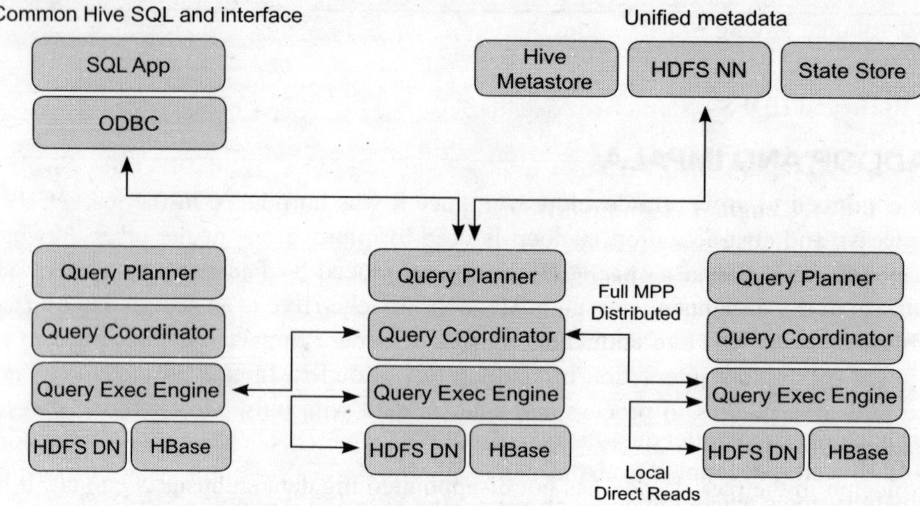

Figure. 19.1: Architecture of Apache Impala

There are many advantages to this approach over alternative approaches for querying Hadoop data, including:

1. Thanks to local processing on data nodes, network bottlenecks are avoided.
2. A single, open, and unified metadata store can be utilized.
3. Costly data format conversion is unnecessary and thus no overhead is incurred.
4. All data is immediately query-able, with no delays for ETL.
5. All hardware is utilized for Impala queries as well as for MapReduce.
6. Only a single machine pool is needed to scale.

19.2.2 Working with Apache Hadoop

The Impala solution is composed of the following components:

1. **Clients** - Entities including Hue, ODBC clients, JDBC clients, and the Impala Shell can all interact with Impala. These interfaces are typically used to issue queries or complete administrative tasks such as connecting to Impala.

2. **Hive Metastore** - Stores information about the data available to Impala. For example, the metastore lets Impala know what databases are available and what the structure of those databases is. As you create, drop, and alter schema objects, load data into tables, and so on through Impala SQL statements, the relevant metadata changes are automatically broadcast to all Impala nodes by the dedicated catalog service introduced in Impala 1.2.

3. **Impala** - This process, which runs on DataNodes, coordinates and executes queries. Each instance of Impala can receive, plan, and coordinate queries from Impala clients. Queries are distributed among Impala nodes, and these nodes then act as workers, executing parallel query fragments.

   HBase and HDFS - Storage for data to be queried.

19.3 CLOUDERA IMPALA

Step aside, the SQL engines claiming to do parallel processing! Impala's open source Massively Parallel Processing (MPP) SQL engine is here, armed with all the power to push you aside. The only condition it needs is data be stored in a cluster of computers running Apache Hadoop, which, given Hadoop's dominance in data warehousing, isn't uncommon. Cloudera Impala was announced on the world stage in October 2012 and after a successful beta run, was made available to the general public in May 2013.[2]

19.3.1 Architecture

Impala is a massively-parallel query execution engine, which runs on hundreds of machines in existing Hadoop clusters. It is decoupled from the underlying storage engine, unlike traditional relational database management systems where the query processing and the underlying storage engine are components of a single tightly-coupled system. Impala's high-level architecture is shown in Figure 19.2.

An Impala deployment is comprised of three services. The Impala daemon (**impalad**) service is dually responsible for accepting queries from client processes and orchestrating their execution across the cluster, and for executing individual query fragments on behalf of other Impala daemons. When an Impala daemon operates in the first role by managing query execution, it is said to be the coordinator for that query.

However, all Impala daemons are symmetric; they may all operate in all roles. This property helps with fault-tolerance, and with load-balancing.

One Impala daemon is deployed on every machine in the cluster that is also running a data node process - the block server for the underlying HDFS deployment - and therefore there is typically one Impala daemon on every machine. This allows Impala to take advantage of data locality, and to read blocks from the filesystem without having to use the network.

The Statestore daemon (statestored) is Impala's metadata publish-subscribe service, which disseminates clusterwide metadata to all Impala processes.

Finally, the Catalog daemon (catalogd), serves as Impala's catalog repository and metadata access gateway. Through the catalogd, Impala daemons may execute DDL commands that are reflected in external catalog stores such as the Hive Metastore. Changes to the system catalog are broadcast via the statestore.

All these Impala services, as well as several configuration options, such as the sizes of the resource pools, the available memory, etc. (see Section 6 for more details about resource and workload management) are also exposed to Cloudera Manager, a sophisticated cluster management application.

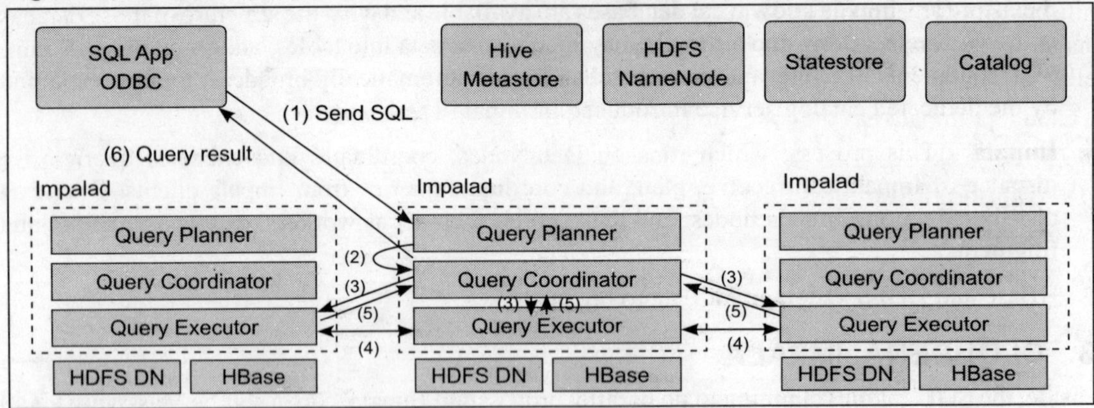

Figure. 19.2: Impala is a distributed query processing system for the Hadoop ecosystem. This figure also shows the flow during query processing.

19.3.3 Handling Queries

Queries executed using Impala are handled as follows:

1. User applications send SQL queries to Impala through ODBC or JDBC, which provide standardized querying interfaces. The user application may connect to any impalad in the cluster. This impalad becomes the coordinator for the query.
2. Impala parses the query and analyzes it to determine what tasks need to be performed by impalad instances across the cluster. Execution is planned for optimal efficiency.
3. Services such as HDFS and HBase are accessed by local impalad instances to provide data.
4. Each impalad returns data to the coordinating impalad, which sends these results to the client.

Impala daemon (also known as impalad) runs on each node where Impala is installed. It accepts the queries from various interfaces like impala shell, hue browser, etc.… and processes them. Whenever a query is submitted to an impalad on a particular node, that node serves as a "coordinator node" for that query.

Whenever a query is submitted to an impalad on a particular node, that node serves as a "coordinator node" for that query. Multiple queries are served by Impalad running on other nodes as well. After accepting the query, Impalad reads and writes to data files and parallelizes the queries by distributing the work to the other Impala nodes in the Impala cluster. When queries are processing on various Impalad instances, all of them return the result to the central coordinating node. Depending on the requirement, queries can be submitted to a dedicated Impalad or in a load balanced manner to another Impalad in your cluster.

Cloudera Impala is an excellent choice for programmers for running queries on HDFS and Apache HBase as it doesn't require data to be moved or transformed prior to processing. Cloudera Impala easily integrates with the Hadoop ecosystem, as its file and data formats, metadata, security and resource management frameworks are the same as those used by MapReduce, Apache Hive, Apache Pig, and other Hadoop software. It is architected specifically to assimilate the strengths of Hadoop and the familiarity of SQL support and multi-user performance of the traditional database. Its unified resource management across frameworks has made it the de facto standard for open-source interactive business intelligence tasks.

Cloudera Impala has the following two technologies that give other processing languages a run for their money:

(1) Columnar Storage

Data is stored in a columnar fashion which achieves a high compression ratio and efficient scanning.

The main benefit of a columnar database is faster performance compared to a row-oriented one. That's because it accesses less memory to output data. Because a columnar database stores data by columns instead of rows, it can store more data in a smaller amount of memory. While a relational database is optimized for storing rows of data, typically for transactional applications, a columnar database is optimized for fast retrieval of columns of data, typically in analytical applications.

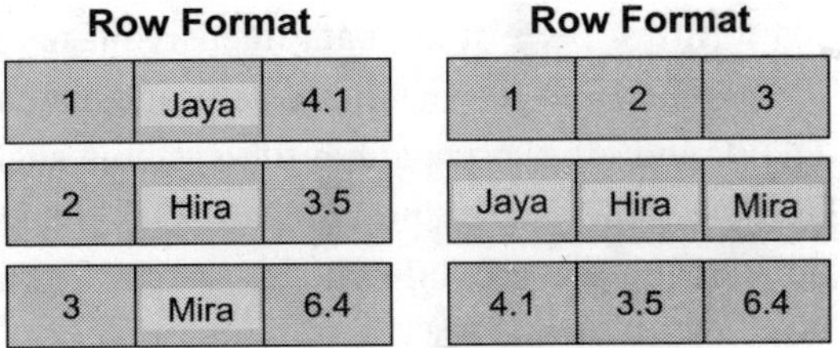

Figure. 19.3: Storing data in columnar fashion

(2) Tree Architecture

This is fundamental to attaining a massively parallel distributed multi–level serving tree for pushing down a query to the tree and then aggregating the results from the leaves.

Impala vs Hive -Apache Hive is a data warehouse infrastructure built on Hadoop whereas Cloudera Impala is open source analytic MPP database for Hadoop.[2]

Impala massively improves on the performance parameters as it eliminates the need to migrate huge

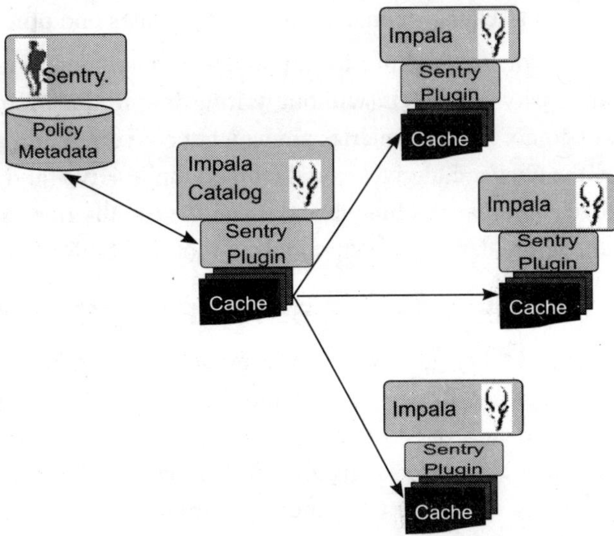

Figure. 19.4 : Massively Parallel data handling structure of Impala (Image Credit:cwiki.apache.org)

data sets to dedicated processing systems or convert data formats prior to analysis. Salient features of Impala include:

1. Hadoop Distributed File System (HDFS) and Apache HBase storage support
2. Recognizes Hadoop file formats, text, LZO, SequenceFile, Avro, RCFile, and Parquet
3. Supports Hadoop Security (Kerberos authentication)
4. Fine – grained, role-based authorization with Apache Sentry
5. Can easily read metadata, ODBC driver, and SQL syntax from Apache Hive
6. Impala's rise within a short span of a little over 2 years can be gauged from the fact that Amazon Web Services and MapR have both added support for it.

19.3.3 Apache Hive

Initially developed by Facebook, Apache Hive is a data warehouse infrastructure build over Hadoop platform for performing data intensive tasks such as querying, analysis, processing and visualization. [2]Apache Hive is versatile in its usage as it supports the analysis of large datasets stored in Hadoop's HDFS and other compatible file systems such as Amazon S3. To keep the traditional database query designers interested, it provides an SQL – like language (HiveQL) with schema on read and transparently converts queries to MapReduce, Apache Tez and Spark jobs. Other features of Hive include:

19.3.4 Indexing for Accelerated Processing

Support for different storage types such as plain text, RCFile, HBase, ORC, and others Metadata storage in RDBMS, bringing downtime to perform semantic checks during query execution Has SQL like queries that get implicitly converted into MapReduce, Tez or Spark jobs Familiar built-in user-defined functions (UDFs) to manipulate strings, dates and other data – mining tools.

If you are looking for an advanced analytics language which would allow you to leverage your familiarity with SQL (without writing MapReduce jobs separately) then Apache Hive is definitely the way to go. HiveQL queries anyway get converted into a corresponding MapReduce job which executes on the cluster and gives you the final output. Hive (and its underlying SQL like language HiveQL) does have its limitations though and if you have really fine-grained, complex processing requirements at hand you would definitely want to take a look at MapReduce.

19.4 DIFFERENCE BETWEEN HIVE AND IMPALA

Hive is written in Java. Hive provides a SQL-like interface to allow querying of data from various databases and file systems within the Hadoop ecosystem. SQL queries have to be implemented in the MapReduce Java API to allow querying of the data. Hive provides an SQL abstraction to perform SQL-like queries(known as HiveQL) in Java without having to implement queries in the low-level Java API. Impala is written in C++ and Java. Impala uses the same syntax as Hive and provides the necessary abstraction to perform SQL-like queries without worrying about the low-level APIs in Java or C++, which run the query execution.[2]

19.4.1 Hive vs Impala - Performance

Hive is built over MapReduce and hence is slower than Impala for less complex queries due to many I/O operations that have to run, for single query execution. Hence, Hive is primarily used for batch processing and ETLs (extract, transform, load). Hive is better able to handle longer-running, more complex queries on much larger datasets. Since Impala is not built over the MapReduce algorithms, the latency is reduced allowing Impala to run faster than Hive. Impala supports in-memory data processing, which means that it accessed data that is stored on the Hadoop data nodes without movement of data. Impala has a very efficient run-time execution framework, inter-process communication, parallel processing and metadata caching.

Impala has been shown to have a performance lead over Hive by benchmarks of both Cloudera (Impala's vendor) and AMPLab. Benchmarks have been observed to be notorious about biasing due to minor software tricks and hardware settings. However, it is worthwhile to take a deeper look at this constantly observed difference. The following reasons come to the fore as possible causes:

1. Cloudera Impala being a native query language, avoids startup overhead which is commonly seen in MapReduce/Tez based jobs (MapReduce programs take time before all nodes are running at full capacity). In Hive, every query has this problem of "cold start" whereas Impala daemon processes are started at boot time itself, always being ready to process a query.
2. Hadoop reuses JVM instances to reduce startup overhead partially but introduces another problem when large haps are in use. Cloudera benchmark have 384 GB memory which is a big challenge for the garbage collector of the reused JVM instances.
3. MapReduce materializes all intermediate results, which enables better scalability and fault tolerance (while slowing down data processing). Impala streams intermediate results between executors (trading off scalability).
4. Hive generates query expressions at compile time whereas Impala does runtime code generation for "big loops".
5. Apache Hive might not be ideal for interactive computing whereas Impala is meant for interactive computing.
6. Hive is batch based Hadoop MapReduce whereas Impala is more like MPP database.
7. Hive supports complex types but Impala does not.
8. Apache Hive is fault-tolerant whereas Impala does not support fault tolerance. When a hive query is run and if the DataNode goes down while the query is being executed, the output of the query will be produced as Hive is fault tolerant. However, that is not the case with Impala. If a query execution fails in Impala it has to be started all over again.

Hive transforms SQL queries into Apache Spark or Apache Hadoop jobs making it a good choice for long-running ETL jobs for which it is desirable to have fault tolerance because developers do not want to re-run a long-running job after executing it for several hours.

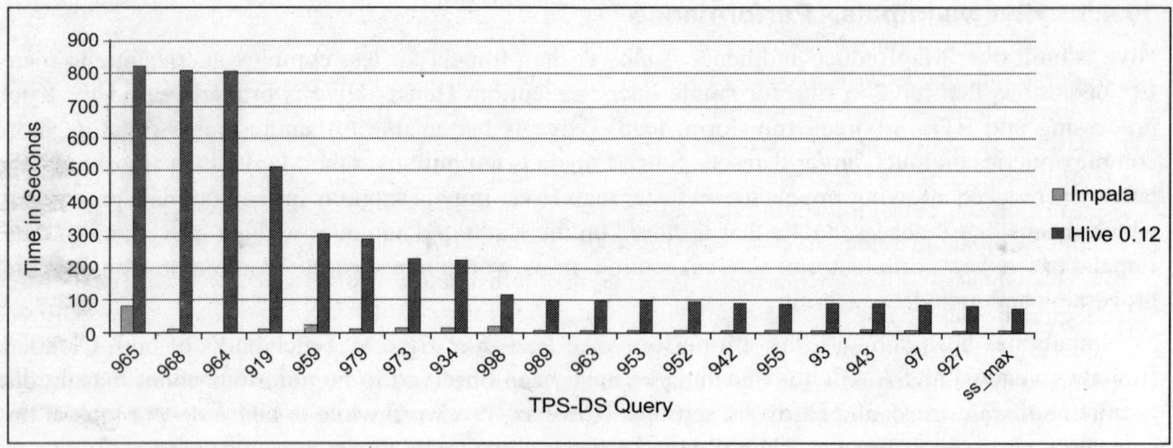

Figure. 19.5 : Time taken for handling queries (Image Credit : csdn.net)

Database benchmarking is a proven and clearly defined method for analysing and comparing the performance characteristics of databases or database management systems (DBMS). Performance and scalability is a hot topic in IT. Data-driven applications and cloud infrastructures are current challenges for databases.

TPC-DS is a decision support benchmark that models several generally applicable aspects of a decision support system, including queries and data maintenance. The benchmark provides a representative evaluation of performance as a general purpose decision support system.

The above graph demonstrates that Cloudera Impala is 6 to 69 times faster than Apache Hive.[2] To conclude, Impala does have a number of performance-related advantages over Hive but it also depends upon the kind of task at hand. That being said, Jamie Thomson has found some really interesting results through dumb querying published on sqlblog.com, especially in terms of execution time. For all its performance related advantages Impala does have few serious issues to consider. Being written in C/C++, it will not understand every format, especially those written in java. If you are starting something fresh then Cloudera Impala would be the way to go but when you have to take up an upgradation project where compatibility becomes as important a factor as (or may be more important than) speed, Apache Hive would nudge ahead.

In practical terms, Apache Hive and Cloudera Impala need not necessarily be competitors. As both-Hive Hadoop, Impala have a MapReduce foundation for executing queries, there can be scenarios where you are able to use them together and get the best of both worlds – compatibility and performance. Hive is the more universal, versatile, and pluggable language. Once data integration and storage has been done, Cloudera Impala can be called upon to unleash its brute processing power and give lightning-fast analytic results.

19.4.2 Hive Vs Impala - Use cases

Apache Impala, supported by the Cloudera Enterprise, was primarily designed for speed. [2] It is written in C++, a CPU-efficient language that allows fast query execution and metadata caching. Impala is optimized to execute queries at low latency. Impala has also been designed with a very efficient execution framework at run-time, as it makes use of code generation, inter-process communication, massive support for parallelism and performs metadata caching. This makes the query engine impala a perfect choice to work on a data mart. A data mart is a subset of a data warehouse that is focused on a specific functional area of an organization. Data warehouses span the entire enterprise, whereas data marts are usually specific to a line of business or a particular department. Due to Impala's efficient run-time execution framework, Impala is a good choice for working with ad-hoc queries and allows exploring the data in an iterative manner. Even if the query is changed several times at a moment's notice, Impala provides a very speedy response time.

Apache Hive was primarily built to handle sophistication. This makes it a little more difficult for beginners to get comfortable with it. However, Hive is very effective when it comes to running complex queries, possibly requiring heavy transformations and/or multiple joins. The latency in Hive is higher since queries take longer to execute since queries go through planning and ramp-up prior to execution. Hive is also very fault-tolerant. If a part of a long-running query fails, Hive will ensure that this part of the query is reassigned and tried again. Hive supports query federation, where queries are allowed to run across several components and databases. Due to the level of sophistication provided by Hive, it is a good choice for the implementation of data warehouses or for EDW (enterprise data warehouse) use cases. EDWs generally demand workloads that require taking multiple dimensions into consideration. In many cases, EDWs are required to process queries that are much more complex than those processed by data marts. These queries involve complex data types, scheduled queries, and orchestration of queries for regular data extraction and to populate data marts. Hive is better able to handle complex queries and longer-running queries on large-scale datasets. Hive's latency is not suitable for ad-hoc queries or for interactive computing, as its latency may slow the queries down when compared to Impala.

19.4.3 Hive Vs Impala v/s Spark

Table 19.1 provides comparison of three big data storage and retrieval Technologies based on certain parameters.

Table 19.1 : Comparison of three big data storage and retrieval Technologies.

	Apache Hive	Cloudera Impala	Apache Spark SQL
Latency	Hive is built on Hadoop's MapReduce and hence has a higher latency when it comes to processing queries. Hive was built mainly for sophistication and not speed.	Impala was built primarily for speed and hence has a very low latency.	Spark is a very fast query execution engineer and can run queries upto 10-100 faster than MapReduce.
Throughput	Among the three, Hive has the lowest throughput.	Among the three, Impala has the highest throughput.	Spark has a higher throughput than Hive, but not as high as that of Impala. Impala's throughput is almost seven times that of Spark.

	Apache Hive	Cloudera Impala	Apache Spark SQL
Use cases	Hive is ideal for situations where multiuser support is required and complex queries which has to span multiple databases are frequently performed.	Impala is best suited for business interactive workloads where a low latency is required, and queries have to be interactive.	Spark SQL is suitable for building Spark pipelines. The data here is primarily used for analytics purposes.
Fault tolerance	Hive can recover from mid-query faults.	Impala is not fault-tolerant. If query execution fails mid-query, then the query has to be executed again.	Spark is able to recover from mid-query faults.
Popularity	As of July 2021, Hive has a total score of 82.68 and is ranked at number 14.	As of July 2021, Impala has a total score of 19.56 and is ranked at number 36.	As of July 2021, Spark SQL has a total score of 21.39 and is ranked at number 34.
Query complexity	Hive is built to handle long running queries which require multiple transformations and joins.	Impala is built to handle shorter queries on large data sets, but due to its low latency, it is ideal for interactive computing.	Spark provides support for both short and long running queries.

References

[1] Apache Impala, From Wikipedia, the free encyclopedia,https://en.wikipedia.org/wiki/Apache_Impala

[2] Impala vs Hive: Difference between Sql on Hadoop components,https://www.projectpro.io/article/impala-vs-hive-difference-between-sql-on-hadoop-components/

CHAPTER

20

Summary of other Emerging Big Data Platforms

20.1 EMERGING BIG DATA PLATFORMS

Other Hadoop-related projects at Apache include:

Ambari™: A web-based tool for provisioning, managing, and monitoring Apache Hadoop clusters which includes support for Hadoop HDFS, Hadoop MapReduce, Hive, HCatalog, HBase, ZooKeeper, Oozie, Pig and Sqoop. Ambari also provides a dashboard for viewing cluster health such as heatmaps and ability to view MapReduce, Pig and Hive applications visually alongwith features to diagnose their performance characteristics in a user-friendly manner.

Avro™: Provides data serialization and data exchange services for Apache Hadoop

Cassandra™: A scalable multi-master database with no single points of failure.

Chukwa™: A data collection system for managing large distributed systems.

Flink : Flink is an open-source, unified stream-processing and batch-processing framework developed by the Apache

Flume : Big Data Realtime streaming. Flume is a distributed, reliable, and available service for efficiently collecting, aggregating, and moving large amounts of log data

HBase™: A scalable, distributed database that supports structured data storage for large tables.

Hive™: A data warehouse infrastructure that provides data summarization and ad hoc querying.

Impala : Apache and IBM Cloudera : Models to apply stream flows and analyze massive amounts of data in real-timeunstructured text, video, audio, geospatial and sensor

JASQL : JSON based structured query Language

Kafka : Kafka is a popular open-source event store and streaming platform

Knox : Apache Knox Gateway effectively hides the Hadoop cluster topology details and integrates with Enterprise LDAP and Kerberos.

Mahout™: A Scalable machine learning and data mining library.

Map reduce : MapReduce that plays a crucial role in transforming the otherwise unmanageable data into a manageable structure.

Ozone™: A scalable, redundant, and distributed object store for Hadoop.

Pig™: A high-level data-flow language and execution framework for parallel computation.

Phonix : Apache Phoenix takes your SQL query, compiles it into a series of HBase scans, and orchestrates the running of those scans to produce regular JDBC result sets.

Runger : Apache Ranger is a framework to enable, monitor, and manage comprehensive data security across the Hadoop platform.

Spark™: A fast and general compute engine for Hadoop data. Spark provides a simple and expressive programming model that supports a wide range of applications, including ETL, machine learning, stream processing, and graph computation.

Scoop : Importing Data from Heterogenous Sources

Storm : Storm is the stream processing engine for processing real-time streaming data

Submarine: A unified AI platform which allows engineers and data scientists to run Machine Learning and Deep Learning workload in distributed cluster.

Tez™: A generalized data-flow programming framework, built on Hadoop YARN, which provides a powerful and flexible engine to execute an arbitrary DAG of tasks to process data for both batch and interactive use-cases. Tez is being adopted by Hive™, Pig™ and other frameworks in the Hadoop ecosystem, and also by other commercial software (e.g. ETL tools), to replace Hadoop™ MapReduce as the underlying execution engine.

Thrift : Thrift is an interface definition language and binary communication protocol used for defining and creating services for numerous programming languages.

ZooKeeper™: A high-performance coordination service for distributed applications.

20.2 APACHE AMBARI

Apache Ambari is a tool for provisioning, managing, and monitoring Apache Hadoop clusters. Ambari consists of a set of RESTful APIs and a browser-based management interface.

Ambari enables System Administrators to:

1. Provision a Hadoop Cluster
2. Ambari provides an easy-to-use, step-by-step wizard for installing Hadoop services across any number of hosts.
3. Ambari handles configuration of Hadoop services for the cluster.
4. Manage a Hadoop Cluster
5. Ambari provides central management for starting, stopping, and reconfiguring Hadoop services across the entire cluster.

20.2.1 Monitor a Hadoop Cluster

Ambari provides a dashboard for monitoring health and status of the Hadoop cluster.

Ambari will send emails when your attention is needed (e.g., a node goes down, remaining disk space is low, etc).

Apache Ambari is an open-source administration tool deployed on top of Hadoop clusters, and it is responsible for keeping track of the running applications and. Apache Ambari can be referred to as a web-based management tool that manages, monitors, and provisions the health of Hadoop clusters.

It provides a highly interactive dashboard that allows administrators to visualize the progress and status of every application running over the Hadoop cluster. [1]

Its flexible and scalable user interface allows a range of tools such as Pig, MapReduce, Hive, etc. to be installed on the cluster and administers their performances in a user-friendly fashion. Some of the key features of this technology can be highlighted as:

1. Instantaneous insight into the health of the Hadoop cluster using preconfigured operational metrics
2. User-friendly configuration providing an easy step-by-step guide for installation
3. Installation of Apache Ambari is possible through Hortonworks Data Platform (HDP)
4. Monitoring dependencies and performances by visualizing and analyzing jobs and tasks
5. Authentication, authorization, and auditing by installing Kerberos-based Hadoop clusters
6. Flexible and adaptive technology fitting perfectly in the enterprise environment

ZooKeeper performs similar kinds of tasks. But, there is a huge difference between tasks performed by these two technologies if looked closely. The Table 20.1 provides comparison between the two.

Table 20.1 : Comparison between Apache Ambari and Apache ZooKeeper

Difference	Apache Ambari	Apache ZooKeeper
Basic Task	Monitoring, provisioning, and managing Hadoop clusters	Maintaining configuration information, naming, and synchronizing clusters
Nature	Web interface	Open-source server
Status Maintenance	Status maintained through APIs	Status maintained through znodes

As an Apache Ambari Administrator, you will be creating and managing Ambari users and groups.

The genesis of Apache Ambari traces back to the emergence of Hadoop when its distributed and scalable computing took the world by storm. Since the inception of Hadoop, more and more technologies were incorporated into its existing infrastructure. Gradually, Hadoop got overloaded, and it became difficult to maintain multi-node clusters and applications simultaneously. That is when Apache Ambari came into the picture to make distributed computing easier.

20.2.2 Apache Ambari Architecture

Ambari provides intuitive and REST APIs that automate operations in the Hadoop cluster. Its consistent and secure interface allows it to be fairly efficient in operational control. Its easy and user-friendly interface efficiently diagnoses the health of the Hadoop cluster using an interactive dashboard.

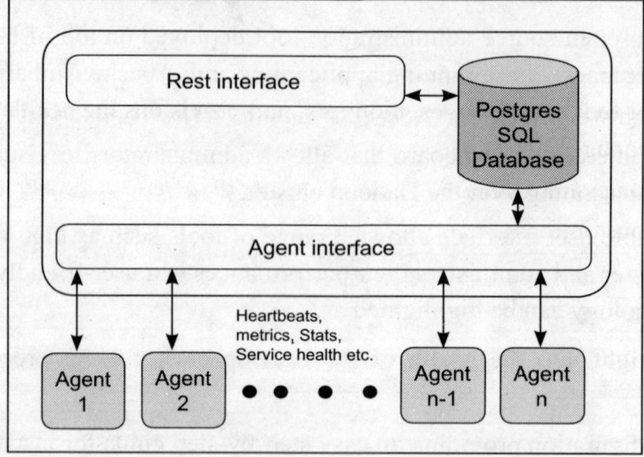

Figure. 20.1: Architecture of Apache Ambari Application

To have a better understanding of how Ambari works, let's look at the detailed architecture of Apache Ambari in the Figure 20.2:

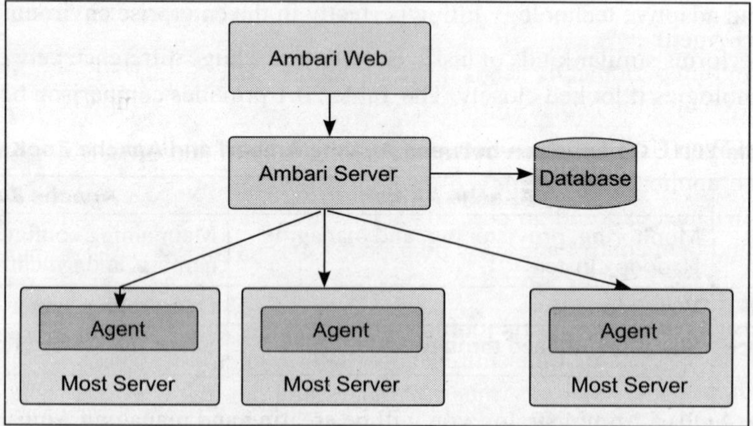

Figure. 20.2: Detailed Architecture of Apache Ambari

20.2.3 Applications of Apache Ambari Core

1. Ambari Server
2. Ambari Agent
3. Ambari Web UI
3. Database

(1) **Ambari Server :** The entry point for all administrative activities on the master server is known as Ambari Server. It is a shell script. Internally, this script uses Python code, ambari-server.py, and routes all requests to it. Ambari Server consists of several entry points that are available when passed different parameters to the Ambari Server program. They are:

1. Daemon management
2. Software upgrade
3. Software setup
4. LDAP (Lightweight Direct Access Protocol)/PAM (Pluggable Authentication Module) / Kerberos management
5. Ambari backup and restore
6. Miscellaneous options

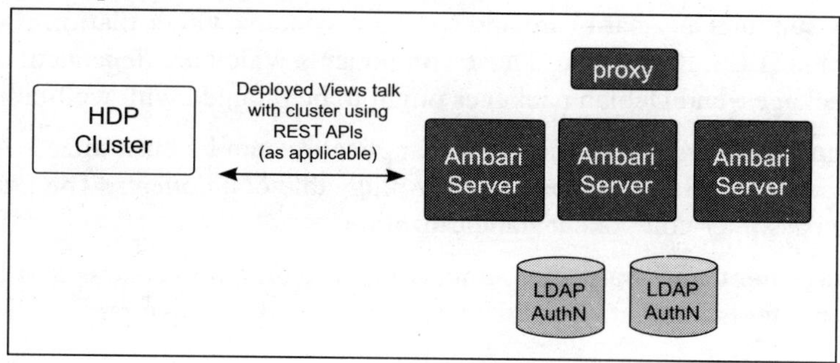

Figure. 20.3 : HDP Cluster

(2) **Ambari Agent :** Ambari Agent runs on all the nodes that you want to manage with Ambari. This program periodically sends heartbeats to the master node. By using Ambari Agent, Ambari Server executes many tasks on the servers.

(3) **Ambari Web User Interface :** Ambari Web UI is one of the powerful features of Apache Ambari. The web application is deployed through the server of Ambari program which is running on the master host exposed on port 8080. This application is protected by authentication. You can access and then control and view all aspects of your Hadoop cluster, once you log in to the web portal.

(4) **Database :** Ambari supports multiple RDBMS (Relational Database Management Systems) to keep track of the state of the entire Hadoop infrastructure. You can choose the database you want to use during the setup of Ambari. Ambari supports these following databases at the time of writing (2022):

1. PostgreSQL
2. Oracle
3. MySQL or MariaDB
4. Embedded PostgreSQL
5. Microsoft SQL Server
6. SQL Anywhere
7. Berkeley DB

This technology is preferred by the Big Data Developers as it is quite handy and comes with a step-by-step guide allowing easy installation on the Hadoop cluster. Its preconfigured key operational metrics provide a quick look into the health of the Hadoop core, i.e., HDFS and MapReduce, along with the additional components such as Hive, HBase, HCatalog, etc. Ambari sets up a centralized security system by incorporating Kerberos and Apache Ranger into the architecture. The RESTful APIs monitor the information and integrate the operational tools. Its user-friendliness and interactivity have made it enter the list of top 10 open-source technologies for the Hadoop cluster.

20.2.4 Features of Apache Ambari

Following are some of the features of Ambari. Read on to understand how the tool is expertly used in the Big Data.

1. **Platform independent:** Apache Ambari runs in Windows, Mac, and many other platforms as it architecturally supports any hardware and software systems. Other platforms on which Ambari runs are Ubuntu, SLES, RHEL, etc. Those components which are dependent on a platform like Yum, RPM packages, and Debian packages ought to be plugged with well-defined interfaces.
2. **Pluggable component:** Any current Ambari application can be customized. Any specific tools and technologies ought to be encapsulated by pluggable components. The goal of pluggability doesn't encompass inter-component standardization.
3. **Version management and upgrade**: Ambari itself maintains versions and hence there is no need for external tools like Git. It is fairly easy to upgrade any Ambari application, or Ambari itself.
4. **Extensibility:** You can extend the functionality of the existing Ambari applications by simply adding different view components.
5. **Failure recovery**: Assume, you are working on an Ambari application and something goes wrong. Then, the system should gracefully recover from it. If you are a Windows user, you can relate to this well. You might have faced this issue while working on a Word file, when suddenly there is a power outage and your system gets switched off. When you turn on the system, there will be an autosaved version of the document as you run the MS Word.
5. **Security:** Apache Ambari comes with robust security, and it can sync with LDAP over the active directory.

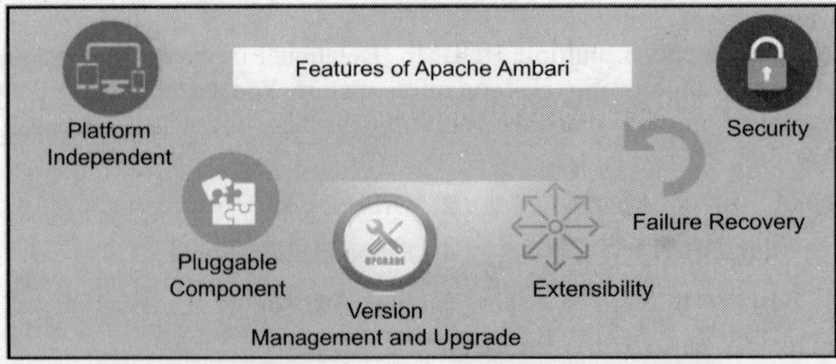

Figure. 20.4 : Various Features of Apache Ambari

20.2.5 Benefits of Using Apache Ambari

This is given with respect to Hortonworks Data Platform (HDP). Ambari eliminates the need for the manual tasks that used to watch over Hadoop operations. It gives a simple and secure platform for provisioning, managing, and monitoring HDP deployments. Ambari is an easy to use Hadoop management UI and is solidly backed by REST APIs. The benefits of using Apache Ambari are mentioned below.

1. **Simplified installation, configuration, and management of the Hadoop cluster**: Ambari can efficiently create Hadoop clusters at scale. Its wizard-driven approach lets the configuration be automated as per the environment so that the performance is optimal. Master–slave and client components are assigned to configuring services. It is also used to install, start, and test the cluster.
2. **Configuration blueprints** give recommendations to those seeking a hands-on approach. The blueprint of an ideal cluster is stored. How it is provisioned is clearly traced. This is then used to automate the creation of successive clusters without any user interaction. Blueprints also preserve and ensure the application of best practices across different environments.
3. **Ambari provides a rolling upgrade feature** where running clusters can be updated on the go with maintenance releases and feature-bearing releases, and therefore there is no unnecessary downtime. When there are large clusters involved, rolling updates are simply not possible, in which case express updates are used. Unlike the previous case, here, there is downtime involved but is minimum as when the update is manual. Both rolling and express updates are free of manual updates.
4. **Centralized security and application:** The complexity of cluster security configuration and administration is greatly reduced by Ambari which is among the components of the Hadoop ecosystem. The tool also helps the automated setup of the advanced security constructs like Kerberos and Ranger.
5. **Complete visibility to your cluster's health**: Through this tool, you can monitor your cluster's health and availability. An easily customized web-based dashboard has metrics that give status information for each service in the cluster like HDFS, YARN, and HBase. The tool also helps with garnering and visualizing critical operational metrics for troubleshooting and analysis. Ambari predefines alerts that are integrated with the existing enterprise monitoring tools that monitor cluster components and hosts as per the specified check intervals. Through the browser interface, users can browse alerts for their clusters, search, and filter alerts. They can also view and modify alert properties and alert instances.
6. **Metrics visualization and dashboarding:** It provides a scalable low-latency storage system for Hadoop component metrics. Picking the metrics of Hadoop which truly matter requires considerable expertise and understanding of how the components work with each other. Grafana is a leading graph and dashboard builder that simplifies the metrics reviewing process. This is included with Ambari Metrics, along with HDP.
7. **Extensibility and customization**: Ambari lets a developer work on Hadoop gracefully in his/her enterprise setup. Ambari leverages the large innovative community which improves upon the tool and it also eliminates vendor lock-in. REST APIs along with Ambari Stacks and Views allows extensive flexibility for customization of HDP implementation.

Ambari Stacks wraps the life cycle control layer used to rationalize operations over a broad set of services. This includes a consistent approach that Ambari uses to manage different types of services like install, start, configure, status, and stop. When provisioning, cluster install experience is rationalized across a set of services by Stacks technology. A natural extension point for operators is provided by Stacks to plug in newly created services that can perform alongside Hadoop.

Third parties can plug in their views through Ambari Views. A view is an application that is deployed into an Ambari container where it offers UI capabilities to be plugged in to give out custom visualization, management, and monitoring features.

20.3 AVRO (BIG DATA)

Avro is an open source project that provides data serialization and data exchange services for Apache Hadoop. These services can be used together or independently. Avro facilitates the exchange of big data between programs written in any language. These services can be used together or independently. Avro facilitates the exchange of big data between programs written in any language. With the serialization service, programs can efficiently serialize data into files or into messages. The data storage is compact and efficient. Avro stores both the data definition and the data together in one message or file. [2]

Avro stores the data definition in JSON format making it easy to read and interpret; the data itself is stored in binary format making it compact and efficient. Avro files include markers that can be used to split large data sets into subsets suitable for Apache MapReduce processing. Some data exchange services use a code generator to interpret the data definition and produce code to access the data. Avro doesn't require this step, making it ideal for scripting languages.

A key feature of Avro is robust support for data schemas that change over time — often called schema evolution. Avro handles schema changes like missing fields, added fields and changed fields; as a result, old programs can read new data and new programs can read old data. Avro includes APIs for Java, Python, Ruby, C, C++ and more. Data stored using Avro can be passed from programs written in different languages, even from a compiled language like C to a scripting language like Apache Pig.

Avro is a row-oriented remote procedure call and data serialization framework developed within Apache's Hadoop project. Its primary use is in Apache Hadoop, where it can provide both a serialization format for persistent data, and a wire format for communication between Hadoop nodes, and from client programs to the Hadoop services.

Avro implementations for C, C++, C#, Java, PHP, Python, and Ruby can be downloaded from the Apache Avro™ Download page.

Avro provides:

1. Rich data structures.
2. A compact, fast, binary data format.
3. A container file, to store persistent data.
4. Remote procedure call (RPC).
5. Simple integration with dynamic languages.

Code generation is not required to read or write data files nor to use or implement RPC protocols. Code generation as an optional optimization, only worth implementing for statically typed languages like *C,C++,C#, Elixir,Go,Haskell,Java,Javascript,Perl,PHP,Python,Ruby,Rust,Scala*. Though theoretically any language could use Avro, the following languages have APIs written for them: [3]

20.3.1 Avro Object Container File

An Avro Object Container File consists of:

1. A file header, followed by
2. one or more file data blocks.

A file header consists of:

1. Four bytes, ASCII 'O', 'b', 'j', followed by the Avro version number which is 1 (0x01) (Binary values 0x4F 0x62 0x6A 0x01).
2. File metadata, including the schema definition.
3. The 16-byte, randomly-generated sync marker for this file.

For data blocks Avro specifies two serialization encodings: binary and JSON. Most applications will use the binary encoding, as it is smaller and faster. For debugging and web-based applications, the JSON encoding may sometimes be appropriate.

20.3.2 Schema Definition

Avro schemas are defined using JSON. Schemas are composed of primitive types (null, boolean, int, long, float, double, bytes, and string) and complex types (record, enum, array, map, union, and fixed).

Example of Simple schema :

```
{
  "namespace": "example.avro",
  "type": "record",
  "name": "User",
  "fields": [
     {"name": "name", "type": "string"},
     {"name": "favorite_number",  "type": ["null", "int"]},
     {"name": "favorite_color", "type": ["null", "string"]}
  ]
}
```

20.3.3 Serializing and Deserializing

Data in Avro might be stored with its corresponding schema, meaning a serialized item can be read without knowing the schema ahead of time.

Example serialization and deserialization code in Python

```
import avro.schema
from avro.datafile import DataFileReader, DataFileWriter
from avro.io import DatumReader, DatumWriter
schema = avro.schema.parse(open(“user.avsc”, “rb”).read())  # need to know the schema to write. According to 1.8.2 of Apache Avro
writer = DataFileWriter(open(“users.avro”, “wb”), DatumWriter(), schema)
writer.append({“name”: “Alyssa”, “favorite_number”: 256})
writer.append({“name”: “Ben”, “favorite_number”: 8, “favorite_color”: “red”})
writer.close()
```

File “users.avro” will contain the schema in JSON and a compact binary representation of the data:

```
$ od -v -t x1z users.avro
0000000 4f 62 6a 01 04 14 61 76 72 6f 2e 63 6f 64 65 63  >Obj...avro.codec<
0000020 08 6e 75 6c 6c 16 61 76 72 6f 2e 73 63 68 65 6d  >.null.avro.schem<
0000040 61 ba 03 7b 22 74 79 70 65 22 3a 20 22 72 65 63  >a..{“type”: “rec<
0000060 6f 72 64 22 2c 20 22 6e 61 6d 65 22 3a 20 22 55  >ord”, “name”: “U<
0000100 73 65 72 22 2c 20 22 6e 61 6d 65 73 70 61 63 65  >ser”, “namespace<
0000120 22 3a 20 22 65 78 61 6d 70 6c 65 2e 61 76 72 6f  >”: “example.avro<
0000140 22 2c 20 22 66 69 65 6c 64 73 22 3a 20 5b 7b 22  >”, “fields”: [{“<
0000160 74 79 70 65 22 3a 20 22 73 74 72 69 6e 67 22 2c  >type”: “string”,<
0000200 20 22 6e 61 6d 65 22 3a 20 22 6e 61 6d 65 22 7d  > “name”: “name”}<
0000220 2c 20 7b 22 74 79 70 65 22 3a 20 5b 22 69 6e 74  >, {“type”: [“int<
0000240 22 2c 20 22 6e 75 6c 6c 22 5d 2c 20 22 6e 61 6d  >”, “null”], “nam<
0000260 65 22 3a 20 22 66 61 76 6f 72 69 74 65 5f 6e 75  >e”: “favorite_nu<
0000300 6d 62 65 72 22 7d 2c 20 7b 22 74 79 70 65 22 3a  >mber”}, {“type”:<
0000320 20 5b 22 73 74 72 69 6e 67 22 2c 20 22 6e 75 6c  > [“string”, “nul<
```

Continued on page 633

```
0000340 6c 22 5d 2c 20 22 6e 61 6d 65 22 3a 20 22 66 61  >l"], "name": "fa<
0000360 76 6f 72 69 74 65 5f 63 6f 6c 6f 72 22 7d 5d 7d  >vorite_color"}]}<
0000400 00 05 f9 a3 80 98 47 54 62 bf 68 95 a2 ab 42 ef  >......GTb.h...B.<
0000420 24 04 2c 0c 41 6c 79 73 73 61 00 80 04 02 06 42  >$.,.Alyssa.....B<
0000440 65 6e 00 10 00 06 72 65 64 05 f9 a3 80 98 47 54  >en....red.....GT<
0000460 62 bf 68 95 a2 ab 42 ef 24                       >b.h...B.$<
0000471
```


References

[1] Introduction to Apache Ambari, https://intellipaat.com/blog/what-is-apache-ambari/

[2] What is Avro?,https://www.ibm.com/in-en/topics/avro

[3] phunt. "GitHub - phunt/avro-rpc-quickstart: Apache Avro RPC Quick Start. Avro is a subproject of Apache Hadoop". GitHub.

Index

OTHER USEFUL BOOKS

DATA STRUCTURES

Theory, Problems and Algorithms

Table of Content

Chapter 1: Introduction to Data Structures, **Chapter 2:** Introduction to Algorithms, **Chapter 3:** Arrays, **Chapter 4:** Linked Lists, **Chapter 5:** Stacks, **Chapter 6:** Queues, **Chapter 7:** Trees, **Chapter 8:** Heaps, **Chapter 9:** Graphs, **Chapter 10:** Hashing And Hash Tables, **Chapter 11:** Sorting Algorithms, **Chapter 12:** Files, Appendix, Index

Edition : Second **ISBN : 9789382609582** **Pages (Approx.) : 420**

DESIGN AND ANALYSIS OF ALGORITHMS

Salient Features

- This book is intended for those students who want to have the basic to advance knowledge of the Design and Analysis of Algorithms.
- The book discusses various features of Algorithm Design.
- More and more algorithms are added, last year papers are solved in the chapters, few algorithms which were difficult to understand in the previous edition are presented in the easier form.

Edition : Third **ISBN : 9788190698856** **Pages (Approx.) : 630**

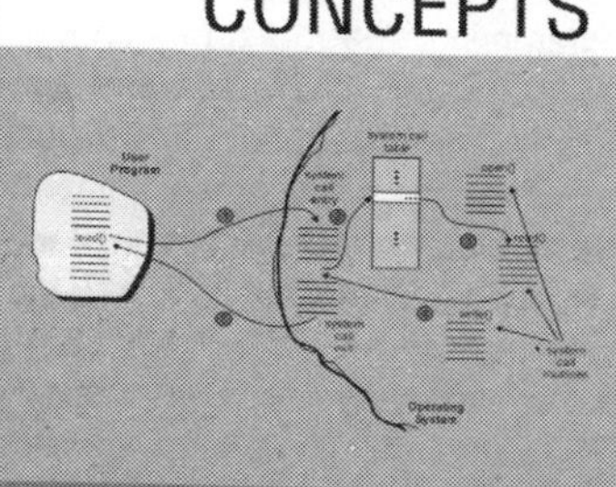

OPERATING SYSTEM CONCEPTS

Salient Features

- Includes simple illustrations to explain difficult concepts.
- Discusses operating systems for handheld devices.
- Discusses Multiprocessing and Real time CPU scheduling algorithms.
- Contains solutions to the selected exercises of individual chapters.
- Contains Question bank and solutions.
- In accordance with syllabi of various under graduate and post graduate courses throughout India.

Edition : Second **ISBN : 9789380016658** **Pages (Approx.) : 365**